STATUTORY

INSTRUMENTS

1984

PART III
(in two sections)

SECTION 2

Published by Authority

LONDON
HER MAJESTY'S STATIONERY OFFICE
1985

Price for two sections £120 net

Printed in the UK for HMSO
by Hobbs the Printers of Southampton
Dd483006 C8 11/85 (942)

ISBN 0 11 840242 0

Contents of the Edition

PART I
(in two sections)

PART II
(in two sections)

PART III
(in two sections)

STATUTORY INSTRUMENTS

1984 No. 1838

LEGAL AID AND ADVICE, ENGLAND AND WALES

The Legal Aid (Financial Conditions) Regulations 1984

Made - - - -	16*th October* 1984
Laid before Parliament	31*st October* 1984
Coming into Operation	26*th November* 1984

The Lord Chancellor, in exercise of the powers conferred on him by sections 6, 9(2) and 20 of the Legal Aid Act 1974 (**a**) , hereby makes the following Regulations:—

1.—(1) These Regulations may be cited as the Legal Aid (Financial Conditions) Regulations 1984 and shall come into operation on 26th November 1984.

(2)   In these Regulations, "the Act" means the Legal Aid Act 1974.

2.   For the yearly sum of £4,925 specified in section 6(1) of the Act, there shall be substituted the sum of £5,155.

3.   For the capital sum of £4,500 specified in section 6(1)*(a)* of the Act, there shall be substituted the sum of £4,710.

4.   For the yearly sum of £2,050 specified in section 9(1)*(a)* of the Act (**b**), there shall be substituted the yearly sum of £2,145.

Hailsham of St. Marylebone, C.

Dated 16th October 1984.

(**a**)   1974 c.4; section 6 was amended by the Legal Aid Act 1979 (c.26), Schedule 1, paragraph 12 and by S.I. 1983/1783 and section 9(2) by the Legal Aid Act 1979, Schedule 1, paragraph 13.
(**b**)   Section 9(1)*(a)* was amended by S.I. 1983/1783.

EXPLANATORY NOTE

(This Note is not part of the Regulations.)

These Regulations increase the financial limits of eligibility for legal aid under Part I of the Legal Aid Act 1974.

The income limits are increased to make legal aid available to those with disposable incomes of not more than £5,155 a year and available without payment of a contribution to those with disposable incomes of £2,145 a year or less.

The capital limit is increased to make the upper limit of disposable capital above which legal aid may be refused if it appears that the applicant could afford to proceed without legal aid, £4,710; the lower limit of disposable capital, below which no contribution in respect of capital may be required, remains £3,000.

STATUTORY INSTRUMENTS

1984 No. 1843

INDUSTRIAL DEVELOPMENT

The Regional Development Grant (Prescribed Percentage, Amount and Limit) Order 1984

Made - - -	26*th November* 1984
Laid before Parliament -	28*th November* 1984
Coming into Operation	29*th November* 1984

The Secretary of State, in exercise of his powers under section 5(1)(*b*), (*c*) and (*d*) and section 5(5)(*a*) of the Industrial Development Act 1982(**a**), and with the consent of the Treasury, hereby makes the following Order:—

Citation and commencement

1. This Order may be cited as the Regional Development Grant (Prescribed Percentage, Amount and Limit) Order 1984 and shall come into operation on 29th November 1984.

Interpretation

2. In this Order "the 1982 Act" means the Industrial Development Act 1982 as amended by the Co-operative Development Agency and Industrial Development Act 1984.

Prescribed Percentage

3. The prescribed percentage (for capital expenditure on the provision of assets) for the purposes of section 4 of the 1982 Act shall be 15 per cent.

Prescribed Amount

4. The prescribed amount (for jobs provided) for the purposes of section 4 of the 1982 Act shall be £3,000.

(**a**) 1982 c.52; a new Part II of that Act as set out in Part I of Schedule 1 to the Co-operative Development Agency and Industrial Development Act 1984 (c.57) was inserted by virtue of section 5(1) of the latter Act.

Prescribed Limit

5.—(1) The prescribed limit (on the amount of grant payable in respect of capital expenditure on the provision of assets) for the purposes of section 4 of the 1982 Act shall be —

(*a*) in the case of a large undertaking —

　(i) where the project in question provides jobs, £10,000 multiplied by the approved number of jobs;

　(ii) where the project in question does not provide jobs, £500;

(*b*) in the case of any other undertaking —

　(i) where the project in question provides jobs, the larger of £75,000 and £10,000 multiplied by the approved number of jobs;

　(ii) where the project in question does not provide jobs, £75,000.

(2) For the purposes of this Article, a large undertaking is an undertaking which at the qualifying date under section 3(3) of the 1982 Act for the project in question employed, employs or will employ more than 200 employees each normally required to work 30 or more hours per week ("full-time employees").

6. For the purposes of Article 5(2) above —

(*a*) any two employees who are not full-time employees but are normally required to work 15 or more hours per week shall be counted as one full-time employee for the purpose of determining the number of full-time employees of an undertaking; and

(*b*) the employees of an undertaking shall include the employees of any associated undertaking.

7. For the purposes of Article 6(*b*) above, "associated undertaking" —

(*a*) in relation to any undertaking which is carried on by one or more companies, includes all other undertakings carried on by companies which are members of the same group of companies; and

(*b*) in relation to any undertaking which is carried on under the direct or indirect control of one or more persons (including companies which are not members of the same group of companies as defined below for the purposes of this Article), includes them and any other undertaking carried on under their direct or indirect control, and in this Article "group of companies" means a company and all other companies which are its subsidiaries within the meaning of section 154 of the Companies Act 1948(a).

Norman Lamont,
Minister of State,
Department of Trade and Industry.

26th November 1984.

We consent to the making of this Order.

Ian B. Lang,
John Major,
Two of the Lords Commissioners of
Her Majesty's Treasury.

26th November 1984.

EXPLANATORY NOTE

(This Note is not part of the Order.)

This Order contains provisions relating to the amounts payable under the new scheme of regional development grants in Part II of the Industrial Development Act 1982 as amended by the Co-operative Development Agency and Industrial Development Act 1984. This new scheme will enable grants to be paid towards capital expenditure on the provision of assets under, or in respect of the provision of jobs by, certain projects of investment. The percentage of capital expenditure applicable for the purposes of grant is fixed at 15 per cent of that expenditure. The amount of grant in respect of jobs provided is fixed at £3,000 for each job. A limit of £10,000 applies in respect of each job provided and operates as a ceiling on the amount of grant otherwise payable in respect of capital expenditure on the provision of assets, except that for this purpose a minimum limit of £75,000 is fixed for projects of small undertakings, and a limit of £500 for projects of large undertakings which do not provide jobs.

(a) 1948 c.38.

STATUTORY INSTRUMENTS

1984 No. 1844

INDUSTRIAL DEVELOPMENT

The Assisted Areas Order 1984

Made - - -	*26th November* 1984
Laid before Parliament	*28th November* 1984
Coming into Operation	*29th November* 1984

The Secretary of State, in exercise of his powers under section 1(1) and 1(3) to (5) of the Industrial Development Act 1982(**a**) hereby makes the following Order:—

Citation and commencement

1. This Order may be cited as the Assisted Areas Order 1984 and shall come into operation on 29th November 1984 ("the appointed day").

Interpretation

2. In this Order, "the 1982 Act" means the Industrial Development Act 1982 as amended by the Co-operative Development Agency and Industrial Development Act 1984, and "the 1979 Order" means the Assisted Areas Order 1979(**b**).

Revocation and savings

3. Subject to Article 4 below, the 1979 Order is hereby revoked.

4. Articles 5, 5A, 5B, 5C and 5D of the 1979 Order as in force immediately prior to the appointed day shall continue to have effect in relation to areas specified or designated by the 1979 Order as so in force in respect of the periods stated in Articles 4(1) and (2) thereof (in the case of areas referred to in those Articles) or commencing on 1st August 1982 and ending with the appointed day (in the case of areas referred to in Article 4(3) thereof).

Designations

5. In this Order the designation of an area as a development area or intermediate area is for the purposes of section 1 of the 1982 Act and section 1 of the Derelict Land Act 1982(**c**).

(**a**) 1982 c.52; a new section 1(4) was inserted by section 4 of the Co-operative Development Agency and Industrial Development Act 1984 (c.57).
(**b**) S.I. 1979/837, as amended by S.I. 1979/1642, 1980/1110 and 1982/934.
(**c**) 1982 c.42.

6. On and after the appointed day —

(*a*) the areas described in Schedule 1 hereto shall be development areas; and

(*b*) the areas described in Schedule 2 hereto shall be intermediate areas.

7.—(1) In Schedules 1 and 2 hereto, any reference to a travel to work area shall be a reference to that area as it existed on 27th September 1984.

(2) In Schedule 2 hereto —

(*a*) any reference to a ward shall be a reference to that ward as it existed on 5th April 1981, save that in the case of wards within the City of Salford any reference to such a ward shall be a reference to that ward as it existed on 6th May 1982; and

(*b*) the reference to the Borough of Tameside shall be a reference to that Borough as it existed on 5th April 1981.

Norman Lamont,
Minister of State,
Department of Trade & Industry.

26th November 1984.

SCHEDULE 1   *Article 6(a)*

DEVELOPMENT AREAS

Scotland

The travel to work areas of:—

Arbroath
Bathgate
Cumnock and Sanquhar
Dumbarton
Dundee
Glasgow
Greenock
Irvine
Kilmarnock
Lanarkshire

Wales

The travel to work areas of:—

Aberdare
Cardigan
Ebbw Vale and Abergavenny
Flint and Rhyl
Holyhead
Lampeter and Aberaeron
Merthyr and Rhymney
Neath and Port Talbot
Pontypridd and Rhondda
South Pembrokeshire
Wrexham

England

The travel to work areas of:—

Bishop Auckland
Corby
Falmouth
Hartlepool
Helston
Liverpool
Middlesbrough
Newcastle-upon-Tyne
Newquay
Penzance and St Ives
Redruth and Camborne
Rotherham and Mexborough
Scunthorpe
South Tyneside
Stockton-on-Tees
Sunderland
Whitby
Widnes and Runcorn
Wigan and St Helens
Wirral and Chester
Workington

Article 6(b)

SCHEDULE 2

INTERMEDIATE AREAS

Scotland

The travel to work areas of:—

Alloa
Ayr
Badenoch
Campbeltown
Dunfermline
Dunoon and Bute
Falkirk
Forres
Girvan
Invergordon and Dingwall
Kirkcaldy
Lochaber
Newton Stewart
Skye and Wester Ross
Stewartry
Stranraer
Sutherland
Western Isles
Wick

Wales

The travel to work areas of:—

Bangor and Caernarfon
Bridgend
Cardiff
Fishguard
Haverfordwest
Llanelli
Newport
Pontypool and Cwmbran
Porthmadoc and Ffestiniog
Pwllheli
Swansea

England

The travel to work areas of:—

Accrington and Rossendale
Barnsley
Birmingham
Blackburn
Bodmin and Liskeard
Bolton and Bury
Bradford
Bude
Cinderford and Ross-on-Wye
Coventry and Hinckley
Darlington
Doncaster
Dudley and Sandwell
Durham
Gainsborough
Grimsby
Hull
Kidderminster
Morpeth and Ashington
Oldham
Plymouth
Rochdale
Sheffield
Telford and Bridgnorth
Walsall
Wolverhampton

The following wards of the Borough of Bury as listed in the Schedule to the Borough of Bury (Electoral Arrangements) Order 1978(**a**):—

Holyrood
St Mary's
Sedgley

The following wards of the City of Manchester as described in Part II of the Schedule to the City of Manchester (Wards) Order 1971(**b**) and as modified in the case of the ward of Moss Side by the Manchester and Trafford (Areas) Order 1980(**c**):—

Alexandra
Ardwick
Beswick
Blackley
Bradford
Charlestown
Cheetham
Collegiate Church
Crumpsall
Gorton North
Gorton South
Harpurhey
Hulme
Levenshulme
Lightbowne
Lloyd Street
Longsight
Miles Platting
Moss Side
Moston
Newton Heath
Rusholme

The following wards of the Borough of Oldham as listed in Schedule 1 to the Borough of Oldham (Electoral Arrangements) Order 1978(**d**):—

Failsworth East
Failsworth West

The following wards of the Borough of Rochdale as listed in Schedule 1 to the Borough of Rochdale (Electoral Arrangements) Order 1979 (**e**):—

Middleton Central
Middleton East
Middleton North
Middleton South
Middleton West

(**a**) S.I. 1978/1722.　　　　　(**b**) S.I. 1971/387.　　　　　(**c**) S.I. 1980/1920.
(**d**) S.I. 1978/1605.　　　　　　　　　　　　　　　　　　　(**e**) S.I. 1979/1341.

The following wards of the City of Salford as listed in the Schedule to the City of Salford (Electoral Arrangements) Order 1980(**a**):—

Blackfriars
Broughton
Claremont
Eccles
Kersal
Langworthy
Ordsall
Pendlebury
Pendleton
Swinton North
Swinton South
Weaste and Seedley
Worsley and Boothstown

The Borough of Tameside, specified as District (*k*) in column (2) of Part I of Schedule 1 to the Local Government Act 1972(**b**) and named in column (3) of the Schedule to the Metropolitan Districts (Names) Order 1973(**c**).

The following wards of the Borough of Trafford as listed in Schedule 1 to the Borough of Trafford (Electoral Arrangements) Order 1979(**d**) and as modified in the case of the ward of Clifford by the Manchester and Trafford (Areas) Order 1980:—

Clifford
Davyhulme East
Park
Talbot

(**a**) S.I. 1980/63.   (**b**) 1972 c.70.   (**c**) S.I. 1973/137.
(**d**) S.I. 1979/1028.

EXPLANATORY NOTE

(This Note is not part of the Order.)

This Order provides that for the purposes of section 1 of the Industrial Development Act 1982 (the 1982 Act) and section 1 of the Derelict Land Act 1982, and as from 29th November 1984, the areas described in Schedule 1 will be development areas, and the areas described in Schedule 2 will be intermediate areas. The Order revokes all earlier Assisted Areas Orders with appropriate saving provisions.

2. Description of the new areas is largely by reference to travel to work areas (areas mentioned in section 1(4) of the 1982 Act as inserted by section 4 of the Co-operative Development Agency and Industrial Development Act 1984). These are areas by reference to which the Secretary of State publishes unemployment statistics, and are listed in heavy type in Appendix 4 to Occasional Supplement No 3 to the Employment Gazette published by the Department of Employment (Volume 92 No 9 of September 1984). Copies of this are available from branches of Her Majesty's Stationery Office.

3. As respects Scotland, information as to the geographical extent of the travel to work areas in question is available from the Industry Department for Scotland at Alhambra House, 45 Waterloo Street, Glasgow G2 6AT; as respects Wales, from the Welsh Office Industry Department at Cathays Park, Cardiff CF1 3NQ; and as respects the region of England for which it is responsible, from the appropriate Regional Office of the Department of Trade and Industry.

4. In Schedule 2, intermediate areas within the Metropolitan County of Greater Manchester are described by reference to electoral wards and, in the case of the Borough of Tameside, by reference to that area in its entirety. A map showing the geographical extent of all areas so described is available for inspection at the North Western Regional Office of the Department of Trade and Industry at Sunley Building, Piccadilly Plaza, Manchester M1 4BA. The Orders referred to in Schedule 2 are available from branches of Her Majesty's Stationery Office, except the City of Manchester (Wards) Order 1971 which is available for inspection at the North Western Regional Office.

5. Areas described in the Schedules are as they existed on the dates given in Article 7 of the Order.

STATUTORY INSTRUMENTS

1984 No. 1845 (c.46)

INDUSTRIAL DEVELOPMENT

The Co-operative Development Agency and Industrial Development Act (Commencement) Order 1984

Made - - - *26th November* 1984

The Secretary of State, in exercise of his powers under section 7(1) (*b*), (2) and (3) of the Co-operative Development Agency and Industrial Development Act 1984 (**a**) hereby makes the following Order:—

Citation
1. This Order may be cited as the Co-operative Development Agency and Industrial Development Act (Commencement) Order 1984.

Interpretation
2. In this Order "the 1982 Act" means the Industrial Development Act 1982 (**b**) as in operation immediately prior to the appointed day, "the amended Act of 1982" means the Industrial Development Act 1982 as in operation on and after the appointed day, "the 1984 Act" means the Co-operative Development Agency and Industrial Development Act 1984, and "the 1979 Order" means the Assisted Areas Order 1979 (**c**).

Appointed day
3. Part II of the 1984 Act shall come into operation on 29th November 1984 ("the appointed day").

Transitional provisions
4.—(1) In relation to an area which immediately prior to the appointed day was a special development area or a development area (areas which for the purposes of Article 9 below are described in Schedule 1 or 2 hereto respectively), grant may be paid in accordance with Part II of the 1982 Act at the rate appropriate to that area at that time towards expenditure incurred in providing an asset if —

    (*a*) the asset is provided within the period of one year beginning with the appointed day; or

    (*b*) the expenditure is defrayed before the appointed day; or

    (*c*) subject to paragraph (2) below, the asset is provided by or as part of a project for which an application for financial assistance under section 7

(**a**) 1984 c.57.
(**b**) 1982 c.52.
(**c**) S.I. 1979/837, as amended by S.I. 1979/1642, 1980/1110 and 1982/934.

or 8 of the 1982 Act, section 5 of the Science and Technology Act 1965 (**a**) or section 8 of the Highlands and Islands Development (Scotland) Act 1965 (**b**) was made before 1st February 1984, an offer of such financial assistance in respect of that project is made before the appointed day, and that offer is accepted (whether before or after the appointed day),

and where in a case falling within sub-paragraphs (*a*) or (*b*) (but not (*c*)) above, grant is paid by virtue of those provisions in accordance with Part II of the 1982 Act, no grant may be paid in accordance with Part II of the amended Act of 1982.

(2) Where an offer of financial assistance under the provisions of the Acts referred to in paragraph (1)(*c*) above is made in respect of any project and that offer —

(*a*) is made before the appointed day and accepted (whether before or after the appointed day); and

(*b*) is not an offer (however expressed) under which the amount of financial assistance payable is to be varied by reference to the amount of regional development grant payable in respect of that project,

then no grant shall be paid in respect of that project in accordance with Part II of the amended Act of 1982 unless the conditions in Article 6(1) below are satisfied.

5. For the purposes of Article 4(1) (*c*) and 4(2) above —

(*a*) the reference to financial assistance under section 5 of the Science and Technology Act 1965 is a reference to financial assistance for a project in respect of which an offer has been made by the Secretary of State for Industry, the Secretary of State for Trade or the Secretary of State for Trade and Industry; and

(*b*) references to financial assistance do not include assistance provided under the small firms loan guarantee scheme, being the scheme under which the Secretary of State for Industry or the Secretary of State for Trade and Industry provides or provided financial assistance under section 8 of the 1982 Act solely by means of guarantees given to banks and other financial institutions to secure loans to small businesses; and

(*c*) references to an offer of financial assistance include offers made before the appointed day and subsequently amended (whether before or after the appointed day), if the amended offer so specifies for the purposes of this paragraph.

6.—(1) In relation to any offer of financial assistance as described in Article 4(2) above, the conditions referred to in that Article are that —

(*a*) it is agreed that any grant remaining to be paid thereunder shall not be paid; and

(*b*) any grant already paid thereunder is repaid; and

(**a**) 1965 c.4.
(**b**) 1965 c.46, as amended by the Highlands and Islands Development (Scotland) Act 1968 (c.51).

(c) if the Secretary of State so requires, any other benefit or facility given or agreed to be given thereunder to the person to whom the offer is made, being a benefit or facility specified in whole or in part for the purposes of the requirement, is cancelled withdrawn or forgone by agreement between him and the Secretary of State; and

(d) in the case of any benefit or facility not falling within sub-paragraphs (a) (b) or (c) of this paragraph (including a benefit or facility to the extent not wholly specified for the purposes of any requirement under the said sub-paragraph (c)) and if the Secretary of State so requires, the person to whom the offer is made indemnifies the Secretary of State in respect of all his costs and expenses of and in connection with any such benefit or facility as may be specified in whole or in part for the purposes of the last mentioned requirement.

(2) In paragraph (1) above as it applies to any offer of financial assistance under section 8 of the Highlands and Islands Development (Scotland) Act 1965, references to the Secretary of State shall be taken as references to the Highlands and Islands Development Board.

7.—(1) Where an application for approval of a project for grant under Part II of the amended Act of 1982 is made to the Secretary of State and the project in respect of which that application is made is partly carried out by the appointed day, the jobs or assets which have been or are to be provided by the project shall be apportioned as between the period before and the period beginning with the appointed day, and grant shall be payable under Part II of the amended Act of 1982 only in respect of expenditure on the provision of assets and jobs apportioned to the latter period.

(2) For the purposes of paragraph (1) above, apportionment shall be carried out —

(a) in the case of assets, by reference to the date of their provision, save that where an asset is provided on or after the appointed day any expenditure on its provision defrayed before that day shall be apportioned to the period before that day; and

(b) in the case of jobs, so as to apportion them in the same proportion as that which in the case of assets (as respects expenditure thereon) is produced by applying sub-paragraph (a) above.

8. Where —

(a) grant is paid in accordance with Part II of the 1982 Act towards expenditure incurred in providing an asset within the period of one year beginning with the appointed day; and

(b) that expenditure is incurred for the purposes of a project in respect of which an application for approval of that project for grant under Part II of the amended Act of 1982 is made to the Secretary of State; and

(c) that project is a project for which the qualifying date under section 3(3) of the amended Act of 1982 falls within the period mentioned in paragraph (a) above, then no grant shall be paid under Part II of the amended Act of 1982 towards any expenditure referred to in the said paragraph (*a*) or in respect of any jobs (whether provided before or after the end of the said period) which are attributable to that expenditure.

9. For the purposes only of section 7 and 13 of the 1982 Act and subject to Article 11 below, for the period of four months beginning with the appointed day ("the prescribed period") —

(*a*) the areas described in Schedule 1 hereto shall continue to be special development areas;

(*b*) the areas described in Schedule 2 hereto shall continue to be development areas; and

(*c*) the areas described in Schedule 3 hereto shall continue to be intermediate areas.

10. In the Schedules hereto, any reference to an employment office area (an area formerly specified by the Manpower Services Commission as an area for which a specified office of the Commission exercised functions) shall be construed as a reference to that area as it existed on the date on which, by virtue of the 1979 Order and section 1(4) of the 1982 Act, it first had the status which it will continue to have by virtue of Article 9 above.

11. Where by virtue of Article 9 above financial assistance may be provided under section 7 or 13 of the 1982 Act, and during the prescribed period the area in question is in an area which is an assisted area of a particular category by virtue of this Order but of another category by virtue of the Assisted Areas Order 1984(**a**), that area shall for the purposes of the said section 7 and 13 be of the category having the higher status.

12. For the purposes of Article 11 above —

(*a*) a special development area has the highest status;

(*b*) a development area has the next highest status; and

(*c*) an intermediate area has the lowest status.

Norman Lamont,
Minister of State,
Department of Trade and Industry.

26th November 1984.

(**a**) S.I. 1984/1844.

SCHEDULE 1   *Article 9(a)*

SPECIAL DEVELOPMENT AREAS

Scotland

The employment office areas of:—

Airdrie	Govan	Maryhill
Alexandria	Greenock	Motherwell
Arbroath	Hamilton	Paisley
Ayr	Helensburgh	Parkhead
Barrhead	Hillington	Partick
Bellshill	Irvine	Port Glasgow
Blantyre	Johnstone	Renfrew
Cambuslang	Kilbirnie	Rutherglen
Carluke	Kilmarnock	Saltcoats (excluding
Clydebank	Kilsyth	the Isle of Arran)
Coatbridge	Kilwinning	Sanquhar
Cumbernauld	Kinning Park	Shawlands
Cumnock	Kirkintilloch	Shotts
Dumbarton	Lanark	Springburn
Dundee	Largs (excluding the	Troon
Easterhouse	Isles of Cumbrae)	Uddingston
East Kilbride	Larkhall	Wishaw
Glasgow Central	Lesmahagow	

The area designated by the New Town (Glenrothes) Designation Order 1948(a) as the site of a new town and the area designated by the New Town (Livingston) Designation Order 1962(b), as varied by the New Town (Livingston) Designation Amendment Order 1978(c), as the site of a new town.

Wales

The employment office areas of:—

Abertillery	Ebbw Vale	Porth (Tonypandy)
Amlwch	Ferndale	Porthcawl
Bargoed	Flint	Port Talbot
Beaumaris	Holyhead	Shotton
Blackwood	Holywell	Tredegar
Bridgend	Llangefni	Treorchy
Brynmawr	Maesteg	Wrexham
Cefn Mawr	Mold	Ystrad Mynach
Cymmer	Pontlottyn	

Northern Region

The employment office areas of:—

Billingham	Jarrow and Hebburn	Shields Road
Birtley	Lanchester	South Shields
Blaydon-on-Tyne	Loftus	Southwick
Chester-le-Street	Middlesbrough	Stanley
Consett	Newburn	Stockton and Thornaby
East Boldon	Newcastle-upon-Tyne	Sunderland
Eston	North Shields	Wallsend
Felling	Peterlee	Washington
Gateshead	Prudhoe	West Moor
Guisborough	Redcar	Whitley Bay
Hartlepool	Saltburn	Wingate
Houghton-le-Spring	Seaham	Yarm

(a) S.I. 1948/1528.   (b) S.I. 1962/814.   (c) S.I. 1978/1012.

North West Region

The employment office areas of:—

Allerton	Kirkby
Bebington	Liverpool
Belle Vale	Neston
Birkenhead	Old Swan
Bootle	Prescot
Crosby	Runcorn
Ellesmere Port	Wallasey
Garston	Walton
Hoylake	Widnes

The area designated by the Skelmersdale New Town (Designation) Order 1961(a), as varied by the Skelmersdale New Town (Designation) Amendment Order 1969(b), as the site of a proposed new town.

South West Region

The employment office areas of:—

Camborne
Falmouth
Hayle
Redruth

(a) S.I. 1961/1918.   (b) S.I. 1969/127.

SCHEDULE 2   *Article 9(b)*

DEVELOPMENT AREAS

Scotland

The employment office areas of:—

Bathgate	Fort William	Lochgilphead
Blairgowrie	Girvan	Newton Stewart
Bo'ness	†Glenrothes	Oban
Broxburn	Grangemouth	Portree
Campbeltown	Invergordon	Rothesay
Cowdenbeath	Inverness	Saltcoats (Isle of Arran)
Denny	Kirkcaldy	Stornoway
Dingwall	Largs (Isles of Cumbrae)	Stranraer
Dunfermline	Leven and Methil	Thurso
Dunoon	††Livingston	Wick
Falkirk		

†excluding that area designated by the New Town (Glenrothes) Designation Order 1948 as the site of a new town.

††excluding that area designated by the New Town (Livingston) Designation Order 1962 as varied by the New Town (Livingston) Designation Amendment Order 1978 as the site of a new town.

Wales

The employment office areas of:—

Aberdare	Garnant	Penarth
Abergavenny	Haverfordwest	Penygroes
Ammanford	Kidwelly	Pontardawe
Bangor	Lampeter	Pontypool
Barry	Llandyssul	Pontypridd
Bethesda	Llanelli	Porthmadog
Blaenau Ffestiniog	Llantrisant	Pwllheli
Blaenavon	Llantwit Major	Resolven
Caernarvon	Merthyr Tydfil	Rhyl
Caerphilly	Milford Haven	Risca
Cardiff	Neath	Tonyrefail
Cardigan	Newbridge	Treharris
Chepstow	Newport	Tumble
Cwmbran	Pembroke Dock	Ystradgynlais
Fishguard		

Northern Region

The employment office areas of:—

Ashington	Cockermouth	Millom
Aspatria	Cramlington	Morpeth
Bedlington	Crook	Spennymoor
Blyth	Durham	Whitehaven
Cleator Moor	Maryport	Workington

North West Region

The employment office areas of:—

Ashton-in-Makerfield	Rawtenstall
Bacup	Rochdale
Haslingden	St Helens
Hindley	Wigan

Yorkshire and Humberside Region

The employment office areas of:—

Barton-on-Humber	Hessle
Beverley	Hull
Bransholme	Mexborough
Goldthorpe	Rotherham
Grimsby	Scunthorpe

South West Region

The employment office areas of:—

Bodmin	Launceston	Plympton
Bude	Liskeard	St Austell
Camelford	Looe	St Ives
Devonport	Newquay	Saltash
Helston	Penzance	Tavistock
Ilfracombe	Plymouth	Truro
		Wadebridge

East Midlands Region

The employment office area of Corby.

SCHEDULE 3

Article 9(c)

INTERMEDIATE AREAS

Scotland

The employment office areas of:—

Alloa	Kirkwall
Anstruther	Lerwick
Castle Douglas	Nairn
Forres	Stirling

Wales

The employment office areas of:—

Colwyn Bay	Llangollen
Conwy	Llanrwst
Denbigh	Monmouth
Gorseinon	Morriston
Llandudno	Swansea
	Tenby

Northern Region

The employment office areas of:—

Alnwick
Amble
Bishop Auckland
Darlington
Newton Aycliffe

North West Region

The employment office areas of:—

Atherton	Horwich	Morecambe
Blackpool Central	Kirkham	Northwich
Blackpool South	Lancaster	Southport
Bolton	Leigh	St Annes
Farnworth	Lytham	Thornton
Fleetwood	Middlewich	Westhoughton
		Winsford

Yorkshire and Humberside Region

The employment office areas of:—

Barnsley	Goole	Shipley
Bingley	Hoyland	Thorne
Bradford	Maltby	Whitby
Bridlington	Richmond	Wombwell
Doncaster	Scarborough	

South West Region

The employment office areas of:—

Ashburton	Brixham	Paignton
Barnstaple	Dartmouth	Teignmouth
Bideford	Kingsbridge	Torquay
Bovey Tracey	Newton Abbot	Totnes

East Midlands Region

The employment office areas of:—

Gainsborough
Mablethorpe
Skegness

EXPLANATORY NOTE

(This Note is not part of the Order.)

This Order brings into force Part II of the Co-operative Development Agency and Industrial Development Act 1984 and Schedule 1 thereto, which substitutes a new Part II of the Industrial Development Act 1982 and introduces a new scheme of regional development grants. The Order also contains appropriate transitional provisions dealing with the change from the old to the new scheme of regional development grants, and to enable financial assistance under section 7 and 13 of the 1982 Act to continue to be given on the basis of the old map of assisted areas for a period of four months after the appointed day. (A new map of assisted areas is brought into force on the appointed day by the Assisted Areas Order 1984 (S.I. 1984/1844)).

STATUTORY INSTRUMENTS

1984 No. 1846

INDUSTRIAL DEVELOPMENT

The Regional Development Grant (Qualifying Activities) Order 1984

Made - - -	*26th November* 1984
Laid before Parliament	*28th November* 1984
Coming into Operation	*29th November* 1984

The Secretary of State, in exercise of his powers under section 5(1)(*a*) and (2)(*a*) of the Industrial Development Act 1982(**a**), and with the consent of the Treasury, hereby makes the following Order:—

1. This Order may be cited as the Regional Development Grant (Qualifying Activities) Order 1984 and shall come into operation on 29th November 1984.

Interpretation

2. In this Order "the 1982 Act" means the Industrial Development Act 1982 as amended by the Co-operative Development Agency and Industrial Development Act 1984.

Qualifying Activities

3. The qualifying activities defined in section 5(1)(*a*) of the 1982 Act shall for the purposes of section 3 of that Act be the activities specified in the Schedule to this Order.

4. In this Order, "the SIC" (by reference to which some qualifying activities are specified) means the 1980 revision of the 1979 edition of the publication entitled "Standard Industrial Classification", "the SIC indexes" means the 1980 revision of the indexes to the SIC, and "Division" means a Division of the SIC.

5. For the purposes of this Order, the SIC and the SIC indexes have effect without regard to any other purpose (whether statutory or not) for which they are or may be applied.

Norman Lamont,
Minister of State,
Department of Trade and Industry.

26th November 1984.

We consent to the making of this Order.

Ian, B. Lang,
John Major,
Two of the Lords Commissioners of
Her Majesty's Treasury.

26th November 1984.

(**a**) 1982 c.52; a new Part II of that Act as set out in Part I of Schedule 1 to the Co-operative Development Agency and Industrial Development Act 1984 (c.57) was inserted by virtue of section 5(1) of the latter Act.

Article 3   SCHEDULE

1. Subject to paragraph 16 below, the following activities listed in the SIC or in the SIC indexes shall be qualifying activities:

DIVISION 1   ENERGY AND WATER SUPPLY INDUSTRIES
Activity 1115   Manufacture of solid fuels.
Activity 1200   Coke ovens.
Activity 1300 (part)   Extraction of mineral oil and natural gas (operation of land terminals for stabilization, separation and storage, and the activity of retorting of oil shale only).
Activity 1401   Mineral oil refining.
Activity 1402   Other treatment of petroleum products (excluding petrochemicals manufacture).
Activity 1520   Nuclear fuel production (excluding disposal of nuclear waste).

DIVISION 2   EXTRACTION OF MINERALS AND ORES OTHER THAN FUELS; MANUFACTURE OF METALS, MINERAL PRODUCTS AND CHEMICALS
All of Division 2 except Class 21 (extraction and preparation of metalliferous ores) and Class 23 (extraction of minerals not elsewhere specified).

DIVISION 3   METAL GOODS, ENGINEERING AND VEHICLES INDUSTRIES
All of Division 3 except Activity 3480 (electrical equipment installation).

DIVISION 4   OTHER MANUFACTURING INDUSTRIES
All of Division 4.

DIVISION 7   TRANSPORT AND COMMUNICATION
Activity 7700/2 (part) Freight brokers and other agents facilitating freight transport, not including porterage or messenger services.

DIVISION 8   BANKING, FINANCE, INSURANCE, BUSINESS SERVICES AND LEASING
Activity 8150/1 (part) Institutions specialising in the granting of credit (export finance companies not licensed under the Banking Act 1979(a) only).
Activity 8370/2   Technical services not elsewhere specified.
Activity 8380 (part)   Advertising (excluding bill posting agencies and window dressers).
Activity 8394   Computer services.
Activity 8395/1, 2   Management consultants and market research and public relations consultants.

DIVISION 9   OTHER SERVICES
Activity 9400 (part)   Research and development work in the industrial field carried out in specialised research establishments only.
Activity 9791/2 (part) Football pools only.

2. In addition to the activities specified in paragraph 1 above, and subject to paragraph 16 below, the activities specified in paragraphs 3 to 15 below shall be qualifying activities.

3. The activity of processing coal mined or extracted from deep coal mines and opencast coal workings and mined or extracted metalliferous ores where that processing activity (such as crushing or grinding) can be identified separately from the activity of mining or extraction, together with activities (such as cleaning, washing or grading) which are ancillary and subsequent to that processing activity.

4. The processing of scrap and waste materials.

5. Scientific research relating to any other qualifying activity and whether or not also within SIC Activity 9400 to the extent specified in paragraph 1 above.

_____

(a) 1979 c.37.

6. The repair or maintenance of any machinery or plant save for that falling within either SIC Class 67 (repair of consumer goods and vehicles) or Activity 9812 (dry cleaning and allied services).

7. The repair or maintenance of premises used wholly or mainly for qualifying activities, including, for the purposes of this paragraph, this activity.

8. The training of staff for work in any other qualifying activity.

9.—(1) Central services provided from a single location by an undertaking (the principal activities of which are carried out at more than one place) exclusively to itself in respect of a principal activity of that undertaking which is carried out on an international, national or regional basis.

(2) Without prejudice to the generality of sub-paragraph (1) above, central services include those relating to management and planning of the undertaking's operations, accounting, audit and records, personnel, computer services, data and word processing, typing, internal telecommunications, marketing, market research and advertising, but do not include distribution, transport of goods or persons or the production or distribution of energy for heating or other purposes.

(3) For the purpose of sub-paragraph (1) above, "undertaking" has the same meaning as in section 2(7) of the 1982 Act.

10.—(1) The provision of a service which consists of the conveyance of messages by means of a telecommunication system together with the provision of an additional service by means of that telecommunication system other than—
    (*a*) switching incidental to that conveyance; or
    (*b*) a directory information service.

(2) In sub-paragraph (1) above—
"directory information service" means a service as described in section 4(3) of the Telecommunications Act 1984(**a**);
"messages" means anything falling within paragraphs (*a*) to (*d*) of section 4(1) of that Act;
"telecommunication system" means a system as defined in the said section 4(1).

11. The provision of a cable programme service as defined in section 2(1) of the Cable and Broadcasting Act 1984(**b**) if that service is also a licensable service as defined in section 2(2) of that Act.

12. Refurbishment of manufactured goods for resale or exchange.

13. The provision of goods or services by mail order, whether or not as part of a mixed retail business.

14. The provision of venture capital to industry by specialist institutions which do not take deposits.

15. The issuing of credit cards and the provision of credit card services where these activities are the sole or principal activities of the provider at the location at which they are carried on.

16. For the purpose of determining whether an activity is a qualifying activity the following ancillary or associated activities shall not be regarded as part of that activity:—
    (*a*) haulage;
    (*b*) distribution;
    (*c*) storage;
    (*d*) production and distribution of energy and heating;
but office work, including accountancy, audit, advertising and market research, where it is ancillary to or associated with any other activity, shall be regarded as part of that activity.

(**a**) 1984 c.12.   (**b**) 1984 c.46.

EXPLANATORY NOTE

(This Note is not part of the Order.)

This Order sets out the qualifying activities for the purposes of the new scheme of regional development grants in Part II of the Industrial Development Act 1982 as amended by the Co-operative Development Agency and Industrial Development Act 1984. The qualifying activities are specified mainly but not exclusively by reference to the Standard Industrial Classification and its indexes as revised in 1980 (published by Her Majesty's Stationery Office on behalf of the Central Statistical Office).

STATUTORY INSTRUMENTS

1984 No. 1847

LIBRARIES

The Public Lending Right Scheme 1982 (Amendment) Order 1984

Made - - - -	*20th November* 1984
Laid before Parliament	*6th December* 1984
Coming into Operation	*28th December* 1984

The Lord President of the Council, in exercise of powers conferred by section 3(7) of the Public Lending Right Act 1979(**a**) and now vested in him (**b**) and after consulting with representatives of authors and library authorities and of others who appear likely to be affected, hereby makes the following Order:—

Citation, commencement and interpretation

1.— (1) This Order may be cited as the Public Lending Right Scheme 1982 (Amendment) Order 1984 and shall come into operation on 28th December 1984.

(2) In this Order "the Scheme" means the Public Lending Right Scheme 1982(**c**).

Authors

2. There shall be substituted for Article 4 of the Scheme the following Article:—

"**4.**(1) Subject to paragraph (2), a person shall be treated as an author of a book for the purpose of this Scheme if he is either—

(*a*) a writer of the book, including without prejudice to the generality of that expression,

(i) a translator thereof, and

(ii) an editor or compiler thereof, who in either case has contributed more than ten per cent of the contents of the book or more than ten pages of the contents, whichever is the less; or

(*b*) an illustrator thereof, which for this purpose includes the author of a photograph (within the meaning of section 48 of the Copyright Act 1956).

(**a**) 1979 c.10.
(**b**) S.I. 1979/907, 1981/207, 1983/879.
(**c**) The Scheme is set out in the Appendix to S.I. 1982/719. It has been amended by S.I. 1983/480, 1688.

(2) Notwithstanding paragraph (1), a person shall not be treated as an author of a book unless the fact that he is an author within the meaning of paragraph (1) is evidenced by his being named on the title page of the book.".

Eligible persons

3. Article 5 of the Scheme shall be amended by substituting for paragraph (1) the following paragraph:—

"(1) For the purposes of the Scheme, and in relation to each application by a person relating to an eligible book, the applicant is an eligible person if he is an author (within the meaning of Article 4) of that book who at the date of the application has his only or principal home in one of the countries specified in Schedule 5, or, if he has no home, has been present in one of those countries for not less than twelve months out of the preceding twenty-four months.".

Eligible books

4. Article 6 of the Scheme shall be amended as follows:—

"*(a)* by substituting for paragraph (2) the following paragraph:—

"(2) In paragraph (1) "book" means a printed and bound publication (including a paper-back edition) but does not include—

(a) a book bearing, in lieu of the name of an author who is a natural person, the name of a body corporate or an unincorporated association;

(b) a book with four or more authors, but for the purpose of this sub-paragraph a translator, editor or compiler shall not be treated as an author of the book unless each of his co-authors is a translator, editor or compiler;

(c) a book which is wholly or mainly a musical score;

(d) a book the copyright of which is vested in the Crown;

(e) a book which has not been offered for sale to the public; or

(f) a serial publication including, without prejudice to the generality of that expression, a newspaper, magazine, journal or periodical.";

(b) by deleting paragraph (3).".

Registration

5. Article 9 of the Scheme shall be amended:—

(a) by substituting for paragraph (1) the following paragraph—

"(1) Public Lending Right in respect of a book may, and may only, be registered if—

(a) the book is an eligible book, and

(b) application in that behalf is made in accordance with Articles 14 and 17.";

(b) in paragraph (3) by substituting for sub-paragraph *(b)* the following sub-paragraph:—

    "(b) application in that behalf is made in accordance with Articles 14 and 17.".

Shares in Public Lending Right

6. The following new Article shall be inserted in the Scheme after Article 9:—

"Shares in Public Lending Right

9A.— (1) Subject to the following paragraphs an eligible person's registered share of Public Lending Right in respect of a book of which he is author shall be the whole of that Right or, where a book has two or more authors (including any who are not eligible persons), such share of the Public Lending Right as may be specified in accordance with Article 17(1)*(c)* in the application for first registration of the Right.

(2) A translator's share of Public Lending Right in respect of a book shall be thirty per cent of that Right, or if there is more than one translator (including any who are not eligible persons), an equal share of thirty per cent, but this paragraph shall not apply where a translator is an author of the book in another capacity unless he makes an application in accordance with Article 17(1)*(c)*(ii).

(3) An editor's or compiler's share of Public Lending Right in respect of a book shall be

    (a) twenty per cent of that Right, or

    (b) if he satisfies the Registrar that he has contributed more than twenty per cent of the contents of the book, the percentage equal to that percentage contribution, or

    (c) if there is more than one editor or compiler (including any who are not eligible persons), an equal share of twenty per cent or the higher percentage attributable to the editors or compilers in accordance with sub-paragraph *(b)*.

(4) Where a book has two or more authors (including any who are not eligible persons) and the Registrar is satisfied that one or more of them is dead or cannot be traced at the date of application, despite all reasonable steps having been taken to do so, the Public Lending Right shall be apportioned amongst all the authors equally (including any who are not eligible persons), subject to—

    (a) the prior application of paragraphs (2) and (3), and

    (b) where the book is illustrated, the attribution of twenty per cent of the Public Lending Right to the illustrator, or if there is more than one illustrator, (including any who are not eligible persons), the attribution of an equal share of twenty per cent to each illustrator.

(5) Where paragraph 4*(b)* applies, an illustrator who is also an author of the book in another capacity shall, in addition to any share of Public Lending Right to which he is entitled under that sub-paragraph, be entitled to any further share of the Right which is attributable to him as author in that other capacity.

(6) Where all the authors who are party to an application under Article 17(1)(c) and who are entitled under paragraph (4) to a share of a percentage of Public Lending Right in respect of the relevant book specify in accordance with Article 17(1)(c) that the said percentage shall be apportioned in a manner other than that provided for by paragraph (4) the specified apportionment shall apply if the Registrar is satisfied that it is reasonable in that case.".

Payments consequent upon amendment

7. Article 13 of the Scheme shall be amended by inserting "or 17A" after "Article 12".

Application for first registration

8. Article 17 of the Scheme shall be amended in paragraph (1) by substituting for sub-paragraph *(c)* the following sub-paragraph:—

"*(c)* where the book has two or more authors (including any who are not eligible persons), shall specify the proposed shares of each of them and for that purpose each of those authors who is alive at the date of application shall be a party to the application, unless

    (i) the Registrar is satisfied that he cannot be traced, despite all reasonable steps having been taken to do so, or

    (ii) the application is made by the translator or editor or compiler of the book and he specifies that he is making the application only in his capacity as such.".

Transitional provisions for translators, editors and compilers

9. The following new Article shall be inserted in the Scheme after Article 17:—

"Transitional provisions for translators, editors and compilers"

17A.— (1) Where an application for first registration of Public Lending Right in respect of a book was made before 28th December 1984 and a translator, editor or compiler thereof would have been party to the said application if it had been made on or after that date he may, if he is an eligible person, make an application for the registered shares of the Right to be revised.

(2) Subject to the following paragraphs, the provisions of this Scheme shall apply to an application under paragraph (1) as though it were an application for first registration of Public Lending Right.

(3) Where a successful application is made under paragraph (1)—

    (a) the applicant's share of the Public Lending Right shall be that prescribed in Article 9A(2) or (3) as the case may be, and

    (b) the relevant shares of his co-authors, one to another, shall remain unaltered, unless all the authors who were party to the original application before 28th December 1984 are party to the application under paragraph (1) and specify an apportionment of their shares in a different manner and the Registrar is satisfied that such apportionment is reasonable.

(4) Where a successful application is made in accordance with paragraph (1) the Registrar shall amend the Register accordingly.".

Evidence required in connection with the application

10. There shall be substituted for Article 18 of the Scheme the following Article:—

"18. The Registrar may require the submission of evidence to satisfy him that—

(*a*) a book is an eligible book,

(*b*) a person applying as author for the first registration of Public Lending Right, or the registration of a share of the Right, is in fact the author of that book and is an eligible person, or

(*c*) that any co-author who is not a party to an application for first registration of Public Lending Right is dead or cannot be traced despite all reasonable steps having been taken to do so,

and may for the purpose of obtaining any such evidence require a statutory declaration to be made by any person.".

Designation of sampling points

11. Article 38 of the Scheme shall be amended by substituting for paragraph (2) the following paragraphs:—

"(2) The Registrar shall so exercise his powers under this Article as to secure, subject to paragraph (4), that—

(*a*) at all times there shall be 20 operative sampling points comprising—

   (i) 5 points falling within Group B in Schedule 2, including, subject to paragraph (3), a principal service point and an ordinary service point, and

   (ii) 3 points falling within each of Groups A, C and F, in each case, subject to paragraph (3), including a principal service point and an ordinary service point, and

   (iii) 2 points falling within each of the other groups, being, subject to paragraph (3), a principal service point and an ordinary service point respectively;

(*b*) at all times one of the 2 operative sampling points falling within Group E in Schedule 2 shall be within either the County of Dyfed or that of Gwynedd;

(*c*) at all times at least one of the 3 operative sampling points falling within Group F in Schedule 2 shall be outside the Metropolitan Districts of Edinburgh and Glasgow;

(*d*) with effect from the beginning of each sampling year at least 5 out of the 20 operative sampling points shall be replaced by new such points, and

(*e*) no service point shall remain an operative sampling point for a continuous period of more than four years.".

Method of determining the number of notional loans

12. Article 42 of the Scheme shall be amended in paragraph (3) by substituting the word "six" for the word "twelve".

Determination of the sum due in respect of Public Lending Right

13. Article 46 of the Scheme shall be amended in paragraph (1)*(a)* by substituting "0.92p" for "1.02p",

Information to be provided in connection with applications

14. Schedule 1 to the Scheme shall be amended in Part I by substituting for paragraphs 5, 6 and 7 the following paragraphs:—

"**5.** A statement signed by each applicant that in each case the conditions as to eligibility specified in Part II of the Scheme are satisfied at the date of application, accompanied, when the applicant has not previously made an application under Article 17 of this Scheme, by a certificate signed by a Member of Parliament, Justice of the Peace, Minister of Religion, lawyer, bank officer, school teacher, police officer, doctor or other person accepted by the Registrar as being of similar standing and stating that he has known the applicant for at least two years, that he is not related to the applicant and that to the best of his knowledge the contents of the statement by the applicant are true.

6. In the case of a work by more than one author—

    (a) a statement signed by all the authors who are alive and can be traced at the date of application specifying—

        (i) the agreed share in the Public Lending Right of each author, and

        (ii) whether any author is translator, editor, compiler or, if any author is dead or untraced at the date of application, illustrator of the book and, if so, whether he is also an author of the book in another capacity, or

    (b) a statement by the applicant that he is translator, editor or compiler of the book and that his claim to the Public Lending Right in respect thereof is limited to the percentage precribed in Article 9A(2) or (3) as the case may be.

7. Where an editor or compiler of a book wishes to claim, or claim an equal share of, more than twenty per cent of the Public Lending Right in accordance with Article 9A(3), particulars indicating evidence of the percentage that he has, or where there are two or more editors or compilers that they have jointly, contributed to the contents of the book.

8. In the case of an author not of full age, a declaration by the applicant that he is the parent or guardian, as the case may be, of the author, and a copy of the author's birth certificate.".

Specified countries

15. There shall be added after Schedule 4 to the Scheme the following new Schedule:—

"Article 5 SCHEDULE 5

SPECIFIED COUNTRIES

Federal Republic of Germany
United Kingdom. ".

Revocations

16. Orders specified in the Schedule hereto are hereby revoked to the extent specified in column 3 of the Schedule.

SCHEDULE

REVOCATIONS

Column 1 Orders revoked	Column 2 References	Column 3 Extent of Revocation
The Public Lending Right Scheme 1982 (Commencement) Order 1982.	S.I. 1982/719	Article 45 and 52 of and Schedule 3 to the Scheme.
The Public Lending Right Scheme 1982 (Amendment) Order 1983.	S.I. 1983/480	The Whole Order.
The Public Lending Right Scheme 1982 (Amendment) (No. 2) Order 1983.	S.I. 1983/1688	Article 2*(a)*.

Whitelaw,
Lord President of the Council.

20th November 1984.

EXPLANATORY NOTE
(This Note is not part of the Order.)

This Order, which comes into force on 28th December 1984, amends the Public Lending Right Scheme 1982.

Article 2 extends the definition of "author" in the Scheme so that translators and editors and compilers can now benefit from Public Lending Right.

Article 3 removes the nationality requirement for benefit under the Scheme and with Article 15 extends the residential requirement so that residence in the Federal Republic of Germany (which has a reciprocal Scheme) is treated in the same way as residence in the United Kingdom.

Article 4 removes the requirement for an eligible book to contain a minimum number of pages.

Article 5 removes the requirement for all the authors of a book to be alive at the date of application for registration of Public Lending Right in the book.

Article 6 specifies the way in which Public Lending Right is to be apportioned where there are joint authors and provides for where an author is an editor, compiler or translator or is dead or cannot be traced at the date of application.

Articles 8 and 10 make amendments to the rules relating to the registration of Public Lending Right.

Article 9 provides transitional provisions where a translator, editor or compiler is the co-author of a book in which the Public Lending Right has been registered before 28th December 1984 and Article 7 makes a consequential amendment.

Article 14 makes amendments as to the material which must be supplied by each applicant.

Articles 11 and 12 amend the way in which the number of loans of a book is ascertained.

Article 13 reduces the sum attributable to each qualifying loan from 1.02p to 0.92p.

STATUTORY INSTRUMENTS

1984 No. 1848 (S.143)

SHERIFF COURT, SCOTLAND

The Confirmation to Small Estates (Scotland) Order 1984

Made - - - - -	*8th November* 1984
Laid before Parliament	*6th December* 1984
Coming into Operation	*27th December* 1984

In exercise of the powers conferred on me by section 1(3) of the Confirmation to Small Estates (Scotland) Act 1979**(a)**, and of all other powers enabling me in that behalf, I hereby make the following order:—

1. This order may be cited as the Confirmation to Small Estates (Scotland) Order 1984 and shall come into operation on 27th December 1984.

2. In each of the following provisions of the Intestates Widows and Children (Scotland) Act 1875**(b)**, namely:—

(*a*) section 3 (confirmation to small intestate estate);

(*b*) Schedule A (form of inventory and relative oath); and

(*c*) Schedule B (form of confirmation),

for the words "£10,000" there shall be substituted the words "£13,000".

3. In each of the following provisions of the Small Testate Estates (Scotland) Act 1876 **(c)**, namely:—

(*a*) section 3 (confirmation to small testate estate); and

(*b*) Schedule A (form of inventory and relative oath),

for the words "£10,000" there shall be substituted the words "£13,000".

New St Andrew's House,
Edinburgh.
8th November 1984.

George Younger,
One of Her Majesty's
Principal Secretaries of State.

(**a**) 1979 c. 22.

(**b**) 1875 c. 41; section 3 was amended by the Small Estates (Representation) Act 1961 (c. 37), section 1(1) and Schedule 1, paragraph 1(1), by the Administration of Estates Act 1971 (c. 25), section 12(1) and Schedule 2, Part I, and by the Finance Act 1975 (c. 7), sections 52(2), 59(5) and Schedule 13, Part I; section 3 was further amended and Schedules A and B were amended by section 1(1) of the Confirmation to Small Estates (Scotland) Act 1979.

(**c**) 1876 c. 24; section 3 was amended by the Small Estates (Representation) Act 1961, section 1(1) and Schedule 1, paragraph 2(1) and by the Administration of Estates Act 1971, section 12(1) and Schedule 2, Part I; section 3 was further amended and Schedule A was amended by section 1(2) of the Confirmation to Small Estates (Scotland) Act 1979.

EXPLANATORY NOTE

(This Note is not part of the Order.)

This order increases from £10,000 to £13,000 the limit of value of a deceased person's estate at or below which confirmation of executors may be obtained by the simplified procedures prescribed by the Intestates Widows and Children (Scotland) Act 1875 (for small intestate estates) and by the Small Testate Estates (Scotland) Act 1876 (for small testate estates).

STATUTORY INSTRUMENTS

1984 No. 1849

OFFSHORE INSTALLATIONS

The Offshore Installations (Safety Zones) (Revocation) (No. 67) Order 1984

Made - - - -	*26th November* 1984
Coming into Operation	*28th November* 1984

The Secretary of State, in exercise of the power conferred on him by section 21(1) of the Oil and Gas (Enterprise) Act 1982(**a**), and of all other powers enabling him in that behalf, hereby makes the following Order:—

1. This Order may be cited as the Offshore Installations (Safety Zones) (Revocation) (No. 67) Order 1984 and shall come into operation on 28th November 1984.

2. The Offshore Installations (Safety Zones) (No. 71) Order 1984(**b**) is hereby revoked.

Alick Buchanan-Smith,
Minister of State,
Department of Energy.

26th November 1984.

EXPLANATORY NOTE

(This Note is not part of the Order.)

This Order revokes the Offshore Installations (Safety Zones) (No. 71) Order 1984. The installation known as Glomar Biscay II which was protected by the safety zone established by that Order has been removed and accordingly that Order is no longer required.

(**a**) 1982 c. 23.   (**b**) S.I. 1984/1602.

STATUTORY INSTRUMENTS

1984 No. 1850

MUSEUMS AND GALLERIES

The Armed Forces Museums (Designation of Institutions) No. 2 Order 1984

Made - - - - -	*26th November* 1984
Laid before Parliament	*28th November* 1984
Coming into Operation	*19th December* 1984

Whereas the institutions specified in this Order are of a kind mentioned in section 30(1) of the National Heritage Act 1983 **(a)** ("the 1983 Act") and were, immediately before the making of this Order, staffed by persons at least one of whom was employed in the civil service of the State;

Now, therefore, the Secretary of State, in exercise of the powers conferred on him by section 31(1) of the 1983 Act and of all other powers enabling him in that behalf, hereby makes the following Order:—

Citation and commencement

1. This Order may be cited as the Armed Forces Museums (Designation of Institutions) No. 2 Order 1984 and shall come into operation on the 19th December 1984.

Designation of institutions

2. For the purposes of section 31 of the 1983 Act there are hereby designated, as institutions to which Schedule 2 of that Act shall have effect, the following institutions:—

The charity established by deed of trust dated 4th October 1973 as "the Portsmouth Royal Naval Museum".

The charity established by deed of trust dated 11th September 1963 as "the Submarine Branch Collection".

Michael Heseltine,
One of Her Majesty's Principal
Secretaries of State.

Dated 26th November 1984.

(a) 1983 c. 47.

EXPLANATORY NOTE

(This Note is not part of the Order.)

By Schedule 2 to the National Heritage Act 1983 the governing body of an institution, which has been duly designated by the Secretary of State under that Act, is required to offer, by such date as the Secretary of State may determine, employment to each person who was immediately before the date of designation employed in the civil service of the State for the purposes of that institution.

The terms of employment offered have to be such, that taken as a whole, they are no less favourable to the employee than those held by him in the civil service, and the offer has to remain open for 3 months. If the person does so change his employment he then enjoys continuity of employment and his employment with the designated institution is included as one to which a scheme under section 1 of the Superannuation Act 1972 (c. 11) can apply, and the Schedule to that Act is accordingly construed as if it included a reference to the institution. Disputes as to whether terms taken as a whole are less favourable may be referred to the industrial tribunal.

The institution may not be designated unless is satisfies the conditions provided for by section 31 of the Act that it has as a main object the collection, exhibition or retention of articles relating to the history and traditions of some section of the armed forces of the Crown, and that immediately prior to designation at least one of its staff was employed in the civil service.

This Order effects the necessary designation in the case of the Portsmouth Royal Naval Museum and the Royal Navy Submarine Museum.

STATUTORY INSTRUMENTS

1984 No. 1857

INCOME TAX

The Income Tax (Sub-contractors in the Construction Industry) Regulations 1984

Made - - - - 26th November 1984

Laid before the
House of Commons 29th November 1984

Coming into operation in accordance with Regulation 1

The Commissioners of Inland Revenue, in exercise of the powers conferred on them by sections 69 and 70 of the Finance (No. 2) Act 1975(**a**) and of all other powers enabling them in that behalf, hereby make the following Regulations:—

Citation and commencement

1.—(1) These Regulations may be cited as the Income Tax (Sub-contractors in the Construction Industry) Regulations 1984.

(2) These Regulations shall come into operation on 1st January 1985, with the exception of Regulation 4, which shall come into operation on 6th April 1985.

Interpretation

2. In these Regulations "the Principal Regulations" means the Income Tax (Sub-contractors in the Construction Industry) Regulations 1975(**b**).

Amendments to the Principal Regulations

3. In Regulation 9(1) of the Principal Regulations the words "(*a*) the greatest such amount which shall be recoverable summarily as a civil debt shall be £100 instead of £50; (*b*)" shall be omitted.

4. In Regulation 10(1) of the Principal Regulations, after the words "shall render to the" there shall be inserted:

"Inspector or, if so required, to the".

J. M. Green,
A. J. G. Isaac,
Two of the Commissioners of
Inland Revenue.

26th November 1984.

(**a**) 1975 c. 45.
(**b**) S.I. 1975/1960; a relevant amending instrument is S.I. 1982/1391.

EXPLANATORY NOTE

(This Note is not part of the Regulations.)

These Regulations: (1) abolish, with effect from 1st January 1985, the special limit previously provided in the Subcontractors in the Construction Industry Regulations for the amount recoverable by the Collector in the Magistrates' Courts in respect of deductions by contractors from payments to uncertificated subcontractors; this special limit was £100 instead of any amount less than £50 as provided for assessed tax generally by section 65, Taxes Management Act 1970 (c. 9); section 57, Finance Act 1984 (c. 43) amends section 65 by substituting £250 for £50 and these Regulations bring recovery by the Collector of deductions from subcontractors' payments into line with this new limit.

(2) provide that, with effect from 6th April 1985, the contractor's end-of-year return in respect of sub-contractors is to be rendered to the Inspector unless required to be rendered to the Collector (to whom all such returns are at present rendered).

STATUTORY INSTRUMENTS

1984 No. 1858

INCOME TAX

The Income Tax (Employments) (No. 14) Regulations 1984

Made - - - -   *26th November* 1984

Laid before the
House of Commons   *29th November* 1984

Coming into operation in accordance with Regulation 1

The Commissioners of Inland Revenue, in exercise of the powers conferred upon them by section 204 of the Income and Corporation Taxes Act 1970(a) and of all the powers enabling them in that behalf, hereby make the following Regulations:—

Citation and commencement

1.—(1) These Regulations may be cited as the Income Tax (Employments) (No. 14) Regulations 1984.

(2) These Regulations shall come into operation on 1st January 1985, with the exception of Regulation 4, which shall come into operation on 6th April 1985.

Interpretation

2. In these Regulations "the Principal Regulations" means the Income Tax (Employments) Regulations 1973(b).

Amendments to the Principal Regulations

3. In Regulation 28(1) of the Principal Regulations the words "(a) the greatest such amount which shall be recoverable summarily as a civil debt shall be £100 instead of £50; and (b)" shall be omitted.

4.—(1) In Regulation 30(1) of the Principal Regulations, after the words "shall render to the" there shall be inserted:

"Inspector or, if so required, to the".

(2) In Regulation 51(5) of the Principal Regulations, after the words "forthwith render to the" there shall be inserted:

"Inspector or, if so required, to the".

(a) 1970 c. 10.
(b) S.I. 1973/334; relevant amending instruments are S.I. 1981/44, 1982/66.

(3) In Regulation 51(6) of the Principal Regulations, after the words "render to the" there shall be inserted:

"Inspector, or if so required, to the".

J. M. Green,
A. J. G. Isaac,
Two of the Commissioners
of Inland Revenue.

26th November 1984.

EXPLANATORY NOTE

(This Note is not part of the Regulations.)

These Regulations: (1) abolish, with effect from 1st January 1985, the special limit previously provided in the PAYE Regulations for the amount of PAYE tax recoverable by the Collector from the employer in the Magistrates' Courts; this special limit was £100 instead of any amount less than £50 as provided for assessed tax generally by section 65, Taxes Management Act 1970 (c. 9); section 57, Finance Act 1984 (c. 43) amends section 65 by substituting £250 for £50 and these Regulations bring PAYE Collection into line with this new limit.

(2) provide that, with effect from 6th April 1985, the employer's end-of-year PAYE returns, and, where an employee's PAYE tax is being collected direct under the alternative procedure, that employee's returns, are to be rendered to the Inspector unless required to be rendered to the Collector (to whom these returns are at present rendered).

STATUTORY INSTRUMENTS

1984 No. 1859

COMPANIES

The Companies (Accounts and Audit) Regulations 1984

Made - - -	*28th November* 1984
Laid before Parliament	*3rd December* 1984

The Secretary of State, in exercise of his powers under section 454(1)*(b)* of the Companies Act 1948 (**a**), hereby makes the following Regulations:

1. These Regulations may be cited as the Companies (Accounts and Audit) Regulations 1984.

2.—(1) In paragraph 74A in Part VA of Schedule 8 to the Companies Act 1948(**b**), after subparagraph (3), there shall be added the following subparagraph—

"(4) Where in pursuance of the arrangement in question shares are allotted on different dates, the time of allotment for the purposes of subparagraphs (1)*(e)* and (3)*(a)* above shall be taken to be—

(*a*) if the other company becomes a subsidiary of the company as a result of the arrangement—

    (i) if the arrangement becomes binding only upon the fulfilment of a condition, the date upon which that condition is fulfilled; and

    (ii) in any other case, the date on which the other company becomes a subsidiary of the company;

(*b*) if the other company is a subsidiary of the company when the arrangement is proposed, the date of the first allotment pursuant to that arrangement."

(2) The subparagraph inserted in paragraph 74A of Schedule 8 by paragraph (1) of this Regulation shall also be inserted in paragraph 26A in Part IIIA of Schedule 8A to the Companies Act 1948 (**c**) as subparagraph (4) thereof.

Alexander Fletcher,
Parliamentary Under-Secretary of State,
Department of Trade and Industry.

28th November 1984.

(**a**) 1948 c.38; section 454(1) was substituted by the Companies Act 1981 (c.62).
(**b**) Part VA was inserted by S.I. 1982/1092.
(**c**) Part IIIA was inserted by S.I. 1982/1092.

EXPLANATORY NOTE

(This Note is not part of the Regulations.)

These Regulations determine the 'time of allotment' of shares for the purpose of calculating profits or losses of the allottee company which are required by paragraph 74A of Schedule 8 and paragraph 26A of Schedule 8A to the Companies Act 1948 to be disclosed in the accounts of the company making the allotment.

Those paragraphs require a company which enters into an arrangement for the acquisition of shares in another company to which section 37 of the Companies Act 1981 (merger relief) applies, to disclose certain particulars of the transaction, and of profits and losses of the other company. There are also requirements for the disclosure of particulars of disposals of fixed assets or shares in the other company, or disposals of shares in another company holding such assets or shares.

STATUTORY INSTRUMENTS

1984 No. 1860

COMPANIES

The Companies (Accounts) Regulations 1984

Made - - - -	*27th November* 1984
Laid before Parliament	*3rd December* 1984

The Secretary of State, in exercise of his powers under section 454(1)(*b*) of the Companies Act 1948(**a**), hereby makes the following Regulations:

1.—(1) These Regulations may be cited as the Companies (Accounts) Regulations 1984.

(2) In these Regulations, "the Act" means the Companies Act 1980(**b**).

2. At the end of section 54 of the Act there shall be added as subsections (8) and (9)—

"(8) Neither subsection (1)(*c*) nor subsection (2)(*c*) above applies in relation to any transaction or arrangement if—

(*a*) each party to the transaction or arrangement which is a member of the same group of companies (as defined in section 50(1) of this Act) as the company entered into the transaction or arrangement in the ordinary course of business, and

(*b*) the terms of the transaction or arrangement are not less favourable to any such party than it would be reasonable to expect if the interest mentioned in that subsection had not been an interest of a person who was a director of the company or of its holding company.

(9) Neither subsection (1)(*c*) nor subsection (2)(*c*) above applies in relation to any transaction or arrangement if:

(*a*) the company is a member of a group of companies (as defined in section 50(1) of this Act), and

(*b*) either the company is a wholly-owned subsidiary or no body corporate (other than the company or a subsidiary of the company) which is a member of the group of companies which includes the company's ultimate holding company was a party to the transaction or arrangement, and

---

(**a**) 1948 c. 38; section 454(1) was substituted by the Companies Act 1981 (c. 62).
(**b**) 1980 c. 22.

(c) the director in question was at some time during the relevant period associated with the company, and

(d) the material interest of the director in question in the transaction or arrangement would not have arisen if he had not been associated with the company at any time during the relevant period."

3.—(1) Section 55 of the Companies Act 1980 shall be renumbered as subsection (1).

(2) At the beginning of subsection (1) there shall be inserted—

"Subject to subsection (2) below".

(3) After subsection (1) there shall be added as subsection (2)—

"(2) Paragraphs (c) to (f) of subsection (1) do not apply in the case of a loan or quasi-loan made or agreed to be made by a company to or for a body corporate which is either—

(a) a body corporate of which that company is a wholly-owned subsidiary, or

(b) a wholly-owned subsidiary of a body corporate of which that company is a wholly-owned subsidiary, or

(c) a wholly-owned subsidiary of that company,

if particulars of that loan, quasi-loan or agreement therefor would not have been required to be included in that company's annual accounts if the first-mentioned body corporate had not been associated with a director of that company at any time during the relevant period."

Alexander Fletcher,
Parliamentary Under-Secretary of State,
Department of Trade and Industry.

27th November 1984.

EXPLANATORY NOTE

(This Note is not part of the Regulations.)

These Regulations:

(*a*) amend section 54 of the Companies Act 1980 so as to exempt from disclosure:

    (i) any transaction in which a director has a material interest if that transaction is entered into at arm's length and in the ordinary course of business;

    (ii) any transaction between members of a group of companies which would have been disclosable only because of a director's being associated with the contracting companies, provided no minority interests in the reporting company are affected;

(*b*) amend section 55 of the Companies Act 1980 to reduce the disclosure required when one member of a group of companies carries out certain financial transactions on behalf of other members of the group.

STATUTORY INSTRUMENTS

1984 No. 1861

MEDICINES

The Medicines (Exemptions from Restrictions on the Retail Sale or Supply of Veterinary Drugs) Order 1984

Made - - - -	*26th November* 1984
Laid before Parliament	*5th December* 1984
Coming into Operation	*1st January* 1985

The Secretary of State concerned with health in England, the Secretaries of State respectively concerned with health and with agriculture in Scotland and in Wales, the Minister of Agriculture, Fisheries and Food, the Department of Health and Social Services for Northern Ireland, and the Department of Agriculture for Northern Ireland, acting jointly, in exercise of the powers conferred by sections 57(1), (2), (2A) and 129(4) of the Medicines Act 1968 (a) and now vested in them (b), and of all the powers enabling them in that behalf, after consulting such organisations as appear to them to be representative of interests likely to be substantially affected by the following order in accordance with section 129(6) of the said Act and with the consent of the Treasury, hereby make the following order:—

Title and commencement

1. This order may be cited as the Medicines (Exemptions from Restrictions on the Retail Sale or Supply of Veterinary Drugs) Order 1984 and shall come into operation on 1st January 1985.

Interpretation

2.—(1) In this order, unless the context otherwise requires—

"the Act" means the Medicines Act 1968;

"agricultural requisites" means things used in the cultivation of the soil or in the keeping of animals for the production of food or as game and equipment used in or for the collection of produce from animals kept for the production of food and things used for the maintenance of such equipment, and includes any protective clothing but does not include any other kind of human apparel;

"the Department" means the Department of Health and Social Services for Northern Ireland;

"the Department's register" means the register of merchants in veterinary drugs kept by the Department under Article 3(7);

(a) 1968 c.67; section 57(2A) was inserted by section 14 of the Animal Health and Welfare Act 1984 (c.40).

(b) In the case of the Secretaries of State concerned with health in England and Wales by virtue of S.I. 1969/388, in the case of the Secretary of State concerned with agriculture in Wales by virtue of S.I. 1978/272 and in the case of the Northern Ireland Departments by virtue of section 40 of, and Schedule 5 to, the Northern Ireland Constitution Act 1973 (c.36) and section 1(3) of, and paragraph 2(1)(b) of, Schedule 1 to, the Northern Ireland Act 1974 (c.28).

"dosage unit" means—

(a) where a veterinary drug is in the form of a tablet or capsule or is an article in some other pharmaceutical form that tablet, capsule or other similar article, and

(b) where a veterinary drug is not in any such form, the quantity of the drug which is used as the unit by reference to which the dose of the drug is measured;

"external use" means application to the skin, hair, fur, feathers, scales, hoof, horn, ear, eye, mouth or mucosa of the throat or prepuce, when local action only is necessary and extensive systemic absorption is unlikely to occur;

"maximum strength" means either the maximum quantity of the substance by weight or volume contained in a dosage unit of a veterinary drug or the maximum percentage of the substance contained in a veterinary drug calculated in terms of weight in weight, weight in volume, volume in weight or volume in volume, as appropriate;

"the Minister" means the Minister of Agriculture, Fisheries and Food;

"qualifying business" means a business in respect of which more than one half of the total sales for its last accounting period was derived from the retail sale of agricultural requisites;

"self-service methods" means any method of sale which allows a purchaser to help himself on or before payment;

"sell by retail" includes offer or expose for sale by retail and supply in circumstances corresponding to retail sale, and cognate expressions shall be construed accordingly;

"the Society" means the Pharmaceutical Society of Great Britain;

"the Society's register" means the register of merchants in veterinary drugs kept by the Society under Article 3(7);

"a specially authorised person" means, in relation to a veterinary drug, either—

(a) a person specially authorised, by virtue of a direction of the licensing authority under Article 3(1) of the Medicines (Exemptions from Licences) (Special and Transitional Cases) Order 1971 **(a)** , to assemble that drug otherwise than in accordance with a manufacturer's licence; or

(b) a person specially authorised by the product licence in respect of that drug to sell the drug under the alternative product name specified in the licence;

"veterinary drug on a general sale list" means a veterinary drug of a description, or falling within a class, specified in an order under section 51 of the Act which is for the time being in force.

(2) A reference in this order to a numbered Article or Schedule is to the Article of, or Schedule to, this order which bears that number.

Exemption for merchants in veterinary drugs

3.—(1) The restrictions imposed by section 52 of the Act (restrictions on sale or supply of medicinal products not on a general sale list) shall not apply to the sale by retail of any veterinary drug not on a general sale list by the

---

(a) S.I. 1971/1450.

holder of the product licence in respect thereof, by a specially authorised person or by a person who is for the time being carrying on a qualifying business, if—

   (*a*) that veterinary drug either—

      (i) is a veterinary drug consisting of or contained in a medicinal product in respect of which there has been granted a product licence, being a licence of right and is not on a general sale list by reason of its consisting of or containing one or more of the substances classified in the first column and specified in the second column of Part A of Schedule 1, or

      (ii) is specified in the second column of Part B of Schedule 1, and

   (*b*) the conditions contained in this Article are complied with.

(2) No veterinary drug such as is described in paragraph (1)(*a*) (i) or (ii) above shall be sold by retail except—

   (*a*) in the container in which it was made up for sale by the manufacturer or, as the case may be, the assembler of the drug;

   (*b*) in a container which has not been opened since the drug was made up for sale in it;

   (*c*) on premises which are occupied by, and under the control of, the seller at the time of sale and which are capable of being closed so as to exclude the public; and

   (*d*) to a person whom the seller knows, or has reasonable cause to believe, to be a person who has in his charge or maintains animals for the purposes of, and in the course of carrying on, a business, either as his sole business activity or as a part of his business activities;

except that, when a person has lawfully purchased a veterinary drug on the premises of the seller, condition *(c)* above shall not apply to the subsequent delivery of that drug to/that person.

(3) No veterinary drug such as is described in paragraph (1)(*a*) (i) or (ii) above shall be sold by retail by self-service methods.

(4) Where in relation to a veterinary drug containing one or more of the substances classified in the first column and listed in the second column of Part A of Schedule 1—

   (*a*) a maximum strength or concentration is specified in the third column of the said Part A, that drug shall not be sold by retail except in containers or packages labelled so as to show a strength or concentration not exceeding that so specified;

   (*b*) a pharmaceutical form is specified in the fourth column of the said Part A, that drug shall not be sold by retail except in the form so specified;

   (*c*) a form of administration is specified in the said fourth column, that drug shall not be sold by retail except for use in the form so specified;

   (*d*) any other restriction is specified in the fifth column of the said Part A, that drug shall not be sold by retail except in compliance with the restriction so specified.

(5)(*a*) In respect of any sale by retail of any veterinary drug such as is described in paragraph (1)(*a*) (i) or (ii) above the seller shall make a record of the sale containing the particulars specified in sub-paragraph *(b)* below and shall keep such record for a period of two years from the date of the sale.

(b) The particulars referred to in sub-paragraph *(a)* above are—

  (i) the date on which the veterinary drug was sold;

  (ii) the name, quantity and, except where it is apparent from the name, the pharmaceutical form and strength of the veterinary drug sold; and

  (iii) the name and address of the person to whom the veterinary drug was sold.

(6) No person shall, in the course of a qualifying business carried on by him, sell by retail any veterinary drug such as is described in paragraph (1)*(a)* (i) or (ii) above unless his name is entered in the Society's register or the Department's register in respect of the premises on which the drug is sold.

(7) The Society and the Department shall keep, for the purposes of paragraph (6) above, a register of persons as being persons entitled, in the course of qualifying businesses carried on by them, to sell by retail on premises in respect of which their names are entered in the register, any veterinary drug such as is described in paragraph (1)*(a)* (i) or (ii) above free from the restrictions imposed by section 52 of the Act, if and so long as the conditions contained in this Article are complied with.

(8) Where a person who, whilst carrying on a qualifying business elsewhere than in Northern Ireland, makes an application in writing to the Society for his name to be entered in the Society's register in respect of any premises on which any veterinary drug such as is described in paragraph (1)*(a)* (i) or (ii) above is to be sold by him in the course of that qualifying business, the Society, shall, subject to paragraphs (12) and (13) below, enter his name in the Society's register in respect of those premises.

(9) Where a person who, whilst carrying on a qualifying business in Northern Ireland, makes an application in writing to the Department for his name to be entered in the Department's register in respect of any premises on which any veterinary drug such as is described in paragraph (1)*(a)* (i) or (ii) above is to be sold by him in the course of that qualifying business, the Department shall, subject to paragraphs (12) and (13) below, enter his name in the Department's register in respect of those premises.

(10) Subject to paragraphs (14) and (15) below a person whose name is entered in the Society's register or the Department's register in respect of any premises shall, in order to retain his name on the register in respect of those premises in any year subsequent to the year in which his name is first entered in it, in the month of January in any such year make an application in writing to the Society or the Department (as the case may be) for his name to be retained in the Society's register or the Department's register (as the case may be) in respect of those premises.

(11) There shall be paid to the Society or the Department in respect of the entry or the retention in the Society's register or the Department's register (as the case may be) of the name of any person in respect of any premises a fee of £55.00.

(12) The Society or the Department shall refuse to enter in the Society's register or the Department's register (as the case may be) the name of any person in respect of any premises unless that person—

  (a) has paid to the Society or the Department (as the case may be) the fee specified in paragraph (11) above for the entry of his name in the register; and

(b) has given to the Society or the Department (as the case may be) an undertaking in writing that he will comply with the provisions of the Code of Practice for Merchants Selling or Supplying Veterinary Drugs dated 30th October 1984 and published by the Ministry of Agriculture, Fisheries and Food (being a code relating to the sale or supply of such veterinary drugs as are described in paragraphs (1)(a) (i) and (ii) above).

(13) The Society, with the approval of the Minister, or the Department, with the approval of the Department of Agriculture for Northern Ireland, may refuse to enter in the Society's register or the Department's register (as the case may be) the name of any person in respect of any premises if, in the opinion of the Society or the Department (as the case may be), the premises are unsuitable for the storage or safekeeping of any veterinary drug such as is described in paragraph (1)(a) (i) or (ii) above.

(14) The Society or the Department shall refuse to retain in the Society's register or the Department's register (as the case may be) the name of any person in respect of any premises unless that person has paid to the Society or the Department (as the case may be) the fee specified in paragraph (11) above for the retention of his name in the register.

(15) The Society, with the approval of the Minister, or the Department, with the approval of the Department of Agriculture for Northern Ireland, may refuse to retain in, or may remove from, the Society's register or the Department's register (as the case may be) the name of any person in respect of any premises if, in the opinion of the Society or the Department (as the case may be),—

(a) that person has failed to observe any of the provisions of the code of practice referred to in paragraph (12)(b) above; or

(b) the conditions under which any veterinary drug such as is described in paragraph (1)(a) (i) or (ii) above is sold by retail on the premises or under which it is stored on the premises prior to retail sale thereon, are unsuitable for that purpose.

(16) In paragraph (2)(c) above "premises" includes a stall of a permanent nature situated at a market or an agricultural showground.

Exemptions in respect of veterinary drugs to be incorporated in animal feeding stuffs

4.—(1) The restrictions imposed by section 52 of the Act shall not apply to the sale by retail of any veterinary drug not on a general sale list by the holder of the product licence in respect thereof, by a specially authorised person or by a person for the time being carrying on a business wholly or mainly comprising either the manufacture of animal feeding stuffs for sale or the sale or supply in bulk of veterinary drugs, if—

(a) that veterinary drug either—

(i) is a veterinary drug consisting of or contained in a medicinal product in respect of which there has been granted a product licence, being a licence of right and is not on a general sale list by reason only of its consisting of or containing one or more substances classified in the first column and specified in the second column of Part A of Schedule 2 or specified in Part A of Schedule 3, or

(ii) is specified in the second column of Part B of Schedule 2 or the second column of Part B of Schedule 3, and *(b)* the conditions set out in paragraphs (2) to (6) below are complied with.

(2) No veterinary drug such as is described in paragraph (1)*(a)* (i) or (ii) above shall be sold by retail except—

  (a) for incorporation in animal feeding stuffs; and

  (b) to a person whom the seller knows, or has reasonable cause to believe, to be a person carrying on a business wholly or mainly comprising the manufacture of animal feeding stuffs for sale.

(3) No veterinary drug such as is described in paragraph (1)*(a)* (i) or (ii) above shall be sold by retail by self-service methods.

(4)*(a)* In respect of any sale by retail of any veterinary drug such as is described in paragraph (1)*(a)* (i) or (ii) above the seller shall make a record of the sale containing the particulars specified in sub-paragraph *(b)* below and shall keep such record for a period of two years from the date of the sale.

  (b) The particulars referred to in sub-paragraph *(a)* above are—

    (i) the date on which the veterinary drug was sold;

    (ii) the name, quantity and, except where it is apparent from the name, the pharmaceutical form and strength of the veterinary drug sold; and

    (iii) the name and address of the person to whom the veterinary drug was sold.

(5) No person shall, in the course of a business carried on by him, sell by retail any veterinary drug such as is described in paragraph (1)*(a)* (i) or (ii) above unless—

  (a) before making any such sale he, or a previous owner of the business, has notified the Society, or in the case of a business carried on in Northern Ireland, the Department, of the relevant particulars;

  (b) every twelve months after the first notification, whether made by him or by a previous owner, he notifies the Society or the Department, as appropriate, of the relevant particulars; and

  (c) he notifies the Society or the Department, as appropriate, of any change in the relevant particulars which has occurred since the last notification thereof as soon after such change occurs as is reasonably practicable.

(6) In paragraph (5) above "the relevant particulars", in relation to a business, means the name of the business and the address, or, where appropriate, the location of every premises on which, during the course of the carrying on of that business, veterinary drugs such as are described in paragraph (1)*(a)* (i) or (ii) above are being, or are during the next twelve months to be, sold.

Exemptions for merchants in horse wormers

5.—(1) The restrictions imposed by section 52 of the Act shall not apply during the period referred to in paragraph (15) below to the sale by retail of any veterinary drug not on general sale list by the holder of the product licence in respect thereof, by a specially authorised person or by a person who is for the time being carrying on a qualifying business or a saddlery business if—

(a) that veterinary drug is specified in the second column of Schedule 4, and

(b) the conditions contained in this Article are complied with.

(2) No veterinary drug such as is described in paragraph (1)(a) above shall be sold by retail except—

(a) in the container in which it was made up for sale by the manufacturer or, as the case may be, the assembler of the drug;

(b) in a container which has not been opened since the drug was made up for sale in it;

(c) on premises which are occupied by, and under the control of, the seller at the time of sale and which are capable of being closed so as to exclude the public; and

(d) to a person whom the seller knows, or has reasonable cause to believe, to be a person who has in his charge horses or ponies;

except that, where a person has lawfully purchased a veterinary drug on the premises of the seller, condition (c) above shall not apply to the subsequent delivery of that drug to that person.

(3) No veterinary drug such as is described in paragraph (1)(a) above shall be sold by retail by self-service methods.

(4)(a) In respect of any sale by retail of any veterinary drug such as is described in paragraph (1)(a) above the seller shall make a record of the sale containing the particulars specified in sub-paragraph (b) below and shall keep such record for a period of two years from the date of the sale.

(b) The particulars referred to in sub-paragraph (a) above are—

(i) the date on which the veterinary drug was sold; and

(ii) the name, quantity and, except when it is apparent from the name, the pharmaceutical form and strength of the veterinary drug sold.

(5) No person shall, in the course of a qualifying business or a saddlery business carried on by him, sell by retail any veterinary drug such as is described in paragraph (1)(a) above unless his name is entered in the register kept by the Society or the Department under paragraph (6) below in respect of the premises on which the drug is sold.

(6) The Society and the Department shall keep, for the purposes of paragraph (5) above, a register of persons as being persons entitled, in the course of qualifying businesses or saddlery businesses carried on by them, to sell by retail on premises in respect of which their names are entered in the register, any veterinary drug such as is described in paragraph (1)(a) above free from the restrictions imposed by section 52 of the Act, if and so long as the conditions contained in this Article are complied with.

(7) Where a person who, whilst carrying on a qualifying business or a saddlery business elsewhere than in Northern Ireland, makes an application in writing to the Society for his name to be entered in the register kept by the Society under paragraph (6) above in respect of any premises on which any veterinary drug such as is described in paragraph (1)(a) above is to be sold by him in the course of that qualifying business or saddlery business, the Society shall, subject to paragraphs (11) and (12) below, enter his name in that register in respect of those premises.

(8) Where a person who, whilst carrying on a qualifying business or a saddlery business in Northern Ireland, makes an application in writing to the Department for his name to be entered in the register kept by the Department under paragraph (6) above in respect of any premises on which any veterinary drug such as is described in paragraph (1)(a) above is to be sold by him in the course of that qualifying business or saddlery business, the Department shall, subject to paragraphs (11) and (12) below, enter his name in that register in respect of those premises.

(9) Subject to paragraphs (13) and (14) below a person whose name is entered in the register kept by the Society or the Department under paragraph (6) above in respect of any premises shall, in order to retain his name on the register in respect of those premises in any year subsequent to the year in which his name was first entered in it, in the month of January in any such year make an application in writing to the Society or the Department (as the case may be) for his name to be retained on that register in respect of those premises.

(10) There shall be paid to the Society or the Department in respect of the entry in, or the retention in, the register kept by the Society or the Department (as the case may be) under paragraph (6) above of the name of any person in respect of any premises, a fee of £25.00, except that no such fee shall be payable in respect of a person whose name is for the time being entered in the Society's register or the Department's register (as the case may be) in respect of those premises as being a person entitled to sell thereon, during the course of a qualifying business carried on by him, any veterinary drug such as is described in paragraph (1)(a) (i) or (ii) of Article 3.

(11) The Society or the Department shall refuse to enter in the register kept by the Society or the Department (as the case may be) under paragraph (6) above the name of any person in respect of any premises unless that person—

> (a) has paid to the Society or the Department (as the case may be) the fee specified in paragraph (10) above for the entry of his name in the register; and

> (b) has given to the Society or the Department (as the case may be) an undertaking in writing that he will comply with the provisions of the Code of Practice for Saddlers Selling or Supplying Horse Wormers dated 30th October 1984 and published by the Ministry of Agriculture, Fisheries and Food (being a code of practice relating to the sale or supply of such veterinary drugs as are described in paragraph (1)(a) above).

(12) The Society, with the approval of the Minister, or the Department, with the approval of the Department of Agriculture for Northern Ireland, may refuse to enter in the register kept by the Society or the Department (as the case may be) the name of the person in respect of any premises if, in the opinion of the Society or the Department (as the case may be), the premises are unsuitable for the storage or safekeeping of any veterinary drug such as is described in paragraph (1)(a) above.

(13) The Society or the Department shall refuse to retain in the register kept by the Society or the Department (as the case may be) under paragraph (6) above the name of any person in respect of any premises unless that person has paid to the Society or the Department (as the case may be) the fee specified in paragraph (11) above for the retention of his name in the register.

(14) The Society, with the approval of the Minister, or the Department, with the approval of the Department of Agriculture for Northern Ireland,

may refuse to retain in, or may remove from, the register kept by the Society or the Department (as the case may be) under paragraph (6) above the name of any person in respect of any premises if, in the opinion of the Society or the Department (as the case may be),—

(a) that person has failed to observe any of the provisions of the code of practice referred to in paragraph (11)(b) above; or

(b) the conditions under which any veterinary drug such as is described in paragraph (1)(a) above is sold by retail on the premises or under which it is stored on the premises prior to retail sale thereon, are unsuitable for that purpose.

(15) The period referred to in paragraph (1) above is that of 3 years from the date of the coming into operation of this order.

(16) In paragraph (2)(c) above "premises" includes a stall of a permanent nature situated at a market or agricultural showground.

(17) For the purposes of this Article—

(a) "saddlery business" means a business in respect of which more than one half of the total sales for its last accounting period was derived from the retail sale of saddlery requisites; and

(b) "saddlery requisites" means equipment used in the keeping of horses or ponies and things used for the maintenance of such equipment and includes any human apparel used in the keeping of horses or ponies.

Exemption for supply, subsequent to sale, by pharmacists

6. The restrictions imposed by section 52 of the Act on the supply of medicinal products shall not apply to the supply in circumstances corresponding to retail sale of a veterinary drug such as is described in paragraph (1)(a) (i) or (ii) of Article 4 by a pharmacist, or his agent, to the person to whom the pharmacist has, in accordance with the provisions of the said section 52, sold the drug by retail.

Exemption in cases involving another's default

7.—(1) The restrictions imposed by section 52 of the Act shall not apply to the sale by retail, in compliance with the conditions contained in Article 3, of a veterinary drug by a person for the time being carrying on a qualifying business, which drug that person, having exercised all due diligence, on reasonable grounds believes to be a veterinary drug such as is described in paragraph (1)(a) (i) or (ii) of Article 3, but which, due to the act or default of another person, is not such a veterinary drug.

(2) The restrictions imposed by section 52 of the Act shall not apply to the sale by retail, in compliance with the conditions set out in paragraphs (2) to (6) of Article 4, of a veterinary drug by a person for the time being carrying on a business as is described in Article 4(1), which drug that person, having exercised all due diligence, on reasonable grounds believes to be a veterinary drug such as is described in paragraph (1)(a) (i) or (ii) of Article 4 but which, due to the act or default of another person, is not such a veterinary drug.

(3) The restrictions imposed by section 52 of the Act shall not apply to the sale by retail, in compliance with the conditions set out in Article 5, of a veterinary drug by a person for the time being carrying on a qualifying business or a saddlery business (as defined in Article 5(17)), which drug that person, having exercised all due diligence, on reasonable grounds believes to

be a veterinary drug such as is described in paragraph (1)*(a)* of Article 5, but which, due to the act or default of another person is not such a veterinary drug.

Revocation

8. The orders listed in Schedule 5 are hereby revoked.

Norman Fowler,
Secretary of State for
Social Services.

26th November 1984.

George Younger,
Secretary of State for Scotland.

14th November 1984.

Nicholas Edwards,
Secretary of State for Wales.

15th November 1984.

In Witness whereof the Official Seal of the Minister of Agriculture, Fisheries and Food is hereunto affixed on 12th November 1984.

Michael Jopling,
Minister of Agriculture,
Fisheries and Food.

Sealed with the Official Seal of the Department of Health and Social Services for Northern Ireland this 15th day of November 1984.

Maurice N. Hayes,
Permanent Secretary.

Sealed with the Official Seal of the Department of Agriculture for Northern Ireland this 15th day of November 1984.

W. H. Jack,
Permanent Secretary.

We consent,

A. G. Hamilton,
T. Garel Jones,
Two of the Lords Commissioners
of Her Majesty's Treasury.

14th November 1984.

Article 3

SCHEDULE 1

PART A

LICENCE OF RIGHT VETERINARY DRUGS

Group/Class	Substance	Maximum strength or concentration	Pharmaceutical form or route of administration	Other restrictions
1. GROWTH PROMOTERS	Bacitracin Zinc	6,300,000 i.u./kg	Incorporation in feed	
	Bambermycin	30 g/kg	Incorporation in feed	
	Nitrovin		Incorporation in feed	
	Tylosin Phosphate		Incorporation in feed	For pigs
	Virginiamycin	20 g/kg	Incorporation in feed	
2. COCCIDIOSTATS	Amprolium Hydrochloride			
	Clopidol	33%		
	Decoquinate	80 g/kg	Incorporation in feed	
	Diaveridine			
	Dinitolmide	33%		
	Ethopabate			
	Methyl Benzoquate	1.75%	Incorporation in feed	When combined with not more than 20.6% of Clopidol
	Pyrimethamine		Incorporation in feed	For broiler chickens at levels not exceeding 5 ppm
	Robenidine			

Group/Class	Substance	Maximum strength or concentration	Pharmaceutical form or route of administration	Other restrictions
	Sulphaquinoxaline	12%	Incorporation in feed	When combined with not more than 20% of Amprolium hydrochloride and 1% of Ethopabate with or without 1% of Pyrimethamine
3. ANTI-BLACKHEAD PREPARATIONS	Acinitrazole			
	Aminonitrothiazole			
	Nifursol			
4. SHEEP DIPS AND ECTO-PARASITICIDES	Allethrin			
	Amitraz		External use only	
	Benzuldazic Acid, Sodium Salt			
	Benzyl Benzoate		External use only	
	Bromocyclen			
	Bromophos			
	Bucarpolate			
	Butacarb			
	Carbaryl			
	Carbophenothion			
	Chlorfenvinphos			
	Chlorpyrifos			
	Coal Tar Phenols		External use only	
	Coumaphos			
	Crotoxyphos			
	Cresol	4%		

Group/Class	Substance	Maximum strength or concentration	Pharmaceutical form or route of administration	Other restrictions
4. SHEEP DIPS AND ECTO-PARASITICIDES (continued)	Cresylic Acid Derris Resins Diazinon Dichlofenthion Dicophane Dioxathion Dursban Fenchlorphos Fenitrothion Gamma BHC Iodofenphos Lethane Malathion Phosalone Pyractone Pyrimithate Rotenone		External use only	
5. ANTHELMINTICS	Bephenium and its salts Bunamidine and its salts Cyacetazide Dichlorvos Diethyl-carbamazine and its salts			

Group/Class	Substance	Maximum strength or concentration	Pharmaceutical form or route of administration	Other restrictions
	Haloxon			
	Levamisole and its salts			
	Mebendazole			
	Metriphonate			
	Morantel and its salts			
	Naphthalophos			
	Niclosamide			
	Parbendazole			
	Phenothiazine			
	Piperazine Carbon Disulphide Complex			
	Pyrantel and its salts			
	Sodium Glycarsamate			
	Tetramisole and its salts			
	Thiabendazole			
	Thiophanate			
6. MILK FEVER PREPARATIONS	Calcium borogluconate Injection whether or not containing all or any of the following substances:			

Group/Class	Substance	Maximum strength or concentration	Pharmaceutical form or route of administration	Other restrictions
6. MILK FEVER PREPARATIONS (continued)	Dextrose, Magnesium and Phosphorus			
7. WARBLE FLY DRESSINGS	Crufomate Famphur Fenchlorphos Fenthion Metriphonate Prolate			
8. LIVER FLUKE REMEDIES	Brotianide Diamphenethide Hexachloroethane Hexachlorophane Nitroxynil and its salts Oxyclozanide Rafoxanide Tribromsalan			
9. SHEEP AND CATTLE CLOSTRIDIAL VACCINES AND ANTISERA	Black Disease Antisera and Vaccines Blackleg (Blackquarter) Vaccines and Antisera			

Group/Class	Substance	Maximum strength or concentration	Pharmaceutical form or route of administration	Other restrictions
	Braxy Vaccines and Antisera			
	Enterotoxaemia Vaccines and Antisera			
	Lamb Dysentry Antisera and Vaccines			
	Pulpy Kidney Vaccines and Antisera			
	Struck Vaccines and Antisera			
	Tetanus Toxoids			
	Combinations of two or more of Braxy, Blackleg (Black-quarter), Lamb Dysentry, Pulpy Kidney, Enterotoxaemia, Struck, Tetanus, Black Disease and Pasteurella Vaccines			
10. POULTRY VACCINES	Avian Encephalomyelitis Vaccine (Living and Inactivated)			

Group/Class	Substance	Maximum strength or concentration	Pharmaceutical form or route of administration	Other restrictions
10. POULTRY VACCINES (continued)	Duck Hepatitis Vaccines (Living)			
	Fowl Pox Vaccines			
	Fowl Typhoid Vaccines (Salmonella gallinarum)			
	Infectious Bronchitis Vaccines (Living and Inactivated)			
	Infectious Bursal Disease Vaccines			
	Infectious Laryngotracheitis Vaccines (Living)			
	Marek's Disease Vaccines			
	Newcastle Disease Vaccines (Living and Inactivated)			
	Combinations of Newcastle Disease Vaccines and Avian Encephalomyelitis Vaccines			

Group/Class	Substance	Maximum strength or concentration	Pharmaceutical form or route of administration	Other restrictions
	Combinations of Newcastle Disease Vaccines with Infectious Bronchitis Vaccines			
	Pasteurella Vaccines			
11. ERYSIPELAS VACCINES	Avian Erysipelas Vaccines			
	Swine Erysipelas Vaccines			
12. SALMONELLA AND E. COLI VACCINES	E. Coli Vaccines (Killed)			
	Salmonella Vaccines (Killed)			
	E. Coli and Salmonella Sero Vaccines			
13. OTHER SHEEP AND CATTLE VACCINES	Foot Rot Vaccines			
	Louping Ill Vaccines (Killed)			
	Ovine Enzootic Abortion Vaccines			
	Pasteurella Vaccines (Killed)			
	Pneumonia Combined Vaccines (Pasteurella)			

Group/Class	Substance	Maximum strength or concentration	Pharmaceutical form or route of administration	Other restrictions
14. MISCELLANEOUS VACCINES	Botulism Vaccines (Mink) Combinations of E. Coli, Salmonella and Pasteurella Vaccines (Killed) Pigeon Pox Vaccines (Living)			
15. SULPHANILAMIDE SURFACE WOUND DRESSINGS	This group comprises powdered surface wound dressings containing not more than 5% of sulphanilamide for application to farm animals			
16. LOCAL ANAESTHETICS	This group comprises injections containing not more than 5% of procaine hydrochloride, lignocaine, or lignocaine hydrochloride with or without not more than 0.002% of adrenaline,			

Group/Class	Substance	Maximum strength or concentration	Pharmaceutical form or route of administration	Other restrictions
16. LOCAL ANAESTHETICS (continued)	adrenaline acid tartrate or noradrenaline			
17. OTHERS	Ammonia Solution Conc.	4%		
	Broxyquinoline			
	Butafosfan			
	Butyl Amino Benzoate		Non-parenteral use only	
	Butynorate			
	Clioquinol	5%		
	Cobalt Carbonate			For use only in anthelmintics
	Cobalt Oxide			For use only in combination with anthelmintics and in ruminal pellets
	Copper its inorganic salts and organic preparations		Non-parenteral use only	
	Creosote			
	Dextrose Injection			
	Dill, Oil of		Internal use	
	Halquinol	5%		
	Iron organic complexes with or without Vitamin B_{12}			

Group/Class	Substance	Maximum strength or concentration	Pharmaceutical form or route of administration	Other restrictions
17. OTHERS (continued)	Magnesium salts		(1) Subcutaneous injection (2) Slow intravenous injection	(2) When combined with any of calcium borogluconate, phosphorus or dextrose
	Menandione Sodium Bisulphite Menandione Dimethyl Pyrimidinol Bisulphite Phenol Poloxalene Turpentine Vitamin A Vitamin B group	40%	Internal use	
	Vitamin D$_2$ Vitamin D$_3$ Vitamin E Injection			Excluding:— (1) preparations recommended for administration by intravenous route and (2) those recommended for use for conditions requiring a veterinary diagnosis

SCHEDULE 1   Article 3

PART B

VETERINARY DRUGS

Product Licence No.   Name of Product*

1. Growth Promoters
    PL 4131/4000 Advantage with Romensin^R
    PL 0095/4026 { Avotan 50 Avoparcin
                  { Avotan 50
    PL 0095/4036 Avotan 100
    PL 0095/4028 Avotan 50c Avoparcin
    PL 0010/4043 Bayo-n-ox 10% Premix
    PL 3832/4031 Eskalin 100
    PL 0002/4045 } Eskalin 500
    PL 3832/4017
    PL 0002/4055 } Eskalin S-400
    PL 3832/4021
    PL 0029/4102 Fedan 10% Premix
    PL 0086/4124 Flavomycin 40
    PL 0086/4137 Flavomycin 50
    PL 3405/4016 Nitrovin
    PL 3405/4018 Nitrovin – 20
    PL 2592/4075 Nitrozone 25
    PL 4869/4000 Panazone 250–Nitrovin
    PL 0095/4007 Payzone 50 MA Nitrovin Milk Replacer Additive
    PL 4188/4008 Pentazone 250
    PL 0006/4052 Romensin (Monensin Sodium) Premix
    PL 2969/4006 Rumevite with Romensin
    PL 0012/4170 SPIRA 200
    PL 0006/4055 Tylamix Premix 100 g/kg
    PL 0006/4062 Tylamix Premix 250 g/kg
    PL 3405/4007 Tylosin 100 Premix
    PL 3405/4002 ZB 100
    PL 3405/4015 ZB – 100
    PL 3405/4005 ZB 150
    PL 3734/4000 Zinc Bacitracin Dumex Feed Grade
    PL 3734/4001 Zinc Bacitracin "Dumex" 150 Premix
    PL 0109/4001 Zinc Bacitracin Premix

2. Implants
    PL 0829/4119 Ralgro

3. Coccidiostats
    PL 0025/4035 Arpocox
    PL 0031/4011 Avatec Premix
    PL 3405/4017 Clopidol
    PL 0109/4000 Dinormix SR 25
    PL 4188/4004 { Dinitolmide (DOT) 3.5 – Dinitro-ortho-toluamide
                  { Unicox Pure
    PL 4869/4005 DOT
    PL 0109/4002 DOT (dinitolmide)
    PL 1598/4032 DOT Premix 12.5%
    PL 1598/4033 DOT Premix 25%

---

* Alternative product names used by specially authorised persons are not shown.

Items shown in italics did not appear in the Medicines (Exemptions from Restrictions on the Retail Sale or Supply of Veterinary Drugs) Order 1979 as amended.

Product Licence No.   Name of Product

3. Coccidiostats (continued)

PL 0006/4047	{ Elancoban { Elancoban Premix
PL 3405/4006	{ Elancoban Premix { Monensin 200
PL 0621/4015	Lerbek
PL 0006/4061	Monteban 100 Premix
PL 0025/4019	Nicrazin (Premix)
PL 0086/4135	Sacox 60 Premix
PL 0086/4117	Stenorol
PL 0025/4003	Supacox

4. Anti-Blackhead Preparations

PL 3405/4009 Dazole Premix
PL 4869/4003 Dimetridazole BP (Vet)
PL 3636/4001 Dimetridazole – PML Turkeys
PL 0012/4176 'Emtryl' premix
PL 0012/4174 'Emtryl' Pure
PL 0012/4175 'Emtryl' Soluble

5. Sheep Dips and Ectoparasiticides

PL 0010/4041 Asuntol Scab Dip
PL 1300/4010 Barricade
PL 0676/4089 Battles Improved Organo-Phosphorus Single-Dipping Fluid Dip
PL 0676/4088 Battles Improved Special Single-Dipping Fluid Dip
PL 0676/4086 Battles Liquid Summer Fly Dip (Scab Approved)
PL 0676/4087 Battles Organo-Phosphorus Single-Dipping Fluid Dip
PL 2613/4003 Cheviot Sheep Head Ointment
PL 1300/4004 Ciodrin Insecticide
PL 0805/4015 Cooper MD Powder Dip (BHC)
PL 0003/4124 Cooper – Summer Dip 400
PL 0003/4116 Cooper Winter Dip 200
PL 1300/4011 C Tag 97 Fly Tag/Flectron Fly Tag
PL 4149/4001 Deodorised Malathion Premium Grade
PL 1476/4018 Deosan Dysect
PL 1476/4026 Deosan Flectron
PL 1476/4021 Deosan Summer Dip
PL 1476/4020 Deosan Winter Dip
PL 0829/4127 Dermol
PL 1978/4001 Ectoral Tablets No. 1, 2 and 3
PL 4055/4031 Farmers Fly and Tick Dip
PL 0038/4061 Flockcare Fly and Scab Dip
PL 0038/4063 Flockcare Winter Dip
PL 4436/4005 Fly Dip
PL 2759/4006 Killgerm and Marstan Sheep Dip
PL 2759/4009 Killgerm Scab and Fly Sheep Dip
PL 2759/4007 Killgerm Single Dipping Type Liquid – Sheep Dip
PL 4055/4012 Lice and Mange Remedy
PL 1826/4004 Lice Tick and Mange Dressing (LTM)
PL 0430/4001 Lorexane Medicated Shampoo
PL 2759/4007 Marstan Single Dipping Type Liquid – Sheep Dip
PL 3317/4070 Milocide 50%
PL 0015/4003 Nexion (Bromophos) 2% Dusting Powder
PL 1826/4001 Northern Fly Dip
PL 4055/4003 Northern Fly Dip
PL 1728/4055 Nuvanol Vet
PL 1826/4023 Osmond's Wintol Sheep Dip (1–200)
PL 0025/4044 Ovidip Scab Approved Sheep Dip
PL 0028/4068 Porect
PL 0086/4138 Prodip

Product Licence No.   Name of Product

5.   Sheep Dips and Ectoparasiticides (continued)

PL 2100/4034   Rodgers No. 10 Neu-Fly and Tick Dip
PL 0003/4113   Stomoxin
PL 0003/4148   Stomoxin Fly Tags
PL 4055/4001   Supona Fly and Tick Dip
PL 1300/4005   Supona Sheep Dip
PL 4436/4001   Taktic
PL 1345/4040   Taskill
PL 0086/4140   *Tirade Fly Tags*
PL 1728/4070   *Topclip Parasol*
PL 1826/4025   Viper Dip
PL 4055/4000   Viper Winter Dip
PL 4055/4002   Vipex 200 Liquid Dip
PL 4436/4003   Winter Dip
PL 1447/4052   Young's 200 Liquid Tick Dip
PL 1447/4087   Young's 400 Fly Dip
PL 1447/4096   Young's Cypor
PL 1447/4086   Young's Dursban 400 Winter Dip
PL 1447/4080 {   Young's Ectomort Sheep Dip
            Young's Scab Approved Summer Dip
PL 1447/4015   Young's Powder Fly Dip
PL 1447/4058   Young's Scab Approved 200 Liquid Tick Dip
PL 1447/4050   Young's Scab Approved 200 Winter Dip
PL 1447/4063   Young's Scab Approved 400 Fly Dip
PL 1447/4068   Young's Scab Approved Bromophos Winter Dip
PL 1447/4085   Young's Scab Approved Diazinon Winter Dip
PL 1447/4071   Young's Scab Approved Dursban 400 Winter Dip
PL 1447/4070   Young's Scab Approved Dursban Winter Dip
PL 1447/4103   *Young's Scab Approved Ectomort Summer Dip*
PL 1447/4073   Young's Scab Approved Iodofenphos Winter Dip
PL 1447/4055   Young's Scab Approved Killtick Liquid Tick Dip
PL 1447/4041   Young's Scab Approved Liquid Fly Dip
PL 1447/4056   Young's Scab Approved Powder Fly Dip
PL 1447/4056   Young's Scab Approved Summer Mycotic Dip
PL 1447/4060   Young's Sheep Blowfly Spray
PL 1447/4083   Young's SP Fly Spray
PL 1447/4015   Young's Summer Mycotic Dip
PL 3893/4069   *Zeprox*

6.   Anthelminitics

PL 0829/4135   Action Paranil Pellets
PL 0029/4103   'Amatron' Cattle Drench
PL 0029/4105   'Amatron' Sheep Drench
PL 1447/4092   Anthelpor
PL 4318/4003   Ashmintic Drench
PL 4318/4013   Ashmintic Injection
PL 1732/4059   *Astrobot 5*
PL 1732/4060   *Astrobot 10*
PL 0010/4054   Bayverm L.V. Paste
PL 0010/4058   *Bayverm Pellets 1.9%*
PL 0010/4049   Bayverm Premix 0.6%
PL 0010/4050   Bayverm Premix 2.4%
PL 0010/4047   Bayverm Suspension 2.5%
PL 0010/4048   Bayverm Suspension 10%
PL 3974/4021   *Cevasol Injection*
PL 3974/4020   *Cevasol Worm Drench*
PL 0095/4040   *Cyverm 11.5% Gel*
PL 0095/4038   Cyverm Levamisole 3.2% Drench
PL 0095/4037   Cyverm Levamisole 7.5% Injection
PL 1861/4055   Day's Worm Drench

Product Licence No. Name of Product

6. Anthelminitics (continued)

PL 0100/4047 Dicarocide Forte Injection
PL 0010/4046 Droncit
PL 1596/4071 Duphamisole 7.5% Oral
PL 0025/4023 Equiben
PL 0002/4074 ⎱Equitac
PL 3832/4012 ⎰
PL 0829/4044 Equivurm Plus
PL 0829/4058 Equivurm Plus Paste
PL 0025/4027 Equizole Pony Paste
PL 0025/4042 Eqvalan Paste for Horses
PL 0829/4120 Flubenol
PL 0829/4131 Flubenol Pellets
PL 0010/4055 Flukombin
PL 3763/4000 Gapex
PL 0002/4004 Helmatac In-Feed Wormer
PL 0002/4014 ⎱Helmatac Wormer Pellets
PL 3832/4051 ⎰
PL 2592/4076 Helminate Sow Wormer Pellets
PL 0025/4041 Ivomec Drench
PL 0025/4043 Ivomec Injection for Pigs
PL 2000/4054 Levacide – C Worm Drench
PL 2000/4049 Levacide Injection
PL 2000/4050 Levacide Worm Drench
PL 1447/4091 Levanthel
PL 3832/4066 Loditac 3% Wormer Pellets
PL 0829/4126 Mebatreat
PL 0829/4113 Mebenvet (1.2%)
PL 0829/4123 Mebenvet (5%)
PL 0010/4026 Neguvon
PL 0012/4003 Nemafax Drench
PL 0012/4150 Nemafax P Wormer Pellets
PL 0012/4149 Nemafax 5
PL 0012/4149 Nemafax 14
PL 0012/4151 Nemafax Cattle, Sheep and Goat Wormer Pellets
PL 0012/4151 Nemafax Sow
PL 0012/4153 Nemafax Wettable Powder
PL 0029/4101 Nemicide Cattle Drench
PL 1345/4069 Nilvax Under 30 kg
PL 0029/4100 ⎰Nilverm C. Small Dose Cattle Drench
⎱Nilverm C. Cattle Drench
PL 0029/4101 Nilverm Cattle Special
PL 0029/4114 Nilverm Plus Drench
PL 0029/4118 Nilverm Super
PL 0029/4098 Nilzan C
PL 0029/4115 'Nilzan' Drench Plus
PL 0029/4117 'Nilzan' Drench Super
PL 0829/4114 Ovitelmin
PL 0829/4162 Ovitelmin Bolus
PL 0829/4163 Ovitelmin SC
PL 0086/4121 Panacur 1.5% Pellets
PL 0086/4105 Panacur 2.5% Sheep Wormer
PL 0086/4105 Panacur 2.5% Suspension
PL 0086/4110 Panacur 4% Paste
PL 0086/4106 Panacur 10% Suspension
PL 0086/4107 Panacur 22% Granules
PL 0086/4119 Panacur Paste
PL 0086/4130 ⎰Panacur SC
⎱Panacur SC Sheep Wormer
PL 0086/4136 Panacur SC Cattle Wormer

Product Licence No.   Name of Product

6.   Anthelminitics (continued)

PL 0057/4075 Paratect Sustained Release Bolus
PL 0025/4031 Porcam
PL 0025/4038 Ranizole Paste
PL 0829/4150 Ripercol
PL 0829/4133 Ripercol 3.2% Oral Solution
PL 0829/4140 Ripercol 5% Injectable Solution
PL 0829/4151 Ripercol 7.5% Injectable
PL 0829/4132 Ripercol 15% Injectable Solution
PL 0086/4115 Rumevite Wormablok with Panacur for Cattle
PL 0086/4114 Rumevite Wormablok with Panacur for Sheep
PL 1447/4094 Rycovet Horse and Pony Wormer
PL 0029/4099 Spectril
PL 0057/4060 Strongid-P (Granules)
PL 0057/4062 Strongid-P Paste
PL 0057/4063 Suiminth (Morantel Tartrate)
PL 0286/4032 Synanthic
PL 0286/4034 Synanthic DC
PL 0286/4039 Synanthic Horse Paste
PL 0286/4035 Synanthic Horse Pellets
PL 0003/4127 Systamex Paste 18.5% Cattle and Horse Wormer
PL 0003/4127 Systamex Paste 18.5% Horse and Pony Wormer
PL 0003/4121 Systamex 906 Concentrated Cattle Wormer
PL 0003/4112 Systamex Worm Drench for Cattle and Sheep
PL 1300/4002 Task
PL 0829/4112 Telmin KH
PL 0829/4114 Telmin Liquid
PL 4462/4002 Tetramisole Hydrochloride BP (Vet)
PL 0025/4024 {Thibenzole 50% Paste
             {Thibenzole Paste
PL 1728/4060 Topclip Wormer
PL 1728/4061 Topclip Wormer Pellets
PL 0829/4136 Triban Drench
PL 0002/4061 }Valbazen 2.5% Total Spectrum Wormer
PL 3832/4022}
PL 0002/4062 }Valbazen 10% Total Spectrum Wormer
PL 3832/4023}
PL 3832/4015 Valbazen 40% Paste
PL 3832/4025 Valbazen C 10% Total Spectrum Wormer
PL 3832/4026 Valbazen SC 2.5% Total Spectrum Wormer
PL 3832/4016 Valbazen Cattle Wormer Pellets
PL 0012/4172 Vermadex
PL 0086/4139 Wormex
PL 1447/4091 Young's Anthelpor 20
PL 1447/4075 {Young's Anthelworm
             {*Rycovet Widespec*
PL 1447/4090 Young's Anthelworm Feed Pellets
PL 1447/4076 Young's Anthelworm L
PL 1447/4100 Young's Endozal
PL 1447/4079 Young's Nemtrem

7.   Milk Fever Preparations

PL 4134/4003 Astracalc (Calcium Borogluconate 20%) No. 1
PL 4134/4004 Astracalc (Calcium Borogluconate 40%) No. 2
PL 4134/4005 Astracalc (Calcium Borogluconate PM) No. 3
PL 4134/4006 Astracalc (Calcium Borogluconate PM 29) No. 4
PL 4134/4007 Astracalc (Calcium Borogluconate PM 40) No. 5
PL 4134/4008 Astracalc (Calcium Borogluconate PMD) No. 6
PL 4134/4009 Astracalc (Calcium Borogluconate M) No. 7
PL 0100/4028 Boracalinate 20 Injection

Product Licence No.   Name of Product

7. Milk Fever Preparations (continued)

PL 0100/4027 Boracalinate 40 Injection
PL 0100/4025 Boracalinate MP Injection
PL 0100/4048 Boracalinate MPD Injection
PL 0123/4034 Calcibor C.B.G. 20% w/v
PL 0123/4035 Calcibor C.B.G. 40% w/v
PL 0123/4036 Calcibor C.M.P. 20
PL 0123/4037 Calcibor C.M.P. 30
PL 0123/4038 Calcibor C.M.P. 40
PL 0123/4039 Calcibor C.M.P. and D
PL 2324/4077 Calcium Borogluconate 30% and Magnesium Hypophosphite 2.2% Solution CMP 30
PL 0829/4118 Calcium Borogluconate 40% with Magnesium and Phosphorus
PL 2848/4018 Calcium Borogluconate Injection B Vet C 20%
PL 2848/4019 Calcium Borogluconate Injection B Vet C 30%
PL 2848/4020 Calcium Borogluconate Injection B Vet C 40%
PL 2324/4076 Calcium Borogluconate Solution CBG 20
PL 4134/4003 Flexopax (Calcium Borogluconate 20%) No. 1
PL 4134/4004 Flexopax (Calcium Borogluconate 40%) No. 2
PL 4134/4005 Flexopax (Calcium Borogluconate PM) No. 3
PL 4134/4008 Flexopax (Calcium Borogluconate PMD) No. 6
PL 2324/4079 Glucose Saline Injection
PL 2324/4078 Injection of Calcium Borogluconate 40% and Magnesium Hypophosphite 2.2% Solution CMP 40
PL 4134/4012 Novocalc
PL 1345/4007 TVL Calcium Borogluconate "Borocal"

8. Warble Fly Dressings

PL 0003/4115 Cooper Warble Fly Liquid
PL 0829/4127 Dermol
PL 0010/4045 Neguvon Spot-on
PL 0038/4062 Orbisect Warble Fly Liquid and Louse Liquid for Cattle
PL 0621/4013 Trolene FM
PL 0095/4024 Warbex 16.7% Famphur Pour-on
PL 4436/4000 Warbexol – Ready to Use Systemic Warble Fly Dressing
PL 1447/4059 Young's Concentrated Poron
PL 1447/4074 Young's New Poron
PL 1447/4077 Young's Poron 20

9. Liver Fluke Remedies

PL 0010/4031 Dirian
PL 0025/4036 Flukanide
PL 1826/4000 Hexol
PL 0002/4061
PL 3832/4022 } Valbazen 2.5% Total Spectrum Wormer
PL 0002/4062
PL 3832/4023 } Valbazen 10% Total Spectrum Wormer
PL 3832/4025 Valbazen C 10% Total Spectrum Wormer
PL 3832/4026 Valbazen SC 2.5% Total Spectrum Wormer
PL 1447/4065 Young's Flukol
PL 1447/4101 Young's New Flukol

10. Sheep and Cattle Clostridial Vaccines and Antisera

PL 0086/4132 Heptavac P
PL 1345/4063 Nilvax
PL 1345/4069 Nilvax under 30 kg
PL 0086/4129 Ovivac P
PL 1345/4062 Tasvax 8
PL 1728/4066 Topclip Ewe Vaccine 8 in 1

Product Licence No.   Name of Product

11. Poultry Vaccines

PL 1531/4001	Addervax ND Vaccine (Living) HB 1
PL 3359/4024	Avian Encephalomyelitis Vaccine Delvax AE
PL 1598/4001	Avian Encephalomyelitis Vaccine (Living) Calnek Strain
PL 1708/4133	Avian Encephalomyelitis Vaccine (Living) Nobilis
PL 3317/4086	Avivac-Avian Encephalomyelitis Vaccine (Live)
PL 0002/4053 PL 3832/4033	Bronchimune IB Vaccine *Infectious Bronchitis Vaccine (Living) Strain HL Massachusetts type (Bronchimune)*
PL 0002/4034	Combimune
PL 1598/4029	Combined ND (HB1) and IB (Massachusetts MM) Vaccine (Living)
PL 1598/4028	Combined ND La Sota and IB Vaccine (Living)
PL 3359/4004	Delvax IB H52
PL 3359/4003	Delvax IB H120
PL 3359/4001	Delvax Marek THV Freeze-dried
PL 3359/4035	Delvax ND Hitchner
PL 3359/4006	Delvax ND La Sota
PL 3359/4005	Delvax ND HB1
PL 2592/4055	Eavax
PL 3317/4083	Fowl Laryngotracheitis Vaccine (Modified Live Virus)
PL 1598/4055	Fowl Pox Vaccine Poxine
PL 1598/4053	Fowl Pox Vaccine Poxinet
PL 1708/4139	Gumboro Disease Vaccine (Living) Nobilis
PL 4978/4004	Iblin Emulsion
PL 2592/4037	Ibvax
PL 0002/4002 PL 3832/4056	IB Vaccine (Living) Massachusetts H52 Strain
PL 0002/4003 PL 3832/4036	IB Vaccine (Living) Massachusetts H120 Strain
PL 1708/4135	Inactivated ND Vaccine (oil emulsion) Newcavac Nobilis
PL 1598/4056	Infectious Laryngotracheitis Vaccine (LT-VAC)
PL 2592/4074	Ivamarek Marek's Disease Vaccine
PL 2592/4044	Lentogen HB1
PL 2592/4043	Lentogen La Sota
PL 0086/4004	Marek's Disease Vaccine, Behringwerke
PL 0002/4001 PL 3832/4039	Marek's Disease Vaccine (Living) THV (Marimune) *Marek's Disease Vaccine (Living) THV (Strain FC 126) Freeze-dried (Marimune)*
PL 3317/4085	Marek's Disease Vaccine (Live) THV
PL 1598/4026	Marek's Disease Vaccine MD-VAC (Living) THV (Winter Strain) Frozen (Wet)
PL 1598/4027	Marek's Disease Vaccine (Lyophilised) MD-VAC
PL 1708/4141	Marexine MD
PL 1708/4169	Marexine THV/CA
PL 4978/4005	Maternalin Emulsion
PL 4978/4003	Myxilin Emulsion
PL 2592/4033	Newcastle Disease Vaccine (Inactivated) Oil Emulsion (Layer Plus)
PL 0039/4040 PL 4978/4002	Newcadin Day Old
PL 3317/4087	Newcastle Disease Vaccine K2C (Inactivated)
PL 1708/4142	Newcastle Disease Vaccine (Living) Nobilis Clone 30
PL 3317/4086	Newcastle Disease Vaccine (Live) La Sota Strain
PL 1708/4150	Newcavac + EDS'76 Vaccine
PL 1598/4000	NDV (Living) La Sota
PL 0020/4000	ND Vaccine (Living) La Sota
PL 0039/4000 PL 4978/4000	ND Vaccine (Living) HB 1 Strain (Newcadin L)
PL 0039/4029 PL 4978/4001	ND Oil Adjuvant Vaccine (Inactivated) (Newcadin Emulsion)

Product Licence No.   Name of Product

11. Poultry Vaccines (continued)

PL 3318/4000 ND Vaccine (Inactivated) Oil Emulsion
PL 1708/4143 Nobi-Vac Egg Drop Syndrome 76 Vaccine BC14 (Inactivated)
PL 1708/4155 Nobi-Vac Gumboro Inactivated
PL 1596/4034 Poulvac AE
PL 1596/4040 Poulvac EDS
PL 1596/4029 Poulvac IB Vaccine H52 (Living)
PL 1596/4030 Poulvac IB Vaccine H120 (Living)
PL 1596/4045 Poulvac Marek HVT Vaccine
PL 1596/4025 Poulvac Marek THV
PL 1596/4026 Poulvac ND Vaccine (Living) HB 1
PL 1596/4027 Poulvac ND Vaccine (Living) La Sota
PL 0002/4005⎫
PL 3832/4024⎭ Tremimune

12. Erysipelas Vaccines

PL 1531/4012 Ferrovac Ery Vaccine
PL 3317/4110 Swine Erysipelas Vaccine (Inactivated)
PL 1345/4004 Swine Erysipelas Vaccine, Inactivated (Oil Adjuvant) Erysivax

13. Salmonella and E. coli Vaccines

PL 0086/4134 Coliovac
PL 3832/4009 Ecopig
PL 0003/4110 Gletvax K88-Porcine E. coli Vaccine (Polyvalent)
PL 0003/4110 Gletvax-Porcine E. coli Vaccine (Polyvalent)
PL 0003/4110 Gletvax-Porcine E. coli Vaccine (Polyvalent) + K88
PL 0086/4113 Porcovac AT
PL 3832/4004 Scourguard I

14. Other Sheep and Cattle Vaccines

PL 0003/4135 Ovine Enzootic Abortion (Improved) Vaccine
PL 0086/4133 Ovipast

15. Miscellaneous Vaccines

PL 1708/4152 Nobi-Vac L.T. K88
PL 3317/4088 Pigeon Pox Vaccine (Live Virus-Chicken Embryo Origin)

16. Sulphanilamide Surface Wound Dressings

PL 2428/4002 Sulphonamide Wound and Navel Dressing Powder

17. Local Anaesthetics

PL 3317/4049 Lignavet Plus Injection
PL 2324/4074 Lignocaine Anaesthetic Injection
PL 2000/4029 Lignocaine and Adrenalin Injection
PL 2428/4021 Lignocaine Injection
PL 0123/4052 Lignol
PL 1599/4005 Ruby Freezaject
PL 0123/4068 Willcain

18. Others

PL 4318/4002 Ashfer 100
PL 4134/4010 Astracalc (Glucose (Dextrose) 40%) No. 8
PL 4134/4011 Astracalc (Magnesium Sulphate 25%) No. 9
PL 2428/4026 Bactasorb Tablets
PL 0002/4043⎫
PL 3832/4034⎭ Bloat Guard
PL 0002/4054 Bloat Guard Drench
PL 0002/4051⎫
PL 3832/4065⎭ Bloat Guard Liquid
PL 3514/4002 Boar Mate

Product Licence No.   Name of Product

18. Others (continued)

PL 4261/4000 Bovinyl
PL 1754/4003 Calf Intagen Premix
PL 2613/4000 Cheviot Veterinary Oil
PL 2545/4009 Codifer 10
PL 0010/4009 Coforta 10
PL 0676/4091 Colostrene Watery Mouth Drench for Young Lambs
PL 3317/4010 Copavet
PL 2987/4003 Copper (Cupric) Carbonate
PL 0038/4088 Copporal 2 g
PL 0038/4089 Copporal 4 g
PL 0038/4078 Copprite 2 g
PL 0038/4084 Copprite 4 g
PL 1345/4012 Cujec
PL 2987/4002 Cupric Oxide
PL 2987/4001 Cuprous Chloride
PL 3656/4012 Dio-Iron
PL 1596/4031 Ducrofer
PL 1532/4026 Ferriphor
PL 3317/4041 Ferrofax 10
PL 0113/4005 Fisons Multivitamin Injection
PL 0113/4006 Fisons Vitamin A, D & E Injection
PL 3026/4009 "Flex Flac" Pack for infusion 25% Dextrose Injection BP
PL 0113/4007 Gleptosil
PL 2324/4079 Glucose Saline Injection
PL 0100/4031 Glucose Saline Injection
PL 1708/4121 Haemalift
PL 1754/4009 HI-FAT Baby Calf Food 'Intagen'
PL 0100/4029 Injection Magnesium Sulphate 25%
PL 0100/4022 Injection of Dextrose 40%
PL 1754/4000 Intagen Premix
PL 2000/4017 Intravit 12
PL 0829/4117 Iron Dextran 10% (Pharmacosmos)
PL 0025/4040 Ivomec Injection
PL 0043/4000 Leodex
PL 0043/4042 Leodex 20%
PL 0043/4036 Leodex Plus
PL 2000/4043 Magnesium Sulphate Injection 25% w/v
PL 4127/4000 Micro Anti-Bloat Premix
PL 2592/4059 Microdex
PL 0101/4001 MS 222 Sandoz
PL 3317/4069 Multivet Soluble Powder
PL 0676/4090 Orfoids – Capsules for Orf
PL 0032/4060 Pegasus DE Mineral Mixture
PL 0032/4041 Pegasus Minerals JGW 343
PL 0032/4087 Pegasus OCU Mineral Mixture
PL 1345/4042 Permaco C
PL 1345/4041 Permaco S
PL 1345/4051 Permasel-C
PL 1345/4052 Permasel-S
PL 0295/4000 Poudre Armoricaine
PL 4134/4000 Proviton
PL 4262/4000 Quay-Iron
PL 0829/4133 Ripercol 3.2% Oral
PL 0829/4140 Ripercol 5% Injectable Solution
PL 0829/4132 Ripercol 15% Injectable
PL 2100/4032 Rogers 1–80 Purl Dip
PL 1011/4001 Roscofer 10% Vet
PL 1011/4000 Roscoral Vet
PL 3317/4077 Sildex

Product Licence No.   Name of Product

18. Others (continued)

PL 1754/4002 Sow Intagen 0/I
PL 3317/4022 Super Suntax
PL 1599/4004 Swipoul
PL 0032/4039 Telmin Pellet JGW 343
PL 0829/4117 Tendex
PL 5923/4002 *Tracerglass C*
PL 2686/4000 Vache Ointment
PL 2428/4000 Vetrion 200
PL 3317/4047 Vetrivite Plus
PL 0829/4121 Vital Multivitamin Solution
PL 0038/4060 Vitament Vitamin A, D_3 & E Injection
PL 1532/4020 Vitamin AD_3 E Oral
PL 3317/4069 Vitapol
PL 2969/4001 Vituramag
PL 2969/4005 Vituramol 60 with Romensin
PL 0038/4057 Whitmoyer V – Mix
PL 1447/4036 Young's Swaycop

SCHEDULE 2   Article 4

PART A

LICENCE OF RIGHT VETERINARY DRUGS

Group/Class   Substance

1. GROWTH PROMOTERS   Bacitracin Zinc
                                      Bambermycin
                                      Nitrovin
                                      Tylosin Phosphate
                                      Virginiamycin

2. COCCIDIOSTATS   Amprolium Hydrochloride
                                      Clopidol
                                      Decoquinate
                                      Diaveridine
                                      Dinitolmide
                                      Ethopabate
                                      Pyrimethamine
                                      Robenidine

3. ANTI-BLACKHEAD   Acinitrazole
   PREPARATIONS   Aminonitrothiazole
                                      Nifursol

4. ANTHELMINTICS   Haloxon
                                      Mebendazole
                                      Parbendazole
                                      Phenothiazine
                                      Piperazine Carbon Disulphide Complex
                                      Tetramisole
                                      Thiabendazole

5. OTHERS   Menandione Dimethyl Pyrimidinol Bisul-
                                      phite
                                      Menandione Sodium Bisulphite

Article 4 SCHEDULE 2

PART B

VETERINARY DRUGS

Product Licence No. Name of Product*

1. Growth Promoters

PL 0095/4026	{ Avotan 50 Avoparcin { Avotan 50
PL 0095/4028	Avotan 50c Avoparcin
PL 0095/4036	*Avotan 100*
PL 0010/4043	Bayo-n-ox 10% Premix
PL 3832/4031	Eskalin 100
PL 0002/4045 *PL 3832/4017*	} Eskalin 500
PL 0002/4055 PL 3832/4021	} Eskalin S-400
PL 0029/4102	Fedan 10% Premix
PL 0086/4124	Flavomycin 40
PL 0086/4137	Flavomycin 50
PL 3405/4016	Nitrovin
PL 3405/4018	*Nitrovin – 20*
PL 2592/4075	Nitrozone 25
PL 4869/4000	Panazone 250 Nitrovin
PL 0095/4007	Payzone 50 MA Nitrovin Milk Replacer Additive
PL 4188/4008	Pentazone 250
PL 2969/4006	Rumevite with Romensin
PL 0006/4052	Romensin (Monensin Sodium) Premix
PL 0012/4170	SPIRA 200
PL 0006/4055	Tylamix Premix 100 g/kg
PL 0006/4062	Tylamix Premix 250 g/kg
PL 3405/4007	Tylosin 100 Premix
PL 3734/4000	Zinc Bacitracin Dumex Feed Grade
PL 3734/4001	Zinc Bacitracin "Dumex" 150 Premix
PL 0109/4001	Zinc Bacitracin Premix
PL 3405/4015	*ZB-100*
PL 3405/4002	ZB100
PL 3405/4005	ZB150

2. Coccidiostats

PL 0025/4035	Arpocox
PL 0031/4011	Avatec Premix
PL 3405/4017	Clopidol
PL 0012/4056	"Deccox" Pure
PL 0109/4000	Dinormix SR 25
PL 4188/4004	{ Dinitolmide (DOT) 3.5-Dinitro-ortho-toluamide { Unicox Pure
PL 4869/4005	*DOT*
PL 0109/4002	DOT (dinitolmide)
PL 1598/4032	DOT Premix 12.5%
PL 1598/4033	DOT Premix 25%
PL 0006/4047	{ Elancoban { Elancoban Premix
PL 3405/4006	{ Elancoban Premix { Monensin 200

* Alternative product names used by specially authorised persons are not shown.

Items shown in italics did not appear in the Medicines (Exemptions from Restrictions on the Retail Sale or Supply of Veterinary Drugs) Order 1979 as amended.

Product Licence No.   Name of Product

2. Coccidiostats (continued)

PL 0621/4015 Lerbek
PL 0006/4061 Monteban 100 Premix
PL 0025/4019 Nicrazin (Premix)
PL 0025/4010 Pancoxin
PL 0086/4135 Sacox 60 Premix
PL 1598/4036 Salcostat
PL 0086/4117 Stenorol
PL 0025/4003 Supacox

3. Anti-Blackhead Preparations

PL 4869/4003 Dimetridazole BP (Vet)
PL 3636/4001 Dimetridazole – PML Turkeys
PL 3405/4009 Dazole Premix
PL 0012/4176 'Emtryl' Premix
PL 0012/4174 'Emtryl' Pure
PL 0012/4175 'Emtryl' Soluble

4. Anthelmintics

PL 0010/4049 Bayverm Premix 0.6%
PL 0010/4050 Bayverm Premix 2.4%
PL 0829/4131 Flubenol Pellets
PL 0002/4004 Helmatac In-Feed Wormer
PL 0829/4113 Mebenvet (1.2%)
PL 0829/4123 Mebenvet (5%)
PL 0012/4149 Nemafax 5
PL 0012/4149 Nemafax 14
PL 0012/4153 Nemafax Wettable Powder

5. Others

PL 0002/4043 ⎫
PL 3832/4034 ⎬ Bloat Guard
PL 1754/4003 Calf Intagen Premix
PL 1754/4009 HI-FAT Baby Calf Food 'Intagen'
PL 1754/4000 Intagen Premix
PL 4127/4000 Micro Anti-Bloat Premix
PL 0032/4041 Pegasus Minerals JGW 343
PL 1754/4002 Sow Intagen O/I
PL 0032/4039 Telmin Pellet JGW 343
PL 2969/4005 Vituramol 60 with Romensin
PL 0038/4057 Whitmoyer V – Mix

Article 4   SCHEDULE 3

PART A

LICENCE OF RIGHT OF VETERINARY DRUGS

Aklomide
Ampicillin Trihydrate
Arsanilic Acid
Benzylpenicillin
Chlortetracycline
Erythromycin
Framycetin Sulphate
Furazolidone
4 hydroxy-3 nitrophenyl arsonic acid
Lincomycin Hydrochloride
Methyl Benzoquate
Nitrofurazone
Oxytetracycline
Procaine Penicillin
Sulphadimidine
Sulphanitran
Sulphaquinoxaline
Tylosin Phosphate

SCHEDULE 3   Article 4

PART B

VETERINARY DRUGS

Product Licence No.   Name of Product*

PL 0006/4053	Apralan Soluble Powder
PL 0006/4057	Apralan 20 Premix
PL 0006/4058	Apralan 100 Premix
PL 4188/4002	Chlortetracycline Feedgrade Auromix 100
PL 0095/4029	Cycostat 66R Robenidine Feed Additive
PL 3405/4010	*Dazole Prescription Premix*
PL 3636/4002	*Dimetridazole – POM Swine and Turkeys*
PL 0034/4031	Dynamutilin 2% Premix
PL 0006/4063	Elancoban for Turkeys and Replacement Chickens
PL 0012/4159	'Emtryl' Prescription Premix
PL 0012/4160	'Emtryl' Prescription Pure
PL 0012/4161	'Emtryl' Prescription Soluble
PL 0012/4158	Emtrymore
PL 1596/4018	Engemycin 5% Soluble Powder
PL 3832/4018	*Eskalin 20 POM for laying and breeding hens*
PL 0002/4071 *PL 3832/4019*	'Eskalin' 500 POM for laying and breeding hens
PL 0057/4068	Fortigro S Premix
PL 1654/4012	Fortracin BMD^R
PL 3317/4023	Framomycin Feed Additive
PL 3317/4031	Framomycin Soluble Powder 25%
PL 3405/4018	*Furazolidone – 200*
PL 3405/4012	Furazolidone BP
PL 0131/4002	Furazolidone BPC 68
PL 4188/4003	Furazolidone BPC 68 or USNF 13 Unidone
PL 3058/4000	Furazolidone NF BVC
PL 2592/4036	Furazolidone Premix
PL 0006/4050	Granulated Tylosin Concentrate
PL 0032/4084	Lincocin Premix
PL 2592/4065	Micro-Bio Sulphadimidine Premix
PL 3832/4060	*Neftin 200*
PL 0364/4003	Neftin Premix
PL 0364/4004	Neftin Supplement
PL 1598/4037	Nifulidone Premix 11.6%
PL 1598/4037	Nifulidone Premix 22.4%
PL 1598/4037	Nifulidone Premix 44.8%
PL 4188/4001	Oxytetracycline HCI Feedgrade
PL 0034/4001	Quixalud Feed Additive
PL 0034/4026	Quixalud Premix 12%
PL 0025/4028	Ridzol 12% Premix
PL 1728/4041	Sermix
PL 0086/4120	Stenorol for Turkeys
PL 4219/4000	Sulphadimidine
PL 3405/4003	*Sulphadimidine*
PL 3405/4020	*Sulphadimidine – 100*
PL 0057/4061	Terramycine Concentrate 20%
PL 0057/4031	Terramycine 5% Feed Supplement

---

* Alternative product names used by specially authorised persons are not shown.

Items shown in italics did not appear in the Medicines (Exemptions from Restrictions on the Retail Sale or Supply of Veterinary Drugs) Order 1979 as amended.

Product Licence No.	Name of Product
PL 0057/4065	Terramycine 20% Feed Supplement
PL 0003/4105	Tribrissen Powder
PL 0006/4045	Tylan Premix 20 g/kg
PL 0006/4001	Tylasul Premix Veterinary Tylasul Premix
PL 0006/4064	Tylasul Premix 100
PL 4188/4000	Unidim
PL 0131/4008	Unidim
PL 4188/4007	Unidim 100
PL 4188/4012	Unizole S Soluble – For Pigs
PL 4188/4011	Unizole S – For Pigs and Poultry
PL 3317/4076	Vi-Mycin Soluble Powder
PL 0038/4037	Whitsyn 10
PL 0038/4047	Whitsyn – S

SCHEDULE 4   Article 5

HORSE WORMERS

Product Licence No.   Name of Product*

PL 1732/4059 Astrobot 5
PL 1732/4060 Astrobot 10
PL 0010/4054 Bayverm LV Paste
PL 1745/4005 Equigard 5
PL 1745/4006 Equigard 10
PL 0829/4043 Equilox
PL 0002/4074 ⎫
PL 3832/4012 ⎬ Equitac
PL 0829/4044 Equivurm Plus
PL 0829/4058 Equivurm Plus Paste
PL 0829/4043 Equivurm Syringe
PL 0025/4004 Equizole Feed Pellets
PL 0025/4027 Equizole Pony Paste
PL 0025/4005 Equizole Powder
PL 0025/4042 Eqvalan Paste for Horses
PL 0844/4055 Multiwurma (Horses)
PL 0086/4109 Panacur 22% Granules
PL 0086/4119 Panacur Paste
PL 1599/4001 Ruby Horse Wormer
PL 1447/4094 Rycovet Horse and Pony Wormer Paste
PL 0057/4060 Strongid P (Granules)
PL 0057/4062 Strongid P Paste
PL 0286/4039 Synanthic Horse Paste
PL 0286/4035 Synanthic Horse Pellets
PL 0003/4127 Systamex Paste 18.5% Horse and Pony Wormer
PL 0829/4058 Telmin
PL 0829/4044 Telmin Granules

---

* Alternative product names used by specially authorised persons are not shown.

Items shown in italics did not appear in the Medicines (Exemptions from Restrictions on the Retail Sale or Supply of Veterinary Drugs) Order 1979 as amended.

Article 8 SCHEDULE 5

REVOCATION

Orders revoked	References
The Medicines (Exemptions from Restrictions on the Retail Sale or Supply of Veterinary Drugs) Order 1979	S.I. 1979/45
The Medicines (Exemptions from Restrictions on the Retail Sale or Supply of Veterinary Drugs) (Amendment) Order 1979	S.I. 1979/1008
The Medicines (Exemptions from Restrictions on the Retail Sale or Supply of Veterinary Drugs) (Amendment) Order 1980	S.I. 1980/283
The Medicines (Exemptions from Restrictions on the Retail. Sale or Supply of Veterinary Drugs) (Amendment) (No. 2) Order 1980	S.I. 1980/1650
The Medicines (Exemptions from Restrictions on the Retail Sale or Supply of Veterinary Drugs) (Amendment) Order 1981	S.I. 1981/793
The Medicines (Exemptions from Restrictions on the Retail Sale or Supply of Veterinary Drugs) (Amendment) (No. 2) Order 1981	S.I. 1981/1872
The Medicines (Exemptions from Restrictions on the Retail Sale or Supply of Veterinary Drugs) (Amendment) Order 1982	S.I. 1982/1019
The Medicines (Exemptions from Restrictions on the Retail Sale or Supply of Veterinary Drugs) (Amendment) (No. 2) Order 1982	S.I. 1982/1805
The Medicines (Exemptions from Restrictions on the Retail Sale or Supply of Veterinary Drugs) (Amendment) Order 1983	S.I. 1983/274
The Medicines (Exemptions from Restrictions on the Retail Sale or Supply of Veterinary Drugs) (Amendment) (No. 2) Order 1983	S.I. 1983/1156
The Medicines (Exemptions from Restrictions on the Retail Sale or Supply of Veterinary Drugs) (Amendment) Order 1984	S.I. 1984/349

EXPLANATORY NOTE

(This Note is not part of the Order.)

This order re-enacts, with amendments, the provisions of the Medicines (Exemptions from Restrictions on the Retail Sale or Supply of Veterinary Drugs) Order 1979 and its amending instruments, which are revoked.

The order continues to provide for certain exemptions from the restrictions imposed by section 52 of the Medicines Act 1968. Section 52 restricts the retail sale or supply of medicinal products not on a general sale list (a general sale list being a list of freely sellable medicinal products specified in an order made under section 51 of the Act) to sale or supply from a registered pharmacy by or under the supervision of a pharmacist.

Article 3 of the order exempts from the restrictions imposed by section 52 the sale or supply of any veterinary drug described in Article 3(1)*(a)* of the order by (1) the product licence holder, (2) a specially authorised person (as defined in the order) or (3) a person carrying on a qualifying business (that is to say, a business in respect of which more than one half of the total sales for its last accounting period was derived from the retail sale of agricultural requisites) provided, in each case, that the relevant conditions contained in Article 3 are complied with.

These conditions include a requirement that a person who, in the course of carrying on a qualifying business, wishes to sell any veterinary drug described in Article 3(1)*(a)* must have his name and details of the relevant premises entered in a register of merchants in veterinary drugs ("the Register"). The Register is kept by the Pharmaceutical Society of Great Britain ("the Society") and the Department of Health and Social Services for Northern Ireland ("the Department"). A fee of £55 is to be paid to the Society or the Department for the initial entry in the Register of the name of a person in respect of any premises and a further fee of £55 will be payable annually for the retention of a person's name in the Register in respect of any premises.

A person's name will not be entered in the Register unless he has paid the prescribed fee and has given an undertaking that he will comply with the provisions of the Code of Practice for Merchants Selling or Supplying Veterinary Drugs dated 30th October 1984. This Code is published by the Ministry of Agriculture, Fisheries and Food.

In addition, the Society (with the prior approval of the Minister of Agriculture, Fisheries and Food) or the Department (with the prior approval of the Department of Agriculture for Northern Ireland) may refuse to retain in, or may remove from, its Register, the name of any person in respect of any premises if that person has failed to observe any of the provisions of the Code of Practice referred to above or, if the conditions under which any veterinary drug described in Article 3(1)*(a)* is sold by retail on the premises, or under which it is stored on the premises prior to retail sale, are unsuitable for that purpose.

Article 4 of the order exempts from the restrictions imposed by section 52 the sale or supply of any veterinary drug described in Article 4(1)*(a)* of the order by (1) the product licence holder, (2) a specially authorised person or (3) a person carrying on a business comprising either the manufacture of animal feeding-stuffs for sale or the sale or supply in bulk of veterinary drugs provided, in each case, that the conditions contained in Article 4 are complied with.

Article 5 of the order exempts from the restrictions imposed by section 52 the sale by retail of any veterinary drug (being a horse wormer) described in Article 5(1)*(a)* of the order by (1) the product licence holder, (2) a specially authorised person and (3) a person carrying on a qualifying business or a saddlery business (that is to say, a business in respect of which more than one half of its total sales for its last accounting period was derived from the retail sale of saddlery requisites) provided, in each case, that the conditions contained in Article 5 are complied with.

These conditions are similar to those contained in Article 3 except that horse wormers may only be sold by retail to keepers of horses and ponies. The code of practice to be complied with is the Code of Practice for Saddlers Selling or Supplying Horse Wormers dated 30th October 1984 (published by the Ministry of Agriculture, Fisheries and Food) and the registration and retention fee is £25. (This fee is not payable by a person carrying on a qualifying business on premises in respect of which his name is entered in the Register for the purposes of the exemption contained in Article 3.)

The exemption contained in Article 5 will apply for a period of three years from 1st January 1985.

Article 6 of the order provides for exemptions from the restrictions imposed by section 52 in the case of the supply, subsequent to retail sale, of veterinary drugs described in Article 4(1)*(a)* by pharmacists and Article 7 provides for further exemptions from the restrictions imposed by section 52 in cases involving another person's default.

The changes of substance made by this order are:—

(1) The inclusion of a registration requirement as one of the conditions of the exemption contained in Article 3(Article 3(6)) and of ancilliary provisions relating to that requirement (Article 3(7) to (15)) including conditions in respect of the inclusion and the retention of persons in the registers kept by the Society and the Department for the purposes of that exemption and in respect of the payment of registration and retention fees;

(2) the inclusion, in Article 5, of an exemption for sellers of horse wormers subject to certain conditions being complied with. Such conditions include a registration requirement (Article 5(5)) and conditions in respect of the inclusion and the retention of persons in the registers kept by the Society and the Department for the purposes of the exemption and in respect of registration and retention fees;

(3) the inclusion of a requirement that persons registered in accordance with Article 3(1)*(a)* and Article 5(1)*(a)* have to comply with the provisions of the relevant Codes of Practice (Article 3(12)*(b)* and Article 5(11)*(b))*.

(These Codes of Practice are priced publications and are available from MAFF Publications Unit, Willowburn Estate, Alnwick, Northumberland, NE66 2PF).

STATUTORY INSTRUMENTS

1984 No. 1862

MEDICINES

The Medicines (Veterinary Drugs) (Prescription Only) (Amendment) Order 1984

Made - - - - -	*26th November* 1984
Laid before Parliament	*5th December* 1984
Coming into Operation	*1st January* 1985

The Secretary of State concerned with health in England, the Secretaries of State respectively concerned with health and with agriculture in Scotland and in Wales, the Minister of Agriculture, Fisheries and Food, the Department of Health and Social Services for Northern Ireland, and the Department of Agriculture for Northern Ireland, acting jointly, in exercise of powers conferred by sections 58(1) and (4) and 129(4) of the Medicines Act 1968(a) and now vested in them(b) and of all other powers enabling them in that behalf, after consulting such organisations as appear to them to be representative of interests likely to be substantially affected by the following order in accordance with section 129(6) of the said Act, and after consulting and taking into account the advice of the Veterinary Products Committee in accordance with sections 58(6) and 129(7) of the said Act, hereby make the following order:—

Title, commencement and interpretation

1.—(1) This order may be cited as the Medicines (Veterinary Drugs) (Prescription Only) (Amendment) Order 1984 and shall come into operation on 1st January 1985.

(2) In this order "the principal order" means the Medicines (Veterinary Drugs) (Prescription Only) Order 1983(c).

(a) 1968 c. 67.

(b) In the case of the Secretaries of State concerned with health in England and Wales by virtue of S.I. 1969/388, in the case of the Secretary of State concerned with agriculture in Wales by virtue of S.I. 1978/272 and in the case of the Northern Ireland Departments by virtue of section 40 of, and Schedule 5 to, the Northern Ireland Constitution Act 1973 (c. 36) and section 1(3) of, and paragraph 2(1)(b) of Schedule 1 to, the Northern Ireland Act 1974 (c. 28).

(c) S.I. 1983/1213, amended by S.I. 1983/1506, 1792.

Amendment of principal order

2. The principal order shall be amended as follows—

(*a*) in Article 1(2)(*a*) (interpretation) for the definition of "the Veterinary Drugs Exemption Order" there shall be substituted the following definition—

" "the Veterinary Drugs Exemption Order" means the Medicines (Exemptions from Restrictions on the Retail Sale or Supply of Veterinary Drugs) Order 1984" **(a)**;

(*b*) in Part I of Schedule 1 (which lists substances which render a veterinary drug a prescription only medicine except in circumstances also listed)—

(i) there shall be inserted in column 1, at the appropriate places in alphabetical order, the substances specified in column 1 of the Schedule to this order and there shall be inserted in column 3, in relation to the substance Clioquinol, the entry specified in column 3 of the Schedule to this order,

(ii) there shall be inserted in column 1, after the substance Joint Ill Vaccine listed under the heading Vaccines, the entry "Orf Vaccines (live)", and

(iii) the entries specified in column 3 in relation to the substances Carbon Tetrachloride and Chlorprothixene listed in column 1 shall be omitted;

(*c*) in Part II of Schedule 1 (which specifies certain veterinary drugs which are prescription only medicines) the following entries shall be omitted—

"Quixalud Feed Additive

0034/4001

Quixalud Premix

0034/4026"

(*d*) in Schedule 2 (which lists substances which exclude a veterinary drug for parenteral administration from being a prescription only medicine in circumstances also listed)—

(i) the substance "Azaperone" listed in column 1 and the entry specified in column 3 in relation to that substance shall be omitted, and

(ii) for the entry specified in column 2 in relation to the substance Procaine Hydrochloride listed in column 1 there shall be substituted the entry "5.0 per cent"; and

(*e*) in Part I of Schedule 3 (which lists persons exempted from the restrictions on the sale and supply of prescription only medicines imposed by section 58(2)(*a*) of the Medicines Act 1968 when they sell or supply a prescription only medicine listed in column 2 of that Part of that Schedule if the conditions specified in column 3 of that

---

(a) S.I. 1984/1861.

Part of that Schedule are fulfilled), for the entry numbered 4 in column 3 there shall be substituted the following entry—

"4. The sale or supply shall be subject to the conditions specified in Article 3 of the Veterinary Drugs Exemption Order".

Norman Fowler,
Secretary of State for Social Services.

26th November 1984.

George Younger,
Secretary of State for Scotland.

14th November 1984.

Nicholas Edwards,
Secretary of State for Wales.

15th November 1984.

In Witness whereof the Official Seal of the Minister of Agriculture, Fisheries and Food is hereunto affixed on 12th November 1984.

Michael Jopling,
Minister of Agriculture, Fisheries and Food.

Sealed with the Official Seal of the Department of Health and Social Services for Northern Ireland this 15th day of November 1984.

Maurice N. Hayes,
Permanent Secretary.

Sealed with the Official Seal of the Department of Agriculture for Northern Ireland this 15th day of November 1984.

W. H. Jack,
Permanent Secretary.

Article 2*(b)*(i)   SCHEDULE

ENTRIES ADDED TO PART I OF SCHEDULE 1 TO THE PRINCIPAL ORDER(a)

| Column 1 | Circumstances excluding medicinal products from the class of prescription only medicines | | |
	Column 2	Column 3	Column 4
Substances	Maximum strength	Use, pharmaceutical form or route of administration	Maximum dose and maximum daily dose
Broxyquinoline Clioquinol		Treatment of enteritis in livestock	
Dimethyl Sulphoxide Etisazole Etisazole Hydrochloride Halquinol Tetanus anti-toxins			

(a) Note: all columns appearing in the principal order are set out in this order, although no entries are added by this order to columns 2 or 4.

EXPLANATORY NOTE

(This Note is not part of the Order.)

This order further amends the Medicines (Veterinary Drugs) (Prescription Only) Order 1983 ("the principal order") which specifies descriptions and classes of medicinal products (being veterinary drugs) for the purposes of section 58 of the Medicines Act 1968 and states that veterinary surgeons and veterinary practitioners are to be appropriate practitioners for the purposes of that section in relation to such products. By virtue of section 58 such products may be sold or supplied by retail only in accordance with a prescription given by a veterinary surgeon or veterinary practitioner and may be administered only by or in accordance with the directions of such a person.

Amendments made by Article 2 of this order—

(1) add certain substances to the list of substances in Part I of Schedule 1 to the principal order which, if contained in a veterinary drug, make that drug a prescription only medicine except in circumstances also listed;

(2) delete from Part I of Schedule 1 to the principal order the circumstances in which a veterinary drug containing the substances Carbon Tetrachloride or Chlorprothixene is excluded from being a prescription only medicine;

(3) delete two veterinary drugs from Part II of Schedule 1 to the principal order which specifies veterinary drugs which are prescription only medicines;

(4) delete the substance Azaperone from the list of substances in Schedule 2 to the principal order which, if contained in a veterinary drug for parenteral administration, exclude that drug from being a prescription only medicine; and

(5) vary the circumstances listed in Schedule 2 to the principal order in which a veterinary drug for parenteral administration containing the substance Procaine Hydrochloride is excluded from being a prescription only medicine.

STATUTORY INSTRUMENTS

1984 No. 1863

LOCAL GOVERNMENT, ENGLAND AND WALES

The Local Government (Supplementary Grants for Transport Purposes Specified Descriptions) Order 1984

Approved by both Houses of Parliament

Made - - - - -	18*th October* 1984
Laid before Parliament	22*nd October* 1984
Coming into Operation	28*th November* 1984

The Secretary of State for Transport as respects England and the Secretary of State for Wales as respects Wales, in exercise of the powers conferred by section 51(2), (3), (4) and (6) of the Local Government, Planning and Land Act 1980(a) and now vested in them(b), and of all other enabling powers, hereby make the following order:

1. This order may be cited as the Local Government (Supplementary Grants for Transport Purposes Specified Descriptions) Order 1984 and shall come into operation on the day after the day on which it is approved by resolution of each House of Parliament.

2. The Local Government (Supplementary Grants for Transport Purposes Specified Descriptions) (Wales) Order 1981(c) is hereby revoked.

3. In this order—

"the 1974 Act" means the Local Government Act 1974(d);

"the 1980 Act" means the Local Government, Planning and Land Act 1980; and

"year" means a period of twelve months beginning with 1st April.

4. For the year 1985–86 and each subsequent year no supplementary grants for transport purposes shall be paid by the Secretary of State to county councils in England or the Greater London Council under section 6 of the 1974 Act except in respect of their estimated expenditure of the description specified in Schedule 1 to this order.

(a) 1980 c. 65.
(b) As to the Secretary of State for Transport by S.I. 1981/238.
(c) S.I. 1981/1770.
(d) 1974 c. 7.

5. For the year 1985-86 and each subsequent year no supplementary grants for transport purposes shall be paid by the Secretary of State to county councils in Wales under section 6 of the 1974 Act except in respect of their estimated expenditure of the description specified in Schedule 2 to this order.

6. Section 6 of the 1974 Act (Supplementary grants for transport purposes) shall be amended as follows:

(*a*) in subsection (1) for the words from "to county councils" to the end of the subsection there shall be substituted—

"(*a*) to county councils in England and the Greater London Council in respect of their estimated expenditure in connection with—

(i) highways and

(ii) the regulation of traffic, and

(*b*) to county councils in Wales in respect of their estimated expenditure in connection with—

(i) public transport

(ii) highways and

(iii) the regulation of traffic

and in this section "transport matters" means, in England, the matters specified in paragraphs (*a*)(i) and (ii) above and, in Wales, the matters specified in paragraphs (*b*)(i) to (iii) above";

(*b*) in subsection (2) after the words "for the purposes of this section" there shall be inserted the words "as it applies in Wales";

(*c*) in subsection (4) the words "in England", and "the extent (if any) to which" and from "exceeds a level" to the end of the subsection shall be omitted;

(*d*) subsection (4A) shall be omitted; and

(*e*) for subsections (5) and (5A) there shall be substituted—

"(5) For the purposes of subsection (4) above—

(*a*) the Secretary of State may treat the estimated expenditure of the London borough councils and the Common Council of the City of London in connection with transport matters as forming part of the estimated expenditure in connection with those matters of the Greater London Council;

(*b*) the Secretary of State may treat the estimated expenditure of a district council in connection with transport matters as forming part of the estimated expenditure in connection with those matters of the council of the county in which that district is situated; and

(*c*) "accepted", in relation to the estimated expenditure of a council, means so much of their estimated expenditure as the Secretary of State may determine to be appropriate to be taken into account for the purposes of this section;

and in making a determination under paragraph (c) above, in relation to the estimated expenditure of a council, the Secretary of State shall have regard to the progress which appears to him to have been made by the council in formulating and implementing suitable policies to meet the needs of their area in connection with transport matters.".

Nicholas Ridley,
Secretary of State for Transport.

17th October 1984.

Nicholas Edwards,
Secretary of State for Wales.

18th October 1984.

Article 4 ## SCHEDULE 1

DESCRIPTION OF EXPENDITURE (ENGLAND)

Expenditure in connection with highways and the regulation of traffic which is, in accordance with the provisions of Schedule 12 to the 1980 Act and the Local Government (Prescribed Expenditure) Regulations 1983 **(a)**, prescribed expenditure for the purposes of Schedule 2 to the London Government Act 1963 **(b)** or Part VIII of the 1980 Act.

Article 5 ## SCHEDULE 2

DESCRIPTION OF EXPENDITURE (WALES)

Expenditure in connection with public transport, highways and the regulation of traffic which is, in accordance with the provisions of Schedule 12 to the 1980 Act and the Local Government (Prescribed Expenditure) Regulations 1983, prescribed expenditure for the purposes of Part VIII of the 1980 Act.

(a) S.I. 1983/296.   **(b)** 1963 c. 33.

EXPLANATORY NOTE

(This Note is not part of the Order.)

This order revokes the Local Government (Supplementary Grants for Transport Purposes Specified Descriptions) (Wales) Order 1981 and makes new provision specifying descriptions of expenditure for which supplementary grants for transport purposes shall be paid respectively in England and Wales under the provisions of section 6 of the Local Government Act 1974 from 1st April 1985 onwards.

In England the descriptions relate only to capital expenditure on highways and the regulation of traffic. In Wales the descriptions relate only to capital expenditure on public transport, highways and the regulation of traffic.

The order also makes amendments to section 6 of the 1974 Act which are consequential upon the specification in the order of descriptions of expenditure.

STATUTORY INSTRUMENTS

1984 No. 1865 (S.146)

LEGAL AID AND ADVICE, SCOTLAND

The Legal Aid (Scotland)
(Financial Conditions) Regulations 1984

Approved by both Houses of Paliament

Made - - - - -   24th October 1984

Laid before Parliament   31st October 1984

Coming into Operation   26th November 1984

In exercise of the powers conferred on me by sections 2, 3 and 15 of the Legal Aid (Scotland) Act 1967(a), and of all other powers enabling me in that behalf, I hereby make the following regulations:—

1.—(1) The regulations may be cited as the Legal Aid (Scotland) (Financial Conditions) Regulations 1984 and shall come into operation on 26th November 1984.

(2) In these regulations, "the Act" means the Legal Aid (Scotland) Act 1967.

2. For the purposes of section 2(1) of the Act, there is hereby prescribed the yearly figure of disposable income of £5,155 in place of the yearly figure of £4,925 prescribed by the Legal Aid (Scotland) (Financial Conditions) (No. 2) Regulations 1983(b).

3. For the purposes of section 2(1) of the Act, there is hereby prescribed the figure of disposable capital of £4,710 in place of the figure of £4,500 prescribed by the Legal Aid (Scotland) (Financial Conditions) (No. 2) Regulations 1983.

4. For the yearly sum of £2,050 specified in section 3(1)(a) of the Act there shall be substituted the yearly sum of £2,145.

(a) 1967 c. 43; section 2(1) was amended by the Legal Aid Act 1979 (c. 26), section 13(1) and Schedule 1, paragraph 1; section 3(1) was amended by section 9 of the said Act of 1979 and by S.I. 1983/1835; section 3(1A) was inserted by, and section 15 amended by, section 26 of the Law Reform (Miscellaneous Provisions) (Scotland) Act 1980 (c. 55).

(b) S.I. 1983/1835.

5. The Legal Aid (Scotland) (Financial Conditions) (No. 2) Regulations 1983 are hereby revoked.

George Younger,
New St Andrew's House,   One of Her Majesty's Principal
Edinburgh.   Secretaries of State.
24th October 1984.

EXPLANATORY NOTE

(This Note is not part of the Regulations.)

These regulations increase certain of the financial limits of eligibility for legal aid under the Legal Aid (Scotland) Act 1967.

The income limits are increased to make legal aid available to persons with disposable incomes of not more than £5,155 a year (instead of £4,925) and available without payment of a contribution to those with disposable incomes of less than £2,145 a year (instead of £2,050).

The upper limit of disposable capital, above which legal aid may be refused if it appears that the applicant could afford to proceed without legal aid is increased to £4,710 (instead of £4,500). The lower limit of disposable capital below which no contribution in respect of capital may be required remains at £3,000.

STATUTORY INSTRUMENTS

1984 No. 1866 (S.147)

LEGAL AID AND ADVICE, SCOTLAND

The Legal Advice and Assistance (Scotland) (Financial Conditions) Regulations 1984

Approved by both Houses of Parliament

Made - - - - -	24*th October* 1984
Laid before Parliament	31*st October* 1984
Coming into Operation	26*th November* 1984

In exercise of the powers conferred on me by section 15 of the Legal Aid (Scotland) Act 1967 (a) and sections 1 and 11 of the Legal Advice and Assistance Act 1972 (b), and of all other powers enabling me in that behalf, I hereby make the following regulations:—

1.—(1) These regulations may be cited as the Legal Advice and Assistance (Scotland) (Financial Conditions) Regulations 1984 and shall come into operation on 26th November 1984.

(2) In these regulations, "the Act" means the Legal Advice and Assistance Act 1972.

2. For the purposes of section 1(a) of the Act, there is hereby prescribed the weekly sum of £108 in place of the weekly sum of £103 prescribed by the Legal Advice and Assistance (Scotland) (Financial Conditions) (No. 3) Regulations 1983 (c).

3. For the purposes of section 1 of the Act, there is hereby prescribed the capital sum of £765 in place of the capital sum of £730 prescribed by the Legal Advice and Assistance (Scotland) (Financial Conditions) (No. 3) Regulations 1983.

(a) 1967 c. 43; section 15 was extended by section 6 of the Legal Advice and Assistance Act 1972 (c. 50).

(b) 1972 c. 50; section 1 was amended by the Legal Aid Act 1979 (c. 26), section 13(1) and Schedule 1, paragraph 5; section 11(1) was amended by the said Act of 1979, section 13(1) and Schedule 1, paragraph 7.

(c) S.I. 1983/1836.

4. The Legal Advice and Assistance (Scotland) (Financial Conditions) (No. 3) Regulations 1983 are hereby revoked.

New St Andrew's House,
Edinburgh.
24th October 1984.

George Younger,
One of Her Majesty's Principal
Secretaries of State.

EXPLANATORY NOTE

(This Note is not part of the Regulations.)

These regulations increase the disposable income limit for eligibility for legal advice and assistance under the Legal Advice and Assistance Act 1972 from £103 a week to £108 a week and increase the disposable capital limit from £730 to £765.

STATUTORY INSTRUMENTS

1984 No. 1867 (S. 148)

CHILDREN AND YOUNG PERSONS

The Children's Hearings (Scotland) (Amendment—Secure Accommodation) (No. 2) Rules 1984

Made   -   -   -   *22nd November* 1984

Coming into Operation   16*th December* 1984

In exercise of the powers conferred on me by section 35(4) and (5) of the Social Work (Scotland) Act 1968(**a**) and of all other powers enabling me in that behalf, and after consultation with the Council on Tribunals, I hereby make the following Rules:—

Citation and commencement
1. These Rules may be cited as the Children's Hearings (Scotland) (Amendment—Secure Accommodation) (No. 2) Rules 1984 and shall come into operation on 16th December 1984.

Interpretation
2. In these Rules "the principal Rules" means the Children's Hearings (Scotland) Rules 1971(**b**).

Amendment of rule 7 of the principal Rules
3. After sub-paragraph (*aa*) of rule 7(1) of the principal Rules (notification of hearings to children) there shall be inserted the following sub-paragraph:—

"(*aaa*) to consider the case of a child detained in a place of safety where a warrant for detention involving secure accommodation has been granted under section 58E(1) of the Act(**c**); or".

George Younger,
New St Andrew's House,   One of Her Majesty's Principal
Edinburgh.   Secretaries of State.
22nd November 1984.

(**a**) 1968 c.49.   (**b**) 1971/492, amended by S.I. 1983/1424 and 1984/100.
(**c**) Section 58E(1) was inserted by the Health and Social Services and Social Security Adjudications Act 1983 (c.41), section 8(4).

EXPLANATORY NOTE

(This Note is not part of the Rules.)

These Rules provide for a further amendment to the Children's Hearings (Scotland) Rules 1971 in addition to the amendments made by the Children's Hearings (Scotland) (Amendment—Secure Accommodation etc.) Rules 1984. They change the requirement for the period of notice of a children's hearing to be given where a warrant for a child's detention in a place of safety has been granted and that warrant relates to the use of secure accommodation.

STATUTORY INSTRUMENTS

1984 No. 1870

OFFSHORE INSTALLATIONS

The Offshore Installations (Safety Zones) (No. 90) Order 1984

Made - - - -	*28th November* 1984
Coming into Operation	*30th November* 1984

The Secretary of State, in exercise of the powers conferred on him by section 21(1), (2) and (3) of the Oil and Gas (Enterprise) Act 1982 (a) (hereinafter referred to as "the Act"), and of all other powers enabling him in that behalf, hereby makes the following Order:—

1. This Order may be cited as the Offshore Installations (Safety Zones) (No. 90) Order 1984 and shall come into operation on 30th November 1984.

2.—(1) A safety zone is hereby established around the installation specified in Column 1 of the Schedule hereto (being an installation maintained in waters in an area designated under section 1(7) of the Continental Shelf Act 1964 (b)) having a radius of five hundred metres from the point as respects that installation which has the co-ordinates of latitude and longitude according to European Datum (1950) specified in Columns 2 and 3 of the Schedule.

(2) The prohibition under section 21(3) of the Act on a vessel entering or remaining in a safety zone without the consent of the Secretary of State shall not apply to a vessel entering or remaining in the safety zone established under paragraph (1) above—

(a) in connection with the laying, inspection, testing, repair, alteration, renewal or removal of any submarine cable or pipe-line in or near that safety zone;

(b) to provide services for, to transport persons or goods to or from, or under the authority of a government department to inspect, any installation in that safety zone;

(c) if it is a vessel belonging to a general lighthouse authority performing duties relating to the safety of navigation;

(d) in connection with the saving or attempted saving of life or property;

(e) owing to stress of weather; or

(f) when in distress.

Alastair Goodlad,
Parliamentary Under Secretary of State,
Department of Energy.

28th November 1984.

(a) 1982 c.23.   (b) 1964 c.29.

SCHEDULE   Article 2(1)

SAFETY ZONE

1	2	3
Name or other designation of the offshore installation	Latitude North	Longitude East
Glomar Biscay II	57° 28′ 24.31″	02° 05′ 33.95″

EXPLANATORY NOTE

(*This Note is not part of the Order.*)

This Order establishes, under section 21 of the Oil and Gas (Enterprise) Act 1982, a safety zone, having a radius of 500 metres from a specified point, around the installation known as Glomar Biscay II maintained in waters in an area designated under section 1(7) of the Continental Shelf Act 1964.

Vessels (which includes hovercraft, submersible apparatus and installations in transit) are prohibited from entering or remaining in the safety zone except with the consent of the Secretary of State or in the circumstances mentioned in Article 2(2) of the Order.

STATUTORY INSTRUMENTS

1984 No. 1871

PLANT HEALTH

The Chrysanthemum (Temporary Prohibition on Landing) (Great Britain) Order 1984

Made - - - -	29th November 1984
Laid before Parliament	30th November 1984
Coming into Operation	1st December 1984

The Minister of Agriculture, Fisheries and Food in relation to England, the Secretary of State for Scotland in relation to Scotland and the Secretary of State for Wales in relation to Wales, in exercise of the powers conferred by sections 2 and 3(1) and (2) of the Plant Health Act 1967 (a), as read with section 20 of the Agriculture (Miscellaneous Provisions) Act 1972 (b), and now vested in them (c), and every other power enabling them in that behalf, hereby make the following order:—

Title, extent, commencement and duration

1. This order may be cited as the Chrysanthemum (Temporary Prohibition on Landing) (Great Britain) Order 1984, shall apply to Great Britain, shall come into operation on 1st December 1984 and shall cease to have effect on 31st March 1985.

Prohibition on landing

2. The landing in Great Britain of florists' chrysanthemum (species, hybrids and cultivars of *Dendranthema* (DC) Desmoul.) grown in Italy is hereby prohibited.

Application of the Import and Export (Plant Health) (Great Britain) Order 1980

3. The provisions of Articles 12 (examination, sampling and marking), 13 and 15 (procedure when plants are landed), 16 (powers of an officer of Customs and Excise), 17 (licences) and 19 (service of notices) of the Import and Export (Plant Health) (Great Britain) Order 1980 (d) shall apply in relation to the prohibition contained in Article 2 of this order.

In Witness whereof the official seal of the Minister of Agriculture, Fisheries and Food is hereunto affixed on 29th November 1984.

(a) 1967 c.8; section 3(2) was amended by the European Communities Act 1972 (c.68), section 4(1) and Schedule 4, paragraph 8.
(b) 1972 c.62.
(c) In the case of the Secretary of State for Wales by virtue of S.I. 1978/272.
(d) S.I. 1980/420, to which there are amendments not relevant to this order.

Michael Jopling,
Minister of Agriculture, Fisheries
and Food.

George Younger,
Secretary of State for Scotland.
29th November 1984.

Nicholas Edwards,
Secretary of State for Wales.
29th November 1984.

EXPLANATORY NOTE

(This Note is not part of the Order.)

This Order prohibits for 4 months from 1st December 1984 the landing in Great Britain of chrysanthemums grown in Italy.

The following provisions of the Import and Export (Plant Health) (Great Britain) Order 1980 apply to the prohibition on landing contained in Article 2:—

(a) an officer of the appropriate Minister authorised for the purposes of that Order has the powers of entry, examination and sampling and powers to enable remedial action to be taken when plants or flowers are landed or are likely to be landed in contravention of this Order (Articles 12 and 13 of that Order);

(b) Officers of Customs and Excise may detain plants and flowers for examination (Article 16 of that Order);

(c) the landing of a plant or flower which is prohibited by this Order may be authorised by licence (Article 17 of that Order).

Any person who lands a plant or flower in contravention of this Order with intent to evade the prohibition contained in it is guilty of an offence under section 50(2) of the Customs and Excise Management Act 1979 (c.2) and may be detained. A person guilty of such offence is liable, on summary conviction, to a penalty of £2,000 or of three times the value of the goods, whichever is the greater, or to imprisonment for a term not exceeding 6 months, or to both, and, on conviction on indictment, to a penalty of any amount, or to imprisonment for a term not exceeding 2 years, or to both.

STATUTORY INSTRUMENTS

1984 No. 1872

SEEDS

The Fodder Plant Seeds (Amendment) Regulations 1984

Made - - - -	*29th November* 1984
Laid before Parliament	*13th December* 1984
Coming into Operation	*4th January* 1985

The Minister of Agriculture, Fisheries and Food, the Secretary of State for Scotland and the Secretary of State for Wales, acting jointly, in exercise of the powers conferred by sections 16(1), (1A) and (8), and 36 of the Plant Varieties and Seeds Act 1964(a) and now vested in them(b) and of all other powers enabling them in that behalf, after consultation in accordance with the said section 16(1) with representatives of such interests as appear to them to be concerned, hereby make the following regulations:—

Title and commencement

1. These regulations may be cited as the Fodder Plant Seeds (Amendment) Regulations 1984 and shall come into operation on 4th January 1985.

Amendment of principal regulations

2. For paragraph 7 of Part I of Schedule 2 to the Fodder Plant Seeds Regulations 1980(c) (which sets out required standards for varietal purity) there shall be substituted the following paragraph—

"*Standards for varietal purity and species purity*

7. The crop shall have sufficient varietal identity and varietal purity. In particular the average level of the following impurities shall not exceed—

	IN CROPS TO PRODUCE	
	basic seeds	certified seeds
(a) recognisable off-types of the same species in grasses and herbage legumes (including Italian or awned ryegrass in perennial ryegrass and perennial or awnless ryegrass in Italian ryegrass) other than apomictic uni-clonal varieties of *Poa* spp	1 plant in 50 sq m	1 plant in 10 sq m
(b) recognisable off-types of apomictic uni-clonal varieties of *Poa* spp	0.3%	2%

(a) 1964 c. 14; section 16 was amended by the European Communities Act 1972 (c. 68), section 4(1) and paragraph 5(1), (2) and (3) of Schedule 4.
(b) In the case of the Secretary of State for Wales by virtue of S.I. 1978/272.
(c) S.I. 1980/899, amended by S.I. 1982/1757.

IN CROPS TO PRODUCE

		basic seeds	certified seeds
(c)	recognisable off-types of the same species in field peas and field beans	0.3%	1%
(d)	recognisable off-types of the same species in swede and fodder kale	0.3%	1%
(e)	recognisable off-types of the same species in vetches, lupins and fodder radish	1 plant in 30 sq m	1 plant in 10 sq m
(f)	plants (other than those classified as off-types) grown from shed seeds in grasses and herbage legumes	1% of seed heads in crop	No standard
(g)	ryegrass in cocksfoot, meadow fescue, red fescue or tall fescue	1 plant in 50 sq m	1 plant in 10 sq m "
(h)	suckling clover (*Trifolium dubium* Sibth.) in white clover		

In Witness whereof the Official Seal of the Minister of Agriculture, Fisheries and Food is hereunto affixed on 26th November 1984.

Michael Jopling,
Minister of Agriculture,
Fisheries and Food.

George Younger,
Secretary of State for Scotland.

27th November 1984.

Nicholas Edwards,
Secretary of State for Wales.

29th November 1984.

EXPLANATORY NOTE

(This Note is not part of the Regulations.)

These regulations, which amend the Fodder Plant Seeds Regulations 1980, give effect to Article 1 of Commission Directive 81/126/EEC (O.J. No. L67, 12.3.81, p.36) and Articles 1 and 2 of Commission Directive 82/287/EEC (O.J. No. L131, 13.5.82, p.24), which amended Council Directive 66/401/EEC (O.J. No. 125, 11.7.66, p.2298/66) on the marketing of seeds of fodder plants.

The regulations lay down revised varietal purity standards which must be achieved by crops grown to produce seeds of fodder plants (other than commercial seeds) for marketing (Regulation 2). The principal changes are to the maximum levels of permitted impurities in crops of vetches, lupins and fodder radish which are defined by reference to the number of plants in an area instead of in percentages.

STATUTORY INSTRUMENTS

1984 No. 1873

SEEDS

The Oil and Fibre Plant Seeds (Amendment) (No. 2) Regulations 1984

Made - - - -	29th November 1984
Laid before Parliament	13th December 1984
Coming into Operation	4th January 1985

The Minister of Agriculture, Fisheries and Food, the Secretary of State for Scotland and the Secretary of State for Wales, acting jointly, in exercise of the powers conferred by sections 16(1), (1A) and (8), and 36 of the Plant Varieties and Seeds Act 1964 (a) and now vested in them (b) and of all powers enabling them in that behalf, after consultation in accordance with the said section 16(1) with representatives of such interests as appear to them to be concerned, hereby make the following regulations:—

Title and commencement

1. These regulations may be cited as the Oil and Fibre Plant Seeds (Amendment) (No. 2) Regulations 1984 and shall come into operation on 4th January 1985.

Amendment of principal regulations

2. For paragraph 8 of Part I of Schedule 2 to the Oil and Fibre Plant Seeds Regulations 1979 (c) (which sets out required standards for varietal purity) there shall be substituted the following paragraph—

"Standards for varietal purity

8. The crop shall have sufficient varietal identity and varietal purity. In particular—

(*a*) for crops of swede rape (other than varieties to be used solely for fodder purposes), turnip rape (other than varieties to be used solely for fodder purposes), soya bean, flax, linseed, sunflower (other than hybrid varieties including their components) and white mustard, the minimum varietal purity standards shall be:

(a) 1964 c.14; section 16 was amended by the European Communities Act 1972 (c.68), section 4(1) and paragraph 5(1), (2) and (3) of Schedule 4.
(b) In the case of the Secretary of State for Wales by virtue of S.I. 1978/272.
(c) S.I. 1979/1005, amended by S.I. 1984/199.

Minimum varietal purity (percentage by number)	Basic seeds	Certified seeds or certified seeds of the first generation	Certified seeds of the second or third generation
Swede rape and Turnip rape‡	99.9	99.7	—
Soya bean	97	95	95
Flax and Linseed	99.7	98	97.5
Sunflower and White mustard	99.7	99	—

‡ For swede rape and turnip rape varieties to be used solely for fodder purposes the minimum varietal purity standards shall be 99.7 per cent for basic seeds and 99 per cent for certified seeds.

(b) In crops of brown mustard and black mustard the number of plants of the crop species which are recognisable as obviously not being true to the variety shall not exceed—

(a) one plant in 30 sq m for the production of basic seeds, and

(b) one plant in 10 sq m for the production of certified seeds."

In Witness whereof the Official Seal of the Minister of Agriculture, Fisheries and Food is hereunto affixed on 26th November 1984.

Michael Jopling,
Minister of Agriculture, Fisheries and Food.

George Younger,
Secretary of State for Scotland.

27th November 1984.

Nicholas Edwards,
Secretary of State for Wales.

29th November 1984.

EXPLANATORY NOTE

(This Note is not part of the Regulations.)

These regulations, which amend the Oil and Fibre Plant Seeds Regulations 1979, give effect to Articles 3 and 4 of Commission Directive 82/287/EEC (O.J. No. L131, 13.5.82, p.24), and Article 1 of Commission Directive 82/859/EEC (O.J. No. L357, 18.12.82, p.31), which amended Council Directive 69/208/EEC (O.J. No. L169, 10.7.69, p.3) on the marketing of seeds of oil and fibre plants.

The regulations lay down revised varietal purity standards which must be achieved by crops grown to produce seeds of oil and fibre plants (other than commercial seeds) for marketing (Regulation 2). The principal changes made are to the varietal purity standards for turnip rape, swede rape, sunflower and white mustard (which are defined in percentages instead of by reference to the number of plants in an area) and for black mustard and brown mustard.

STATUTORY INSTRUMENTS

1984 No. 1874

WATER, ENGLAND AND WALES
WATER SUPPLY, SCOTLAND

The Reservoirs Act 1975 (Supervising Engineers Panel) (Applications and Fees) Regulations 1984

Made - - - - -	*29th November* 1984
Coming into Operation	*20th December* 1984

The Secretary of State having determined, after consultation with the Reservoirs Act Consultative Committee of the Institution of Civil Engineers, that a separate panel of civil engineers shall be constituted for the purposes of section 12 of the Reservoirs Act 1975(a), in exercise of his powers under sections 4(2) and 5 of that Act and of all other powers enabling him in that behalf, makes the following regulations:—

Citation and commencement

1. These regulations may be cited as the Reservoirs Act 1975 (Supervising Engineers Panel) (Applications and Fees) Regulations 1984 and shall come into operation on 20th December 1984.

Applications

2.—(1) An application under section 4(2) of the Reservoirs Act 1975 to be appointed a member of the panel of civil engineers constituted for the purposes of section 12 of the Act shall be in writing, shall include the information set out in the Schedule to these regulations and shall be sent, together with the prescribed fee and a reference from a civil engineer as to the suitability of the applicant for appointment, to the Secretary of State for the Environment.

(2) The prescribed fee to accompany an application referred to in paragraph (1) of this regulation shall be £50.

Regulation 2   SCHEDULE

RESERVOIRS ACT 1975

Information required from applicants for the panel of Supervising Engineers:

1. Full name of applicant.
2. Address of applicant.
3. Date of birth of applicant.
4. Relevant qualifications of applicant.

(a) 1975 c. 23.

5. Applicant's membership of Professional Institutions.

6. Particulars of past and present employment of applicant, including—

i. dates of any appointment,

ii. details of the reservoirs, including their capacity and main dimensions, in connection with the design construction, management, maintenance or repair of which the applicant has been employed,

iii. details of the nature and extent of the applicants responsibility for any reservoir in relation to which he has been employed, that is to say, whether he had responsibility for the design, construction or operation of the reservoir and to what degree of supervision he was subject,

iv. the name and address of any engineer under whose supervision the applicant worked.

Signed by authority of
the Secretary of State

Ian Gow,
Minister for Housing and Construction,
Department of the Environment.

27th November 1984.

Nicholas Edwards,
Secretary of State for Wales.

29th November 1984.

George Younger,
Secretary of State for Scotland.

29th November 1984.

EXPLANATORY NOTE

(*This note is not part of the regulations.*)

The Secretaries of State for the Environment, Wales and Scotland have determined that there shall be a number of different panels of civil engineers for the purposes of the Reservoirs Act 1975. One of these panels will consist of those civil engineers who may be employed under section 12 of the Act, which provides for the supervision of large raised reservoirs. These regulations prescribe the manner in which a civil engineer may apply to be appointed to that panel. They also prescribe the fee which is to accompany such an application.

STATUTORY INSTRUMENTS

1984 No. 1879

SEA FISHERIES

SEA FISH INDUSTRY

The Fishing Vessels (Acquisition and Improvement) (Grants) (Amendment) Scheme 1984

Made - - - -	*29th November* 1984
Laid before Parliament	*3rd December* 1984
Coming into Operation	*1st January* 1985

The Minister of Agriculture, Fisheries and Food and the Secretaries of State respectively concerned with the sea fish industry in Scotland, Wales and Northern Ireland, in exercise of the powers conferred on them by sections 15(1) and (2) and 18(1) of the Fisheries Act 1981(a), and of all other powers enabling them in that behalf, with the approval of the Treasury, hereby make the following scheme:—

Title and commencement

1. This scheme may be cited as the Fishing Vessels (Acquisition and Improvement) (Grants) (Amendment) Scheme 1984 and shall come into operation on 1st January 1985.

Amendment of the Fishing Vessels (Acquisition and Improvement) (Grants) Scheme 1981

2. The Fishing Vessels (Acquisition and Improvement) (Grants) Scheme 1981 (b) is hereby amended by substituting for the date "1st January 1985" in paragraph 7(1)(*a*) the date "1st January 1987".

In Witness whereof the Official Seal of the Minister of Agriculture, Fisheries and Food is hereunto affixed on 29th November 1984.

Michael Jopling,
Minister of Agriculture,
Fisheries and Food.

(a) 1981 c.29.   **(b)** S.I. 1981/1765.

27th November 1984.

George Younger,
Secretary of State for Scotland.

26th November 1984.

Nicholas Edwards,
Secretary of State for Wales.

Douglas Hurd,
Secretary of State for
Northern Ireland.

29th November 1984.

Approved on 27th November 1984.

A. G. Hamilton,
T. Garel-Jones,
Two of the Lords Commissioners
of Her Majesty's Treasury.

EXPLANATORY NOTE

(*This Note is not part of the Scheme.*)

This scheme amends the Fishing Vessels (Acquisition and Improvement) (Grants) Scheme 1981 by extending by two years to the end of 1986 the final date for approval of applications for grant.

STATUTORY INSTRUMENTS

1984 No. 1880

HOUSING, ENGLAND AND WALES

The Grants by Local Authorities (Appropriate Percentage and Exchequer Contribution) (Repairs Grants for Airey Houses) (Variation) Order 1984

Laid before the House of Commons in draft

Made - - -		*29th November* 1984
Coming into Operation		*1st December* 1984

The Secretary of State for the Environment, as respects England, and the Secretary of State for Wales, as respects Wales, in exercise of the powers conferred on them by sections 59, 78(4) and (5) and 128 of the Housing Act 1974(a) and of all other powers enabling them in that behalf, and with the consent of the Treasury, hereby make the following order, a draft of which has been approved by resolution of the House of Commons:—

1.—(1) This order may be cited as the Grants by Local Authorities (Appropriate Percentage and Exchequer Contribution) (Repairs Grants for Airey Houses) (Variation) Order 1984 and shall come into operation on 1st December 1984.

(2) In this order—

"approved applications" means applications for repairs grants approved by local authorities before 1st December 1984;

"the principal order" means the Grants by Local Authorities (Appropriate Percentage and Exchequer Contribution) (Repairs Grants for Airey Houses) Order 1982(b); and

"relevant applications" means applications for repairs grants made to local authorities before 1st December 1984 and not approved by them before that date.

2. The principal order shall cease to have effect except in relation to approved applications and relevant applications.

(a) 1974 c.44; section 59 was substituted by paragraph 4 of Schedule 12 to the Housing Act 1980 (c.51) and section 128 was amended by paragraph 30 of Schedule 25 to that Act.
(b) S.I. 1983/95.

3. In relation to relevant applications, the principal order is hereby varied by the substitution, in article 4, (Contribution by the Secretary of State) for the words "100 per cent." of the words "90 per cent.".

Signed by authority of
The Secretary of State

Ian Gow,
Minister for Housing and Construction,
Department of the Environment.

28th November 1984.

Nicholas Edwards,
Secretary of State for Wales.

28th November 1984.

We consent,

Donald Thompson,
A. G. Hamilton,
Two of the Lords
Commissioners of Her
Majesty's Treasury.

29th November 1984.

EXPLANATORY NOTE

(This note is not part of the order.)

This order provides for the Grants by Local Authorities (Appropriate Percentage and Exchequer Contribution) (Repairs Grants for Airey Houses) Order 1982 ("the 1982 Order") to cease to have effect except in two cases.

In relation to applications for repairs grants for Airey houses and flats, which are made but not approved before 1st December 1984, article 4 of the 1982 Order is varied so as to reduce the percentage contribution by the Secretary of State, towards the expense incurred by local authorities in making a repairs grant for any Airey house or flat, from 100 per cent. to 90 per cent. (article 3).

This order does not affect the operation of the 1982 Order in relation to applications for repairs grants approved before 1st December 1984.

Financial assistance may be available for certain owners of Airey houses and flats by virtue of the Housing Defects Act 1984 (c.50), which comes into operation on 1st December 1984.

STATUTORY INSTRUMENTS

1984 No. 1881 (S.149)

RATING AND VALUATION

The Rating of Caravan Sites (Scotland) Order 1984

approved by the House of Commons

Made - - -	*8th October* 1984
Laid before the House of Commons	17*th October* 1984
Coming into Operation	1*st April* 1985

In exercise of the powers conferred on me by section 3A(1) of the Rating (Caravan Sites) Act 1976(**a**) (hereinafter referred to as "the Act") and of all other powers enabling me in that behalf, I hereby make the following order:—

Citation and commencement

1. This order may be cited as the Rating of Caravan Sites (Scotland) Order 1984 and shall come into operation on 1st April 1985.

2. The rateable value of a caravan site to which section 3A of the Act applies shall be the sum of the following amounts:—

(*a*) the amount produced by deducting from the aggregate net annual value of the caravan pitches on the site (being caravan pitches to which that section applies) 40 per cent of the aggregate net annual value of those caravan pitches;

(*b*) the amount of the net annual value of so much of the site as does not consist of those pitches.

George Younger,
One of Her Majesty's Principal
Secretaries of State.

New St Andrew's House,
Edinburgh.
8th October 1984.

(**a**) 1976 c.15; section 3A was added by section 15 of the Rating and Valuation (Amendment) (Scotland) Act 1984 (c.31).

EXPLANATORY NOTE

(This Note is not part of the Order.)

This order prescribes the method for calculating the rateable value of a caravan site in terms of section 3A of the Rating (Caravan Sites) Act 1976.

STATUTORY INSTRUMENTS

1984 No. 1885 (S. 150)

FOOD

FOOD HYGIENE

The Fresh Meat Export (Hygiene and Inspection) (Scotland) Amendment Regulations 1984

Made - - - -	*29th November* 1984
Laid before Parliament	*10th December* 1984
Coming into Operation	*1st January* 1985

In exercise of the powers conferred on me by section 2(2) of the European Communities Act 1972(a) (being one of the Ministers designated(b) for the purposes of that section in relation to the common agricultural policy of the European Economic Community), and by sections 13 and 56 of the Food and Drugs (Scotland) Act 1956(c), and of all other powers enabling me in that behalf, having in accordance with section 56(6) of the said Act of 1956 consulted with such organisations as appear to me to be representative of interests substantially affected by the regulations, I hereby make the following regulations:—

Citation, commencement and interpretation

1.— (1) These regulations may be cited as the Fresh Meat Export (Hygiene and Inspection) (Scotland) Amendment Regulations 1984 and shall come into operation on 1st January1985.

(2) In these regulations "the principal regulations" means the Fresh Meat Export (Hygiene and Inspection) (Scotland) Regulations 1981(d) and, unless the context otherwise requires, any reference herein to a numbered regulation or schedule shall be construed as a reference to the regulation or schedule bearing that number in the principal regulations.

Amendment of the principal regulations

2.— (1) Regulation 2(1) (interpretation) shall be amended—

(a) 1972 c. 68; section 2 is subject to Schedule 2 to that Act and is to be read with section 289(F) and 289(G) of the Criminal Procedure (Scotland) Act 1975 (c. 21) (as inserted by section 54 of the Criminal Justice Act 1982 (c. 48)), and S.I. 1984/526.
(b) S.I. 1972/1811.
(c) 1956 c. 30.
(d) S.I. 1981/1034; relevant amending instrument is S.I. 1983/703.

(a) by inserting in the definition of "animals" after the words "bovine animals" the words "(including buffalo)";

(b) by substituting in the definition of "cutting up" for the words "quarter carcases" the words "half carcases cut into three wholesale cuts";

(c) by substituting for the definition of "fresh" the following definition:—
" "fresh" as applied to meat means all meat which has not undergone any preserving process and which includes meat vacuum wrapped or wrapped in a controlled atmosphere, however chilled and frozen meat shall be considered to be fresh meat;".

(2) For regulation 3 (exemption) there shall be substituted the following regulation:—

"Exemption

3. These regulations shall not apply to fresh meat which is exported with the authority of the country of destination and intended exclusively as supplies for international organisations and military forces stationed on its territory but serving under another flag.".

(3) In regulation 4(1)*(a)*(i) (approval of premises) for the words "can comply" there shall be substituted the word "complies".

(4) In regulation 4(1)*(a)*(ii) (approval of premises) there shall be added at the end the words "save that such premises shall not be approved if they are situated within the curtilage of a slaughterhouse which is not approved for export.".

(5) In regulation 4(8) (approval of premises) for the words "prior consultation with" there shall be substituted the words "the prior agreement in writing of".

(6) For regulation 6(1) (suspension and revocation of approval) there shall be substituted the following regulation:—

"6.— (1) The Secretary of State may suspend or revoke his approval of any export slaughterhouse, export cutting premises, export cold store or transhipment centre and require the withdrawal of the equipment for the application of the health mark if after an inspection of or an enquiry into, and a report on, the premises by a veterinary officer and, in the case of revocation of approval, after consultation with the local authority and the occupier, he is satisfied in respect of these premises that the requirements of these regulations are no longer or have not been complied with, and no action has been taken to ensure that a similar breach does not recur or that the condition attached to the approval of those premises referred to in regulation 4(8) has not been observed.".

(7) Regulation 10(1) (conditions for export of fresh meat) shall be amended by inserting after the words "quarter carcases" the words "half carcases cut into three wholesale cuts".

(8) Regulation 10(1)*(g)* shall be amended by inserting after the words "Schedule 14" the words "to the country of destination".

(9) Regulation 10(2)*(i)* shall be amended by inserting after the words "Schedule 14" the words "to the country of destination."

(10) For regulation 10(3) (conditions for export of fresh meat) there shall be substituted the following regulation:—

"(3) No person shall export or sell for export for human consumption—

(a) fresh meat of animals in which any form of tuberculosis or any living or dead cysticercus bovis or cysticercus cellulosae have been found;

(b) those parts of carcases or offal showing the traumatic lesions, malformations or changes referred to in paragraph (1)*(d)* of this regulation;

(c) those parts of carcases or offal which have been contaminated;

(d) fresh meat which has been treated with natural or artificial colouring matters;

(e) fresh meat which has been treated with ionizing or ultra-violet radiation.

(4) Except where the country of destination has granted a general authorisation or an authorisation restricted to a specific case, no person shall export or sell for export for human consumption—

(a) fresh meat from cryptorchid or hermaphrodite pigs;

(b) fresh meat from boars;

(c) heads of bovine animals and fresh meat from the heads of bovine animals excluding tongues and brains;

(d) fresh meat from animals to which tenderisers have been administered;

(e) blood;

(f) fresh meat in pieces each weighing less than 100g;

(g) minced meat or meat which is similarly finely divided and mechanically recovered meat.".

(11) Regulation 11 (admission of animals and carcases to an export slaughterhouse) shall be amended by inserting after the words "an official veterinary surgeon may require that the accommodation" the words "or alternative method of operation and facilities" and by adding at the end the following paragraph:—

"(2) Fresh meat from any carcase which has been examined or dressed in accordance with paragraphs 1*(b)* or *(c)* of this regulation shall not be eligible for export.".

(12) In regulation 18 (offences and penalties) for the sum of "£100" there shall be substituted the sum of "£2,000".

(13) In Schedule 1 (conditions for the approval of export slaughterhouses)—

(a) for paragraph 2(a) there shall be substituted the following:—

"(a) a suitable, sufficient and separate room or rooms exclusively reserved for the storage of hides, skins, horns, hooves, pigs bristles and fat not intended for human consumption;";

(b) in paragraph 2(b) after the words "suspected of being diseased or injured" there shall be inserted the words "save that such accommodation need not be provided if—

(i) such diseased animals are slaughtered after completion of the slaughter of animals whose meat is intended for export;

(ii) steps are taken to prevent contamination of such meat;

(iii) the premises are cleaned and disinfected under official supervision before being used again for the slaughtering of animals intended for export; and

(iv) suitable and sufficient facilities are provided for the introduction of the carcase of an injured animal into the slaughterhall in a manner which will not prejudice the hygenic operation of the slaughterhouse;";

(c) for paragraph 2(c) there shall be substituted the following:—

"(c) a suitable and sufficiently large refrigerated room for the cooling of and for the exclusive storage of meat prepared in an export approved slaughterhouse; the room shall be equipped with corrosion resistant fittings capable of preventing meat coming into contact with the floors and walls; and, where a room is used to store meat already cooled, it shall also have a recording thermometer or recording telethermometer;";

(d) after paragraph 2(i) there shall be added the following:—

"(j) doors and door frames made of a hard wearing, non-corrodible material or, if made of wood, faced on both sides with a smooth, impermeable covering;

(k) facilities for the hygienic handling and protection of meat during loading and unloading;

(l) insulation materials which are rotproof and odourless;

(m) a separate room or rooms capable of being securely locked for the retention of meat rejected as being unfit for human consumption; except that where such meat is removed as often as may be necessary and at least daily and the quantities are not sufficient to require the provision of a separate room or rooms then suitable and sufficient receptacles shall be provided which are capable of being securely locked; such receptacles shall be used only for holding meat rejected as being unfit for human consumption and shall be clearly marked to that effect; and any chutes used to transport meat to such receptacles shall be so constructed and installed as to enable them to be kept clean and avoid the risk of contamination of the fresh meat;

(n) suitable refrigeration equipment which will enable the internal temperature of the meat to be maintained at the level prescribed in Schedule 7; such equipment shall include drainage which must present no risk of contamination of the meat;

(o) in the accommodation where persons working in the slaughterhouse may change their clothes, surfaces of walls and floors which are smooth, washable and impermeable;

(p) on all hand washing facilities in changing rooms, and rooms associated with the sanitary conveniences, taps which are not operable by hand or arm;

(q) in the lairage, walls and floors which are durable, impermeable, and easy to clean and disinfect;

(r) a suitable, sufficient and separate room exclusively reserved for the preparation and cleaning of offal other than the emptying and cleaning of stomachs and intestines and the dressing of guts and tripe and which includes a separate area for heads at a sufficient distance from other offal where these operations are carried out in the slaughterhouse other than on the slaughterline;

(s) a suitable and separate place for the packaging of offal in accordance with the requirements of Part II of Schedule 12.";

(e) in paragraph 3—

(i) there shall be inserted at the commencement of the paragraph the following words:—

"Water which is required to be clean and wholesome shall meet the requirements of Council Directive 80/778/EEC(**a**) and records of the results of water tests and any consequent action shall be available at all times to an official veterinary surgeon or to a veterinary officer and shall be kept for a period of not less than 1 year.";

(ii) for the words "shall be painted a distinctive colour and shall not pass through any room which contains meat" there shall be substituted the words "shall clearly be distinguished from those used for potable water and shall present no risk of contamination of the fresh meat".

(14) In Schedule 2 (conditions for the approval of export cutting premises)—

(a) paragraph 1*(c)* of Part I shall be amended by inserting at the end the words "except that cutting, boning, wrapping and packaging of meat may take place in the same room provided that the room is sufficiently large and so arranged that the hygiene of the operation is assured; that the rooms in which packaging and wrapping material are stored are free from dust and vermin and are not connected in any way with rooms containing substances which might contaminate fresh meat; and the requirements of paragraph 1*(k)* of Schedule 9 are observed.";

(b) paragraph 1*(f)* of Part I shall be amended by inserting at the end the words "the surfaces of the walls and floors of such rooms shall be smooth, washable and impermeable.";

(**a**) O.J. No. L229, 30.8.80, p.11.

(c) paragraph 1*(h)* of Part I shall be amended by inserting at the end the words "and any chutes used to transport meat to such receptacles shall be so constructed and installed as to enable them to be kept clean and avoid the risk of contamination of the fresh meat;";

(d) paragraph 1*(i)* of Part I shall be amended by deleting the words "thermometer or" and by inserting after the words "recording thermometer" the words "or recording telethermometer";

(e) after paragraph 1*(k)* of Part I there shall be added the following:—

"(l) doors and door frames made of a hard wearing, non-corrodible material or, if made of wood, faced on both sides with a smooth, impermeable covering;

(m) insulation materials which are rotproof and odourless;

(n) facilities for the hygienic handling and protection of meat during loading and unloading;

(o) suitable refrigeration equipment which will enable the internal temperature of the meat to be maintained at the level prescribed in Schedule 9, such equipment shall include satisfactory drainage which presents no risk of contamination of the meat;

(p) on all hand washing facilities in work rooms, changing rooms, and rooms associated with the sanitary conveniences, taps which are not operable by hand or arm;

(q) a place and adequate equipment for cleansing and disinfecting vehicles;

(r) suitable and sufficient means of ventilation to the external air and where necessary adequate means of steam extraction.";

(f) in paragraph 2—

(i) there shall be inserted at the commencement of the paragraph the following words:—

"Water which is required to be clean and wholesome shall meet the requirements of Council Directive 80/778/EEC and records of the results of water tests and any consequent action shall be available at all times to an official veterinary surgeon or to a veterinary officer and shall be kept for a period of not less than 1 year".

(ii) for the words "shall be painted a distinctive colour and shall not pass through any room which contains meat" shall be substituted the words "shall clearly be distinguished from those used for potable water and shall present no risk of contamination of the fresh meat".

(g) paragraphs *(a)* and *(b)* of Part II shall be amended by inserting after the word "water" the words "within the meaning of Council Directive 80/778/EEC";

(h) paragraph (j) of Part II shall be amended by inserting after the words "impervious material" the words "other than wood".

(15) In Schedule 3 (conditions for the approval of export cold stores)—

(a) for paragraph *(b)* there shall be substituted the following:—

"*(b)* adequate means and procedures, including fixed apparatus for mechanical or electrical recording of temperatures for ensuring that each storage chamber is maintained at the temperatures required by paragraph 3 of Schedule 13;";

(b) paragraph *(d)* shall be amended by inserting at the end the words "the surfaces of the walls and floors of such rooms shall be smooth, washable and impermeable;";

(c) after paragraph *(f)* there shall be added the following:—

"*(g)* interior wall surfaces faced with smooth, durable, impervious and washable material, which shall be of a light colour, up to a height of not less than the usable storage height;

(h) floor surfaces which are waterproof and rotproof;

(i) doors and door frames made of a hard wearing, non-corrodible material and if made of wood, faced on both sides with a smooth, impermeable covering;

(j) insulation materials which are rotproof and odourless;

(k) if applicable, at places readily accessible to the work stations, suitable facilities adequately equipped with hot and cold or warm running water at a suitable temperature for the washing of hands by persons handling meat. Taps supplying these facilities shall not be operable by hand or arm. Disposable towels, which shall only be used once, shall be provided in a suitable container and a receptacle shall be provided for used towels;

(l) in rooms where unwrapped fresh meat is handled or stored, equipment and fittings must be constructed of a durable and impervious material other than wood, resistant to corrosion and capable of being kept clean;

(m) suitable refrigeration equipment which will enable the internal temperature of meat to be maintained at the level prescribed in Schedule 13, such equipment shall include satisfactory drainage which presents no risk of contamination of the meat;

(n) suitable facilities for the exclusive use of the veterinary service;

(o) an adequate number of changing rooms with smooth, waterproof, washable walls and floors, wash basins and flush lavatories, not opening directly on to the work rooms. A sufficient number of wash basins shall be provided close to the lavatories; the wash basins shall have hot and cold running water or water premixed to a suitable temperature. Sufficient materials for cleaning and disinfecting hands, and disposable hand towels which can be used once only shall be provided;

(p) on all hand washing facilities in work rooms, changing rooms and rooms associated with the sanitary conveniences, taps which are not operable by hand or arm;

(q) a sufficient, clean and wholesome supply of water available at an adequate pressure throughout the premises, and a sufficient, clean, constant and wholesome supply of hot water under adequate pressure available in the work rooms during working hours; such water shall meet the requirements of Council Directive

80/778/EEC(a) and records of the results of water tests and any consequent action shall be available at all times to an official veterinary surgeon or to a veterinary officer and shall be kept for a period of not less than 1 year.";

(d) After paragraph 1 there shall be added the following:—

"2. Water which is not clean and wholesome may be used only for the purpose of firefighting or the operation of refrigeration equipment or steam boilers, and pipes carrying such water shall be so arranged as not to allow any such water to be used for any other purpose, and all such pipes shall be clearly distinguished from those used for carrying potable water and shall present no risk of contamination of the fresh meat".

(16) In Schedule 5 (hygiene requirements in relation to staff, premises, equipment and implements in export slaughterhouses, export cutting premises and export cold stores)—

(a) after paragraph 6 of Part I there shall be added the following:—

"7. The occupier shall ensure that no sawdust or any similar substance is spread on floors.";

(b) in paragraph 1 (c) of Part II after the words "cleansed and disinfected" there shall be inserted the words "and then rinsed in clean water.";

(c) after paragraph 1(d) of Part III there shall be added the following:—

"(e) wash his hands with hot water and soap or other detergent frequently during the working day and each time work is started and resumed;

(f) wash his hands and arms with hot water and soap or other detergent immediately after contact with meat which he knows or suspects to be diseased.";

(d) after paragraph 3(d) of Part III there shall be added the following:—

"(e) ensure that all equipment and instruments which come into contact with meat and which are cleansed and disinfected are then rinsed in clean water.".

(17) In Schedule 6 (ante-mortem health inspection)—

(a) in paragraph 1 for the words "more than 24 hours have elapsed since the previous inspection" there shall be substituted the words "the animal has been kept in the lairage overnight";

(b) after paragraph 3(c) there shall be added the following:—

"(d) where there is visible evidence that they have had substances with pharmacological effects administered to them or have consumed any other substances which may make the meat unfit for human consumption.".

(c) in paragraph 4(b) after the words "stressed animals must not" there shall be inserted the words "unless the official veterinary surgeon determines otherwise";

(a) O.J. No. L229, 30.8.80, p.11.

(d) after paragraph 4*(b)* there shall be added the following:—

"*(c)* have been found to have any form of clinical tuberculosis.";

(e) paragraph 5*(b)* shall be amended by inserting at the end the words "and that immediately following slaughtering and dressing of the animal and before the slaughtering of other animals takes place the premises shall be fully cleaned and disinfected in such manner as he shall determine.".

(18) In Schedule 7 (slaughter and dressing practices)—

(a) in paragraph *(c)*(i) after the words "viscera (save that" there shall be inserted the words "the lungs, the heart, the liver, the spleen, the mediastinum and", and after the words "natural connections" there shall be deleted the words "but are" and there shall be inserted the words "save that the kidneys shall be";

(b) in paragraph *(c)* (ii)—

(i) after the words "the hair and bristles" there shall be inserted the words "(which may be removed by use of a debristling agent provided that the carcase is then rinsed by means of a spray system in running water which is clean and wholesome)";

(ii) after the words "viscera (save that" there shall be inserted the words "the lungs, the heart, the liver, the spleen, the mediastinum and" and after the words "natural connections" there shall be deleted the words "but are" and there shall be inserted the words "save that the kidneys shall be";

(iii) after the words "perirenal coverings", there shall be inserted the words "save that, in the case of pigs not intended for export, exposure of the kidneys shall not be compulsory, and if the kidneys of a pig are not exposed, the meat of that pig shall not be eligible for export";

(c) in paragraph *(c)*(iii):—

(i) after the words "viscera (save that" there shall be inserted the words "the lungs, the heart, the liver, the spleen, the mediastinum and" and after the words "natural connections" there shall be deleted the words "but are" and there shall be inserted the words "save that the kidneys shall be";

(ii) after the words "fatty covering" there shall be inserted the words "save that, in the case of sheep and goats not intended for export, exposure of the kidneys shall not be compulsory, and if the kidneys of a sheep or goat are not exposed, the meat of that sheep or goat shall not be eligible for export";

(d) for paragraph *(d)* there shall be substituted the following:—

"*(d)* evisceration must be carried out immediately and completed not later than 45 minutes after stunning or in the case of ritual slaughter, half an hour after bleeding;";

(e) for paragraph *(f)* there shall be substituted the following:—

"*(f)* carcases of solipeds, bovine animals over six months old and pigs over four weeks old are split lengthwise through the spinal column before being submitted for inspection in accordance with

Schedule 8 (save that in the case of pigs over four weeks old not intended for export the carcase need not be so split, and if the carcase of any pig is not so split the meat of that pig shall not be eligible for export). Heads of solipeds shall be split. An authorised officer of the Council may require any carcase or head to be split lengthwise if he considers it necessary for the purpose of carrying out the inspection prescribed in Schedule 8;";

(f) in paragraph (h) after the words "where the blood" there shall be inserted the words "or offal" and after the words "which the blood" there shall be inserted the words "or offal";

(g) in paragraph (i) after the words "quarter carcases" there shall be inserted the words "and half carcases cut into three wholesale cuts";

(h) after paragraph (j) there shall be added the following:—

"(k) bleeding, flaying or removing bristles, dressing and evisceration is carried out in such a way as to avoid contamination of the carcase or offal;

(l) no implement is left in the meat;

(m) fresh meat intended for freezing is only frozen by a rapid method and is stored at a temperature of not more than $-12°C$.".

(19) In Schedule 8 (post-mortem health inspection)—

(a) in paragraph 2(a) of Part I for the words "in the case of mature animals" there shall be substituted the words "where considered necessary by the official veterinary surgeon";

(b) in paragraph 2(b) of Part I the words "such lymph nodes are to be examined in detail" shall be deleted;

(c) for paragraph 3 of Part I there shall be substituted the following:—

"3. Where an authorised officer of the Council considers it necessary, lymph nodes specified in Parts III and IV of this Schedule and any lymph nodes which are not specified in Parts II, III and IV of this Schedule shall be examined in detail.";

(d) in paragraph 6 of the Annex to Part I after the words "of this Annex" there shall be inserted the words "or is contaminated";

(e) in paragraph 1(c) of Part II for the word "perpendicular" there shall be substituted the words "at right angles";

(f) paragraph 1(i) of Part II shall be amended by inserting at the end the words "(save that in the case of bovines not intended for export the examination of the renal lymph nodes shall not be compulsory and if the renal lymph nodes of any bovine are not examined the meat of that bovine shall not be eligible for export)";

(g) for paragraph 2(d) of Part II there shall be substituted the following:—

"(d) the external (masseter) cheek muscles in which at least two deep incisions shall be made and internal (pterygoid) cheek muscles in which at least one deep incision shall be made. All incisions shall be made parallel to the mandible from its upper muscular insertion;";

(h) for paragraph 1(b) of Part III there shall be substituted the following:—

"(b) the head and throat, the tongue having been freed to permit a detailed inspection of the mouth including so far as is practicable the lips and gums, and the fauces: where an authorised officer of the Council considers it necessary the tonsils shall be inspected: the tonsils shall be removed and the submaxillary lymph nodes shall be examined in detail; the retro-pharyngeal and parotid lymph nodes shall be examined (save that in the case of pigs not intended for export, removal of the tonsils and examination of the retro-pharyngeal and parotid lymph nodes shall not be compulsory, and if the tonsils of any pig are not removed or those lymph nodes are not examined, the meat of that pig shall not be eligible for export);";

(i) in paragraph 1*(c)* of Part III for the word "perpendicular" there shall be inserted the words "at right angles"; and the words "(save that the lungs need not be incised if they are to be excluded from human consumption unless an authorised officer of the Council considers it necessary)" shall be inserted at the end;

(j) in paragraph 1*(g)* of Part III the words "in detail" shall be deleted.

(k) in paragraph 1*(i)* of Part III the words "in detail" shall be deleted.

(l) in paragraph 1*(j)* of Part III for the words "in the case of a boar and, if an authorised officer of the Council considers it necessary, in the case of other males" there shall be inserted the words "in the case of all male pigs."

(m) in paragraph 1*(k)* of Part III for the words "in detail;" there shall be inserted the words "and in the case of sows in detail;"

(n) for paragraph 1*(b)* of Part IV there shall be substituted the following:—

"(b) the head and throat with, if an authorised officer of the Council considers it necessary, the tongue having been freed, in order to permit a detailed inspection of the mouth and the fauces including so far as is practicable the lips, gums, and nasal cavities; the tonsils shall be inspected: the retro-pharyngeal, submaxillary, and parotid lymph nodes shall be examined;";

(o) in paragraph 1*(c)* of Part IV for the word "perpendicular" there shall be inserted the words "at right angles";

(p) in paragraph 1*(f)* of Part IV the words after "shall be examined" to the end of the paragraph shall be deleted;

(q) in paragraph 1*(g)* of Part IV the words "where an authorised officer of the Council considers it necessary" and the words "in detail" shall be deleted;

(r) in paragraph 1*(i)* of Part IV the words after "shall be examined" to the end of the paragraph shall be deleted;

(s) paragraph 1*(j)* of Part IV shall be deleted and replaced by the following:—

"(j) the outer surface and substance of the genital organs; in the case of male animals the superficial inguinal lymph nodes shall be examined; in the case of a female animal the uterus shall be opened by means of a lengthwise incision: such incision shall not be carried out in the slaughterhall or in any other part of the premises where it may contaminate meat;";

(20) In Schedule 9 (cutting practices)—

(a) in paragraph 1*(d)* after the words "quarter carcases" there shall be inserted the words "and half carcases cut into three wholesale cuts" and after the words "by means of an extension of the overhead rail system employed in that slaughterhouse" there shall be added the words "or other hygienic transport system";

(b) in paragraph 1*(f)* for the words "+ 10°C" there shall be substituted the words "+ 12°C";

(c) after paragraph 1*(i)* there shall be added the following:—

"*(j)* ensure that no implement is left in the meat;

(k) ensure that when cutting, boning, wrapping and packing operations take place in the same room, the following conditions are observed:—

(i) the packaging and wrapping material shall during storage be contained in a sealed and undamaged protective cover under hygienic conditions in a separate room;

(ii) packaging and wrapping material shall not be stored on the floor;

(iii) packaging material shall be assembled under hygienic conditions before being brought into the cutting room;

(iv) packaging material shall be hygienically brought into the room and shall be used without delay: it shall not be handled by persons who handle fresh meat;

(v) immediately after packing and wrapping the meat shall be placed in the storage rooms referred to in paragraph 1(a)(ii) of part I of Schedule 2;

(l) ensure that fresh meat intended for freezing is only frozen by a rapid method and is stored at a temperature of not more than − 12°C.".

(21) In Schedule 11 (health marking)—

(a) paragraph 2*(a)* shall be amended by inserting after the words "on the upper part" the words "the letters "UK" or";

(b) paragraph 3 shall be amended—

(i) by deleting "60kg" and inserting "65kg";

(ii) after the word "breast" inserting the word "and";

(iii) by deleting the words "and pleura";

(c) paragraph 4 shall be amended by inserting after the word "livers" the words "of bovine animals, swine and solipeds";

(d) paragraph 5 shall be amended by substituting for the words "heads, tongues, hearts and lungs" the words "all the offal" and by inserting after those words the words "unless they are wrapped or packed in accordance with the requirements of Schedule 12";

(e) paragraph 6 shall be amended—

    (i) by deleting "3kg" and inserting "100g each";

    (ii) by inserting after the words "and which do not bear a health mark shall" the words "unless they are wrapped or packed in accordance with the requirements of Schedule 12".

(22) In Schedule 12 (wrapping and packing of cut meat and offal)—

(a) the heading "Requirements applicable in export cutting premises" shall be deleted;

(b) paragraph 1 of Part I shall be amended by inserting at the end the words "except where the wrapping material used conforms to the requirements of paragraph 6 of this Part of this Schedule";

(c) paragraph 2 of Part I shall be amended by inserting at the end the words "it shall not be handled by persons who handle fresh meat";

(d) after paragraph 4 of Part I there shall be inserted the following:—

"5. The occupier shall ensure that all wrapped meat intended for sale bears a reproduction of the health mark bearing the letters "UK" on the wrapping material or on a label affixed to the wrapping material. The health mark shall include the approval number of the export cutting premises except that in the case of offal wrapped in an export approved slaughterhouse it shall bear the approval number of that slaughterhouse.

6. The occupier shall ensure that wrapped meat is packed in accordance with the requirements of Part II of this Schedule, save that where the wrapping material used fulfills the requirement of packaging material in accordance with the provisions of paragraph 1 of Part II of this Schedule it does not in addition require to be packed.";

(e) in paragraph 3 of Part II—

    (i) the words "has a clearly visible label which" shall be deleted;

    (ii) in sub-paragraph (a) at end the words "either on the package itself or on a label affixed to wrapping material which fulfills the requirements of paragraph 6 of Part I of this Schedule.".

(23) In Schedule 13 (storage of meat) paragraph 3(a) shall be amended by deleting the words "an adequately low temperature without undue fluctuation" and inserting the words "a temperature of not more than − 12°C".

(24) For Schedule 14 (health certificate) there shall be substituted the following Schedule:—

"SCHEDULE 14 Regulations 7(5) and (6), 9,
10(1)(g) and (2)(i) and 12(1)

HEALTH CERTIFICATE

1. The official veterinary surgeon shall sign the health certificate which is to

accompany the meat to the country of destination at the time the meat is loaded into the means of transport in which it is to travel.

2. The health certificate shall be provided by the Secretary of State and shall correspond in form to, and contain the information specified in, the model in the Annex to this Schedule. It shall be expressed at least in English and in the language of the country of destination.

ANNEX

Health certificate for fresh meat intended for consignment to a Member State (1) of the EEC

No........(2)

Exporting country ....

Ministry ....

Department ....

Ref (2) ....

  I. Identification of meat:

    Meat of ....
                               (animal species)

    Nature of cuts ....

    Nature of packaging ....

    Number of cuts or packages ....

    Month(s) and year(s) when frozen ....

    Net weight ....

  II. Origin of meat:

    Address(es) and veterinary approval number(s) of the approved slaughterhouse(s)

    ....

    ....

    Address(es) and veterinary approval number(s) of the approved cutting plant(s)

    ....

    ....

    Address(es) and veterinary approval number(s) of the approved store(s)

    ....

    ....

  III. Destination of meat:

    The meat will be sent from ....

    ....
                            (place of loading)

    to ....
                      (country and place of destination)

    ....

    by the following means of transport (3) ....

Name and address of consignor ....

Name and address of consignee ....

IV. Health attestation:

I, the undersigned, official veterinarian, certify that the meat described above was obtained under the conditions governing production and control laid down in Directive 64/433/EEC on health problems affecting intra-Community trade in fresh meat and that it is, therefore, considered as such to be fit for human consumption.

Done at .... on ....

Signature of the official veterinarian

....

(1) Fresh meat: in accordance with the directive referred to in IV of this certificate, all edible parts of domestic bovine animals (including buffalo), swine, sheep and goats and solipeds which have not undergone any preserving process and including meat vacuum wrapped or wrapped in a controlled atmosphere; however, chilled and frozen meat shall be considered to be fresh meat.

(2) Optional.

(3) In the case of trucks and lorries, state the registration number, in the case of aircraft the flight number, and in the case of boats, the name, and where necessary, the number of the container."

(25) In Schedule 15 (transport of fresh meat intended for export)—

(a) in paragraph 1 after the words "1. Fresh meat" there shall be inserted the words "shall be loaded at a temperature of not more than $+7°C$ for carcases and cuts and $+3°C$ for offal and";

(b) in paragraph 3 at the end there shall be inserted the words "except that fittings for hanging such meat shall not be required where the meat is transported by aircraft in which suitable facilities resistant to corrosion have been provided for hygienically loading, holding and unloading the meat";

(c) in paragraph 5, there shall be deleted the words "as any other substance" and there shall be inserted the words "as any other product likely to affect the hygiene of the meat or to contaminate it unless it is transported in such a manner that it will not contaminate the fresh meat";

(d) in paragraph 6 after the words "stomachs shall be scalded" there shall be inserted the words "or cleaned" and after the words "and feet" there shall be inserted the words "and heads";

(e) in paragraph 8 after the words "throughout the period of transport" there shall be inserted the words "except where such meat is transported by aircraft in which suitable facilities resistant to corrosion have been provided for hygienically loading, holding and unloading the meat".

George Younger,
One of Her Majesty's Principal
Secretaries of State.

New St. Andrew's House,
Edinburgh.
29th November 1984.

EXPLANATORY NOTE

(This Note is not part of the Regulations.)

These Regulations which apply to Scotland only further amend the Fresh Meat Export (Hygiene and Inspection) (Scotland) Regulations 1981.

They implement in part the provisions of Council Directive No. 83/90 EEC (O.J. No. L59, 5.3.1983, p. 10) further amending Council Directive No. 64/433/EEC (O.J. No. 121, 29.7.1964, p. 2012/64; OJ/SE 1963–64, p. 185) on health problems affecting intra-Community trade in fresh meat, by modifying and adapting the health provisions to take account of new developments. They prescribe revised conditions which must be satisfied for the production, cutting up, storage and transport of fresh meat of domestic bovine animals (including buffalo), swine, sheep, goats and solipeds when it is intended for export, or for sale for export, to a Member State of the EEC for human consumption.

In particular, the regulations—

(a) provide for revised conditions to be satisfied for the approval of premises by the Secretary of State and for the suspension and revocation of such approval (regulation 2(5) and (6));

(b) increase the fine for contravention of the regulations from £100 to £2,000 in consequence of the coming into operation of the Criminal Justice Act 1982 (c.48) and the Increase of Criminal Penalties etc (Scotland) Order 1984 (S.I. 1984/526) (regulation 2(12));

(c) amend existing conditions for export of fresh meat (regulations 2(7) to (10));

(d) provide revised conditions for the hygiene requirements of staff and premises (regulation 2(16));

(e) amend existing requirements as to ante-mortem and post-mortem health inspection procedures (regulations 2(17) and (19)), slaughter and dressing practices (regulation 2(18)) and cutting practices (regulation 2(20));

(f) amend health marking procedures (regulation 2(21)) and wrapping and packing requirements (regulation 2(22)); and

(g) provide for revised conditions to be satisfied for the transport of fresh meat intended for export (regulation 2(25)).

STATUTORY INSTRUMENTS

1984 No. 1886

MEDICINES

The Medicines (Pharmacies) (Applications for Registration and Fees) Amendment Regulations 1984

Made - - - -	30*th November* 1984
Laid before Parliament	11*th December* 1984
Coming into Operation	1*st January* 1985

The Secretaries of State respectively concerned with health in England, in Wales and in Scotland and the Department of Health and Social Services for Northern Ireland, acting jointly, in exercise of powers conferred by sections 75(1), 76(1), (2) and (6) and 129(5) of the Medicines Act 1968(**a**) and now vested in them(**b**) and of all other powers enabling them in that behalf, after consulting such organisations as appear to them to be representative of interests likely to be substantially affected by these regulations pursuant to section 129(6) of that Act, hereby make the following regulations:

Citation and commencement

1. These regulations may be cited as the Medicines (Pharmacies) (Applications for Registration and Fees) Amendment Regulations 1984 and shall come into operation on 1st January 1985.

Amendment of regulations

2. Regulation 3 of the Medicines (Pharmacies) (Applications for Registration and Fees) Regulations 1973(**c**) is amended as follows:—

(*a*) in paragraph (1) (fee for registration of premises), for "£72" there is substituted "£75" and for "£37" (fee where premises are in Northern Ireland) there is substituted "£38.50";

(*b*) in paragraph (2) (retention fee), for "£43" there is substituted "£45" and for "£31.50" (fee where premises are in Northern Ireland) there is substituted "£33"; and

---

(**a**) 1968 c. 67.
(**b**) In the case of the Secretaries of State concerned with health in England and in Wales by virtue of Article 2(2) of, and Schedule 1 to, the Transfer of Functions (Wales) Order 1969 (S.I. 1969/388), and in the case of the Department of Health and Social Services for Northern Ireland by virtue of section 40 of, and Schedule 5 to, the Northern Ireland Constitution Act 1973 (c. 36), and section 1(3) of, and paragraph 2(1)(*b*) of Schedule 1 to, the Northern Ireland Act 1974 (c. 28).
(**c**) S.I. 1973/1822; relevant amending instruments are S.I. 1980/1806, 1983/1787.

(c) in paragraph (3) (additional sum by way of penalty), for "£46" there is substituted "£50" and for "£33" (sum where premises are in Northern Ireland) there is substituted "£36".

Signed by authority of the Secretary of State for Social Services.

John Patten,
Parliamentary Under-Secretary of State,
Department of Health and Social Security.

22nd November 1984.

Nicholas Edwards,
Secretary of State for Wales.

26th November 1984.

George Younger,
Secretary of State for Scotland.

27th November 1984.

Sealed with the official seal of the Department of Health and Social Services for Northern Ireland this 30th day of November 1984.

Maurice N. Hayes,
Permanent Secretary.

EXPLANATORY NOTE

(This Note is not part of the Regulations.)

These regulations further amend the Medicines (Pharmacies) (Applications for Registration and Fees) Regulations 1973. They increase the fees for registration of premises at which a retail pharmacy business is or is to be carried on, the subsequent annual fees (retention fees) and the penalty (payable in circumstances specified in section 76(2) of the Medicines Act 1968) for failure to pay retention fees.

STATUTORY INSTRUMENTS

1984 No. 1887

MONOPOLIES AND MERGERS

The Monopoly References (Alteration of Exclusions) Order 1984

Made - - - -	*3rd December* 1984
Laid before Parliament	*10th December* 1984
Coming into Operation	*1st January* 1985

The Secretary of State, in exercise of the powers conferred on him by section 50(5) of the Fair Trading Act 1973 (**a**) ("the Act"), hereby makes the following Order:—

1. This Order may be cited as the Monopoly References (Alteration of Exclusions) Order 1984 and shall come into operation on 1st January 1985.

2. Part I of Schedule 7 to the Act (goods and services excluded from section 50) is altered by the substitution for paragraph 7 of the following paragraph—

"7. International carriage by air, otherwise than on a charter flight (that is to say, a flight on which the whole capacity of the aircraft is available for purchase by one or more charterers for his or their own use or for resale)."

Alexander Fletcher,
Parliamentary Under-Secretary of State for
Corporate and Consumer Affairs,
3rd December 1984.   Department of Trade and Industry.

EXPLANATORY NOTE

(*This Note is not part of the Order.*)

This Order alters the exclusion in Schedule 7 to the Fair Trading Act 1973 for the carriage of passengers or goods by air. The effect of the amendment is to enable the Director General of Fair Trading to make monopoly references under the Fair Trading Act in relation to domestic flights and international charter flights. The effect is also, by virtue of section 51(2) of the Fair Trading Act, that monopoly references by the Secretary of State in relation to such flights will no longer be required to be made jointly with another responsible Minister.

(**a**) 1973 c.41.

STATUTORY INSTRUMENTS

1984 No. 1888

COAL INDUSTRY

The Coal Industry (Limit on Deficit Grants) Order 1984

Laid before the House of Commons in draft

Made - - - - - -	30*th November* 1984
Coming into Operation	14*th December* 1984

The Secretary of State, in exercise of the powers conferred upon him by section 3(4) of the Coal Industry Act 1980(a) and with the approval of the Treasury, hereby makes the following Order, a draft of which has been laid before the Commons House of Parliament and approved by a resolution of that House in accordance with the provisions of section 3(5) of the said Act:—

1. This Order may be cited as the Coal Industry (Limit on Deficit Grants) Order 1984 and shall come into operation on 14th December 1984.

2. The limit specified in section 3(4) of the Coal Industry Act 1980 on the aggregate of grants made under that section is hereby increased from £1,200 million to £2,000 million.

David Hunt,
Parliamentary Under Secretary of State,
Department of Energy.

27th November 1984.

We approve

A. G. Hamilton,
Donald Thompson,
Two of the Lords Commissioners
of Her Majesty's Treasury.

30th November 1984.

(a) 1980 c. 50; section 3(4) and (5) were substituted by section 2(2) of the Coal Industry Act 1983 (c. 60).

EXPLANATORY NOTE

(This Note is not part of the Order.)

Section 3(4) of the Coal Industry Act 1980 (as substituted by section 2(2) of the Coal Industry Act 1983) imposes a limit of £1,200 millon on the aggregate amount of grants which may be made by the Secretary of State, with the approval of the Treasury, to the National Coal Board under section 3 of that Act towards eliminating any group deficit of the Board for specified financial years.

Under section 3(4) of the 1980 Act the Secretary of State has power to increase this limit by Order made with the approval of the Treasury. This Order increases the limit to £2,000 million, the maximum permitted by section 3(4).

STATUTORY INSTRUMENTS

1984 No. 1889

COAL INDUSTRY

The Redundant Mineworkers and Concessionary Coal (Payments Schemes) (Amendment) Order 1984

Laid before the House of Commons in draft

Made - - - - -	*27th November* 1984
Coming into Operation	*7th December* 1984

The Secretary of State, in exercise of the powers conferred on him by section 7(1) and (7) of the Coal Industry Act 1977(a), hereby makes the following Order, a draft of which has been laid before the Commons House of Parliament and has been approved by that House in accordance with section 7(7) of that Act:—

Citation and commencement

1. This Order may be cited as the Redundant Mineworkers and Concessionary Coal (Payments Schemes) (Amendment) Order 1984 and shall come into operation on 7th December 1984.

Interpretation

2. In this Order:—

"the 1983 Order" means the Redundant Mineworkers and Concessionary Coal (Payments Schemes) Order 1983(b); and

"the 1984 Order" means the Redundant Mineworkers and Concessionary Coal (Payments Schemes) Order 1984(c).

Amendment of 1983 and 1984 Orders

3. The 1983 and the 1984 Orders shall be varied in their Schedules as follows—

(*a*) In Article 5(2), for the words from "After each period" to "that sum" there shall be substituted the words—

"After each period of 52 weeks from the relevant date, the weekly sum payable to a coal industry employee under paragraph (1)";

(**a**) 1977 c. 39; section 7(1) was amended by the Coal Industry Act 1980 (c. 50), section 7(1), and extended by section 7(2) of that Act and by the Coal Industry Act 1983 (c. 60), section 4(2).
(**b**) S.I. 1983/506, as amended by S.I. 1984/457.   (**c**) S.I. 1984/457.

(b) In Article 10, the word "or" shall be inserted at the end of sub-paragraph (2)(f) and after that sub-paragraph there shall be inserted the following sub-paragraph—

"(g) (except in the case of weekly payments under Article 9 above) the provisions of section 19(1) of the Social Security Act 1975(a),";

(c) In Article 10(5), there shall be inserted in sub-paragraph (a) between "(e)" and "of that paragraph" the words "and (g)" and in sub-paragraph (b) between "(e)" and "of paragraph (2)" the words "and (g)";

(d) In Article 10, after paragraph (5) there shall be inserted the following paragraph—

"(6) Notwithstanding the provisions of paragraph (2) above, the Secretary of State may, if he thinks fit, pay to any coal industry employee a lump sum not exceeding the total amount of weekly payments net of tax (except weekly benefits under Article 9 above) to which that employee would have been entitled under this Scheme before the coming into operation of this paragraph, but for the provisions of section 19(1) of the Social Security Act 1975."

Amendment of 1984 Order
4. The 1984 Order shall be varied in the Schedule as follows—

In Article 1, for the definition of "coking plant operator" there shall be substituted the words—

" "coking plant operator" means a person carrying on in Great Britain a business which consists wholly or mainly of the production in coke ovens of coke by high temperature carbonisation of coal;".

David Hunt,
Parliamentary Under Secretary of State,
Department of Energy.

27th November 1984.

(a) 1975 c. 14; section 19(1) was amended by the Employment Protection Act 1975 (c. 71), Schedule 18.

EXPLANATORY NOTE

(This Note is not part of the Order.)

This Order makes changes in the Redundant Mineworkers Payments Schemes scheduled to the Redundant Mineworkers and Concessionary Coal (Payments Schemes) Order 1983 and the Redundant Mineworkers and Concessionary Coal (Payments Schemes) Order 1984. The 1983 Scheme provides for benefits for certain employees in the coal and coke industry made redundant between 6th April 1983 and 31st March 1984 and the 1984 Scheme makes provisions for those employees made redundant between 1st April 1984 and 28th March 1986.

A further sub-paragraph, (g), has been added to Article 10(2) of the Schedule to both Orders enabling weekly benefits under the Schemes (except unemployment benefit equivalent under Article 9) to be paid to employees becoming redundant during a trade dispute at their place of employment who would otherwise not be entitled to such benefits by reason of section 19(1) of the Social Security Act 1975 (which disqualifies from receipt of unemployment benefit a person who has lost employment because of a trade dispute at his place of work).

A new paragraph, (6), has been added to Article 10 in both Schedules enabling the Secretary of State to compensate employees for loss of weekly benefits (other than unemployment benefit equivalent) before the coming into operation of this Order by reason of section 19(1) of the 1975 Act.

Consequential provision is also made with regard to the up-rating of benefits for inflation.

Finally, the meaning of "coking plant operator" in the 1984 Scheme is clarified.

STATUTORY INSTRUMENTS

1984 No. 1890

HEALTH AND SAFETY

The Freight Containers (Safety Convention) Regulations 1984

Made - - - -	*4th December* 1984
Laid before Parliament	*11th December* 1984
Coming into Operation	*1st January* 1985

ARRANGEMENT OF REGULATIONS

1. Citation and commencement
2. Interpretation
3. Application of Regulations
4. Conditions of use
5. Approval of containers—either by design type or individually
6. Fixing of safety approval plate
7. Examination of containers
8. Exemptions

Schedule—Safety approval plate

The Secretary of State, in exercise of the powers conferred on him by sections 15(1), (2), (4), (5)(*b*), (6)(*b*) and (9), 43(2) and (4), and 82(3) and paragraphs 1(1)(*a*) and (*c*), (2) and (3), 3, 4(1), and 6(1) of Schedule 3 to, the Health and Safety at Work etc. Act 1974(**a**) and of all other powers enabling him in that behalf and for the purpose of giving effect without modifications to the proposals submitted to him by the Health and Safety Commission under section 11(2)(*d*) of that Act, after the carrying out by the said Commission of consultations in accordance with section 50(3) of that Act, hereby makes the following Regulations:—

Citation and commencement

1. These Regulations may be cited as the Freight Containers (Safety Convention) Regulations 1984 and shall come into operation on 1st January 1985.

Interpretation

2.—(1) In these Regulations, unless the context otherwise requires—

"the Convention" means the International Convention for Safe Containers

---

(**a**) 1974 c. 37; sections 15 and 50 were amended by the Employment Protection Act 1975 (c. 71), Schedule 15, paragraphs 6 and 16 respectively.

signed at Geneva on 2nd December 1972 and ratified by the United Kingdom on 8th March 1978;

"container" means an article of transport equipment which is

(*a*) of a permanent character and accordingly strong enough for repeated use, and

(*b*) designed to facilitate the transport of goods by one or more modes of transport without intermediate reloading, and

(*c*) designed to be secured or readily handled or both, having corner fittings for these purposes, and

(*d*) of a size such that the area enclosed by the outer bottom corners is either

    (i) if the container is fitted with top corner fittings, at least 7 square metres, or

    (ii) in any other case, at least 14 square metres,

and includes a container when carried on a chassis but does not include a vehicle or packaging, or any article of transport equipment designed solely for use in air transport, or a swap body except when it is carried by or on board a sea-going ship and is not mounted on a road vehicle or rail wagon;

"corner fittings" means an arrangement of apertures and faces at either the top or the bottom or both at the top and the bottom of the container for the purposes of handling, stacking and securing or any of those purposes;

"maintained" means maintained in an efficient state in efficient working order and in good repair;

"safety approval plate" means a plate in the form and containing the information specified by the Schedule;

"swap body" means a container which is specially designed for carriage by road only or by rail and road only and is without stacking capability and top lift facilities;

"use" means use for the purpose for which the container is designed but shall not include—

(*a*) movement to a place for remedial action provided:

    (i) so far as is reasonably practicable the movement is without risk to the safety of any person, and

    (ii) the remedial action is carried out before the container is repacked with goods,

(*b*) if the container is not loaded with goods,

    (i) transport to a place for testing the container to obtain approval under Regulation 5, or

    (ii) delivery of the container to its purchaser by the vendor or his agent.

(2) Unless the context otherwise requires, any reference in these Regulations to—

(*a*) a numbered Regulation is a reference to the Regulation of these Regulations which bears that number,

(*b*) a numbered paragraph is a reference to that paragraph so numbered in the Regulation in which the reference appears,

(*c*) "the Schedule" is a reference to the Schedule to these Regulations,

(*d*) any document operates as a reference to that document as revised or re-issued from time to time.

Application of Regulations

3. These Regulations apply to—

(*a*) any container used at work, or supplied for use at work, and which is in Great Britain;

(*b*) any container so used or supplied and which is outside Great Britain in circumstances in which sections 1 to 59 and 80 to 82 of the Health and Safety at Work etc. Act 1974 apply by virtue of the Health and Safety at Work etc. Act 1974 (Application outside Great Britain) Order 1977**(a)**.

Conditions of use

4.—(1) The owner or lessee of a container shall not use or permit that container to be used unless—

(*a*) it has valid approval in accordance with Regulation 5, and

(*b*) it has a valid safety approval plate fixed to it in accordance with Regulation 6, and

(*c*) it is properly maintained, and

(*d*) the examination requirements in Regulation 7 are met in respect of that container, and

(*e*) all markings on the container showing maximum gross weight are consistent with the maximum gross weight information on the safety approval plate, except that if construction of the container commenced before 1st January 1984 then compliance with this sub-paragraph is not required before 1st January 1989.

(2) Any other person using or permitting the use of a container shall, so far as is reasonably practicable, ensure that—

(*a*) a valid safety approval plate is fixed to it in accordance with Regulation 6, and

(*b*) all markings on the container showing maximum gross weight are consistent with the maximum gross weight information on the safety

(**a**) S.I. 1977/1232.

approval plate, except that if construction of the container commenced before 1st January 1984 then compliance with this sub-paragraph is not required before 1st January 1989.

(3) Where it is an express term of a bailment of a container that the bailee should be responsible for ensuring that the container is maintained or examined, the bailee shall, in addition to any duty placed on him by paragraph (2), ensure that—

(a) it is properly maintained, and

(b) the examination requirements in Regulation 7 are met in respect of that container.

(4) It shall be a defence to any proceedings for using or permitting to be used a container which does not have a valid approval in accordance with Regulation 5 that at the time of the contravention an approval had been given by an organisation authorised for this purpose by the Health and Safety Executive before these Regulations come into operation and such an approval had not ceased to be valid for the purposes for which it was given.

(5) It shall be a defence to any proceedings for using or permitting a container to be used which had not been properly maintained or examined that at the time of the contravention a bailment or lease was in force in respect of the container and

(a) in the case of an owner, that it was an express term of the bailment or lease that the bailee or lessee, as the case may be, should be responsible for ensuring that the container was maintained or examined,

(b) in the case of a lessee

(i) that it was not an express term of the lease that he should be responsible for ensuring that the container was maintained or examined, or

(ii) that he had become a lessor under a further lease and that it was an express term of the further lease that the further lessee should be responsible for ensuring that the container was maintained or examined,

(c) in the case of a bailee that he had become a bailor under a further bailment and that it was an express term of the further bailment that the further bailee should be responsible for ensuring that the container was maintained or examined.

Approval of containers—either by design type or individually

5.—(1) An approval referred to in Regulation 4(1)(a) (whether relating to a design type or to an individual container) shall be valid only if—

(a) it has been issued:

(i) by the Health and Safety Executive, or

(ii) by a person or body of persons appointed for the time being by the Executive in accordance with paragraph (3), or

(iii) by or under the authority of a Government which has ratified or accepted or approved or acceded to the Convention, and

(b) it has not ceased in accordance with paragraph (2) to be valid.

(2) If—

(a) the person or body of persons which issued the approval states in writing that it is no longer valid, or

(b) the Executive states in writing that the approval is no longer valid, whether or not it was issued by the Executive,

then that approval shall cease to be valid for the purposes of paragraph (1).

(3) The Executive shall appoint in writing such persons and bodies as it considers appropriate for the purpose of issuing approvals under paragraph (1)(a)(ii) and any such appointment may be subject to conditions and limited as to time and may be varied or revoked at any time by the Executive in writing.

Fixing of safety approval plate

6. The container has a valid safety approval plate fixed to it if—

(a) the safety approval plate is marked and fixed to the container in accordance with the Schedule, and

(b) the information on the safety approval plate is correct and relates to a valid approval, and

(c) the safety approval plate is fixed either—

(i) after the container is manufactured and before it is first used, or

(ii) after the container is examined in accordance with Regulation 7 and before it is again used.

Examination of containers

7.—(1) The examination referred to in Regulation 4(1)(d) and (3)(b) shall be in accordance with an examination scheme or programme approved by the Health and Safety Executive for the purposes of this Regulation.

(2) There shall be clearly marked on the container either on or as close as practicable to the safety approval plate all matters which the examination scheme or programme requires to be marked.

(3) A fee of £75 is payable by the applicant to the Executive when any application for approval of a scheme or programme under Regulation 7(1) is made.

(4) Compliance with the procedure adopted by the State where the owner is permanently resident or incorporated shall be deemed to be in compliance with this Regulation provided the procedure has been approved or prescribed by the Government of that State, or by any organisation authorised by such a Government to act on its behalf, for the purpose of the Convention and that Government has ratified accepted approved or acceded to the Convention.

Exemptions

8.—(1) Subject to paragraph (2) below the Health and Safety Executive may by cert: cate in writing exempt any container or class of containers, or any person or class of persons to which these Regulations apply from any requirement or prohibition imposed by these Regulations and any such exemption may be granted subject to conditions and to a limit of time and may be revoked by a certificate in writing at any time.

(2) The Health and Safety Executive shall not grant any such exemption unless, having regard to the circumstances of the case, and in particular to—

(*a*) the conditions, if any, which it proposes to attach to the exemption, and

(*b*) any other requirements imposed by or under any enactments which apply to the case,

it is satisfied that the health and safety of persons who are likely to be affected by the exemption will not be prejudiced because of it.

Signed by order of the Secretary of State.

Peter Bottomley,
Joint Parliamentary Under Secretary of State,
Department of Employment.

4th December 1984.

SCHEDULE   *Regulations 2 and 6*

Safety approval plate

1. The safety approval plate required by Regulation 6 shall be permanently fixed to the container in a position such that it is—

(*a*) readily visible, and

(*b*) adjacent to any other officially approved plate carried on the container, and

(*c*) not likely to be easily damaged.

2. The safety approval plate shall—

(*a*) be in the form prescribed by figure 1 of this Schedule;

(*b*) consist of a permanent, non-corroding, fireproof rectangular plate measuring not less than 200mm by 100mm,

(*c*) be marked with:

(i) the legend 'CSC Safety Approval' in letters of at least 8mm in height, and

(ii) the other legends and information prescribed by sub-paragraph (*d*) and by figure 1 of this Schedule in letters of at least 5mm in height,

and such markings shall be permanent, clear and legible and in at least the English or French language, but nothing in this sub-paragraph shall prevent any markings for the purposes of an examination scheme or programme being by means of a decal.

(*d*) contain the following information in at least the English or French language—

    (i) line 1—the country of approval and approval reference,

    (ii) line 2—the month and year of manufacture,

    (iii) line 3—the manufacturer's identification number in respect of the container, or in the case of containers for which that number is unknown the owner's identification number, or the number allotted by the Government or organisation which has granted the approval,

    (iv) line 4—the maximum gross weight in kilograms and pounds,

    (v) line 5—the allowable stacking weight for 1.8g in kilograms and pounds (that is to say, the designed maximum superimposed static stacking weight),

    (vi) line 6—the transverse racking test load value in kilograms and pounds,

    (vii) line 7—the end wall strength value as a proportion of the maximum permissible payload, which shall not be entered unless the end walls are designed to withstand a load of less or more than 0.4 times the maximum permissible payload,

    (viii) line 8—the side wall strength value as a proportion of the maximum permissible payload, which shall not be entered unless the side walls are designed to withstand a load of less or more than 0.6 times the maximum permissible payload,

    (ix) line 9—on and after 1st January 1987 (if the approved examination scheme or programme so requires)—

        (*a*) a legend indicating that the container is subject to a continuous examination programme, or

        (*b*) the date (expressed in month and year only) before which the container shall next be thoroughly examined.

Lines 7 and 8 may be used for the above purposes (*a*) and (*b*) if they are not required to contain other information.

Figure 1

CSC SAFETY APPROVAL

1 ....

2 ....   DATE MANUFACTURED ....

3 ....   IDENTIFICATION No. ....

4 ....   MAXIMUM GROSS WEIGHT ..... kg .... lb

5 ....   ALLOWABLE STACKING WEIGHT
                                            FOR 1.8g .... kg .... lb

6 ....   RACKING TEST LOAD VALUE ... kg .. lb

7 ....

8 ....

9 ....

EXPLANATORY NOTE

(This Note is not part of the Regulations.)

These Regulations require owners and lessees and others in control of freight containers used at work or supplied for use at work to comply with conditions of use, in accordance with the International Convention for Safe Containers 1972.

The Regulations apply to containers which have top corner fittings and a bottom area of at least 7 square metres or, if they do not have top corner fittings, a bottom area of at least 14 square metres.

Regulations 4 and 5 impose a condition that a container should have a valid approval issued by the Health and Safety Executive or a body which it has appointed for that purpose, or by or under the authority of a foreign Government which has acceded to the Convention. The details of the arrangements for the approval of containers in Great Britain are set out in a document entitled "Arrangements in Great Britain for the Approval of Containers" obtainable from the Health and Safety Executive.

Regulation 4 also imposes a condition that a container should be properly maintained and meet the examination requirements of Regulation 7, in accordance with an examination scheme or programme approved by the Executive. A document entitled "Conditions for Approval of Examination Schemes or Programmes" is obtainable from the Executive.

Regulation 4 imposes a further condition that a container should have a valid safety approval plate fixed to it in accordance with Regulation 6. Detailed requirements as to the safety approval plate are set out in the Schedule.

The Regulations provide for defences to criminal proceedings (Regulation 4) and for the Health and Safety Executive to grant exemptions (Regulation 8).

STATUTORY INSTRUMENTS

1984 No. 1892

PLANT HEALTH

The Import and Export of Trees, Wood and Bark (Health) (Great Britain) (Amendment) Order 1984

Made - - -	*4th December* 1984
Laid before Parliament	*11th December* 1984
Coming into Operation	*1st January* 1985

The Forestry Commissioners, in exercise of the powers conferred on them by sections 2 and 3(1), (2) and (4) of the Plant Health Act 1967 (a), as read with section 20 of the Agriculture (Miscellaneous Provisions) Act 1972 (b), and of all other powers enabling them in that behalf, hereby make the following Order:—

Citation and commencement

1. This Order may be cited as the Import and Export of Trees, Wood and Bark (Health) (Great Britain) (Amendment) Order 1984 and shall come into operation on 1st January 1985.

Amendment of Import and Export of Trees, Wood and Bark (Health) (Great Britain) Order 1980

2. The Import and Export of Trees, Wood and Bark (Health) (Great Britain) Order 1980 (c) shall be further amended in accordance with articles 3 to 6 below.

3. In Schedule 3 thereto (trees and isolated bark the landing of which is prohibited when grown in specified countries):—

(a) in the entry numbered 3 in the second column there shall be substituted for the existing words the words "All countries.";

(b) the entry numbered 8 shall be deleted.

4. In Schedule 4 thereto (special conditions subject to which the landing is permitted in Great Britain of specified trees, wood, isolated bark and soil):—

(a) 1967 c.8; sections 2(1) and 3(1) and (2) were amended by the European Communities Act 1972 (c.68), Schedule 4, paragraph 8; section 3(4) was last amended by the Criminal Justice Act 1982 (c.48), section 42.
(b) 1972 c.62.
(c) S.I. 1980/449; the relevant amending instrument is S.I. 1983/807.

(a) there shall be substituted in the first and second columns for the entry numbered 1 the following entry—

| "1. Wood of conifers *(Coniferae).* | 1. *(a)* The wood shall have been stripped of its bark; or |
| | *(b)* the wood shall have been kiln-dried to a moisture content below 20% expressed as a percentage of the dry matter and there shall have been put on the wood or its packaging the mark "kiln-dried", "KD" or another internationally recognised mark to that effect."; |

(b) the entry numbered 7 shall be deleted.

5. In Schedule 5 thereto (phytosanitary certificates to accompany imported trees, wood, isolated bark and soil):—

(a) in Part II there shall be substituted for the entry numbered 2 the following entry—

"2. Wood of conifers *(Coniferae).*";

(b) in Part II the entry numbered 4 shall be deleted;

(c) in Part III in the entry numbered 2 the word *"Picea"* shall be deleted;

(d) in Part III there shall be substituted for the entry numbered 3 the following entry—

"3. Wood of conifers *(Coniferae).*";.

(e) in Part III the entry numbered 5 shall be deleted.

6. In Schedule 6 thereto (wood and isolated bark the origin of which is to be declared) the entry numbered 3 shall be deleted.

In Witness whereof the Official Seal of the Forestry Commissioners is hereunto affixed on 4th December 1984.

P. J. Clarke,
Secretary to the Forestry Commissioners.

EXPLANATORY NOTE

(This Note is not part of the Order.)

This Order further amends the Import and Export of Trees, Wood and Bark (Health) (Great Britain) Order 1980. The amendments are made in part in accordance with Article 15 of Council Directive No. 77/93/EEC (OJ No. L26, 31.1.77, p.20) on protective measures against the introduction into the Member States of harmful organisms of plants or plant products, which allows Member States to take additional protective measures against the introduction of harmful organisms. The Order also implements Article 4(1) of Council Directive 84/378/EEC (OJ No. L207, 2.8.84, p.1) amending Directive 77/93/EEC to require that coniferous wood originating in non-European countries be stripped of its bark or kiln-dried when introduced into Member States.

The Order—
  (a) extends the prohibition on the landing in Great Britain of isolated bark of conifers to all such bark regardless of country of origin (article 3 *(a)*);
  (b) extends controls for the landing in Great Britain of coniferous wood to all such wood regardless of country of origin and requires the wood either to be stripped of its bark or to be kiln-dried to a moisture content below 20% and in each case to be accompanied by a phytosanitary certificate (articles 4*(a)* and 5*(a)* and *(d)*).

The controls in the 1980 Order relating to the wood and bark of *Picea* are now included in the general controls introduced in the present Order in respect of wood and bark of all coniferous species. Consequential amendments are accordingly made in articles 3*(b)*, 4*(b)* and 5*(b)* and *(c)*. Amendments are also made in articles 5*(e)* and 6 reflecting the total ban on the landing of isolated bark of conifers.

STATUTORY INSTRUMENTS

1984 No. 1895

OFFSHORE INSTALLATIONS

The Offshore Installations (Safety Zones) (Revocation) (No. 68) Order 1984

Made - - - - -	*4th December* 1984
Coming into Operation	*6th December* 1984

The Secretary of State, in exercise of the power conferred on him by section 21(1) of the Oil and Gas (Enterprise) Act 1982**(a)**, and of all other powers enabling him in that behalf, hereby makes the following Order:—

1. This Order may be cited as the Offshore Installations (Safety Zones) (Revocation) (No. 68) Order 1984 and shall come into operation on 6th December 1984.

2. The Offshore Installations (Safety Zones) (No. 74) Order 1984**(b)** is hereby revoked.

Alastair Goodlad,
Parliamentary Under Secretary of State,
Department of Energy.

4th December 1984.

EXPLANATORY NOTE

(*This Note is not part of the Order.*)

This Order revokes the Offshore Installations (Safety Zones) (No. 74) Order 1984. The installation known as Kingsnorth U.K. which was protected by the safety zone established by that Order has been removed and accordingly that Order is no longer required.

(a) 1982 c. 23.   **(b)** S.I. 1984/1624.

STATUTORY INSTRUMENTS

1984 No. 1896

OFFSHORE INSTALLATIONS

The Offshore Installations (Safety Zones) (Revocation) (No. 69) Order 1984

Made - - - -	*4th December* 1984
Coming into Operation	*6th December* 1984

The Secretary of State, in exercise of the power conferred on him by section 21(1) of the Oil and Gas (Enterprise) Act 1982(**a**), and of all other powers enabling him in that behalf, hereby makes the following Order:—

1. This Order may be cited as the Offshore Installations (Safety Zones) (Revocation) (No. 69) Order 1984 and shall come into operation on 6th December 1984.

2. The Offshore Installations (Safety Zones) (No. 62) Order 1984(**b**) is hereby revoked.

Alastair Goodlad,
Parliamentary Under Secretary of State,
Department of Energy.

4th December 1984.

EXPLANATORY NOTE

(*This Note is not part of the Order.*)

This Order revokes the Offshore Installations (Safety Zones) (No. 62) Order 1984. The installation known as Ocean Benloyal which was protected by the safety zone established by that Order has been removed and accordingly that Order is no longer required.

(**a**) 1982 c. 23.   (**b**) S.I. 1984/1444.

STATUTORY INSTRUMENTS

1984 No. 1897

OFFSHORE INSTALLATIONS

The Offshore Installations (Safety Zones) (Revocation) (No. 70) Order 1984

Made - - - -	*4th December* 1984
Coming into Operation	*6th December* 1984

The Secretary of State, in exercise of the power conferred on him by section 21(1) of the Oil and Gas (Enterprise) Act 1982 (**a**), and of all other powers enabling him in that behalf, hereby makes the following Order:—

1. This Order may be cited as the Offshore Installations (Safety Zones) (Revocation) (No. 70) Order 1984 and shall come into operation on 6th December 1984.

2. The Offshore Installations (Safety Zones) (No. 82) Order 1984 (**b**) is hereby revoked.

Alastair Goodlad,
Parliamentary Under Secretary of State,
Department of Energy.

4th December 1984.

EXPLANATORY NOTE

(*This Note is not part of the Order.*)

This Order revokes the Offshore Installations (Safety Zones) (No. 82) Order 1984. The installation known as Ocean Nomad which was protected by the safety zone established by that Order has been removed and accordingly that Order is no longer required.

(**a**) 1982 c.23. (**b**) S.I. 1984/1726.

STATUTORY INSTRUMENTS

1984 No. 1898

OFFSHORE INSTALLATIONS

The Offshore Installations (Safety Zones) (No. 91) Order 1984

Made - - - -	*4th December* 1984
Coming into Operation	*6th December* 1984

The Secretary of State, in exercise of the powers conferred on him by section 21(1), (2) and (3) of the Oil and Gas (Enterprise) Act 1982(a) (hereinafter referred to as "the Act"), and of all other powers enabling him in that behalf, hereby makes the following Order:—

1. This Order may be cited as the Offshore Installations (Safety Zones) (No. 91) Order 1984 and shall come into operation on 6th December 1984.

2.—(1) A safety zone is hereby established around the installation specified in Column 1 of the Schedule hereto (being an installation maintained in waters in an area designated under section 1(7) of the Continental Shelf Act 1964(b)) having a radius of five hundred metres from the point as respects that installation which has the co-ordinates of latitude and longitude according to European Datum (1950) specified in Columns 2 and 3 of the Schedule.

(2) The prohibition under section 21(3) of the Act on a vessel entering or remaining in a safety zone without the consent of the Secretary of State shall not apply to a vessel entering or remaining in the safety zone established under paragraph (1) above—

(*a*) in connection with the laying, inspection, testing, repair, alteration, renewal or removal of any submarine cable or pipe-line in or near that safety zone;

(*b*) to provide services for, to transport persons or goods to or from, or under the authority of a government department to inspect, any installation in that safety zone;

(*c*) if it is a vessel belonging to a general lighthouse authority performing duties relating to the safety of navigation;

(*d*) in connection with the saving or attempted saving of life or property;

(*e*) owing to stress of weather; or

(*f*) when in distress.

Alastair Goodlad,
Parliamentary Under Secretary of State,
Department of Energy.

4th December 1984.

(**a**) 1982 c. 23.   (**b**) 1964 c. 29.

SCHEDULE

Article 2(1)

SAFETY ZONE

1	2	3
Name or other designation of the offshore installation	Latitude North	Longitude East
Bendoran	56° 05′ 54·54″	03° 13′ 37·86″

EXPLANATORY NOTE

(This Note is not part of the Order.)

This Order establishes, under section 21 of the Oil and Gas (Enterprise) Act 1982, a safety zone, having a radius of 500 metres from a specified point, around the installation known as Bendoran maintained in waters in an area designated under section 1(7) of the Continental Shelf Act 1964.

Vessels (which includes hovercraft, submersible apparatus and installations in transit) are prohibited from entering or remaining in the safety zone except with the consent of the Secretary of State or in the circumstances mentioned in Article 2(2) of the Order.

STATUTORY INSTRUMENTS

1984 No. 1899

OFFSHORE INSTALLATIONS

The Offshore Installations (Safety Zones) (No. 92) Order 1984

Made -	-	-	-	*4th December* 1984	
Coming into Operation				*6th December* 1984	

The Secretary of State, in exercise of the powers conferred on him by section 21(1), (2) and (3) of the Oil and Gas (Enterprise) Act 1982(**a**) (hereinafter referred to as "the Act"), and of all other powers enabling him in that behalf, hereby makes the following Order:—

1. This Order may be cited as the Offshore Installations (Safety Zones) (No. 92) Order 1984 and shall come into operation on 6th December 1984.

2.—(1) A safety zone is hereby established around the installation specified in Column 1 of the Schedule hereto (being an installation maintained in waters in an area designated under section 1(7) of the Continental Shelf Act 1964(**b**)) having a radius of five hundred metres from the point as respects that installation which has the co-ordinates of latitude and longitude according to European Datum (1950) specified in Columns 2 and 3 of the Schedule.

(2) The prohibition under section 21(3) of the Act on a vessel entering or remaining in a safety zone without the consent of the Secretary of State shall not apply to a vessel entering or remaining in the safety zone established under paragraph (1) above—

(*a*) in connection with the laying, inspection, testing, repair, alteration, renewal or removal of any submarine cable or pipe-line in or near that safety zone;

(*b*) to provide services for, to transport persons or goods to or from, or under the authority of a government department to inspect, any installation in that safety zone;

(*c*) if it is a vessel belonging to a general lighthouse authority performing duties relating to the safety of navigation;

(*d*) in connection with the saving or attempted saving of life or property;

(*e*) owing to stress of weather; or

(*f*) when in distress.

Alastair Goodlad,
Parliamentary Under Secretary of State,
Department of Energy.

4th December 1984.

(**a**) 1982 c. 23.   (**b**) 1964 c. 29.

SCHEDULE

Article 2(1)

SAFETY ZONE

1	2	3
Name or other designation of the offshore installation	Latitude North	Longitude East
Deep Sea Pioneer	56° 10′ 40·32″	02° 46′ 51·23″

EXPLANATORY NOTE

(*This Note is not part of the Order.*)

This Order establishes, under section 21 of the Oil and Gas (Enterprise) Act 1982, a safety zone, having a radius of 500 metres from a specified point, around the installation known as Deep Sea Pioneer maintained in waters in an area designated under section 1(7) of the Continental Shelf Act 1964.

Vessels (which includes hovercraft, submersible apparatus and installations in transit) are prohibited from entering or remaining in the safety zone except with the consent of the Secretary of State or in the circumstances mentioned in Article 2(2) of the Order.

STATUTORY INSTRUMENTS

1984 No. 1900

OFFSHORE INSTALLATIONS

The Offshore Installations (Safety Zones) (Amendment) (No. 2) Order 1984

Made	-	-	*4th December* 1984
Coming into Operation			*6th December* 1984

The Secretary of State, in exercise of the power conferred on him by section 21(1) of the Oil and Gas (Enterprise) Act 1982(**a**), and of all other powers enabling him in that behalf, hereby makes the following Order:—

1. This Order may be cited as the Offshore Installations (Safety Zones) (Amendment) (No. 2) Order 1984 and shall come into operation on 6th December 1984.

2. The entry numbered 56 in Schedule 1 to the Offshore Installations (Safety Zones) Order 1982(**b**) relating to the Offshore Installation known as Transworld 58 (Argyll) shall be omitted.

Alastair Goodlad,
Parliamentary Under Secretary of State,
Department of Energy.

4th December 1984.

EXPLANATORY NOTE

(This Note is not part of the Order.)

This Order amends the Offshore Installations (Safety Zones) Order 1982 by omitting from Schedule 1 to that Order the safety zone established around the installation Transworld 58 (Argyll). This safety zone is no longer required as the installation has been removed and replaced by the installation Deep Sea Pioneer in respect of which a safety zone has been established by the Offshore Installations (Safety Zones) (No. 92) Order 1984 (S.I. 1984/1899).

(**a**) 1982 c.23.   (**b**) S.I. 1982/1606.

STATUTORY INSTRUMENTS

1984 No. 1901

OFFSHORE INSTALLATIONS

The Offshore Installations (Safety Zones) (Amendment) (No. 3) Order 1984

Made - - - -	*4th December* 1984
Coming into Operation	*6th December* 1984

The Secretary of State, in exercise of the power conferred on him by section 21(1) of the Oil and Gas (Enterprise) Act 1982(**a**), and of all other powers enabling him in that behalf, hereby makes the following Order:—

1. This Order may be cited as the Offshore Installations (Safety Zones) (Amendment) (No. 3) Order 1984 and shall come into operation on 6th December 1984.

2. The entry numbered 3 in Schedule 1 to the Offshore Installations (Safety Zones) Order 1982(**b**) relating to the offshore installation known as 211/18-Thistle-SPM shall be omitted.

Alastair Goodlad,
Parliamentary Under Secretary of State,
Department of Energy.

4th December 1984.

EXPLANATORY NOTE

(*This Note is not part of the Order.*)

This Order amends the Offshore Installations (Safety Zones) Order 1982 by omitting from Schedule 1 to that Order the safety zone established around the installation 211/18-Thistle-SPM. This safety zone is no longer required as the installation has been removed.

(**a**) 1982 c. 23.　　　(**b**) S.I. 1982/1606.

STATUTORY INSTRUMENTS

1984 No. 1902

HEALTH AND SAFETY

The Control of Industrial Major Accident Hazards Regulations 1984

Made - - - - -	*4th December* 1984
Laid before Parliament	*18th December* 1984

Coming into Operation
for the purposes of

Regulations 6 to 10	*8th January* 1985
for all other purposes	*1st April* 1985

ARRANGEMENT OF REGULATIONS

The Secretary of State, being the designated (a) Minister for the purposes of section 2(2) of the European Communities Act 1972 (b) in relation to measures relating to the prevention and limitation of the effects of accidents arising from industrial activities involving dangerous substances, in exercise of the powers conferred on him by the said section 2 and by sections 15(1), (2), (3)(c), (5)(b) and (6)(b), 43(2), (4), (5) and (6) and 82(3)(a) of, and paragraphs 1(1)(b) and (c) and (2), 15(1) and 20 of Schedule 3 to, the Health and Safety at Work etc. Act 1974 (c) ("the 1974 Act") and of all other powers enabling him in that behalf and for the purpose of giving effect with modifications to proposals submitted to him by the Health and Safety Commission under section 11(2)(d) of the 1974 Act after the carrying out by the said Commission of consultations in accordance with section 50(3) of that Act and after consulting the said Commission in accordance with section 50(2) thereof, hereby makes the following Regulations:—

Citation, commencement and powers

1.—(1) These Regulations may be cited as the Control of Industrial Major Accident Hazards Regulations 1984 and shall come into operation—

     (*a*) for the purposes of Regulations 6 to 10, on 8th January 1985;

     (*b*) for all other purposes, on 1st April 1985.

(2) To the extent that any provision of these Regulations is within scope of powers contained in the Health and Safety at Work etc. Act 1974, it is made solely under those powers.

Interpretation

2.—(1) In these Regulations, unless the context otherwise requires—

"the 1974 Act" means the Health and Safety at Work etc. Act 1974;

"dangerous substance" means—

     (*a*) any substance which satisfies any of the criteria laid down in Schedule 1 (which sets out the provisions of Annex IV to the Directive);

     (*b*) any substance listed in column 1 of Schedule 2 (which sets out the provisions of Annex II to the Directive); and

     (*c*) any substance listed in column 1 of Schedule 3 (which sets out the provisions of Annex III to the Directive);

"the Directive" means Council Directive No. 82/501/EEC "on the major-accident hazards of certain industrial activities" (d);

"the Executive" means the Health and Safety Executive;

(**a**) S.I. 1983/603.   (**b**) 1972 c. 68.
(**c**) 1974 c. 37; sections 15 and 43 were amended by the Employment Protection Act 1975 (c. 71), Schedule 15, paragraphs 6 and 12 respectively.
(**d**) OJ No L230, 5.8.82, p. 1.

"industrial activity" means either—

(a) an operation carried out in an industrial installation referred to in Schedule 4 (which sets out the provisions of Annex I to the Directive) involving or liable to involve one or more dangerous substances and includes on-site storage and on-site transport which is associated with that operation unless the operation is incapable of producing a major accident hazard, or

(b) isolated storage;

"isolated storage" means storage of a dangerous substance, other than storage associated with an installation specified in Schedule 4 on the same site, where that storage involves at least the quantities of that substance set out in Schedule 2;

"local authority" means—

(a) for the purposes of Regulations 11 and 15—

(i) in relation to England and Wales, a county council, the Greater London Council or the Council of the Isles of Scilly, or

(ii) in relation to Scotland, a regional or islands council; and

(b) for the purposes of Regulation 12—

(i) in relation to England and Wales, a district council, a London borough council, the Common Council of the City of London, the Sub-Treasurer of the Inner Temple, or the Under-Treasurer of the Middle Temple, or the Council of the Isles of Scilly or

(ii) in relation to Scotland, an islands or district council; and

(c) for the purposes of Regulation 13, any local authority mentioned in sub-paragraph (a) or (b) above;

"major accident" means an occurrence (including in particular, a major emission, fire or explosion) resulting from uncontrolled developments in the course of an industrial activity, leading to a serious danger to persons, whether immediate or delayed, inside or outside the installation, or to the environment, and involving one or more dangerous substances;

"manufacturer" means a person having control of an industrial activity;

"site" means—

(a) the whole of an area of land under the control of a manufacturer and includes a pier, jetty or similar structure, whether floating or not, or

(b) a structure, whether floating or not, which is within the inland waters of Great Britain and which is under the control of a manufacturer.

(2) In these Regulations, unless the context otherwise requires any reference to—

(a) a numbered Regulation or Schedule is a reference to the Regulation or Schedule in these Regulations so numbered; and

(b) a numbered paragraph is a reference to the paragraph so numbered in the Regulation or Schedule in which that reference appears.

Application of these Regulations
3.—(1) These Regulations shall apply to any industrial activity except an industrial activity which is carried on at—

(*a*) a nuclear installation within the meaning of section 44(8) of the 1974 Act;

(*b*) an installation which is under the control of—

(i) the Secretary of State for the purposes of the Ministry of Defence, or

(ii) a headquarters or organisation designated for the purposes of the International Headquarters and Defence Organisations Act 1964**(a)** or of the service authorities of a visiting force within the meaning of any of the provisions of Part I of the Visiting Forces Act 1952**(b)**;

(*c*) a factory, magazine or store licensed under the Explosives Act 1875**(c)**;

(*d*) a mine or a quarry within the meaning of section 180 of the Mines and Quarries Act 1954**(d)**;

(*e*) a site operated by a disposal authority in accordance with section 11(2) of the Control of Pollution Act 1974**(e)** or for which a licence issued in pursuance of section 5 of that Act is in force.

(2) These Regulations shall not apply to Northern Ireland.

Demonstration of safe operation
4.—(1) This Regulation shall apply to—

(*a*) an industrial activity, other than isolated storage, in which a dangerous substance which satisfies any of the criteria laid down in Schedule 1 is or may be involved; and

(*b*) isolated storage in which there is involved a quantity of a dangerous substance listed in Schedule 2 in column 1 which is equal to or more than the quantity specified in the entry for that substance in column 2.

(2) A manufacturer who has control of an industrial activity to which this Regulation applies shall at any time provide evidence including documents to show that he has—

(*a*) identified the major accident hazards; and

(*b*) taken adequate steps to—

(i) prevent such major accidents and to limit their consequences to persons and the environment, and

(ii) provide persons working on the site with the information, training and equipment necessary to ensure their safety.

(**a**) 1964 c. 5.   (**b**) 1952 c. 67.   (**c**) 1875 c. 17.
(**d**) 1954 c. 70.   (**e**) 1974 c. 40.

Notification of major accidents

5.—(1) Where a major accident occurs on a site, the manufacturer shall forthwith notify the Executive of that accident and the Executive shall obtain from the manufacturer who made that notification—

(*a*) the following information relating to the accident as soon as it becomes available—

(i) the circumstances of the accident,

(ii) the dangerous substances involved,

(iii) the data available for assessing the effects of the accident on persons and the environment,

(iv) the emergency measures taken; and

(*b*) a statement of the steps envisaged—

(i) to alleviate medium or long term effects of the accident, if any, and

(ii) to prevent the recurrence of such an accident.

(2) In such a case, the Executive shall—

(*a*) collect, where possible, the information necessary for a full analysis of the major accident; and

(*b*) send to the European Commission the information specified in Schedule 5 (which sets out the provisions of Annex VI to the Directive).

(3) Where a manufacturer has notified a major accident to the Executive in accordance with the requirements of the Notification of Accidents and Dangerous Occurrences Regulations 1980(**a**), he shall be deemed to have complied with the requirement to notify that accident under paragraph (1) of this Regulation.

Industrial activities to which Regulations 7 to 12 apply

6.—(1) Regulations 7 to 12 shall apply to—

(*a*) an industrial activity, other than isolated storage, in which there is involved a quantity of a dangerous substance listed in Schedule 3 in column 1 which is equal to or more than the quantity specified in the entry for that substance in column 2; and

(*b*) isolated storage in which there is involved a quantity of a dangerous substance which is listed in Schedule 2 in column 1 which is equal to or more than the quantity specified in the entry for that substance in column 3.

(2) For the purposes of Regulations 7 to 12—

(*a*) a "new industrial activity" means an industrial activity which—

(i) was commenced after the date of the coming into operation of this Regulation, or

---

(**a**) S.I. 1980/804.

    (ii) if commenced before that date, is an industrial activity in which there has been since that date a modification which would be likely to have important implications for major accident hazards, and that activity shall be deemed to have been commenced on the date on which the change was made;

  (b) an "existing industrial activity" means an industrial activity which is not a new industrial activity.

Reports on industrial activities

7.—(1) Subject to the following paragraphs of this Regulation, a manufacturer shall not undertake any industrial activity to which this Regulation applies, unless he has prepared a written report containing the information specified in Schedule 6 and has sent a copy of that report to the Executive at least 3 months before commencing that activity or before such shorter time as the Executive may agree in writing.

(2) In the case of a new industrial activity which a manufacturer commences, or by virtue of Regulation 6(2)(a)(ii) is deemed to commence, within 6 months after the date of the coming into operation of these Regulations, it shall be a sufficient compliance with paragraph (1) if the manufacturer sends to the Executive a copy of the report required in accordance with that paragraph within 3 months after the coming into operation of the Regulations or within such longer time as the Executive may agree in writing.

(3) In the case of an existing industrial activity, until 8 July 1989 it shall be a sufficient compliance with paragraph (1) if the manufacturer on or before 1st April 1985 sends to the Executive the information specified in Schedule 7 relating to that activity, except that nothing in this paragraph shall require a manufacturer to provide information which he has already provided by a notification made in accordance with the Notification of Installations Handling Hazardous Substances Regulations 1982(a).

(4) Where paragraph (3) applies, the Executive may, by a certificate in writing (which it may revoke in writing at any time), exempt, either unconditionally or subject to conditions, any manufacturer or class of manufacturers from the requirement in paragraph (1) to send to the Executive a copy of the report required under that paragraph.

Updating of reports under Regulation 7

8.—(1) Where a manufacturer has made a report in accordance with Regulation 7(1), he shall not make any modification to the industrial activity to which that report relates which could materially affect the particulars in that report, unless he has made a further report to take account of those changes and has sent a copy of that report to the Executive at least 3 months before making those changes or before such shorter time as the Executive may agree in writing.

(a) S.I. 1982/1357.

(2) Where a manufacturer has made a report in accordance with Regulation 7(1), paragraph (1) of this Regulation or this paragraph, and that industrial activity is continuing, the manufacturer shall within three years of the date of the last such report, make a further report which shall have regard in particular to new technical knowledge which materially affects the particulars in the previous report relating to safety and developments in the knowledge of hazard assessment, and shall within one month, or in such longer time as the Executive may agree, send a copy of the report to the Executive.

(3) A certificate of exemption issued under Regulation 7(4), shall apply to reports or declarations made under this Regulation as it applies to reports made under Regulation 7(1).

Requirement for further information to be sent to the Executive
9.—(1) Where, in accordance with Regulation 7(1), a manufacturer has sent a report relating to an industrial activity to the Executive, the Executive may, by a notice served on the manufacturer, require him to provide such additional information as is specified in the notice and the manufacturer shall send that information to the Executive within such time as is specified in the notice or within such longer time as the Executive may subsequently agree.

(2) The Executive shall not serve a notice under paragraph (1) unless, having regard to all the circumstances of the particular case, the information is reasonably required for the evaluation of the major accident hazards created by the activity.

(3) It shall be a defence in proceedings against any person for an offence consisting of a contravention of paragraph (1), for that person to prove that, at the time the proceedings were commenced—

 (*a*) an improvement notice under section 21 of the 1974 Act relating to the contravention had not been served on him; or

 (*b*) if such a notice had been served on him—

   (i) the period for compliance had not expired, or

   (ii) he had appealed against the notice and that appeal had not been dismissed or withdrawn.

Preparation of on-site emergency plan by the manufacturer
10.—(1) A manufacturer who has control of an industrial activity to which this Regulation applies shall, after consulting such persons as appear to him to be appropriate, prepare and keep up to date an adequate on-site emergency plan detailing how major accidents will be dealt with on the site on which the industrial activity is carried on and that plan shall include the name of the person who is responsible for safety on the site and the names of those who are authorised to take action in accordance with the plan in the case of an emergency.

(2) The manufacturer shall ensure that the emergency plan prepared in accordance with paragraph (1) takes into account any material changes made in the industrial activity and that every person on the site who is affected by the plan is informed of its relevant provisions.

(3) The manufacturer shall prepare the emergency plan required under paragraph (1)—

(a) in the case of a new industrial activity, before that activity is commenced, except that, in the case of a new industrial activity which is commenced or is deemed to have been commenced before a date 3 months after the coming into operation of the Regulations, by that date; or

(b) in the case of an existing industrial activity by 1st April 1985.

Preparation of off-site emergency plan by the local authority
11.—(1) It shall be the duty of the local authority, in whose area there is a site on which a manufacturer carries on an industrial activity to which this Regulation applies, to prepare and keep up to date an adequate off-site emergency plan detailing how emergencies relating to a possible major accident on that site will be dealt with and in preparing that plan the authority shall consult the manufacturer, the Executive and such other persons as appear to the authority to be appropriate.

(2) For the purpose of enabling the local authority to prepare the emergency plan required under paragraph (1), the manufacturer shall provide the authority with such information relating to the industrial activity under his control as the authority may reasonably require, including the nature, extent and likely effects off-site of possible major accidents and the authority shall provide the manufacturer with any information from the off-site emergency plan which relates to his duties under Regulation 10 or this paragraph.

(3) The local authority shall prepare its emergency plan for any industrial activity before that activity is commenced, except that in the case of an existing industrial activity or a new industrial activity commenced or deemed to have been commenced before 1st October 1985, it shall be a sufficient compliance with this Regulation if the local authority prepares its emergency plan by that date or in any case within six months of its being notified by the Executive of the industrial activity, whichever is the later.

Information to be given to persons liable to be affected by a major accident
12.—(1) The manufacturer shall endeavour to enter into an agreement with the local authority in whose area the industrial activity is situated for that local authority to take appropriate steps to inform persons outside the site who are likely to be in an area which, in the opinion of the Executive, might be affected by a major accident at any site on which an industrial activity under his control to which this Regulation applies is carried on—

(a) that the industrial activity is an activity which has been notified to the Executive;

(b) of the nature of the major accident hazard; and

(c) of the safety measures and the correct behaviour which should be adopted in the event of a major accident,

and that agreement shall specify the information that the local authority will provide.

(2) If the manufacturer is unable to enter into an agreement with the local authority in whose area the industrial activity is situated, then the manufacturer shall take appropriate steps to inform persons referred to in paragraph (1) of the information specified in sub-paragraphs (a) to (c) of that paragraph.

(3) The manufacturer shall take the steps required under paragraph (1) or (2) to inform persons about an industrial activity, before that activity is commenced, except that, in the case of an existing industrial activity or a new industrial activity commenced or deemed to have been commenced before 1st January 1986, it shall be a sufficient compliance with those paragraphs if the manufacturer takes those steps by that date.

Disclosure of information notified under these Regulations
13.—(1) Subject to Regulation 5(2)(b) and paragraph (2) of this Regulation, in so far as any provision of Regulations 5 and 7 to 12 is made under section 2(2) of the European Communities Act 1972(a), information notified to the Executive or a local authority under that provision shall be treated as relevant information for the purposes of section 28 of the 1974 Act (which imposes restrictions on the disclosure of information).

(2) Where for the purpose of evaluating information notified under Regulation 5 or Regulations 7 to 12, the Executive or a local authority discloses that information to some other person, that other person shall not use that information for any purpose except a purpose of the Executive or the local authority disclosing it, as the case may be, and before disclosing that information the Executive or the local authority, as the case may be, shall inform that other person of his obligations under this paragraph.

Enforcement
14.—(1) In so far as any provision of these Regulations is made under section 2(2) of the European Communities Act 1972, that provision shall be enforced as if it were a health and safety regulation made under section 15 of the 1974 Act, and the provisions of the 1974 Act (including the provisions relating to the approval of codes of practice and the use of approved codes of practice in criminal proceedings) and any health and safety regulations made under it, shall apply to that provision as they apply to health and safety regulations.

(2) Notwithstanding Regulation 3 of the Health and Safety (Enforcing Authority) Regulations 1977(b) and Regulation 2(1) and (3) of the Petroleum (Consolidation) Act 1928 (Enforcement) Regulations 1979(c), the enforcing authority for the relevant statutory provisions in relation to any industrial activity to which Regulations 7 to 12 of these Regulations apply shall be the Executive.

Charge by the local authority for off-site emergency plan
15.—(1) A local authority which prepares or keeps up to date an off-site emergency plan in pursuance of the duty imposed on it by Regulation 11(1) may charge a fee, determined in accordance with paragraphs (2) to (4), to any manufacturer having control of a site to which the plan relates.

(a) 1972 c. 68.   (b) S.I. 1977/746, amended by S.I. 1980/1744.
(c) S.I. 1979/427.

(2) The fee shall not exceed the sum of the costs reasonably incurred by the local authority in preparing or keeping up to date the off-site emergency plan and, where the plan covers sites under the control of different manufacturers, the fee charged to each manufacturer shall not exceed the proportion of such sum attributable to the part or parts of the plan relating to the site or sites under his control.

(3) In determining the fee no account shall be taken of costs other than the costs of preparing or keeping up to date those parts of the plan which relate to the protection of the health or safety of persons and which were costs incurred after the coming into operation of Regulation 11(1).

(4) The local authority may determine the cost of employing a graded officer for any period on work appropriate to his grade by reference to the average cost to it of employing officers of his grade for that period.

(5) When requiring payment the local authority shall send or give to the manufacturer a detailed statement of the work done and costs incurred including the dates of any site visits and the period to which the statement relates; and the fee, which shall be recoverable only as a civil debt, shall become payable one month after the statement has been sent or given.

Signed by order of the Secretary of State.

Peter Bottomley,
Joint Parliamentary Under Secretary of State,
Department of Employment.

4th December 1984.

Regulations 2(1) and 4(1)   SCHEDULE 1

(WHICH SETS OUT THE PROVISIONS OF ANNEX IV TO THE DIRECTIVE)

INDICATIVE CRITERIA

(a) Very toxic substances:

—substances which correspond to the first line of the table below,

—substances which correspond to the second line of the table below and which, owing to their physical and chemical properties, are capable of producing major accident hazards similar to those caused by the substance mentioned in the first line:

	LD50 (oral)([1]) mg/kg body weight	LD50 (cutaneous)([2]) mg/kg body weight	LC50([3]) mg/l (inhalation)
1	$LD50 \leqslant 5$	$LD50 \leqslant 10$	$LC50 \leqslant 0.1$
2	$5 < LD50 \leqslant 25$	$10 < LD50 \leqslant 50$	$0.1 < LC50 \leqslant 0.5$

([1]) LD50 oral in rats.
([2]) LD50 cutaneous in rats or rabbits.
([3]) LC50 by inhalation (four hours) in rats.

(b) Other toxic substances:

The substances showing the following values of acute toxicity and having physical and chemical properties capable of producing major accident hazards:

LD50 (oral)([1]) mg/kg body weight	LD50 (cutaneous)([2]) mg/kg body weight	LC50([3]) mg/l (inhalation)
$25 < LD50 \leqslant 200$	$50 < LD50 \leqslant 400$	$0.5 < LC50 \leqslant 2$

([1]) LD50 oral in rats.
([2]) LD50 cutaneous in rats or rabbits.
([3]) LC50 by inhalation (four hours) in rats.

(c) Flammable substances:

(i) flammable gases:
substances which in the gaseous state at normal pressure and mixed with air become flammable and the boiling point of which at normal pressure is 20°C or below;

(ii) highly flammable liquids:
substances which have a flash point lower than 21°C and the boiling point of which at normal pressure is above 20°C;

(iii) flammable liquids:
substances which have a flash point lower than 55°C and which remain liquid under pressure, where particular processing conditions, such as high pressure and high temperature, may create major accident hazards.

(d) Explosive substances:
substances which may explode under the effect of flame or which are more sensitive to shocks or friction than dinitrobenzene.

SCHEDULE 2   Regulations 2(1), 4(1) and 6(1)

(WHICH SETS OUT THE PROVISIONS OF ANNEX II TO THE DIRECTIVE)

ISOLATED STORAGE

STORAGE AT INSTALLATIONS OTHER THAN THOSE COVERED BY SCHEDULE 4 (ANNEX I TO THE DIRECTIVE)

The quantities set out below relate to each installation or group of installations belonging to the same manufacturer where the distance between installations is not sufficient to avoid, in foreseeable circumstances, any aggravation of major accident hazards. These quantities apply in any case to each group of installations belonging to the same manufacturer where the distance between the installations is less than 500 metres.

Substances or groups of substances (Column 1)	Quantities (tonnes)	
	For application of Regulation 4 (Column 2)	For application of Regulations 7 to 12 (Column 3)
Acrylonitrile	350	5,000
Ammonia	60	600
Ammonium nitrate	500*	5,000*
Chlorine	10	200
Flammable gases as defined in Schedule 1, paragraph (c)(i)	50	300
Highly flammable liquids as defined in Schedule 1, paragraph (c)(ii)	10,000	100,000
Liquid oxygen	200	2,000*
Sodium chlorate	25	250*
Sulphur dioxide	20	500

* Where this substance is in a state which gives it properties capable of creating a major accident hazard.

Regulations 2(1) and 6(1)   SCHEDULE 3

(WHICH SETS OUT THE PROVISIONS OF ANNEX III TO THE DIRECTIVE)

LIST OF SUBSTANCES FOR THE APPLICATION OF
REGULATIONS 7 TO 12

The quantities set out below relate to each installation or group of installations belonging to the same manufacturer where the distance between the installations is not sufficient to avoid, in foreseeable circumstances, any aggravation of major accident hazards. These quantities apply in any case to each group of installations belonging to the same manufacturer where the distance between the installations is less than 500 metres.

Substance (Column 1)	Quantity (for application of Regulations 7-12) (Column 2)	CAS Number (Column 3)	EEC Number (Column 4)
Group 1—Toxic substances *(quantity ≤ 1 tonne)*			
Aldicarb	100 kilograms	116–06–3	006–017–00–X
4-Aminodiphenyl	1 kilogram	92–67–1	
Amiton	1 kilogram	78–53–5	
Anabasine	100 kilograms	494–52–0	
Arsenic pentoxide, Arsenic (V) acid and salts	500 kilograms		
Arsenic trioxide, Arsenious (III) acid and salts	100 kilograms		
Arsine (Arsenic hydride)	10 kilograms	7784–42–1	
Azinphos-ethyl	100 kilograms	2642–71–9	051–056–00–1
Azinphos-methyl	100 kilograms	86–50–0	015–039–00–9
Benzidine	1 kilogram	92–87–5	612–042–00–2
Benzidine salts	1 kilogram		
Beryllium (powders, compounds)	10 kilograms		
Bis(2-chloroethyl) sulphide	1 kilogram	505–60–2	
Bis(chloromethyl) ether	1 kilogram	542–88–1	603–046–00–5
Carbofuran	100 kilograms	1563–66–2	006–026–00–9
Carbophenothion	100 kilograms	786–19–6	015–044–00–6
Chlorfenvinphos	100 kilograms	470–90–6	015–071–00–3
4-(Chloroformyl)morpholine	1 kilogram	15159–40–7	
Chloromethyl methyl ether	1 kilogram	107–30–2	
Cobalt (powders, compounds)	100 kilograms		
Crimidine	100 kilograms	535–89–7	613–004–00–8
Cyanthoate	100 kilograms	3734–95–0	015–070–00–8
Cycloheximide	100 kilograms	66–81–9	
Demeton	100 kilograms	8065–48–3	
Dialifos	100 kilograms	10311–84–9	015–088–00–6
OO-Diethyl *S*-ethylsulphinylmethyl phosphorothioate	100 kilograms	2588–05–8	
OO-Diethyl *S*-ethylsulphonylmethyl phosphorothioate	100 kilograms	2588–06–9	

SCHEDULE 3 (*continued*)

Substance (Column 1)	Quantity (Column 2)	CAS Number (Column 3)	EEC Number (Column 4)
OO-Diethyl *S*-ethylthio-methyl phosphorothioate	100 kilograms	2600-69-3	
OO-Diethyl *S*-isopropylthio-methyl phosphorodithioate	100 kilograms	78-52-4	
OO-Diethyl *S*-propylthio-methyl phosphorodithioate	100 kilograms	3309-68-0	
Dimefox	100 kilograms	115-26-4	015-061-00-9
Dimethylcarbamoyl chloride	1 kilogram	79-44-7	
Dimethylnitrosamine	1 kilogram	62-75-9	
Dimethyl phosphoramido-cyanidic acid	1 tonne	63917-41-9	
Diphacinone	100 kilograms	82-66-6	
Disulfoton	100 kilograms	298-04-4	015-060-00-3
EPN	100 kilograms	2104-64-5	015-036-00-2
Ethion	100 kilograms	563-12-2	015-047-00-2
Fensulfothion	100 kilograms	115-90-2	015-090-00-7
Fluenetil	100 kilograms	4301-50-2	607-078-00-0
Fluoroacetic acid	1 kilogram	144-49-0	607-081-00-7
Fluoroacetic acid, salts	1 kilogram		
Fluoroacetic acid, esters	1 kilogram		
Fluoroacetic acid, amides	1 kilogram		
4-Fluorobutyric acid	1 kilogram	462-23-7	
4-Fluorobutyric acid, salts	1 kilogram		
4-Fluorobutyric acid, esters	1 kilogram		
4-Fluorobutyric acid, amides	1 kilogram		
4-Fluorocrotonic acid	1 kilogram	37759-72-1	
4-Fluorocrotonic acid, salts	1 kilogram		
4-Fluorocrotonic acid, esters	1 kilogram		
4-Fluorocrotonic acid, amides	1 kilogram		
4-Fluoro-2-hydroxybutyric acid	1 kilogram		
4-Fluoro-2-hydroxybutyric acid, salts	1 kilogram		
4-Fluoro-2-hydroxybutyric acid, esters	1 kilogram		
4-Fluoro-2-hydroxybutyric acid, amides	1 kilogram		
Glycolonitrile (Hydroxyacetonitrile)	100 kilograms	107-16-4	
1,2,3,7,8,9-Hexa-chlorodibenzo-*p*-dioxin	100 kilograms	19408-74-3	
Hexamethylphosphoramide	1 kilogram	680-31-9	
Hydrogen selenide	10 kilograms	7783-07-5	
Isobenzan	100 kilograms	297-78-9	602-053-00-0
Isodrin	100 kilograms	465-73-6	602-050-00-4
Juglone (5-Hydroxynaph-thalene-1,4-dione)	100 kilograms	481-39-0	
4,4'-Methylenebis(2-chloro-aniline)	10 kilograms	101-14-4	

SCHEDULE 3 (continued)

Substance (Column 1)	Quantity (Column 2)	CAS Number (Column 3)	EEC Number (Column 4)
Methyl isocyanate	1 tonne	624-83-9	615-001-00-7
Mevinphos	100 kilograms	7786-34-7	015-020-00-5
2-Naphthylamine	1 kilogram	91-59-8	612-022-00-3
Nickel (powders, compounds)	100 kilograms		
Nickel tetracarbonyl	10 kilograms	13463-39-3	028-001-00-1
Oxydisulfoton	100 kilograms	2497-07-6	015-096-00-X
Oxygen difluoride	10 kilograms	7783-41-7	
Paraoxon (Diethyl 4-nitro-phenyl phosphate)	100 kilograms	311-45-5	
Parathion	100 kilograms	56-38-2	015-034-00-1
Parathion-methyl	100 kilograms	298-00-0	015-035-00-7
Pentaborane	100 kilograms	19624-22-7	
Phorate	100 kilograms	298-02-2	015-033-00-6
Phosacetim	100 kilograms	4104-14-7	015-092-00-8
Phosphamidon	100 kilograms	13171-21-6	015-022-00-6
Phosphine (Hydrogen phosphide)	100 kilograms	7803-51-2	
Promurit (1-(3, 4-Dichloro-phenyl)-3-triazenethio-carboxamide)	100 kilograms	5836-73-7	
1,3-Propanesultone	1 kilogram	1120-71-4	
1-Propen-2-chloro-1,3-diol diacetate	10 kilograms	10118-72-6	
Pyrazoxon	100 kilograms	108-34-9	015-023-00-1
Selenium hexafluoride	10 kilograms	7783-79-1	
Sodium selenite	100 kilograms	10102-18-8	034-002-00-8
Stibine (Antimony hydride)	100 kilograms	7803-52-3	
Sulfotep	100 kilograms	3689-24-5	015-027-00-3
Sulphur dichloride	1 tonne	10545-99-0	016-013-00-X
Tellurium hexafluoride	100 kilograms	7783-80-4	
TEPP	100 kilograms	107-49-3	015-025-00-2
2,3,7,8-Tetrachlorodibenzo-p-dioxin (TCDD)	1 kilogram	1746-01-6	
Tetramethylene-disulphotetramine	1 kilogram	80-12-6	
Thionazin	100 kilograms	297-97-2	
Tirpate (2,4-Dimethyl-1,3-dithiolane-2-carboxalde-hyde O-methyl-carbamoyloxime)	100 kilograms	26419-73-8	
Trichloromethanesulphenyl chloride	100 kilograms	594-42-3	
1-Tri(cyclohexyl)stannyl-1H-1,2,4-triazole	100 kilograms	41083-11-8	
Triethylenemelamine	10 kilograms	51-18-3	
Warfarin	100 kilograms	81-81-2	607-056-00-0

SCHEDULE 3 (*continued*)

Substance (Column 1)	Quantity (Column 2)	CAS Number (Column 3)	EEC Number (Column 4)
Group 2—Toxic substances (quantity > 1 tonne)			
Acetone cyanohydrin (2-Cyanopropan-2-ol)	200 tonnes	75–86–5	608–004–00–X
Acrolein (2-Propenal)	200 tonnes	107–02–8	605–008–00–3
Acrylonitrile	200 tonnes	107–13–1	608–003–00–4
Allyl alcohol (2-Propen-1-ol)	200 tonnes	107–18–6	603–015–00–6
Allylamine	200 tonnes	107–11–9	612–046–00–4
Ammonia	500 tonnes	7664–41–7	007–001–00–5
Bromine	500 tonnes	7726–95–6	035–001–00–5
Carbon disulphide	200 tonnes	75–15–0	006–033–00–3
Chlorine	50 tonnes	7782–50–5	017–001–00–7
Ethylene dibromide (1,2-Dibromoethane)	50 tonnes	106–93–4	602–010–00–6
Ethyleneimine	50 tonnes	151–56–4	613–001–00–1
Formaldehyde (concentration ⩾90%)	50 tonnes	50–00–0	605–001–01–2
Hydrogen chloride (liquefied gas)	250 tonnes	7647–01–0	017–002–00–2
Hydrogen cyanide	20 tonnes	74–90–8	006–006–00–X
Hydrogen fluoride	50 tonnes	7664–39–3	009–002–00–6
Hydrogen sulphide	50 tonnes	7783–06–4	016–001–00–4
Methyl bromide (Bromomethane)	200 tonnes	74–83–9	602–002–00–3
Nitrogen oxides	50 tonnes	11104–93–1	
Phosgene (Carbonyl chloride)	20 tonnes	75–44–5	006–002–00–8
Propyleneimine	50 tonnes	75–55–8	
Sulphur dioxide	1,000 tonnes	7446–09–5	016–011–00–9
Tetraethyl lead	50 tonnes	78–00–2	
Tetramethyl lead	50 tonnes	75–74–1	
Group 3—Highly reactive substances			
Acetylene (Ethyne)	50 tonnes	74–86–2	601–015–00–0
Ammonium nitrate*	5,000 tonnes	6484–52–2	
2,2-Bis(*tert*-butyl-peroxy)butane (concentration ⩾70%)	50 tonnes	2167–23–9	
1,1-Bis(*tert*-butyl-peroxy)cyclohexane (concentration ⩾80%)	50 tonnes	3006–86–8	
tert-Butyl peroxyacetate (concentration ⩾70%)	50 tonnes	107–71–1	
tert-Butyl peroxyisobutyrate (concentration ⩾80%)	50 tonnes	109–13–7	
tert-Butyl peroxy isopropyl carbonate (concentration ⩾80%)	50 tonnes	2372–21–6	
tert-Butyl peroxymaleate (concentration ⩾80%)	50 tonnes	1931–62–0	

SCHEDULE 3 (*continued*)

Substance (Column 1)	Quantity (Column 2)	CAS Number (Column 3)	EEC Number (Column 4)
tert-Butyl peroxypivalate (concentration ⩾77%)	50 tonnes	927-07-1	
Dibenzyl peroxydicarbonate (concentration ⩾90%)	50 tonnes	2144-45-8	
Di-*sec*-butyl peroxydicarbonate (concentration ⩾80%)	50 tonnes	19910-65-7	
Diethyl peroxydicarbonate (concentration ⩾30%)	50 tonnes	14666-78-5	
2,2-Dihydroperoxypropane (concentration ⩾30%)	50 tonnes	2614-76-8	
Di-isobutyryl peroxide (concentration ⩾50%)	50 tonnes	3437-84-1	
Di-*n*-propyl peroxydicarbonate (concentration ⩾80%)	50 tonnes	16066-38-9	
Ethylene oxide	50 tonnes	75-21-8	603-023-00-X
Ethyl nitrate	50 tonnes	625-58-1	007-007-00-8
3,3,6,6,9,9-Hexamethyl-1,2,4,5-tetroxacyclononane (concentration ⩾75%)	50 tonnes	22397-33-7	
Hydrogen	50 tonnes	1333-74-0	001-001-00-9
Methyl ethyl ketone peroxide (concentration ⩾60%)	50 tonnes	1338-23-4	
Methyl isobutyl ketone peroxide (concentration ⩾60%)	50 tonnes	37206-20-5	
Peracetic acid (concentration ⩾60%)	50 tonnes	79-21-0	607-094-00-8
Propylene oxide	50 tonnes	75-56-9	603-055-00-4
Sodium chlorate*	250 tonnes	7775-09-9	017-005-00-9
Group 4—Explosive substances			
Barium azide	50 tonnes	18810-58-7	
Bis(2,4,6-trinitrophenyl)-amine	50 tonnes	131-73-7	612-018-00-1
Chlorotrinitrobenzene	50 tonnes	28260-61-9	610-004-00-X
Cellulose nitrate (containing >12.6% nitrogen)	100 tonnes	9004-70-0	603-037-00-6
Cyclotetramethylene-tetranitramine	50 tonnes	2691-41-0	
Cyclotrimethylene-trinitramine	50 tonnes	121-82-4	
Diazodinitrophenol	10 tonnes	7008-81-3	
Diethylene glycol dinitrate	10 tonnes	693-21-0	603-033-00-4
Dinitrophenol, salts	50 tonnes		609-017-00-3
Ethylene glycol dinitrate	10 tonnes	628-96-6	603-032-00-9
1-Guanyl-4-nitrosamino-guanyl-1-tetrazene	10 tonnes	109-27-3	
2,2',4,4',6,6'-Hexanitro-stilbene	50 tonnes	20062-22-0	

SCHEDULE 3 (continued)

Substance (Column 1)	Quantity (Column 2)	CAS Number (Column 3)	EEC Number (Column 4)
Hydrazine nitrate	50 tonnes	13464-97-6	
Lead azide	50 tonnes	13424-46-9	082-003-00-7
Lead styphnate (Lead 2,4,6-trinitroresorcinoxide)	50 tonnes	15245-44-0	609-019-00-4
Mercury fulminate	10 tonnes	{20820-45-5 / 628-86-4	080-005-00-2
N-Methyl-N,2,4,6-tetranitroaniline	50 tonnes	479-45-8	612-017-00-6
Nitroglycerine	10 tonnes	55-63-0	603-034-00-X
Pentaerythritol tetranitrate	50 tonnes	78-11-5	603-035-00-5
Picric acid (2,4,6-Trinitro-phenol)	50 tonnes	88-89-1	609-009-00-X
Sodium picramate	50 tonnes	831-52-7	
Styphnic acid (2,4,6-Trinitroresorcinol)	50 tonnes	82-71-3	609-018-00-9
1,3,5-Triamino-2,4,6-trinitrobenzene	50 tonnes	3058-38-6	
Trinitroaniline	50 tonnes	26952-42-1	
2,4,6-Trinitroanisole	50 tonnes	606-35-9	609-011-00-0
Trinitrobenzene	50 tonnes	25377-32-6	609-005-00-8
Trinitrobenzoic acid	50 tonnes	{35860-50-5 / 129-66-8	
Trinitrocresol	50 tonnes	28905-71-7	609-012-00-6
2,4,6-Trinitrophenetole	50 tonnes	4732-14-3	
2,4,6-Trinitrotoluene	50 tonnes	118-96-7	609-008-00-4
Group 5—Flammable substances			
Flammable substances as defined in Schedule 1, paragraph (c)(i)	200 tonnes		
Flammable substances as defined in Schedule 1, paragraph (c)(ii)	50,000 tonnes		
Flammable substances as defined in Schedule 1, paragraph (c)(iii)	200 tonnes		

* Where this substance is in a state which gives it properties capable of creating a major accident hazard.

Note (This note does not form part of Annex III to the Directive).

1. CAS Number (Chemical Abstracts Number) means the number assigned to the substance by the Chemical Abstracts Service, details of which can be obtained from the United Kingdom Chemical Information Service, University of Nottingham, Nottingham.

2. EEC Number means the number assigned to the substance by the Commission of the European Communities, details of which can be obtained from its office at 20 Kensington Palace Gardens, London W8 4QQ.

Regulation 2(1)   SCHEDULE 4

(WHICH SETS OUT THE PROVISIONS OF ANNEX I TO THE DIRECTIVE)

INDUSTRIAL INSTALLATIONS WITHIN THE MEANING OF
REGULATION 2(1)

1. (a) Installations for the production or processing of organic or inorganic chemicals using for this purpose, in particular:
—alkylation
—amination by ammonolysis
—carbonylation
—condensation
—dehydrogenation
—esterification
—halogenation and manufacture of halogens
—hydrogenation
—hydrolysis
—oxidation
—polymerization
—sulphonation
—desulphurization, manufacture and transformation of sulphur-containing compounds
—nitration and manufacture of nitrogen-containing compounds
—manufacture of phosphorus-containing compounds
—formulation of pesticides and of pharmaceutical products.

(b) Installations for the processing of organic and inorganic chemical substances, using for this purpose, in particular:
—distillation
—extraction
—solvation
—mixing.

2. Installations for distillation, refining or other processing of petroleum or petroleum products.

3. Installations for the total or partial disposal of solid or liquid substances by incineration or chemical decomposition.

4. Installations for the production or processing of energy gases, for example, LPG, LNG, SNG.

5. Installations for the dry distillation of coal or lignite.

6. Installations for the production of metals or non-metals by a wet process or by means of electrical energy.

SCHEDULE 5　　　　　　　　　　Regulation 5(2)

(WHICH SETS OUT THE PROVISIONS OF ANNEX VI TO THE DIRECTIVE)

INFORMATION TO BE SUPPLIED TO THE COMMISSION OF THE
EUROPEAN COMMUNITIES BY THE MEMBER STATES PURSUANT TO
REGULATION 5(2)

REPORT OF MAJOR ACCIDENT

Member State:
Authority reponsible for report:
Address:

1. General data
　　Date and time of the major accident:
　　Country, administrative region, etc.:
　　Address:
　　Type of industrial activity:

2. Type of major accident
　　Explosion ☐　Fire ☐　Emission of dangerous substance ☐
　　Substance(s) emitted:

3. Description of the circumstances of the major accident

4. Emergency measures taken

5. Cause(s) of major accident
　　Known:
　　(to be specified)
　　Not known:
　　Information will be supplied as soon as possible

6. Nature and extent of damage
　　(a) Within the establishment
　　　　—casualties　　　　　　　　　　　　.........killed
　　　　　　　　　　　　　　　　　　　　　.........injured
　　　　　　　　　　　　　　　　　　　　　.........poisoned

　　　　—persons exposed to the major accident　.........
　　　　—material damage
　　　　—the danger is still present
　　　　—the danger no longer exists
　　(b) Outside the establishment
　　　　—casualties　　　　　　　　　　　　.........killed
　　　　　　　　　　　　　　　　　　　　　.........injured
　　　　　　　　　　　　　　　　　　　　　.........poisoned

　　　　—persons exposed to the major accident　.........
　　　　—material damage
　　　　—damage to the environment
　　　　—the danger is still present
　　　　—the danger no longer exists

7. Medium and long-term measures, particularly those aimed at preventing the recurrence of similar major accidents (to be submitted as the information becomes available).

Regulation 7(1)   SCHEDULE 6

INFORMATION TO BE INCLUDED IN A REPORT UNDER
REGULATION 7(1)

1. The report required under Regulation 7(1) shall contain the following information.

2. Information relating to every dangerous substance involved in the activity in a relevant quantity as listed in Schedule 2 column 3 or Schedule 3, namely—

(a) the name of the dangerous substance as given in Schedule 2 or 3 or, for a dangerous substance included in either of those Schedules under a general designation, the name corresponding to the chemical formula of the dangerous substance;

(b) a general description of the analytical methods available to the manufacturer for determining the presence of the dangerous substance, or references to such methods in the scientific literature;

(c) a brief description of the hazards which may be created by the dangerous substance;

(d) the degree of purity of the dangerous substance, and the names of the main impurities and their percentages.

3. Information relating to the installation, namely—

(a) a map of the site and its surrounding area to a scale large enough to show any features that may be significant in the assessment of the hazard or risk associated with the site;

(b) a scale plan of the site showing the locations and quantities of all significant inventories of the dangerous substance;

(c) a description of the processes or storage involving the dangerous substance and an indication of the conditions under which it is normally held;

(d) the maximum number of persons likely to be present on site;

(e) information about the nature of the land use and the size and distribution of the population in the vicinity of the industrial activity to which the report relates.

4. Information relating to the management system for controlling the industrial activity, namely—

(a) the staffing arrangements for controlling the industrial activity with the name of the person responsible for safety on the site and the names of those who are authorised to set emergency procedures in motion and to inform outside authorities;

(b) the arrangements made to ensure that the means provided for the safe operation of the industrial activity are properly designed, constructed, tested, operated, inspected and maintained;

(c) the arrangements for training of persons working on the site.

5. Information relating to the potential major accidents, namely—

(*a*) a description of the potential sources of a major accident and the conditions or events which could be significant in bringing one about;

(*b*) a diagram of any plant in which the industrial activity is carried on, sufficient to show the features which are significant as regards the potential for a major accident or its prevention or control;

(*c*) a description of the measures taken to prevent, control or minimise the consequences of any major accident;

(*d*) information about the emergency procedures laid down for dealing with a major accident occurring at the site;

(*e*) information about prevailing meteorological conditions in the vicinity of the site;

(*f*) an estimate of the number of people on site who may be exposed to the hazards considered in the report.

SCHEDULE 7
Regulation 7(3)

PRELIMINARY INFORMATION TO BE SENT TO THE EXECUTIVE UNDER REGULATION 7(3)

1. The name and address of the person supplying the information.

2. The full postal address of the site where the industrial activity is being carried on and its ordnance survey grid reference.

3. The area of the site, and of any adjacent site which is required to be taken into account by virtue of Schedule 2 or 3.

4. A statement to the effect that the industrial activity had already commenced on or before 7 January 1985.

5. A general description of the industrial activity carried on at the site or sites.

6. The name and address of the planning authority in whose area the industrial activity is being carried on.

7. The name and maximum quantity liable to be on the site or sites of each dangerous substance involved in the industrial activity concerning which information is being supplied.

EXPLANATORY NOTE

(This Note is not part of the Regulations.)

1. These Regulations implement as respects Great Britain Council Directive 82/501/EEC (OJ No. L230, 5.8.82, p. 1) "on the major-accident hazards of certain industrial activities" and thus introduce new requirements with a view to preventing and limiting the effects of accidents arising from industrial activities involving dangerous substances.

2. Subject to the exceptions contained in Regulation 3, the Regulations apply to any operation in an industrial installation specified in Schedule 4 which involves one or more dangerous substances, unless that operation is incapable of producing a major accident hazard, and to storage of at least specified quantities of the substances listed in Schedule 2 ("isolated storage").

3. Dangerous substances are substances which fulfil the criteria laid down in Schedule 1 for very toxic, toxic, explosive or flammable substances or are substances listed in Schedule 2 or 3.

4. Manufacturers who have control of relevant industrial activities are required by Regulation 4 to be able to demonstrate that they have identified major accident hazards, have taken adequate steps to prevent or limit the consequences of any major accident and have provided suitable information, training and equipment for persons working on the site. By Regulation 5 such manufacturers are required to report any major accident to the Health and Safety Executive which is required to send information about the accident to the Commission of the European Communities.

5. Regulation 6 provides that where a manufacturer has control of an industrial activity other than isolated storage in which at least the quantity of a dangerous substance specified in Schedule 3, or of isolated storage in which at least the quantity specified in Schedule 2 is involved, Regulations 7 to 12 shall apply. He is required by Regulation 7 to send a report containing the particulars specified in Schedule 6 to the Executive. This must be done, in the case of a new activity at least three months before the activity is commenced, or in the case of an existing activity before 8 July 1989. In the latter case he must notify the particulars specified in Schedule 7 by 1 April 1985 unless he has already provided that information by a notification under the Notification of Installations Handling Hazardous Substances Regulations 1982 (S.I. 1982/1357).

6. The Regulations provide for such reports to be kept up to date (Regulation 8) and for the manufacturer to give further information relating to the activity if the Health and Safety Executive requires it (Regulation 9).

7. By Regulation 10, the manufacturer is required to prepare and keep up to date an on-site emergency plan detailing how major accidents will be dealt with on the site where the industrial activity is carried on and by Regulation 11 the local authority is required to prepare and keep up to date an off-site emergency plan on the basis of information to be supplied to it by the manufacturer after consulting him, the Executive and any other appropriate person.

8. Regulation 12 requires the manufacturer to arrange that persons outside the site who may be affected by a major accident are informed of the nature of the hazard and of the safety measures and the correct behaviour that should be adopted if such an accident occurs.

9. The Regulations restrict the use that may be made of the information notified (Regulation 13) and provide for enforcement generally and for the enforcing authority for the relevant statutory provisions in relation to any industrial activity to which Regulations 7 to 12 apply to be the Health and Safety Executive (Regulation 14).

10. Regulation 15 enables a local authority which prepares and keeps up to date an off-site emergency plan to recover from the manufacturer the costs reasonably incurred for that purpose.

STATUTORY INSTRUMENTS

1984 No. 1903

COAL INDUSTRY

The Opencast Coal (Rate of Interest on Compensation) (No. 3) Order 1984

Made - - -	*4th December* 1984
Laid before Parliament	13*th December* 1984
Coming into Operation	2*nd January* 1985

The Treasury, in exercise of the powers conferred upon them by sections 35(8) and 49(4) of the Opencast Coal Act 1958(a), and of all other powers enabling them in that behalf, hereby make the following Order:—

1. This Order may be cited as the Opencast Coal (Rate of Interest on Compensation) (No. 3) Order 1984, and shall come into operation on 2nd January 1985.

2. The rate of interest for the purposes of section 35 of the Opencast Coal Act 1958 shall be 10½ per cent. per annum.

3. The Opencast Coal (Rate of Interest on Compensation) No. 2 Order 1984(**b**) is hereby revoked.

Ian B. Lang,
John Major,
Two of the Lords Commissioners
of Her Majesty's Treasury.

4th December 1984.

EXPLANATORY NOTE

(*This Note is not part of the Order.*)

Section 35 of the Opencast Coal Act 1958 provides that interest shall be payable in addition to compensation in certain circumstances. This Order decreases the rate of interest from 11½ per cent. to 10½ per cent. per annum and revokes the Opencast Coal (Rate of Interest on Compensation) No. 2 Order 1984.

(**a**) 1958 c.69.　　　　　　　　(**b**) S.I. 1984/1049.

STATUTORY INSTRUMENTS

1984 No. 1904

SOCIAL SECURITY

The Social Security (Treasury Supplement to Contributions) (No. 2) Order 1984

Laid before Parliament in draft

Made - - -	*3rd December* 1984
Coming into Operation	*6th April* 1985

Whereas a draft of the following Order was laid before Parliament in accordance with the provisions of section 167(1) of the Social Security Act 1975(a) and approved by resolution of each House of Parliament:

Now, therefore, the Secretary of State for Social Services, with the consent of the Treasury, in exercise of the powers conferred upon him by section 1(5A) of the Social Security Act 1975(b) and of all other powers enabling him in that behalf, hereby makes the following Order:—

Citation and commencement

1. This Order may be cited as the Social Security (Treasury Supplement to Contributions) (No. 2) Order 1984 and shall come into operation on 6th April 1985.

Alteration of Treasury supplement to contributions

2. In section 1(5) of the Social Security Act 1975 (Treasury supplement to contributions to be a fixed percentage of so much of all contributions paid in the year concerned as remains after deducting the appropriate national health service allocation and the appropriate employment protection allocation)(c) for the words "11 per cent."(d) there shall be substituted the words "9 per cent.".

Signed by authority of the Secretary of State for Social Services.

Tony Newton,
Minister of State,
Department of Health and Social
Security.

29th November 1984.

Donald Thompson,
Ian B. Lang,
Two of the Lords Commissioners of
Her Majesty's Treasury.

3rd December 1984.

(a) 1975 c.14; section 167(1) was amended by the Social Security (Contributions) Act 1981 (c.1), section 4(5).

(b) Section 1(5A) was inserted by the Social Security (Contributions) Act 1981, section 2(2), and was amended by the Social Security (Contributions) Act 1982 (c.2), section 2(2).

(c) Section 1(5) was amended by the Social Security (Miscellaneous Provisions) Act 1977 (c.5), section 24(6) and Schedule 2, and by the Employment Protection Act 1975 (c.71), section 40(1).

(d) *See* S.I. 1984/14, article 2.

EXPLANATORY NOTE

(This Note is not part of the Order.)

This Order decreases the Treasury supplement to contributions paid under the Social Security Act 1975 from 11 per cent. to 9 per cent..

STATUTORY INSTRUMENTS

1984 No. 1905

SOCIAL SECURITY

The Social Security (Contributions, Re-rating) (No. 2) Order 1984

Laid before Parliament in draft

Made   -   -   -   *3rd December* 1984

Coming into Operation   *6th April* 1985

Whereas the Secretary of State for Social Services, as a result of carrying out in the tax year 1984–85 a review of the general level of earnings pursuant to subsections (2) and (3) of section 120 of the Social Security Act 1975(**a**), has determined that an order should be made under that section amending Part I of the said Act by altering the rates of Class 2 and Class 3 contributions, the amount of earnings below which an earner may be excepted from liability for Class 2 contributions and the lower and upper limits of profits or gains to be taken into account for Class 4 contributions:

And whereas a draft of the following Order was laid before Parliament in accordance with the provisions of sections 120(4) and 121(2) of that Act and approved by resolution of each House of Parliament:

Now, therefore, the Secretary of State for Social Services, in conjunction with the Treasury so far as relates to matters with regard to which the Treasury has so directed(**b**), in exercise of the powers conferred on him by sections 120(5) and (6) and 121(2) of the said Act and of all other powers enabling him in that behalf, hereby makes the following Order:—

Citation, commencement and interpretation

1.—(1) This Order may be cited as the Social Security (Contributions, Re-rating) (No.2) Order 1984 and shall come into operation on 6th April 1985.

(2) In this Order "the Act" means the Social Security Act 1975.

Rate of, and small earnings exception from, Class 2 contributions

2. In section 7 of the Act (Class 2 contributions)—

(*a*) in subsection (1) (weekly rate) for "£4.60"(**c**) there shall be substituted "£4.75";

(*b*) in subsection (5) (small earnings exception) for "£1,850"(**d**) there shall be substituted "£1,925".

(**a**) 1975 c.14.   (**b**) *See* Social Security Act 1975, section 166(5). (**c**) *See* S.I. 1984/15, article 2(*a*).
(**d**) *See* S.I. 1984/15, article 2(*b*).

Amount of Class 3 contributions
   3. In section 8(1) of the Act (amount of Class 3 contributions) for "£4.50"(a) there shall be substituted "£4.65".

Lower and upper limits for Class 4 contributions
   4. In sections 9(2) and 10(1) of the Act (Class 4 contributions recoverable under Tax Acts and regulations)—

   (a) for "£3,950" (lower limit)(b) wherever that amount appears there shall be substituted in each of those sections "£4,150";

   (b) for "£13,000" (upper limit)(c) there shall be substituted in each of those sections "£13,780".

Signed by authority of the Secretary of State for Social Services.

Tony Newton,
Minister of State,
Department of Health and Social
Security.

29th November 1984.

Donald Thompson,
Ian B. Lang,
Two of the Lords Commissioners of
Her Majesty's Treasury.

3rd December 1984.

EXPLANATORY NOTE

(This Note is not part of the Order.)

   This Order increases the rates of Class 2 and Class 3 contributions payable under the Social Security Act 1975. It increases the amount of earnings below which an earner may be excepted from liability for Class 2 contributions, and the lower and upper limits of profits or gains between which Class 4 contributions are payable.

   In accordance with section 121(1) of the Social Security Act 1975, a copy of the report by the Government Actuary (Cmnd. 9386), giving his opinion on the likely effect on the National Insurance Fund of the making of the Order, was laid before Parliament with a draft of it.

(a) *See* S.I. 1984/15, article 3.   (b) *See* S.I. 1984/15, article 4(a).   (c) *See* S.I. 1984/15, article 4(b).

STATUTORY INSTRUMENTS

1984 No. 1907

PARLIAMENT

The Parliamentary Pensions (Purchase of Added Years) (Amendment) Order 1984

Made - - - -	*5th December* 1984
Laid before the House of Commons	*10th December* 1984
Coming into Operation	*31st December* 1984

The Lord President of the Council, in exercise of the powers conferred on him by section 11(1), (2) and (4) of the Parliamentary Pensions Act 1978(a), and of all other powers enabling him in that behalf, hereby makes the following Order:—

Citation and commencement

1. This Order may be cited as the Parliamentary Pensions (Purchase of Added Years) (Amendment) Order 1984 and shall come into operation on 31st December 1984.

Interpretation

2.—(1) In this Order, "the principal Order" means the Parliamentary Pensions (Purchase of Added Years) Order 1978(b).

(2) Words and expressions defined in Article 3 of the principal Order shall have the same meanings when used in this Order.

Amendment of Article 3 of the principal Order (Interpretation)

3. In Article 3 of the principal Order—

(i) after the definition of "the Act of 1978" there shall be inserted the following definition:

" "the Act of 1984" means the Parliamentary Pensions etc. Act 1984(c);";

(ii) in the definition of "added year", after the words "expressed in days" there shall be inserted the words "and any future added year";

(a) 1978 c. 56.
(b) S.I. 1978/1837, amended by S.I. 1981/800. Supplementary provision is contained in S.I. 1982/1155.
(c) 1984 c. 52.

(iii) after the definition of "aggregate period of reckonable service" there shall be inserted the following definitions:

" "fraction of a year" means a part of a year of reckonable service, expressed as the proportion borne by the number of days in that part to three hundred and sixty-five; and "fraction of an added year" shall be construed accordingly;

"future added year" means with reference to a specified date, an added year in respect of which a Member's application to purchase has been accepted by the Trustees, but—

(i) which, in the case of an added year being purchased by periodical contributions, would not be added to his reckonable service if Article 7(2) of this Order were to apply to him at that date; or

(ii) in respect of which a lump sum payment remains to be made by him;";

(iv) after the definition of "periodical contributions" there shall be inserted the following definitions:

" "previous employment" means in respect of a Member, the period of employment (not being a period of self-employment or a period of service as a Member or as the holder of a qualifying office) which immediately preceded the period of his actual reckonable service during which he applies under Article 14 of this Order, or during which (if earlier) his sixty-fifth birthday occurs;

"previous expectations" means in respect of a Member, the annual value at his sixty-fifth birthday which in the opinion of the Trustees is to be given to the pension benefits to which he would have become entitled under a pension scheme relating to his previous employment, had he remained in that employment and retired from it at the normal retirement age under that scheme;";

(v) for the definition of "retained benefits" there shall be substituted the following definition:

" "retained benefits" means	the annual value at his sixty-fifth birthday which in the opinion of the Trustees is to be given to benefits accrued or accruing to a Member (other than in the Parliamentary Contributory Pension Fund) before his last period of actual reckonable service beginning before that birthday, and being benefits within the classes taken into account by the Commissioners of Inland Revenue in determining maximum benefits for the purposes of their approval of retirement benefit schemes under Chapter II of Part II of the Finance Act 1970;"(a);

(vi) the definition of "retained lump sum benefits" shall be deleted.

Amendment of Article 4 of the principal Order (Purchase of added years by periodical contributions)

4. In Article 4(1) of the principal Order, there shall be substituted for sub-paragraph (i) the following sub-paragraph:—

"(i) the Member will not at his next birthday after the date of the application have attained the age of sixty-five;".

Amendment of Article 7 of the principal Order (Interrupted service)

5. In Article 7 of the principal Order, after paragraph (6) there shall be inserted the following new paragraph:

"(7) Paragraph (2) of this Article shall apply to a Member who becomes Speaker of the House of Commons or Prime Minister and First Lord of the Treasury from the day after the date of his election or appointment as such, as if he were a person who ceases to be a Member in circumstances to which section 2 of the Act of 1978 does not apply, but the other provisions of this Article and Article 8(6) of this Order shall not apply to him.".

Amendment of Article 9 of the principal Order (Lump sum payments)

6. In Article 9(1) of the principal Order, for the words "in accordance with Part 2" there shall be substituted "in accordance with the appropriate table of Part 2".

Amendment of Article 10 of the principal Order (Limits on purchase of added years)

7.—(1) In paragraph (1) of Article 10 of the principal Order, for the words

---

(a) 1970 c. 24.

"Subject to paragraph (1A)" there shall be substituted the words "Subject to paragraphs (1A) to (1C)".

(2) After paragraph (1A) of Article 10 of the principal Order, there shall be inserted the following new paragraphs:—

"(1B) Subject to paragraph (1C) of this Article, paragraph (1) of this Article shall not apply to a Member's periodical contributions which on the date of the passing of the Act of 1984 were payable in accordance with Article 6(1)(*a*), or for a period of five years in accordance with Articles 4(2) or (3) and 6(1)(*b*), of this Order.

(1C) If, after 31st December 1984 a Member applies to the Trustees to purchase added years by periodical contributions, the annual amount of periodical contributions payable by him in accordance with Article 6(1)(*a*), or for a period of five years in accordance with Articles 4(3) and 6(1)(*b*), of this Order shall not be such as to exceed, at any time during the period such contributions would be so payable, the amount (if any) by which for the time being—

(i) the annual amount of his periodical contributions referred to in paragraph (1B) of this Article (if any) aggregated with the annual amount of his contributions under section 3 of the Act of 1972,

is less than—

(ii) the limit under paragraph (1) of this Article.".

(3) For paragraph (3) of Article 10 of the principal Order, there shall be substituted the following paragraph:—

"(3) The maximum added years that a Member with no retained benefits may purchase:

(i) if his prospective actual reckonable service to his sixty-fifth birthday is less than 6 years, shall be nil;

(ii) if his prospective actual reckonable service to his sixty-fifth birthday is 6 years or more, shall be the number of added years, in respect of which the annual pension, calculated in accordance with section 7(3) of the Act of 1972, aggregated with the annual pension so calculated in respect of a period of reckonable service equal to the number of years and any part of a year of that prospective actual reckonable service, is as specified in column (B) below:

(A)	(B)
Prospective actual reckonable service to the Member's 65th birthday	*Aggregate annual pension (expressed as a fraction of relevant terminal salary)*
10 years or more	2/3
9 years	8/15
8 years	6/15
7 years	4/15
6 years	2/15

Where the period of prospective actual reckonable service includes part of a year, the aggregate annual pension appropriate to that period expressed in years and days shall be calculated proportionately by reference to the fraction in column (B)."

(4) For paragraph (4) of Article 10 of the principal Order, there shall be substituted the following paragraph:—

"(4) If a Member has retained benefits or any period of reckonable service as a Member determined in respect of him under section 22(3) of the Act of 1972, the maximum added years that he may purchase shall not exceed the limits under paragraph (3) of this Article and shall not be such that the aggregate annual pension calculated in respect of him under paragraph (3)(ii), when aggregated with the retained benefits and with pension calculated in accordance with section 7(3) of that Act in respect of the period so determined, will exceed 2/3 of the relevant terminal salary."

8. There shall be inserted after Article 12 of the principal Order the following Articles:—

"Applications to reduce added years being purchased

13.—(1) Notwithstanding any of the other Articles of this Order, if within a period of twelve months from 31st December 1984 a Member who was in service as a Member on the date of the passing of the Act of 1984 applies to the Trustees for a reduction, by a specified number, in the number of his future added years on the date of acceptance by them of his application, the Trustees shall accept his application and those future added years shall be reduced by the specified number.

(2) Subject to paragraph (3) of this Article, if a reduction in a Member's future added years is made under paragraph (1) of this Article—

(i) the annual amount of any periodical contributions; and

(ii) the amount of any lump sum payment,

which (apart from the provisions of this Article) would be payable by him on or after the date of the acceptance of his application under paragraph (1) of this Article in respect of those future added years, shall be reduced by the proportion (up to and including 100%) which the specified number under paragraph (1) of this Article bears to the number of his future added years referred to in that paragraph.

(3) If a Member's future added years referred to in paragraph (1) of this Article are being purchased by him under more than one application under this Order, a reduction under paragraph (2) of this Article shall be effected taking those applications in such order as the Trustees shall consider appropriate, having regard to any preferences expressed to them in writing by the Member.

Purchase of added years by reference to earlier service

14.—(1) A Member who was in service as a Member on the date of the passing of the Act of 1984, and who had any actual reckonable service on or after 16th October 1964 and before 20th July 1983, may apply in writing to the Trustees to purchase added years under this Article.

(2) The Trustees shall accept a Member's application to purchase added years under this Article if the following conditions are satisfied:

(i) the application is made within twelve months of 31st December 1984;

(ii) in the case of an application which specifies purchase by periodical contributions, the Member has satisfied the Trustees, in whatever manner the Trustees require, that he is in good health;

(iii) in the case of an application which specifies purchase by a lump sum payment, the Member has not applied to the Trustees under the provisions of section 2 of the Act of 1978 for an early pension because of ill-health;

(iv) the Member has supplied to the Trustees such information and evidence as they may require;

(v) the application specifies whether the purchase of added years is to be by periodical contributions payable until he attains the age of 65 years (if he has not attained that age), by periodical contributions for a period of four or five years (as the Member shall further specify in the application), or by a lump sum payment:

Provided that this condition shall not apply in respect of added years which are subject to a maximum calculated under paragraph (4)(i) of this Article, if on the date of the application a pension calculated in accordance with section 7(3) of the Act of 1972 by reference to an aggregate period of reckonable service consisting of his reckonable service under paragraph (5)(ii)–(iv) of this Article would equal or exceed either two-thirds of the relevant terminal salary or the maximum in respect of the Member under paragraph (5) of this Article.

(3) Notwithstanding anything in the other provisions of this Order, the following only of Articles 4 to 13 of this Order shall apply to the purchase of added years under this Article:

(i) Article 5 (Applications irrevocable after acceptance);

(ii) Article 6 (Payment of periodical contributions), with the substitution:

(a) in Article 6(1)(a), for the words "under Article 4(1) of this Order", of the words "to purchase added years by periodical contributions payable until the age of 65";

(b) in Article 6(1)(b), for the words "under Article 4(2) or (3) of this Order", of the words "to purchase added years by periodical contributions for a period of four or five years";

(iii) Article 7 (Interrupted service), with the substitution, for any reference in that Article to a rate or rates, of a reference to a cost determined in accordance with the provisions of this Article;

(iv) Article 9 (Lump sum payment);

(v) Article 10(1), (1A) and (1B) (Limits on purchase of added years);

(vi) Article 12 (Further applications to purchase added years).

(4) Subject to paragraphs (3)(v) and (5) of this Article, the maximum number of added years that a Member may purchase under this Article shall be calculated, by reference to the period of his actual reckonable service on or after 16th October 1964 and before 20th July 1983, as follows:

(i) one-sixth of that period, expressed in years and any fraction of a year, before his sixty-fifth birthday; and

(ii) one-sixth of that period, so expressed, on or after that birthday.

(5) The maximum added years of a Member calculated under sub-paragraph (4)(i) of this Article shall be such that a pension, calculated under section 7(3) of the Act of 1972 on the date of the acceptance by the Trustees of the Member's application under this Article and by reference to an aggregate period of reckonable service consisting of:

(i) the number of those added years;

(ii) the number of his added years, other than years purchased under this Article;

(iii) his actual reckonable service on that date or before his sixty-fifth birthday (if earlier); and

(iv) any period of reckonable service which has been determined in respect of him under section 22(3)(a) of the Act of 1972,

does not exceed a maximum, being (if the Member has retained benefits) the greater of—

(a) ⅔ of the relevant terminal salary, less his retained benefits; and

(b) his previous expectations less his retained benefits accruing during his previous employment (up to the amount of ⅔ of the relevant terminal salary),

or (if the Member has no retained benefits) ⅔ of the relevant terminal salary.

(6) A Member who has applied to purchase added years under this Article by periodical contributions for a period of four or five years and to whom Article 7(2) of this Order applies, may, in respect of any such applications and subject to the foregoing provisions, apart from paragraph (2), of this Article, apply in writing to the Trustees to purchase by a lump sum payment some or all of the added years comprised in any reduction, in consequence of his ceasing to be a Member, in the number of added years he is able to purchase in full, and the Trustees shall accept his application under this paragraph if:

(i) the Member has not applied to the Trustees under the provisions of section 2 of the Act of 1978 for an early pension because of ill-health;

(ii) the number of added years which the Member applies to purchase does not exceed the maximum permitted under the provisions of this Article;

(iii) the Member has supplied to the Trustees such information and evidence as they may require; and

(iv) the application under this paragraph is made within three months of his ceasing to be a Member.

General

15. The provisions of this Order are without prejudice to any maximum pension imposed in relation to a Member by an order under section 7(3B) of the Act of 1972 (maximum pensions payable).".

Amendment of Schedule

9. For the Schedule to the principal Order there shall be substituted the Schedule to this Order.

Revocations

10. The following are hereby revoked:

(i) Article 11 of the principal Order (Commutation);

(ii) the Parliamentary Pensions (Purchase of Added Years) (Amendment) Order 1982(a).

Whitelaw,
Lord President of the Council.

Dated 5th December 1984.

ARTICLE 9   THE SCHEDULE

CONTRIBUTIONS FOR ADDED YEARS

PART 1 — PERIODICAL CONTRIBUTIONS   Article 6
(of the principal Order).

Tables for the calculation of the cost of purchasing added years by periodical contributions. The contribution due is that percentage of the Member's ordinary salary determined as the appropriate percentage shown in the table opposite the Member's age on his birthday next following the receipt by the Trustees of his application multiplied by the number, in years and fractions of years, of added years being bought.

(a) S.I. 1982/1155.

TABLE A

(for the calculation of the cost of purchasing added years by periodical contributions payable until the Member's 65th birthday pursuant to an application under Article 4(1) or 7(5))

Age next birthday	MALES %	FEMALES %
32	0.71	0.68
33	0.73	0.71
34	0.76	0.74
35	0.79	0.77
36	0.83	0.80
37	0.86	0.84
38	0.90	0.88
39	0.95	0.91
40	1.00	0.95
41	1.05	1.00
42	1.10	1.06
43	1.16	1.12
44	1.23	1.18
45	1.31	1.25
46	1.39	1.33
47	1.48	1.42
48	1.58	1.52
49	1.69	1.63
50	1.81	1.75
51	1.94	1.88
52	2.10	2.03
53	2.28	2.21
54	2.50	2.42
55	2.76	2.70
56	3.07	3.05
57	3.47	3.49
58	4.01	4.07
59	4.70	4.78
60	5.64	5.70
61	7.13	7.26
62	9.64	9.89
63	14.54	15.04
64	28.03	29.10

TABLE B

(for the calculation of the cost of purchasing added years by periodical contributions payable until the Member's 65th birthday pursuant to an application under Article 14(1))

Age next birthday	MALES %	FEMALES %
24	0.23	0.22
25	0.24	0.22
26	0.24	0.23
27	0.24	0.23
28	0.25	0.24
29	0.26	0.24
30	0.26	0.25
31	0.27	0.26
32	0.28	0.27
33	0.29	0.28
34	0.30	0.30
35	0.32	0.31
36	0.33	0.32
37	0.34	0.34
38	0.36	0.35
39	0.38	0.36
40	0.40	0.38
41	0.42	0.40
42	0.44	0.42
43	0.46	0.45
44	0.49	0.47
45	0.52	0.50
46	0.56	0.53
47	0.59	0.57
48	0.63	0.61
49	0.68	0.65
50	0.72	0.70
51	0.78	0.75
52	0.84	0.81
53	0.91	0.88
54	1.00	0.97
55	1.10	1.08
56	1.23	1.22
57	1.39	1.40
58	1.60	1.63
59	1.88	1.91
60	2.26	2.28
61	2.85	2.90
62	3.86	3.96
63	5.82	6.02
64	11.21	11.64

TABLE C

(for the calculation of the cost of purchasing added years by periodical contributions payable for a period of 4 years pursuant to an application under Article 4(3))

Age next birthday	MALES %	FEMALES %
32	4.91	4.73
33	4.95	4.78
34	4.99	4.82
35	5.04	4.87
36	5.10	4.92
37	5.16	4.97
38	5.22	5.02
39	5.28	5.06
40	5.34	5.11
41	5.40	5.17
42	5.47	5.23
43	5.54	5.29
44	5.62	5.36
45	5.70	5.44
46	5.78	5.51
47	5.86	5.58
48	5.92	5.65
49	5.98	5.72
50	6.04	5.80
51	6.10	5.87
52	6.16	5.95
53	6.22	6.04
54	6.28	6.13
55	6.35	6.25
56	6.42	6.40
57	6.52	6.55
58	6.64	6.72
59	6.78	6.90
60	6.95	7.08
61	7.13	7.26
62	7.31	7.45
63	7.48	7.63
64	7.34	7.49
65	7.20	7.34
66	7.06	7.19
67	6.91	7.01
68	6.76	6.80
69	6.59	6.57
70	6.41	6.32
71	6.22	6.07
72	6.00	5.82
73	5.76	5.58
74	5.51	5.34
75	5.27	5.10
76	5.04	4.87
77	4.82	4.66
78	4.62	4.45
79	4.43	4.25
80	4.26	4.06

TABLE D

(for the calculation of the cost of purchasing added years by periodical contributions payable for a period of 4 years pursuant to an application under Article 14(1))

Age next birthday	MALES %	FEMALES %
24	1.87	1.76
25	1.88	1.77
26	1.89	1.78
27	1.90	1.80
28	1.91	1.82
29	1.92	1.83
30	1.94	1.85
31	1.95	1.87
32	1.96	1.89
33	1.98	1.91
34	2.00	1.93
35	2.02	1.95
36	2.04	1.97
37	2.06	1.99
38	2.09	2.01
39	2.11	2.03
40	2.14	2.05
41	2.16	2.07
42	2.19	2.09
43	2.22	2.12
44	2.25	2.14
45	2.28	2.17
46	2.31	2.20
47	2.34	2.23
48	2.37	2.26
49	2.39	2.29
50	2.42	2.32
51	2.44	2.35
52	2.46	2.38
53	2.49	2.42
54	2.51	2.45
55	2.54	2.50
56	2.57	2.56
57	2.61	2.62
58	2.66	2.69
59	2.71	2.76
60	2.78	2.83
61	2.85	2.90
62	2.92	2.98
63	2.99	3.05
64	2.94	3.00
65	2.88	2.94
66	2.82	2.88
67	2.76	2.80
68	2.70	2.72
69	2.64	2.63
70	2.56	2.53

TABLE D continued

Age next birthday	MALES %	FEMALES %
71	2.49	2.43
72	2.40	2.33
73	2.30	2.23
74	2.20	2.14
75	2.11	2.04
76	2.02	1.95
77	1.93	1.86
78	1.85	1.78
79	1.77	1.70
80	1.70	1.62

TABLE E

(for the calculation of the cost of purchasing added years by periodical contributions payable for a period of 5 years pursuant to an application under Article 4(3))

Age next birthday	MALES %	FEMALES %
32	3.97	3.80
33	4.00	3.84
34	4.04	3.88
35	4.08	3.91
36	4.13	3.95
37	4.18	3.98
38	4.22	4.02
39	4.27	4.07
40	4.32	4.12
41	4.38	4.18
42	4.43	4.24
43	4.48	4.30
44	4.54	4.36
45	4.60	4.42
46	4.66	4.48
47	4.72	4.54
48	4.77	4.60
49	4.82	4.66
50	4.87	4.72
51	4.92	4.78
52	4.97	4.84
53	5.02	4.91
54	5.06	4.98
55	5.11	5.06
56	5.17	5.16
57	5.26	5.27

TABLE E continued

Age next birthday	MALES %	FEMALES %
58	5.36	5.39
59	5.50	5.53
60	5.66	5.70
61	5.81	5.88
62	5.95	6.04
63	6.07	6.17
64	5.96	6.05
65	5.86	5.94
66	5.75	5.82
67	5.63	5.68
68	5.51	5.51
69	5.39	5.33
70	5.26	5.14
71	5.11	4.93
72	4.94	4.73
73	4.75	4.54
74	4.55	4.36
75	4.36	4.18
76	4.18	4.00
77	4.01	3.83
78	3.85	3.66
79	3.71	3.50
80	3.58	3.35

TABLE F

(for the calculation of the cost of purchasing added years by periodical contributions payable for a period of 5 years pursuant to an application under Article 14(1))

Age next birthday	MALES %	FEMALES %
24	1.51	1.43
25	1.52	1.44
26	1.53	1.44
27	1.54	1.46
28	1.55	1.47
29	1.56	1.48
30	1.57	1.49
31	1.58	1.51
32	1.59	1.52
33	1.60	1.54
34	1.62	1.55
35	1.63	1.56
36	1.65	1.58

TABLE F continued

Age next birthday	MALES %	FEMALES %
37	1.67	1.59
38	1.69	1.61
39	1.71	1.63
40	1.73	1.65
41	1.75	1.67
42	1.77	1.70
43	1.79	1.72
44	1.82	1.74
45	1.84	1.77
46	1.86	1.79
47	1.89	1.82
48	1.91	1.84
49	1.93	1.86
50	1.95	1.89
51	1.97	1.91
52	1.99	1.94
53	2.01	1.96
54	2.03	1.99
55	2.05	2.02
56	2.07	2.06
57	2.10	2.11
58	2.14	2.16
59	2.20	2.21
60	2.26	2.28
61	2.32	2.35
62	2.38	2.42
63	2.43	2.47
64	2.38	2.42
65	2.34	2.38
66	2.30	2.33
67	2.25	2.27
68	2.20	2.20
69	2.16	2.13
70	2.10	2.06
71	2.04	1.97
72	1.98	1.89
73	1.90	1.82
74	1.82	1.74
75	1.74	1.67
76	1.67	1.60
77	1.60	1.53
78	1.54	1.46
79	1.48	1.40
80	1.43	1.34

PART 2 — LUMP SUM   Article 9
(of the principal Order)

Tables for the calculation of the single payment required to purchase added years. The payment due, calculated as at the date of the receipt by the Trustees of the application, per £100 of pensionable salary of a Member, is the appropiate figure shown in the table opposite the Member's age on his birthday next following, multiplied by the number, in years and fractions of years, of added years being bought.

TABLE A

(for the calculation of the single payment required to purchase added years pursuant to an application under Article 8(1))

Age next birthday	MALES £	FEMALES £
32	18.7	18.0
33	18.9	18.2
34	19.1	18.4
35	19.3	18.6
36	19.5	18.7
37	19.7	18.9
38	19.9	19.1
39	20.2	19.3
40	20.4	19.5
41	20.6	19.7
42	20.9	19.9
43	21.2	20.2
44	21.5	20.5
45	21.8	20.9
46	22.1	21.2
47	22.3	21.5
48	22.6	21.7
49	22.8	22.0
50	23.0	22.2
51	23.3	22.5
52	23.5	22.8
53	23.8	23.2
54	24.0	23.5
55	24.2	23.9
56	24.5	24.4
57	24.8	25.0
58	25.3	25.7
59	25.9	26.5
60	26.5	27.4
61	27.2	28.1
62	27.8	28.9
63	28.3	29.5
64	27.7	28.9
65	27.1	28.3
66	26.5	27.6

TABLE A continued

Age next birthday	MALES £	FEMALES £
67	25.9	26.8
68	25.3	25.9
69	24.6	25.0
70	23.8	24.1
71	22.8	23.1
72	21.8	22.1
73	20.9	21.1
74	19.9	20.1
75	19.0	19.1
76	18.1	18.1
77	17.2	17.2
78	16.3	16.3
79	15.5	15.5
80	14.6	14.6

TABLE B

(for the calculation of the single payment required to purchase added years pursuant to an application under Article 14(1))

Age next birthday	MALES £	FEMALES £
24	7.1	6.8
25	7.2	6.8
26	7.2	6.8
27	7.2	6.9
28	7.3	6.9
29	7.4	7.0
30	7.4	7.1
31	7.4	7.2
32	7.5	7.2
33	7.6	7.3
34	7.6	7.4
35	7.7	7.4
36	7.8	7.5
37	7.9	7.6
38	8.0	7.6
39	8.1	7.7
40	8.2	7.8
41	8.3	7.9
42	8.4	8.0
43	8.5	8.1
44	8.6	8.2
45	8.7	8.4

TABLE B continued

Age next birthday	MALES £	FEMALES £
46	8.8	8.5
47	8.9	8.6
48	9.0	8.7
49	9.1	8.8
50	9.2	8.9
51	9.3	9.0
52	9.4	9.1
53	9.5	9.3
54	9.6	9.4
55	9.7	9.6
56	9.8	9.8
57	9.9	10.0
58	10.1	10.3
59	10.4	10.6
60	10.6	10.9
61	10.9	11.2
62	11.1	11.5
63	11.3	11.8
64	11.1	11.6
65	10.8	11.3
66	10.6	11.0
67	10.4	10.7
68	10.1	10.4
69	9.8	10.0
70	9.5	9.6
71	9.1	9.2
72	8.7	8.8
73	8.4	8.4
74	8.0	8.0
75	7.6	7.6
76	7.2	7.2
77	6.9	6.9
78	6.5	6.5
79	6.2	6.2
80	5.8	5.8

EXPLANATORY NOTE

(This Note is not part of the Order.)

The Parliamentary Pensions (Purchase of Added Years) Order 1978 ("the principal Order") makes provision for Members of the House of Commons to purchase added years of reckonable, pensionable service, by periodical contributions or payment of a lump sum. This Order makes a number of changes to the principal Order, including some related to provisions of the Parliamentary Pensions etc. Act 1984 ("the Act of 1984"). The main changes are as follows:

Article 5 of this Order provides (by amendment of Article 7 of the principal Order) for a Member to cease paying periodical contributions for the purchase of added years on his becoming Prime Minister or Speaker of the House of Commons. Article 5 further provides for his reckonable service to be increased in respect of the contributions already paid by him.

Article 7(2) of this Order provides that the limit on total pension contributions (under Article 10(1) of the principal Order) is not to apply to periodical contributions to purchase added years payable at the date of the passing of the Act of 1984. This provision results from the increase in Members' pension contributions under the Act of 1984. Contributions under the principal Order will continue to count, as before the making of this Order, towards that limit in its application to future purchases of added years. Increases in Members' contributions which are provided for in the Act of 1984 and which would take effect during a period of payment for the purchase of added years will also count towards that limit.

Article 7(3) of this Order provides (by substituting a new Article 10(3) of the principal Order) new limits on the number of added years that may be purchased, related to the basic limit on Members' pensions under the Act of 1984 of two-thirds of final salary.

Article 8 of this Order adds three new Articles to the principal Order:

(i) The new Article 13 of the principal Order entitles persons who were Members on the date of the passing of the Act of 1984 to apply, within twelve months after the coming into operation of this Order, to reduce the number of the added years they have still to pay for and their future payments.

(ii) The new Article 14 of the principal Order entitles the same Members to apply, within the same period of twelve months, to purchase added years under this Article subject to a maximum of one-sixth of the number of years of their actual service from 16th October 1964 to 20th July 1983 (the date from which the new accrual rate of 1/50 applies under the Act of 1984). This maximum is based on the difference between pension benefits which have accrued for the period of service from 16th October 1964 to 20th July 1983 (at a rate of 1/60) and the benefits which would have accrued for that period if the accrual rate had been 1/50. The number of added years that a Member may purchase under this Article is further limited if the pension benefits from them, with those from his other reckonable service, would exceed either the basic two-thirds limit or, if he has retained pension benefits from previous employment, the greater of two-thirds less the amount of those benefits and of his pension expectations from previous employment less benefits retained from that employment (Article 14(5)).

(iii) The new Article 15 of the principal Order provides that the provisions of the principal Order are without prejudice to the limits on pension entitlement which may be imposed by an order under section 7(3B) of the Parliamentary and other Pensions Act 1972.

Article 9 of this Order provides, in a new Schedule to the principal Order, tables for the cost of extra added years under the new Article 14 and new tables for the cost of added years under other provisions of the principal Order. The cost of purchasing added years under Article 14 will be at a rate of 40% of the cost of purchasing added years under the other Articles of the principal Order.

Article 10 of this Order provides for the revocation of Article 11 of the principal Order (Commutation); a power to make provision generally for maximum commutation of Members' pensions is provided in section 6(1) of the Act of 1984. Article 10 also revokes the Parliamentary Pensions (Purchase of Added Years) (Amendment) Order 1982, which provided revised tables of the cost of purchasing certain added years and which are in effect replaced by the new Schedule under Article 9 of this Order.

STATUTORY INSTRUMENTS

1984 No. 1908

PARLIAMENT

The Parliamentary Pensions (Added Years and Rates of Accrual) (Further Provisions) Order 1984

Made - - -	*5th December* 1984
Laid before Parliament	10*th December* 1984
Coming into Operation	31*st December* 1984

The Lord President of the Council, in exercise of the powers conferred on him by section 5(1) and (2) of the Parliamentary Pensions etc. Act 1984(a), hereby makes the following Order:—

Citation and commencement

   1. This Order may be cited as the Parliamentary Pensions (Added Years and Rates of Accrual) (Further Provisions) Order 1984 and shall come into operation on 31st December 1984.

Interpretation

   2. In this Order, unless the context otherwise requires:—

"the Act of 1972" means	the Parliamentary and other Pensions Act 1972(b);
"the Act of 1978" means	the Parliamentary Pensions Act 1978(c);
"the Act of 1984" means	the Parliamentary Pensions etc. Act 1984;
"actual reckonable service" means	the aggregate period of reckonable service as a Member, excluding any additional period determined under section 22 of the Act of 1972 and excluding any added years;
"added year" means	any year or part of a year of reckonable service purchased under the provisions of an order under section 11 of the Act of 1978(d), including any future added year;
"aggregate period of reckonable service" means	the aggregate period of reckonable service as a Member determined in accordance with the provisions of the Acts of 1972 and 1978;

(a) 1984 c.52.   (b) 1972 c.48.   (c) 1978 c.56.

(d) The present scheme for the purchase of added years is contained in the Parliamentary Pensions (Purchase of Added Years) Order 1978 (S.I. 1978/1837), as amended by S.I. 1981/800 and by the Parliamentary Pensions (Purchase of Added Years) (Amendment) Order 1984 (S.I. 1984/1907), made on the same day as this Order.

"excess number" means	(in Article 4 of this Order) in respect of a Member's added years, the number of those added years annual pension in respect of which, calculated in accordance with section 7(3) of the Act of 1972, would equal the amount by which his prospective pension exceeds his allowable pension;
"fraction of a year" means	a part of a year of reckonable service, expressed as the proportion borne by the number of days in that part to three hundred and sixty-five;
"future added year" means	with reference to a specified date, an added year in respect of which a Member's application to purchase has been accepted by the Trustees, but:

(i) which, in the case of an added year being purchased by periodical contributions, would not be added to his reckonable service if Article 7(2) of the Parliamentary Pensions (Purchase of Added Years) Order 1978(a) were to apply to him at that date; or

(ii) in respect of which a lump sum payment remains to be made by him;

"Member" means	a Member of the House of Commons;
"payment for the purchase of added years" means	such a payment whether payable periodically or by way of a single lump sum;
"prospective actual reckonable service" means	in respect of a Member:

(i) at a date falling before his sixty-fifth birthday, his actual reckonable service before and after that date, assuming continuous actual reckonable service by him from that date until his sixty-fifth birthday;

(ii) at a date falling on or after his sixty-fifth birthday, his actual reckonable service at his sixty-fifth birthday;

(a) S.I. 1978/1837, amended by S.I. 1981/800.

"prospective pension" means | in respect of a Member, the annual amount of a pension calculated in accordance with section 7(3) of the Act of 1972 by reference to an aggregate period of reckonable service as a Member consisting of the number of his added years at the relevant date and a period of actual reckonable service equal to his prospective actual reckonable service at that date;

"reckonable service" means reckonable service as a Member or holder of a qualifying office (as the case may be) under the provisions of the Acts of 1972 and 1978;

"the relevant date" means the date of the coming into operation of this Order.

PART I

ADDED YEARS OF RECKONABLE SERVICE

3. Where on the relevant date a Member has added years for which periodical contributions are or have been, or a lump sum payment is or has been, payable by him, the provisions of Article 4 of this Order shall apply in relation to him.

Effect of increased accrual rate on added years
4.—(1) If, in consequence of section 7(5A)(a) of the Act of 1972, a Member's prospective pension exceeds his allowable pension, determined in accordance with the Schedule to this Order, the excess number of his added years shall be cancelled as stated below:

(i) so many of his future added years on the relevant date (if any) as are in total not more than the excess number;

(ii) so many of his added years, other than future added years, on the relevant date, as are not more than the excess number as reduced in accordance with sub-paragraph (i) above.

(2) In respect of the cancellation of a Member's future added years under paragraph (1)(i) of this Article —

(i) the annual amount of any payment for the purchase of added years which (apart from the provisions of this Order) would be payable by him after the relevant date, shall be reduced by the proportion (up to and including 100%) which the number of his future added years cancelled bears to the number of his future added years on the relevant date.

(a) Section 7(5A) of the Act of 1972, which was inserted by section 1(4) of the Parliamentary Pensions etc. Act 1984 (c.52), provides for a higher accrual rate of one-fiftieth.

(ii) If the Member's future added years are being purchased by him under more than one application in accordance with an order under section 11 of the Act of 1978, the cancellation shall be effected taking those applications in such order as the Trustees shall consider appropriate, having regard to any preferences expressed to them in writing by the Member.

(3) In respect of the cancellation under paragraph (1)(ii) of this Article of any of a Member's added years on the relevant date, the Trustees shall refund to the Member, with interest, a proportion (up to and including the whole) of the payments for the purchase of added years which he has made up to and including the relevant date, the proportion being that which the number cancelled of those added years bears to the number of those added years.

(4) The interest payable under paragraph (3) of this Article shall be calculated:

(i) at the annual rate specified below for the year of payment during which a payment for the purchase of added years to be wholly or partly refunded under that paragraph was made by the Member, assuming for the purposes of this paragraph that the refund under paragraph (3) is of individual payments for the purchase of added years in reverse order of their payment by the Member, starting with the payment last made by him on or before the relevant date:

Year of Payment	Annual Rate (per cent)
1979	12.7
1980	12.8
1981	12.3
1982	11.7
1983	10.8
1984	10.9;

(ii) in respect of any year or fraction of a year from the date on which the payment refunded, or assumed to be refunded under sub-paragraph (i), was made by the Member until the date of the refund under paragraph (3) of this Article.

Applications by Members to reduce added years

5.—(1) Subject to the following provisions of this Article, if a Member applies to the Trustees, in accordance with an order under section 11 of the Act of 1978 which provides for a reduction in his future added years at the date of the acceptance by the Trustees of his application, and the Trustees are satisfied that the reduction in his added years made under such provision is, in consequence of its being limited to his future added years at that date, less than each of —

(i) the appropriate reduction under paragraph (5) of this Article, and

(ii) the reduction in the number of his added years desired by the Member at that date,

the following provisions of this Article shall apply in relation to him.

(2) If a Member has added years which were future added years on the date of the passing of the Act of 1984, but which are no longer future added years at the date referred to in paragraph (1) of this Article, the number of those added years shall be reduced by the number by which the lesser of the reductions under paragraph (1)(i) and (1)(ii) of this Article exceeds the reduction in his added years, made under the provisions of an order under section 11 of the Act of 1978 and referred to in paragraph (1) of this Article.

(3) In respect of the reduction under paragraph (2) of this Article in the number of a Member's added years referred to in that paragraph, the Trustees shall refund to the Member with interest a proportion (up to and including the whole) of the payments for the purchase of added years which he has made between the date of the passing of the Act of 1984 and the date referred to in paragraph (1), the proportion being that which the number of the reduction bears to the number of his added years referred to in paragraph (2).

(4) The interest payable under paragraph (3) of this Article shall be calculated at the annual rate of 12 per cent in respect of any year or fraction of a year from the date on which each payment to be wholly or partly refunded under that paragraph was made by the Member until the date of its refund, assuming for the purposes of this paragraph that the refund under paragraph (3) is of individual payments in reverse order of their payment by the Member, starting with the payment last made by him before the date referred to in paragraph (1) of this Article.

(5) The appropriate reduction shall be such reduction in the number of a Member's future added years at the date of the passing of the Act of 1984 as in the opinion of the Trustees is appropriate in consequence of the provisions of sections 1 to 3 of that Act, having regard to such matters as are in their opinion relevant, including (without prejudice to the generality of the foregoing) any cancellation required under Article 4 of this Order of the excess number of the Member's added years.

6.—(1) If within a period of 12 months from the date of the coming into operation of this Order a Member who had future added years on the date of the passing of the Act of 1984 makes an application in writing to the Trustees for a reduction under this Article in the number of those added years, and on the date of that application he no longer has any future added years, the following provisions of this Article shall apply in relation to him.

(2) If the Trustees are satisfied in respect of a Member that a reduction in the number of his added years is appropriate in consequence of any provision of sections 1 to 3 of the Act of 1984, they shall, unless he has made an application referred to in Article 5(1) of this Order, accept the application and the number of his future added years at the date of the passing of the Act of 1984 shall be reduced by the lesser of:

(i) the appropriate reduction under Article 5(5) of this Order;
   and

(ii) any reduction in the number of his added years requested, or stipulated as a maximum, by the Member in his application under paragraph (1) of this Article.

(3) In respect of the reduction under paragraph (2) of this Article in the number of a Member's added years referred to in paragraph (1) of this Article, the Trustees shall refund to the Member with interest a proportion (up to and including the whole) of the payments for the purchase of added years which he made between the date of the passing of the Act of 1984 and the date of his application under paragraph (1), the proportion being that which the number of the reduction bears to the number of his added years referred to in paragraph (1).

(4) The interest payable under paragraph (3) of this Article shall be calculated at the annual rate of 12 per cent in respect of any year or fraction of a year from the date on which each payment to be wholly or partly refunded under that paragraph was made by the Member until the date of its refund, assuming for the purposes of this paragraph that the refund under paragraph (3) is of individual payments in reverse order of their payment by the Member, starting with the payment last made by him before the date of his application under paragraph (1) of this Article.

Refunds of contributions in certain further circumstances
7.—(1) If a Member applies to the Trustees to purchase added years and —
  (i) a number of those added years is (under the provisions of an order under section 11 of the Act of 1978) subject to a maximum calculated by reference to the period of the Member's actual reckonable service which fell both on or after 16th October 1964 and before 20th July 1983 and before his sixty-fifth birthday, and
  (ii) at the date of the acceptance by the Trustees of his application he has any added years, but does not have any future added years,
the following provisions of this Article shall apply in relation to him.

(2) If the number of added years referred to in sub-paragraph (1)(i) of this Article in respect of a Member (within the maximum referred to in that sub-paragraph) exceeds any maximum, further to that referred to in sub-paragraph (1)(i) of this Article, imposed on the number of those added years by the provisions of an order under section 11 of the Act of 1978, the Trustees shall:
  (i) determine the number of the Member's added years referred to in sub-paragraph (1)(ii) of this Article, pension in respect of which, calculated under section 7(3) of the Act of 1972, would not be more than pension so calculated in respect of a period of his reckonable service beginning after 20th July 1983 equal to the excess under this paragraph; and
  (ii) refund to the Member with interest a part of the payments for the purchase of added years which in the opinion of the Trustees (having regard to the terms of the purchase of those added years) were made by him in respect of the number of his added years determined under sub-paragraph (i) above and identified in accordance with the assumption (applied in respect of a refund under this paragraph) in Article 4(4)(i) of this Order.

(3) The part of the payments for the purchase of added years refundable under sub-paragraph (2)(ii) of this Article shall be the amount of those payments less the amount which would be payable under the order referred to in sub-paragraph (1)(i) of this Article to purchase a number, of the added years referred to in sub-paragraph (1)(i), equal to the number of the excess under paragraph (2).

(4) Article 4(4) (which relates to interest on refunds) of this Order shall apply to a refund under this Article with the substitution of a reference to paragraph (2)(ii) of this Article for any reference to paragraph (3) of Article 4.

8.—(1) The provisions of this Article shall apply in relation to a Member within sub-paragraph (i) and (ii) of Article 7(1) of this Order, if, on application as referred to in Article 7(1), he also applies in writing to the Trustees under this Article for a refund of a part of the payments made by him for the purchase of a number, specified by him in his application under this Article, of his added years referred to in Article 7(1)(ii) of this Order —

(i) the payments for the purchase of which are not refundable under the provisions of Article 7 of this Order; and

(ii) pension in respect of which, calculated under section 7(3) of the Act of 1972, would not be more than the relevant amount under paragraph (2) of this Article.

(2) The relevant amount shall be the amount by which a pension, calculated under section 7(3) of the Act of 1972 by reference to an aggregate period of reckonable service consisting of —

(i) the number of added years referred to in sub-paragraph (i) of Article 7(1) of this Order in respect of the Member (within the maximum referred to in that sub-paragraph);

(ii) the number of his added years referred to in Article 7(1)(ii) of this Order;

(iii) his prospective actual reckonable service on the date referred to in Article 7(1)(ii) of this Order; and

(iv) any period of reckonable service as a Member which on that date has been determined in respect of him under section 22(3) of the Act of 1972,

exceeds any maximum pension, by reference to which a maximum, further to that referred to in sub-paragraph (i) of Article 7(1) of this Order, has been imposed on the number of the added years under that sub-paragraph by the provisions of an order under section 11 of the Act of 1978.

(3) The Trustees shall accept a Member's application in accordance with paragraph (1) of this Article and shall refund to the Member with interest a part of the payments which in the opinion of the Trustees (having regard to the terms of the purchase of the relevant added years) were made by him in respect of the number of added years specified in accordance with paragraph (1) in that application and identified in accordance with the assumption (applied in respect of a refund under this paragraph) in Article 4(4)(i) of this Order, the part so refundable being the amount of those payments less the amount which would be payable under the order referred to in sub-paragraph (i) of Article 7(1) of this

Order to purchase the number of the added years which are referred to in that sub-paragraph, pension in respect of which, calculated under section 7(3) of the Act of 1972, would be equal to the pension so calculated in respect of the number of added years specified in his application in accordance with paragraph (1) of this Article.

(4) Article 4(4) (which relates to interest on refunds) of this Order, shall apply to a refund under this Article with the substitution of a reference to paragraph (3) of this Article for any reference to paragraph (3) of Article 4.

(5) There shall be cancelled the number referred to in paragraph (3) of this Article of the added years referred to in Article 7(1)(i) of this Order.

Reckonability of added years purchased by reference to previous actual service
9. If a Member purchases a number of added years subject (under the provisions of an order under section 11 of the Act of 1978) to a maximum calculated by reference to the period of his actual reckonable service which fell both on or after 16th October 1964 and before 20th July 1983 and before his sixty-fifth birthday, the number of those added years (within that maximum) shall, for the purposes of section 7(3A) and of any order under 7(3B) of the Act of 1972(**a**), be treated as a period of reckonable service ending before the date of the Member's sixty-fifth birthday.

PART II

RATE OF ACCRUAL OF PENSION

10.—(1) For the purposes of the appropriate fraction under section 7(3) and 7(5A)(**b**) of the Act of 1972 (calculation and rate of accrual of Members' pensions) a period of reckonable service —

(i) an application to purchase which, under the provisions of an order under section 11 of the Act of 1978 (added years), was accepted by the Trustees before the date of the coming into operation of this Order; or

(ii) attributable to a determination under section 22(3) of the Act of 1972 (transfers from other pension schemes) made before the date of the coming into operation of this Order; or

(iii) of a person who ceased to be a Member before 20th July 1983, being reckonable service attributable to the provisions of section 2(4) of the Act of 1978 (increase of service for purposes of ill-health pension),

shall be treated as a period ending before 20th July 1983; and a period of reckonable service —

(*a*) an application to purchase which is, under the provisions of an order under section 11 of the Act of 1978, accepted by the Trustees on or after the date of the coming into operation of this Order; or

(*b*) attributable to a determination under section 22(3) of the Act of 1972 made on or after the date of the coming into operation of this Order; or

---

(**a**) Section 7(3A) and section 7(3B) were inserted in the Act of 1972 by section 1(2) of the Parliamentary Pensions etc. Act 1984 and relate to maximum pension.
(**b**) Section 7(3) of the Act of 1972 was substituted, and section 7(5A) was inserted, by section 1(2) and section 1(4) respectively of the Parliamentary Pensions etc. Act 1984.

(c) of a person who ceased or ceases to be a Member on or after 20th July 1983, being reckonable service attributable to the provisions of section 2(4) of the Act of 1978,

shall be treated as a period beginning after 20th July 1983.

(2) For the purposes of the appropriate fraction under section 10(3) and 10(3A)(a) of the Act of 1972 (calculation and rate of accrual of office-holders' pensions) a year of reckonable service which is the subject of a determination under section 22(4)(a) of the Act of 1972 (transfers from other pension schemes) shall:

(i) if the determination is made before the date of the coming into operation of this Order, be treated as a year ending before 1st April 1983;

(ii) if the determination is made on or after the date of the coming into operation of this Order, be treated as a year beginning after 31st March 1984.

Whitelaw,
Lord President of the Council.

Dated 5th December 1984.

(a) Section 10(3) of the Act of 1972 was amended and section 10(3A) was inserted, by section 2(4) and section 2(5) respectively of the Parliamentary Pensions etc. Act 1984.

Article 4
THE SCHEDULE

ALLOWABLE PENSION

1. Subject to paragraph 2 below, the allowable pension of a Member shall be of the annual amount specified in column (B) below in relation to the Member's prospective actual reckonable service at the date of the last acceptance by the Trustees before the relevant date of an application by him to purchase added years:

(A) *Prospective actual reckonable service*	(B) *Allowable pension (expressed as a fraction of relevant terminal salary under section 7(5) of the Act of 1972)*
10 years or more	2/3
9 years	8/15
8 years	6/15
7 years	4/15
6 years	2/15

Where the period of prospective actual reckonable service includes part of a year, the allowable pension appropriate to that period expressed in years and days shall be calculated proportionately by reference to the fraction in column (B).

2. The allowable pension of a Member with retained benefits or any period of reckonable service as a Member determined in respect of him under section 22(3) of the Act of 1972 shall not exceed the pension calculated in accordance with paragraph 1 above and, when aggregated with the retained benefits and with pension calculated in accordance with section 7(3) of that Act in respect of the period so determined, shall not exceed $\frac{2}{3}$ of the relevant terminal salary.

EXPLANATORY NOTE

(This Note is not part of the Order.)

This Order makes provision in connection with the main provisions of the Parliamentary Pensions etc. Act 1984 ("the Act of 1984"), in particular the new rates of contribution, the new annual accrual rate (of one-fiftieth instead of one-sixtieth) and the abolition of the qualifying period of reckonable service for entitlement to pension benefits.

The provisions of Part I of the Order are in connection further with the scheme for the purchase by Members of added years of reckonable service contained in the Parliamentary Pensions (Purchase of Added Years) Order 1978 and by the Parliamentary Pensions (Purchase of Added Years) (Amendment) Order 1984 ("the 1984 Order"), made on the same day as this Order.

Article 4 of the Order provides for the cancellation of added years purchased and the refund with interest of payments already made in respect of them to the extent that, in consequence of the increase in the rate of accrual of Members' pensions (under section 1(4) of the Act of 1984, amending section 7 of the Parliamentary and other Pensions Act 1972), the number of a Member's added years represents the excess of his prospective pension at the higher accrual rate over a maximum pension based on a specified fraction of his final salary.

Articles 5 and 6 supplement new provisions (under the 1984 Order) of the added years scheme, by providing for the cancellation of certain added years purchased and refunds with interest of payments made for them, where the Member has requested it and the Trustees consider it appropriate in consequence of the main changes in the Act of 1984.

Article 7 makes supplementary provision for the refund with interest of a part of payments made to purchase added years (but without reduction in the number of years purchased) where a Member is unable, because of limits under the added years scheme, to purchase further added years at a reduced price to the extent provided for, by reference to his actual service from 16th October 1964 to 20th July 1983, under new provisions (added by the 1984 Order) of the added years scheme.

Article 8 allows a Member to apply for such a refund with interest (as an alternative to the purchase of added years at the reduced price to the full amount which would not result immediately in his pension exceeding the maximum applicable to his pension) to the extent that the purchase of further added years would (assuming he continues in service as a member until his sixty-fifth birthday) lead to his pension exceeding the maximum. Under Articles 7 and 8 the amount of the refund is related to the difference between the cost to him of added years for which a refund is available and that of added years at the reduced price. In respect of the reduced-price added years *Article 9* provides that those purchased by reference to service before the Member is aged 65 are to count towards maximum pension for service before that age.

Part II of the Order deals with the accrual rate in respect of reckonable service other than actual service. The Act of 1984 (sections 1(4) and 2(5)) specifies the accrual rate only for years of service ending before or beginning after specified dates, and enables years of reckonable service other than actual service to be treated, as provided by order, as if they were years beginning after or ending before a certain date.

Article 10 provides that (in the case of Members) added years purchased under applications accepted by the Trustees after the coming into operation of the Order and enhancements of service made after 20th July 1983 on retirement on ill-health and (for Members and office-holders) transfers from other schemes after the operative date of the Order shall be treated as years of service beginning after 20th July 1983 (for which an accrual rate of one-fiftieth is specified in the Act of 1984). Other years of the same categories of reckonable service are to be treated as years of service beginning before that date (for which an accrual rate of one-sixtieth is specified in the Act of 1984).

STATUTORY INSTRUMENTS

1984 No. 1909

PARLIAMENT

The Parliamentary Pensions (Maximum and Abated Pensions and Pension Commutation) Order 1984

Made - - - -	*5th December* 1984
Laid before Parliament	*10th December* 1984
Coming into Operation	*31st December* 1984

The Lord President of the Council, in exercise of the powers conferred on him by sections 7(3B) and 10(3C) of the Parliamentary and other Pensions Act 1972(a) and by sections 1(5), 2(8), 4(3) and 4(4) and subsections (1) to (3) of section 6 of the Parliamentary Pensions etc. Act 1984(b), hereby makes the following Order:—

Citation and commencement

1.— (1) This Order may be cited as the Parliamentary Pensions (Maximum and Abated Pensions and Pension Commutation) Order 1984 and shall come into operation on 31st December 1984.

(2) Part I of this Order shall be treated as having come into operation on 20th July 1983 in relation to pensions first payable on or after that date.

Interpretation

2.— (1) In this Order, unless the context otherwise requires:—

"Act of 1972" means the Parliamentary and Other Pensions Act 1972;

"Act of 1978" means the Parliamentary Pensions Act 1978(c);

"actual reckonable service" means (in respect of a pension under section 7 of the 1972 Act) the aggregate period of reckonable service as a Member or (in respect of a pension under section 9 of the Act of 1972) such period as an office-holder, but excluding (in respect of the former) any increase in that period by virtue of section 2(4) of the Act of 1978 and any period of reckonable service purchased in pursuance of an order under section 11 of the Act of 1978, and excluding (in respect of either) any additional period determined under section 22 of the Act of 1972;

(a) 1972 c. 48; sections 7(3B) and 10(3C) were inserted respectively by sections 1(2) and 2(5) of the Parliamentary Pensions etc. Act 1984 (c. 52). They relate to Part I of this Order.
(b) 1984 c. 52. Sections 1(5) and 2(8) relate to Part I of this Order, section 4(3) and (4) to Part II, and section 6(1) to (3) to Part III.
(c) 1978 c. 56.

"aggregate period of reckonable service" means the aggregate period of reckonable service as a Member or office-holder (as the case may be) determined in accordance with the provisions of the Act of 1972 and the Act of 1978;

"appropriate period" means in respect of a relevant person, the period until the relevant date or his sixty-fifth birthday (if earlier) from the date on which he began a period of actual reckonable service during which pension in respect of him calculated in accordance with section 7(3) or 10(1) to (3) (as appropriate) of the Act of 1972 would reach:

    (i) (if he is within Article 6(2)(i)) the greater of the maximum pensions under Article 6(2)(i)(*a*) and (*b*);

    (ii) (if he is within Article 6(2)(ii)) the greater of the maximum pensions under Article 6(2)(ii)(*a*) and (*b*);

"fraction of a year" means a part of a year of actual reckonable service expressed as the proportion borne by the number of days in that part to three hundred and sixty-five;

"Member" means a Member of the House of Commons;

"month" means

    (i) for the purpose of aggregating under Article 8 of this Order any periods of less than a month, a period of 30 days; and

    (ii) in all other cases, a calendar month;

"the multiple" means

    (*a*) in respect of a pension under section 7 of the Act of 1972 of a relevant person, the relevant terminal salary under section 7(5) of that Act;

    (*b*) in respect of a pension under section 9 of the Act of 1972 of a relevant person, the relevant terminal salary under section 10(6) of that Act multiplied by the average of all the contribution factors under Part I of the Act of 1972 calculated in relation to him:

        (i) in the case of Article 6(2)(i)(*a*) of this Order, for his actual reckonable service before the relevant date;

        (ii) in all other cases under Part I of this Order, for the part of his actual reckonable service, pension in respect of which is, under a provision of that Part, subject to a maximum referring to "the multiple";

        (iii) in Part III of this Order, for the period of his actual reckonable service;

"N" means in respect of the pension of a relevant person, the period in years and any fraction of a year of his actual reckonable service before the relevant date or (if earlier) his sixty-fifth birthday;

"NS" means in respect of the pension of a relevant person, the lesser of 40 years and the period in years and any fraction of a year of his prospective actual reckonable service at the relevant date;

"national insurance pension" means in respect of a relevant person, the annual amount payable at the weekly rate, applicable on the date from which a pension becomes payable to him by virtue of Article 8(1) of this

Order, under section 6(1)(*a*) of the Social Security Pensions Act 1975(**a**) (basic component of a national insurance Category A retirement pension), not being a "specified sum" within section 1(1)(*c*) of the Social Security (No. 2) Act 1980(**b**);

"office-holder" means the holder of a qualifying office;

"pension" means (except in "national insurance pension" and any reference thereto) a pension, expressed as an annual amount, under section 7 (Members' pensions) or section 9 (office-holders' pensions) of the Act of 1972, as the case may be; and "maximum pension" shall be construed accordingly;

"previous employment" means, in respect of a relevant person, the period of employment (not being a period of self-employment or a period of service as a Member or office-holder) which immediately preceded the last period of his actual reckonable service beginning before the relevant date or his sixty-fifth birthday (if earlier);

"previous expectations" means, in respect of a relevant person, the annual value at his sixty-fifth birthday which in the opinion of the Trustees is to be given to the pension benefits to which he would have become entitled under a pension scheme relating to his previous employment, had he remained in that employment and retired from it at the normal retirement age under that scheme;

"prospective actual reckonable service" means in respect of a relevant person:

(i) if the relevant date falls before his sixty-fifth birthday, his actual reckonable service before and after that date, assuming continuous actual reckonable service by him from that date until his sixty-fifth birthday;

(ii) if the relevant date falls on or after his sixty-fifth birthday, his actual reckonable service at his sixty-fifth birthday;

"reckonable service" means reckonable service as a Member or office-holder (as the case may be) under the provisions of the Acts of 1972 and 1978:

"relevant date" means the relevant date for the determination under any provision of the Act of 1972 or the Act of 1978 of the pension of a relevant person;

"relevant person" means a person in respect of whom a pension falls to be determined;

"retained benefits" means in respect of a relevant person, the annual value at his sixty-fifth birthday which in the opinion of the Trustees is to be given to benefits accrued or accruing to him (other than in the Parliamentary Contributory Pension Fund) before his last period of actual reckonable service beginning before that birthday, ånd being benefits within the classes taken into account by the Commissioners of Inland Revenue in determining maximum benefits for the purposes of their approval of retirement benefit schemes under Chapter II of Part II of the Finance Act 1970(**c**);

"retained lump sum benefits" means retained benefits which are payable as

---

(**a**) 1975 c. 60. The amount of the basic component was increased most recently by the Social Security Benefits Up-rating Order 1984 (S.I. 1984/1104).
(**b**) 1980 c. 39.
(**c**) 1970 c. 24.

single payments whether by way of commutation of accrued pension rights, refund of contributions or otherwise;

"Y" means

(i) (in respect of a pension under section 7 of the Act of 1972 of a relevant person) the period in years and any fraction of a year of his reckonable service, pension in respect of which is, under a provision of this Order, subject to a maximum referring to "Y";

(ii) (in respect of a pension under section 9 of the Act of 1972 of a relevant person) the number of years beginning in each case on 1st April, during which he has any actual reckonable service and pension in respect of which is, under a provision of this Order, subject to a maximum referring to "Y";

"year" means for the purpose of aggregating under Article 8 of this Order any periods of less than a year, a period of 365 days.

(2) Any reference in this Order to the beginning of a period of actual reckonable service of a person or of a relevant person means any such beginning on his becoming a Member or office-holder (as the case may be) other than after an interval in his actual reckonable service occurring on a dissolution of Parliament.

(3) Any reference in this Order to a person or relevant person being or no longer being a Member or office-holder shall be construed as a reference to whichever of those circumstances is applicable to the calculation of his pension.

PART I

MAXIMUM PENSIONS

3. This Part of this Order shall apply to the calculation of the maximum pension of a relevant person at the relevant date.

Less than Six Years' Actual Reckonable Service

4.— (1) Subject to the following paragraphs of this Article, if at any date the prospective actual reckonable service of a relevant person is less than six years, the pension payable to him shall be subject to a maximum, of Y/60 of the multiple, in respect of his actual reckonable service from that date until the relevant date or (if earlier) his sixty-fifth birthday, and in respect (in the case of a Member) of any increase by virtue of section 2(4) of the Act of 1978 in his aggregate period of reckonable service.

(2) Subject to paragraph (4) of this Article, if, in addition to the circumstances specified in paragraph (1) of this Article—

(i) the relevant person was a Member or office-holder on his sixty-fifth birthday, or he is entitled to a pension by virtue of section 2 or 3 of the Act of 1978 (ill-health pension), or he dies while he is a Member or office-holder and before his sixty-fifth birthday; and

(ii) in the opinion of the Trustees, if the maximum pension of that person in respect of his actual reckonable service at the relevant date or (if earlier) his sixty-fifth birthday, and in respect (in the case of a Member) of any increase by virtue of section 2(4) of the Act of 1978 in his aggregate period of reckonable service, were the amount of his previous expectations less his retained benefits (if any) accruing during his previous employment, his pension would be greater than if calculated subject to the maximum under paragraph (1) of this Article,

the maximum allowing the greater pension shall apply.

(3) Subject to paragraph (4) of this Article, if, in addition to the circumstances specified in paragraph (1) of this Article—

    (i) either the relevant person is no longer a Member or office-holder and the relevant date falls on his sixty-fifth birthday or he has not yet reached his sixty-fifth birthday; and

    (ii) he is not within paragraph (2)(i) of this Article; and

    (iii) in the opinion of the Trustees, if the maximum pension of that person in respect of his actual reckonable service at the relevant date were the product of N/NS and the amount mentioned in paragraph (2)(ii) of this Article, his pension would be greater than if calculated subject to the maximum under paragraph (1) of this Article,

the maximum allowing the greater pension shall apply.

(4) Notwithstanding the provisions of paragraphs (1), (2) and (3) of this Article, if at the relevant date a relevant person has in aggregate six or more years of actual reckonable service before or after his sixty-fifth birthday, his pension shall not be subject to a maximum under this Article.

More than 33 1/3 Years' Prospective Actual Reckonable Service

5.— (1) Subject to paragraph (2) of this Article and to Article 6, if at the relevant date—

    (i) a relevant person has more than 33 years and 4 months of prospective actual reckonable service; and

    (ii) either he is no longer a Member or office-holder and the relevant date falls on his sixty-fifth birthday or he has not yet reached his sixty-fifth birthday,

his pension shall be subject to whichever of the following, in the opinion of the Trustees, is the greater:

    (a) a maximum, of the product of N/NS and 2/3 of the multiple, in respect of his actual reckonable service at the relevant date;

    (b) a maximum of the product of N/NS and his previous expectations (if any), in respect of that service at that date.

(2) Notwithstanding the provisions of paragraph (1) of this Article, the pension of a relevant person shall not be subject to a maximum under this Article if at the relevant date that person is entitled to a pension under section 2 or 3 of the Act of 1978, or he dies on that date while he is a Member or office-holder and before his sixty-fifth birthday.

Retained Benefits

6.— (1) If a relevant person has any retained benefits, his pension shall, unless it is subject to a maximum under Article 4, be subject to the appropriate maximum in accordance with paragraph (2) of this Article.

(2)(i) If either the relevant person was a Member or office-holder on his sixty-fifth birthday or he is entitled to a pension by virtue of section 2 or 3 of the Act of 1978, or he dies while he is a Member or office-holder and before his sixty-fifth birthday, his pension shall be subject to whichever of the following will, in the opinion of the Trustees, allow him the greatest pension:

(*a*) a maximum, of the amount of 2/3 of the multiple, less the amount of his retained benefits, in respect of his aggregate period of reckonable service at his sixty-fifth birthday;

(*b*) a maximum, of his previous expectations (if any) less his retained benefits accruing during his previous employment, in respect of his aggregate period of reckonable service at his sixty-fifth birthday;

(*c*) a maximum, of Y/60 of the multiple, in respect of his actual reckonable service during the appropriate period and (in the case of a Member) in respect of any increase in his aggregate period of reckonable service by virtue of section 2(4) of the Act of 1978.

(ii) Unless the relevant person is within sub-paragraph (i) of this paragraph, if either he is no longer a Member or office-holder and the relevant date falls on his sixty-fifth birthday or he has not yet reached his sixty-fifth birthday, his pension shall be subject to whichever of the following will, in the opinion of the Trustees, allow him the greatest pension:

(*a*) a maximum of the product of N/NS and the amount under paragraph (2)(i)(*a*) of this Article, in respect of his actual reckonable service before the relevant date;

(*b*) a maximum of the product of N/NS and the amount under paragraph (2)(i)(*b*) of this Article, in respect of his actual reckonable service before the relevant date;

(*c*) a maximum of Y/60 of the multiple, in respect of his actual reckonable service during the appropriate period.

Office-holders' Pensions where Entitlement under Part II

7. If a person becomes entitled to a pension under section 9 of the Act of 1972 (pensions for office-holders) and has, by virtue of Article 8(1) of this Order, become entitled to a pension under section 7(4A) of that Act, the maximum pension payable to him under section 9 shall be a pension calculated in respect of him under section 10(1) to (3B) of that Act in accordance with the foregoing provisions of this Order, reduced from such date as his pension under section 7(4A) shall be abated under the provisions of Part II of this Order by the percentage by which that pension shall for the time being be abated under the provisions of that Part of this Order.

PART II

ENTITLEMENT TO EARLY, ABATED PENSIONS

8.— (1) If, in the case of the dissolution of Parliament on 13th May 1983 or any subsequent dissolution, a person—

   (i) has satisfied the conditions in section 7(4A)(*a*) and (*c*) of the Act of 1972 but has not satisfied, or has satisfied only in part, the conditions in section 7(4A)(*b*) of that Act; and

   (ii) at the dissolution has attained the age of 57 and been a Member for a period of not less than sixteen years, or for two or more periods amounting in the aggregate to not less than sixteen years (which period or periods in aggregate in respect of a person are hereinafter referred to as "the relevant period"); and

   (iii) applies in writing to the Trustees under this Article within a period of six months (in the case of the dissolution of Parliament on 13th May 1983) from the date of the coming into operation of this Order or (in the case of any subsequent dissolution) beginning with the day of the dissolution,

and the Trustees are satisfied that he does not intend to stand and, in the case of the dissolution of 13th May 1983, has not stood since the general election consequent upon that dissolution for re-election to the House of Commons, he shall be entitled to a pension under section 7(4A) of the Act of 1972.

(2) Subject to the following paragraphs of this Article, the pension to which a person is entitled by virtue of paragraph (1) of this Article shall be abated—

   (i) from the date from which that pension is payable (under section 7(4A) of the Act of 1972) by the percentage specified in the appropriate table of Part A of Schedule 1 to this Order in relation to both the person's age at the relevant dissolution referred to in paragraph (1) of this Article and the relevant period; or

   (ii) (in the case of a person who has so requested in his application referred to in paragraph (1) of this Article)—

     (*a*) from the date from which that pension is payable until (in the case of a man) his sixty-fifth birthday or (in the case of a woman) her sixtieth birthday, by the percentage specified in column A of the appropriate table of Part B of Schedule 1 to this Order in relation both to the person's age at the relevant dissolution referred to in paragraph (1) of this Article and to the relevant period; and

     (*b*) from the date of the relevant birthday referred to in (*a*) above, by the percentage specified in column B of the appropriate table of Part B of that Schedule in relation both to that age and that period.

(3) If the relevant period or a person's age at the relevant dissolution referred to in paragraph (1) of this Article includes a part of a year—

   (i) for the purposes of this Article that period or that age (as the case may be) shall be rounded down to the nearest complete month;

   (ii) subject to paragraph (4) of this Article, the percentage by which his pension is, under any provision of paragraph (2) of this Article, to be abated shall be a percentage calculated proportionately by reference to the figures in the appropriate table or the specified column of that table of Part A or B of Schedule 1 to this Order (as provided in paragraph (2) of this Article).

(4) Where a person's pension is under paragraph (2)(ii) of this Article to be abated, for the year or part of a year beginning on the date, or the anniversary of the date, from which that pension becomes payable, and during which year or part of a year—

    (i) that pension is payable to that person; and

    (ii) his sixty-fifth or her sixtieth birthday (as the case may be) falls,

that pension shall be abated—

    (a) from the beginning of that year or part of a year until the date of that birthday, by the percentage (if any) provided for under paragraph (2)(ii)(a), or calculated proportionately under paragraph (3), of this Article, reduced by the fraction of a year (beginning on the same date as that year or part of a year) which will fall on or after the date of that birthday; and

    (b) from the date of that birthday, by the percentage provided for under paragraph (2)(ii)(b), or calculated proportionately under paragraph (3), of this Article, reduced by the fraction of that year or part of a year which falls before the date of that birthday.

(5) If, in a case within paragraph (2)(ii) of this Article, the difference between the amounts by which a person's pension under section 7(4A) of the Act of 1972 would (apart from this paragraph) be abated under paragraph (2)(ii)(a) and under paragraph (2)(ii)(b) respectively is greater than the national insurance pension, the pension under section 7(4A) shall be abated by a percentage before, and a percentage after, that person reaches (in the case of a man) his sixty-fifth birthday or (in the case of a woman) her sixtieth birthday—

    (i) such that the difference between the amount by which that pension shall be abated before, and the amount after, the date of that birthday shall be equal to the national insurance pension; and

    (ii) which in the opinion of the Trustees will together provide pension benefits before and after that date equivalent to the person's pension under section 7(4A) abated before that date under paragraph (2)(ii)(a), and after that date under paragraph (2)(ii)(b), of this Article.

Part III

Maximum Commutation of Pensions

9. If a person—

    (i) has given notice in accordance with section 11 of the Act of 1972 in respect of the commutation of his pension, and at the date of the coming into operation of this Order no determination has been made by the Trustees under subsection (2) of that section in respect of that notice; or

    (ii) gives such notice after the date of the coming into operation of this Order, the permitted maximum for the purposes of subsection (4) of that section (referred to in this Part of this Order as "the permitted maximum") shall be an amount calculated in accordance with this Part of this Order, instead of an amount determined under subsection (5) of that section.

Members' Pensions

10. In the case of a person entitled to a pension under section 7 of the Act of 1972:

(1) who has no retained lump sum benefits and who either was a Member on his sixty-fifth birthday or is so entitled by virtue of section 2 of the Act of 1978 (ill-health pensions), the amount of the permitted maximum shall be the aggregate of:

(i) the amount of:

(*a*) the number of eightieths of the multiple, either specified in the table in Schedule 2 to this Order in relation to the number of complete years of his actual reckonable service or (if the period of that service includes a fraction of a year) calculated proportionately by reference to the numbers specified in that table; and

(*b*) the product of three-eightieths of the multiple and any period, expressed in years and any fraction of a year, determined in respect of him under section 22(3) of the Act of 1972 (Transfers from other pension schemes),

subject to a maximum of the amount of 120/80 of the multiple; and

(ii) the amount of the product of three-eightieths of the multiple and the period, expressed in years and any fraction of a year and subject to a maximum of five years, being his actual reckonable service in excess of forty years and occurring after his sixty-fifth birthday;

(2) who has no retained lump sum benefits, was no longer a Member on his sixty-fifth birthday and is not entitled to a pension by virtue of section 2 of the Act of 1978, the amount of the permitted maximum, subject to a maximum of 120/80 of the multiple, shall be whichever is the greater of:

(i) the amount of the product of N/NS and the number of eightieths of the multiple, either specified in the table in Schedule 2 to this Order in relation to the number of complete years of his prospective actual reckonable service or (if the period of that service includes a fraction of a year) calculated proportionately as under sub-paragraph (i)(*a*) of paragraph (1) of this Article; and

(ii) the amount of the product of three-eightieths of the multiple and the period, expressed in years and any fraction of a year, of his actual reckonable service,

aggregated with the amount referred to in paragraph (1)(i)(*b*) of this Article;

(3) who has retained lump sum benefits, but would otherwise be within paragraph (1) of this Article, the amount of the permitted maximum shall be as provided in that paragraph, subject, in respect of the amount under sub-

paragraph (i) of that paragraph, to a maximum instead of that provided for in that sub-paragraph, of whichever is the greater of:

    (i) the amount of 120/80 of the multiple, less the amount of his retained lump sum benefits; and

    (ii) the amount of the product of three-eightieths of the multiple and the aggregate, expressed in years and any fraction of a year subject to a maximum of forty years, of his actual reckonable service and of any period determined in respect of him under section 22(3) of the Act of 1972;

(4) who has retained lump sum benefits but would otherwise be within paragraph (2) of this Article, the amount of the permitted maximum shall be whichever is the greater of:

    (i) the aggregate of:

        (a) the amount referred to in paragraph (2)(i) of this Article, subject to a maximum of the product of N/NS and the amount referred to in paragraph (3)(i) of this Article; and

        (b) the amount referred to in paragraph (1)(i)(b) of this Article,

    subject to a maximum of the amount of 120/80 of the multiple, less his retained lump sum benefits; and

    (ii) the amount referred to in paragraph (3)(ii) of this Article.

Office-holders' pensions

11. In the case of a person entitled to a pension under section 9 of the Act of 1972:

(1) who has no retained lump sum benefits and who either was an office-holder on his sixty-fifth birthday or is so entitled by virtue of section 3 of the Act of 1978 (ill-health pensions), the amount of the permitted maximum shall be the aggregate of:

    (i) the amount of:

        (a) the number of eightieths of the multiple, specified in the table in Schedule 2 to this Order in relation to the number of years, each beginning on 1st April, during which he had any actual reckonable service; and

        (b) the product of three-eightieths of the multiple and any period, expressed in years and any fraction of a year, determined in respect of him under section 22(4) of the Act of 1972,

    subject to a maximum of the amount of 120/80 of the multiple; and

    (ii) the amount of the product of—

        (a) subject to a maximum of five, the number of years, each beginning on 1st April, during which he had any actual reckonable service, being years in excess of the first 40 such years and beginning after his sixty-fifth birthday; and

        (b) three-eightieths of the relevant terminal salary under section 10(6) of the Act of 1972; and

(c) the average of all the contribution factors under Part I of the Act of 1972 in relation to him for the years under (a) above or (where the maximum under (a) applies) the first five of those years;

(2) who has no retained lump sum benefits, was no longer an office-holder on his sixty-fifth birthday and is not entitled to a pension by virtue of section 3 of the Act of 1978, the amount of the permitted maximum, subject to a maximum of 120/80 of the multiple, shall be whichever is the greater of:

(i) the amount of the product of N/NS and the number of eightieths of the multiple, specified in the table in Schedule 2 to this Order in relation to the number of years, each beginning on 1st April, during which any part of his prospective actual reckonable service falls; and

(ii) the amount of the product of three-eightieths of the multiple and the number of years, each beginning on 1st April, during which he has any actual reckonable service,

aggregated with the amount referred to in paragraph 1(i)(b) of this Article;

(3) who has retained lump sum benefits, but would otherwise be within paragraph (1) of this Article, the amount of the permitted maximum shall be as provided in that paragraph, subject, in respect of the amount under sub-paragraph (i) of that paragraph, to a maximum, instead of that provided for in that sub-paragraph, of whichever is the greater of:

(i) the amount of 120/80 of the multiple, less his retained lump sum benefits; and

(ii) the amount of the product of three-eightieths of the multiple and, subject to a maximum of forty years, the aggregate of:

(a) the number of years, each beginning on 1st April, during which he has any actual reckonable service; and

(b) the number of years (if any) determined in respect of him under section 22(4) of the Act of 1972;

(4) who has retained lump sum benefits but would otherwise be within paragraph (2) of this Article, paragraph (4) of Article 10 of this Order shall apply in respect of him, as if set out in this Article.

Whitelaw,
Lord President of the Council

Dated 5th December 1984.

Article 8   SCHEDULE 1

PERCENTAGE ABATEMENT OF PENSION ENTITLEMENT UNDER SECTION 7(4A) OF
THE ACT OF 1972

PART A—ABATEMENT BY SINGLE PERCENTAGE FROM DATE PENSION PAYABLE

TABLE 1—MEN

Age at dissolution (years)	Service (years)				
	20 or more	19	18	17	16
65	0	0	0	0	0
64	0	2	4	$5\frac{1}{2}$	$7\frac{1}{2}$
63	0	$3\frac{1}{2}$	7	$10\frac{1}{2}$	14
62	0	5	10	$15\frac{1}{2}$	$20\frac{1}{2}$
61	0	$6\frac{1}{2}$	13	$19\frac{1}{2}$	26
60	0	$7\frac{1}{2}$	15	23	$30\frac{1}{2}$
59	14	19	24	29	35
58	28	31	34	37	39
57	$42\frac{1}{2}$	$42\frac{1}{2}$	$42\frac{1}{2}$	$42\frac{1}{2}$	$42\frac{1}{2}$

TABLE 2—WOMEN

Age at dissolution (years)	Service (years)				
	20 or more	19	18	17	16
65	0	0	0	0	0
64	0	$1\frac{1}{2}$	3	$4\frac{1}{2}$	6
63	0	3	6	9	12
62	0	$4\frac{1}{2}$	9	13	$17\frac{1}{2}$
61	0	$5\frac{1}{2}$	11	$16\frac{1}{2}$	22
60	0	7	$13\frac{1}{2}$	20	$26\frac{1}{2}$
59	12	$16\frac{1}{2}$	21	26	$30\frac{1}{2}$
58	25	$27\frac{1}{2}$	30	32	34
57	$37\frac{1}{2}$	$37\frac{1}{2}$	$37\frac{1}{2}$	$37\frac{1}{2}$	$37\frac{1}{2}$

PART B—ABATEMENT BY DIFFERENT PERCENTAGES BEFORE AND AFTER THE 65TH OR 60TH BIRTHDAY

TABLE 1—MEN

The figures specified below are (in column A) the percentage abatement until the 65th birthday of the person entitled to a pension and (column B) the percentage abatement from that birthday.

Age at dissolution (years)	30 or more		29		28		27		26		25		24		23		22		21		20		19		18		17		16	
	A	B	A	B	A	B	A	B	A	B	A	B	A	B	A	B	A	B	A	B	A	B	A	B	A	B	A	B	A	B
65	0.0	0.0	0.0	0.0	0.0	0.0	0.0	0.0	0.0	0.0	0.0	0.0	0.0	0.0	0.0	0.0	0.0	0.0	0.0	0.0	0.0	0.0	0.0	0.0	0.0	0.0	0.0	0.0	0.0	0.0
64	0.0	0.0	0.0	0.0	0.0	0.0	0.0	0.0	0.0	0.0	0.0	0.0	0.0	0.0	0.0	0.0	0.0	0.0	0.0	0.0	0.0	0.0	0.0	2.2	0.0	4.4	0.0	6.0	0.0	8.2
63	0.0	0.0	0.0	0.0	0.0	0.0	0.0	0.0	0.0	0.0	0.0	0.0	0.0	0.0	0.0	0.0	0.0	0.0	0.0	0.0	0.0	0.0	0.0	4.1	0.0	8.3	0.0	12.4	0.0	16.5
62	0.0	0.0	0.0	0.0	0.0	0.0	0.0	0.0	0.0	0.0	0.0	0.0	0.0	0.0	0.0	0.0	0.0	0.0	0.0	0.0	0.0	0.0	0.0	6.4	0.0	12.8	0.0	19.8	0.0	26.2
61	0.0	0.0	0.0	0.0	0.0	0.0	0.0	0.0	0.0	0.0	0.0	0.0	0.0	0.0	0.0	0.0	0.0	0.0	0.0	0.0	0.0	0.0	0.0	8.9	0.0	17.9	0.0	26.8	0.6	35.8
60	0.0	22.3	0.0	22.3	0.0	22.3	0.0	22.3	0.0	22.3	0.0	22.3	0.0	22.3	0.0	22.3	0.0	22.3	0.0	22.3	0.0	22.3	0.0	11.1	0.0	22.2	0.0	34.1	0.6	44.9
59	0.0	37.8	0.0	38.1	0.0	38.4	0.0	38.8	0.0	39.3	0.0	39.7	0.0	40.2	0.0	40.7	0.0	41.3	0.0	41.9	0.0	42.6	0.0	30.2	0.0	38.1	2.8	44.5	7.1	51.4
58	14.1	53.1	13.6	53.5	13.1	53.9	12.6	54.3	12.0	54.8	11.4	55.3	10.7	55.8	9.9	56.4	9.1	57.0	8.2	57.7	7.2	58.5	9.1	46.4	10.9	50.3	12.5	54.2	13.0	57.3
57	29.5	53.1	29.1	53.5	28.6	53.9	28.1	54.3	27.5	54.8	26.9	55.3	26.3	55.8	25.6	56.4	24.8	57.0	24.0	57.7	23.0	58.5	22.0	59.3	20.9	60.2	19.6	61.3	18.2	62.5

TABLE 2—WOMEN

The figures specified below are (in column A) the percentage abatement until the 60th birthday of the person entitled to a pension and (column B) the percentage abatement from that birthday.

Age at dissolution (years)	30 or more A	30 or more B	29 A	29 B	28 A	28 B	27 A	27 B	26 A	26 B	25 A	25 B	24 A	24 B	23 A	23 B	22 A	22 B	21 A	21 B	20 A	20 B	19 A	19 B	18 A	18 B	17 A	17 B	16 A	16 B
65	0.0	0.0	0.0	0.0	0.0	0.0	0.0	0.0	0.0	0.0	0.0	0.0	0.0	0.0	0.0	0.0	0.0	0.0	0.0	0.0	0.0	0.0	0.0	0.0	0.0	0.0	0.0	0.0	0.0	0.0
64	0.0	0.0	0.0	0.0	0.0	0.0	0.0	0.0	0.0	0.0	0.0	0.0	0.0	0.0	0.0	0.0	0.0	0.0	0.0	0.0	0.0	0.0	0.0	1.5	0.0	3.0	0.0	4.5	0.0	6.0
63	0.0	0.0	0.0	0.0	0.0	0.0	0.0	0.0	0.0	0.0	0.0	0.0	0.0	0.0	0.0	0.0	0.0	0.0	0.0	0.0	0.0	0.0	0.0	3.0	0.0	6.0	0.0	9.0	0.0	12.0
62	0.0	0.0	0.0	0.0	0.0	0.0	0.0	0.0	0.0	0.0	0.0	0.0	0.0	0.0	0.0	0.0	0.0	0.0	0.0	0.0	0.0	0.0	0.0	4.5	0.0	9.0	0.0	13.0	0.0	17.5
61	0.0	0.0	0.0	0.0	0.0	0.0	0.0	0.0	0.0	0.0	0.0	0.0	0.0	0.0	0.0	0.0	0.0	0.0	0.0	0.0	0.0	0.0	0.0	5.5	0.0	11.0	0.0	16.5	0.0	22.0
60	0.0	12.7	0.0	12.7	0.0	12.7	0.0	12.7	0.0	12.7	0.0	12.7	0.0	12.7	0.0	12.7	0.0	12.7	0.0	12.7	0.0	12.7	0.0	7.0	0.0	13.5	0.0	20.0	0.0	26.5
59	0.0	27.6	0.0	27.7	0.0	27.8	0.0	27.9	0.0	28.0	0.0	28.1	0.0	28.1	0.0	28.1	0.0	28.1	0.0	28.1	0.0	28.1	0.0	17.5	0.0	22.3	0.0	27.6	0.0	32.4
58	4.0	41.3	3.3	41.4	2.5	41.5	1.6	41.7	0.7	41.8	0.0	42.0	0.0	42.2	0.0	42.4	0.0	42.6	0.0	42.9	0.0	43.1	0.0	30.9	0.0	33.7	0.0	36.0	0.0	38.2
57	17.6		16.9		16.2		15.4	41.7	14.6		13.7		12.7		11.6		10.4		9.1		7.7		6.1	43.4	4.4	43.8	2.4	44.1	0.2	44.5

SCHEDULE 2   Articles 10 and 11

MAXIMUM COMMUTATION OF PENSIONS

TABLE

Number of years	Number of eightieths
1	3
2	6
3	9
4	12
5	15
6	18
7	21
8	24
9	30
10	36
11	42
12	48
13	54
14	63
15	72
16	81
17	90
18	99
19	108
20 or more	120

EXPLANATORY NOTE

(This Note is not part of the Order.)

The Parliamentary Pensions etc. Act 1984 (c. 52) made new provision in respect of the parliamentary contributory pension scheme for Members of Parliament and the supplementary scheme for ministerial and other office-holders. These provisions include a new annual accrual rate for benefits of one-fiftieth, a basic limit on pension of two-thirds of final salary for Members (with equivalent provision for office-holders), and provision for the extension of entitlement to early pension for Members leaving at a dissolution of Parliament and for laying down a new permitted maximum lump sum payable by way of commutation of pension.

Part I of this Order makes provision for Members' and office-holders' pensions to be subject in certain circumstances to a maximum further to the basic limit referred to above. Under powers in sections 1(5) and 2(8) of the 1984 Act, the Order provides *(Article 1(2))* for the new maxima to apply to pensions which fall to be determined after 19th July 1983.

Under *Article 4* of the Order, if at any date (in practice at the start of a period of service) a Member's or office-holder's prospective actual reckonable service (namely his total actual reckonable service assuming that he will serve from that date until his sixty-fifth birthday) is less than six years, his pension will be subject to a maximum, in respect of his actual reckonable service during the period from that date until that birthday (but not in respect of any earlier service). The maximum is based on an assumed rate of accrual of one-sixtieth, or (if greater) on his previous pension expectations from other employment. If his actual reckonable service before and after age 65 is in total six years or more, the maximum provided by the Order does not apply.

The Order further provides (*Article 5*) that where, on a determination of his pension, a person has ceased to be a Member or office-holder before the age of 65, but prospectively he has more than 33 1/3 years of actual reckonable service (had he continued in service until that age), his maximum pension is the proportion of the basic two-thirds limit that the length of his actual reckonable service bears to that prospective service or (if greater) that proportion of his previous expectations from other employment. The limit under Article 5 does not apply to ill-health pensions.

Article 6 of the Order provides for the basic two-thirds limit to be reduced by the amount of any benefits a Member or office-holder retains from other employment. Article 6 also provides for the maximum pension not to be less than a maximum based on an assumed accrual rate of one-sixtieth, and for a maximum based on his previous expectations in other employment to apply if this will be higher.

Article 7 of the Order provides for the pension to which an office-holder becomes entitled before reaching the age of 65, where he has become entitled under Part II of the Order to an early Member's pension, to be subject to a maximum which reduces it by the same percentage as his Member's pension is abated under Part II.

Part II of the Order *(Article 8)* extends entitlement to an early Member's pension to Members who leave the House of Commons at a dissolution (including that of 13th May 1983) but have not met part or all of the requirements for such a pension (the age of 60 and 20 years of service at the dissolution) under section 7(4A) of the Parliamentary and other Pensions Act 1972. Entitlement is extended to Members who at the relevant dissolution are at least 57 years old and have been a Member for at least 16 years. The amount of the pension to which they become entitled is abated at a constant percentage from the date of entitlement or, if the Member requests it, mainly or entirely from (in the case of a man) his sixty-fifth birthday or (in the case of a woman) her sixtieth birthday. The percentage abatement provided for in general decreases in accordance with the Member's greater age and length of service at the relevant dissolution. The percentage abatement of the annual amount of the Member's pension is provided for in tables in Schedule 1 to the Order and by further provision in Article 8 for its calculation by reference to the nearest completed month of age and period of service. In a case where the difference between the amount of the abatements provided for before and after age sixty-five or sixty would exceed the basic national insurance retirement pension, other rates of abatement are to apply such that the difference is equal to the basic national insurance retirement pension.

Part III *(Articles 9 to 11)* of the Order provides for the new permitted maximum for the lump sum payable by way of commutation of pension. The amount of the maximum is to vary depending in general on whether a person is still a Member or office-holder at his sixty-fifth birthday, on whether he has retained any lump sum pension benefits from other employment, and on the length of his actual reckonable service and of any period of service transferred from another scheme. Different provision is made in respect of Members' pensions *(Article 10)* and those of office-holders *(Article 11)* because of the different methods of calculating the amounts of these pensions.

STATUTORY INSTRUMENTS

1984 No. 1911

OFFSHORE INSTALLATIONS

The Offshore Installations (Safety Zones) (Revocation) (No. 71) Order 1984

Made - - - -	*6th December* 1984
Coming into Operation	*8th December* 1984

The Secretary of State, in exercise of the power conferred on him by section 21(1) of the Oil and Gas (Enterprise) Act 1982(a), and of all other powers enabling him in that behalf, hereby makes the following Order:—

1. This Order may be cited as the Offshore Installations (Safety Zones) (Revocation) (No. 71) Order 1984 and shall come into operation on 8th December 1984.

2. The Offshore Installations (Safety Zones) (No. 83) Order 1984(**b**) is hereby revoked.

David Hunt,
Parliamentary Under Secretary of State,
Department of Energy.
6th December 1984.

EXPLANATORY NOTE

(*This Note is not part of the Order.*)

This Order revokes the Offshore Installations (Safety Zones) (No. 83) Order 1984. The installation known as Dundee Kingsnorth which was protected by the safety zone established by that Order has been removed and accordingly that Order is no longer required.

(**a**) 1982 c. 23. (**b**) S.I. 1984/1774.

STATUTORY INSTRUMENTS

1984 No. 1912

OFFSHORE INSTALLATIONS

The Offshore Installations (Safety Zones) (No. 93) Order 1984

Made - - - - -	*6th December* 1984
Coming into Operation	*8th December* 1984

The Secretary of State, in exercise of the powers conferred on him by section 21(1), (2) and (3) of the Oil and Gas (Enterprise) Act 1982(a) (hereinafter referred to as "the Act"), and of all other powers enabling him in that behalf, hereby makes the following Order:—

1. This Order may be cited as the Offshore Installations (Safety Zones) (No. 93) Order 1984 and shall come into operation on 8th December 1984.

2.—(1) A safety zone is hereby established around the installation specified in Column 1 of the Schedule hereto (being an installation maintained in waters in an area designated under section 1(7) of the Continental Shelf Act 1964(b)) having a radius of five hundred metres from the point as respects that installation which has the co-ordinates of latitude and longitude according to European Datum (1950) specified in Columns 2 and 3 of the Schedule.

(2) The prohibition under section 21(3) of the Act on a vessel entering or remaining in a safety zone without the consent of the Secretary of State shall not apply to a vessel entering or remaining in the safety zone established under paragraph (1) above:

(*a*) in connection with the laying, inspection, testing, repair, alteration, renewal or removal of any submarine cable or pipe-line in or near that safety zone;

(*b*) to provide services for, to transport persons or goods to of from, or under the authority of a government department to inspect, any installation in that safety zone;

(*c*) if it is a vessel belonging to a general lighthouse authority performing duties relating to the safety of navigation;

(*d*) in connection with the saving or attempted saving of life or property;

(*e*) owing to stress or weather; or

(*f*) when in distress.

David Hunt,
Parliamentary Under Secretary of State,
Department of Energy.

6th December 1984.

(a) 1982 c. 23.   (b) 1964 c. 29.

SCHEDULE

Article 2(1)

SAFETY ZONE

1	2	3
Name or other designation of the offshore installation	Latitude North	Longitude West
Benvrackie	58°24'10·33"	00°07'20·69"

EXPLANATORY NOTE

(*This Note is not part of the Order.*)

This Order establishes, under section 21 of the Oil and Gas (Enterprise) Act 1982, a safety zone, having a radius of 500 metres from a specified point, around the installation known as Benvrackie maintained in waters in an area designated under section 1(7) of the Continental Shelf Act 1964.

Vessels (which includes hovercraft, submersible apparatus and installations in transit) are prohibited from entering or remaining in the safety zone except with the consent of the Secretary of State or in the circumstances mentioned in Article 2(2) of the Order.

STATUTORY INSTRUMENTS

1984 No. 1913

OFFSHORE INSTALLATIONS

The Offshore Installations (Safety Zones) (No. 94) Order 1984

Made - - - - -	*6th December* 1984
Coming into Operation	*8th December* 1984

The Secretary of State, in exercise of the powers conferred on him by section 21(1), (2) and (3) of the Oil and Gas (Enterprise) Act 1982**(a)** (hereinafter referred to as "the Act"), and of all other powers enabling him in that behalf, hereby makes the following Order:—

1. This Order may be cited as the Offshore Installations (Safety Zones) (No. 94) Order 1984 and shall come into operation on 8th December 1984.

2.—(1) A safety zone is hereby established around the installation specified in Column 1 of the Schedule hereto (being an installation maintained in waters in an area designated under section 1(7) of the Continental Shelf Act 1964**(b)**) having a radius of five hundred metres from the point as respects that installation which has the co-ordinates of latitude and longitude according to European Datum (1950) specified in Columns 2 and 3 of the Schedule.

(2) The prohibition under section 21(3) of the Act on a vessel entering or remaining in a safety zone without the consent of the Secretary of State shall not apply to a vessel entering or remaining in the safety zone established under paragraph (1) above:

   (*a*) in connection with the laying, inspection, testing, repair, alteration, renewal or removal of any submarine cable or pipe-line in or near that safety zone;

   (*b*) to provide services for, to transport persons or goods to or from, or under the authority of a government department to inspect, any installation in that safety zone;

   (*c*) if it is a vessel belonging to a general lighthouse authority performing duties relating to the safety of navigation;

   (*d*) in connection with the saving or attempted saving of life or property;

   (*e*) owing to stress of weather; or

   (*f*) when in distress.

David Hunt,
Parliamentary Under Secretary of State,
Department of Energy.

6th December 1984.

(a) 1982 c. 23.   **(b)** 1964 c. 29.

SCHEDULE   Article 2(1)

SAFETY ZONE

1	2	3
Name or other designation of the offshore installation	Latitude North	Longitude East
Kingsnorth U.K.	57°54'12·96"	00°01'55·95"

EXPLANATORY NOTE

(*This Note is not part of the Order.*)

This Order establishes, under section 21 of the Oil and Gas (Enterprise) Act 1982, a safety zone, having a radius of 500 metres from a specified point, around the installation known as Kingsnorth U.K. maintained in waters in an area designated under section 1(7) of the Continental Shelf Act 1964.

Vessels (which includes hovercraft, submersible apparatus and installations in transit) are prohibited from entering or remaining in the safety zone except with the consent of the Secretary of State or in the circumstances mentioned in Article 2(2) of the Order.

STATUTORY INSTRUMENTS

1984 No. 1914

OFFSHORE INSTALLATIONS

The Offshore Installations (Safety Zones) (No. 95) Order 1984

Made - - - - -	*6th December* 1984
Coming into Operation	*8th December* 1984

The Secretary of State, in exercise of the powers conferred on him by section 21(1), (2) and (3) of the Oil and Gas (Enterprise) Act 1982(**a**) (hereinafter referred to as "the Act"), and of all other powers enabling him in that behalf, hereby makes the following Order:—

1. This Order may be cited as the Offshore Installations (Safety Zones) (No. 95) Order 1984 and shall come into operation on 8th December 1984.

2.—(1) A safety zone is hereby established around the installation specified in Column 1 of the Schedule hereto (being an installation maintained in waters in an area designated under section 1(7) of the Continental Shelf Act 1964(**b**)) having a radius of five hundred metres from the point as respects that installation which has the co-ordinates of latitude and longitude according to European Datum (1950) specified in Columns 2 and 3 of the Schedule.

(2) The prohibition under section 21(3) of the Act on a vessel entering or remaining in a safety zone without the consent of the Secretary of State shall not apply to a vessel entering or remaining in the safety zone established under paragraph (1) above—

(*a*) in connection with the laying, inspection, testing, repair, alteration, renewal or removal of any submarine cable or pipe-line in or near that safety zone;

(*b*) to provide services for, to transport persons or goods to or from, or under the authority of a government department to inspect, any installation in that safety zone;

(*c*) if it is a vessel belonging to a general lighthouse authority performing duties relating to the safety of navigation;

(*d*) in connection with the saving or attempted saving of life or property;

(*e*) owing to stress of weather; or

(*f*) when in distress.

David Hunt,
Parliamentary Under Secretary of State,
Department of Energy.

6th December 1984.

(**a**) 1982 c. 23.   (**b**) 1964 c. 29.

SCHEDULE   Article 2(1)

SAFETY ZONE

1	2	3
Name or other designation of the offshore installation	Latitude North	Longitude East
Maersk Endeavour	53°22′21·00″	01°33′53·00″

EXPLANATORY NOTE

(*This Note is not part of the Order.*)

This Order establishes, under section 21 of the Oil and Gas (Enterprise) Act 1982, a safety zone, having a radius of 500 metres from a specified point, around the installation known as Maersk Endeavour maintained in waters in an area designated under section 1(7) of the Continental Shelf Act 1964.

Vessels (which includes hovercraft, submersible apparatus and installations in transit) are prohibited from entering or remaining in the safety zone except with the consent of the Secretary of State or in the circumstances mentioned in Article 2(2) of the Order.

STATUTORY INSTRUMENTS

1984 No. 1915

NORTHERN IRELAND

The Northern Ireland Loans (Increase of Limit) Order 1984

Laid before the House of Commons in draft

Made - - - - *4th December* 1984

Coming into Operation *7th January* 1985

Whereas a draft of this Order has been approved by a resolution of the House of Commons:

Now, therefore, in pursuance of section 1(5) of the Northern Ireland (Loans) Act 1975(a), I hereby make, with the approval of the Treasury, the following Order:—

1. This Order may be cited as the Northern Ireland Loans (Increase of Limit) Order 1984 and shall come into operation on 7th January 1985.

2. The limit in section 1(2) of the Northern Ireland (Loans) Act 1975 is hereby increased by the sum of £200 million (and, accordingly, that limit shall be £1,000 million).

Douglas Hurd,
One of Her Majesty's Principal
Secretaries of State.

Northern Ireland Office.
3rd December 1984.

(a) 1975 c.83.

We approve,

T. *Garel-Jones,*
Donald Thompson,
Two of the Lords Commissioners of
Her Majesty's Treasury.

4th December 1984.

EXPLANATORY NOTE
(*This Note is not part of the Order.*)

Section 1(2) of the Northern Ireland (Loans) Act 1975 specifies a maximum of £800 million for the aggregate amount outstanding by way of principal in respect of certain loans (namely, loans by the Secretary of State to the Consolidated Fund of Northern Ireland under section 1(1) of, and loans under the enactments specified in section 1(3) of, that Act). Section 1(5) of the Act gives the Secretary of State power to raise the maximum, on not more than one occasion, by not more than £200 million. This Order exercises that power so as to raise the maximum by £200 million.

STATUTORY INSTRUMENTS

1984 No. 1916

CIVIL AVIATION

The Civil Aviation (Joint Financing) (Second Amendment) Regulations 1984

Made - - - -	*7th December* 1984
Laid before Parliament	*10th December* 1984
Coming into Operation	*1st January* 1985

The Secretary of State for Transport, in exercise of his powers under sections 73 and 74 of the Civil Aviation Act 1982(a) and of all other powers enabling him in that behalf, and with the consent of the Treasury, hereby makes the following Regulations:—

1. These Regulations may be cited as the Civil Aviation (Joint Financing) (Second Amendment) Regulations 1984 and shall come into operation on 1st January 1985.

2. Regulation 4(1) of the Civil Aviation (Joint Financing) Regulations 1982(b) shall be further amended by substituting respectively for the sums £41.37, £12.11 and £29.26 the sums £32.10, £8.84 and £23.26.

Nicholas Ridley,
Secretary of State for Transport.

6th December 1984.

We consent to the making of these Regulations.

T. Garel-Jones,
John Major,
Lord Commissioners of Her Majesty's Treasury.

7th December 1984.

(a) 1982 c. 16; section 73(4) was amended by section 3(2) of the Civil Aviation (Eurocontrol) Act 1983 (c. 11).

(b) S.I. 1982/1784, amended by S.I. 1983/1833.

EXPLANATORY NOTE

(This Note is not part of the Regulations.)

These Regulations further amend the Civil Aviation (Joint Financing) Regulations 1982.

The charge payable by operators of aircraft to the Civil Aviation Authority in respect of crossings between Europe and North America is decreased by a decision of the Council of the International Civil Aviation Organisation. The element of the charge payable in respect of air navigation services provided by the Government of Denmark is decreased from £12.11 to £8.84. The element of the charge payable in respect of air navigation services provided by the Government of Iceland is decreased from £29.26 to £23.26. The total charge is thus decreased from £41.37 to £32.10.

The charges are payable in pursuance of the Agreements on the Joint Financing of certain Air Navigation Services respectively in Greenland and the Faroe Islands and in Iceland, opened for signature in Geneva on 25th September 1956 (Cmnd. Nos 677 and 678) as amended by the Protocols opened for signature at Montreal on 3rd November 1982 (Cmnd. Nos 8844 and 8845).

The charges are required by the Regulations to be remitted to the Governments of Denmark and Iceland subject to the deduction of a fee not exceeding 5 per cent for the Authority's expenses in billing and collection.

STATUTORY INSTRUMENTS

1984 No. 1917

FOOD

FOOD HYGIENE

The Imported Food (Northern Ireland) Regulations 1984

Made - - - -	*7th December* 1984
Laid before Parliament	*10th December* 1984
Coming into Operation	*1st January* 1985

ARRANGEMENT OF REGULATIONS

PART I

PRELIMINARY

PART II

ALL IMPORTED FOOD

PART III

MEAT AND MEAT PRODUCTS

PART IV

GENERAL

SCHEDULES

The Secretary of State for the Home Department, the Secretary of State for Social Services and the Minister of Agriculture, Fisheries and Food, acting jointly, being designated (a) Ministers for the purposes of section 2(2) of the European Communities Act 1972 (b) in relation to the common agricultural policy of the European Economic Community, in exercise of the powers conferred upon them by the said section 2(2), and by sections 13 and 118 of the Food Act 1984 (c) , as applied to Northern Ireland by section 135 of that Act, and of all other powers enabling them in that behalf, after consultation with such organisations as appear to them to be representative of interests substantially affected by the regulations, hereby make the following regulations:—

PART I

PRELIMINARY

Citation and commencement

1. These regulations may be cited ´as the Imported Food (Northern Ireland) Regulations 1984 and shall come into operation on 1st January 1985.

Interpretation

2.—(1) In these regulations—

"the Act" means the Food and Drugs Act (Northern Ireland) 1958 (d) ;

(a) S.I. 1972/1811.   (b) 1972 c.68.   (c) 1984 c.30.
(d) 1958 c.27 (N.I.).

"authorised officer" means an authorised officer of an enforcing authority, and for the purposes of these regulations has the meaning otherwise assigned to it by section 30 of the Act;

"competent authority" means an authority having power under the laws in force in any country to examine food and to certify as to its fitness for human consumption;

"the Department" means the Department of Health and Social Services for Northern Ireland;

"district" means the district of a district council, and includes the waters of any customs port abutting on any part of the district;

"district council" means a district council within the meaning of the Local Government Act (Northern Ireland) 1972 (a);

"enforcing authority" means the authority responsible for the enforcement and execution of these regulations under regulation 4;

"food" includes drink, chewing gum and other products of a like nature and use, and articles and substances used as ingredients in the preparation of food or drink or of such products, but does not include—

(a) water, live animals or birds,

(b) articles and substances used only as drugs, or

(c) milk, which has the meaning given to it in the Importation of Milk Regulations (Northern Ireland) 1983 (b);

"fresh meat" means the flesh or other edible parts of a mammal or bird, which has not been subjected to any treatment or process other than chilling, freezing, vacuum packing or packing in a controlled atmosphere and includes minced, chopped or mechanically recovered meat, and meat treated by the addition of seasonings;

"hovercraft" has the meaning assigned to it by section 4(1) of the Hovercraft Act 1968 (c);

"importer", in relation to imported food, includes any person who, whether as owner, consignor, consignee, agent or broker, is in possession of the food or in any way entitled to the custody or control of it;

"master", in relation to a ship, aircraft or hovercraft, includes the officer or any other person for the time being in charge or command of the ship, aircraft or hovercraft;

"officer of Customs and Excise" includes any person acting under the authority of the Commissioners of Customs and Excise.

(2) Subject to the provisions of paragraph 4 of the Second Schedule to the Act the Interpretation Act (Northern Ireland) 1954 (d) shall apply to the interpretation of these regulations as it applies to a Measure of the Northern Ireland Assembly.

Presumption as to food commonly used for human consumption

3. For the purposes of these regulations, any food commonly used for human consumption shall, if imported for sale or for use in the preparation of food for sale, be presumed, until the contrary is proved, to have been imported for sale, or, as the case may be, for use in the preparation of food for sale, for human consumption.

(a) 1972 c.9 (N.I.). (b) S.R. (N.I.) 1983 No. 338. (c) 1968 c.59.
(d) 1954 c.33 (N.I.).

Enforcement authorities

4.—(1) Subject to the provisions of this regulation and to such of the provisions of these regulations as prescribe functions to be exercised by officers of Customs and Excise, the authority responsible for the enforcement of these regulations shall be,—

(a) in relation to imported food which is in, or unloaded in, a district, and—

    (i) which is liable to immediate customs examination, the district council for that district,

    (ii) where the customs examination is deferred until the food reaches a place of destination in Northern Ireland, the district council in whose district the place of destination lies;

(b) in relation to imported food which is unloaded in England, Wales or Scotland, the district council in whose district the food is deposited for customs examination.

(2) Where imported food is unloaded in a district, and—

(a) customs examination of the food has been completed; and

(b) an authorised officer of the district council for that district nevertheless considers it expedient (having regard to the nature of the container in which the food is imported) that—

    (i) any examination of the food for the purposes of these regulations should be deferred until the food reaches a specified place of destination elsewhere in Northern Ireland, or

    (ii) any examination of the food should take place under England and Wales or Scotland regulations when the food reaches a specified place of destination in England, Wales or Scotland; and

(c) the importer gives to the district council in whose district the port, airport or other place of entry is situated an undertaking in writing that the container has been sealed and will not be opened until it reaches the place of destination specified in the undertaking,

the authorised officer shall, by the most expeditious means available, notify the receiving authority that the food (so described as to enable it to be identified) has not, by reason of the matters referred to in sub-paragraph *(b)*, been examined under these regulations at the port, airport or other place of entry and send them a copy of the undertaking referred to in sub-paragraph *(c)*; and where the receiving authority are a district council within the meaning of these regulations that district council shall thereupon become responsible for the execution and enforcement of these regulations in relation to that food.

(3) Where under any provision corresponding to paragraph (2) contained in England and Wales or Scotland regulations a district council receive notification that imported food which has not been examined under those regulations has been or is being sent to a place of destination in their district, they shall thereupon become responsible for the execution and enforcement of these regulations in relation to that food.

(4) Where imported food is in, or unloaded in, a district and customs examination is deferred until the food reaches a place of destination elsewhere in the United Kingdom, the district council shall so inform the receiving authority.

(5) In this regulation—

"England and Wales or Scotland regulations" means regulations with respect to imported food in force in England and Wales or Scotland, as the case may be;

"receiving authority" means an authority within the United Kingdom in whose district is situated the place of destination of any imported food, being an authority with enforcement functions under these regulations or the England and Wales or Scotland regulations, namely—

(a) where that place is in England or Wales, a local authority within the meaning of the Food Act 1984;

(b) where that place is in Scotland, a local authority within the meaning of the Food and Drugs (Scotland) Act 1956 (**a**) ;

(c) where that place is in Northern Ireland, a district council within the meaning of the Local Government Act (Northern Ireland) 1972.

PART II

ALL IMPORTED FOOD

Prohibition on importation of unfit food

5.—(1) No person shall import into Northern Ireland any food intended for sale for human consumption—

(a) which has been rendered injurious to health by means of any operation described in section 1(1) of the Act;

(b) which has been examined by a competent authority and found at the time of examination not to be fit for human consumption;

(c) which is otherwise unfit for human consumption or is unsound or unwholesome; or

(d) in the preparation of which any such food as aforesaid has been used.

(2) In any proceedings for an offence against paragraph (1)*(c)*, it shall be a defence for the defendant to prove that at the time when he imported the food he did not know, and could not with reasonable diligence have ascertained, that it was unfit for human consumption or unsound or unwholesome.

Examination of imported food

6.—(1) An authorised officer may at all reasonable times examine any food intended for sale for human consumption which is imported into Northern Ireland, and where on examination it appears to the authorised officer that any such food is being or has been imported in contravention of regulation 5, he may by notice in writing to the importer and to any other person in possession of the food require that, until the food has been dealt with by a justice of the peace, it shall not, without the consent of the authorised officer, be moved from the place of examination or from any other place specified in the notice.

(2) If on such examination being made it appears to an authorised officer that the food is being or has been imported in contravention of regulation 5, he may deal with it as food falling within section 9(1) of the Act (which relates to the examination and seizure of suspected food); and subsections (2) to (5)

(**a**) 1956 c.30.

of that section shall apply in relation to such food and to regulation 5 as they apply in relation to food seized under that section and to section 8 of the Act (which relates to offences).

(3) If the food is fresh meat, or is a meat product as defined in regulation 10(1), the following further provisions shall apply.

(a) Every notice served under paragraph (1) shall—

    (i) specify the grounds upon which it is based, and

    (ii) inform the person to whom it is addressed of his right to serve a counter-notice in accordance with subparagraph *(d)*, if the food is subject to any of the directives specified in subparagraph *(b)*.

(b) The directives referred to in subparagraph *(a)* are—

Council Directive 64/433/EEC on health problems affecting intra-Community trade in fresh meat (**a**) ;

Council Directive 71/118/EEC on health problems affecting trade in fresh poultrymeat (**b**) ; and

Council Directive 77/99/EEC on health problems affecting intra-Community trade in meat products (**c**) .

(c) The authorised officer shall after service of the notice provide the Department, for transmission to the Minister, with full details of the food and the reasons for its rejection or condemnation.

(d) A person served with a notice under paragraph (1) may, within seven days of receipt thereof, serve a counter-notice in writing on the authorised officer, stating that the food is subject to one of the directives specified in subparagraph *(b)*, and requiring him, before the food is dealt with by a justice of the peace, to obtain the opinion of an independent veterinary expert, to be nominated by the Department after consultation with the Minister, as to the condition of the food and the validity of any matter specified in the notice as a ground on which it is based.

(e) Upon receipt of such a counter-notice the authorised officer shall inform the Department, for transmission to the Minister, of its contents and request the nomination of an independent veterinary expert for the said purpose.

(f) If it appears to the Department, after consultation with the Minister, that the food is food which is not subject to any of the directives specified in subparagraph *(b)*, it shall so inform the person serving the notice under subparagraph *(d)*, whereupon the food shall be dealt with by a justice of the peace.

(g) If it appears to the Department, after consultation with the Minister, that the food is food which is subject to any of the directives specified in subparagraph *(b)*, the Minister shall consult the Commission of the European Economic Community as to the nomination of an appropriate independent veterinary expert, who shall be a national of a member state of the said Community other than the exporting country or the United Kingdom.

(h) The Department, after consultation with the Minister, shall nominate an independent veterinary expert, acting on the advice of the Commission of the European Economic Community, to determine—

    (i) whether the food is being, or has been, imported in contravention of regulation 5, and

(a)   O.J. No. L121, 29.7.1964, p.23.   (b)   O.J. No. L55, 8.3.1971, p.23.
(c)   O.J. No. L26, 31.1.1977, p.85.

    (ii) the accuracy and relevance of any matter specified under subparagraph *(a)*(i) as a ground on which the notice served under paragraph (1) was based.

(i) The independent veterinary expert so nominated shall examine the food and determine the matters referred to in subparagraph *(h)* and shall give his written opinion thereon to the authorised officer.

(j) Within seven days of receipt by him of that written opinion the authorised officer—

    (i) shall make it available to the person who, under subparagraph *(d)*, has required it to be obtained, and

    (ii) may rescind the notice given by him under paragraph (1) by serving written notice to that effect on that person.

(k) If, within seven days after receipt by him of that written opinion, the authorised officer has not rescinded the notice given by him under paragraph (1), the food shall be dealt with by a justice of the peace.

Special examination

7.—(1) Where an authorised officer is of the opinion that a special procedure is necessary for the examination of food, or where at the request of the importer he has recourse to such special procedure, the importer shall provide all such facilities as the authorised officer may reasonably require for the examination of such food.

(2) An authorised officer may by notice in writing to the importer or to any other person in possession of the imported food prohibit or restrict the removal or delivery of the food during any period, not exceeding 6 days (exclusive of Saturdays, Sundays and public holidays), which may reasonably be required for the examination of the food; and the notice shall specify the period and the procedure required for that examination.

(3) When a notice under paragraph (2) has been given to an importer or to any other person in possession of the imported food he may appeal against the notice to a court of summary jurisdiction, and the court may direct that the notice be withdrawn or that such shorter period be fixed as appears reasonable in the circumstances.

Consent of officer of Customs and Excise

8. Where the duties of an officer of Customs and Excise with regard to the examination of a cargo or consignment comprising food have not been wholly discharged, no examination of the food shall be made or sample procured for the purposes of these regulations without his consent; but every officer of Customs and Excise shall afford such facilities as the circumstances require for such examination of the food to be made or sample to be taken.

Powers of officer of Customs and Excise

9.—(1) An authorised officer may request an officer of Customs and Excise (either orally or in writing) to prohibit the removal of imported food which has not been cleared from customs charge until it has been examined by an authorised officer, and such a request may be made in relation to a particular consignment of food or in relation to food of any class or description specified in the request. A request made orally under this paragraph shall be confirmed in writing.

(2) Where a request has been made under paragraph (1), the officer of Customs and Excise shall by notice in writing given to the importer or master of the ship, aircraft or hovercraft, or to the driver of the road vehicle, in which the food is imported require that, until the food has been examined by an authorised officer, it shall not be removed from the place specified in the notice, and he shall at the same time inform the enforcing authority of the effect of the notice.

(3) An authorised officer shall, without undue delay, examine any food in respect of which a notice has been given by an officer of Customs and Excise under this regulation and shall send to that officer a copy of any notice or certificate issued by him in accordance with these regulations, or a statement in writing of any action taken by him under any other provision of these regulations in respect of that food.

(4) Where an officer of Customs and Excise has given notice under paragraph (2) forbidding removal of any food, such food shall not, prior to its inspection by an authorised officer, be removed by any person contrary to the terms of the notice except with the written permission of either such officer.

PART III

MEAT AND MEAT PRODUCTS

Interpretation and application of Part III

10.—(1) In this Part—

"bulk lard" means lard or any other rendered mammal or poultry fat transported unpackaged in the tank of a ship, aircraft, hovercraft or road vehicle;

"carcase" means the whole body of a slaughtered animal or bird after bleeding, skinning (except pigs) or plucking, evisceration (including removal of the thick skirt and kidneys) and removal of the limbs at the carpus (except birds) and tarsus, the head, the tail (except birds) and the udder;

"designated person" means a person having power under the laws in force in a country of origin to examine food and to certify as to its fitness for human consumption;

"health mark" means a label, mark, seal, brand, stamp or other voucher;

"meat product" means any product prepared wholly or partly from fresh meat (which has undergone treatment to ensure a certain degree of preservation) but excluding fresh meat and those products specified in Schedule 1;

"offal" means fresh meat other than that of the carcase as defined in this paragraph, whether or not naturally connected to the carcase;

"package" means an outer container of any material into which any fresh meat or meat product is placed, but shall not include a bulk container which may become part of a road vehicle or of a trailer to such a vehicle;

"pig" includes a boar, sow and hog;

"poultry" means domestic fowls, turkeys, guinea fowls, ducks and geese;

"scraps and trimmings" means small pieces and trimmings, being muscular or other tissues or fat weighing less than one hundred grammes, which have been removed from an animal during the preparation of wholesale cuts, the boning, cutting or trimming of fresh meat or the preparation of fresh meat for the retail trade;

"transport" means the movement or conveyance of any fresh meat or meat product from one place to another place;

"wrapping" means the protection of fresh meat or meat product by the use of an initial wrapping of any material or initial container in direct contact with the fresh meat or meat product concerned, and also the initial wrapping material or initial container itself.

(2) This Part applies to any fresh meat or meat product, but does not apply to any article of food specified in Schedule 1.

Requirements as to health marks etc for imported meat

11.—(1) No person shall import into Northern Ireland for sale for human consumption any fresh meat, meat product or bulk lard unless it bears a health mark which—

(a) shall be so placed as to be legible and clearly visible;

(b) conforms to the requirements of Schedule 3; and

(c) is recognised by the Department in accordance with paragraph (3).

(2) No person shall import into Northern Ireland for sale for human consumption any fresh meat or meat product unless it has been wrapped and packed, and is transported, in accordance with the requirements of Schedule 4.

(3) The Department, after consultation with the Minister, shall recognise a health mark which appears to show—

(a) that the fresh meat to which it relates, or the meat from which the meat product to which it relates was prepared, was derived from mammals or birds inspected before and immediately after death, or in the case of mammals or birds killed when wild, was derived from mammals or birds inspected immediately after death only, and passed in accordance with criteria satisfactory to the Department; and

(b) that the dressing, packing and other preparation of the fresh meat or meat product was carried out with all necessary precautions for the prevention of danger to health,

by means of a notice published in the Belfast Gazette, and the recognition may be made subject to conditions which shall be specified in the notice; and any such recognition or condition may be varied or revoked by a subsequent notice so published.

(4) In relation to any fresh meat of a description specified in Schedule 5, there shall be included in the notice referred to in paragraph (3) a statement to the effect that the recognition conferred by the notice extends to that description of fresh meat; and any such notice which does not contain a statement to that effect shall be deemed not to confer any recognition in respect of any description of meat set out in Schedule 5.

Requirements as to health certificates

12.—(1) No person shall import into Northern Ireland for sale for human consumption any fresh meat which is derived from domestic bovine animals (including buffalo), swine, sheep, goats, solipeds or poultry, or any meat product (other than a product listed in Schedule 2) in the preparation of which any such fresh meat was used, unless it is accompanied by a health certificate which is valid in accordance with the requirements of paragraph (2).

(2) A health certificate is valid if,—

(a) in the case of a certificate which relates to fresh meat which is derived from domestic bovine animals (including buffalo), swine, sheep, goats or solipeds imported from the Channel Islands or from any member state of the European Economic Community, it corresponds in form and content to the model in Schedule 6 and contains the information specified in that model;

(b) in the case of a certificate which relates to fresh meat which is derived from domestic bovine animals (including buffalo), swine, sheep, goats or solipeds imported from any country not being the Channel Islands or a member state of the European Economic Community, it corresponds in form and content to the model in Schedule 7 and contains the information specified in that model;

(c) in the case of a certificate which relates to meat products imported from the Channel Islands or any country of the European Economic Community, it corresponds in form and content to the model in Schedule 8 and contains the information specified in that model;

(d) in the case of a certificate which relates to meat products imported from any country not being the Channel Islands or a member state of the European Economic Community, it corresponds in form and content to the model in Schedule 9 and contains the information specified in that model;

(e) in the case of a certificate which relates to poultry meat, it corresponds in form and content to the model in Schedule 10 and contains the information specified in that model;

(f) it is expressed at least in the English language; and

(g) it is issued by a designated person.

Lost, damaged or defective health marks and certificates

13.—(1) In any case where the importation into Northern Ireland of any fresh meat or meat product is not permitted by an authorised officer, having regard to the provisions of regulation 11 or 12, he may forthwith notify the Department to that effect, and shall furnish to it all relevant information in his possession.

(2) On receipt of such notification and information the Department shall consult with the Minister, and shall make such enquiries as he considers appropriate, and shall communicate the results of his enquiries to the Department, for transmission to the authorised officer.

(3) If, after taking into consideration the results of the Minister's enquiries, and after consultation with the Department, the authorised officer is satisfied that—

(a) the fresh meat or meat product originally came from a country in respect of which a health mark is for the time being recognised by the Department pursuant to regulation 11;

(b) the fresh meat, or meat from which the meat product was prepared, was derived from mammals or birds, as the case may be, inspected before and immediately after death, or in the case of mammals or birds killed while wild, was derived from mammals or birds inspected immediately after death only, by a designated person and passed in accordance with criteria satisfactory to the Department; and

(c) the dressing, packing and other preparation of the fresh meat or meat product were carried out with all necessary precautions for the prevention of danger to health,

and notifies the Department in writing to that effect, the provisions of regulations 11 and 12 shall have effect in relation to the fresh meat or meat product as if it had been accompanied by a health mark or certificate or both in compliance with the relevant requirements of those regulations.

Disposal of meat imported contrary to the regulations

14.—(1) If upon examination of any food an authorised officer is of the opinion that it comprises any fresh meat or meat product imported into Northern Ireland in contravention of the provisions of regulation 11 or 12 or that it comprises any fresh meat or meat product to which regulation 13(1) applies, he shall notify in writing the importer, or the master of the ship, aircraft or hovercraft or the driver of the road vehicle in which the food is so imported that any such meat or meat product must not be removed for any purposes other than its exportation from Northern Ireland.

(2) Unless the authorised officer proposes to notify the Department under regulation 13(1), any notice served under paragraph (1) shall—

(a) specify the grounds upon which it is based;

(b) notify the person to whom it is addressed of his right to serve a counter-notice in accordance with subparagraph (5)(b), if the food is subject to any of the directives specified in regulation 6(3)(b); and

(c) notify the person to whom it is addressed that the food may be destroyed or disposed of, so that it cannot be used for human consumption, unless—

(i) within the time specified in the notice, being not less than 7 days after receiving the notice, the importer gives a written undertaking to the authorised officer to export the food at his own expense within 14 days from the date of the undertaking, or to prove in proceedings before a justice of the peace that the importation or removal of the food into Northern Ireland is not contrary to regulation 11 or 12,

(ii) within 7 days after the written opinion of an independent veterinary expert has been made available to him under paragraph (14), the importer gives a written undertaking to the authorised officer in the terms required under subparagraph (c)(i), or

(iii) the authorised officer rescinds the notice.

(3) In the case of food in respect of which the authorised officer proposes to notify the Department under regulation 13(1), the notice referred to in paragraph (2) shall be given if, after completion of the enquiries and consultation required under regulation 13(3), the authorised officer fails to notify the Department that he is satisfied as to the matters set out in regulation 13(3).

(4) The authorised officer shall, after service of a notice under paragraph (2), provide the Department, for transmission to the Minister, with full details of the food and the reasons for its rejection or condemnation.

(5) A person served with a notice under paragraph (2), may—

(a) within the time specified in the notice, give an undertaking in writing to the authorised officer—

    (i) to export the food to which the notice relates, at his own expense, within 14 days after the date of the undertaking, or

    (ii) to prove in proceedings before a justice of the peace that the importation or removal of the food into Northern Ireland is not contrary to regulation 11 or 12; or

(b) within 7 days after service of the notice, serve a counter-notice in writing upon the authorised officer, stating that the food is food which is subject to one of the directives specified in regulation 6(3)(b), and requiring him to obtain the opinion of an independent veterinary expert, to be nominated by the Department, after consultation with the Minister, as to the condition of the food and the validity of any matter specified in the notice as a ground on which it is based.

(6) If within the time specified in any notice given under paragraph (2) the authorised officer has not received either a counter-notice or such written undertaking as described in the notice, or if within that time the authorised officer has received an undertaking that the importer will, at his own expense, export the food and the importer has failed to export it within 14 days after receipt of the undertaking, the authorised officer may supervise its destruction or disposal by such means and in such manner as to prevent it from being used for human consumption.

(7) Where in pursuance of this regulation, the importer has given an undertaking to prove that the importation or removal of the food into Northern Ireland is not contrary to regulation 11 or 12, the authorised officer shall, within 24 hours after receipt of the undertaking, take steps to obtain the decision of a justice of the peace with respect thereto.

(8) If upon examination of any food in respect of which an officer of Customs and Excise has given a notice under regulation 9, an authorised officer is of the opinion that its importation or removal into Northern Ireland is not contrary to regulation 11 or 12, he shall give a certificate authorising its removal unless he takes action in respect of it under any other provision of these regulations.

(9) Upon receipt of a counter-notice served under paragraph (5)(b) the authorised officer shall inform the Department of its contents. The Department shall then inform the Minister, and request the nomination of an independent veterinary expert for the said purpose.

(10) If it appears to the Department that the food is food which is not subject to any of the directives specified in regulation 6(3)(b), it shall so inform the person serving the notice under paragraph (5)(b), whereupon the importer may give an undertaking in accordance with paragraph 2(c)(i), failing which the authorised officer may take appropriate action under paragraph (6).

(11) If it appears to the Department that the food is food which is subject to any of the directives specified in regulation 6(3)(b), it shall arrange for the Commission of the European Economic Community to be consulted as to the nomination of an appropriate independent veterinary expert, who shall be a national of a member state of the said Community other than the exporting country or the United Kingdom.

(12) The Department shall nominate an independent veterinary expert, acting on the advice of the Commission of the European Economic Community, to determine—

(a) whether the food is being, or has been, imported in contravention of regulation 11 or 12; and

(b) the accuracy and relevance of any matter specified under paragraph (2)*(b)* as a ground on which the notice served under paragraph (2) was based.

(13) The independent veterinary expert so nominated shall examine the food and determine the matters referred to in paragraph (2)*(a)*, and shall give his written opinion thereon to the authorised officer.

(14) Within 7 days of receipt by him of the written opinion, the authorised officer—

(i) shall make it available to the person who, under paragraph (5)*(b)*, has required it to be obtained, and

(ii) may rescind the notice given by him under paragraph (2) by serving written notice to that effect on that person.

(15) If, within 7 days after receiving the written opinion, the authorised officer has not rescinded the notice given by him under paragraph (2), the importer may give to the authorised officer a written undertaking in accordance with paragraph (2)*(c)*(ii), failing which the authorised officer may take appropriate action under paragraph (6).

(16) Where, in pursuance of paragraph (1), an authorised officer has given a notice forbidding the removal of any food, it shall not be removed by any person contrary to the terms of the notice except with the written permission of the authorised officer.

Powers of a justice of the peace

15.—(1) Where, in pursuance of regulation 14, an application is made to a justice of the peace in respect of any fresh meat or meat product and he is satisfied that the importer has failed to prove that the importation or removal into Northern Ireland of the fresh meat or meat product was not contrary to the provisions of regulation 11 or 12, he shall condemn the fresh meat or meat product and order it to be destroyed or disposed of under the supervision of an authorised officer by such means and in such manner as to prevent it from being used for human consumption.

(2) Where on such application the justice of the peace is satisfied that the importation or removal into Northern Ireland of the fresh meat or meat product is not contrary to the provisions of regulation 11 or 12 he shall order the rescission of the notice prohibiting its removal.

Prohibition on the importation of meat required to be exported

16. No person shall land in Northern Ireland any fresh meat or meat product in respect of which a notice has been given under regulation 14(1) or any other regulation to the like effect then in force in any part of the United Kingdom, the Channel Islands or the Isle of Man.

PART IV

GENERAL

Record to be kept of food destroyed

17. Where in pursuance of these regulations any food is destroyed or otherwise disposed of under the supervision of an authorised officer, the enforcing authority, before the destruction or other disposal of the food, shall cause a description of, and such other details as will suffice to identify, the food to be recorded and shall keep the record in their custody for a period of not less than 12 months from the date of destruction or other disposal of the food.

Offences and penalties

18. If any person contravenes any of the provisions of these regulations, he shall be guilty of an offence and shall be liable—

(a) on summary conviction, to a fine not exceeding £2,000; and

(b) on conviction on indictment, to a fine or imprisonment for a term not exceeding two years,

or to both such fine and such imprisonment.

Court may include a justice who has examined the food

19. The justice of the peace before whom any food is brought under regulation 6 or 14 may, but need not, be a member of the court before which a person is charged with an offence under regulation 5, 11 or 12, as the case may be, in relation to the food.

Disputes as to compensation

20. Any dispute as to compensation arising under these regulations shall be determined, and any compensation awarded thereunder shall be recoverable, in like manner as if the dispute had arisen or the award had been made under the Act, and section 54 of the Act (which relates to disputed compensation) shall apply accordingly.

Protection for officers

21. Section 62 of the Act (which relates to protection for district council officers acting in good faith) shall have effect for the purposes of these regulations as if references therein to that Act were references to these regulations.

Application of various provisions of the Act

22.—(1) Subject to paragraph (2), the following provisions of the Act shall apply for the purposes of these regulations as if references therein to proceedings, or a prosecution, under or taken or brought under the Act included references to proceedings, or a prosecution, as the case may be, taken or brought for an offence under these regulations—

(a) section 46(7) and (8) (which relates to prosecutions);

(b) section 48(1) and (2) (which relates to evidence of analysis);

(c) section 50 (which relates to the power of a court to require analysis by the Government Chemist);

(d) section 51 (which relates to a contravention due to some person other than the person charged);

(e) section 52(2) (which relates to the conditions under which a warranty may be pleaded as a defence);

(f) section 53 (which relates to offences in relation to warranties and certificates of analysis).

(2) Section 50 of the Act shall apply for the purposes of these regulations as if the reference therein to section 46(8) of the Act included a reference to that subsection as applied by paragraph (1).

Revocations

23. The regulations specified in Schedule 12 are hereby revoked.

In Witness whereof the Official Seal of the Minister of Agriculture, Fisheries and Food is hereunto affixed on 26th November 1984.

Michael Jopling,
Minister of Agriculture, Fisheries and Food.

Norman Fowler,
Secretary of State for Social Services.

7th December 1984.

Leon Brittan,
Secretary of State for the Home Department.

23rd November 1984.

SCHEDULE 1   Regulation 10(1) and (2)

ARTICLES OF FOOD TO WHICH PART III DOES NOT APPLY

Vitamin concentrates containing meat.
Pharmaceutical products containing meat.
Gelatine.
Rennet.
Meat products, of which meat is not a principal ingredient and which do not contain fragments of meat.

SCHEDULE 2   Regulation 12(1)

MEAT PRODUCTS WHICH ARE EXEMPT FROM THE REQUIREMENTS OF REGULATION 12

1.   Meat extracts, meat consommé and stock, meat sauces and similar products not containing fragments of meat;

2.   Whole, broken or crushed bones, meat peptones, meat powder, pork-rind powder, blood plasma, dried blood, dried blood plasma, cellular proteins, bone extracts and similar products;

3.   Fats melted down from animal tissues;

4.   Stomachs, bladders and intestines, cleaned and bleached, salted or dried;

5.   Products containing fragments of meat, but which contain a quantity of meat or meat product not exceeding ten per cent of the total weight of the final product ready for use, after preparation in accordance with the instructions for use issued by the manufacturer.

SCHEDULE 3   Regulation 11(1)

REQUIREMENTS AS TO HEALTH MARKS FOR IMPORTED MEAT

1.   The meat of all solipeds, ruminating animals and swine, and venison shall bear a health mark as specified below.

(a)   A health mark shall before importation have been applied to the meat on all carcases, half-carcases, quarter-carcases and half-carcases cut into no more than 3 pieces and to livers. The health mark shall have been applied either by hot branding or stamping with marking ink, and shall have been applied in the following places—

   (i)   the external surface of the thighs, loins, back, breast and shoulder of each carcase weighing more than 65 kilograms; and

   (ii)   the external surface of the thighs and on the shoulders of all other carcases.

(b)   Livers of bovine animals, swine and solipeds shall bear a health mark which has been applied by hot-branding.

(c)   If meat has been wrapped and packaged in accordance with Schedule 4, the packaging shall bear a health mark; in addition such meat may also bear a health mark.

(d)   Cuts of meat and offal, other than livers, which have not been wrapped or packaged, shall bear a health mark which has been applied by hot branding or by stamping with marking ink.

(e)   Meat, including pieces weighing less than 100 grammes, shall be wrapped and packaged and a health mark shall be borne on both the wrapping and packaging.

(f)   Portions of meat wrapped for direct retail sale shall bear a health mark on both the wrapping and packaging.

2.   Poultry meat shall bear a health mark in the manner following—

(a)   large packages containing poultry carcases which may be consigned from a poultry slaughterhouse to either—

(i) a poultry cutting plant for cutting the carcases, or

(ii) restaurants, canteens, institutions or similar outlets for direct supply to a final consumer after preparation of the poultry meat by a process involving the application of heat,

or similar packages of poultry carcases which may be consigned from a poultry cutting plant to a meat products plant for treatment, shall bear a health mark and also a label in the form which is described in Schedule 11;

(b) individual carcases shall bear a health mark on the wrapping or on the carcase in such a manner that it is clearly visible under the wrapping, and also on any packaging;

(c) large packages containing cuts of poultry meat and offal which may be consigned from a poultry slaughterhouse or a poultry cutting plant to a meat products establishment for treatment shall bear a health mark and also a label in the form which is described in Schedule 11;

(d) the wrapping and packaging of individual cuts of poultry meat and offal shall bear a health mark.

3. Fresh meat, other than that to which paragraph 1 or paragraph 2 applies, shall bear a health mark which shall have been applied—

(a) either to the meat or to the wrapping thereof; and

(b) to any packaging thereof.

4. Meat products shall bear a health mark which shall have been applied—

(a) either to the meat product or to the wrapping thereof; and

(b) to any packaging thereof.

5. Bulk lard shall be presumed to bear a health mark in the following circumstances—

(a) a health mark shall accompany any bulk lard which is transported in any ship, aircraft, hovercraft or road vehicle;

(b) the health mark shall indicate the position of any tank containing lard, to which it may relate, in any ship, aircraft or hovercraft in which such lard is transported;

(c) the health mark shall state the quantity of lard carried in any tank containing such lard; and

(d) a health mark shall contain a certificate to the effect that any tank, pipe and pump which may have been used for the loading of such lard into the tank had been inspected and found to be clean before the loading of the lard into the tank.

6. In all cases where a health mark has been applied to packaging, or is printed on packaging, it shall have been applied or printed in such a manner so that the health mark shall be destroyed when the package is opened, unless the packaging is not capable of being used again as packaging.

Regulation 11(2)   SCHEDULE 4

REQUIREMENTS AS TO WRAPPING, PACKAGING AND TRANSPORT OF IMPORTED MEAT

1. The wrapping of fresh meat or meat products shall comply with the following conditions—

(a) it shall be transparent and colourless, unless it fulfils, at the same time, the protective requirements of packaging;

(b) it shall not alter the organoleptic characteristics of the meat;

(c) it shall not be capable of transmitting to the meat any substances harmful to human health;

(d) it shall not be used again for wrapping meat, but earthenware containers for meat products and wrappings which fulfil the protective requirements of packaging may be used again after cleaning and disinfection.

2. Poultry carcases, parts of poultry or poultry offal shall be suitably enclosed in wrapping.

3. The packaging of fresh meat or meat products shall comply with the following conditions—

(a) it shall be strong enough to ensure the effective protection of the meat during transportation and handling;

(b) it shall not contain fresh meat of more than one species of animal;

(c) it shall not be used again for a similar purpose, unless it is made of impervious and corrosion-resistant materials, which are easy to clean, and it has first been cleansed and disinfected.

4. Fresh meat and meat products shall be transported in sealed means of transport, designed and equipped in such a manner so that the following temperatures for the meat are maintained during the course of transport—

(a) for carcases and cuts (excluding rabbit meat, hare meat and poultry meat) — not higher than +7°C (chilled) — not higher than –12°C (frozen)

(b) for offals (excluding rabbit offals, hare offals and poultry offals) — not higher than +3°C

(c) for rabbit meat, hare meat, poultry meat, rabbit offals, hare offals and poultry offals — not higher than +4°C

(d) for meat products — temperature as specified on the label (when appropriate)

5. Fresh meat shall not be transported in a vehicle or container which is not clean or has not been disinfected before use. Vehicles or containers used for this purpose shall not show any evidence of having been used for the transport of live animals or birds.

6. Fresh meat and meat products shall not be transported in a vehicle or container with any other products likely to contaminate or to affect the hygiene of the meat, unless appropriate precautions are taken to prevent such an occurrence.

SCHEDULE 5 Regulation 11(4)

MEAT OR POULTRY MEAT IN RESPECT OF WHICH SPECIFIC RECOGNITION IS REQUIRED

1. Fresh meat comprising, or forming part of, the head of any animal or bird.

2. Any part of a carcase which has been chopped or minced, with or without the addition of any spices, cereal products, salt, flavourings, vegetables or other ingredient.

3. Scraps and trimmings.

4. Boneless veal appearing to an authorised officer to be from calves less than three months old.

Regulation 12(2)(*a*)

SCHEDULE 6

HEALTH CERTIFICATE

for fresh meat for consignment to a Member State(1) of the EEC

No (2)....................

Exporting country ....

Ministry ....

Department ....

Ref. ....

(Optional)

I. Identification of meat
Meat of ....
(Animal species)

Nature of cuts ....
Nature of packaging ....
Number of cuts or packages ....
Month(s) and year(s) when frozen ....
Net weight ....

II. Origin of meat
Address(es) and veterinary approval number(s) of the approved slaughter-house(s) ....
....
Address(es) and veterinary approval number(s) of the approved cutting plant(s)
....
Address(es) and veterinary approval number(s) of the approved store(s) ....
....

III. Destination of meat
The meat will be sent from ....
(Place of loading)
to ....
(Country and place of destination)
by the following means of transport (3) ....
Name and address of consignor ....
....
Name and address of consignee ....
....

IV. Health attestation

'I, the undersigned official veterinarian, certify that the meat described above was obtained under the conditions governing production and control laid down in Directive 64/433/EEC on health problems affecting intra-Community trade in fresh meat and that it is, therefore, considered as such to be fit for human consumption.'

Done at ....on ....

....
(Signature of the official veterinarian)

(1) Fresh meat: in accordance with the Directive referred to in IV of this certificate, this means all parts fit for human consumption from domestic bovine animals, swine, sheep and goats and solipeds which have not undergone any preserving process; however, chilled and frozen meat shall be considered to be fresh meat.

(2) Optional.

(3) In the case of rail trucks and lorries, state the registration number, in the case of aircraft the flight number, and in the case of boats the name, and where necessary the number of the container.

SCHEDULE 7 Regulation 12(2)(b)

PUBLIC HEALTH CERTIFICATE

for fresh meat(1) intended for ....(Name of EEC Member State)

No ....(2)

Exporting country ....
Ministry ....
Department ....
Ref. ....

(Optional)

I. Identification of meat:

Meat of ....

(Animal species)

Nature of cuts..
Nature of packaging ....
Number of cuts or packages ....
Month(s) and year(s) when frozen ....
Net weight ....

II. Origin of meat:

Address(es) and veterinary approval number(s) of the approved slaughter-house(s) ....

....

Address(es) and veterinary approval number(s) of the approved cutting plant(s)

....

....

Address(es) and veterinary approval number(s) of the approved store(s) ....

....

III. Destination of meat:

The meat will be sent from: ....

(Place of loading)

to: ....

(Country and place of destination)

by the following means of transport (3) ....

Name and address of consignor ....

....

Name and address of consignee ....

....

IV. Health attestation

I, the undersigned, official veterinarian, certify that:

(a) the meat described above (4),

the label affixed to the packages of meat described above (4),

bear(s) (4) a mark to the effect that the meat comes wholly from animals slaughtered in slaughterhouses approved for exporting to the country of destination;

(b) the meat was obtained under the conditions governing production and control contained in Council Directive 72/462/EEC and that it is therefore considered as such to be fit for human consumption;

(c) the meat has been cut in an approved cutting plant (4);

(d) the meat has/has not been subject to an examination for trichinosis or, where Article 3 of Directive 77/96/EEC applies, has undergone cold treatment;

(e) the means of transport and the loading conditions of meat of this consignment meet the hygiene requirements laid down in respect of export to the country of destination.

Done at ....on ....

....

(Signature of the official veterinarian)

(1) Fresh meat within the meaning of Article 2(b) of Directive 64/433/EEC.

(2) Optional.

(3) For railway wagons or goods vehicles the registration number should be given, for aircraft the flight number and for ships the name.

(4) Delete as appropriate.

SCHEDULE 8   Regulation 12(2)*(c)*

HEALTH CERTIFICATE FOR MEAT PRODUCTS (1) INTENDED FOR CONSIGNMENT TO A MEMBER STATE OF THE EEC

No (2)............................

Exporting country ....

Ministry ....

Department concerned ....

Ref (2) ....

I.   Identification of meat products:

     Products manufactured with meat from ....

                                               (Animal species)

     Nature of products (3) ....

     Nature of packaging ....

     Number of individual items or packages ....

     Storage and transport temperature (4) ....

     Storage life (4) ....

     Net weight ....

II.   Meat products from:

     Address(es) and veterinary approval number(s) of approved processing establishment(s) ....

     ....

III. Destination of meat products

     The meat products will be sent from ....

                                               (Place of loading)

     to ....

     by the following means of transport (5) ....

     Name and address of consignor ....

     ....

     Name and address of consignee ....

     ....

IV. Health attestation

     I, the undersigned, certify that:

     (a) the meat products described above were manufactured from fresh meat or meat products under conditions that comply with the standards laid down in Directive 77/99/EEC (6);

     (b) the said meat products, their wrappings or packaging, bear a mark proving that they have all come from approved establishments (6);

     (c) the fresh pigmeat used in the manufacture of the meat products has/has not been (6) subjected to a trichinae detection test;

(d) the transport vehicles and equipment and the loading conditions of this consignment comply with the hygiene requirements laid down in Directive 77/99/EEC.

Done at ....on ....

(Signature) ....

Stamp   (Name in capital letters)

(1) Under Article 2 of Directive 77/99/EEC.
(2) Optional.
(3) Possible indication of ionizing radiation for medical reasons.
(4) Where an indication is given in accordance with Article 4 of Directive 77/99/EEC.

(5) Indicate the registration number (railway, wagons and trucks); the flight number (aircraft) or the name (ship).

(6) Delete as appropriate.

Regulation 12(2)(d)   SCHEDULE 9

HEALTH CERTIFICATE FOR MEAT PRODUCTS INTENDED FOR CONSIGNMENT TO THE UNITED KINGDOM

No (1) ....

Exporting country ....
Ministry ....
Department concerned ....
Ref (1) ....

I.   Identification of meat products
     Products manufactured with meat from ....
                                        (Animal species)

     Nature of products (2) ....
     Nature of packaging ....
     Number of individual items or of packages ....
     Storage and transport temperature (3) ....
     Net weight ....

II. Meat products from

     Address(es) and veterinary approval number(s) of approved processing establishment(s) ....
     ....

III. Destination of meat products

     The meat products will be sent from ....
                                        (Place of loading)

     by the following means of transport (4) ....
     Name and address of consignor ....
     ....
     Name and address of consignee ....
     ....

IV. Health attestation

I, the undersigned, certify that:

(a) the meat products described above were manufactured from fresh meat or meat products under conditions that comply with the standards laid down in the Explanatory Memorandum on the Importation of Meat Products into the United Kingdom;

(b) the said meat products, their wrappings or packaging, bear a mark proving that they have all come from approved establishments;

(c) the fresh pigmeat used in the manufacture of the meat products has/has not been (5) subject to a trichinae detection test;

(d) the transport vehicles and equipment and the loading conditions of this consignment comply with the hygiene requirements laid down in the Explanatory Memorandum on the Importation of Meat Products into the United Kingdom.

Done at .... on...............................

(Signature) ....

Stamp   (Name in capital letters)

---

(1) Optional.

(2) Possible indication of ionizing radiation for medical reasons.

(3) Where an indication is given in accordance with Section E, paragraph 23 of the Explanatory Memorandum on the Importation of Meat Products into the United Kingdom.

(4) Indicate the registration number (railway, wagons and trucks); the flight number (aircraft) or the name (ship).

(5) Delete as appropriate.

SCHEDULE 10   Regulation 12(2)(e)

HEALTH CERTIFICATE

for fresh poultrymeat (1) intended for consignment to a Member State of the EEC

No (2) ....

Exporting country ....

Ministry ....

Competent service ....

Ref (2) ....

I.   Identification of meat:

Meat of ....

(animal species)

Nature of cuts ....

Nature of packaging ....

Number of packages ....

Net weight ....

II. Origin of meat:

   Address(es) and veterinary approval number(s) of the slaughterhouse(s) (4) ....

   ....

   Address(es) and veterinary approval number(s) of the approved cutting premises

   (4) ....

   ....

III. Destination of meat:

   The meat will be sent

   from ....
                              (place of loading)

   to ....
                        (Country and place of destination)

   by the following means of transport (3) ....

   Name and address of consignor ....

   Name and address of consignee ....

IV. Health attestation

   I, the undersigned, official veterinarian, certify that:

   (a)— the poultry meat described (4)

      — the packaging of the meat described above (4)

      bears a mark proving that

      — the meat comes from animals slaughtered in approved slaughterhouses (4);

      — the meat was cut in approved cutting premises (4);

   (b) this meat has been passed as fit for human consumption following a veterinary
      inspection carried out in accordance with the Council Directive of 15
      February 1971 on health problems affecting trade in fresh poultry meat;

   (c) the transport vehicles or containers and the loading conditions of this
      consignment meet the hygiene requirements laid down in that Directive.

Done at .... on..............................

                                        ....
                                        (Signature of official veterinarian)

(1) Fresh poultry meat: fresh meat from the following species—live domestic hens,
turkeys, guinea fowls, ducks and geese which have not been treated to ensure their
preservation; however, poultry meat which has been chilled or frozen shall be
considered to be fresh.

(2) Optional.

(3) For railway wagons and lorries the registration number, for aircraft the flight
number and for ships the name should be given.

(4) Delete as appropriate.

SCHEDULE 11

LABEL TO BE AFFIXED TO LARGE PACKAGES OF POULTRY MEAT INTENDED FOR A CERTAIN DESTINATION

INTENDED USE: CUTTING/TREATMENT (1)
ADDRESS OF DESTINATION
(1) Delete as appropriate

SCHEDULE 12

Regulation 23

REVOCATIONS

Column 1 Regulation revoked	Column 2 References
The Imported Food (Northern Ireland) Regulations 1968	S.I. 1968/98
The Imported Food (Northern Ireland) (Amendment) Regulations 1973	S.I. 1973/1350
The Imported Food (Northern Ireland) (Amendment) Regulations 1979	S.I. 1979/1427
The Imported Food (Northern Ireland) (Amendment) Regulations 1981	S.I. 1981/1084

EXPLANATORY NOTE

(*This Note is not part of the Regulations.*)

1. These regulations contain measures for the protection of public health in relation to imported food. They supersede the Imported Food (Northern Ireland) Regulations 1968 and consolidate them with their amending regulations.

2. Further amendments are made in implementation of—

(*a*) Council Directive 64/433/EEC on health problems affecting intra-Community trade in fresh meat (O.J. No. 121, 29.7.64, p.2012/64), as last amended by the Council Directive 83/90/EEC (O.J. No. L59, 5.3.83, p.10);

(*b*) Council Directive 71/118/EEC on health problems affecting trade in fresh poultrymeat (O.J. No. L55, 8.3.71, p.23), as last amended by the Council Directive 82/532/EEC (O.J. No. L234, 9.8.82, p.12);

(*c*) Council Directive 72/462/EEC on health and veterinary inspection problems upon importation of bovine animals and swine and fresh meat from third countries (O.J. No. L302, 31.12.72, p.28), as last amended by the Council Directive 83/91/EEC (O.J. No. L59, 5.3.83, p.34);

(*d*) Council Directive 77/99/EEC on health problems affecting intra-Community trade in meat products (O.J. No. L26, 31.1.77, p.85), as amended by the Council Directive 80/214/EEC (O.J. No. L47, 21.2.80, p.3).

Details are given in paragraph 7 below.

3. Part I of the regulations contains definitions and specifies the authorities by whom the regulations are to be enforced and provides for the deferred examination of imported food in certain circumstances (regulations 2 to 4).

4. Part II deals with imported food generally, and prohibits the importation of food which is unfit for human consumption, or is unsound or unwholesome (regulation 5). Imported food may be examined by authorised officers of an enforcing authority (regulation 6), and provision is made for special procedures for the examination of food (regulation 7) and for the co-operation of authorised officers of enforcing authorities with officers of Customs and Excise (regulations 8 and 9).

5. Part III deals with imported meat and meat products (including lard), which may not be imported for sale for human consumption unless they bear a health mark and are wrapped, packed and transported as specified. Provision is made for the official recognition of health marks (regulation 11). This Part contains requirements as to health certificates for fresh meat and meat products (regulation 12) and provisions as to lost, damaged or defective health marks and certificates (regulation 13), the disposal of meat imported contrary to the regulations (regulations 14 and 16) and the powers of a justice of the peace in respect of meat so imported (regulation 15).

6. Part IV makes general supplementary provisions, including—

(*a*) a requirement for records to be kept by enforcing authorities of food destroyed or disposed of in pursuance of the regulations (regulation 17);

(*b*) offences and penalties (regulation 18);

(c) provision that a justice of the peace may be a member of a court before which a person is charged with an offence under the regulations notwithstanding his prior dealings with the food concerned in the offence charge (regulation 19);

(d) disputes as to compensation (regulation 20);

(e) protection for authorised officers of enforcing authorities (regulation 21);

(f) the application for the purposes of the regulations of various provisions of the Food and Drugs Act (Northern Ireland) 1958 (regulation 22); and

(g) the revocation of the superseded regulations (regulation 23).

7.   The amendments made of the superseded regulations comprise—

(a) the provisions of regulations 6(3) and 14(5) as to the service of notices and counter-notices and the procedure to be followed when a counter-notice is served;

(b) new requirements for health marks, and the wrapping, packaging and transport of meat prescribed by regulation 11(1) and (2), as read with Schedules 3 and 4;

(c) new forms of health certificate, prescribed by regulation 12(2) as read with Schedules 6 to 10;

(d) the application of Part III in full to meat imported from the Republic of Ireland and the Channel Islands, and the non-application of Part III to meat imported from the Isle of Man;

(e) the inclusion of the meat of rabbits, hares and birds other than poultry among the meats subject to Part III of the regulations.

The provisions referred to in subparagraphs (a), (b), (c) and (d) above are made in implementation of the directives referred to in paragraph 2 above.

STATUTORY INSTRUMENTS

1984 No. 1918

FOOD

FOOD HYGIENE

The Imported Food Regulations 1984

Made - - - - -	*7th December* 1984
Laid before Parliament -	10*th December* 1984
Coming into Operation -	
Regulations 4(7), (8) *and*	
(9) *and* 5 - - - -	1*st July* 1985
Remainder	1*st January* 1985

ARRANGEMENT OF REGULATIONS

PART I

PRELIMINARY

PART II

ALL IMPORTED FOOD

PART III

MEAT AND MEAT PRODUCTS

16. Disposal of meat imported contrary to the regulations.
17. Powers of a justice of the peace.
18. Prohibition on the importation of meat required to be exported.

PART IV

GENERAL

19. Record to be kept of food destroyed.
20. Offences and penalties.
21. Court may include a justice who has examined the food.
22. Examination outside business hours.
23. Disputes as to compensation.
24. Protection for officers.
25. Application of various provisions of Food Act 1984.
26. Revocations.

SCHEDULES

The Minister of Agriculture, Fisheries and Food, the Secretary of State for Social Services and the Secretary of State for Wales, acting jointly, in exercise of the powers conferred by sections 13 and 118 of the Food Act 1984(a) and now vested in them(b), and of all other powers enabling them in that behalf; and the Minister of Agriculture, Fisheries and Food and the Secretary of State, being Ministers designated(c) for the purposes of section 2(2) of the European

(a) 1984 c. 30.
(b) In the case of the Secretary of State for Social Services by virtue of S.I. 1968/1699, and in the case of the Secretary of State for Wales by virtue of S.I. 1978/272.
(c) S.I. 1972/1811.

Communities Act 1972(**a**) in relation to the common agricultural policy of the European Economic Community, in exercise of the powers conferred on them by the said section 2(2), and of all other powers enabling them in that behalf;

hereby make the following regulations, after consultation in accordance with section 118(6) of the said Act of 1984 with such organisations as appear to them to be representative of interests substantially affected by the regulations (in so far as the regulations are made in exercise of the powers conferred by the said sections 13 and 118):—

PART I

PRELIMINARY

Title and commencement

1. These regulations may be cited as the Imported Food Regulations 1984 and shall come into operation as follows:—

(a) regulations 4(7), (8) and (9) and 5 shall come into operation on 1st July 1985, and

(b) this regulation and the remaining provisions of these regulations shall come into operation on 1st January 1985.

Interpretation

2. In these regulations unless the context otherwise requires—

"the Act" means the Food Act 1984;

"appropriate Minister" means, as respects importation into England, the Minister of Agriculture, Fisheries and Food, and as respects importation into Wales, the Secretary of State for Wales;

"authorised officer" means an authorised officer of an enforcing authority, and for the purposes of these regulations has the meaning otherwise assigned to it by Section 73 of the said Act of 1984;

"competent authority" means an authority having power under the laws in force in any country to examine food and to certify as to its fitness for human consumption;

"district" means the district of a local authority, and includes the waters of any customs port abutting on any part of the district so far as such waters are not within a port health district;

"enforcing authority" means the authority responsible for the enforcement and execution of these regulations under regulation 4;

"food" includes drink, chewing gum and other products of a like nature and use, and articles and substances used as ingredients in the preparation of food or drink or of such products, but does not include—

(a) water, live animals or birds,

(b) articles and substances used only as drugs, or

(a) 1972 c. 68; section 2 is subject to Schedule 2 to that Act and is to be read with section 40 of the Criminal Justice Act 1982 (c. 48).

(c) milk, which has the meaning given to it in the Importation of Milk Regulations 1983(a);

"fresh meat" means the flesh or other edible parts of a mammal or bird, which has not been subjected to any treatment or process other than chilling, freezing, vacuum packing or packing in a controlled atmosphere and includes minced chopped or mechanically recovered meat, and meat treated by the addition of seasonings;

"hovercraft" has the meaning assigned to it by section 4(1) of the Hovercraft Act 1968(b);

"importer", in relation to imported food, includes any person who, whether as owner, consignor, consignee, agent or broker, is in possession of the food or in any way entitled to the custody of or control of it;

"master", in relation to a ship, aircraft or hovercraft, includes the officer or any other person for the time being in charge or command of the ship, aircraft or hovercraft;

"officer of Customs and Excise" includes any person acting under the authority of the Commissioners of Customs and Excise.

Presumption as to food commonly used for human consumption

3. For the purposes of these regulations, any food commonly used for human consumption shall, if imported for sale or for use in the preparation of food for sale, be presumed, until the contrary is proved, to have been imported for sale, or, as the case may be, for use in the preparation of food for sale, for human consumption.

Enforcement authorities

4.— (1) Subject to the provisions of this regulation and to such of the provisions of these regulations as prescribe functions to be exercised by officers of Customs and Excise, the authority responsible for the enforcement of these regulations shall be—

(a) in relation to imported food which is in or unloaded in a port health district and—

(i) which is liable to immediate customs examination, the port health authority; or

(ii) where the customs examination is deferred until the food reaches a place of destination in England and Wales, the local authority in whose district the place of destination lies;

(b) in relation to imported food which is unloaded—

(i) elsewhere than in a port health district, or

(a) S.I. 1983/1563.
(b) 1968 c. 59.

(ii) in Scotland or Northern Ireland,

the local authority in whose district the food is deposited for customs examination.

(2) Where immediately prior to the commencement of these regulations the Imported Food Regulations 1968(a) were enforced and executed by a local authority in any part of a port health district, these regulations shall to the same extent be enforced and executed by that authority or by any other authority to whom the functions of the first named authority have been transferred.

(3) Where imported food is unloaded in the district of a port health authority or of a local authority and—

    (a) customs examination of the food has been completed; and

    (b) an authorised officer of such authority nevertheless considers it expedient (having regard to the nature of the container in which the food is imported) that—

        (i) any examination of the food for purposes of these regulations should be deferred until the food reaches a specified place of destination elsewhere in England or Wales, or

        (ii) any examination of the food should take place under Scotland or Northern Ireland regulations when the food reaches a specified place of destination in Scotland or Northern Ireland; and

    (c) the importer gives to the port health authority or local authority of the port or airport of entry an undertaking in writing that the container has been sealed and will not be opened until it reaches the place of destination specified in the undertaking,

the authorised officer shall, by the most expeditious means available, notify the receiving authority that the food (so described as to enable it to be identified) has not, by reason of the matters referred to in sub-paragraph *(b)* hereof, been examined under these regulations at the port or airport of entry and send them a copy of the undertaking referred to in sub-paragraph *(c)* hereof; and where the receiving authority are a local authority within the meaning of these regulations that authority shall thereupon become responsible for the execution and enforcement of these regulations in relation to that food.

(4) Where under any provision corresponding to the last foregoing paragraph contained in Scotland or Northern Ireland regulations a local authority receive notification that imported food which has not been examined under those regulations has been or is being sent to a place of destination in their district, they shall thereupon become responsible for the execution and enforcement of these regulations in relation to that food.

(5) Where imported food is unloaded in a district or port health district, and customs examination is deferred until the food reaches a place of destination elsewhere in the United Kingdom, the local authority or port health authority shall so inform the receiving authority.

(6) In this regulation—

    "Scotland or Northern Ireland regulations" means regulations with

---

(a) S.I. 1968/97, to which there are amendments not relevant to these regulations.

respect to imported food in force in Scotland or Northern Ireland, as the case may be;

"receiving authority" means an authority within the United Kingdom in whose area or district is situated the place of destination of any imported food, being an authority with enforcement functions under these regulations or the Scotland or Northern Ireland regulations, namely—

(a) where that place is in England or Wales, a local authority within the meaning of these regulations;

(b) where that place is in Scotland, a local authority within the meaning of the Food and Drugs (Scotland) Act 1956(a);

(c) where that place is in Northern Ireland, a district council within the meaning of the Local Government Act (Northern Ireland) 1972(b).

(7) On the day on which this paragraph comes into operation paragraphs (1) to (6) of this regulation shall be revoked, and paragraphs (8) and (9) below and regulation 5 shall come into operation.

(8) Subject to the provisions of this regulation and to such provisions of these regulations as prescribe functions to be exercised by officers of Customs and Excise, the authority responsible for the enforcement and execution of these regulations shall be—

(a) in relation to all fresh meat of mammalian origin which is in, or unloaded in—

(i) a port health district, the port health authority, or

(ii) elsewhere than in a port health district, the local authority in whose district the food is or is unloaded;

(b) in relation to imported food other than fresh meat of mammalian origin, which is in, or unloaded in, a port health district and—

(i) which is liable to immediate customs examination, the port health authority; or

(ii) where the customs examination is deferred until the food reaches a place of destination in England and Wales, the local authority in whose district the place of destination lies;

(c) in relation to imported food other than fresh meat of mammalian origin which enters the United Kingdom elsewhere than in a port health district, the local authority in whose district the food is deposited for customs examination;

(d) in relation to imported food which enters the United Kingdom in Scotland or Northern Ireland, the local authority in whose district the food is deposited for customs examination.

(9) Where immediately prior to the commencement of these regulations the Imported Food Regulations 1968 were enforced and executed by a local authority in any part of a port health district, these regulations shall to the same extent be enforced and executed by that authority or by any other authority to whom the functions of the first named authority have been transferred.

(a) 1956 c. 30.
(b) 1972 c. 9. (N.I.).

Deferred examination

5.— (1) *(a)* Subject to the exception in sub-paragraph *(b)* below, paragraphs (2) and (3) shall not apply to any imported food to which Part III applies;

   (b) paragraph (3) of this regulation shall apply to any food to which Part III applies, where examination is deferred under Northern Ireland regulations.

(2) Where imported food is unloaded in the district of a port health authority or of a local authority and—

   (a) customs examination of the food has been completed; and

   (b) an authorised officer nevertheless considers it expedient (having regard to the nature of the container in which the food is imported) that—

      (i) any examination of the food for the purposes of these regulations should be deferred until the food reaches a specified place of destination elsewhere in England or Wales; or

      (ii) any examination of the food should take place under Scotland or Northern Ireland regulations when the food reaches a specified place of destination in Scotland or Northern Ireland; and

   (c) the importer gives to the port health authority or local authority of the port or airport of entry an undertaking in writing that the container has been sealed and will not be opened until it reaches the place of destination specified in the undertaking,

the authorised officer shall, by the most expeditious means available, notify the receiving authority that the food (so described as to enable it to be identified) has not, by reason of the matters referred to in sub-paragraph *(b)* hereof, been examined under these regulations at the port or airport of entry and send them a copy of the undertaking referred to in sub-paragraph *(c)* hereof; and where the receiving authority are a local authority within the meaning of these regulations that authority shall thereupon become responsible for the execution and enforcement of these regulations in relation to that food.

(3) Where under any provision corresponding to the last foregoing paragraph contained in Scotland or Northern Ireland regulations a local authority receive notification that imported food which has not been examined under those regulations has been or is being sent to a place of destination in their district, they shall thereupon become responsible for the execution and enforcement of these regulations in relation to that food.

(4) Where imported food is unloaded in a district or port health district, and customs examination is deferred until the food reaches a place of destination elsewhere in the United Kingdom, the local authority or port health authority shall so inform the receiving authority.

(5) In this regulation—

   "Scotland and Northern Ireland regulations" means regulations with respect to imported food in force in Scotland or Northern Ireland, as the case may be;

   "receiving authority" means an authority within the United Kingdom in whose area or district is situated the place of destination of any imported food, being an authority with enforcement functions under these regulations or the Scotland or Northern Ireland regulations, namely—

(a) where that place is in England or Wales, a local authority within the meaning of section 72 of the Act;

(b) where that place is in Scotland, a local authority within the meaning of the Food and Drugs (Scotland) Act 1956(**a**);

(c) where that place is in Northern Ireland, a district council within the meaning of the Local Government Act (Northern Ireland) 1972(**b**).

PART II

ALL IMPORTED FOOD

Prohibition on importation of unfit food

6.— (1) No person shall import into England and Wales any food intended for sale for human consumption—

(a) which has been rendered injurious to health by means of any operation described in section 1(1) of the Act;

(b) which has been examined by a competent authority and found at the time of examination not to be fit for human consumption;

(c) which is otherwise unfit for human consumption or is unsound or unwholesome; or

(d) in the preparation of which any such food as aforesaid has been used.

(2) In any proceedings for an offence against paragraph (1)*(c)* of this regulation, it shall be a defence for the defendant to prove that at the time when he imported the food he did not know, and could not with reasonable diligence have ascertained, that it was unfit for human consumption or unsound or unwholesome.

Examination of imported food

7.— (1) An authorised officer may at all reasonable times examine any food intended for sale for human consumption which is imported into England and Wales, and where on examination it appears to the authorised officer that any such food is being or has been imported in contravention of regulation 6, he may by notice in writing to the importer and to any other person in possession of the food require that, until the food has been dealt with by a justice of the peace, it shall not, without the consent of the authorised officer, be moved from the place of examination or from any other place specified in the notice.

(2) If on such examination being made it appears to an authorised officer that the food is being or has been imported in contravention of regulation 6, he may deal with it as food falling within section 9(1) of the Act (which relates to the examination and seizure of suspected food); and subsections (2) to (4) of that section shall apply in relation to such food and to regulation 6 as they

---

(**a**) 1956 c. 30.
(**b**) 1972 c. 9. (N.I.).

apply in relation to food seized under that section and to section 8 of the Act (which relates to offences).

(3) If the food is fresh meat, or is a meat product as defined in regulation 12(1), the following further provisions shall apply.

(a) Every notice served under paragraph (1) shall—

(i) specify the grounds upon which it is based, and

(ii) inform the person to whom it is addressed of his right to serve a counter-notice in accordance with subparagraph (d) below, if the food is subject to any of the directives specified in subparagraph (b) below.

(b) The directives referred to in subparagraph (a) are—

Council Directive 64/433/EEC on health problems affecting intra-Community trade in fresh meat(a);

Council Directive 71/118/EEC on health problems affecting trade in fresh poultrymeat(b);

and Council Directive 77/99/EEC on health problems affecting intra-Community trade in meat products(c).

(c) The authorised officer shall after service of the notice provide the appropriate Minister with full details of the food and the reasons for its rejection or condemnation.

(d) A person served with a notice under paragraph (1) above may, within seven days of receipt thereof, serve a counter-notice in writing on the authorised officer, stating that the food is subject to one of the directives specified in subparagraph (b) above, and requiring him, before the food is dealt with by a justice of the peace, to obtain the opinion of an independent veterinary expert, to be nominated by the appropriate Minister, as to the condition of the food and the validity of any matter specified in the notice as a ground on which it is based.

(e) Upon receipt of such a counter-notice the authorised officer shall inform the appropriate Minister of its contents and request the nomination by him of an independent veterinary expert for the said purpose.

(f) If it appears to the appropriate Minister that the food is food which is not subject to any of the directives specified in subparagraph (b) above, he shall so inform the person serving the notice under subparagraph (d), whereupon the food shall be dealt with by a justice of the peace.

(g) If it appears to the appropriate Minister that the food is food which is subject to any of the directives specified in subparagraph (b) above, he shall consult the Commission of the European Economic Community as to the nomination of an appropriate independent veterinary expert, who shall be a national of a member state of the said Community other than the exporting country or the United Kingdom.

(h) The appropriate Minister shall nominate an independent veterinary

(a) O.J. No. L121, 29.7.1964, p.23.
(b) O.J. No. L55, 8.3.1971, p.23.
(c) O.J. No. L26, 31.1.1977, p.85.

expert, acting on the advice of the Commission of the European Economic Community, to determine—

    (i) whether the food is being, or has been, imported in contravention of regulation 6, and

    (ii) the accuracy and relevance of any matter specified under subparagraph *(a)*(i) above as a ground on which the notice served under paragraph (1) above was based.

(i) The independent veterinary expert so nominated shall examine the food and determine the matters referred to in subparagraph *(h)* above, and shall give his written opinion thereon to the authorised officer.

(j) Within seven days of receipt by him of that written opinion the authorised officer—

    (i) shall make it available to the person who, under subparagraph (d) above, has required it to be obtained, and

    (ii) may rescind the notice given by him under paragraph (1) above by serving written notice to that effect on that person.

(k) If, within seven days after receipt by him of that written opinion the authorised officer has not rescinded the notice given by him under paragraph (1) above, the food shall be dealt with by a justice of the peace.

Analysis of samples

8. In any case where under section 78 of the Act (which confers powers of sampling) a sample has been procured for the purposes of these regulations by an authorised officer of a port health authority and submitted for analysis to a public analyst, section 79 of the Act (which relates to the analysis of samples) shall apply as though the sample had been procured within the area of the food and drugs authority which appointed the public analyst to whom it is submitted.

Special examination

9.— (1) Where an authorised officer is of the opinion that a special procedure is necessary for the examination of food, or where at the request of the importer he has recourse to such special procedure, the importer shall provide all such facilities as the authorised officer may reasonably require for the examination of such food.

(2) An authorised officer may by notice in writing to the importer or to any other person in possession of the imported food prohibit or restrict the removal or delivery of the food during any period, not exceeding six days (exclusive of Saturdays, Sundays and public holidays), which may reasonably be required for the examination of the food; and the notice shall specify the period and the procedure required for that examination.

(3) When a notice under paragraph (2) of this regulation has been given to an importer or to any other person in possession of the imported food he may appeal against the notice to a magistrates' court, and the court may direct that the notice be withdrawn or that such shorter period be fixed as appears reasonable in the circumstances.

Consent of officer of Customs and Excise

10. Where the duties of an officer of Customs and Excise with regard to the examination of a cargo or consignment comprising food have not been wholly discharged, no examination of the food shall be made or sample procured for the purposes of these regulations without his consent; but every officer of Customs and Excise shall afford such facilities as the circumstances require for such examination of the food to be made or sample to be taken.

Powers of officer of Customs and Excise

11.— (1) An authorised officer may request an officer of Customs and Excise (either orally or in writing) to prohibit the removal of imported food which has not been cleared from customs charge until it has been examined by an authorised officer, and such a request may be made in relation to a particular consignment of food or in relation to food of any class or description specified in the request. A request made orally under this paragraph shall be confirmed in writing.

(2) Where a request has been made under the last preceding paragraph, the officer of Customs and Excise shall by notice in writing given to the importer or master of the ship, aircraft or hovercraft in which the food is imported require that, until the food has been examined by an authorised officer, it shall not be removed from the place specified in the notice, and he shall at the same time inform the enforcing authority of the effect of the notice.

(3) An authorised officer shall, without undue delay, examine any food in respect of which a notice has been given by an officer of Customs and Excise under this regulation and shall send to that officer a copy of any notice or certificate issued by him in accordance with these regulations, or a statement in writing of any action taken by him under any other provision of these regulations in respect of that food.

(4) Where an officer of Customs and Excise has given notice under paragraph (2) of this regulation forbidding removal of any food, such food shall not, prior to its inspection by an authorised officer, be removed by any person contrary to the terms of the notice except with the written permission of either such officer.

PART III

MEAT AND MEAT PRODUCTS

Interpretation and application of Part III

12.— (1) In this Part—

"bulk lard" means lard or any other rendered mammal or poultry fat transported unpackaged in the tank of a ship, aircraft, hovercraft or road vehicle;

"carcase" means the whole body of a slaughtered animal or bird after bleeding, skinning (except pigs) or plucking, evisceration (including removal of the thick skirt and kidneys) and removal of the limbs at the carpus (except birds) and tarsus, the head, the tail (except birds) and the udder;

"designated person" means a person having power under the laws in force in a country of origin to examine food and to certify as to its fitness for human consumption;

"health mark" means a label, mark, seal, brand, stamp or other voucher;

"meat product" means any product prepared wholly or partly from fresh meat (which has undergone treatment to ensure a certain degree of preservation) but excluding fresh meat and those products specified in Schedule 1;

"Ministers" means the Minister of Agriculture, Fisheries and Food and the Secretary of State for Wales acting jointly;

"offal" means fresh meat other than that of the carcase as defined in this paragraph, whether or not naturally connected to the carcase;

"package" means an outer container of any material into which any fresh meat or meat product is placed, but shall not include a bulk container which may become part of a road vehicle or of a trailer to such a vehicle; and "packaging" shall be construed accordingly;

"pig" includes a boar, sow and hog;

"poultry" means domestic fowls, turkeys, guinea fowls, ducks and geese;

"scraps and trimmings" means small pieces and trimmings being muscular or other tissues or fat weighing less than one hundred grammes, which have been removed from an animal during the preparation of wholesale cuts, the boning, cutting or trimming of fresh meat or the preparation of fresh meat for the retail trade;

"transport" means the movement or conveyance of any fresh meat or meat product from one place to another place;

"wrapping" means the protection of fresh meat or meat product by the use of an initial wrapping of any material or initial container in direct contact with the fresh meat or meat product concerned, and also the initial wrapping material or initial container itself, and "wrapped" shall be construed accordingly.

(2) This Part applies to any fresh meat, or meat product, but does not apply to any article of food specified in Schedule 1.

Requirements as to health marks etc for imported meat

13.— (1) No person shall import into England and Wales for sale for human consumption any fresh meat, meat product or bulk lard unless it bears a health mark which—

(a) shall be so placed as to be legible and clearly visible;

(b) conforms to the requirements of Schedule 3; and

(c) is recognised by the Ministers in accordance with paragraph (3) of this regulation.

(2) No person shall import into England and Wales for sale for human consumption any fresh meat or meat product unless it has been wrapped and packed, and is transported, in accordance with the requirements of Schedule 4.

(3) The Ministers shall recognise a health mark which appears to them to show—

(a) that the fresh meat to which it relates, or the meat from which the meat product to which it relates was prepared, was derived from mammals or birds inspected before and immediately after death, or in the case of mammals or birds killed when wild, was derived from mammals or birds inspected immediately after death only, and passed in accordance with criteria satisfactory to the Ministers; and

(b) that the dressing, packing and other preparation of the fresh meat or meat product was carried out with all necessary precautions for the prevention of danger to health,

by means of a notice published in the London Gazette, and the recognition may be made subject to conditions which shall be specified in the notice; and any such recognition or condition may be varied or revoked by a subsequent notice so published.

(4) In relation to any fresh meat of a description specified in Schedule 5, there shall be included in the notice referred to in paragraph (3) of this regulation a statement to the effect that the recognition conferred by the notice extends to that description of fresh meat; and any such notice which does not contain a statement to that effect shall be deemed not to confer any recognition in respect of any description of meat set out in Schedule 5.

Requirements as to health certificates

14.— (1) No person shall import into England and Wales for sale for human consumption any fresh meat which is derived from domestic bovine animals (including buffalo), swine, sheep, goats, solipeds or poultry, or any meat product (other than a product listed in Schedule 2) in the preparation of which any such fresh meat was used, unless it is accompanied by a health certificate which is valid in accordance with the requirements of paragraph (2) of this regulation.

(2) A health certificate is valid if—

(a) in the case of a certificate which relates to fresh meat which is derived from domestic bovine animals (including buffalo), swine, sheep, goats or solipeds imported from the Channel Islands or from any member state of the European Economic Community it corresponds in form and content to the model in Schedule 6, and it contains the information specified in that model;

(b) in the case of a certificate which relates to fresh meat which is derived from domestic bovine animals (including buffalo), swine, sheep, goats or solipeds imported from any country not being the Channel Islands or a member state of the European Economic Community, it corresponds in form and content to the model in Schedule 7, and it contains the information specified in that model;

(c) in the case of a certificate which relates to meat products imported from the Channel Islands or any country of the European Economic Community, it corresponds in form and content to the model in Schedule 8 and it contains the information specified in that model;

(d) in the case of a certificate which relates to meat products imported from any country not being the Channel Islands or a member state of the European Economic Community, it corresponds in form and content to the model in Schedule 9 and it contains the information specified in that model;

(e) in the case of a certificate which relates to poultry meat, it corresponds in form and content to the model in Schedule 10 and contains the information specified in that model;

(f) it is expressed at least in the English language; and

(g) it is issued by a designated person.

Lost, damaged or defective health marks and certificates

15.— (1) In any case where the importation into England and Wales of any fresh meat or meat product is not permitted by an authorised officer, having regard to the provisions of regulation 13 or 14, he may forthwith notify the appropriate Minister to that effect, and in that case shall furnish him with all relevant information in his possession.

(2) On receipt of such notification and information the appropriate Minister shall make such enquiries as he considers appropriate, and shall communicate the results of his enquiries to the authorised officer.

(3) If, after taking into consideration the results of the appropriate Minister's enquiries, and after consultation with the appropriate Minister, the authorised officer is satisfied that—

(a) the fresh meat or meat product originally came from a country in respect of which a health mark is for the time being recognised by the Ministers pursuant to regulation 13;

(b) the fresh meat or meat from which the meat product was prepared, was derived from mammals or birds, as the case may be, inspected before and immediately after death, or in the case of mammals or birds killed while wild, was derived from mammals or birds inspected immediately after death only, by a designated person and passed in accordance with criteria satisfactory to the Ministers; and

(c) the dressing, packing and other preparation of the fresh meat or meat product were carried out with all necessary precautions for the prevention of danger to health,

and notifies the appropriate Minister in writing to that effect, the provisions of regulations 13 and 14 shall have effect in relation to the fresh meat or meat product as if it had been accompanied by a health mark or certificate or both in compliance with the relevant requirements of those regulations.

Disposal of meat imported contrary to the regulations

16.— (1) If upon examination of any food an authorised officer is of the opinion that it comprises any fresh meat or meat product imported into England and Wales in contravention of the provisions of regulation 13 or 14 or that it comprises any fresh meat or meat product to which regulation 15(1) applies, he shall notify in writing the importer, or the master of the ship, aircraft or hovercraft or the driver of the road vehicle in which the food is so imported that any such meat or meat product must not be removed for any purposes other than its exportation from England and Wales.

(2) Unless the authorised officer proposes to notify the appropriate Minister under regulation 15(1), any notice served under paragraph (1) shall—

(a) specify the grounds upon which it is based;

(b) notify the person to whom it is addressed of his right to serve a counter-notice in accordance with subparagraph (5)(b) below, if the food is subject to any of the directives specified in regulation 7(3)(b); and

(c) notify the person to whom it is addressed that the food may be destroyed or disposed of, so that it cannot be used for human consumption, unless—

(i) within a time specified in the notice, being not less than seven days after receiving the notice, the importer gives a written undertaking to the authorised officer to export the food at his own expense within fourteen days from the date of the undertaking, or to prove in proceedings before a justice of the peace, that the importation or removal of the food into England and Wales is not contrary to regulations 13 or 14;

(ii) within seven days after the written opinion of an independent veterinary expert has been made available to him under paragraph (14) below, the importer gives a written undertaking to the authorised officer in the terms required under subparagraph (c) (i) above; or

(iii) the authorised officer rescinds the notice.

(3) In the case of food in respect of which the authorised officer proposes to notify the appropriate Minister under regulation 15(1), the notice referred to in paragraph (2) above shall be given if, after completion of the enquiries and consultation required under regulation 15(3), the authorised officer fails to notify the appropriate Minister that he is satisfied as to the matters set out in regulation 15(3).

(4) The authorised officer shall, after service of a notice under paragraph (2) above, provide the appropriate Minister with full details of the food and the reasons for its rejection or condemnation.

(5) A person served with a notice under paragraph (2) above, may—

(a) within the time specified in the notice, give an undertaking in writing to the authorised officer—

(i) to export the food to which the notice relates, at his own expense, within fourteen days after the date of the undertaking; or

(ii) to prove in proceedings before a justice of the peace that the importation or removal of the food into England and Wales is not contrary to regulations 13 or 14; or

(b) within seven days after service of the notice, serve a counter-notice in writing upon the authorised officer, stating that the food is food which is subject to one of the directives specified in regulation 7(3)(b), and requiring him to obtain the opinion of an independent veterinary expert, to be nominated by the appropriate Minister, as to the condition of the food and the validity of any matter specified in the notice as a ground on which it is based.

(6) If within the time specified in any notice given under paragraph (2) above, the authorised officer has not received either a counter-notice or such written undertaking as described in the notice, or if within that time, the authorised officer has received an undertaking that the importer will, at his own expense, export the food and the importer has failed to export it within fourteen days after receipt of the undertaking, the authorised officer may supervise its destruction or disposal by such means and in such manner as to prevent it from being used for human consumption.

(7) Where in pursuance of this regulation, the importer has given an undertaking to prove that the importation or removal of the food into England and Wales is not contrary to regulations 13 or 14, the authorised officer shall, within 24 hours after receipt of the undertaking, take steps to obtain the decision of a justice of the peace with respect thereto.

(8) If upon examination of any food in respect of which an officer of Customs and Excise has given a notice under regulation 11, an authorised officer is of the opinion that its importation or removal into England and Wales is not contrary to regulations 13 or 14, he shall give a certificate authorising its removal unless he takes action in respect of it under any other provision of these regulations.

(9) Upon receipt of a counter-notice served under paragraph (5)(b) above, the authorised officer shall inform the appropriate Minister of its contents and request the nomination by him of an independent veterinary expert for the said purpose.

(10) If it appears to the appropriate Minister that the food is food which is not subject to any of the directives specified in regulation 7(3)(b), he shall so inform the person serving the notice under paragraph (5)(b) above, whereupon the importer may give an undertaking in accordance with paragraph (2)(c)(i) above, failing which the authorised officer may take appropriate action under paragraph (6) above.

(11) If it appears to the appropriate Minister that the food is food which is subject to any of the directives specified in regulation 7(3)(b), he shall consult the Commission of the European Economic Community as to the nomination of an appropriate independent veterinary expert, who shall be a national of a member state of the said Community other than the exporting country or the United Kingdom.

(12) The appropriate Minister shall nominate an independent veterinary expert, acting on the advice of the Commission of the European Economic Community to determine—

(a) whether the food is being, or has been, imported in contravention of regulations 13 or 14; and

(b) the accuracy and relevance of any matter specified under paragraph (2)(b) above as a ground on which the notice served under paragraph (2) above was based.

(13) The independent veterinary expert so nominated shall examine the food and determine the matters referred to in paragraph (2)(a) above, and shall give his written opinion thereon to the authorised officer.

(14) Within seven days of receipt by him of the written opinion, the authorised officer—

 (i) shall make it available to the person who, under paragraph (5)*(b)* above, has required it to be obtained, and

 (ii) may rescind the notice given by him under paragraph (2) above by serving written notice to that effect on that person.

(15) If, within seven days after receiving the written opinion, the authorised officer has not rescinded the notice given by him under paragraph (2) above, the importer may give to the authorised officer a written undertaking in accordance with paragraph (2)*(c)*(ii) above, failing which the authorised officer may take appropriate action under paragraph (6) above.

(16) Where, in pursuance of paragraph (1) above, an authorised officer has given a notice forbidding the removal of any food, it shall not be removed by any person contrary to the terms of the notice except with the written permission of the authorised officer.

Powers of a justice of the peace

17.— (1) Where, in pursuance of regulation 16, an application is made to a justice of the peace in respect of any fresh meat or meat product and he is satisfied that the importer has failed to prove that the importation or removal into England and Wales of the fresh meat or meat product was not contrary to the provisions of regulation 13 or 14, he shall condemn the fresh meat or meat product and order it to be destroyed or disposed of under the supervision of an authorised officer by such means and in such manner as to prevent it from being used for human consumption.

(2) Where on such application the justice of the peace is satisifed that the importation or removal into England and Wales of the fresh meat or meat product is not contrary to the provision of regulation 13 or 14 he shall order the rescission of the notice prohibiting its removal.

Prohibition on the importation of meat required to be exported

18. No person shall land in England and Wales any fresh meat or meat product in respect of which a notice has been given under regulation 16(1) or any other regulation to the like effect then in force in any part of the United Kingdom, the Channel Islands or the Isle of Man.

PART IV

GENERAL

Record to be kept of food destroyed

19. Where in pursuance of these regulations any food is destroyed or otherwise disposed of under the supervision of an authorised officer, the enforcing authority, before the destruction or other disposal of the food, shall cause a description of, and such other details as will suffice to identify, the food to be recorded and shall keep the record in their custody for a period of not less than 12 months from the date of destruction or other disposal of the food.

Offences and penalties

20. If any person contravenes or fails to comply with any of the provisions of these regulations, he shall be guilty of an offence and shall be liable:—

   (a) on summary conviction to a fine not exceeding £2,000, and

   (b) on conviction on indictment, to a fine or imprisonment for a term not exceeding two years or both.

Court may include a justice who has examined the food

21. The justice of the peace before whom any food is brought under regulation 7 or 16 may, but need not, be a member of the court before which a person is charged with an offence under regulation 6, 13 or 14, as the case may be, in relation to the food.

Examination outside business hours

22.— (1) The provisions of this regulation shall apply to an enforcing authority responsible under regulation 4 for the enforcement of these regulations at any port or airport which, by virtue of the implementation of Article 5 of Council Directive Number 83/643/EEC(**a**) on the facilitation of physical inspections and administrative formalities in respect of the carriage of goods between Member States, is required to be open.

(2) Where an importer specifically requests an enforcing authority, to which this regulation applies, during the business hours of that authority, and for sound reasons, to carry out for the purposes of these regulations at a specified time outside business hours any examination of food intended for sale for human consumption which is imported into England or Wales from a Member State, the enforcing authority shall arrange for an authorised officer to carry out such examination as he may consider necessary at that time.

(3) An enforcing authority may, in respect of any examination carried out in pursuance of paragraph (2) of this regulation, make such charge (if any) as the authority considers reasonable for that service.

(4) Any charge made by an enforcing authority by virtue of paragraph (3) of this regulation shall be payable by the importer making the request.

(5) Any charge due to an enforcing authority by virtue of this regulation may (without prejudice to any other method of recovery) be recovered summarily as a civil debt.

Disputes as to compensation

23. Any dispute as to compensation arising under these regulations shall be determined, and any compensation awarded thereunder shall be recoverable, in like manner as if the dispute had arisen or the award had been made under the Act, and section 121 of the Act (which relates to disputed compensation) shall apply accordingly.

(**a**) O.J. No. L359, 22.12.1983, p.8.

Protection for officers

24. Section 128 of the Act (which relates to protection for local government officers acting in good faith) shall have effect for the purposes of these regulations as if references therein to that Act were references to these regulations.

Application of various provisions of Food Act 1984

25.— (1) Subject to paragraph (2) of this regulation, the following provisions of the Act shall apply for the purposes of these regulations as if references therein to proceedings, or a prosecution, under or taken or brought under the Act included references to proceedings, or a prosecution, as the case may be, taken or brought for an offence under these regulations:—

(a) section 95(5) and (6) (which relates to prosecutions);

(b) section 97(1), (2) and (3) (which relates to evidence of analysis);

(c) section 99 (which relates to the power of a court to require analysis by the Government Chemist);

(d) section 100(1) and (2) (which relates to a contravention due to some person other than the person charged);

(e) section 102(2) (which relates to the conditions under which a warranty may be pleaded as a defence);

(f) section 103 (which relates to offences in relation to warranties and certificates of analysis).

(2) Section 99 of the Act shall apply for the purposes of these regulations as if the reference therein to section 95(6) of the Act included a reference to that subsection as applied by paragraph (1) of this regulation.

Revocations

26. The regulations specified in Schedule 12 are hereby revoked.

In Witness whereof the Official Seal of the Minister of Agriculture, Fisheries and Food is hereunto affixed on 26th November 1984.

(L.S.)

Michael Jopling,
Minister of Agriculture, Fisheries and Food.

Norman Fowler,
7th December 1984.   Secretary of State for Social Services.

Nicholas Edwards,
26th November 1984.   Secretary of State for Wales.

SCHEDULE 1   Regulation 12(1) and (2)

ARTICLES OF FOOD TO WHICH PART III

DOES NOT APPLY

Vitamin concentrates containing meat.

Pharmaceutical products containing meat.

Gelatine.

Rennet.

Meat products, of which meat is not a principal ingredient and which do not contain fragments of meat.

SCHEDULE 2   Regulation 14(1)

MEAT PRODUCTS WHICH ARE EXEMPT FROM

THE REQUIREMENTS OF REGULATION 14

1. Meat extracts, meat consommé and stock, meat sauces and similar products not containing fragments of meat;

2. Whole, broken or crushed bones, meat peptones, meat powder, pork-rind powder, blood plasma, dried blood, dried blood plasma, cellular proteins, bone extracts and similar products;

3. Fats melted down from animal tissues;

4. Stomachs, bladders and intestines, cleaned and bleached, salted or dried;

5. Products containing fragments of meat, but which contain a quantity of meat or meat product not exceeding ten per cent of the total weight of the final product ready for use, after preparation in accordance with the instructions for use issued by the manufacturer.

SCHEDULE 3   Regulation 13(1)

REQUIREMENTS AS TO HEALTH MARKS

FOR IMPORTED MEAT

1. The meat of all solipeds, ruminating animals and swine, and venison shall bear a health mark as specified below.

    (a) A health mark shall before importation have been applied to the meat on all carcases, half-carcases, quarter-carcases and half-carcases cut into no more than three pieces and to livers. The health mark shall have been applied either by hot branding or stamping with marking ink, and shall have been applied in the following places:

        (i) the external surface of the thighs, loins, back, breast and shoulder of each carcase weighing more than sixty-five kilograms;

and

(ii) the external surface of the thighs and on the shoulders of all other carcases.

(b) Livers of bovine animals, swine and solipeds shall bear a health mark which has been applied by hot-branding.

(c) If meat has been wrapped and packaged in accordance with Schedule 4, the packaging shall bear a health mark; in addition such meat may also bear a health mark.

(d) Cuts of meat and offal, other than livers, which have not been wrapped or packaged, shall bear a health mark which has been applied by hot branding or by a stamping with marking ink.

(e) Meat including pieces weighing less than 100 grammes, shall be wrapped and packaged and a health mark shall be borne on both the wrapping and packaging.

(f) Portions of meat wrapped for direct retail sale shall bear a health mark on both the wrapping and packaging.

2. Poultry meat shall bear a health mark in the manner following:—

(a) large packages containing poultry carcases which may be consigned from a poultry slaughterhouse to either:

(i) a poultry cutting plant for cutting the carcases,

or,

(ii) restaurants, canteens, institutions or similar outlets for direct supply to a final consumer after preparation of the poultry meat by a process involving the application of heat,

or similar packages of poultry carcases which may be consigned from a poultry cutting plant to a meat products plant for treatment, shall bear a health mark and also a label in the form which is described in Schedule 11;

(b) individual carcases shall bear a health mark on the wrapping or on the carcase in such a manner that it is clearly visible under the wrapping, and also on any packaging;

(c) large packages containing cuts of poultry meat and offal which may be consigned from a poultry slaughterhouse or a poultry cutting plant to a meat products establishment for treatment shall bear a health mark and also a label in the form which is described in Schedule 11;

(d) the wrapping and packaging of individual cuts of poultry meat and offal shall bear a health mark.

3. Fresh meat, other than that to which paragraph 1 or paragraph 2 applies, shall bear a health mark which shall have been applied:

(a) either to the meat or to the wrapping thereof,

and

(b) to any packaging thereof.

4. Meat products shall bear a health mark which shall have been applied:

(a) either to the meat product or to the wrapping thereof

and

(b) to any packaging thereof.

5. Bulk lard shall be presumed to bear a health mark in the following circumstances:—

(a) a health mark shall accompany any bulk lard which is transported in any ship, aircraft, hovercraft or road vehicle;

(b) the health mark shall indicate the position of any tank containing lard, to which it may relate, in any ship, aircraft or hovercraft in which such lard is transported;

(c) the health mark shall state the quantity of lard carried in any tank containing such lard;

and

(d) a health mark shall contain a certificate to the effect that any tank, pipe and pump which may have been used for the loading of such lard into the tank had been inspected and found to be clean before the loading of the lard into the tank.

6. In all cases where a health mark has been applied to packaging, or is printed on packaging, it shall have been applied or printed in such a manner so that the health mark shall be destroyed when the package is opened, unless the packaging is not capable of being used again as packaging.

SCHEDULE 4   Regulation 13(2)

REQUIREMENTS AS TO WRAPPING,

PACKING AND TRANSPORT OF

IMPORTED MEAT

1. The wrapping of fresh meat or meat products shall comply with the following conditions:—

(a) it shall be transparent and colourless, unless it fulfils, at the same time, the protective requirements of packaging;

(b) it shall not alter the organoleptic characteristics of the meat;

(c) it shall not be capable of transmitting to the meat any substances harmful to human health;

(d) it shall not be used again for wrapping meat, but earthenware containers for meat products and wrappings which fulfil the protective requirements of packaging may be used again after cleaning and disinfection.

2. Poultry carcases, parts of poultry or poultry offal shall be suitably enclosed in wrapping;

3. The packaging of fresh meat or meat products shall comply with the following conditions:—

(a) it shall be strong enough to ensure the effective protection of the meat during transportation and handling;

(b) it shall not contain fresh meat of more than one species of animal;

(c) it shall not be used again for a similar purpose, unless it is made of impervious and corrosion-resistant materials, which are easy to clean, and it has first been cleansed and disinfected.

4. Fresh meat and meat products shall be transported in sealed means of transport, designed and equipped in such a manner so that the following temperatures for the meat are maintained during the course of transport:—

(a) for carcases and cuts (excluding rabbit meat, hare meat and poultry meat) —not higher than + 7°C (chilled)

—not higher than − 12°C (frozen)

(b) for offals (excluding rabbit offals, hare offals and poultry offals) —not higher than + 3°C

(c) for rabbit meat, hare meat, poultry meat, rabbit offals, hare offals and poultry offals —not higher than + 4°C

(d) for meat products —temperature as specified on the label (when appropriate)

5. Fresh meat shall not be transported in a vehicle or container which is not clean or has not been disinfected before use. Vehicles or containers used for this purpose shall not show any evidence of having been used for the transport of live animals or birds.

6. Fresh meat and meat products shall not be transported in a vehicle or container with any other products likely to contaminate or to affect the hygiene of the meat, unless appropriate precautions are taken to prevent such an occurrence.

Regulation 13(4) SCHEDULE 5

MEAT OR POULTRY MEAT IN RESPECT OF WHICH SPECIFIC

RECOGNITION IS REQUIRED

1. Fresh meat comprising, or forming part of, the head of any animal or bird.

2. Any part of a carcase which has been chopped or minced, with or without the addition of any spices, cereal products, salt, flavouring, vegetables or other ingredient.

3. Scraps and trimmings.

4. Boneless veal appearing to an authorised officer to be from calves less than three months old.

SCHEDULE 6   Regulation 14(2)(*a*)

HEALTH CERTIFICATE

for fresh meat for consignment to a Member State (1) of the EEC

No (2) ....

Exporting country ....

Ministry ....

Department ....

Ref. ....
(Optional)

I. Identification of meat
    Meat of ....
(Animal species)

     Nature of cuts ....

     Nature of packaging ....

     Number of cuts or packages ....

     Month(s) and year(s) when frozen ....

     Net weight ....

II. Origin of meat
    Address(es) and veterinary approval number(s) of the approved slaughterhouse(s)

    ....

    Address(es) and veterinary approval number(s) of the approved cutting plant(s)

    ....

    Address(es) and veterinary approval number(s) of the approved store(s)

    ....

III. Destination of meat
     The meat will be seen from ....
(Place of loading)

            to ....
(Country and place of destination)
     by the following means of transport (3) ....

     Name and address of consignor ....

     ....

     Name and address of consignee ....

IV. Health attestation
     'I, the undersigned official veterinarian, certify that the meat described above was
     obtained under the conditions governing production and control laid down in

Directive 64/443/EEC on health problems affecting intra-Community trade in fresh meat and that it is, therefore, considered as such to be fit for human consumption.'

Done at.. on..

....
(Signature of the official veterinarian)

---

(1) Fresh meat: in accordance with the Directive referred to in IV of this certificate, this means all parts fit for human consumption from domestic bovine animals, swine, sheep and goats and solipeds which have not undergone any preserving process; however, chilled and frozen meat shall be considered to be fresh meat.
(2) Optional.
(3) In the case of rail trucks and lorries, state the registration number, in the case of aircraft the flight number, and in the case of boats the name, and where necessary the number of the container.

Regulation 14(2)(*b*)   SCHEDULE 7

PUBLIC HEALTH CERTIFICATE

for fresh meat (1) intended for ....(Name of EEC Member State)

No ....(2)

Exporting country...

Ministry ....

Department..

Ref. ....
(Optional)

I. Identification of meat:
   Meat of..
(Animal species)

Nature of cuts ....

Nature of packaging..

Number of cuts or packages ....

Month(s) and year(s) when frozen...

Net weight ....

II. Origin of meat:
   Address(es) and veterinary approval number(s) of the approved slaughterhouse(s)

....

Address(es) and veterinary approval number(s) of the approved cutting plant(s)

....

Address(es) and veterinary approval number(s) of the approved store(s)
....

III. Destination of meat:
The meat will be sent from: ....
(Place of loading)
to: ....
(Country and place of destination)
by the following means of transport (3) ....

Name and address of consignor...

....

Name and address of consignee...

....

IV. Health attestation
I, the undersigned, official veterinarian, certify that:
a) — the meat described above (4),
— the label affixed to the packages of meat described above (4), bear(s)(4) a
mark to the effect that the meat comes wholly from animals slaughtered in
slaughterhouses approved for exporting to the country of destination;
b) the meat was obtained under the conditions governing production and
control contained in Council Directive 72/462/EEC and that it is therefore
considered as such to be fit for human consumption;
c) the meat has been cut in an approved cutting plant (4);
d) the meat has/has not been subject to an examination for trichinosis or,
where Article 3 of Directive 77/96/EEC applies, has undergone cold
treatment;
e) the means of transport and the loading conditions of meat of this
consignment meet the hygiene requirements laid down in respect of export
to the country of destination.

Done at .... on ....

....
(Signature of the official veterinarian)

_____

(1) Fresh meat within the meaning of Article 2(b) of Directive 64/433/EEC.
(2) Optional.
(3) For railway wagons or goods vehicles the registration number should be given, for aircraft the
flight number and for ships the name.
(4) Delete as appropriate.

SCHEDULE 8   Regulation 14(2)(c)

HEALTH CERTIFICATE FOR MEAT PRODUCTS(1) INTENDED FOR CONSIGNMENT

TO A MEMBER STATE OF THE EEC

No (2).............

Exporting country: ....

Ministry: ....

Department concerned: ....

Ref. (2)...

I. Identification of meat products
   Products manufactured with meat from:...
                         (Animal species)

   Nature of products (3): ....

   Nature of packaging: ....

   Number of individual items or of packages:..

   Storage and transport temperature (4): ....

   Storage life (4): ....

   Net weight:...

II. Meat products from
   Address(es) and veterinary approval number(s) of approved processing establish-

   ment(s):...

   ....

III. Destination of meat products
    The meat products will be seen from: ....
                         (Place of loading)

    to: ....

    by the following means of transport (5): ....

    Name and address of consignor: ....

    ....

    Name and address of consignee: ....

    ....

IV. Health attestation
    'I, the undersigned, certify that:
    (a)   the meat products described above were manufactured from fresh meat or
           meat products under conditions that comply with the standards laid down in
           Directive 77/99/EEC(6):
    (b)   the said meat products, their wrappings or packaging, bear a mark proving
           that they have all come from approved establishments (6):
    (c)   the fresh pigmeat used in the manufacture of the meat products has/has not
           been(6) subjected to a trichinae detection test;
    (d)   the transport vehicles and equipment and the loading conditions of this
           consignment comply with the hygiene requirements laid down in Directive
           77/99/EEC.

           Done at... on ....

                                        (Signature)
           Stamp   (Name in capital letters)

(1) Under Article 2 of Directive 77/99/EEC.
(2) Optional.
(3) Possible indication of ionizing radiation for medical reasons.
(4) Where an indication is given in accordance with Article 4 of Directive 77/99/EEC.

(5) Indicate the registration number (railway, wagons and trucks); the flight number
(aircraft) or the name (ship).
(6) Delete as appropriate.

SCHEDULE 9   Regulation 14(2)(*d*)

HEALTH CERTIFICATE FOR MEAT PRODUCTS INTENDED FOR CONSIGNMENT

TO THE UNITED KINGDOM

No. (1)..............

Exporting country:...

Ministry:..

Department concerned ....

Ref.(1):...

I. Identification of meat products
Products manufactured with meat from: ....
(Animal species)

Nature of products (2):...

Nature of packaging: ....

Number of individual items or of packages:...

Storage and transport temperature (3):...

Net weight:..

II. Meat products from
Address(es) and veterinary approval number(s) of approved processing

establishment(s):...

....

III. Destination of meat products
The meat products will be seen from: ....
(Place of loading)
by the following means of transport (4): ....

Name and address of consignor: ....

....

Name and address of consignee: ....

....

IV. Health attestation
'I, the undersigned certify that:
(a) the meat products described above were manufactured from fresh meat or
meat products under conditions that comply with the standards laid down in
the Explanatory Memorandum on the Importation of Meat Products into
the United Kingdom;

(b)   the said meat products, their wrappings or packaging, bear a mark proving that they have all come from approved establishments;

(c)   the fresh pigmeat used in the manufacture of the meat products has/has not been(5) subject to a trichinae detection test;

(d)   the transport vehicles and equipment and the loading conditions of this consignment comply with the hygiene requirements laid down in the Explanatory Memorandum on the Importation of Meat Products into the United Kingdom.

Done at.. on ....

(Signature)
Stamp   (Name in capital letters)

(1) Optional.
(2) Possible indication of ionizing radiation for medical reasons.
(3) Where an indication is given in accordance with Section E, paragraph 23 of the Explanatory Memorandum on the Importation of Meat Products into the United Kingdom.
(4) Indicate the registration number (railway, wagons and trucks); the flight number (aircraft) or the name (ship).
(5) Delete as appropriate.

Regulation 14(2)(e)   **SCHEDULE 10**

HEALTH CERTIFICATE

for fresh poultrymeat (1) intended for consignment to a Member State of the EEC

No.(2) ....

Exporting country...

Ministry ....

Competent service ....

Ref.(2)..

I. Identification of meat
Meat of...
(animal species)

Nature of cuts ....

Nature of packaging..

Number of packages ....

Net weight ....

II. Origin of meat
Address(es) and veterinary approval number(s) of the slaugherhouse(s) (4)

....

Address(es) and veterinary approval number(s) of the approved cutting

premises (4)..

....

III. Destination of meat
    The meat will be sent

from...
                         (place of loading)

to ....
          (Country and place of destination)

by the following means of transport (3)...

Name and address of consignor...

Name and address of consignee..

IV. Health attestation
    I, the undersigned, offical veterinarian, certify that:
    (a) —the poultry meat described (4)
         — the packaging of the meat described above (4) bears a mark proving that
         — the meat comes from animals slaughteered in approved slaughterhouses (4);
         — the meat was cut in approved cutting premises (4);
    (b)   this meat has been passed as fit for human consumption following a
          veterinary inspection carried out in accordance with the Council Directive
          of 15 February 1971 on health problems affecting trade in fresh poultry
          meat;
    (c)   the transport vehicles or containers and the loading conditions of this
          consignment meet the hygiene requirements laid down in that Directive.

    Done at.. on ....

    (...)
                   (Signature of official veterinarian)
(1) Fresh poultry meat: fresh meat from the following species—live domestic hens, turkeys, guinea fowls, ducks and geese which have not been treated to ensure their preservation; however, poultry meat which has been chilled or frozen shall be considered to be fresh.
(2) Optional.
(3) For railway wagons and lorries the registration number, for aircraft the flight number and for ships the name should be given.
(4) Delete as appropriate.

SCHEDULE 11

LABEL TO BE AFFIXED TO LARGE PACKAGES OF POULTRY MEAT INTENDED FOR
A CERTAIN DESTINATION

INTENDED USE: CUTTING/TREATMENT(1) ADDRESS OF DESTINATION:
(1) Delete as appropriate

Regulation 26 SCHEDULE 12

REVOCATIONS

Column 1 Regulation revoked	Column 2 References
The Imported Food Regulations 1968	S.I. 1968/97
The Imported Food (Amendment) Regulations 1973	S.I. 1973/1351
The Imported Food (Amendment) Regulations 1979	S.I. 1979/1426
The Imported Food (Amendment) Regulations 1981	S.I. 1981/1085

EXPLANATORY NOTE

(This Note is not part of the Regulations.)

1. These regulations, which apply to England and Wales only, contain measures for the protection of public health in relation to imported food. They supersede the Imported Food Regulations 1968 and consolidate them with their amending regulations.

2. Further amendments are made in implementation of:—

(a) Council Directive 64/433/EEC on health problems affecting intra-Community trade in fresh meat (O.J. No. 121, 29.7.64, p. 2012/64), as last amended by the Council Directive 83/90/EEC (O.J. No. L59, 5.3.83, p.10);

(b) Council Directive 71/118/EEC on health problems affecting trade in fresh poultrymeat (O.J. No. L55, 8.3.71, p.23), as last amended by the Council Directive 82/532/EEC (O.J. No. L234, 9.8.82, p.12);

(c) Council Directive 72/462/EEC on health and veterinary inspection problems upon importation of bovine animals and swine and fresh meat from third countries (O.J. No. L302, 31.12.72, p.28), as last amended by the Council Directive 83/91/EEC (O.J. No. L59, 5.3.83, p.34);

(d) Council Directive 77/99/EEC on health problems affecting intra-Community trade in meat products (O.J. No. L26, 31.1.77, p.85), as amended by the Council Directive 80/214/EEC (O.J. No. L47, 21.2.80, p.3); and

(e) Council Directive 83/643/EEC on the facilitation of physical inspections and administrative formalities in respect of the carriage of goods between member states (O.J. No. L359, 22.12.83, p.8).

Details are given in paragraph 7 below.

3. Part I of the regulations contains definitions and specifies the authorities by whom the regulations are to be enforced (regulation 4). Provision is made

for the deferred examination of imported food in certain circumstances (regulation 5).

4. Part II deals with imported food generally, and prohibits the importation of food which is unfit for human consumption, or is unsound or unwholesome (regulation 6). Imported food may be examined by authorised officers of an enforcing authority (regulation 7), and provision is made for the analysis of samples by the public analyst of an authority other than the port authority in whose district they were procured (regulation 8), special procedures for the examination of food (regulation 9) and the co-operation of authorised officers of enforcing authorities with officers of Customs and Excise (regulation 10 and 11).

5. Part III deals with imported meat and meat products (including lard), which may not be imported for sale for human consumption unless they bear a health mark and are wrapped, packed and transported as specified. Provision is made for the official recognition of health marks (regulation 13). This Part contains requirements as to health certificates for fresh meat and meat products (regulation 14) and provisions as to lost, damaged or defective health marks and certificates (regulation 15), the disposal of meat imported contrary to the regulations (regulations 16 and 18) and the powers of a justice of the peace in respect of meat so imported (regulation 17).

6. Part IV makes general supplementary provisions, including—

    (a) a requirement for records to be kept by enforcing authorities of food destroyed or disposed of in pursuance of the regulations (regulation 19);

    (b) offences and penalties (regulation 20);

    (c) provision that a justice of the peace may be a member of a court before which a person is charged with an offence under the regulations notwithstanding his prior dealings with the food concerned in the offence charged (regulation 21);

    (d) arrangements for the examination of food outside business hours (regulation 22);

    (e) disputes as to compensation (regulation 23);

    (f) protection for authorised officers of enforcing authorities (regulation 24);

    (g) the application for the purposes of the regulations of various provisions of the Food Act 1984; and

    (h) the revocation of the superseded regulations (regulation 26).

7. The amendments made of the superseded regulations comprise—

    (a) the provisions of regulation 4(8) and (9) prescribing enforcement authorities;

    (b) the provisions of regulation 5 permitting the deferment of the examination of food until its arrival at its place of destination;

    (c) the provisions of regulations 7(3) and 16(5) as to the service of notices and counter-notices and the procedure to be followed when a counter-notice is served;

(d) new requirements for health marks, and the wrapping, packaging and transport of meat prescribed by regulation 13(1) and (2), as read with Schedules 3 and 4;

(e) new forms of health certificate, prescribed by regulation 14(2) as read with Schedule 6 to 10;

(f) the application of Part III in full to meat imported from the Republic of Ireland and the Channel Islands, and the non-application of Part III to meat imported from the Isle of Man;

(g) the provisions of regulation 22 as to the examination of food outside business hours;

(h) the inclusion of the meat of rabbits, hares and birds other than poultry among the meats subject to Part III of the regulations.

The provisions referred to in subparagraphs (c), (d), (e), (f) and (g) above are made in implementation of the directives referred to in paragraph 2 above.

STATUTORY INSTRUMENTS

1984 No. 1919

COMPETITION

The Anti-Competitive Practices (Exclusions) (Amendment) Order 1984

Approved by Parliament

Made - - - - -	10*th December* 1984
Laid before Parliament	10*th December* 1984
Coming into Operation	1*st January* 1985

The Secretary of State, in exercise of the powers conferred on him by section 2(3) of the Competition Act 1980**(a)**, and of all other powers enabling him in that behalf, hereby makes the following Order:—

1. This Order may be cited as the Anti-Competitive Practices (Exclusions) (Amendment) Order 1984 and shall come into operation on 1st January 1985.

2. Paragraph 4 of Schedule 1 to the Anti-Competitive Practices (Exclusions) Order 1980**(b)** (which describes certain courses of conduct relating to international carriage by air which are excluded from constituting anti-competitive practices) is amended—

(*a*) by the addition, in subparagraphs (1) and (2), after the words "international carriage by air" of the words "otherwise than on a charter flight"; and

(*b*) by the substitution for subparagraph (3) of the following subparagraph—

"(3) In this paragraph, "air transport undertaking" has the same meaning as in the Air Navigation Order 1980**(c)** and "charter flight" means a flight on which the whole capacity of the aircraft is available for purchase by one or more charterers for his or their own use or for resale.".

Alexander Fletcher,
Parliamentary Under-Secretary of State for Corporate
and Consumer Affairs,
Department of Trade and Industry.

10th December 1984.

(a) 1980 c. 21.   **(b)** S.I. 1980/979.   **(c)** S.I. 1980/1965.

EXPLANATORY NOTE

(*This Note is not part of the Order.*)

This Order amends the exclusion in the Anti-Competitive Practices (Exclusions) Order 1980 for certain courses of conduct relating to international carriage by air. The effect of the amendment is to end the exclusion for international charter flights. Courses of conduct relating to such flights become capable of constituting anti-competitive practices under the Competition Act 1980. They accordingly become subject to investigation and control under that Act.

1984 No. 1920

CIVIL AVIATION

The Civil Aviation (Route Charges for Navigation Services) Regulations 1984

Made - - - -	*9th December* 1984
Laid before Parliament	*10th December* 1984
Coming into Operation	*1st January* 1985

Whereas in pursuance of tariffs approved under the Eurocontrol Convention(a) and under the Multilateral Agreement relating to the Collection of Route Charges concluded at Brussels on 8th September 1970(b) (being international agreements to which the United Kingdom is a party), the Secretary of State for Transport has determined rates of charges, as specified in the following Regulations, payable to the Eurocontrol Organisation in respect of navigation services provided for aircraft in the airspace hereinafter specified:

Now, therefore, the Secretary of State for Transport in exercise of his powers under sections 73 and 74 of the Civil Aviation Act 1982(c) and of all other powers enabling him in that behalf, hereby makes the following Regulations:—

Citation and Operation

1. These Regulations may be cited as the Civil Aviation (Route Charges for Navigation Services) Regulations 1984 and shall come into operation on 1st January 1985.

Revocation

2. The Civil Aviation (Route Charges for Navigation Services) Regulations 1983(d) are hereby revoked.

Interpretation

3.— (1) In these Regulations—

"AIP" in relation to a country other than the United Kingdom means a document in force at the date of the making of these Regulations, entitled

---

(a) Cmnd. 2114.
(b) Cmnd. 4916.
(c) 1982 c. 16; section 73(4) was amended by section 3(2) of the Civil Aviation (Eurocontrol) Act 1983 (c. 11).
(d) S.I. 1983/1797.

"Aeronautical Information Publication" or "AIP" and published by a public authority of that country;

"Authorised person" means any person authorised by the Authority (whether by name or by class or description) either generally or in relation to a particular case or class of cases;

"FIR" means "Flight Information Region";

"Offshore installation" means any installation which is maintained, or is intended to be established, for underwater exploitation or exploration;

a "specified airspace" means the airspace of a FIR described as set forth in columns 1 and 2 of Schedule 1 hereto;

"United Kingdom Air Pilot" means a document so entitled in force at the date of the making of these Regulations and published by the Civil Aviation Authority.

(2) Expressions used in these Regulations shall, unless the context otherwise requires, have the same respective meanings as in the Air Navigation Order 1980(a).

Charge to be paid to Eurocontrol

4.— (1) Subject to the provisions of these Regulations the operator of any aircraft (in whatsoever State it is registered) for which navigation services (not being navigation services provided in connection with the use of an aerodrome) are made available in a specified airspace shall pay to the Organisation, in respect of each flight by that aircraft in that airspace, a charge for those services (hereinafter referred to as "the charge") at the appropriate rate calculated in accordance with Regulation 6 or 7 of these Regulations, whichever shall apply in the circumstances.

(2) If the Organisation is unable, after taking reasonable steps, to ascertain who is the operator, it may give notice to the owner of the aircraft that it will treat him as the operator until he establishes to the reasonable satisfaction of the Organisation that some other person is the operator; and from the time when the notice is given the Organisation shall be entitled, for so long as the owner is unable to establish as aforesaid that some other person is the operator, to treat the owner as if he were the operator, and for that purpose the provisions of these Regulations (other than this paragraph) shall apply to the owner of the aircraft as if he were the operator.

(3) The operator of an aircraft shall not be required to pay any charge to the Organisation under these Regulations in respect of a flight if he has previously paid to the Organisation in respect of that flight a charge of the same or a greater amount under the law of a country specified in Column 1 of Schedule 1 hereto.

Payment

5.— (1) The amount of the charge shall be payable to the Organisation at its principal office in Brussels and shall be paid in United States dollars.

_____

(a) S.I. 1980/1965, to which there are amendments not relevant to these Regulations.

(2) Without prejudice to any existing rule of law relating to the payment, under an order of the Court, of a debt expressed in foreign currency, the equivalent in Sterling of the charge may be recovered in any Court of competent jurisdiction in the United Kingdom.

(3) Nothing in this Regulation shall prevent the Organisation from accepting as a good discharge payment in currencies other than United States dollars or at places other than the principal office of the Organisation.

Calculation of the Charge

6.— (1) Except in the case of flights specified in Regulation 7 of these Regulations, the charge shall be calculated in United States dollars according to the following formula:—

$$r = N \times U$$

where r is the charge for the flight, N is the number of service units relating to that flight and U is the appropriate unit rate specified in column 3 of Schedule 1 hereto in relation to the specified airspace through which the flight is made, increased or decreased as the case may be by the same percentage as the relevant national currency has increased or decreased against the United States dollar as compared with the rate of exchange specified in column 4 of the said Schedule in relation to that airspace.

(2) For the purpose of the preceding paragraph, the number of service units relating to a flight shall be calculated in accordance with the following formula:—

$$N = d \times p$$

where d is the distance factor for the flight in the specified airspace in question and p is the weight factor for the aircraft concerned.

(3) For the purposes of the preceding paragraph—

(a) the distance factor shall be the number of kilometres in the great circle distance between the points specified in paragraph (4) of this Regulation minus 20 kilometres for each landing and take-off in the specified airspace in question, divided by 100 and expressed to two places of decimals, and

(b) the weight factor, subject to the provisions of paragraph (6) of this Regulation, shall be equal to the square root of the quotient obtained by dividing by 50 the number of metric tonnes of the maximum total weight authorised of the aircraft and shall be expressed to two places of decimals.

(4) The points referred to in paragraph (3) of this Regulation are:

(a) the aerodrome of departure within the specified airspace in question or, if there is no such aerodrome, the point specified in paragraph (5) of this Regulation as the standard point of entry into that airspace for the route in question or in the case specified in the proviso to that paragraph, the actual point of entry into that airspace; and

(b) the aerodrome of first destination within the specified airspace in question or, if there is no such aerodrome, the point specified in paragraph (5) of this Regulation as the standard point of exit from that airspace for the route in question or, in the case specified in the proviso to that paragraph, the actual point of exit from that airspace.

(5) The standard points of entry and exit referred to in paragraph (4) of this Regulation are the points, as described in the United Kingdom Air Pilot or relevant AIP as the case may be, where the median line of the appropriate airway or upper Air Traffic Service route so described crosses the boundary of the airspace.

For the purposes of this paragraph, the appropriate airway or route, in the case of a flight made between 1st April and 31st March in any year, shall be:—

(a) the airway or route between the aerodrome of departure and the aerodrome of first destination which appears to the Organisation on 1st April of that year to be the most frequently used such airway or route; or

(b) if the Organisation is unable to ascertain on 1st April of that year which such airway or route is the most frequently used, the shortest such airway or route:

Provided that in the case of a flight in respect of which the aerodrome of departure or the aerodrome of first destination is situated in one of the zones specified in column 1 of Schedule 2 to these Regulations but that aerodrome is not specified in column 2 of the said Schedule the point of entry into or, as the case may be, of exit from the said airspace shall be the actual point where the flight in question crosses the lateral limits of that airspace as described in the United Kingdom Air Pilot or relevant AIP as the case may be.

(6) The weight factor for an aircraft of any type shall be calculated by reference to the maximum total weight authorised of the heaviest aircraft of that type;

Provided that where an operator has indicated to the Organisation, within the period of one year immediately preceding the flight, the composition of the fleet of aircraft of which he disposes and that it includes two or more aircraft which are different versions of the same type of aircraft, the weight factor shall be calculated by reference to the average of the maximum total weight authorised of all his aircraft of that type so indicated to the Organisation.

7. The charge in relation to a flight which enters a specified airspace and in respect of which the aerodrome of departure or the aerodrome of first destination, as the case may be, is specified in column 2 of Schedule 2 hereto and the aerodrome of first destination or the aerodrome of departure, as the case may be, is situated in any one of the zones specified in column 1 of that Schedule shall be calculated in United States dollars according to the following formula:—

$$C = Z \times p$$

where C is the charge payable, Z is the charge specified in column 3 of the said Schedule (appropriate to the maximum total weight authorised of 50 metric tonnes) increased or decreased as the case may be by the same percentage as the relevant national currencies have increased or decreased against the United States dollar as compared with the rate of exchange specified in column 4 of

Schedule 1 hereto in relation to that airspace and p is the weight factor of the aircraft concerned determined in accordance with Regulations 6(3)*(b)* and 6(6) of these Regulations.

8.— (1) For the purposes of Regulations 6 and 7 the rate of exchange of the United States dollar to a national currency shall be the average monthly rate of exchange of the United States dollar to that national currency established by the International Monetary Fund and publication in the International Financial Statistics of the International Monetary Fund for the month preceding the month during which the flight takes place shall be conclusive evidence of that matter; and a document purporting to be the International Financial Statistics published by the International Monetary Fund shall in any proceedings be received in evidence and, unless the contrary is proved, be deemed to be such a document.

(2) In the event that the International Monetary Fund does not publish the International Financial Statistics for the month preceding the month during which the flight takes place, a certificate given by or on behalf of the Treasury stating the average monthly rate of exchange of the United States dollar to a national currency for the month preceding the month during which the flight takes place shall be conclusive evidence of that matter; and a document purporting to be such a certificate shall in any proceedings be received in evidence and, unless the contrary is proved, be deemed to be such a certificate.

Exempt Flights

9. (1) These Regulations shall not apply to the following flights:—

(i) flights by military aircraft;

(ii) flights made for the purposes of search and rescue operations;

(iii) flights by aircraft of which the maximum total weight authorised is 5700 kg or less made entirely in accordance with the Visual Flight Rules in the Rules of the Air and Air Traffic Control Regulations 1981(**a**);

(iv) flights terminating at the aerodrome from which the aircraft has taken off;

(v) flights other than the flights referred to in paragraph (i) of this Regulation made by aircraft which are the property of a State (including customs and police aircraft) and which are not made for commercial purposes;

(vi) flights made exclusively for the purpose of checking or testing equipment used or intended to be used as aids to air navigation;

(vii) flights made exclusively for the purpose of instruction or testing of flight crew;

(viii) flights made exclusively for the purpose of enabling an aircraft to qualify for the issue or renewal of a Certificate of Airworthiness or of the validation thereof or the approval of a modification of the aircraft,

---

(**a**) S.I. 1981/34, to which there are amendments not relevant to these Regulations.

after an application has been made for such issue, renewal, validation or approval as the case may be;

(ix) flights made by aircraft of which the maximum total weight authorised is less than two metric tonnes;

(x) flights made by helicopters between any point in the United Kingdom and an offshore installation within the area bounded by straight lines joining successively the following points—
62°00′N04°00′W; 62°00′N04°00′E; 56°00′N04°00′E; 56°00′N01°00′W; 57°40′N01°00′W; 57°40′N04°00′W; 62°00′N04°00′W;

(xi) flights between points within the specified airspace of Austria;

(xii) flights between points within the specified airspace of France.

Detention and sale of the aircraft for unpaid charges

10. Where default is made in the payment of charges incurred in respect of any aircraft under these Regulations the Organisation may require the Authority to act on behalf of the Organisation in accordance with the provisions of Regulations 11–14 or any of them.

11. Where such a requirement has been made, the Authority or an authorised person may on behalf of the Organisation, subject to the provisions of this and the following Regulations, take such steps as are necessary to detain pending payment, either,

(a) The aircraft in respect of which the charges were incurred (whether or not they were incurred by the person who is the operator of the aircraft at the time when the detention begins); or

(b) any other aircraft of which the person in default is the operator at the time when the detention begins;

and if the charges are not paid within 56 days of the date when the detention begins, the Authority may sell the aircraft on behalf of the Organisation in order to satisfy the charges.

12. The Authority or the authorised person concerned shall not detain, or continue to detain, an aircraft on behalf of the Organisation under these Regulations by reason of any alleged default in the payment of charges payable under these Regulations if the operator of the aircraft or any other person claiming an interest therein—

(a) disputes that the charges, or any of them, are due or, if the aircraft is detained under Regulation 10*(a)* of these Regulations, that the charges in question were incurred in respect of that aircraft; and

(b) gives to the Organisation, pending the determination of the dispute, sufficient security for the payment of the charges which are alleged to be due.

13. The Authority shall not sell an aircraft on behalf of the Organisation under these Regulations without the leave of the court; and the court shall not give leave except on proof that a sum is due to the Organisation for charges under these Regulations, that default has been made in the payment thereof and that the aircraft which the Authority seeks leave to sell on behalf of the Organisation is liable to sale under these Regulations by reason of the default.

14. The Authority shall, before applying to the court for leave to sell an aircraft on behalf of the Organisation under these Regulations, take such steps for bringing the proposed application to the notice of interested persons and for affording them an opportunity of becoming a party to the proceedings as are set forth in Schedule 3 to these Regulations. If such leave is given, the Authority shall secure that the aircraft is sold on behalf of the Organisation for the best price that can reasonably be obtained; but failure to comply with any requirement of this Regulation or of the said Schedule in respect of any sale, while actionable as against the Authority at the suit of any person suffering loss in consequence thereof, shall not, after the sale has taken place, be a ground for impugning its validity.

15. The proceeds of any sale under these Regulations shall be applied as follows, and in the following order, that is to say:—

(a) in payment of any customs duty which is due in consequence of the aircraft having been brought into the United Kingdom;

(b) in payment of the expenses incurred by the Authority in detaining, keeping and selling the aircraft, including its expenses in connection with the application to the court;

(c) in payment of any airport charges incurred in respect of any aircraft which are due from the operator of the aircraft to the person owning or managing the aerodrome at which the aircraft was detained under these Regulations;

(d) in payment of any other charge in respect of the aircraft which is due by virtue of these or any other Regulations under section 73 of the Civil Aviation Act 1982;

and the surplus, if any, shall be paid to or among the person or persons whose interests in the aircraft have been divested by reason of the sale.

16. The power of detention and sale conferred by these Regulations in respect of an aircraft extends to the equipment of the aircraft and any stores for use in connection with its operation (being equipment and stores carried in the aircraft) whether or not the property of the person who is its operator, and references to the aircraft in Regulations 10 to 14 of these Regulations include, except where the context otherwise requires, references to any such equipment and stores.

17. The power of detention conferred by these Regulations in respect of an aircraft extends to any aircraft documents carried in it, and any such documents may, if the aircraft is sold under these Regulations, be transferred by the Authority to the purchaser.

18. The power conferred by these Regulations to detain an aircraft may be exercised on any occasion when the aircraft is on an aerodrome to which section 88 of the Civil Aviation Act 1982 for the time being applies.

19. Nothing in these Regulations shall prejudice any right of the Organisation to recover any charges, or any part thereof, by action.

Nicholas Ridley,
9th December 1984   Secretary of State of Transport.

SCHEDULE 1   Regulations 3(1), 6(1) and 7

SPECIFIED AIRSPACES

(1)	(2)	(3)	(4)
Country	Publication in which FIRS are described	Unit Rate in US $	Established at a Rate of exchange of
Austria	AIP Austria	38.40	1 US $ = 19.990 Sch
Belgium et Luxembourg	AIP Belgique	33.21	1 US $ = 57.697 BF
France	AIP France (France Metropolitaine)	35.01	1 US $ = 8.7396 FF
Germany	AIP Germany	35.70	1 US $ = 2.8471 DM
Federal Republic of Ireland	AIP Ireland	17.14	1 US $ = 0.92818 £1r
Republic of Netherlands	AIP Netherlands	31.63	1 US $ = 3.2135 G
Portugal	AIP Portugal*	26.85	1 US $ = 147.343 Esc
Spain	AIP Espana	Madrid and Barcelona FIRS–22.06 Canaries FIRS–14.50	1 US $ = 161.25 Pts
Switzerland	AIP Switzerland	43.34	1 US $ = 2.4071 SF
United Kingdom	United Kingdom Air Pilot†	43.36	1 US $ = £0.75740

*Excluding Santa Maria FIR.
†Excluding Shanwick FIR.

Regulation 7 ·   SCHEDULE 2

Aerodromes of departure (or of first destination) situated	Aerodromes of first destination (or of departure)	Amount of the charge in US $
(1)	(2)	(3)
ZONE I —between 14°W and 110°W and North of 55°N with the exception of Iceland	Copenhagen	163.47
	Frankfurt	652.66
	London	424.92
	Prestwick	222.44
ZONE II —between 30°W and 110°W and 28°N and 55°N	Amsterdam	425.34
	Athens	556.00
	Belfast	94.76
	Belgrade	722.43
	Bergen-Flesland	253.22
	Berlin-Schonefeld	407.08
	Birmingham	256.90
	Bordeaux	273.22
	Brussels	412.41
	Cairo	565.31
	Casablanca	93.17
	Cologne–Bonn	489.12
	Copenhagen	398.95
	Dakar	1.02
	Dhahran	685.03
	Dublin	92.65
	Dusseldorf	483.25
	Frankfurt	533.16
	Geneva	448.85
	Glasgow	146.63
	Helsinki	269.27
	Jeddah	601.68
	Lagos	126.01
	Las Palmas (Canary Islands)	76.27
	Lisbon	140.69
	Ljubljana	695.27
	London	280.03
	Luxembourg	452.49
	Lyons	422.37
	Madrid	206.89
	Malaga	250.91
	Manchester	220.60
	Marseilles	482.13
	Milan	487.68
	Moscow	298.02
	Munich	606.64
	Newcastle	232.40
	Nice	509.52
	Oslo	293.44
	Paris	337.92
	Pisa	470.62
	Prague	624.37
	Prestwick	146.63
	Rome	546.60
	Santiago	82.73
	Shannon	65.99

SCHEDULE 2 *(continued)*   Regulation 7

Aerodromes of departure (or of first destination) situated	Aerodromes of first destination (or of departure)	Amount of the charge in US $
(1)	(2)	(3)
ZONE II *(continued)*		
	Stuttgart	523.21
	Tel-Aviv	631.43
	Tenerife	49.01
	Venice	611.98
	Vienna	728.84
	Warsaw	337.53
	Zagreb	722.43
	Zurich	514.67
ZONE III —West of 110°W and between 28°N and 55°N	Amsterdam	475.03
	Dusseldorf	559.53
	Frankfurt	589.61
	London	393.66
	Luxembourg	562.65
	Manchester	310.67
	Paris	501.03
	Prestwick	212.90
	Shannon	62.05
ZONE IV —West of 30°W and between the equator and 28°N	Amsterdam	407.01
	Berlin—Schonefeld	416.53
	Bordeaux	269.36
	Brussels	381.89
	Cologne–Bonn	452.14
	Dusseldorf	462.39
	Frankfurt	476.75
	Las Palmas (Canary Islands)	136.01
	Lisbon	139.35
	London	260.08
	Lyons	408.11
	Madrid	251.33
	Marseilles	454.60
	Milan	473.08
	Paris	323.47
	Porto Santo (Madeira)	44.30
	Prague	590.65
	Shannon	70.45
	Tenerife	120.93
	Zurich	469.10

Regulation 14   **SCHEDULE 3**

Steps to be taken to bring proposed application to court to notice of interested persons and afford them an opportunity of becoming a party to the proceedings.

1. The Authority, if it proposes to apply to the court for leave to sell an aircraft on behalf of the Organisation under these Regulations, shall take such of the following steps for bringing the proposed application to the notice of persons whose interests may be affected by the determination of the court thereon and for affording to any such person an opportunity of becoming a party to the proceedings on the application as are applicable to the aircraft:—

(1) At least 21 days before applying to the court, the Authority shall publish—

    (i) in the London Gazette and also if the aircraft is detained in Scotland, in the Edinburgh Gazette, or if it is detained in Northern Ireland, in the Belfast Gazette; and

    (ii) in one or more local newspapers circulating in the locality in which the aircraft is detained

such notice as is prescribed in paragraph 2 of this Schedule, and shall also, unless in that case it is impracticable to do so, serve such a notice, in the manner so prescribed, on each of the following persons:

    (a) the person in whose name the aircraft is registered;

    (b) the person, if any, who appears to the Authority to be the owner of the aircraft;

    (c) any person who appears to the Authority to be a charterer of the aircraft whether or not by demise;

    (d) any person who appears to the Authority to be the operator of the aircraft;

    (e) H. P. Information Ltd., being a company incorporated under the Companies Acts 1948 to 1981;

    (f) any person who is registered as a mortgagee of the aircraft under an Order in Council made under section 86 of the Civil Aviation Act 1982 or who appears to the Authority to be a mortgagee of the aircraft under the law of any country other than the United Kingdom;

    (g) any other person who appears to the Authority to have a proprietary interest in the aircraft.

(2) If any person who has been served with a notice in accordance with sub-paragraph (1) of this paragraph informs the Authority in writing within 14 days of the service of the notice of his desire to become a party to the proceedings the Authority shall make that person a defendant to the application.

Content and service of the notice under paragraph 1.

2.— (1) A notice under paragraph 1 of this Schedule shall—

    (a) state the nationality and registration marks of the aircraft;

    (b) state the type of aircraft;

(c) state that by reason of default in the payment of a sum due to the Organisation for charges imposed by these Regulations, the Authority, on a date which shall be specified in the notice, detained the aircraft under these Regulations and, unless payment of the sum so due is made within a period of 56 days from the date when the detention began, or within 21 days of the date of service of the notice, whichever shall be the later, will apply to the court for leave to sell the aircraft;

(d) invite the person to whom the notice is given to inform the Authority within 14 days of the service of the notice if he wishes to become a party to the proceedings on the application.

(2) A notice under paragraph 1 of this Schedule shall be served—

(a) by delivering it to the person to whom it is to be sent; or

(b) by leaving it at his usual or last known place of business or abode; or

(c) by sending it by post in a prepaid registered letter, or by recorded delivery service, addressed to him at his usual or last known place of business or abode; or

(d) if the person to whom it is to be sent is an incorporated company or body, by delivering it to the secretary, clerk or other appropriate officer of the company or body at their registered or principal office, or sending it by post in a prepaid registered letter, or by the recorded delivery service, addressed to the secretary, clerk or officer of the company or body at that office.

(3) Any notice which is sent by post in accordance with the preceding paragraph to a place outside the United Kingdom shall be sent air mail or by some other equally expeditious means.

EXPLANATORY NOTE
(This Note is not part of the Regulations.)

These Regulations revoke and replace the Civil Aviation (Route Charges for Navigation Services) Regulations 1983.

In addition to some minor and drafting amendments, the following changes of substance are made:—

(1) Provisions for the detention and sale of aircraft for unpaid charges due to the Eurocontrol Organisation are introduced in pursuance of an Agreement between the United Kingdom and the Organisation relating to the collection of route charges signed in Brussels on 8th September 1970 as amended by an agreement contained in an exchange of notes dated 29th November 1984 whereby the Organsation can have recourse to the UK authorities for the recovery of debts owed to the Organisation by the detention of aircraft on its behalf. This will be carried out by the Civil Aviation Authority on behalf of the Organisation.

(2) Revised charges are introduced reflecting forecasts of costs and traffic for 1985 and taking into account the balance of over and under recoveries of revenue as compared with costs experienced by the countries participating in the Eurocontrol charging system in 1983.

The unit rates in United States dollars set out in Schedule 1 and the amount of the charges in United States dollars set out in Schedule 2 are calculated by reference to the costs of provision of en route navigation services in the participating countries in the Eurocontrol charges system, the amount of the traffic using each country's airspace and the relationship of each country's currency to the United States dollar over a period agreed by Ministers of the participating countries. The inter-action of these elements varies in each country. In calculating the revised charges the average of the exchange rates between the United States dollar and the currencies of the participating countries obtaining in the month of July 1984 have been used.

The unit rate in United States dollars for Belgium, France, the Grand Duchy of Luxembourg and Portugal has increased by an average of 7.4%.

The unit rate in United States dollars for Austria, the Federal Republic of Germany, the Republic of Ireland, the Netherlands, Spain and Switzerland has decreased by an average of 22.7%.

The unit rate in United States dollars for the United Kingdom has decreased by 20.5%

The United Kingdom Air Pilot and the foreign Aeronautical Information Publications referred to in the Regulations can be purchased from the Civil Aviation Authority, Greville House, 37 Gratton Road, Cheltenham, Glos. GL50 2BN and can be inspected at major aerodromes in the United Kingdom. The International Financial Statistics published by the International Monetary Fund can be inspected at the Civil Aviation Authority Central Library, CAA House, 45–59 Kingsway, London WC2B 6TE.

STATUTORY INSTRUMENTS

1984 No. 1921

PENSIONS

The Contracting-out (Protection of Pensions) Regulations 1984

Made - - - - -	*7th December* 1984
Laid before Parliament	*11th December* 1984
Coming into Operation	*1st January* 1985

The Secretary of State for Social Services, in exercise of the powers conferred upon him by section 168(1) of, and Schedule 20 to, the Social Security Act 1975**(a)** and sections 41C(7) and 66(3) and (4) of the Social Security Pensions Act 1975**(b)**, and of all other powers enabling him in that behalf, by this instrument, which contains only provisions consequential on Schedule 6 to the Health and Social Security Act 1984**(c)** and regulations made under section 41C of the Social Security Pensions Act 1975, makes the following regulations:—

Citation, commencement and interpretation

1.—(1) These regulations may be cited as the Contracting-out (Protection of Pensions) Regulations 1984 and shall come into operation on 1st January 1985.

(2) In these regulations—

"the Act" means the Social Security Pensions Act 1975 and references to sections are to sections of that Act **(d)**;

"the Board" means the Occupational Pensions Board;

"relevant employment", in relation to a scheme, means any employment with an employer who contributes or is liable to contribute to the resources of the scheme, or with any successor to such an employer;

"scheme" means an occupational pension scheme as defined in section 66(1);

and other expressions have the same meanings as in the Act.

(a) 1975 c. 14. *See* definitions of "prescribe" and "regulations" in Schedule 20. Section 168(1) applies, by virtue of section 66(2) of the Social Security Pensions Act 1975 (c. 60), to the exercise of certain powers conferred by that Act.

(b) 1975 c. 60; section 41C was inserted by section 20 of, and Schedule 6 to, the Health and Social Security Act 1984 (c. 48).

(c) 1984 c. 48.

(d) Sections 41A to 41E were inserted into the Act by section 20 of, and Schedule 6 to, the Health and Social Security Act 1984.

(3) Except so far as the context otherwise requires, any reference in these regulations to a numbered regulation is to the regulation in these regulations bearing that number.

Schemes which provide benefit equal to or larger than short service benefit for certain members before normal pension age
2. In a case where—

(*a*) under the provisions of a scheme a benefit equal to or larger than that which would be required to constitute short service benefit may be paid earlier than at normal pension age to or in respect of a member who has left relevant employment; and

(*b*) such a benefit is payable earlier than at normal pension age to such a member at his request or by his consent,

sections 41A and 41B shall not apply to any pension payable under that scheme to or in respect of that member.

Limitation of increases in certain cases
3.—(1) This regulation applies to cases to which regulation 2 does not apply and in which short service benefit falls to be paid, by virtue of regulation 26 of the Occupational Pension Schemes (Preservation of Benefit) Regulations 1984 **(a)**, at a higher rate than that which would apply apart from that regulation; and the difference between the 2 rates is referred to in this regulation as "the regulation 26 increase".

(2) In a case where the excess mentioned in section 41A(1)(*c*) and (ii) is equal to or less than the regulation 26 increase, section 41A shall not apply.

(3) In a case where the excess mentioned in section 41A(1)(*c*) and (ii) is greater than the regulation 26 increase, section 41A shall be so modified as to have effect as if subsection (1)(ii) of that section referred to the difference between the excess mentioned in subsection (1)(*c*) and the regulation 26 increase.

Widows of persons granted alternatives to short service benefit
4. In a case where a member of a scheme is provided with an alternative to short service benefit by virtue of paragraph 9(2)(*b*) of Schedule 16 to the Social Security Act 1973 **(b)** but his widow is provided with short service benefit, section 41B shall not apply to the pension payable to that widow.

Pensions reduced on attainment of pensionable age by the beneficiary
5. Subject to regulations 2 and 3, in a case where—

(*a*) a scheme makes provision for pensions to be payable to persons before they attain pensionable age;

(*b*) its provision for pensions payable to persons on or after attaining that age is made by virtue of paragraph (*b*), or the words following paragraph (*b*), in section 34(9); and

(*c*) those provisions may have the effect that the pension payable to a particular person is reduced on or after his attainment of pensionable age,

section 41A(1) shall be so modified as to operate without prejudice to those provisions.

(a) S.I. 1984/614.   **(b)** 1973 c. 38.

Schemes with alternative methods of calculation of pensions

6.—(1) Subject to regulations 2 and 3, in a case where a scheme provides for the annual rate of an earner's pension to be whichever is the greater of the following rates, namely—

(*a*) a rate which is related to the earner's average annual salary or final salary (as the case may be) in the manner specified in section 34; and

(*b*) some other rate which is not directly related to the salaries mentioned in section 34,

and the rate referred to in sub-paragraph (*b*) of this paragraph is the greater, section 41A(3) shall be so modified as to require the relevant sum to be ascertained as if the rate referred to in sub-paragraph (*a*) of this paragraph were the annual rate of the earner's pension.

(2) Subject to regulations 2 and 4, in a case where a scheme provides for the annual rate of a widow's pension to be whichever is the greater of the following rates, namely—

(*a*) a rate which is related to the earner's average annual salary or final salary (as the case may be) in the manner specified in sections 36 and 37; and

(*b*) some other rate which is not directly related to the salaries mentioned in sections 36 and 37,

and the rate referred to in sub-paragraph (*b*) of this paragraph is the greater, section 41B(3) shall be so modified as to require the relevant sum to be ascertained as if the rate referred to in sub-paragraph (*a*) of this paragraph were the annual rate of the widow's pension.

Widows' pensions increased during early widowhood

7. Subject to regulations 2 and 4, in a case where, apart from the provisions of section 41B, the weekly rate of the pension of a deceased earner's widow is increased for a period ending not later than the later of the following dates, namely—

(*a*) the date 6 months later than the date of the earner's death; and

(*b*) the date 10 years later than the date on which the earner's pension became payable,

subsection (3) of section 41B shall have effect as if that increase were excluded from the weekly rate referred to in that subsection.

Benefit analogous to short service benefit

8. Subject to regulations 2 and 3, in a case where a scheme contains rules under which there may be provided benefit to which section 41A(3)(*b*) applies but which is not short service benefit, section 41C(3) shall be so modified as to have effect as if the definition of "protected provision" included any provision the inclusion of which in a scheme would be by virtue of one or more of the provisions of Schedule 16 to the Social Security Act 1973 which are mentioned in section 41C(3)(*a*)(i) if that benefit were short service benefit.

Transfers agreed but not implemented before 1*st January* 1985

9. In a case where an enforceable agreement for the transfer from one scheme to another of accrued rights to or the liability for the payment of benefits was entered into before 1st January 1985 (whether or not subject to further agreement about the rates of benefits to be paid to or in respect of individuals) but the transfer becomes or became effective on or after that date, sections 41A(6) (subject to regulations 2 and 3) and 41B(5) (subject to regulations 2 and 4) shall be modified so as to have effect as if the references to any transfer before the commencement of the section included a reference to that transfer.

Meaning of expressions "*member*", "*prospective member*" *and* "*employer*" *in relation to a scheme*

10.—(1) The following provisions of this regulation shall apply for the purposes of section 41E.

(2) Any person is to be regarded as a member of a scheme if he is or has been a person whose service in relevant employment is or was such that at the time it is or was given it either—

(*a*) qualifies or qualified him for benefits under the scheme; or

(*b*) is or was certain so to qualify him subsequently if it continues or continued for a sufficiently long time and the rules of the scheme and the terms of his contract of service remain or remained unaltered during that time,

or if she is the widow of such a person.

(3) There are to be regarded as prospective members of a scheme any persons in relevant employment who are not members but—

(*a*) who, by virtue of the terms of their contracts of service, are able to become members at their own option or the option of any other person; or

(*b*) who, by virtue of the terms of their contracts of service, will become so able, if their service in relevant employment continues for a sufficiently long time and the terms of their contracts of service remain unaltered during that time; or

(*c*) who, by virtue of the rules of the scheme or the terms of their contracts of service, will become members in any event, if their service in relevant employment continues for a sufficiently long time and the rules of the scheme or, as the case may be, the terms of their contracts of service remain unaltered during that time.

(4) Any person, government department, public authority or body of persons who under the Social Security Act 1975**(a)** is, or is to be treated as, the secondary Class 1 contributor shall be treated as the employer of the earner in respect of whom the Class 1 contributions are payable.

(a) 1975 c. 14.

(5) Without prejudice to paragraph (4) of this regulation, there shall be treated as the employer of a self-employed earner to whom a scheme applies any person (other than that self-employed earner), government department, public authority or body of persons who makes or is to make payments towards the resources of that scheme in respect of that self-employed earner (either under actual or contingent legal obligation or in the exercise of a power conferred, or duty imposed, on a Minister of the Crown, government department or any other person, being a power or duty which extends to the disbursement or allocation of public money).

Signed by authority of the Secretary of State for Social Services.

Tony Newton,
Minister of State,
Department of Health and Social Security.

7th December 1984.

EXPLANATORY NOTE

(This Note is not part of the Regulations.)

These regulations are all either made under section 41C of the Social Security Pensions Act 1975 or consequential on Schedule 6 to the Health and Social Security Act 1984, and are made before the expiry of the period of 6 months beginning with the commencement (on 1st January 1985) of that Schedule. Consequently, by virtue of section 22(4)(*d*) of the Health and Social Security Act 1984, the provisions of section 61(2) and (3) of the Social Security Pensions Act 1975 (which require reference to the Occupational Pensions Board of, and a report by the Board on, proposals to make regulations for certain purposes of that Act) do not apply to them.

The regulations make miscellaneous modifications of sections 41A, 41B and 41C (protection of pensions) of the Social Security Pensions Act 1975 and define "member", "prospective member" and "employer" in relation to an occupational pension scheme for the purposes of section 41E. Sections 41A to 41E were inserted into the Social Security Pensions Act 1975 by section 20 of, and Schedule 6 to, the Health and Social Security Act 1984.

The modifications of sections 41A to 41C relate to cases of schemes which provide benefit equal to or larger than short service benefit for certain members before normal pension age; cases where short service benefit is required to be increased in order to compare reasonably with contributions paid; cases where a scheme member is provided with an alternative to short service benefit but his widow is not; cases where an occupational pension is reduced on the beneficiary's attaining pensionable age for the purposes of the state scheme; cases where there are alternative methods of calculation of pensions; cases where a widow's pension is increased during early widowhood; cases where schemes provide benefit analogous to short service benefit for persons who do not qualify, on grounds of age or length of service, for short service benefit; and cases where a transfer of accrued rights from one scheme to another was agreed but not implemented before 1st January 1985.

STATUTORY INSTRUMENTS

1984 No. 1922

AGRICULTURE

HORTICULTURE

The Agriculture and Horticulture Development (Amendment) (No. 2) Regulations 1984

Made - - - -	*6th December* 1984
Laid before Parliament	*11th December* 1984
Coming into Operation	*12th December* 1984

The Minister of Agriculture, Fisheries and Food and the Secretary of State, acting jointly, being Ministers designated for the purposes of section 2(2) of the European Communities Act 1972(a) in relation to the common agricultural policy of the European Economic Community(b), in exercise of the powers conferred upon them by the said section 2(2) and of all other powers enabling them in that behalf, hereby make the following regulations:—

Citation and commencement

1. These regulations may be cited as the Agriculture and Horticulture Development (Amendment) (No. 2) Regulations 1984 and shall come into operation on 12th December 1984.

Saving

2. These regulations shall not apply in relation to—

(*a*) any work, facility or transaction included in an application received by the appropriate Minister before 12th December 1984 for approval of a development plan or for a variation of a development plan approved for the purposes of the Agriculture and Horticulture Development Regulations 1980(c) (hereinafter called "the principal regulations"); or

(*b*) any claim for grant towards expenditure incurred for the purposes of those regulations before that date;

and these regulations shall not affect the operation of the principal regulations in relation to any such work, facility or transaction or claim for grant.

(a) 1972 c. 68.   (b) S.I. 1972/1811.
(c) S.I. 1980/1298; the relevant amending instruments are S.I. 1983/1763, 1984/618.

Amendment of principal regulations

3. The principal regulations shall be further amended in accordance with regulations 4 and 5 of these regulations.

4. In regulation 7(1) thereof (farm development and related grants) there shall be substituted for subparagraph (*a*) the following subparagraph—

"(*a*) has been incurred in respect of any work, facility or transaction of a kind specified in any of paragraphs 1 to 11, 12(i), 12(ii), 12(iii) and 13 to 21 of column 1 of the Schedule or, in relation to Northern Ireland only, paragraph 12(iv) thereof, and".

5. In the Schedule thereto—

(*a*) in paragraph 1(ii) thereof in column 1 there shall be substituted for the words "designed and intended solely for the drying or storage of grain for consumption by livestock" the words "designed and intended for the drying or storage of grain for consumption solely by livestock";

(*b*) in paragraph 7(i) thereof in columns 2, 3 and 4 there shall be substituted for the existing figures the figures "32.5", "50" and "32.5" respectively;

(*c*) in paragraph 8 thereof in column 3 there shall be inserted after the figure "50" the symbol "*" and there shall be inserted at the end of the Schedule the following footnote—

"* In accordance with regulation 8(1) this rate of grant is available only to agricultural businesses situated on severely disadvantaged land.";

(*d*) in paragraph 10(i) and (ii) thereof in column 1 there shall be substituted for the existing descriptions the following descriptions—

"10. (i) Provision, replacement or improvement of hedges, walls and dykes (where the walls and dykes are built of materials traditional in the locality) and associated gates.

(ii) Provision, replacement or improvement of permanent fences, walls and dykes (where the walls and dykes are not built of materials traditional in the locality) and associated gates.";

(*e*) for paragraph 12 thereof there shall be substituted the following paragraph in columns 1, 2, 3 and 4—

"12. (i) Reseeding and regeneration of grassland, laying down of permanent pasture and bracken control, including as part of a complete programme of work the application of lime or fertilizer.	32.5	Nil	Nil
(ii) Reseeding and regeneration of grassland and laying down of permanent pasture; bracken control;	Nil	50	Nil

application of lime or fertilizer (other than normal husbandry applications) for the benefit of grassland.	Nil	50	Nil
(iii) Burning heather or grass or making muirburn or regenerating heather by cutting.	32.5	50	32.5
(iv) In Northern Ireland only, reclamation of land, including the removal of obstructions to cultivation.	32.5	50	32.5"

In Witness whereof the Official Seal of the Minister of Agriculture, Fisheries and Food is hereunto affixed on 6th December 1984.

Michael Jopling,
Minister of Agriculture, Fisheries and
Food.

George Younger,
One of Her Majesty's Principal
Secretaries of State.

6th December 1984.

EXPLANATORY NOTE

(This Note is not part of the Regulations.)

These regulations amend the Agriculture and Horticulture Development Regulations 1980, as amended ("the principal regulations") (implementing Council Directive No. 72/159/EEC (OJ No. L96, 23.4.72, p.1 (OJ/SE 1972 (II) p.324)) on the modernisation of farms and Council Directive No. 75/268/ EEC (OJ No. L128, 19.5.75, p.1) on mountain and hill farming and farming in certain less-favoured areas).

In relation to any work, facility or transaction included in an application for a development plan, or for a variation of such a plan, received on or after 12th December 1984 and to claims for grant towards expenditure incurred on or after that date the regulations—

(*a*) reduce the rates of grant in relation to the provision, replacement or improvement of field drainage (regulations 2 and 5(*b*));

(*b*) introduce revised descriptions in respect of paragraph 1(ii) (main framework of bulk dry stores or silos), paragraphs 10(i) and 10(ii) (hedges, walls, dykes and gates) and paragraphs 12(i), 12(ii), 12(iii) and 12(iv) (grassland) of the Schedule to the principal regulations (regulations 2, 5(*a*), 5(*d*) and 5(*e*)).

In Great Britain grant is no longer available in relation to the clearance and reclamation of land, but in Northern Ireland grant is available for reclamation of land and the removal of other obstructions to cultivation.

The regulations also insert a footnote into the Schedule to the principal regulations to make it clear that the higher rate of grant in respect of roads, paths and other permanent ways, grids, hard standings, fords, bridges, culverts, railway crossings, creeps, piers, jetties or slips is available only to agricultural businesses situated on severely disadvantaged land (regulation 5(*c*)).

STATUTORY INSTRUMENTS

1984 No. 1923

AGRICULTURE

HORTICULTURE

The Agriculture and Horticulture Grant (Variation) (No. 2) Scheme 1984

Made - - - - -	6th December 1984
Laid before Parliament	11th December 1984
Coming into Operation	12th December 1984

The Minister of Agriculture, Fisheries and Food, the Secretary of State for Scotland and the Secretary of State for Wales, acting jointly, in exercise of the powers conferred upon them by sections 28 and 29 of the Agriculture Act 1970(a) and of all other powers enabling them in that behalf, with the approval of the Treasury, hereby make the following scheme:—

Citation and commencement

1. This scheme may be cited as the Agriculture and Horticulture Grant (Variation) (No. 2) Scheme 1984 and shall come into operation on 12th December 1984.

Saving

2. This scheme shall not apply in relation to any claim for grant towards expenditure incurred for the purposes of the Agriculture and Horticulture Grant Scheme 1980(b) (hereinafter called "the principal scheme") before 12th December 1984; and this scheme shall not affect the operation of the principal scheme in relation to any such claim for grant.

Variation of principal scheme

3. The principal scheme shall be further varied in accordance with paragraphs 4 to 8 of this scheme.

(a) 1970 c. 40.
(b) S.I. 1980/1072; the relevant amending instruments are S.I. 1983/1764, 1984/619.

4. In paragraph 3(1) thereof (payment of grant) there shall be substituted for subparagraph (*a*) the following subparagraph—

> "(*a*) has been incurred in respect of any work, facility or transaction of a kind specified in—
>
>> (i) any of paragraphs 1 to 6, 7(i), 7(ii), 8 to 11, 12(i), 12(ii) and 13 to 17 of column 1 of the Schedule;
>>
>> (ii) in relation to Scotland only, paragraph 7(iii) of column 1 of the Schedule;
>>
>> (iii) in relation to Northern Ireland only, paragraph 12(iii) of column 1 of the Schedule;".

5. In paragraph 6(1) thereof (restrictions on payment of grant) there shall be substituted for the amount "52,599 ECU" the amount "40,000 ECU" and there shall be inserted at the end the words "except to the extent that such excess expenditure or excess aggregate expenditure has been incurred in relation to any work, facility or transaction of a kind specified in paragraph 2(ii), 13(ii), 13(iii) or 16(ii) of column 1 of the Schedule and does not exceed the further sum of 39,379 ECU".

6. In paragraph 7(1) thereof (restrictions on payment of grant) there shall be substituted for the words from "exceeds 160,000 ECU" to the end the words "exceeds 80,000 ECU, that Minister shall not pay grant towards so much of that expenditure or, as the case may be, that aggregate as exceeds that figure except to the extent that such excess expenditure or excess aggregate expenditure has been incurred in relation to any work, facility or transaction—

> (i) of a kind specified in paragraph 2(ii) or 16(ii) of column 1 of the Schedule and does not exceed the further sum of 130,000 ECU; or
>
> (ii) of a kind specified in paragraph 13(ii) or 13(iii) of column 1 of the Schedule and does not exceed the further sum of 80,000 ECU.".

7. In paragraph 9(1) thereof (amounts of grant)—

> (*a*) in subparagraph (*a*) there shall be substituted for the words "paragraphs 1 to 5, 7(iii) and 13 to 16" the words "paragraphs 2, 3, 7(iii) and 13 to 16";
>
> (*b*) in subparagraph (*b*) there shall be substituted for the words "paragraphs 6, 7(i), 7(ii) and 8 to 12" the words "paragraphs 1, 4 to 6, 7(i), 7(ii) and 8 to 12";
>
> (*c*) in subparagraph (*b*A)(ii) there shall be substituted for the words "paragraphs 6, 7(i), 7(ii) and 9 to 12" the words "paragraphs 1, 4 to 6, 7(i), 7(ii) and 9 to 12".

8. The Schedule to this scheme shall be substituted for the Schedule to the principal scheme (eligible works, facilities and transactions and rates of grant).

In Witness whereof the Official Seal of the Minister of Agriculture, Fisheries and Food is hereunto affixed on 6th December 1984.

(L.S.)

Michael Jopling,
Minister of Agriculture, Fisheries and Food.

George Younger,
Secretary of State for Scotland.

6th December 1984.

Nicholas Edwards,
Secretary of State for Wales.

6th December 1984.

We approve,

T. Garel-Jones,
Donald Thompson,
Two of the Lords Commissioners
of Her Majesty's Treasury.

6th December 1984.

SCHEDULE   Paragraph 8

CONTAINING NEW SCHEDULE TO THE PRINCIPAL SCHEME

"SCHEDULE

ELIGIBLE WORKS, FACILITIES AND TRANSACTIONS AND RATES OF GRANT

Column 1	Column 2	Column 3	Column 4
Kind of work or facility or transaction	Agricultural business. Rate of grant. Per cent.	Agricultural business in Less-Favoured Area. Rate of grant. Per cent.	Horticultural production business. Rate of grant. Per cent.
1. (i) Provision, replacement, improvement, alteration, enlargement or reconditioning of the main framework of permanent buildings (except living accommodation or such buildings designed and intended for the drying or storage of grain (see paragraph 1(ii) of this Schedule) or for the production of horticultural produce (see paragraph 2(i) of this Schedule)), permanently sited durable structures for cladding with plastic (except such structures designed and intended for the production of horticultural produce (see paragraph 2(i) of this Schedule)), bulk dry stores or silos (except such stores or silos designed and intended for the drying or storage of grain (see paragraph 1(ii) of this Schedule)), yards, loading platforms, ramps or banks.	15	20*	15
(ii) Provision, replacement, improvement, alteration, enlargement or reconditioning of the main framework of permanent buildings, bulk dry stores or silos designed and intended for the drying or storage of grain for consumption solely by livestock kept on the land used in connection with the carrying on of the agricultural business to which the claim for grant relates.	15	20*	Nil

* In accordance with paragraph 9(1) these rates of grant are available only to agricultural businesses with an income per labour unit less than the comparable income.

Column 1	Column 2	Column 3	Column 4
Kind of work or facility or transaction	Agricultural business. Rate of grant. Per cent.	Agricultural business in Less-Favoured Area. Rate of grant. Per cent.	Horticultural production business. Rate of grant. Per cent.
2. (i) Replacement, reconstruction, alteration, reconditioning or other improvement to the main framework of permanent buildings, of glasshouses (except glasshouses of a kind specified in paragraph 2(ii) of this Schedule) or of durable structures for cladding with plastic (except the outer cladding of such structures unless this outer cladding is of adequate durability) where such buildings, glasshouses or structures are designed and intended for production of horticultural produce.	Nil	Nil	15
(ii) Replacement, reconstruction, alteration, reconditioning or other improvement (including the supply and installation of permanent thermal insulation) of heated glasshouses in existence on 1st December 1983 being heated internally by means of permanent installations for the consumption of fuel.	Nil	Nil	37.5
3. Supply and installation of permanent thermal insulation, vapour sealing or gas sealing for the control of temperature or atmosphere in buildings designed and intended for horticultural use.	Nil	Nil	15
4. Provision, replacement or improvement of systems for the disposal of agricultural waste.	15	20*	15
5. Provision, replacement or improvement of facilities for the supply of electricity or gas for agricultural purposes.	15	20*	15

* In accordance with paragraph 9(1) these rates of grant are available only to agricultural businesses with an income per labour unit less than the comparable income.

Column 1	Column 2	Column 3	Column 4
Kind of work or facility or transaction	Agricultural business. Rate of grant. Per cent.	Agricultural business in Less-Favoured Area. Rate of grant. Per cent.	Horticultural production business. Rate of grant. Per cent.
6. Provision, replacement or improvement of facilities for the supply or storage of water for agricultural purposes.	15	30*	15
7. (i) Provision, replacement or improvement of field drainage including under-drainage and ditching but excluding any hedge removal.	15	30*	15
(ii) Works and facilities to prevent the flooding of agricultural land by watercourses.	15	30*	15
(iii) In Scotland only, making, improvement or alteration of the banks or channels of watercourses or other agricultural flood protection works to provide or improve the drainage of agricultural land or to prevent or mitigate the flooding or erosion of agricultural land.	40	50	Nil
8. Provision, replacement or improvement of roads, paths and other permanent ways, grids, hard standings, fords, bridges, culverts, railway crossings, creeps, piers, jetties or slips.	15	20*†	15
9. Provision, replacement or improvement of pens, dips, stells or other facilities designed and intended for use in connection with the gathering, treatment or feeding of livestock or to provide a shelter, in an area removed from other farm buildings, which allows the livestock to move in or out	15	30*	Nil

* In accordance with paragraph 9(1) these rates of grant are available only to agricultural businesses with an income per labour unit less than the comparable income.

† In accordance with paragraph 9(1) this rate of grant is available only to agricultural businesses situated on severely disadvantaged land.

Column 1	Column 2	Column 3	Column 4
Kind of work or facility or transaction	Agricultural business. Rate of grant. Per cent.	Agricultural business in Less-Favoured Area. Rate of grant. Per cent.	Horticultural production business. Rate of grant. Per cent.
without restriction in periods of adverse weather, but not suitable for permanent housing or for in-wintering.			
10. (i) Provision, replacement or improvement of hedges, walls and dykes (where the walls and dykes are built of materials traditional in the locality) and associated gates.	30	60*	30
(ii) Provision, replacement or improvement of permanent fences, walls and dykes (where the walls and dykes are not built of materials traditional in the locality) and associated gates.	15	30*	15
11. Provision, replacement or improvement of shelter belts.	Nil	60*	15
12. (i) Reseeding and regeneration of grassland and laying down of permanent pasture; bracken control; application of lime or fertilizer (other than normal husbandry applications) for the benefit of grassland.	Nil	30*	Nil
(ii) Burning heather or grass or making muirburn or regenerating heather by cutting.	Nil	30*	Nil
(iii) In Northern Ireland only, reclamation of land, including the removal of obstructions to cultivation.	Nil	30*	Nil
13. (i) Orchard grubbing.	15	15	15
(ii) Replacement of apple orchards (other than apple	22.5	22.5	22.5

* In accordance with paragraph 9(1) these rates of grant are available only to agricultural businesses with an income per labour unit less than the comparable income.

Column 1	Column 2	Column 3	Column 4
Kind of work or facility or transaction	Agricultural business. Rate of grant. Per cent.	Agricultural business in Less-Favoured Area. Rate of grant. Per cent.	Horticultural production business. Rate of grant. Per cent.
orchards consisting of trees producing cider apples) which have been grubbed up after 7th November 1982 by an equal or smaller area of apple orchards consisting of— (a) the varieties of apple trees known as Cox's Orange Pippin apple, Bramley's Seedling apple or Spartan apple; (b) any other named varieties of apple trees required for pollination (other than varieties producing cider apples) not exceeding in total one third of the number of trees of the varieties specified in sub-paragraph (a); (c) any species of crab apple tree and any hybrid varieties of crab apple tree required for pollination.			
(iii) Replacement of pear orchards (other than pear orchards consisting of trees producing perry pears) which have been grubbed up after 7th November 1982 by an equal or smaller area of pear orchards consisting of— (a) the varieties of pear trees known as Conference pear or Doyenne du Comice pear; (b) any other named varieties of pear trees required for pollination (other than varieties producing perry pears) not exceeding in total one third of the number of trees of the varieties specified in subparagraph (a).	22.5	22.5	22.5

Column 1	Column 2	Column 3	Column 4
Kind of work or facility or transaction	Agricultural business. Rate of grant. Per cent.	Agricultural business in Less-Favoured Area. Rate of grant. Per cent.	Horticultural production business. Rate of grant. Per cent.
14. Provision, replacement or improvement of stakes and wirework for—			
(i) hop gardens;	15	15	Nil
(ii) cane fruit.	Nil	Nil	15
15. Provision, replacement, improvement, alteration, enlargement or reconditioning of watercress beds.	Nil	Nil	15
16. (i) Plant or equipment designed and intended for the preparation for market of harvested horticultural produce.	Nil	Nil	15
(ii) Provision, installation or replacement of glasshouse heating systems including boilers.	Nil	Nil	15
17. Any work, facility or transaction incidental to the carrying out or provision of any work, facility or transaction specified in any of paragraphs 1 to 16 of this Schedule or necessary or proper in carrying out or providing it or securing the full benefit thereof.	The rate appropriate to that work, facility or transaction in accordance with the provisions of this scheme."		

EXPLANATORY NOTE

(This Note is not part of the Scheme.)

This scheme varies the Agriculture and Horticulture Grant Scheme 1980, as varied, ("the principal scheme") and applies in relation to claims for grant towards expenditure incurred on or after 12th December 1984 (paragraph 2 of the scheme).

The scheme substitutes a new Schedule of eligible works, facilities and transactions and rates of grant for the existing Schedule to the principal scheme (paragraph 8 of the scheme). New rates of grant are specified for most items, and revised descriptions are introduced in respect of paragraph 1(ii) (main framework of bulk dry stores or silos), paragraphs 10(i) and 10(ii) (hedges, walls, dykes and gates) and paragraphs 12(i), 12(ii) and 12(iii) (grassland). In Great Britain grant is no longer available in relation to the clearance and reclamation of land, but in Northern Ireland grant is available for reclamation of land and removal of other obstructions to cultivation. The higher rates of grant in relation to the items specified in paragraphs 1(i) (main framework of permanent buildings and structures not intended for horticultural production), 1(ii), 4 (waste disposal systems) and 5 (facilities for supply of electricity or gas) are available only to agricultural businesses with an income per labour unit less than the comparable income (paragraph 7 of the scheme).

The maximum limit on expenditure in respect of an agricultural business which is eligible for grant over a 2 year period is reduced to 40,000 ECU per labour unit required in carrying on the business, except in relation to works of a kind specified in paragraphs 2(ii) (heated glasshouses), 13(ii), 13(iii) (restructuring of orchards) or 16(ii) (glasshouse heating systems) of the Schedule where the maximum limit is 79,379 ECU per labour unit (paragraph 5 of the scheme).

The maximum limit on expenditure in respect of an agricultural business which is eligible for grant over a 6 year period is reduced to 80,000 ECU, except in relation to works of a kind specified in paragraph 2(ii) or 16(ii) of the Schedule where the limit remains at 210,000 ECU and in respect of works of a kind specified in paragraph 13(ii) or 13(iii) of the Schedule where the limit remains at 160,000 ECU (paragraph 6 of the scheme).

STATUTORY INSTRUMENTS

1984 No. 1924

AGRICULTURE

HORTICULTURE

The Farm and Horticulture Development (Amendment) (No. 2) Regulations 1984

Made - - -	*6th December* 1984
Laid before Parliament	*11th December* 1984
Coming into Operation	*12th December* 1984

The Minister of Agriculture, Fisheries and Food and the Secretary of State, acting jointly, being Ministers designated for the purposes of section 2(2) of the European Communities Act 1972(a) in relation to the common agricultural policy of the European Economic Community(b), in exercise of the powers conferred upon them by the said section 2(2) and of all other powers enabling them in that behalf, hereby make the following regulations:—

Citation and commencement

1. These regulations may be cited as the Farm and Horticulture Development (Amendment) (No. 2) Regulations 1984 and shall come into operation on 12th December 1984.

Saving

2. These regulations shall not apply in relation to—

(a) any work, facility or transaction included in an application received by the appropriate Minister before 12th December 1984 for a variation of a development plan approved for the purposes of the Farm and Horticulture Development Regulations 1981(c) (hereinafter called "the principal regulations"); or

(b) any claim for grant towards expenditure incurred for the purposes of those regulations before that date;

and these regulations shall not affect the operation of the principal regulations in relation to any such work, facility or transaction or claim for grant.

(a) 1972 c.68.   (b) S.I. 1972/1811.
(c) S.I. 1981/1707; the relevant amending instruments are S.I. 1983/1762, 1984/620.

Amendment of principal regulations

3. The principal regulations shall be further amended in accordance with regulations 4 and 5 of these regulations.

4. In regulation 3(1) thereof (farm development grants) there shall be substituted for subparagraph (a) the following subparagraph—

"(*a*) has been or is to be incurred in respect of any work or facility, or part thereof, or transaction of a kind specified in—

   (i) column 1 of Schedule 1;

   (ii) paragraphs 1 to 13, 14(i), 14(ii), 14(iii) and 15 to 28 of column 1 of Schedule 2;

   (iii) in relation to Northern Ireland only, paragraph 14(iv) of column 1 of Schedule 2, and".

5. In Schedule 2 thereto—

(*a*) in paragraph 1(ii) thereof in column 1 there shall be substituted for the words "designed and intended solely for the drying or storage of grain for consumption by livestock" the words "designed and intended for the drying or storage of grain for consumption solely by livestock".

(*b*) in paragraph 7 thereof in columns 2, 3 and 4 there shall be substituted for the existing figures the figures "32.5", "50" and "32.5" respectively;

(*c*) in paragraph 9 thereof in column 3 there shall be inserted after the figure "50" the symbol "*" and there shall be inserted at the end of that Schedule the following footnote—

   "*In accordance with regulation 12(2) this rate of grant is available only to agricultural businesses situated on severely disadvantaged land.";

(*d*) in paragraph 12(i) and (ii) thereof in column 1 there shall be substituted for the existing descriptions the following descriptions—

   "12. (i) Provision, replacement or improvement of hedges, walls and dykes (where the walls and dykes are built of materials traditional in the locality) and associated gates.

   (ii) Provision, replacement or improvement of permanent fences, walls and dykes (where the walls and dykes are not built of materials traditional in the locality) and associated gates.".

(*e*) for paragraph 14 thereof there shall be substituted the following paragraph in columns 1, 2, 3 and 4—

"14 (i) Reseeding and regeneration of grassland, laying down of permanent pasture and bracken control, including as part of a complete programme of work the application of lime or fertilizer.	32.5	Not Applicable	Not Applicable
(ii) Reseeding and regeneration of grassland and laying down of permanent pasture; bracken control; application of lime or fertilizer (other than normal husbandry applications) for the benefit of grassland.	Not Applicable	50	Not Applicable
(iii) Burning heather or grass or making muirburn or regenerating heather by cutting.	32.5	50	32.5
(iv) In Northern Ireland only, reclamation of land, including the removal of obstructions to cultivation.	32.5	50	32.5"

In Witness whereof the Official Seal of the Minister of Agriculture, Fisheries and Food is hereunto affixed on 6th December 1984.

Michael Jopling,
Minister of Agriculture, Fisheries and Food.

George Younger,
One of Her Majesty's Principal
Secretaries of State.

6th December 1984.

EXPLANATORY NOTE

(This Note is not part of the Regulations.)

These regulations amend the Farm and Horticulture Development Regulations 1981, as amended ("the principal regulations") (implementing Council Directive No. 72/159/EEC (OJ No. L96, 23.4.72, p.1 (OJ/SE 1972 (II) p.324)) on the modernisation of farms and Council Directive No. 75/268/EEC (OJ No. L128, 19.5.75, p.1) on mountain and hill farming and farming in certain less-favoured areas).

In relation to any work, facility or transaction included in an application for a variation of an approved development plan received on or after 12th December 1984 and to claims for grant towards expenditure incurred on or after that date the regulations—

(*a*) reduce the rates of grant in relation to the provision, replacement or improvement of field drainage (regulations 2 and 5(b));

(*b*) introduce revised decriptions in respect of paragraph 1(ii) (main framework of bulk dry stores or silos), paragraphs 12(i) and 12(ii) (hedges, walls, dykes and gates) and paragraphs 14(i), 14(ii), 14(iii) and 14(iv) (grassland) of Schedule 2 to the principal regulations (regulations 2, 5(a), 5(d) and 5(e)).

In Great Britain grant is no longer available in relation to the clearance and reclamation of land, but in Northern Ireland grant is available for reclamation of land and the removal of other obstructions to cultivation.

The regulations also insert a footnote into Schedule 2 to the principal regulations to make it clear that the higher rate of grant in respect of roads, paths and other permanent ways, hard standings, fords, bridges, culverts, railway crossings, creeps, piers, jetties or slips is available only to agricultural businesses situated on severely disadvantaged land (regulation 5(c)).

STATUTORY INSTRUMENTS

1984 No. 1925

ROAD TRAFFIC

The Heavy Goods Vehicles (Drivers' Licences) (Amendment) (No. 2) Regulations 1984

Made - - -	*6th December* 1984
Laid before Parliament	*19th December* 1984
Coming into Operation	*10th January* 1985

The Secretary of State for Transport, in exercise of the powers conferred by sections 114(3), 119 and 124 of the Road Traffic Act 1972(**a**), and now vested in him (**b**), and of all other enabling powers, and after consultation with representative organisations in accordance with the provisions of section 199(2) of that Act, hereby makes the following Regulations:—

1. These Regulations shall come into operation on 10th January 1985 and may be cited as the Heavy Goods Vehicles (Drivers' Licences) (Amendment) (No. 2) Regulations 1984.

2. The Heavy Goods Vehicles (Drivers' Licences) Regulations 1977(**c**) shall be further amended in accordance with the following provisions of these Regulations.

3. In Regulation 2 (Interpretation), in paragraph (1), after the definition of "ordinary driving licence" insert the following new definition —

"PSV operator's licence" and "public service vehicle" have the meanings given by section 82(1) of the Public Passenger Vehicles Act 1981(**d**);".

4. In Regulation 4 (which deals with qualifications of applicants) —

(*a*) for sub-paragraph (*b*) substitute the following new sub-paragraphs:—

"(*b*) he shall not at any time since he attained the age of 5 years have had an epileptic attack;

(*bb*) he shall be fit to hold the licence having regard to his health and any disability which he may suffer;

(**a**) 1972 c.20; section 119 was amended by paragraph 10 of Schedule 1 to the Road Traffic (Drivers' Ages and Hours of Work) Act 1976 (c.3).
(**b**) S.I. 1979/571 and 1981/238.
(**c**) S.I. 1977/1309; the relevant amending Instruments are S.I. 1982/429, 1983/1232.
(**d**) 1981 c.14.

(*bbb*) he shall, having regard to his conduct (including conduct in Northern Ireland) as the driver of a motor vehicle, be a fit person to hold such a licence;"; and

(*b*) for sub-paragraph (*d*) substitute the following sub-paragraph:—

"(*d*) in the case of an applicant for a hgv trainee driver's licence he shall be a registered employee of a registered employer and —

(i) if he has not previously held any hgv driver's licence, the licence referred to in sub-paragraph (*c*) above shall not have endorsed on it

— if it is an ordinary driving licence, any penalty points or disqualifications, or

— if it is a Northern Ireland (ordinary) driving licence, any relevant endorsements or,

(ii) in any other case, the licence referred to in sub-paragraph (*c*) above shall not have endorsed on it

— if it is an ordinary driving licence, more than 3 penalty points or any disqualification or,

— if it is a Northern Ireland (ordinary) driving licence, more than one relevant endorsement

so, however, that there shall be disregarded for this purpose any number of penalty points exceeding 3 endorsed on or after 1st November 1982 but before 13th September 1983 in consequence of there having been committed on any occasion a single offence or several offences.".

5. For Regulation 6 (Form of licences) substitute the following Regulation:—

"**6.** A hgv driver's licence shall indicate —

(*a*) whether it is a provisional licence or a full licence,

(*b*) whether it is a hgv trainee driver's licence or a standard hgv driver's licence,

(*c*) whether it is the licence originally granted, or a duplicate licence issued under Regulation 14,

(*d*) the classes of vehicle which the holder of the licence is thereby authorised to drive, and

(*e*) such other particulars as the Secretary of State considers to be appropriate.".

6. In Regulation 9 (Provisional standard licences) add the following paragraph:—

"(5) A person to whom a full standard licence has been issued which states that the holder is entitled to drive vehicles in Class 4 only, vehicles in Class 4A only, or vehicles in both those classes, shall be treated as holding a provisional standard licence to drive vehicles in Class 1, 1A, 2, 2A, 3 and 3A for such time as the full standard licence enures.".

7. In Regulation 10 (HGV trainee drivers' licences) —

(*a*) for paragraphs (1) and (2) substitute the following paragraph:—

"(1) Save as provided in paragraph (8) below, every hgv trainee driver's licence shall be subject to the condition that the holder shall not drive a heavy goods vehicle of any class for which the licence is issued or for which, by virtue of paragraph (3) below, the licence is treated as a provisional licence unless the holder is the registered employee of a registered employer named in the licence and either —

    (*a*) (i) the vehicle is a heavy goods vehicle of a class to which the holder's training agreement applies and which is stated in the licence; and

        (ii) the vehicle is owned by that registered employer or by a registered hgv driver training establishment named in the licence; or

    (*b*) the holder is a part-time member of the armed forces of the Crown and the vehicle is owned by the Secretary of State for Defence and used for naval, military or air force purposes."; and

(*b*) in paragraph (6) delete sub-paragraph (*a*) (i).

8. In Regulation 22 (Production of vehicle for test etc.), add the following new paragraph:—

"(3) Where a person submitting himself for a test provides a vehicle which complies with the requirements specified in paragraph (1) (*a*) above he shall allow to travel in the vehicle (so far as the construction of the vehicle so allows) —

(*a*) the examiner, and

(*b*) any person authorised by the Secretary of State to attend the test for the purpose of supervising it or otherwise.".

9. In Regulation 29 (which deals with exemptions from the requirements to hold a hgv drivers' licence) —

(*a*) in paragraph (1) —

(i) for the words "shall not apply to heavy goods vehicles of the following classes" substitute the words "does not apply in respect of the driving of heavy goods vehicles of any of the following classes";

(ii) for sub-paragraph (*g*) substitute the following sub-paragraph:—

"(*g*) industrial tractors;";

(iii) for sub-paragraph (*h*) substitute the following sub-paragraph:—

"(*h*) agricultural motor vehicles;";

(iv) for sub-paragraph (*l*) substitute the following sub-paragraph:—

"(*l*) public service vehicles;"

(v) in sub-paragraph (*o*) after the word "headquarters" add the words "as defined in the Visiting Forces and International Headquarters (Application of Law) Order 1965(**a**);";

(vi) in sub-paragraph (*r*) for "15 cwt" substitute "2 tons";

(**a**) S.I. 1965/1536.

(vii) for sub-paragraph (*t*) substitute the following sub-paragraph:—

"(*t*) any vehicle (not being an articulated vehicle combination) which —

   (i) has an unladen weight not exceeding 10 tons,

   (ii) is being operated by the holder of a PSV operator's licence,

   (iii) is being driven by a person who is licensed for the purpose of driving the vehicle as a public service vehicle under section 22 of the Public Passenger Vehicles Act 1981, and

   (iv) is being used for the purpose of —

— proceeding to, or returning from, a place where assistance is to be, or has been, given to a disabled public service vehicle, or

— giving assistance to or moving a disabled public service vehicle or moving a wreck which, immediately before it became a wreck, was a public service vehicle;"; and

(*b*) for paragraph (2) substitute the following paragraph:—

"(2) In this Regulation —

"digging machine" has the same meaning as in Schedule 3 to the Vehicles (Excise) Act 1971(**a**);

"agricultural motor vehicle", "engineering plant", "industrial tractor", "track laying" and "works truck" have the same meanings as in Regulation 3(1) of the Motor Vehicles (Construction and Use) Regulations 1978(**b**);

"play equipment for children" includes articles required in connection with the use of such equipment by children; and

"road construction vehicle" and "road construction machinery" have the same meanings as in section 4(2) of the Vehicles (Excise) Act 1971.".

10. In Schedule 2 —

(*a*) delete —

   (i) in column 2 in Class 1, the words "other than a vehicle combination coming within Class 4";

   (ii) in column 2 in Class 1A, the words "other than a vehicle combination coming within Class 4A"; and

   (iii) the last two items; and

(*b*) in column 3 in Class 1 and Class 1A, for the words "3A, 4 and 4A" and "3A and 4A" respectively, substitute the words "and 3A".

11. Schedule 3 (Form of heavy goods vehicle full driver's licence and provisional driver's licence) and Schedule 4 (Form of heavy goods vehicle trainee driver's full licence and provisional licence) are revoked.

Nicholas Ridley,
Secretary of State for Transport.

6th December 1984.

(**a**) 1971 c.10.   (**b**) S.I. 1978/1017; the relevant amending Instrument is S.I. 1984/1809.

EXPLANATORY NOTE

(This Note is not part of the Regulations.)

These Regulations further amend the Heavy Goods Vehicles (Drivers' Licences) Regulations 1977 as follows:—

(1) the expressions "PSV Operator's licence" and "public service vehicle" are defined (Regulation 3);

(2) the provisions about qualifications of applicants are amended so that in assessing whether or not an applicant has the necessary qualifications, experience and knowledge the licensing authority shall have regard to his conduct as the driver of a motor vehicle (Regulation 4(*a*));

(3) the provisions about qualifications for applicants are further amended so that disqualifications relating to ordinary driving licences and Northern Ireland (ordinary) driving licences are to be taken into account and the provisions relating to endorsed penalty points are modified to take account of a gap which occurred between the coming into operation on 1st November 1982 of section 19 of the Transport Act 1982 (c.49) and the coming into operation on 13th September 1983 of consequent amendments to these Regulations (Regulation 4(*b*));

(4) the provisions about the forms of licences are amended so that forms are no longer prescribed but matters to be indicated on licences are prescribed (Regulations 5 and 11);

(5) provision is made to extend the validity of licences granted for defunct Classes 4 and 4A (Regulation 6);

(6) provision is made to facilitate the driving by a part-time member of forces of the Crown of vehicles in a class other than that for which his trainee's licence was issued (Regulation 7);

(7) to the provisions that a person submitting himself for the test shall provide a suitable vehicle there is added a requirement that he shall allow to travel in the vehicle the examiner and any person appointed to attend the test (Regulation 8);

(8) the exemptions from the requirements to hold a hgv driver's licence are amended chiefly to replace obsolete references (Regulation 9); and

(9) two of the classes of vehicle to which a licence may relate are abolished (Regulation 10).

STATUTORY INSTRUMENTS

1984 No. 1926 (S. 151)

LOCAL GOVERNMENT, SCOTLAND

The Local Statutory Provisions (Postponement of Repeal) (Scotland) Order 1984

Made - - - -	*5th December* 1984
Laid before Parliament	*12th December* 1984
Coming into Operation	*31st December* 1984

In exercise of the powers conferred on me by section 225(6)(*b*) of the Local Government (Scotland) Act 1973(**a**) and of all other powers enabling me in that behalf, I hereby make the following Order:—

1. This Order may be cited as the Local Statutory Provisions (Postponement of Repeal) (Scotland) Order 1984 and shall come into operation on 31st December 1984.

2. The date on which all local statutory provisions applying to the whole or any part of the local government areas specified in the Schedule to this Order, so far as they so apply, are to cease to have effect is hereby postponed to 31st December 1985.

New St Andrew's House,
Edinburgh.
5th December 1984.

George Younger,
One of Her Majesty's Principal
Secretaries of State.

SCHEDULE

Grampian Region	City of Dundee District
Lothian Region	City of Edinburgh District
Strathclyde Region	City of Glasgow District
City of Aberdeen District	East Lothian District

(**a**) 1973 c. 65; section 225(6) was amended by section 134(1) of the Civic Government (Scotland) Act 1982 (c. 45).

EXPLANATORY NOTE

(This Note is not part of the Order.)

Section 225(6) of the Local Government (Scotland) Act 1973 provides that all local statutory provisions to which the subsection applies shall cease to have effect at the end of 1984. This Order postpones until the end of 1985 the date on which all local statutory provisions applying to the local government areas or parts thereof listed in the Schedule are to cease to have effect.

STATUTORY INSTRUMENTS

1984 No. 1927

ROAD TRAFFIC

The Motor Vehicles (Type Approval) (Amendment) Regulations 1984

Made - - - -	10*th December* 1984
Laid before Parliament	19*th December* 1984
Coming into Operation	10*th January* 1985

The Secretary of State for Transport, being a Minister designated(a) for the purposes of section 2(2) of the European Communities Act 1972(b) in relation to the regulation of the type, description, construction or equipment of vehicles, and of components of vehicles, and in particular any vehicle type approval scheme, in exercise of the powers conferred on him by the said section 2(2) and of all other enabling powers, hereby makes the following Regulations:—

1. These Regulations shall come into operation on 10th January 1985, and may be cited as the Motor Vehicles (Type Approval) (Amendment) Regulations 1984.

2. The Motor Vehicles (Type Approval) Regulations 1980(c) are hereby amended so that in Part I of Schedule 2—

(a) in item 1, in the entry in column 2, there is added:—

" or 70/157/EEC as amended by 73/350/EEC, 77/212/EEC, 81/334/EEC and 84/372/EEC	3 July 1984	O.J. L196, 26.7.1984, p. 47
or 70/157/EEC as amended by 73/350/EEC, 77/212/EEC, 81/334/EEC, 84/372/EEC and 84/424/EEC	3 September 1984	O.J. L238, 6.9.1984, p. 31";

(a) S.I. 1972/1811.   (b) 1972 c.68.
(c) S.I. 1980/1182, as amended by S.I. 1982/7 and 623.

(*b*) in item 2, in the entry in column 2, there is added:—

" or 70/220/EEC as amended by 74/290/EEC, 77/102/EEC, 78/665/EEC and 83/351/EEC	16 June 1983	O.J. L197, 20.7.1983, p. 1";

(*c*) in item 7, in the entry in column 2(a), there is added "as corrected by corrigenda published in O.J. L329, 25.11.1982, p. 31";

(*d*) in item 18, in the entry in column 2(a), after "76/114/EEC", in both places where it occurs there is inserted "as corrected by corrigenda published in O.J. L329, 25.11.1982, p. 31";

(*e*) in item 20, in column 2, there is added:—

| " or 76/756/EEC as amended by 80/233/EEC, 82/244/EEC and 83/276/EEC | 26 May 1983 | O.J. L151, 9.6.1983, p. 47 |
| or 76/756/EEC as amended by 80/233/EEC, 82/244/EEC, 83/276/EEC and 84/8/EEC as corrected in O.J. L135, 22.5.1984, p. 27 | 14 December 1983 | O.J. L9, 12.1.1984, p. 24"; and |

(*f*) in item 38, in the entry in column 2(a), after "78/932/EEC" there is added "as corrected by corrigenda published in O.J. L329, 15.11.1982, p. 31".

10th December 1984.

Nicholas Ridley,
Secretary of State for Transport.

EXPLANATORY NOTE

(This Note is not part of the Regulations.)

1. These Regulations amend the Motor Vehicles (Type Approval) Regulations 1980 so that—

(1) the type approval requirements relating to the permissible sound level and the exhaust system of motor vehicles are, alternatively to the existing requirements, the requirements of Council Directive 70/157/EEC as amended by Commission Directive 73/350/EEC, Council Directive 77/212/EEC and Commission Directives 81/334/EEC and 84/372/EEC or the requirements of Council Directive 70/157/EEC as so amended and as further amended by Council Directive 84/424/EEC;

(2) the type approval requirements relating to measures to be taken against air pollution by gases from positive ignition engines of motor vehicles are, alternatively to the existing requirements, the requirements of Council Directive 70/220/EEC as amended by Council Directive 74/290/EEC, Commission Directives 77/102/EEC and 78/665/EEC and Council Directive 83/351/EEC;

(3) the type approval requirements relating to the installation of lighting and light signalling devices on motor vehicles and their trailers are, alternatively to the existing requirements, the requirements of Council Directive 76/756/EEC as amended by Commission Directives 80/233/EEC and 82/244/EEC and Council Directive 83/276/EEC or the requirements of Council Directive 76/756/EEC as so amended and as further amended by Commission Directive 84/8/EEC as corrected; and

(4) corrections to the type approval requirements relating to—

　　(a) audible warning devices for motor vehicles,

　　(b) statutory plates and inscriptions for motor vehicles and their trailers and their location and method of attachment, and

　　(c) head restraints of seats of motor vehicles

are incorporated.

2. Copies of the Council Directives and Commission Directives referred to in these Regulations may be obtained from Her Majesty's Stationery Office.

STATUTORY INSTRUMENTS

1984 No. 1932

LANDLORD AND TENANT

The Landlord and Tenant Act 1954 (Appropriate Multiplier) Order 1984

Made - - - -	11*th December* 1984
Laid before Parliament	20*th December* 1984
Coming into Operation	7*th May* 1985

The Secretary of State for the Environment, as respects England, and the Secretary of State for Wales, as respects Wales, in exercise of the powers conferred on them by section 37(8) of the Landlord and Tenant Act 1954(**a**), and of all other powers enabling them in that behalf, hereby make the following Order:—

1. This Order may be cited as the Landlord and Tenant Act 1954 (Appropriate Multiplier) Order 1984 and shall come into operation on 7th May 1985.

2. The appropriate multiplier for the purposes of paragraphs (*a*) and (*b*) of section 37(2)(**b**) of the Landlord and Tenant Act 1954 shall be 3.

3. The previous instrument made in the exercise of the above-mentioned powers and known as the Landlord and Tenant Act 1954 (Appropriate Multiplier) Regulations 1981(**c**) is hereby revoked.

Patrick Jenkin,
Secretary of State for the Environment.

7th December 1984.

Nicholas Edwards,
Secretary of State for Wales.

11th December 1984.

(**a**) 1954 c. 56; section 37(8) was inserted by paragraph 4 of Schedule 33 to the Local Government, Planning and Land Act 1980 (c. 65).
(**b**) Section 37(2) was amended by paragraph 4 of Schedule 33 to the Local Government, Planning and Land Act 1980.
(**c**) S.I. 1981/69.

EXPLANATORY NOTE

(This Note is not part of the Order.)

This Order increases, from 2¼ to 3, the appropriate multiplier to be used in calculating the amount of compensation to which a tenant may be entitled, under Part II of the Landlord and Tenant Act 1954, where an order for a new tenancy is precluded on certain grounds. The amount of compensation is arrived at by multiplying either the rateable value of the holding or twice the rateable value of the holding, as the case may be, by the figure prescribed. The previous multiplier was prescribed by S.I. 1981/69, which is revoked by the Order.

STATUTORY INSTRUMENTS

1984 No. 1933

HIGHWAYS, ENGLAND AND WALES

The Builders' Skips (Markings) Regulations 1984

Made - - - -	11*th December* 1984
Laid before Parliament	20*th December* 1984
Coming into Operation	21*st January* 1985

The Secretary of State for Transport, as regards England, and the Secretary of State for Wales, as regards Wales, in exercise of the powers conferred by section 139(4) of the Highways Act 1980(a), and of all other enabling powers, hereby makes the following Regulations:—

1. These Regulations shall come into operation on 21st January 1985, and may be cited as the Builders' Skips (Markings) Regulations 1984.

2.— (1) In these Regulations, unless the context otherwise requires, a reference to a Regulation or a Schedule followed by a number is a reference to the Regulation or Schedule bearing that number in these Regulations.

(2) In these Regulations a reference to an end of a builder's skip shall, in a case where the skip is placed on a highway sideways, be construed as a reference to a side of the skip.

3. On and after 1st January 1986 each end of every builder's skip any part of which is placed on any part of a highway except a footway or a verge shall be marked with a marking which complies with—

(a) the specifications about design set out in the diagrams and notes in Schedule 1, and

(b) the requirements specified in Schedule 2.

4.— (1) Save as provided in paragraph (2) below, the whole of every marking with which a builder's skip is required by these Regulations to be marked shall be—

(a) clean and efficient, and

(b) clearly visible for a reasonable distance to persons using the highway on which the skip is placed.

(a) 1980 c.66; section 139 of that Act has been amended by section 65 of the Transport Act 1982 (c.49).

(2) The requirement specified in paragraph (1)*(b)* above does not apply in respect of a marking, or part of a marking, on any door of a builder's skip whilst that door is required to be open for the purpose of loading or unloading the skip.

Nicholas Ridley,
Secretary of State for Transport.

9th December 1984.

Nicholas Edwards,
Secretary of State for Wales.

11th December 1984.

(Regulation 3)   SCHEDULE 1

Specifications about design

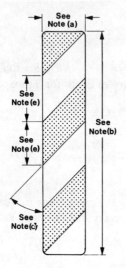 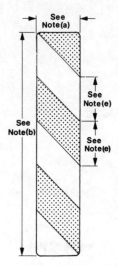

Notes:

(a) The width of each half of the marking shall be not less than 140 millimetres nor more than 280 millimetres.

(b) The length of each half of the marking shall be not less than 350 millimetres nor more than 700 millimetres.

(c) The angle of each stripe shall be not less than 40 degrees to the vertical nor more than 50 degrees to the vertical.

(d) Each half of the marking shall have a minimum area of 980 square centimetres.

(e) The breadth of each stripe shall be not less than 133 millimetres nor more than 147 millimetres.

SCHEDULE 2 (Regulation 3)

Requirements as to markings

1. The marking specified in Schedule 1 shall consist of two plates of equal size and the same shape as one another.

2. Each such plate shall comply with the requirements specified in the British Standard Specification for Rear Marking Plates for Vehicles issued by the British Standards Institution and published on 1st April 1970 under number BS AU 152: 1970 and shall be marked as provided in paragraph 5 of that Standard.

3. The two plates comprising the marking shall be securely attached to the end of the builder's skip in such a manner that—

 (a) each plate is as near to an outer edge of the skip as the construction of the skip allows, so, however, that no part of any plate projects beyond an outer edge of the end of the skip;

 (b) the innermost edge of each plate is parallel to and the same distance from the vertical plane passing through the longitudinal axis of the skip;

 (c) the upper edge of each plate is parallel to and the same distance from the upper edge of the end of the skip;

 (d) no part of either plate is attached to—

  (i) any lid, or

  (ii) any door except in a case where a door is the only place to which the plate can possibly or conveniently be fixed; and

 (e) the upper edge of each plate is—

  (i) not more than 1.5 metres from the ground, and

  (ii) not lower than the upper edge of the skip save in so far as this may be necessary on account of the construction of the skip, the provisions of Regulation 4 or the provisions of sub-paragraph (i) above.

4. The stippled areas in the diagram in Schedule 1 shall be of red fluorescent material, and the unstippled areas in that diagram shall be of yellow reflex reflecting material.

EXPLANATORY NOTE

(This Note is not part of the Regulations.)

1. By these Regulations the power conferred by section 139 of the Highways Act 1980 as amended by section 65 of the Transport Act 1982 to require builder's skips to be marked in a prescribed manner is exercised.

2. These Regulations require each end of every builder's skip to be marked as specified in Schedules 1 and 2 (Regulation 3).

3. Those requirements apply to each end of every builder's skip any part of which is placed on any part of a highway except a footway or a verge (Regulation 3).

4. Every marking with which a builder's skip is required to be marked by these Regulations shall be clean and efficient and (except when fitted to a door which is required to be open for the purpose of loading or unloading the skip) shall be clearly visible for a reasonable distance t persons using the highway on which the skip is placed (Regulation 4).

5. Copies of the British Standard mentioned in paragraph 2 of Schedule 2 may be obtained from any of the sales outlets operated by the British Standards Institution, or by post from that Institution at Linford Wood, Milton Keynes, MK14 6LE (telephone number Milton Keynes (STD 0908) 320066).

STATUTORY INSTRUMENTS

1984 No. 1935

SEA FISHERIES

CONSERVATION OF SEA FISH

The Sole (Bristol Channel and South-east of Ireland) (Prohibition of Fishing) (Revocation) Order 1984

Made - - - -	*10th December* 1984
Laid before Parliament	*19th December* 1984
Coming into Operation	*1st January* 1985

The Minister of Agriculture, Fisheries and Food and the Secretaries of State respectively concerned with the sea fishing industry in Scotland, Wales and Northern Ireland, acting jointly, in exercise of the powers conferred on them by sections 5(1), 15(3) and 20(1) of the Sea Fish (Conservation) Act 1967(**a**), and of all other powers enabling them in that behalf, hereby make the following Order:—

Title and commencement

1. This Order may be cited as the Sole (Bristol Channel and South-east of Ireland) (Prohibition of Fishing) (Revocation) Order 1984, and shall come into operation on 1st January 1985.

Revocation

2. The Sole (Bristol Channel and South-east of Ireland) (Prohibition of Fishing) Order 1984(**b**) is hereby revoked.

(**a**) 1967 c. 84; section 5(1) was substituted by section 22(1) of the Fisheries Act 1981 (c. 29) and, by virtue of S.I. 1973/238, section 5 applies in relation to British fishing boats registered in the Isle of Man as it applies in relation to British fishing boats registered in the United Kingdom; section 15(3) was substituted by paragraph 38(3) of Schedule 1 to the Sea Fisheries Act 1968 (c. 77), and amended by paragraph 16(1) of Schedule 2 to the Fishery Limits Act 1976 (c. 86); the definition of "the Ministers" in section 22(2) was amended by sections 19(2) and 45 of the Fisheries Act 1981.
(**b**) S.I. 1984/1627.

In Witness whereof the Official Seal of the Minister of Agriculture, Fisheries and Food is hereunto affixed on 3rd December 1984.

Michael Jopling,
Minister of Agriculture, Fisheries and Food.

George Younger,
Secretary of State for Scotland.

6th December 1984.

Nicholas Edwards,
Secretary of State for Wales.

10th December 1984.

Douglas Hurd,
Secretary of State for Northern Ireland.

10th December 1984.

EXPLANATORY NOTE

(This Note is not part of the Order.)

This Order revokes the Sole (Bristol Channel and South-east of Ireland) (Prohibition of Fishing) Order 1984.

STATUTORY INSTRUMENTS

1984 No. 1936 (S. 152)

ROAD TRAFFIC

The Parking Meters (Description and Testing) (Scotland) Revocation Order 1984

Made - - - -	*5th December* 1984
Laid before Parliament	*21st December* 1984
Coming into Operation	*11th January* 1985

In exercise of the powers conferred on me by paragraph 11(2) of Schedule 10 to the Road Traffic Regulation Act 1984(a), and of all other powers enabling me in that behalf, I hereby make the following Order:—

1. This Order may be cited as the Parking Meters (Description and Testing) (Scotland) Revocation Order 1984 and shall come into operation on 11th January 1985¹.

2. The Parking Meters (Description and Testing) (Scotland) Order 1959(b) is hereby revoked.

	George Younger,
New St Andrew's House,	One of Her Majesty's
Edinburgh.	Principal Secretaries of State.
5th December 1984.	

EXPLANATORY NOTE

(This Note is not part of the Order.)

This Order revokes the Parking Meters (Description and Testing) (Scotland) Order 1959.

(a) 1984 c. 27.　　　　(b) S.I. 1959/1348.

STATUTORY INSTRUMENTS

1984 No. 1943

ANIMALS

ANIMAL HEALTH

The Tuberculosis (England and Wales) Order 1984

Made - - - -	*6th December* 1984
Laid before Parliament	*21st December* 1984
Coming into Operation	*12th January* 1985

The Minister of Agriculture, Fisheries and Food in relation to England, and the Secretary of State in relation to Wales, in exercise of the powers conferred by sections 1, 7(1), 8(1), 10(1) and (2), 15(4), 25, 32(2), 83(2), 87(2) and 88(2) of the Animal Health Act 1981(a), and of all other powers enabling them in that behalf, hereby make the following Order:—

Title and commencement

1. This Order may be cited as the Tuberculosis (England and Wales) Order 1984 and shall come into operation on 12th January 1985.

Interpretation

2.—(1) In this Order, unless the context otherwise requires:—

"the Act" means the Animal Health Act 1981;

"affected animal" means a cow which is affected with tuberculosis of the udder or is giving tuberculous milk, or a bovine animal which is affected with tuberculous emaciation, or is excreting or discharging tuberculous material, or is affected with a chronic cough and shows clinical signs of tuberculosis, and includes a reactor, and "suspected animal" shall be construed accordingly;

"appropriate Minister" in relation to England means the Minister, and in relation to Wales means the Secretary of State;

"appropriate officer" means a veterinary inspector or in relation to England, another officer of the Ministry, or in relation to Wales, an officer of the Secretary of State;

"approved disinfectant" means a disinfectant listed in the Diseases of Animals (Approved Disinfectants) Order of 1978(b) as being approved for the time being for use against tuberculosis;

"bovine animal" means a bull, cow, steer, heifer or calf;

(a) 1981 c. 22.
(b) S.I. 1978/32; relevant amending instruments are S.I. 1984/55, 1338.

"carcase" means the carcase of a bovine animal, and includes part of a carcase and the flesh, bones, hide, skin, hooves, offal or other part of a bovine animal, separately or otherwise, or any portion thereof;

"cow" includes a heifer that has calved;

"the Divisional Veterinary Officer" means the veterinary inspector appointed by the Minister to receive information about animals or carcases affected or suspected of being affected with specified diseases, for the area in which the animal or carcase is;

"milk" includes cream and separated or skimmed milk;

"the Minister" and "the Ministry" mean respectively the Minister and the Ministry of Agriculture, Fisheries and Food;

"premises" includes land with or without buildings but does not include any part or parts of any premises used for the temporary detention of animals, as a market, sale-yard, fairground, slaughterhouse lair or place of exhibition;

"reactor" means a bovine animal which gives rise to a reaction consistent with its being affected with tuberculosis when tested for that disease either by or on behalf of the appropriate Minister or otherwise, as the case may be, provided that in the case of a test otherwise so carried out the result thereof has been reported to the appropriate Minister;

"slaughterhouse" means a slaughterhouse or knacker's yard as defined in section 34 of the Slaughterhouses Act 1974(a);

"veterinary inspector" means a veterinary inspector appointed by the Minister;

"veterinary surgeon" means a person registered in the register of veterinary surgeons or the supplementary veterinary register.

(2) References in this Order to notices served in Form A or Form B shall be construed as references to notices served in the forms respectively so headed in Schedule 1 to this Order, or in forms substantially to the like effect.

Extension of definition of "disease" and power to slaughter on account of tuberculosis

3. For the purposes of the Act, the definition of "disease" in section 88(1) of the Act is hereby extended so as to include tuberculosis, and section 32 of the Act (power to slaughter animals) shall apply to that disease.

Application of the Order

4. The provisions of this Order shall not apply in relation to approved premises, within the meaning of the Importation of Animals Order 1977(b) and shall apply in relation to imported animals only—

    (*a*) from the time specified in the licence issued in respect of those animals under article 11(5) of that Order; or

---

(**a**) 1974 c. 3.   (**b**) S.I. 1977/944.

(*b*) where the existence or suspected existence of disease in any part of Great Britain makes it expedient that no such licence should be issued for the time being, from the time when those animals have completed the period of detention in quarantine required under the provisions of that Order, or as the case may be, have been rested in an approved reception centre for the period so required.

Notification of disease in bovine animals

5.—(1) A person who has in his possession or under his charge on any premises an affected animal (other than a reactor) or a suspected animal and a veterinary surgeon who, in the course of his practice, examines any such animal shall, with all practicable speed, give notice of the fact to a constable of the police force for the area in which the animal is or to an inspector of the local authority or to the Divisional Veterinary Officer.

(2) Where notice under paragraph (1) above is given to a constable or to an inspector of the local authority, he shall immediately transmit the information contained therein by the most expeditious means to the Divisional Veterinary Officer.

(3) A person who has in his possession or under his charge an affected or suspected animal as is described in paragraph (1) above shall forthwith detain it on the premises where it then is and isolate it as far as practicable from other bovine animals, and shall adopt precautions with respect to milk produced by the affected or suspected animal as if a notice in Form A had already been served upon him under article 7 below in respect of that animal.

Notification of disease in carcases

6.—(1) A person who has in his possession or under his charge on any premises a carcase which is affected with or suspected of being affected with tuberculosis, and—

(*a*) a veterinary surgeon who, in the course of his practice, examines any such carcase, and

(*b*) a person who in the course of his duties under the Meat Inspection Regulations 1963(a), or whilst inspecting meat for any other purpose, inspects any such carcase,

shall with all practicable speed, give notice of the fact to the Divisional Veterinary Officer.

(2) A person who has in his possession or under his charge a carcase to which paragraph (1) above applies shall detain it, or so much of it as is affected with or suspected of being affected with tuberculosis, on the premises where it then is until it has been examined by a veterinary inspector.

Veterinary enquiry as to the existence of disease

7.—(1) Where by reason of information received, whether under article 5 or article 6 above or otherwise, there is reason to believe that there is on any

---

(a) S.I. 1963/1229, to which there are amendments not relevant to this Order.

premises an affected animal (other than a reactor) or a suspected animal or a carcase which is affected with or suspected of being affected with tuberculosis, a veterinary inspector shall, with all practicable speed, take such steps as may be necessary to establish the correctness of that information. For the purpose of carrying out his duties under the foregoing provisions of this paragraph a veterinary inspector may examine any bovine animal or carcase on the premises and take such samples as may be required for the purpose of diagnosis from any such bovine animal or carcase.

(2) A veterinary inspector shall serve a notice in Form A on the owner or person in charge of any bovine animal examined by him which in his opinion is an affected or suspected animal.

(3) The person on whom a notice in Form A has been served under this article shall comply with the notice and such notice shall remain in force until—

(a) the animal to which it relates has died, or has been slaughtered pursuant to section 32 of the Act; or

(b) withdrawn by a notice in writing served by a veterinary inspector on the person on whom the notice in Form A was served.

Tuberculin tests and valuation

8.—(1) The owner or person in charge of any bovine animal shall comply with all reasonable requirements of an appropriate officer with a view to facilitating the examination of that animal by a veterinary inspector, or the application to it of any diagnostic test for tuberculosis or the valuation of the animal in a case where the appropriate Minister intends to cause it to be slaughtered under section 32 of the Act in its application to tuberculosis, and in particular shall arrange for the collection, penning and securing of any such animal if so required.

(2) No person shall test a bovine animal with tuberculin except with the consent of the appropriate Minister and a person to whom any such consent is given shall, as soon as he knows the result of the test, forthwith report it to the appropriate Minister.

(3) If any person fails to comply with any reasonable requirement of an appropriate officer made in accordance with the provisions of paragraph (1) above the appropriate Minister may, without prejudice to any proceedings for an offence arising out of such default, take or cause to be taken all such steps as may be necessary to facilitate the examination and valuation of such animal, or the application to it of any diagnostic test for tuberculosis, and the amount of any expenses reasonably incurred by the appropriate Minister for the purpose of making good the default shall be recoverable by him as a civil debt from the person in default.

Prohibition on vaccination and therapeutic treatment

9.—(1) No person shall vaccinate a bovine animal against tuberculosis.

(2) No person shall treat a bovine animal for tuberculosis.

III/2m

Notification of intended slaughter of animals

10.—(1) Where the appropriate Minister intends to cause a bovine animal to be slaughtered under section 32 of the Act in its application to tuberculosis, a veterinary inspector may serve a notice in Form B on the owner or person in charge of the animal informing him of the intended slaughter and requiring him to detain the animal pending such slaughter (or pending its surrender and removal for such slaughter) on such part of the premises as is specified in the notice and to isolate it as far as practicable from such other animals as are so specified.

(2) The person on whom such a notice has been served—

    (*a*) shall comply with the notice; and

    (*b*) shall not move the animal, or cause or permit it to be moved, off that part of the premises on which it is required to be detained, except under the authority of a licence issued by an appropriate officer.

Precautions against spread of infection

11.—(1) Where the appropriate Minister is satisfied that any bovine animal kept on any premises is an affected animal or a reactor—

    (*a*) a veterinary inspector may, by notice in writing served on the owner or person in charge of any such animal, require him to take such steps as may be reasonably practicable to prevent any bovine animal kept on the premises from infecting by contact any bovine animal kept on any adjoining premises; and

    (*b*) an appropriate officer may, by notice in writing served on the owner or person in charge of any such animal, require him—

        (i) to arrange for the isolation of any animal or animals which may be specified in the notice on any part or parts of the premises so specified.

        (ii) to ensure that any part or parts of the premises specified in the notice shall not be used by any animal on the premises, or by such animal or animals as may be so specified;

        (iii) at his own expense, and within such time and in such manner as may be specified in the notice, to cleanse and disinfect such part or parts of the premises as may be so specified;

        (iv) to treat and store manure or slurry from any place which has been used by such animal in accordance with the requirements of the notice;

        (v) not to spread any manure or to spray or spread any slurry from any place which has been used by any such animal otherwise than in accordance with the requirements of the notice;

        (vi) to cleanse and wash all utensils and other articles used for or about an animal to which the notice relates within such time and in such manner as may be specified in the notice.

(2) Where an appropriate officer reasonably believes that any bovine animal which is on, or which has been on, any premises which are used for any show,

exhibition, market, sale or fair, is an affected animal or has been exposed to the infection of tuberculosis, he may, by notice in writing served on the occupier of such premises, require him—

(*a*) to ensure that any part or parts of the premises specified in the notice shall not be used by any other bovine animal for such period as may be specified in the notice;

(*b*) at his own expense, and within such time and in such manner as may be specified in the notice—

    (i) to cleanse and disinfect such part or parts of the premises as may be specified in the notice;

    (ii) to dispose of any manure, slurry or other animal waste, straw, litter or other matter which has or might have come into contact with such animal.

(3) If any person on whom a notice is served under paragraphs (1)(*b*) or (2) above fails to comply with the requirements of the notice, the appropriate Minister may, without prejudice to any proceedings arising out of such default, carry out or cause to be carried out the requirements of the notice, and the amount of any expenses reasonably incurred by the appropriate Minister for the purpose of making good the default shall be recoverable by him as a civil debt from the person in default.

(4) A notice served under paragraph 1(*b*)(i) or (ii) above shall remain in force until withdrawn by a further notice in writing served by an appropriate officer on the owner or person in charge of the bovine animal to which that notice relates.

Prohibition on movement of bovine animals

12.—(1) A veterinary inspector may by notice in writing served on the owner or person in charge of bovine animals kept on such premises as are specified in the notice, prohibit the movement of bovine animals on to or off such premises, except under the authority of a licence issued by an appropriate officer and in accordance with any conditions subject to which the licence is issued.

(2) Such notice shall remain in force until withdrawn by a further notice in writing served by a veterinary inspector on the owner or person in charge of the bovine animals to which that notice relates.

Manure, slurry etc.

13. Where a notice has been served on the owner or person in charge of bovine animals kept on any premises under the provisions of article 12(1) above which prohibits the movement of bovine animals off such premises except under the authority of a licence, no manure, slurry or other animal waste shall be removed from such premises except under the authority of a licence issued by the appropriate officer and in accordance with any conditions subject to which such licence is issued.

Suspected animals in markets, shows and sales

14.—(1) Where a veterinary inspector reasonably believes that a bovine animal on any premises at which a show, exhibition, market, sale or fair is being held, is infected with, or has been exposed to the infection of tuberculosis, he may require that animal to be removed from those premises, and (as the owner or person in charge of the animal may elect) taken either—

    (*a*) to a slaughterhouse for immediate slaughter; or

    (*b*) back to the premises from which the animal was brought to the show, exhibition, market, sale or fair; or

    (*c*) to such other premises as may be approved by the appropriate officer for the purpose.

(2) A bovine animal shall only be moved in accordance with the provisions of subparagraph (*b*) or (*c*) of paragraph (1) above on condition that it is immediately put into isolation for a period to be terminated by a notice in writing served on the owner or person in charge of the said animal by an appropriate officer.

Control of infection from other animals

15.—(1) Where a veterinary inspector reasonably believes that an animal kept on any premises is, or may be, infected with tuberculosis, he may by notice in writing served on the occupier of such premises, require him to keep the animal under control in such manner as may be specified in the notice or to confine it to such part of the premises as may be so specified.

(2) A notice served under paragraph (1) above in respect of an animal kept on any premises shall remain in force until such time as the animal dies or it is withdrawn by a further notice in writing served by a veterinary inspector on the occupier of such premises.

(3) For the purposes of paragraphs (1) and (2) above "animal" means any kind of mammal except man.

Identification of bovine animals

16.—(1) Subject to paragraph (2) below, the owner of a bovine animal kept on any premises shall mark or identify the animal in a manner approved by the appropriate Minister and shall thereafter maintain such mark or identification so as to be clearly legible.

(2) The requirement in paragraph (1) above shall not apply in relation to any bovine animal less than 14 days old that is not removed, or is removed only to a slaughterhouse from such premises, within such period of 14 days.

Restriction on the sale of unidentified bovine animals in markets

17. The owner of a bovine animal shall not expose the animal for sale or cause or permit it to be exposed for sale in any market or sale-yard unless—

(*a*) the animal has been marked or identified in accordance with the provisions of Article 16(1) above; and

(*b*) such mark or identification is so maintained as to be clearly legible.

Marking of bovine animals

18.—(1) If so required in writing by an appropriate officer the owner or person in charge of bovine animals kept on any premises shall mark such animals in the manner required by the appropriate officer.

(2) The appropriate officer may paint, stamp, clip, tag or otherwise mark bovine animals kept on any premises.

(3) No person shall alter, remove, obliterate or deface, or attempt to alter, remove, obliterate or deface any such mark or identification as is referred to in the foregoing provisions of this article or in article 16(1) above.

Production of licences

19. Where a bovine animal is moved under the authority of a licence issued under this Order—

(*a*) the animal shall be accompanied throughout such movement by the licence; and

(*b*) the person in charge of the animal being so moved shall, on demand made under this Order by an appropriate officer, or by an inspector of the local authority or a constable, furnish his name and address and shall produce the licence and allow a copy thereof or extract therefrom to be taken.

Enforcement by local authority

20. This Order shall, except where otherwise expressly provided, be executed and enforced by the local authority.

Offences

21. Any person who, without lawful authority or excuse, proof of which shall lie on him—

(*a*) contravenes any provision of this Order or of a licence issued or of a notice served under this Order; or

(*b*) fails to comply with any such provision or with any condition of any such licence or notice or with any requirement made under this Order; or

(*c*) causes or permits any such contravention or non-compliance,

commits an offence against the Act.

Revocation

22. The Orders listed in Schedule 2 are hereby revoked.

In Witness whereof the Official Seal of the Minister of Agriculture, Fisheries and Food is hereunto affixed on 4th December 1984.

Michael Jopling,
Minister of Agriculture, Fisheries
and Food.

Nicholas Edwards,
Secretary of State for Wales.

6th December 1984.

SCHEDULE 1

FORM A

ANIMAL HEALTH ACT 1981

TUBERCULOSIS (ENGLAND AND WALES) ORDER 1984

(Article 7)

Notice requiring detention and isolation of affected or suspected animals, adoption of precautions with respect to milk and prohibiting movement of bovine animals

To   of

I, the undersigned, being a veterinary inspector appointed by the Minister of Agriculture, Fisheries and Food hereby give you notice as the owner/person in charge* of the following bovine animal, namely,   on the under-mentioned premises which is an affected or suspected animal for the purposes of the above Order, requiring you—

(1) to detain the animal on the said premises and to keep the animal isolated as far as practicable from other bovine animals;

(2) to take steps to ensure that the milk produced by the animal shall not be mixed with other milk and to ensure that all such milk shall forthwith be boiled or otherwise sterilised, and that any utensil with which such milk has been in contact before being so treated shall be thoroughly cleansed and scalded with steam or boiling water before being used again; and

(3) to ensure that no bovine animals are moved on to or off the premises except under the authority of a licence issued by a veterinary inspector and in accordance with any conditions subject to which the licence is issued.

This notice remains in force until the animal to which it relates has died or has been slaughtered pursuant to the above-mentioned Act, or until it is cancelled by a subsequent notice served by a veterinary inspector on the owner or person in charge of the animal.

(Signed)...
Veterinary Inspector of the Ministry of Agriculture,
Fisheries and Food.

Dated   19

Description of premises on which the animal is to be detained and isolated.

Note. The veterinary inspector is with all practicable speed to send a copy of this notice to the Divisional Veterinary Officer, and to the local authority.

* Delete as appropriate

FORM B

ANIMAL HEALTH ACT 1981

TUBERCULOSIS (ENGLAND AND WALES) ORDER 1984

(Article 10)

NOTICE OF INTENDED SLAUGHTER

Herd Ref No ....

To ....

of ....

....

....

....

I, the undersigned, being a veterinary inspector appointed by the Minister of Agriculture, Fisheries and Food, hereby give notice that the Minister/Secretary of State for Wales* proposes to cause the following bovine animals to be slaughtered with all convenient speed under the powers conferred by section 32 of the above Act in its application to tuberculosis, namely

    (*a*) affected animals and reactors (see Note 2 below)

    ....

    kept at ....

    (*b*) other animals (see Note 2 below)

    ....

    kept at ....

I require you, pending such slaughter (or pending surrender and removal for such slaughter), to detain the animal(s) specified above in ....

....

being part of the premises where it is/they are* now kept, and to keep it/them* isolated as far as practicable from other bovine animals.

Signed..

Veterinary Inspector of the Ministry of Agriculture,
Fisheries and Food.

Dated 19

Note 1: In accordance with Article 11(1) of the Tuberculosis (England and Wales) Order 1984 you are required to take such steps as may be reasonably practicable to prevent the infection of bovine animals kept on adjoining premises by contact with bovine animals kept on your premises.

Note 2: The Brucellosis and Tuberculosis (England and Wales) Compensation Order 1978 (as amended) defines affected animals and reactors and fixes rates of compensation for them and for other bovine animals which are slaughtered as a result of being exposed to the infection of tuberculosis.

* Delete as appropriate

SCHEDULE 2 Article 22

Orders revoked	References
The Tuberculosis Order 1964	S.I. 1964/1151
The Tuberculosis (Amendment) Order 1973	S.I. 1973/2030
The Tuberculosis (Amendment) Order 1977	S.I. 1977/948

EXPLANATORY NOTE

(*This Note is not part of the Order.*)

This Order, which applies to England and Wales, consolidates, with amendments, the provisions of the Tuberculosis Order 1964 and its amending instruments.

The provisions of the 1964 Order relating to the application of what is now section 32 of the Animal Health Act 1981 (power to slaughter animals) to tuberculosis, to the compulsory notification of tuberculosis and to the investigation by a veterinary inspector into the existence of that disease are continued in force (Articles 3, 5, 6 and 7(1)). So are other provisions which enable precautionary measures to be required to be taken when a bovine animal is affected, or suspected of being affected, with tuberculosis (Article 7(2) and (3)), which prohibit the vaccination of a bovine animal against tuberculosis (Article 9) and which enable precautions to be required to be taken against the spread of tuberculosis (such as the isolation of animals and the cleansing and disinfection of premises) (Articles 10, 11, 12, 13 and 14).

The changes of substance made by the Order are—

(1) the inclusion of a default power enabling the appropriate Minister (as defined in the Order) to carry out the requirements of a notice served on the occupier of premises used for any show, exhibition, market, sale or fair and on which there is or has been an animal suspected of being infected with tuberculosis, where such person fails to comply with its requirements, and to recover the cost of doing so from the person in default (Article 11(3));

(2) the extension of a veterinary inspector's power to require pigs and goats, which are believed to be infected with tuberculosis to be confined to certain parts of the premises on which they are kept in order to prevent the risk of the spread of the disease, so that it applies to animals of any species where they are suspected of being infected with tuberculosis (Article 15); and

(3) the inclusion of a prohibition on the exposure for sale in a market of a bovine animal by its owner unless it has been marked or identified in accordance with the provisions of the Order and the mark or identification is clearly legible (Article 17).

STATUTORY INSTRUMENTS

1984 No. 1945

INCOME TAX

The Income Tax (Interest Relief) (Qualifying Lenders) Order 1984

Made -   -   -   -   13*th December* 1984

The Treasury, in exercise of the powers conferred on them by paragraph 14(2) of Schedule 7 to the Finance Act 1982(**a**), as amended by section 17(3) and (4) of the Finance Act 1983(**b**), hereby make the following Order:—

1. This Order may be cited as the Income Tax (Interest Relief) (Qualifying Lenders) Order 1984.

2. The following bodies are prescribed for the purposes of Part IV of Schedule 7 to the Finance Act 1982:—

> Banco Urquijo Hispano Americano Limited
> Bestlane Limited
> Bretton Financial Services Limited
> Business Mortgages Trust p.l.c.
> Canada Permanent Trust Company (U.K.) Limited
> Canadian Imperial Bank of Commerce
> Central Bank of India
> Cheshire Commercial Finance Limited
> Confederation Mortgage Services Limited
> E.T. Trust Limited
> Guinness Mahon & Co. Limited
> Guinness Mahon Financial Services Limited
> Kleinwort, Benson Limited
> Komburg Investment Company Limited,
> Lombard Home Loans Limited
> London and Manchester (Home Loans) Limited
> Morgan Grenfell (Housing Finance) Limited
> National Mutual Home Loans Limited
> N.M. Rothschild & Sons Limited
> Premium Life Finance Limited
> South Notts Finance Limited
> Sterling Trust Limited
> Thames Trust Limited
> Wafthurst Credit Limited

John Major,
Donald Thompson,
Two of the Lords Commissioners
of Her Majesty's Treasury

13th December 1984.

(**a**) 1982 c. 39.   (**b**) 1983 c. 28.

EXPLANATORY NOTE

(This Note is not part of the Order.)

By this Order the bodies listed are prescribed as qualifying lenders so that interest on qualifying loans made by them may be paid to them under deduction of tax under the tax deduction scheme introduced by the Finance Act 1982.

STATUTORY INSTRUMENTS

1984 No. 1946

NATIONAL HEALTH SERVICE, ENGLAND AND WALES

The Family Practitioner Committees (Establishment) Order 1984

Made	11*th December* 1984
Laid before Parliament	2*nd January* 1985
Coming into Operation	23*rd January* 1985

The Secretary of State for Social Services, as respects England, and the Secretary of State for Wales, as respects Wales, in exercise of powers conferred on them by section 10(1), (2) and (3) of the National Health Service Act 1977(**a**), and of all other powers enabling them in that behalf, hereby make the following order:—

Citation, commencement and interpretation

1.— (1) This order may be cited as the Family Practitioner Committees (Establishment) Order 1984 and shall come into operation on 23rd January 1985.

(2) In Part I of the Schedule to this order a reference to a London borough is to that borough as determined on 23rd January 1985, a reference to a county or district is to that county or district as determined under the Local Government Act 1972(**b**)—

> *(a)* on 31st December 1982 in the case of the counties of Cleveland and Durham;
>
> *(b)* on 16th March 1983 in the case of the counties of Avon and Somerset;
>
> *(c)* on 23rd January 1985 in any other case,

and no account shall be taken for the purposes of that Part of any subsequent change effected under that Act in the boundaries of any of those boroughs, counties or districts.

(3) In Part II of the Schedule to this order a reference to a county is to that county as determined under the Local Government Act 1972; and in particular regulation 40(1)(*b*) of the Local Government Area Changes Regulations 1976(**c**) (statutory definitions of areas) shall apply to those counties.

Family Practitioner Committees and their localities

2.— (1) There are hereby established a number of authorities, called Family Practitioner Committees, equal to the total number of entries in column 1 of Parts I and II of the Schedule to this order.

(**a**) 1977 c.49; section 10 was substituted by section 5 of the Health and Social Security Act 1984 (c.48).
(**b**) 1972 c.70.
(**c**) S.I. 1976/246, to which there are no amendments relevant to the subject matter of this order.

(2) Each authority established by paragraph (1) of this Article by virtue of an entry in column 1 of Part I or II of the Schedule to this order—

(a) shall be known by a name consisting of the words comprising that entry followed by the words "Family Practitioner Committee"; and

(b) shall (as from the date to be specified by order made under section 5(5) of the Health and Social Security Act 1984(**a**)) act for the locality specified in relation to that entry in column 2 of Part I or II of that Schedule, localities specified in Part I of that Schedule being in England and localities specified in Part II of that Schedule being in Wales.

Signed by authority of the Secretary of State for Social Services.

John Patten,
Parliamentary Under-Secretary of State,
Department of Health and Social Security.

11th December 1984.

Nicholas Edwards,
Secretary of State for Wales.

11th December 1984.

(**a**) 1984 c.48.

NATIONAL HEALTH SERVICE,
ENGLAND AND WALES

Article 2

SCHEDULE

FAMILY PRACTITIONER COMMITTEES AND THEIR LOCALITIES
PART I—ENGLAND

Column 1	Column 2
NAME OF FAMILY PRACTITIONER COMMITTEE	LOCALITY
Avon	The county of Avon
Barking and Havering	The London boroughs of Barking and Dagenham and Havering
Barnet	The London borough of Barnet
Barnsley	The borough of Barnsley in South Yorkshire
Bedfordshire	The county of Bedfordshire
Birmingham	The City of Birmingham in West Midlands
Bolton	The borough of Bolton in Greater Manchester
Brent and Harrow	The London boroughs of Brent and Harrow
Bromley	The London borough of Bromley
Bury	The borough of Bury in Greater Manchester
Calderdale	The borough of Calderdale in West Yorkshire
Cambridgeshire	The county of Cambridgeshire
City and East London	The City of London, the Inner Temple, the Middle Temple and the London boroughs of Hackney, Newham and Tower Hamlets
Cleveland	The county of Cleveland
Cornwall and Isles of Scilly (a)	The county of Cornwall and the Isles of Scilly
Coventry	The City of Coventry in West Midlands
Croydon	The London borough of Croydon
Cumbria	The county of Cumbria
Derbyshire	The county of Derbyshire
Devon	The county of Devon
Doncaster	The borough of Doncaster in South Yorkshire
Dorset	The county of Dorset
Dudley	The borough of Dudley in West Midlands

(a) The National Health Service Act 1977 was extended to the Isles of Scilly by the Isles of Scilly (National Health Service) Order 1981 (S.I. 1981/1473).

FAMILY PRACTITIONER COMMITTEES AND THEIR LOCALITIES

PART I—ENGLAND (*cont.*)

Column 1	Column 2
NAME OF FAMILY PRACTITIONER COMMITTEE	LOCALITY
Durham	The county of Durham
East Sussex	The county of East Sussex
Enfield and Haringey	The London boroughs of Enfield and Haringey
Essex	The county of Essex
Gateshead	The borough of Gateshead in Tyne and Wear
Gloucestershire	The county of Gloucestershire
Greenwich and Bexley	The London boroughs of Bexley and Greenwich
Hampshire	The county of Hampshire
Hereford and Worcester	The county of Hereford and Worcester
Hertfordshire	The county of Hertfordshire
Hillingdon	The London borough of Hillingdon
Humberside	The county of Humberside
Isle of Wight	The county of Isle of Wight
Kent	The county of Kent
Kirklees	The borough of Kirklees in West Yorkshire
Lambeth Southwark and Lewisham	The London boroughs of Lambeth, Lewisham and Southwark
Leeds	The City of Leeds in West Yorkshire
Leicestershire	The county of Leicestershire
Lincolnshire	The county of Lincolnshire
Liverpool	The City of Liverpool in Merseyside
Manchester	The City of Manchester in Greater Manchester
Newcastle	The City of Newcastle upon Tyne in Tyne and Wear
Norfolk	The county of Norfolk
Northamptonshire	The county of Northamptonshire
North Tyneside	The borough of North Tyneside in Tyne and Wear
Northumberland	The county of Northumberland
Nottinghamshire	The county of Nottinghamshire
Oldham	The borough of Oldham in Greater Manchester

FAMILY PRACTITIONER COMMITTEES AND THEIR LOCALITIES

PART I—ENGLAND (*cont.*)

Column 1	Column 2
NAME OF FAMILY PRACTITIONER COMMITTEE	LOCALITY
Redbridge and Waltham Forest	The London boroughs of Redbridge and Waltham Forest
Rotherham	The borough of Rotherham in South Yorkshire
St Helens and Knowsley	The boroughs of Knowsley and St Helens in Merseyside
Salford	The City of Salford in Greater Manchester
Sandwell	The borough of Sandwell in West Midlands
Sefton	The borough of Sefton in Merseyside
Sheffield	The City of Sheffield in South Yorkshire
Shropshire	The county of Shropshire
Solihull	The borough of Solihull in West Midlands
Somerset	The county of Somerset
South Tyneside	The borough of South Tyneside in Tyne and Wear
Staffordshire	The county of Staffordshire
Stockport	The borough of Stockport in Greater Manchester
Suffolk	The county of Suffolk
Sunderland	The borough of Sunderland in Tyne and Wear
Tameside	The borough of Tameside in Greater Manchester
Trafford	The borough of Trafford in Greater Manchester
Wakefield	The City of Wakefield in West Yorkshire
Walsall	The borough of Walsall in West Midlands
Warwickshire	The county of Warwickshire
West Sussex	The county of West Sussex
Wigan	The borough of Wigan in Greater Manchester
Wiltshire	The county of Wiltshire
Wolverhampton	The borough of Wolverhampton in West Midlands

PART II—WALES

Column 1	Column 2
NAME OF FAMILY PRACTITIONER COMMITTEE	LOCALITY
Clwyd	The county of Clwyd
Dyfed	The county of Dyfed
Gwent	The county of Gwent
Gwynedd	The county of Gwynedd
Mid-Glamorgan	The county of Mid-Glamorgan
Powys	The county of Powys
South Glamorgan	The county of South Glamorgan
West Glamorgan	The county of West Glamorgan

EXPLANATORY NOTE

(This Note is not part of the Order.)

This order establishes 83 new Family Practitioner Committees, names those Committees and specifies the localities for which they are to act. Other Family Practitioner Committees remain to be established by further order. Under section 5(5) and (6) of the Health and Social Security Act 1984 none of the Committees will start to act for its locality until such date (not later than 1st April 1985) as the Secretary of State specifies by order; until such date the existing Family Practitioner Committees established or adopted by District Health Authorities will continue to act.

STATUTORY INSTRUMENTS

1984 No. 1947

OFFSHORE INSTALLATIONS

The Offshore Installations (Safety Zones) (No. 96) Order 1984

Made - - - -	12*th December* 1984
Coming into Operation	14*th December* 1984

The Secretary of State, in exercise of the powers conferred on him by section 21(1), (2) and (3) of the Oil and Gas (Enterprise) Act 1982(**a**) (hereinafter referred to as "the Act"), and of all other powers enabling him in that behalf, hereby makes the following Order:—

1. This Order may be cited as the Offshore Installations (Safety Zones) (No. 96) Order 1984 and shall come into operation on 14th December 1984.

2.—(1) A safety zone is hereby established around the installation specified in Column 1 of the Schedule hereto (being an installation maintained in waters in an area designated under section 1(7) of the Continental Shelf Act 1964(**b**)) having a radius of five hundred metres from the point as respects that installation which has the co-ordinates of latitude and longitude according to European Datum (1950) specified in Columns 2 and 3 of the Schedule.

(2) The prohibition under section 21(3) of the Act on a vessel entering or remaining in a safety zone without the consent of the Secretary of State shall not apply to a vessel entering or remaining in the safety zone established under paragraph (1) above—

(*a*) in connection with the laying, inspection, testing, repair, alteration, renewal or removal of any submarine cable or pipe-line in or near that safety zone;

(*b*) to provide services for, to transport persons or goods to or from, or under the authority of a government department to inspect, any installation in that safety zone;

(*c*) if it is a vessel belonging to a general lighthouse authority performing duties relating to the safety of navigation;

(*d*) in connection with the saving or attempted saving of life or property;

(*e*) owing to stress of weather; or

(*f*) when in distress.

Alick Buchanan-Smith,
Minister of State,
Department of Energy.

12th December 1984.

(**a**) 1982 c. 23.   (**b**) 1964 c. 29.

SCHEDULE   Article 2(1)

SAFETY ZONE

1	2	3
Name or other designation of the offshore installation	Latitude North	Longitude East
Byford Dolphin	59° 52' 35·42"	02° 02' 34·27"

EXPLANATORY NOTE

(*This Note is not part of the Order.*)

This Order establishes, under section 21 of the Oil and Gas (Enterprise) Act 1982, a safety zone, having a radius of 500 metres from a specified point, around the installation known as Byford Dolphin maintained in waters in an area designated under section 1(7) of the Continental Shelf Act 1964.

Vessels (which includes hovercraft, submersible apparatus and installations in transit) are prohibited from entering or remaining in the safety zone except with the consent of the Secretary of State or in the circumstances mentioned in Article 2(2) of the Order.

STATUTORY INSTRUMENTS

1984 No. 1948

OFFSHORE INSTALLATIONS

The Offshore Installations (Safety Zones) (No. 97) Order 1984

Made	- - -	*12th December* 1984
Coming into Operation		*14th December* 1984

The Secretary of State, in exercise of the powers conferred on him by section 21(1), (2) and (3) of the Oil and Gas (Enterprise) Act 1982(**a**) (hereinafter referred to as "the Act"), and of all other powers enabling him in that behalf, hereby makes the following Order:—

1. This Order may be cited as the Offshore Installations (Safety Zones) (No. 97) Order 1984 and shall come into operation on 14th December 1984.

2.—(1) A safety zone is hereby established around the installation specified in Column 1 of the Schedule hereto (being an installation maintained in waters in an area designated under section 1(7) of the Continental Shelf Act 1964(**b**)) having a radius of five hundred metres from the point as respects that installation which has the co-ordinates of latitude and longitude according to European Datum (1950) specified in Columns 2 and 3 of the Schedule.

(2) The prohibition under section 21(3) of the Act on a vessel entering or remaining in a safety zone without the consent of the Secretary of State shall not apply to a vessel entering or remaining in the safety zone established under paragraph (1) above—

(*a*) in connection with the laying, inspection, testing, repair, alteration, renewal or removal of any submarine cable or pipe-line in or near that safety zone;

(*b*) to provide services for, to transport persons or goods to or from, or under the authority of a government department to inspect, any installation in that safety zone;

(*c*) if it is a vessel belonging to a general lighthouse authority performing duties relating to the safety of navigation;

(*d*) in connection with the saving or attempted saving of life or property;

(*e*) owing to stress of weather; or

(*f*) when in distress.

Alick Buchanan-Smith,
Minister of State,
Department of Energy.

12th December 1984.

(**a**) 1982 c.23.　　　　　(**b**) 1964 c.29.

SCHEDULE   Article 2(1)

SAFETY ZONE

1	2	3
Name or other designation of the offshore installation	Latitude North	Longitude East
Ocean Kokuei	60° 38′ 43·40″	01° 01′ 06·10″

EXPLANATORY NOTE

(This Note is not part of the Order.)

This Order establishes, under section 21 of the Oil and Gas (Enterprise) Act 1982, a safety zone, having a radius of 500 metres from a specified point, around the installation known as Ocean Kokuei maintained in waters in an area designated under section 1(7) of the Continental Shelf Act 1964.

Vessels (which includes hovercraft, submersible apparatus and installations in transit) are prohibited from entering or remaining in the safety zone except with the consent of the Secretary of State or in the circumstances mentioned in Article 2(2) of the Order.

STATUTORY INSTRUMENTS

1984 No. 1955 (S.157)

SUMMARY JURISDICTION, SCOTLAND

Act of Adjournal (Applications to District Court under s. 49 of Civic Government (Scotland) Act 1982) 1984

Made - - - - -	13*th December* 1984
Coming into Operation	7*th January* 1985

The Lord Justice General, Lord Justice Clerk and Lords Commissioners of Justiciary, under and by virtue of the powers conferred upon them by section 457 of the Criminal Procedure (Scotland) Act 1975**(a)** as applied by section 4(2) of the District Courts (Scotland) Act 1975**(b)** and of all other powers enabling them in that behalf, do hereby enact and declare:—

Citation and commencement

1.—(1) This Act of Adjournal may be cited as the Act of Adjournal (Applications to District Court under s. 49 of Civic Government (Scotland) Act 1982) 1984 and shall come into operation on 7th January 1985.

(2) This Act of Adjournal shall be inserted in the Books of Adjournal.

Applications to District Court in respect of annoying creatures

2.—(1) An application to a District Court under section 49(3) of the Civic Government (Scotland) Act 1982**(c)** (annoying creatures) shall be made in the form set out in the Schedule to this Act of Adjournal, or as nearly as may be in that form.

(2) On the lodging of any such application, the District Court shall make an order for service of a copy of the application on any person mentioned in the application as having the creature so mentioned in his charge or keeping the creature, and fixing a date and time for the hearing of the application.

(3) A copy of the application and of the order made under sub-paragraph (2) shall be served on any such person by recorded delivery at the normal place of residence or place of business of that person, and such service shall be treated as sufficient notice to that person of the terms of the application and the order for the purposes of subparagraph (4).

(a) 1975 c. 21.   (b) 1975 c. 20.   (c) 1982 c. 45.

(4) If any person upon whom service has been made in accordance with sub-paragraph (3) fails to appear or be represented at the time and date of the hearing specified in the order without reasonable excuse, the Court may proceed to hear and decide the application in his absence.

(5) Where the Court makes an order in respect of any person under section 49(2) of the said Act of 1982, the clerk of court shall, within 7 days of the date on which the order was made, serve on that person by recorded delivery at the normal place of residence or place of business of that person, a copy of the order and a notice setting out the terms of section 49(4) of the said Act.

Emslie,
Lord Justice General
I.P.D.

Edinburgh,
13th December 1984.

SCHEDULE

FORM OF APPLICATION UNDER s. 49 OF CIVIC GOVERNMENT (SCOTLAND) ACT 1984

IN THE DISTRICT COURT OF

APPLICATION
under
The Civic Government (Scotland) Act 1982,
Section 49(2) and (3)
I.C.
A.B. (name and design),

Complainer:

against
C.D. (name and design),

Respondent:

Humbly Sheweth:

1. That A.B. is resident at (specify address).

2. That C.D. occupies premises at (specify address or place) being in the vicinity of (specify A.B.'s address).

3. That at said premises C.D. keeps (here identify the creature and describe the circumstances in which said creature is kept).

4. (Here describe in detail the circumstances in which it is alleged said creature is causing annoyance).

> May it therefore please the Court to order service of a copy of this application upon the said C.D.; to fix a date for the hearing of this application not earlier than 14 days after such service and thereafter to make an Order upon the said C.D. to take within such period as may be specified in the Order such steps (short of destruction of the creature) as may be so specified to prevent the continuance of the annoyance.

> (Signed)/

> (complainer, or his solicitor, name, address, Tel. No.)

EXPLANATORY NOTE

(*This Note is not part of the Act of Adjournal.*)

This Act of Adjournal makes provision for the procedure in an application to the District Court under section 49(3) of the Civic Government (Scotland) Act 1982 relating to annoying creatures.

STATUTORY INSTRUMENTS

1984 No. 1956

SEA FISHERIES

COMMUNITY RESTRICTIONS

The Sea Fishing (Enforcement of Community Conservation Measures) (Amendment) Order 1984

Made - - - -	13*th December* 1984
Laid before Parliament	18*th December* 1984
Coming into Operation	8*th January* 1985

The Minister of Agriculture, Fisheries and Food and the Secretaries of State respectively concerned with sea fishing in Scotland, Wales and Northern Ireland, in exercise of the powers conferred on them by section 30(2) of the Fisheries Act 1981 (**a**) and of all other powers enabling them in that behalf, hereby make the following order:—

Title and commencement

1. This order may be cited as the Sea Fishing (Enforcement of Community Conservation Measures) (Amendment) Order 1984 and shall come into operation on 8th January 1985.

Amendment of the Sea Fishing (Enforcement of Community Conservation Measures) Order 1983

2. The Sea Fishing (Enforcement of Community Conservation Measures) Order 1983 (**b**) is hereby further amended in accordance with articles 3 to 5 of this order.

Amendment of article 2

3. In article 2 (interpretation) for the definition of "the Council Regulation" there shall be substituted the following definition:—

' "the Council Regulation" means Council Regulation (EEC) No. 171/83 laying down certain technical measures for the conservation of fishery resources (**c**) , as amended by Council Regulations (EEC) Nos. 2931/83 (**d**) , 1637/84 (**e**) , 2178/84 (**f**) and 2664/84 (**g**) , and as read with Council Regulation (EEC) No. 2665/84 (**h**) ;'.

(**a**) 1981 c.29.
(**b**) S.I. 1983/256, as amended by S.I. 1983/1818.
(**c**) O.J. No. L24, 27.1.83, p.14.
(**d**) O.J. No. L288, 21.10.83, p.l.
(**e**) O.J. No. L156, 13.6.84, p.l.
(**f**) O.J. No. L199, 28.7.84, p.l.
(**g**) O.J. No. L253, 21.9.84, p.l.
(**h**) O.J. No. L253, 21.9.84, p.4.

Amendment of articles 4, 5 and 7

4. In articles 4*(a)*, 5*(a)* and 7(6)*(a)* (maximum penalties on summary conviction of certain offences relating to undersized fish, to salmon and to obstruction of officers) for "£1,000" there shall be substituted "£2,000".

Amendment of Schedule

5.—(1) In column 3 of items 5, 8 and 14 of the Schedule (maximum penalties on summary conviction) for "£1,000" there shall be substituted "£2,000".

(2) For items 11 to 13 of the Schedule there shall be substituted the following items:—

In column 1 (Provision of the Council Regulation)	In column 2 (Subject Matter)	In column 3 (Maximum Penalty)
" 11. Article 15(1), first sub-paragraph	Prohibition on retaining on board mackerel caught in specified waters in the western English Channel, the Bristol Channel and the Celtic Sea	£2,000
12. Article 15(1), sixth sub-paragraph	Notification requirement relating to intention to fish in waters specified in article 15(1), first sub-paragraph	£2,000
13. Article 15(1), seventh sub-paragraph	Notification requirement relating to quantity of mackerel on board and requirement to submit log-book and catch	£2,000
13A. Article 15(1), eighth sub-paragraph	Notification requirement relating to trans-shipment of mackerel	£2,000".

In Witness whereof the Offical Seal of the Minister of Agriculture, Fisheries and Food is hereunto affixed on 12th December 1984.

L.S.

Michael Jopling,
Minister of Agriculture, Fisheries and Food.

George Younger,
Secretary of State for Scotland.

13th December 1984.

Nicholas Edwards,
Secretary of State for Wales.

13th December 1984.

Douglas Hurd,
Secretary of State for Northern
Ireland.

13th December 1984.

EXPLANATORY NOTE

(This Note is not part of the Order.)

This order further amends the Sea Fishing (Enforcement of Community Conservation Measures) Order 1983 so as to—

(a) provide for the enforcement of Council Regulations (EEC) Nos. 1637/84, 2178/84, and 2664/84 amending Council Regulation (EEC) No. 171/83 (O.J. No. L 24, 27.1.83, p.14) (which lays down certain technical measures for the conservation of fishery resources) and Council Regulation (EEC) No. 2665/84 establishing, by derogation from Council Regulation (EEC) No. 171/83, a temporary measure concerning by-catches in the fishery for Norway pout in the North Sea (articles 3 and 5(2) of the order); and

(b) increase maximum penalties of £1,000 on summary conviction of offences that are triable either on indictment or summarily to £2,000 (articles 4 and 5(1) of the order).

The principal changes effected by the enforcement of the Council Regulations mentioned above are—

(a) a change in the rules for measuring crustaceans (Council Regulation (EEC) No. 2178/84);

(b) changes in the rules relating to fishing for mackerel off south-west England (Council Regulation (EEC) No. 2664/84); and

(c) a temporary relaxation of the rules relating to by-catches caught in the course of fishing for Norway pout in the North Sea (Council Regulation (EEC) No. 2665/84).

STATUTORY INSTRUMENTS

1984 No. 1960

SOCIAL SECURITY

The Child Benefit (Claims and Payments) Regulations 1984

Made - - - -	14*th December* 1984
Laid before Parliament	21*st December* 1984
Coming into Operation	21*st January* 1985

ARRANGEMENT OF REGULATIONS

PART I

GENERAL

PART II

CLAIMS

PART III

PAYMENTS

PART IV

MISCELLANEOUS PROVISIONS

The Secretary of State for Social Services, in exercise of the powers conferred upon him by sections 6(1) and (3) to (5), 7(1)*(b)*, 11(2) and 22(1)*(b)* of the Child Benefit Act 1975(**a**) , and of all other powers enabling him in that behalf and for the purposes only of consolidating the regulations revoked by this instrument, hereby makes the following regulations:—

PART I

GENERAL

Citation, commencement and interpretation

1.—(1) These regulations may be cited as the Child Benefit (Claims and Payments) Regulations 1984 and shall come into operation on 21st January 1985.

(2) In these regulations, unless the context otherwise requires—

"the Act" means the Child Benefit Act 1975;

"the Social Security Act" means the Social Security Act 1975(**b**) ;

"benefit" means child benefit under the Act;

"claim" means a claim to benefit and "claiming" shall be construed accordingly;

"the Department" means the Department of Health and Social Security;

"determining authority" means, as the case may require, the Chief or any other adjudication officer, a social security appeal tribunal, the Chief or any other Social Security Commissioner or a tribunal of three such Commissioners constituted in accordance with section 116 of the Social Security Act, as applied to appeals concerning child benefit by regulation 73(1)*(a)* of the Social Security (Adjudication) Regulations 1984 (**c**).

"increase" means an increase in the weekly rate of benefit under regulation 2(2) of the Child Benefit and Social Security (Fixing and Adjustment of Rates) Regulations 1976 (**d**);

"instrument of payment" means a serial order or any other instrument whatsoever which is intended to enable a person to obtain payment of benefit;

"serial order" means one of a series of orders for the payment of sums on account of benefit which is or has been contained in a book of such orders,

and other expressions have the same meanings as in the Act.

(3) A separate claim shall be required for an increase, except that where a person claims benefit other than an increase in respect of a child having previously claimed for an increase in respect of that child his claim for an increase shall be regarded as a claim to benefit including an increase.

(4) Unless the context otherwise requires, any reference in these regulations to—

    (a) a numbered regulation is a reference to the regulation bearing that number in these regulations and any reference in a regulation to a numbered paragraph is a reference to the paragraph of that regulation bearing that number;

(**a**) 1975 c.61.
(**b**) 1975 c.14.
(**c**) S.I. 1984/451, to which there are amendments not relevant to these regulations.
(**d**) S.I. 1976/1267; relevant amending instruments are S.I. 1980/110, 1984/1106.

(b) any provision made by or contained in any enactment or instrument shall be construed as a reference to that provision as amended or extended by any enactment or instrument and as including a reference to any provision which may re-enact or replace it with or without modification.

PART II

CLAIMS

Manner in which claims are to be made

2.—(1) Every claim shall be made in writing to the Secretary of State on a form approved by the Secretary of State or in such other manner, being in writing, as the Secretary of State may, in his discretion, accept as sufficient in the circumstances of any particular case or class of cases, and shall be delivered or sent to an office of the Department.

(2) The date on which a claim is made shall be the date on which it is received in an office of the Department (hereafter in this paragraph referred to as "the relevant date"), so however that if the Secretary of State is aware that a claim which has been sent by post has not been delivered in the ordinary course of post he may treat the claim as having been made on a date earlier than the relevant date, being, whichever is the later, the date on which the claim would have been made had it been delivered in the ordinary course of post or a date 13 weeks before the relevant date.

(3) Forms of claim shall be supplied without charge by such persons as the Secretary of State may appoint or authorise for that purpose.

(4) If a claim on the form approved is defective at the date when it is received at an office of the Department or has been made otherwise than on the form approved for the time being, the Secretary of State may, in his discretion, refer the claim to the person making it or, as the case may be, supply him with the approved form, and if the form is returned properly completed within one month from the date on which it is so referred or supplied the Secretary of State shall treat the claim as if it had been duly made in the first instance.

(5) A person who has made a claim may amend his claim at any time before a determination has been made on it by a notice in writing delivered or sent to an office of the Department and any claim so amended may be treated as if it had been made as so amended in the first instance.

(6) A person who has made a claim may withdraw it at any time before a determination has been made on it by a notice in writing delivered or sent to an office of the Department and the said notice shall have effect when it is received in the Department.

(7) Any reference in the Act or in regulations to the date on which a claim is made shall, in the case of a claim which is treated—

(a) as having been made on a date earlier than the relevant date under paragraph (2), be construed as a reference to that earlier date; and

(b) as if it had been duly made in the first instance under paragraph (4) or (5), be construed as a reference to the date on which it was first received in an office of the Department.

Information in support of claim

3.—(1) Every person making a claim shall furnish such certificates, documents, information and evidence in connection with the claim as may be required by the Secretary of State and, if reasonably so required, shall for that purpose attend at such office of the Department or other place as the Secretary of State may direct.

(2) Where, in the case of a husband and wife residing together, a claim is made by the husband and not by the wife, the Secretary of State may require the husband to furnish him with a written statement, signed by the wife, that she does not wish to make a claim.

Advance claims and awards

4.—(1) If on the date on which a claim is made by a person in respect of a child that person does not satisfy the requirements for entitlement to benefit in respect of that child but the determining authority is of the opinion that that person is likely to satisfy those requirements for a period beginning on a day (hereafter in this regulation referred to as "the relevant day") not more than 56 days after the date on which the claim is made, then that determining authority may—

(a) treat the claim as if made for a period beginning with the relevant day; and

(b) award benefit accordingly, subject to the condition that the person satisfies the requirements for entitlement when benefit becomes payable under the award.

(2) An award under paragraph (1)*(b)* may be reviewed by the determining authority if the requirements for entitlement are found not to have been satisfied on the relevant day.

Interchange with claims for benefit under the Social Security Act

5.—(1) Where it appears that a person who in accordance with these regulations has claimed child benefit in respect of a child may be entitled alternatively or in addition to any benefit specified in Schedule 1 to these regulations in respect of the same child, the Secretary of State may, in his discretion, treat the claim to child benefit as a claim by that person for the benefit in question specified in the said Schedule.

(2) Where it appears that a person who in accordance with regulations made under the Social Security Act has claimed any benefit specified in the said Schedule in respect of a child may be entitled alternatively or in addition to child benefit in respect of the same child, the Secretary of State may, in his discretion, treat the claim for the benefit in question as a claim by that person to child benefit.

PART III

PAYMENTS

Payment of benefit

6.—(1) Subject to the provisions of this regulation and of regulations 7 and 8, benefit shall be payable as follows:—

(a) in a case where the person entitled to benefit elects to receive payment weekly, in accordance with the provisions of regulation 8, benefit shall be payable weekly from the first convenient date after the election has been made;

(b) in any other case benefit shall be payable in the last week of each successive period of four weeks of the period of entitlement.

(2) Subject to paragraph (3) and regulation 7(3), benefit payable weekly or four-weekly shall be payable on Mondays or Tuesdays (as the Secretary of State may in his discretion in any case determine) by serial orders.

(3) In such cases or class of cases as the Secretary of State may, in his discretion, determine, benefit shall be payable otherwise than—

(a) by means of serial orders, or

(b) on Mondays or Tuesdays, or

(c) at weekly or four-weekly intervals,

and where benefit is being paid at four-weekly intervals in accordance with paragraph 1 *(b)* the Secretary of State shall arrange for it to be paid weekly if satisfied that payment at intervals of four weeks is causing hardship.

(4) The Secretary of State shall take steps to notify persons to whom benefit is payable of the arrangements he has made for payment so far as those arrangements affect such persons.

(5) Instruments of payment and books of serial orders issued by the Secretary of State shall remain his property; and any person having such an instrument of payment or book of serial orders shall, on ceasing to be entitled to the benefit to which such instrument or book relates or when so required by the Secretary of State, deliver the instrument or book to the Secretary of State or to such other person as he may direct.

Payment of benefit by direct credit transfer

7.—(1) Subject to the provisions of this regulation, benefit may, on the application of the person claiming, or entitled to it, and with the consent of the Secretary of State, be paid by way of automated or other direct credit transfer into a bank or other account—

(a) in the name of the person entitled to benefit, or his spouse, or a person acting on his behalf, or

(b) in the joint names of the person entitled to benefit and his spouse, or the person entitled to benefit and a person acting on his behalf.

(2) An application for the benefit to be paid in accordance with paragraph (1)—

(a) shall be in writing on a form approved for the purpose by the Secretary of State or in such other manner, being in writing, as he may accept as sufficient in the circumstances, and

(b) shall contain a statement or be accompanied by a written statement made by the applicant declaring that he has read and understood the conditions applicable to payment of benefit in accordance with this regulation and in particular that he has understood the effect that paragraph (6) would have in the event of any overpayment of benefit.

(3) Benefit shall be paid in accordance with paragraph (1) within seven days of the last day of each successive period of entitlement of four weeks.

(4) In respect of benefit which is the subject of an arrangement for payment under this regulation, the Secretary of State may make a particular payment by credit transfer otherwise than is provided by paragraph (3) if it appears to him appropriate to do so for the purpose of—

    (a) paying any arrears of benefit, or

    (b) making a payment in respect of a terminal period of an award, or of the period covered by the arrangement, where that terminal period is one of less than four weeks, or

for any similar purpose.

(5) The arrangement for benefit to be payable in accordance with this regulation may be terminated—

    (a) by the person entitled to benefit or a person acting on his behalf by notice in writing delivered or sent to an office of the Department, or

    (b) by the Secretary of State if the arrangement seems to him to be no longer appropriate to the circumstances of the particular case.

(6) In relation to payments of benefit which in pursuance of this regulation have been credited to a bank or other account under an arrangement made with the agreement of the person entitled to benefit, if in respect of that arrangement he made a statement in accordance with paragraph (2)*(b)* that he had read and understood the conditions applicable to payment of benefit in accordance with this regulation, section 119 of the Social Security Act, as applied to child benefit by section 8(1) of the Act, shall have effect as if there were omitted from the said section 119 (repayment of overpaid benefit not required where due care and diligence is shown)—

    (a) subsection (2), and

    (b) the words in subsection (2A) from "unless it is shown" to the end of that subsection.

(7) Where the Secretary of State certifies that it appears to him—

    (a) that an overpayment or any specified part thereof is not materially due to the arrangement to receive benefit provided for in this regulation; or

    (b) that in the particular circumstances of the case it would be inappropriate to apply the provisions of paragraph (6) to an overpayment or any specified part thereof,

the question whether repayment of the overpayment or, as the case may be, the specified part of the overpayment is required shall be determined in accordance with the said section 119 of the Social Security Act without the application of paragraph (6) of this regulation.

Election to receive payment weekly

8.—(1) A person to whom benefit is payable for an uninterrupted period beginning before and ending after 15th March 1982 may make an election, in accordance with paragraph (3), that benefit be payable weekly after that date, if either

    (a) he makes the election before the end of the 26th week from the day on which benefit was payable for the first four weeks in respect of which the Secretary of State made arrangements for four-weekly payment to the person entitled in accordance with regulation 6(1)*(b)* or regulation 7; or

(b) he was absent from Great Britain on the 15th March 1982 for one of the reasons specified in paragraph (4) and he makes the election before the end of the 26th week of the period beginning with the first week in respect of which benefit became payable to him in Great Britain on his return.

(2) Subject to paragraph (5), a person entitled to benefit may make an election, in accordance with paragraph (3), that benefit be paid weekly if he satisfies either of the following conditions:

(a) he satisfies the conditions specified in regulation 2(2)*(a)*, *(b)* and *(c)* of the Child Benefit and Social Security (Fixing and Adjustment of Rates) Regulations 1976 **(a)** (conditions for increase of child benefit for person living alone), or

(b) he, or his spouse residing with him or the person with whom he is living as husband and wife, is receiving—

    (i) a supplementary pension or allowance under the Supplementary Benefits Act 1976 **(b)**, or

    (ii) a supplement under the Family Income Supplements Act 1970 **(c)**.

(3) An election for benefit to be payable weekly under paragraphs (1) or (2) shall be effected by giving notice in writing to the Secretary of State delivered or sent to an office of the Department and shall be made when it is received.

(4) An election may not be made under paragraph (1)*(b)* unless the person's absence abroad on the 15th March 1982 was by reason of his being—

(a) a serving member of the forces, as defined by regulation 1(2) of the Social Security (Contributions) Regulations 1979 **(d)**, or

(b) the spouse of such a member, or

(c) a person living with such a member as husband and wife.

(5) Every person making an election for benefit to be paid weekly under paragraph (2) shall furnish such certificates, documents and such other information of facts as the Secretary of State may, in his discretion, require, affecting his right to receive payment of benefit weekly and in particular shall notify the Secretary of State in writing of any change of circumstances which he might reasonably be expected to know might affect the right to receive payment of benefit weekly, as soon as reasonably practicable after the occurrence thereof.

(6) Where a person makes an election, in accordance with this regulation, for benefit to be paid weekly, it shall continue to be so payable—

(a) in the case of an election under paragraph (1), so long as that person remains continually entitled to benefit, or

(b) in the case of an election under paragraph (2), so long as that person remains continually entitled to benefit and the conditions specified in that paragraph continue to be satisfied.

(7) A person who has made an election that benefit be payable weekly may cancel it at any time by a notice in writing delivered or sent to an office of the Department; and effect shall be given to such a notice as soon as is convenient.

(a) S.I. 1976/1267; relevant amending instrument is S.I. 1980/110.
(h) 1976 c.71.
(c) 1970 c.55.
(d) S.I. 1979/591, to which there are amendments not relevant to these regulations.

Information concerning elections

9.   The Secretary of State shall take steps to notify—

(a) persons to whom regulation 8(1) applies of their rights under that regulation; and

(b) persons to whom benefit is payable of the effect of regulation 8(2).

Further information and notification of change of circumstances

10.   Every person claiming benefit, or to whom benefit has been awarded, or to whom benefit is payable, shall furnish in such manner and at such times as the Secretary of State may determine such certificates and other documents and such information of facts affecting the person's right to benefit or, as the case may be, to its receipt, as the Secretary of State may, in his discretion, require (either as a condition on which any sum or sums shall be payable or otherwise) and in particular shall notify the Secretary of State in writing of any change of circumstances which he might reasonably be expected to know might affect the right to benefit, or to its receipt, as soon as reasonably practicable after the occurrence thereof.

Extinguishment of right to payment of sums on account of benefit

11.—(1) Subject to paragraph (2), the right to payment of any sum on account of benefit shall be extinguished where payment thereof is not obtained within the period of 12 months from the date on which the right is to be treated as having arisen; and for the purposes of this regulation the right shall be treated as having arisen—

(a) in relation to any such sum contained in an instrument of payment which has been given or sent for the purpose of making payment thereof to the payee or to an approved place for collection by him (whether or not received or collected, as the case may be) and notwithstanding that that sum is greater or less than the sum to which the payee has the right to payment—

    (i) on the date on the said instrument of payment; or

    (ii) if a further instrument of payment has been so given or sent as a replacement for an instrument of payment previously given or sent, on the date on the last such instrument of payment;

(b) in relation to any such sum to which sub-paragraph *(a)* of this paragraph does not apply, but where notice is given (whether orally or in writing) or is sent that the sum contained in the notice is available for collection and notwithstanding that that sum is greater or less than the sum to which the payee has the right to payment—

    (i) if written notice is sent through the post, on the date on which it would be delivered in the ordinary course of post; and

    (ii) in any other case, on the date of the notice,

and if in any case more than one such notice is given or sent, on the date determined by reference to the first such notice;

(c) in relation to any such sum to which neither sub-paragraph *(a)* nor sub-paragraph *(b)* of this paragraph applies, on such date as the Secretary of State, in his discretion, determines.

(2) Where a question arises whether the right to payment of any sum on account of benefit has been extinguished by the operation of this regulation and the determining authority is satisfied that—

(a) after the expiration of the said period of 12 months the Secretary of State has received written notice requesting payment of that sum; and

(b) throughout a period commencing within the said period of 12 months and continuing up to the date on which the said notice was given there was good cause for not giving that notice,

the said period of 12 months shall be extended to the date on which the determining authority decides that question and for the purposes of the operation of this regulation thereafter the right to payment of that sum shall, notwithstanding the provisions of paragraph (1), be treated as having arisen on that date.

(3) In this regulation—

"payee" means a person to whom sums on account of benefit are payable; and

"approved place" means a place approved by the Secretary of State for the purpose of making payment of sums on account of benefit.

PART IV

MISCELLANEOUS PROVISIONS

Modification of section 6(3) of the Act

12.   A person shall not be disentitled to benefit in respect of a child for any week by virtue of the provisions of section 6(3) of the Act (except where regulations otherwise provide, no person to be entitled to benefit for any week on a claim made by him after that week if benefit in respect of the same child has already been paid for that week to another person, whether or not that other person was entitled to it) if in respect of that week—

(a) the determining authority has decided that the benefit that has already been paid in respect of that child is required to be repaid and, where that determining authority is one from whose decision an appeal lies, the time for appealing has expired and no appeal has been made; or

(b) the benefit already paid to the other person has been voluntarily repaid to or recovered by the Department in a case where the determining authority has decided that that benefit while not properly payable is not required to be repaid.

Persons unable to act

13.—(1) In the case of any person to whom benefit is payable or who is alleged to be entitled to benefit, or by whom or on whose behalf a claim has been made, if he is for the time being unable to act and either—

(a) no receiver has been appointed by the Court of Protection with power to claim or as the case may be to receive benefit on his behalf; or

(b) in Scotland, his estate is not being administered by any curator or other guardian acting or appointed in terms of law,

the Secretary of State may, upon written application made to him by a person over the age of 18, appoint that person to exercise, on behalf of the person who is unable to act, any right to which the latter may be entitled under the Act and to receive and deal on his behalf with any sums payable to him.

(2) Where the Secretary of State has made an appointment under paragraph (1)—

(a) he may at any time in his discretion revoke any such appointment;

(b) the person appointed may resign his office after having given one month's notice in writing to the Secretary of State of his intention to do so;

(c) any such appointment shall terminate when the Secretary of State is notified that a receiver or other person to whom paragraph (1)(a) or (b) applies has been appointed.

(3) Anything required by these regulations to be done by or to any such person as aforesaid who is for the time being unable to act may be done by or to the receiver, curator or other guardian, if any, or by or to the person appointed under this regulation to act on his behalf, and the receipt of any person appointed under this regulation shall be a good discharge to the Secretary of State for any sum paid.

Payment to a person under age 18

14. Where a person who is awarded benefit is under the age of 18, his signature on any instrument of payment shall be a sufficient discharge to the Secretary of State for any sum paid under such instrument.

Payments on death

15.—(1) On the death of a person who has made a claim or who is alleged to have been entitled to benefit, the Secretary of State may appoint such person as he may think fit to proceed with or to make the claim; and the provisions of these regulations shall apply, subject to the necessary modifications, to any such claim.

(2) Subject to the provisions of paragraph (4), any sum payable by way of benefit which is payable under an award on a claim proceeded with or made under paragraph (1) may be paid or distributed by the Secretary of State to or amongst persons over the age of 16 claiming as personal representatives, legatees, next of kin, or creditors of the deceased (or, where the deceased was illegitimate, to or amongst other persons over the age of 16), and the provisions of regulation 11 shall apply to any such payment or distribution; and—

(a) the receipt of any such person shall be a good discharge to the Secretary of State for any sum so paid; and

(b) where the Secretary of State is satisfied that any such sum or part thereof is needed for the benefit of any person under the age of 16, he may obtain a good discharge therefor by paying the sum or part thereof to a person over that age (who need not be a person specified in this paragraph) who satisfies the Secretary of State that he will apply the sum so paid for the benefit of the person under the age of 16.

(3) Subject as aforesaid, any sum payable by way of benefit to the deceased, payment of which he had not obtained at the date of his death, may, unless the right thereto was already extinguished at that date, be paid or distributed to or amongst such persons as are mentioned in paragraph (2), and the provisions of regulation 11 shall apply to any such payment or distribution; so however that, for the purpose of regulation 11, the period of 12 months shall be calculated from the date on which the right to payment of any sum is treated as having arisen in relation to any such person and not from the date on which that right is treated as having arisen in relation to the deceased.

(4) Paragraphs (2) and (3) shall not apply in any case unless written application for the payment of any such sum is made to the Secretary of State within 12 months from the date of the deceased's death or within such longer period as the Secretary of State may allow in any particular case.

(5) The Secretary of State may dispense with strict proof of the title of any person claiming in accordance with the provisions of this regulation.

(6) In paragraph (2) "next of kin" means—

(a) in England and Wales, the persons who would take beneficially on an intestacy; and

(b) in Scotland, the persons entitled to the moveable estate of the deceased on intestacy.

Payment to a third party and to a spouse as alternative payee

16.—(1) In any case where—

(a) it appears to the Secretary of State to be necessary for protecting the interests of a person entitled to benefit, or of a child in respect of whom benefit is payable, that arrangements should be made whereby that benefit should be paid to another person on behalf of the person entitled to it; or

(b) a person entitled to benefit in respect of a child requests the Secretary of State to make that benefit payable to another person on his behalf; or

(c) such a person as is mentioned in regulation 6 of the Child Benefit (Residence and Persons Abroad) Regulations 1976 (a) is in fact absent from Great Britain;

the Secretary of State may, in his discretion, make arrangements whereby the benefit payable to the person entitled to it may be paid to another person on his behalf.

(2) Without prejudice to paragraph (1), where one of two spouses residing together is entitled to benefit the Secretary of State may make arrangements whereby that benefit, as well as being payable to the spouse entitled to it, may, in the alternative, be paid to the other spouse on behalf of the spouse entitled to it.

Breach of regulations

17. Any person who contravenes a requirement of regulation 6(5) or 10 shall be guilty of an offence and shall be liable, on summary conviction, to a fine not exceeding £200.

Revocations

18. The revocations specified in column (1) of Schedule 2 to these regulations are hereby revoked to the extent mentioned in column (3) of that Schedule.

(a) S.I. 1976/963, to which there are amendments not relevant to these regulations.

Signed by authority of the Secretary of State for Social Services.

Tony Newton,
Minister of State,
Department of Health and Social Security.
14th December 1984.

SCHEDULE 1   Regulation 5

BENEFITS UNDER THE SOCIAL SECURITY ACT CLAIMS FOR WHICH MAY BE INTER-
CHANGED WITH A CLAIM TO CHILD BENEFIT

Child's special allowance

Guardian's allowance

Maternity benefit claimed after confinement

Industrial death benefit by virtue of section 70

Increase for child dependant by virtue of sections 41, 49, 64 and 76, or regulations
made under section 39(4).

SCHEDULE 2   Regulation 18

REVOCATIONS

Regulations revoked (1)	Reference (2)	Extent of revocation (3)
The Child Benefit (Claims and Payments) Regulations 1976	S.I.1976/964	The whole of the regulations.
The Child Benefit (Miscellaneous Minor Amendments) Regulations 1976	S.I. 1976/1758	Regulation 2.
The Child Benefit (Miscellaneous Amendments) Regulations 1978	S.I. 1978/540	Regulation 3.
The Child Benefit (Claims and Payments) Amendment Regulations 1981	S.I. 1981/1772	The whole of the regulations.
The Child Benefit (Claims and Payments) Amendment Regulations 1982	S.I. 1982/1242	Regulations 2 and 4.
The Social Security Adjudication (Consequential Amendments) Regulations 1984	S.I. 1984/458	Regulation 9.

EXPLANATORY NOTE

(This Note is not part of the Regulations.)

These regulations are made for the purpose only of consolidating the Child Benefit (Claims and Payments) Regulations 1976 with subsequent amending regulations, all of which they revoke. They are accordingly not required to be referred to the Social Security Advisory Committee: Social Security Act 1980 (c.30) section 10(2) and paragraph 20 of Schedule 3.

The regulations are in the same general form as those which they replace, the main substance being in Parts II and III. These deal, respectively, with the making of claims to child benefit and with the payment of benefit. Part IV of the regulations contains miscellaneous provisions. Part V of the 1976 Regulations, which set out transitional arrangements, is no longer needed.

STATUTORY INSTRUMENTS

1984 No. 1963

PROTECTION OF WRECKS

The Protection of Wrecks (Designation No. 3) Order 1984

Made - - - -	*17th December* 1984
Laid before Parliament	*10th January* 1985
Coming into Operation	*1st February* 1985

The Secretary of State for Transport, being satisfied that the site identified in Article 2 of this Order is, or may prove to be, the site of a vessel believed lying wrecked on or in the sea bed and that, on account of the historical and archaeological importance of the vessel, the site ought to be protected from unauthorised interference, and that the case is one in which an Order should be made as a matter of immediate urgency, in exercise of the powers conferred upon him by section 1(1), (2) and (4) of the Protection of Wrecks Act 1973(**a**), hereby orders as follows:—

1. This Order may be cited as the Protection of Wrecks (Designation No. 3) Order 1984 and shall come into operation on 1st February 1985.

2.—(1) The site where a vessel lies, or is supposed to lie, and in respect of which this Order is made, is in position Latitude 50° 42.52′ North, Longitude 1° 29.597′ West.

(2) The area within a distance of 50 metres of the said position, but excluding any part of that area which lies above high-water mark of ordinary spring tides, shall be a restricted area for the purposes of the Protection of Wrecks Act 1973.

3. The Protection of Wrecks (Designation No. 1) Order 1984(**b**) is hereby revoked.

Nicholas Ridley,
Secretary of State for Transport.

17th December 1984.

(**a**) 1973 c. 33.   (**b**) S.I. 1984/521.

EXPLANATORY NOTE

(This Note is not part of the Order.)

This Order designates as a restricted area for the purposes of the Protection of Wrecks Act 1973 an area near the Isle of Wight round the site of what is, or may prove to be, the wreck of a vessel which is of historical and archaeological importance.

This Order corrects an error in the position of the centre of the site of an historic wreck to which the Protection of Wrecks (Designation No. 1) Order 1984 was intended to relate: that Order is accordingly revoked.

STATUTORY INSTRUMENTS

1984 No. 1965

HOUSING, ENGLAND, AND WALES
HOUSING, SCOTLAND
RATING AND VALUATION

The Housing Benefits Amendment (No. 4) Regulations 1984

Made - - -	*17th December* 1984
Laid before Parliament	*18th December* 1984
Coming into Operation	*19th December* 1984

The Secretary of State for Social Services, with the consent of the Treasury(**a**), in exercise of the powers conferred on him by section 28(1) of the Social Security and Housing Benefits Act 1982(**b**), after consultation with organisations appearing to him to be representative of authorities concerned(**c**), the Social Security Advisory Committee having agreed that the proposals to make regulation 2(2), (3), (4) and (7) should not be referred to it, but without having referred the proposals to make regulation 2(5) and (6) to the Committee since it appears to the Secretary of State that, by reason of urgency, it is inexpedient to do so(**d**), hereby makes the following regulations:—

Citation and commencement
1. These regulations, which may be cited as the Housing Benefits Amendment (No. 4) Regulations 1984, shall come into operation on 19th December 1984.

Amendment of the Housing Benefits Regulations 1982
2.—(1) The Housing Benefits Regulations 1982(**e**) shall be amended in accordance with the following provisions of this regulation.

(2) In regulation 2(1) (interpretation) in the definition of "rent", after paragraph (*c*) there shall be inserted the following new paragraph:—

"(*cc*) payments in respect of or in consequence of use and occupation of a dwelling,".

(3) In regulation 6 (eligibility for rate rebate) the following paragraph shall be substituted for paragraph (2):—

"(2) Notwithstanding paragraph (1) —

(**a**) *See* section 28(1) of the Social Security and Housing Benefits Act 1982 (c.24).
(**b**) 1982 c.24.
(**c**) *See* section 36(1) of the Social Security and Housing Benefits Act 1982.
(**d**) *See* sections 9(7) and 10 of the Social Security Act 1980 (c.30) as amended by section 48(5) of and paragraph 30 of Schedule 4 to the Social Security and Housing Benefits Act 1982.
(**e**) S.I. 1982/1124; the relevant amending instruments are S.I. 1519, 1984/104.

(a) subject to regulation 8A, a boarder on supplementary benefit is not eligible for a rate rebate in respect of the dwelling at which he boards; and

(b) a person who is entitled to supplementary benefit but who is not treated under sub-paragraph (a) of regulation 14(3) of the Requirements Regulations as responsible for housing expenditure is not eligible for a rate rebate in respect of that housing expenditure.".

(4) In regulation 8(3) (eligibility for rent allowance) —

(a) in sub-paragraph (a) the word "and" shall be omitted;

(b) in sub-paragraph (b) after "he boards" there shall be inserted "; and"; and

(c) the following sub-paragraph shall be inserted after sub-paragraph (b) —

"(c) a person who is entitled to supplementary benefit but who is not treated under sub-paragraph (a) of regulation 14(3) of the Requirements Regulations as responsible for housing expenditure is not eligible for a rent allowance in respect of that housing expenditure.".

(5) In regulation 11 (joint occupiers) —

(a) in paragraph (1) for "paragraph (2)" there shall be substituted "paragraphs (2) and (3); and

(b) the following paragraph shall be inserted after paragraph (2):—

"(3)   If a joint occupier of his dwelling was, at any time during the period of eight weeks prior to the creation of the joint tenancy or other agreement giving rise to the joint liability to pay rent or, as the case may be, to make payments by way of rates, a non-dependant of one or more of the other joint occupiers of that dwelling, he shall not be eligible for housing benefit in respect of that dwelling unless the appropriate authority is satisfied that that joint tenancy or other agreement was not created to take advantage of the rate rebate scheme, the rent rebate scheme or the rent allowance scheme, as the case may be.".

(6)   In regulation 18 (deductions for non-dependants) the following paragraph shall be inserted after paragraph (3):—

"(3A)   For the purposes of this regulation, where a person who is a joint occupier of his dwelling is not eligible for a housing benefit by virtue of regulation 11(3), he shall be treated as a non-dependant in respect of whom a deduction falls to be made in calculating any housing benefit payable to any of the other joint occupiers of that dwelling.".

(7)   The following regulation shall be substituted for regulation 23 (disentitlement for rent allowance and rate rebate):—

"Disentitlement to rent allowance and rate rebate
    23.—(1)   A person shall not be entitled to a rent allowance or, as the case may be, a rate rebate where it appears to the appropriate authority

that the tenancy or other agreement to pay rent or, as the case may be, to make payments by way of rates was created to take advantage of the rent allowance scheme, or insofar as the tenancy or other agreement relates to payments by way of rates, the rate rebate scheme, so however that this provision shall not apply to a person who was, for any period within the eight weeks prior to the creation of the tenancy or other agreement to pay rent or, as the case may be, to make payments by way of rates, otherwise liable to pay rent in respect of the same dwelling.

(2) A person shall not be entitled to a rent allowance or, as the case may be, a rate rebate where —

(*a*) he resides with the person to whom he is liable to pay rent or, as the case may be, to make payments by way of rates in respect of the dwelling; and

(*b*) either that person is a close relative or the tenancy or other agreement between them is other than on a commercial basis.

(3) For the purposes of paragraph (2), "close relative" means a parent, son, daughter, step-parent, step-son, step-daughter, father-in-law, mother-in-law, son-in-law, daughter-in-law, brother, sister, brother-in-law or sister-in-law.".

Norman Fowler,
Secretary of State for Social Services.

17th December 1984.

We consent,

T. Garel-Jones,
A. G. Hamilton,
Two of the Lords Commissioners of
Her Majesty's Treasury.

17th December 1984.

EXPLANATORY NOTE

(This Note is not part of the Regulations.)

These regulations amend the Housing Benefits Regulations 1982 ("the principal regulations"). The definition of rent in regulation 2 of the principal regulations is amended to include payments in respect of or in consequence of use and occupation of a dwelling. Regulations 6 and 8 of the principal regulations are amended to provide that a person who is treated as a non-householder (a person not responsible for housing expenditure) for the purposes of the Supplementary Benefit (Requirements) Regulations 1983 (S.I. 1983/1399) is not eligible for a rate rebate or rent allowance in respect of the dwelling in which he is treated as a non-householder.

Regulation 11 of the principal regulations is amended to provide that where a joint tenancy or other joint agreement to pay rent or rates is entered into within eight weeks of one of the joint occupiers being a non-dependant in the same dwelling, the person who was previously a non-dependant is not eligible for housing benefit. Regulation 18 of the principal regulations is amended to provide that the other joint occupiers are still treated as liable to a non-dependant deduction in the calculation of their housing benefit.

A new regulation is substituted for regulation 23 of the principal regulations. The new regulation provides that a person not previously liable to pay rent for a dwelling is not entitled to a rate rebate or a rent allowance in respect of that dwelling if the agreement to pay rates or rent was entered into in order to take advantage of the housing benefits scheme. It also provides that a person who resides with a close relative as defined or who is paying rates or rent other than on a commercial basis to the person with whom he resides is not entitled to a rate rebate or rent allowance.

Regulation 2(5) and (6) will be referred to the Social Security advisory Committee under sub-section (7) of section 10 of the Social Security Act 1980 unless the Committee agrees that that sub-section shall not apply. The Committee agreed that the proposals to make the other regulations in this Instrument should not be referred to it.

STATUTORY INSTRUMENTS

1984 No. 1966

TAXES

The Capital Gains Tax (Gilt-edged Securities) Order 1984

Made - - - 17*th December* 1984

The Treasury, in exercise of the powers conferred on them by paragraph 1 of Schedule 2 to the Capital Gains Tax Act 1979(**a**), hereby make the following Order:

1. This Order may be cited as the Capital Gains Tax (Gilt-edged Securities) Order 1984.

2. The following securities are hereby specified for the purposes of Schedule 2 to the Capital Gains Tax Act 1979:

2½% Exchequer Stock 1986
3% British Transport Stock 1978–88
9½% Treasury Convertible Stock 1989
10% Exchequer Stock 1989 "A"
11% Exchequer Stock 1989
2% Index-linked Treasury Stock 1990
10% Treasury Convertible Stock 1990
10½% Treasury Convertible Stock 1992
9¾% Exchequer Stock 1998
10¼% Conversion Stock 1999
9¾% Conversion Stock 2001
9½% Conversion Stock 2002
10% Conversion Stock 2002
9½% Conversion Stock 2004

John Major,
Donald Thompson,
Two of the Lords Commissioners of
Her Majesty's Treasury.

17th December 1984.

(**a**) 1979 c.14.

EXPLANATORY NOTE

(This Note is not part of the Order.)

This Order specifies gilt-edged securities which are exempt from tax on capital gains if held for more than twelve months.

Other specified gilt-edged securities which enjoy like exemption are listed in the Capital Gains Tax (Gilt-edged Securities) Order 1983 (S.I. 1983/1774) and in the Explanatory Note to that Order. The British Transport 3% Stock 1978–88 now specified was issued under section 12 of the National Loans Act 1968 (c.13) on the same terms and conditions as those currently applying to stock of the same name which was issued under section 89 of the Transport Act 1947 (c.49). The latter stock is now a liability of the National Loans Fund by virtue of section 36 of the Transport Act 1962 (c.46) and was specified in Part II of Schedule 2 to the Capital Gains Tax Act 1979.

STATUTORY INSTRUMENTS

1984 No. 1967

ACQUISITION OF LAND

COMPENSATION

The Acquisition of Land (Rate of Interest after Entry) (No. 4) Regulations 1984

Made - - - -	*17th December* 1984
Laid before Parliament	*20th December* 1984
Coming into Operation	*9th January* 1985

The Treasury, in exercise of the powers conferred upon them by section 32(1) of the Land Compensation Act 1961(**a**), and of all other powers enabling them in that behalf, hereby make the following Regulations:—

1. These Regulations may be cited as the Acquisition of Land (Rate of Interest after Entry) (No. 4) Regulations 1984, and shall come into operation on 9th January 1985.

2. The rate of interest on any compensation in respect of the compulsory acquisition of an interest in any land on which entry has been made before the payment of the compensation shall be 10⅞ per cent. per annum.

3. The Acquisition of Land (Rate of Interest after Entry) (No. 3) Regulations 1984(**b**) are hereby revoked.

John Major,
Donald Thompson,
Two of the Lords Commissioners
of Her Majesty's Treasury.

17th December 1984.

(**a**) 1961 c. 33.   (**b**) S.I. 1984/1647.

EXPLANATORY NOTE

(This Note is not part of the Regulations.)

These Regulations decrease from 11½ per cent. to 10⅞ per cent. per annum, in respect of any period after the coming into operation of these Regulations, the rate of interest payable where entry is made, before payment of compensation, on land in England and Wales which is being purchased compulsorily, and revoke the Acquisition of Land (Rate of Interest after Entry) (No. 3) Regulations 1984.

STATUTORY INSTRUMENTS

1984 No. 1968

ACQUISITION OF LAND

COMPENSATION

The Acquisition of Land (Rate of Interest after Entry) (Scotland) (No. 4) Regulations 1984

Made - - -	*17th December* 1984
Laid before Parliament	*20th December* 1984
Coming into Operation	*9th January* 1985

The Treasury, in exercise of the powers conferred upon them by section 40(1) of the Land Compensation (Scotland) Act 1963(**a**), and of all other powers enabling them in that behalf, hereby make the following Regulations:—

1. These Regulations may be cited as the Acquisition of Land (Rate of Interest after Entry) (Scotland) (No. 4) Regulations 1984, and shall come into operation on 9th January 1985.

2. The rate of interest on any compensation in respect of the compulsory acquisition of an interest in any land on which entry has been made before the payment of the compensation shall be $10\frac{7}{8}$ per cent. per annum.

3. The Acquisition of Land (Rate of Interest after Entry) (Scotland) (No. 3) Regulations 1984(**b**) are hereby revoked.

John Major,
Donald Thompson,
Two of the Lords Commissioners of
Her Majesty's Treasury.

17th December 1984.

(**a**) 1963 c.51.   (**b**) S.I. 1984/1648.

EXPLANATORY NOTE

(This Note is not part of the Regulations.)

These Regulations decrease from 11½ per cent. to 10⅞ per cent. per annum, in respect of any period after the coming into operation of these Regulations, the rate of interest payable where entry is made, before payment of compensation, on land in Scotland which is being purchased compulsorily, and revoke the Acquisition of Land (Rate of Interest after Entry) (Scotland) (No. 3) Regulations 1984.

STATUTORY INSTRUMENTS

1984 No. 1969

CUSTOMS AND EXCISE

The Customs Duties (ECSC) (Amendment No. 7) Order 1984

Made - - - -	*18th December* 1984
Laid before the House of Commons	*21st December* 1984
Coming into Operation	*1st January* 1985

The Treasury, by virtue of the powers conferred on them by section 5(1) and (3) of the European Communities Act 1972 (**a**) and of all other powers enabling them in that behalf, on the recommendation of the Secretary of State, hereby make the following Order:—

1. This Order may be cited as the Customs Duties (ECSC) (Amendment No. 7) Order 1984 and shall come into operation on 1st January 1985.

2. The Customs Duties (ECSC) Order 1981 (**b**) shall be further amended as follows:—

    (*a*) in Article 2 (which provides that the Order shall apply to goods covered by the E.C.S.C. Treaty included in the Schedule of Customs Duties forming part of the common customs tariff of the European Economic Community and referred to in that Order and in this Order as "the CCT Schedule") the reference to the CCT Schedule shall be a reference to the CCT Schedule annexed to Council Regulation (EEC) No. 950/68 (**c**) as last amended by Council Regulation (EEC) No. 3400/84 (**d**);

    (*b*) in Part II of Schedule 1

      (i) before the word "Niger" there shall be inserted the word "Mozambique".

      (ii) after the word "Rwanda" there shall be inserted the words "Saint Christopher and Nevis";

      (iii) after the words "British Virgin Islands" the word "Brunei" shall be deleted;

      (iv) in the entry relating to "Falkland Islands and Dependencies" the words "and Dependencies" shall be deleted;

      (v) before the words "French Polynesia" there shall be inserted the words "Falkland Island Dependencies".

      (vi) after the words "French Southern and Antarctic Territories" there shall be inserted the word "Greenland";

      (vii) in the entry relating to "St Helena and Dependencies" the words "and Dependencies" shall be deleted;

(**a**) 1972 c.68; section 5(3) was amended by the Customs and Excise Duties (General Reliefs) Act 1979 (c.3), Schedule 2, para. 3.
(**b**) S.I. 1981/1769, amended by S.I. 1982/1773, 1983/342, 1782, 1802, 1984/1306, 1452.
(**c**) OJ No. L172, 22.7.1968, p.l. (OJ/SE 1968(I)p.275).
(**d**) OJ No. L320, 10.12.1984.

(viii) before the words "Turks and Caicos Islands" there shall be inserted the words "St Helena Dependencies";

(ix) the entry relating to "West Indies Associated States (St Kitts-Nevis)" shall be deleted.

John Major,
A. G. Hamilton,
Two of the Lords Commissioners,
of Her Majesty's Treasury.

18th December 1984.

EXPLANATORY NOTE

(This Note is not part of the Order.)

This Order, which comes into operation on 1st January 1985, further amends the Customs Duties (ECSC) Order 1981. Under that Order, which charges customs duties in accordance with the unified ECSC tariff on certain ECSC products imported into the United Kingdom, the rates of duty are charged by reference to the Schedule of Customs Duties ("CCT Schedule") forming part of the common customs tariff of the EEC. The ECSC unified tariff has been amended with effect from 1st January 1985 to take account of the reductions in customs duties to be made by member states of the ECSC under the Geneva (1979) Protocol to the General Agreement on Tariffs and Trade (Cmnd. 7668) during 1985 and the CCT Schedule contained in the Annex to Regulation (EEC) No. 950/68 (OJ/SE 1968(I) p.275) has been amended accordingly by Regulation (EEC) No. 3400/84 (OJ No. L320, 10.12.1984). This Order updates the reference to the CCT Schedule.

This Order also amends the 1981 Order to take account of (1) the gaining of independence of Brunei and Saint Christopher and Nevis; (2) the accession of Mozambique and Saint Christopher and Nevis to the Lomé Convention and (3) the change of status of Greenland which is now one of the Overseas Countries and Territories to which Part IV of the EEC Treaty applies.

STATUTORY INSTRUMENTS

1984 No. 1970 (S. 158)

NATIONAL HEALTH SERVICE, SCOTLAND

The National Health Service (Superannuation—Special Provisions) (Scotland) Regulations 1984

Made - - - -	10*th December* 1984
Laid before Parliament	9*th January* 1985
Coming into Operation	30*th January* 1985

In exercise of the powers conferred on me by sections 10 and 12 of the Superannuation Act 1972(**a**) and of all other powers enabling me in that behalf, after consulting with such representatives of persons likely to be affected by these regulations as appear to me to be appropriate, in accordance with section 10(4) of that Act, and with the consent of the Treasury(**b**), I hereby make the following regulations:—

Citation and commencement

1. These regulations may be cited as the National Health Service (Superannuation—Special Provisions) (Scotland) Regulations 1984 and shall come into operation on 30th January 1985 and shall take effect from 1st April 1974.

Interpretation

2. In these regulations, unless the context otherwise requires—

"average remuneration" has the same meaning as in regulation 38 of the National Health Service (Superannuation) (Scotland) Regulations 1980(**c**) as if the employee concerned was subject to those regulations;

"dependant" means a person who the Secretary of State is satisfied is wholly or mainly supported by the employee;

"employee" means a person formerly in local government service and at the effective date of these regulations in the paid employment of an employing authority;

(**a**) 1972 c. 11; section 10(1)(*a*) was amended by the National Health Service (Scotland) Act 1972 (c. 58), Schedule 7, Part II.

(**b**) *See* the Transfer of Functions (Minister for the Civil Service and Treasury) Order 1981 (S.I. 1981/1670), article 2.

(**c**) S.I. 1980/1177, amended by S.I. 1981/1680, 1983/272.

"employing authority" means a Regional Hospital Board, an Executive Council or a joint committee of Executive Councils constituted under section 32(4) of the National Health Service (Scotland) Act 1947(**a**), a Health Board, the Common Services Agency for the Scottish Health Service, a State Hospital Management Committee constituted under section 90(2) of the Mental Health (Scotland) Act 1960(**b**) and any such other body constituted under the National Health Service (Scotland) Act 1947, the National Health Service (Scotland) Act 1972(**c**), the National Health Service (Scotland) Act 1978(**d**) or any other Act relating to the provision of health services as the Secretary of State may approve;

"local government service" means employment under a scheduled body within the meaning of the Local Government Superannuation (Scotland) Regulations 1974(**e**), a local authority, or a local Act authority within the meaning of section 34(1) of the Local Government Superannuation (Scotland) Act 1937(**f**);

"relevant local authority" in relation to any employee, means the local authority by which he was employed immediately before he was transferred to the employment of an employing authority under the National Health Service (Scotland) Act 1972;

"the superannuation regulations" means the National Health Service (Superannuation) (Scotland) Regulations 1980.

Persons to whom the regulations apply

3. These regulations shall apply to an employee who ceases to be in the employment of an employing authority at or after the age at which he would have received superannuation benefits had he been subject to the superannuation regulations or who attains the age of 70 years while in the employment of an employing authority and who—

(*a*) was transferred to the employment of an employing authority on 1st April 1974 by virtue of an order made under sections 31, 32 or 34 of the National Health Service (Scotland) Act 1972; and

(*b*) in his local government service immediately prior to that transfer had reasonable expectation of receiving a gratuity to be paid in accordance with the provisions of section 18 of the Local Government Superannuation Act 1953(**g**); and

(*c*) has remained in the employment of an employing authority without a continuous break of 12 months or more (disregarding, in calculating the length of any break, any period during which the Secretary of State is satisfied that he could not be employed through illness or some other cause); and

(*d*) is not eligible for benefits under the superannuation regulations;

(**a**) 1947 c. 27.
(**b**) 1960 c. 61; section 90(2) was substituted by the Mental Health (Amendment) (Scotland) Act 1983 (c. 39), section 26(1).
(**c**) 1972 c. 58.   (**d**) 1978 c. 29.
(**e**) S.I. 1974/812; relevant amending instruments are S.I. 1975/638, 1984/1232.
(**f**) 1937 c. 69.
(**g**) 1953 c. 25.

or where the said employee dies while in the employment of an employing authority, to his widow or any other dependant.

Payment of benefit

4. The Secretary of State may pay to any person to whom these regulations apply a benefit either—

(*a*) by way of a lump sum of an amount not exceeding twice the amount of the average remuneration of the employee in his employment under an employing authority; or

(*b*) by way of periodical payments not exceeding in aggregate the amount aforesaid; or

(*c*) by way of an annuity the capital value of which does not exceed the amount aforesaid; or

(*d*) by way of a combination of (*a*) and (*b*) above provided the payment does not exceed in aggregate the amount aforesaid.

Benefit payable to widow or other dependant

5. Where the Secretary of State has granted a benefit to an employee under regulation 3 where either—

(*a*) the benefit was by way of periodical payments and the employee dies before all the payments are completed; or

(*b*) the benefit was by way of an annuity and the employee dies before receiving an aggregate amount equal to the capital value of the annuity,

the Secretary of State may grant a benefit to the widow or any other dependant of the employee and for that purpose the said regulation 3 shall have effect as if the employee had died while in the employment of an employing authority but as if for the amount specified in that regulation there were substituted the aggregate amount of the periodical payments outstanding at the employee's death or, as the case may be, the difference between the capital value of the annuity and the aggregate amount of the payments made to the employee before his death.

Conditions for payment of benefit

6.—(1) Any benefit paid under these regulations shall not exceed the gratuity which, in the reasonable expectation of an employee to whom these regulations apply, might have been received by him in respect of his local government service up to 1st April 1974.

(2) In assessing the reasonable expectations of an employee as aforesaid and in making payment of any benefit under these regulations the Secretary of State shall have regard to the terms of any scheme for the payment of gratuities operated by the local authority in whose service the employee was at the time of his transfer.

(3) Employment with an employing authority on or after 1st April 1974 shall be reckonable for the purposes of determining eligibility for a benefit but not for the purposes of calculating the amount of that benefit.

(4) Where an employee ceases to be in the employment of an employing authority on or after attaining the age at which he could have received superannuation benefits had he been subject to the superannuation regulations ("the earlier age") but before attaining the age at which the relevant local authority would have granted the gratuity ("the later age"), then for the purposes of regulation 4 the assumption shall be made that he has attained the later age, but the amount of benefit payable shall, except where the person retired by reason of permanent ill-health or infirmity of mind or body, be reduced by such amount as may be determined by the Government Actuary, to allow for the difference between the earlier age and the later age.

George Younger,
New St Andrew's House,   One of Her Majesty's Principal
Edinburgh.   Secretaries of State.
6th December 1984.

We consent,

A. G. Hamilton,
Donald Thompson,
Two of the Lords Commissioners of
Her Majesty's Treasury.

10th December 1984.

EXPLANATORY NOTE

(This Note is not part of the Regulations.)

These regulations provide for the payment of a benefit to an employee, or the widow or dependant of an employee, who was transferred from local government employment to the employment of the National Health Service in Scotland by virtue of an order under sections 31, 32 or 34 of the National Health Service (Scotland) Act 1972 and who in their local government service had expectation of receiving a gratuity under section 18 of the Local Government Superannuation Act 1953.

Regulations 3, 4 and 6 lay down the conditions necessary to qualify for a benefit and the various methods of calculation and payment of such a benefit. Regulation 5 provides that in the event of the death of an employee entitled to an annuity or periodical payments, payment may be made to the widow or dependant.

In exercise of the powers contained in section 12(1) of the Superannuation Act 1972 these regulations have effect from 1st April 1974 (regulation 1).

STATUTORY INSTRUMENTS

1984 No. 1971

SAVINGS BANKS

The Trustee Savings Banks (Interest-bearing Receipts) (No. 2) Order 1984

Made - - -	18*th December* 1984
Laid before Parliament	20*th December* 1984
Coming into Operation	21*st January* 1985

The Treasury, in exercise of the powers conferred on them by paragraph 2(1) of Schedule 5 to the Trustee Savings Banks Act 1981(**a**) and of all other powers enabling them in that behalf, hereby make the following Order:—

Citation and commencement

1. This Order may be cited as the Trustee Savings Banks (Interest-bearing Receipts) (No. 2) Order 1984 and shall come into operation on 21st January 1985.

Rate of Interest

2. Receipts issued under section 34(1) of the Trustee Savings Banks Act 1969(**b**) or any corresponding earlier enactment in respect of payments into the Fund for the Banks for Savings before 21st November 1979 shall carry interest at the rate of £10.25 per cent. per annum.

Revocation

3. The Trustee Savings Banks (Interest-bearing Receipts) Order 1984(**c**) is hereby revoked.

John Major,
A. G. Hamilton,
Two of the Lords Commissioners
of Her Majesty's Treasury.

18th December 1984.

(**a**) 1981 c.65.
(**b**) 1969 c.50, repealed by Schedule 8 to the Trustee Savings Banks Act 1981.
(**c**) S.I. 1984/612.

EXPLANATORY NOTE

(This Note is not part of the Order.)

This Order increases the rate of interest payable on receipts issued under Section 34(1) of the Trustee Savings Banks Act 1969 or any corresponding earlier enactment. The receipts relate to sums paid into the Fund for the Banks for Savings by trustee savings banks before 21st November 1979.

The increase in the rate of interest is from £9.75 to £10.25 per cent. per annum.

STATUTORY INSTRUMENTS

1984 No. 1972

SOCIAL SECURITY

The Pneumoconiosis etc. (Workers' Compensation) (Payment of Claims) (Amendment) Regulations 1984

Laid before Parliament in draft

Made - - - -	18*th December* 1984
Coming into Operation	1*st January* 1985

The Secretary of State in exercise of the powers conferred on him by sections 1, 4(1) and 7 of the Pneumoconiosis etc. (Workers' Compensation) Act 1979(**a**) ("the Act") and of all other powers enabling him in that behalf hereby makes the following Regulations, of which a draft has been approved by resolution of each House of Parliament.

Citation, commencement and revocation

1.—(1) These Regulations may be cited as the Pneumoconiosis etc. (Workers' Compensation) (Payment of Claims) (Amendment) Regulations 1984 and shall come into operation on 1st January 1985.

(2) Subject to Regulation 4, the Pneumoconiosis etc. (Workers' Compensation) (Payment of Claims) (Amendment) Regulations 1983 (**b**) ("the 1983 Regulations") are revoked.

Interpretation

2. In these Regulations the "principal Regulations" means the Pneumoconiosis etc. (Workers' Compensation) (Payment of Claims) Regulations 1979 (**c**) as amended by the 1983 Regulations.

Amendment of the principal Regulations

3. The principal Regulations shall be amended—

   (a) by the substitution of the Schedule to these Regulations for the Schedule to those Regulations, and

   (b) by the substitution of the amount of £1,109 for the amount of £1,066 in Regulations 5(1) and 8 of those Regulations and of the amount of £2,293 for the amount of £2,205 in Regulation 6(1) of those Regulations,

in any case in which a person first becomes entitled to a payment under the Act as a person disabled by a disease to which the Act applies or as a dependant of a person who immediately before he died was disabled by a disease to which the Act applies, as the case may be, on or after the date upon which these Regulations come into operation.

(**a**) 1979 c.41.   (**b**) S.I. 1983/1861.   (**c**) S.I. 1979/1726.

Transitional provision

4. Notwithstanding the revocation of the 1983 Regulations, those Regulations shall continue to have effect as provided by those Regulations in any case in which a person first becomes entitled to a payment under the Act as a person disabled by a disease to which the Act applies or as a dependant of a person who immediately before he died was disabled by a disease to which the Act applies, as the case may be, before the date upon which these Regulations come into operation.

Signed by order of the Secretary of State.

Peter Bottomley,
Joint Parliamentary Under Secretary of State,
Department of Employment.

18th December 1984.

Regulation 3   SCHEDULE
                               TABLE 1

(1)   Table 1 is for the determination of payments to disabled persons under Regulation 3 (or Regulation 6), and for the determination of payments to dependants of deceased sufferers under Regulation 4(1).

(2)   The relevant period is the period specified in Regulation 3(2) or 3(3) or, in the case of a disabled person to whom Regulation 6 applies (Payment where pneumoconiosis is accompanied by tuberculosis), the period specified in paragraph (1)(b) of that Regulation.

(3)   The age to be taken for the purpose of determining the amount payable to a disabled person is his age on the date specified in Regulation 3(2) or 3(3) or, in the case of a disabled person to whom Regulation 6 applies (Payment where pneumoconiosis is accompanied by tuberculosis), his age on the date specified in paragraph (1) of that Regulation. With a view to determining the amount payable to a dependant of a disabled person under Regulation 4(1), the age to be taken for the purpose of calculating the sum to be deducted from the amount which would have been payable to the disabled person had he still been alive is the age of the deceased at his last birthday preceding his death.

PART A

PAYMENTS TO DISABLED PERSONS TO WHOM IS PAYABLE DISABLEMENT BENEFIT UNDER SECTION 76 OF THE SOCIAL SECURITY ACT 1975 OR UNDER ANY CORRESPONDING PROVISION OF THE FORMER INDUSTRIAL INJURIES ACTS.

Age of disabled person	Percentage assessment for the relevant period									
	10% or less	11%–20%	21%–30%	40%	50%	60%	70%	80%	90%	100%
	£	£	£	£	£	£	£	£	£	£
37 and under	12,842	22,932	26,907	27,671	28,436	29,047	29,659	30,270	30,882	31,493
38	12,475	22,015	26,097	27,030	27,824	28,436	29,047	29,659	30,270	30,882
39	12,108	21,097	25,287	26,387	27,213	27,824	28,436	29,047	29,659	30,270
40	11,742	20,180	24,476	25,745	26,601	27,213	27,824	28,436	29,047	29,659
41	11,374	19,263	23,666	25,102	25,990	26,601	27,213	27,824	28,436	29,047
42	11,007	18,346	22,856	24,461	25,378	25,990	26,601	27,213	27,824	28,436
43	10,457	17,275	22,045	23,972	24,950	25,684	26,295	26,907	27,518	28,130
44	9,907	16,205	21,235	23,482	24,522	25,378	25,990	26,601	27,213	27,824
45	9,356	15,135	20,425	22,993	24,094	25,072	25,684	26,295	26,907	27,518
46	8,806	14,065	19,614	22,504	23,666	24,767	25,378	25,990	26,601	27,213
47	8,256	12,995	18,804	22,015	23,238	24,461	25,072	25,684	26,295	26,907
48	7,781	12,566	18,163	21,036	22,504	23,605	24,216	24,828	25,439	26,051
49	7,308	12,139	17,520	20,057	21,770	22,749	23,360	23,972	24,584	25,195
50	6,834	11,710	16,878	19,080	21,036	21,892	22,504	23,115	23,727	24,338
51	6,360	11,283	16,235	18,101	20,303	21,036	21,648	22,259	22,871	23,482
52	5,886	10,854	15,594	17,123	19,569	20,180	20,792	21,403	22,015	22,626
53	5,442	10,090	14,615	16,267	18,834	19,569	20,180	20,792	21,403	22,015
54	4,999	9,326	13,636	15,411	18,101	18,957	19,569	20,180	20,792	21,403
55	4,556	8,561	12,659	14,554	17,367	18,346	18,957	19,569	20,180	20,792
56	4,112	7,797	11,680	13,698	16,634	17,734	18,346	18,957	19,569	20,180
57	3,669	7,032	10,702	12,842	15,900	17,123	17,734	18,346	18,957	19,569
58	3,379	6,391	9,556	11,527	14,309	15,441	16,098	16,741	17,367	17,978
59	3,088	5,748	8,408	10,213	12,719	13,759	14,462	15,135	15,777	16,388
60	2,798	5,106	7,262	8,897	11,130	12,078	12,826	13,530	14,188	14,799
61	2,507	4,464	6,115	7,583	9,540	10,396	11,190	11,925	12,598	13,209
62	2,217	3,822	4,969	6,268	7,950	8,714	9,556	10,320	11,007	11,619
63	2,064	3,455	4,464	5,604	7,071	7,827	8,623	9,356	10,029	10,640
64	1,912	3,088	3,959	4,938	6,192	6,941	7,690	8,393	9,050	9,662
65	1,759	2,722	3,455	4,273	5,312	6,054	6,757	7,430	8,072	8,684
66	1,606	2,355	2,950	3,608	4,434	5,168	5,825	6,467	7,094	7,705
67	1,453	1,987	2,446	2,943	3,555	4,281	4,892	5,504	6,115	6,727
68	1,414	1,926	2,362	2,820	3,432	4,112	4,701	5,335	5,924	6,528
69	1,376	1,865	2,278	2,699	3,310	3,945	4,510	5,168	5,734	6,329
70	1,337	1,804	2,193	2,576	3,188	3,776	4,319	4,999	5,542	6,131
71	1,300	1,743	2,110	2,453	3,065	3,608	4,128	4,831	5,351	5,932
72	1,262	1,682	2,026	2,332	2,943	3,440	3,936	4,663	5,159	5,734
73	1,230	1,652	1,995	2,286	2,897	3,363	3,860	4,541	5,007	5,565
74	1,200	1,620	1,965	2,240	2,852	3,287	3,784	4,418	4,854	5,397
75	1,170	1,590	1,934	2,193	2,805	3,210	3,708	4,296	4,701	5,228
76	1,139	1,559	1,903	2,148	2,759	3,135	3,631	4,174	4,548	5,061
77 and over	1,109	1,529	1,873	2,102	2,713	3,058	3,555	4,052	4,395	4,892

PART B

PAYMENTS TO DISABLED PERSONS TO WHOM IS PAYABLE AN ALLOWANCE UNDER A SCHEME MADE OR HAVING EFFECT AS IF MADE UNDER SECTION 5 OF THE INDUSTRIAL INJURIES AND DISEASES (OLD CASES) ACT 1975 OR UNDER ANY CORRESPONDING PROVISION OF THE FORMER OLD CASES ACTS.

Age of disabled person	Extent of incapacity for the relevant period	
	Partial	Total
	£	£
37 and under	22,932	31,493
38	22,015	30,882
39	21,097	30,270
40	20,180	29,659
41	19,263	29,047
42	18,346	28,436
43	17,275	28,130
44	16,205	27,824
45	15,135	27,518
46	14,065	27,213
47	12,995	26,907
48	12,566	26,051
49	12,139	25,195
50	11,710	24,338
51	11,283	23,482
52	10,854	22,626
53	10,090	22,015
54	9,326	21,403
55	8,561	20,792
56	7,797	20,180
57	7,032	19,569
58	6,391	17,978
59	5,748	16,388
60	5,106	14,799
61	4,464	13,209
62	3,822	11,619
63	3,455	10,640
64	3,088	9,662
65	2,722	8,684
66	2,355	7,705
67	1,987	6,727
68	1,926	6,528
69	1,865	6,329
70	1,804	6,131
71	1,743	5,932
72	1,682	5,734
73	1,652	5,565
74	1,620	5,397
75	1,590	5,228
76	1,559	5,061
77 and over	1,529	4,892

TABLE 2

(1) *Table 2 is for the determination of additional payments to dependants of deceased sufferers who died as a result of the disease under Regulation 4(2) or Regulation 4(6).*

(2) *The relevant period is the period specified in Regulation 3(2) or 3(3) or, in the case of a disabled person to whom Regulation 6 applies (Payment where pneumoconiosis is accompanied by tuberculosis), the period specified in paragraph (1)(b) of that Regulation.*

PART A

PAYMENTS TO DEPENDANTS TO WHOM DEATH BENEFIT UNDER SECTION 76 OF THE SOCIAL SECURITY ACT 1975 IS PAYABLE, OR TO DEPENDANTS OF PERSONS TO WHOM DISABLEMENT BENEFIT UNDER THAT SECTION OR UNDER ANY CORRESPONDING PROVISION OF THE FORMER INDUSTRIAL INJURIES ACTS WAS PAYABLE, IN CIRCUMSTANCES WHERE THE DISABLED PERSON DIED AS A RESULT OF PNEUMOCONIOSIS OR BYSSINOSIS.

Age of disabled person at his last birthday preceding death	Percentage assessment for the relevant period				
	10% or less	11% – 20%	21% to 30%	40%	50% and over
	£	£	£	£	£
37 and under	6,039	11,772	13,453	13,912	14,295
38	5,855	11,252	12,995	13,453	13,942
39	5,672	10,732	12,536	12,995	13,591
40	5,488	10,213	12,078	12,536	13,239
41	5,305	9,693	11,619	12,078	12,888
42	5,122	9,173	11,160	11,619	12,536
43	4,792	8,500	10,747	11,206	12,200
44	4,464	7,827	10,334	10,793	11,860
45	4,135	7,155	9,922	10,380	11,527
46	3,806	6,482	9,509	9,967	11,190
47	3,478	5,809	9,097	9,556	10,854
48	3,226	5,626	8,791	9,234	10,442
49	2,973	5,442	8,485	8,913	10,029
50	2,722	5,259	8,180	8,591	9,616
51	2,469	5,075	7,874	8,271	9,203
52	2,217	4,892	7,568	7,950	8,791
53	2,102	4,464	6,987	7,507	8,454
54	1,987	4,036	6,405	7,063	8,118
55	1,873	3,608	5,825	6,620	7,781
56	1,759	3,180	5,244	6,177	7,445
57	1,643	2,752	4,663	5,734	7,109
58	1,536	2,446	3,998	4,954	6,177
59	1,429	2,140	3,333	4,174	5,244
60	1,323	1,835	2,668	3,394	4,311
61	1,216	1,529	2,003	2,615	3,379
62	1,109	1,223	1,337	1,835	2,446
63	1,109	1,200	1,292	1,689	2,179
64	1,109	1,177	1,246	1,544	1,912
65	1,109	1,154	1,200	1,399	1,643
66	1,109	1,132	1,154	1,253	1,376
67 and over	1,109	1,109	1,109	1,109	1,109

PART B

PAYMENTS TO DEPENDANTS TO WHOM DEATH BENEFIT UNDER A SCHEME MADE OR HAVING EFFECT AS IF MADE UNDER SECTION 5 OF THE INDUSTRIAL INJURIES AND DISEASES (OLD CASES) ACT 1975 HAS BEEN PAID, OR TO DEPENDANTS OF PERSONS TO WHOM AN ALLOWANCE UNDER SUCH A SCHEME OR UNDER A SCHEME MADE OR HAVING EFFECT AS IF MADE UNDER ANY CORRESPONDING PROVISION OF THE FORMER OLD CASES ACTS WAS PAYABLE, IN CIRCUMSTANCES WHERE THE DISABLED PERSON DIED AS A RESULT OF PNEUMOCONIOSIS OR BYSSINOSIS.

Age of disabled person at his last birthday preceding death	Extent of incapacity for the relevant period	
	Partial	Total
	£	£
37 and under	11,772	14,295
38	11,252	13,942
39	10,732	13,591
40	10,213	13,239
41	9,693	12,888
42	9,173	12,536
43	8,500	12,200
44	7,827	11,863
45	7,155	11,527
46	6,482	11,190
47	5,809	10,854
48	5,626	10,442
49	5,442	10,029
50	5,259	9,616
51	5,075	9,203
52	4,892	8,791
53	4,464	8,454
54	4,036	8,118
55	3,608	7,781
56	3,180	7,445
57	2,752	7,109
58	2,446	6,177
59	2,140	5,244
60	1,835	4,311
61	1,529	3,379
62	1,223	2,446
63	1,200	2,179
64	1,177	1,912
65	1,154	1,643
66	1,132	1,376
67 and over	1,109	1,109

PART C

PAYMENTS TO DEPENDANTS OF PERSONS WHO DIED AS A RESULT OF DIFFUSE MESOTHELIOMA.

Age of disabled person at his last birthday preceding death	Payment
	£
37 and under	14,295
38	13,942
39	13,591
40	13,239
41	12,888
42	12,536
43	12,200
44	11,863
45	11,527
46	11,190
47	10,854
48	10,442
49	10,029
50	9,616
51	9,203
52	8,791
53	8,454
54	8,118
55	7,781
56	7,445
57	7,109
58	6,177
59	5,244
60	4,311
61	3,379
62	2,446
63	2,179
64	1,912
65	1,643
66	1,376
67 and over	1,109

EXPLANATORY NOTE

(This Note is not part of the Regulations.)

The Pneumoconiosis etc. (Workers' Compensation) (Payment of Claims) Regulations 1979, as amended by the Pneumoconiosis etc. (Workers' Compensation) (Payment of Claims) (Amendment) Regulations 1983, prescribe the amount of payments to be made under the Pneumoconiosis etc. (Workers' Compensation) Act 1979 to persons disabled by a disease to which the Act applies (namely pneumoconiosis, byssinosis and diffuse mesothelioma) or to dependants of persons who immediately before they died were disabled by such a disease. These Regulations amend those Regulations by increasing the amount of those payments in any case in which a person first becomes entitled to a payment on or after the date when these Regulations come into operation. The increase is in each case 4%, rounded up or down to the nearest £1 as appropriate. The 1983 Regulations are revoked.

STATUTORY INSTRUMENTS

1984 No. 1975

NURSES, MIDWIVES AND HEALTH VISITORS

The Nursing and Midwifery Qualifications (EEC Recognition) Amendment Order 1984

Made - - - - -	*19th December* 1984
Laid before Parliament	*8th January* 1985
Coming into Operation	*29th January* 1985

At the Court at Buckingham Palace, the 19th day of December 1984

Present,

The Queen's Most Excellent Majesty in Council

Her Majesty, in exercise of the powers conferred upon Her by section 2(2) of the European Communities Act 1972**(a)**, is pleased, by and with the advice of Her Privy Council, to order, and it is hereby ordered, as follows:—

Citation and commencement

1. This Order may be cited as the Nursing and Midwifery Qualifications (EEC Recognition) Amendment Order 1984 and shall come into operation on 29th January 1985.

Amendment of section 11(3A) of the Nurses, Midwives and Health Visitors Act 1979

2. In section 11(3A) of the Nurses, Midwives and Health Visitors Act 1979**(b)** (inserted by Article 3 of the Nursing and Midwifery Qualifications (EEC Recognition) Order 1983**(c)**) there shall be inserted after the words "prescribed conditions" the words "required by a directive issued by the Council of the European Communities".

G. I. de Deney,
Clerk of the Privy Council.

(a) 1972 c. 68.   **(b)** 1979 c. 36.   **(c)** S.I. 1983/884.

EXPLANATORY NOTE

(This Note is not part of the Order.)

This Order amends section 11(3A) of the Nurses, Midwives and Health Visitors Act 1979 so as to limit the prescribed conditions referred to in that section to those which are required by directives issued by the Council of the European Communities.

STATUTORY INSTRUMENTS

1984 No. 1976

CHARITIES

The Exempt Charities Order 1984

Made - - - -	*19th December* 1984
Coming into Operation	*8th January* 1985

At the Court at Buckingham Palace, the 19th day of December 1984

Present,

The Queen's Most Excellent Majesty in Council

Her Majesty, in pursuance of paragraph (c) of Schedule 2 to the Charities Act 1960(a), is pleased, by and with the advice of Her Privy Council, to order, and it is hereby ordered, as follows:—

1. This Order may be cited as the Exempt Charities Order 1984 and shall come into operation on 8th January 1985.

2. University of Wales College of Medicine (Coleg Meddygaeth Prifysgol Cymru) is hereby declared to be an exempt charity for the purposes of the Charities Act 1960.

G. I. de Deney,
Clerk of the Privy Council.

(a) 1960 c. 58.

EXPLANATORY NOTE

(This Note is not part of the Order.)

By a Supplemental Royal Charter granted on 12th July 1984 the Welsh National School of Medicine, declared to be an exempt charity by the Exempt Charities Order 1962 (S.I. 1962/1343), was reconstituted as the University of Wales College of Medicine (Coleg Meddygaeth Prifysgol Cymru), a Constituent Institution of that University.

This Order declares the University of Wales College of Medicine to be an exempt charity within the meaning of the Charities Act 1960.

An exempt charity is not required to be registered with the Charity Commissioners and the Charity Commissioners cannot exercise any of their powers under that Act in relation to an exempt charity except at the request of the charity.

STATUTORY INSTRUMENTS

1984 No. 1977

INTERNATIONAL IMMUNITIES AND PRIVILEGES

The Commonwealth Countries and Republic of Ireland (Immunities and Privileges) (Amendment) Order 1984

Made - - - -	19*th December* 1984
Laid before Parliament	8*th January* 1985
Coming into Operation	30*th January* 1985

At the Court at Buckingham Palace, the 19th day of December 1984

Present,

The Queen's Most Excellent Majesty in Council

Her Majesty, by virtue and in exercise of the powers conferred on Her by sections 12 and 14 of the Consular Relations Act 1968(a), or otherwise in Her Majesty vested, is pleased, by and with the advice of Her Privy Council, to order, and it is hereby ordered, as follows:—

1. This Order may be cited as the Commonwealth Countries and Republic of Ireland (Immunities and Privileges) (Amendment) Order 1984 and shall come into operation on 30th January 1985.

2. Schedule 1 to the Commonwealth Countries and Republic of Ireland (Immunities and Privileges) Order 1971(b) (hereinafter referred to as the Order) shall be amended as follows:

(*a*) the entry
"Malawi
    The Chief Agent, London"
shall be deleted; and

(*b*) for the entry "Assistant Commissioners for Bangladesh" there shall be substituted "Assistant High Commissioners for Bangladesh".

(a) 1968 c. 18; section 12 was amended by section 4 of the Diplomatic and other Privileges Act 1971 (c.64).

(b) S.I. 1971/1237; relevant amending instructions are S.I. 1974/109, 1976/51, 1977/1627.

3. In Schedule 2 to the Order for the entry
  "Cyprus
     The Honorary Commissioner, Glasgow"
shall be substituted the entry
  "Cyprus
     The Honorary Commissioner, Birmingham
     The Honorary Commissioner, Bristol
     The Honorary Commissioner, Glasgow
     The Honorary Commissioner, Manchester".

4. Article 8A of the Order shall be amended by adding at the end the words "and to the office and the residence respectively of the Falkland Islands Government Representative in London.".

G. I. de Deney,
Clerk of the Privy Council.

EXPLANATORY NOTE

(This Note is not part of the Order.)

This Order further amends the Commonwealth Countries and Republic of Ireland (Immunities and Privileges) Order 1971 by making its provisions no longer applicable to the Chief Agent for Malawi, which office has ceased to exist. It also takes account of the new designation of the former Assistant Commissioners for Bangladesh, and makes provision for new Honorary Commissioners for Cyprus. Finally, it extends partial relief from general rates to the office and residence of the Falkland Islands Government Representative in London.

STATUTORY INSTRUMENTS

1984 No. 1978

CONSULAR RELATIONS

The Consular Relations (Privileges and Immunities) (People's Republic of China) Order 1984

Laid before Parliament in draft

Made   -   -   -   *19th December* 1984

Coming into Operation   *On a date to be notified in the London, Edinburgh and Belfast Gazettes*

At the Court at Buckingham Palace, the 19th day of December 1984

Present,

The Queen's Most Excellent Majesty in Council

Whereas a draft of this Order has been laid before Parliament in accordance with section 14(1) of the Consular Relations Act 1968(**a**) (hereinafter referred to as "the Act of 1968") and has been approved by a resolution of each House of Parliament:

Now, therefore, Her Majesty, by virtue and in exercise of the powers conferred on Her by sections 1(11) and 3(1) of the Act of 1968, or otherwise in Her Majesty vested, is pleased, by and with the advice of Her Privy Council, to order and it is hereby ordered, as follows:—

Citation, commencement and interpretation

1.—(1) This Order may be cited as the Consular Relations (Privileges and Immunities) (People's Republic of China) Order 1984, and shall come into operation on a date to be notified in the London, Edinburgh and Belfast Gazettes.

(2) In this Order, "the Act of 1964" means the Diplomatic Privileges Act 1964(**b**).

Members of a Consular Post and their Families

2.—(1) Subject to the provisions of paragraph (2) of this Article and of Article 5 —

   (*a*) the second sentence of Article 29 in Schedule 1 to the Act of 1964 (exemption from liability to arrest or detention) shall be extended to members of a consular post of the People's Republic of China and to members of their families forming part of their households, except that

---

(**a**) 1968 c.18.   (**b**) 1964 c.81.

in the said second sentence the words "any form of arrest or detention" shall be deleted, and the words "arrest or detention pending trial" shall be substituted therefor;

(b) the third sentence of Article 29 in Schedule 1 to the Act of 1964 (protection) shall be extended to consular officers of the People's Republic of China;

(c) the first sentence of paragraph 1 of Article 31 in Schedule 1 to the Act of 1964 (immunity from criminal jurisdiction) shall be extended to members of a consular post of the People's Republic of China and to members of their families forming part of their households;

(d) the second sentence of paragraph 1 (including sub-paragraphs (a), (b) and (c)) of Article 31 in Schedule 1 to the Act of 1964 (immunity from civil and administrative jurisdiction), with the omission of the word "real" in sub-paragraph (a), shall be extended to members of the service staff of a consular post of the People's Republic of China, except that the immunity from jurisdiction:—

   (i) shall apply only in respect of any act performed by them in the exercise of consular functions; and

   (ii) shall not apply to a civil action either:

      (A) arising out of a contract concluded by the member of the service staff in which he did not contract, expressly or impliedly, on behalf of the People's Republic of China; or

      (B) by a third party for damage arising from an accident in the United Kingdom caused by a vehicle, vessel or aircraft;

(e) paragraph 2 of Article 31 in Schedule 1 to the Act of 1964 (exemption from duty to give evidence) shall be extended to members of the families of consular officers of the People's Republic of China forming part of their households;

(f) paragraph 3 of Article 31 in Schedule 1 to the Act of 1964 (exemption from liability to measures of execution) shall be extended to members of a consular post of the People's Republic of China and to members of their families forming part of their households, except that the reference in the said paragraph 3 to sub-paragraph (a) of paragraph 1 of Article 31 shall be taken to be a reference to that sub-paragraph as if the word "real" had been omitted therefrom.

(2) The provisions of paragraph (1) of this Article shall not apply to any person who satisfies the conditions referred to in Article 4 below.

3. Subject to the provisions of Article 5, consular employees of the People's Republic of China and members of the service staff of a consular post of the People's Republic of China, even if they satisfy the conditions referred to in Article 4, shall nevertheless enjoy the immunity provided for in paragraph 3 of Article 44 in Schedule 1 to the Act of 1968 (exemption from liability to give certain evidence).

4. The conditions referred to in Articles 2 and 3 are that the person in question is:—

(a) permanently resident in the United Kingdom; or

(*b*) a British citizen, a British Dependent Territories citizen, a British Overseas citizen, a person who under the British Nationality Act 1981(**a**) is a British subject, or a British protected person (within the meaning of the said Act of 1981).

5.—(1) Any privilege or immunity conferred by the provisions of Article 2 or 3 may be waived by the People's Republic of China. Waiver must always be express. A waiver shall be deemed to have been expressed by the People's Republic of China if it has been expressed by the head, or any person for the time being performing the functions of head, of the diplomatic mission in the United Kingdom of the People's Republic of China or, if there is no such mission, of the consular post concerned. Waiver of immunity in respect of civil or administrative proceedings shall not be held to imply waiver of immunity in respect of execution of the judgment, for which separate waiver shall be required.

(2) Nothing in the provisions of Article 2 or 3 shall be construed as in any way prejudicing the question whether, and in what circumstances, immunity from jurisdiction can be claimed by or on behalf of the People's Republic of China.

Premises and Residences
6.—(1) Subject to the provisions of paragraph (3) of this Article, paragraphs 1 and 2 of Article 22 in Schedule 1 to the Act of 1964 (inviolability and protection of premises) shall be extended to any consular premises of the People's Republic of China.

(2) Subject to the provisions of paragraph (3) of this Article, paragraph 1 of Article 30 in Schedule 1 to the Act of 1964 (inviolability of private residence), with the omission of the words "and protection", shall be extended to the residences of consular officers of the People's Republic of China.

(3) The premises referred to in paragraph (1) and the residences referred to in paragraph (2) may be entered by the authorities of the United Kingdom with the consent of the head of the consular post or the head of the diplomatic mission in the United Kingdom of the People's Republic of China or of a person designated by either of them.

G. I. de Deney,
Clerk of the Privy Council.

(**a**) 1981 c.61.

EXPLANATORY NOTE

(This Note is not part of the Order.)

This Order, which is made pursuant to the Consular Relations Act 1968, provides, with respect to consular posts of the People's Republic of China and persons connected with them, for according privileges and immunities additional to those accorded by Schedule 1 to the Act, namely —

(i) diplomatic protection for consular officers;

(ii) exemption from liability to arrest pending trial, diplomatic immunity from criminal jurisdiction and exemption from liability to measures of execution for certain members of a consular post and members of their families forming part of their households;

(iii) immunity from civil and administrative jurisdiction in respect of acts performed in the exercise of consular functions for certain members of the service staff of a consular post;

(iv) an exemption from the duty to give evidence for certain members of the families of consular officers, and an exemption from the duty to give certain types of evidence for certain persons who would otherwise not be entitled to it on account of their nationality of, or permanent residence in, the United Kingdom;

(v) diplomatic inviolability for consular premises and residences of consular officers.

It gives effect to the relevant provisions of the Agreement between the Government of the United Kingdom of Great Britain and Northern Ireland and the Government of the People's Republic of China on the Establishment of a British Consulate-General at Shanghai and a Chinese Consulate-General at Manchester (Cmnd. 9247).

STATUTORY INSTRUMENTS

1984 No. 1979

DIPLOMATIC SERVICE

The Consular Fees (Amendment No. 3) Order 1984

Made - - - -	*19th December* 1984
Coming into Operation	*1st January* 1985

At the Court at Buckingham Palace, the 19th day of December 1984

Present,

The Queen's Most Excellent Majesty in Council

Her Majesty, in exercise of the power conferred upon Her by section 1(1) of the Consular Fees Act 1980 **(a)**, is pleased, by and with the advice of Her Privy Council, to order, and it is hereby ordered, as follows:—

1. This Order shall come into operation on 1st January 1985 and may be cited as the Consular Fees (Amendment No. 3) Order 1984.

2. Part II of the table of consular fees in the Schedule annexed to the Consular Fees Order 1983 **(b)**, as amended by the Consular Fees (Amendment No. 2) Order 1984 **(c)**, shall be amended by substituting for Fee 22 the following:—

"22 Granting a visa, entry certificate or entry permit— £

for an ordinary visa, entry certificate or entry permit 10.00

for a transit visa, entry certificate or permit 8.00

for a multiple entry visa, entry certificate or permit 20.00

or for any visa, entry certificate or entry permit such sums, being the equivalents of fees charged by the authorities of any State for granting a visa, entry certificate or entry permit to a British citizen, as the Secretary of State, with the consent of the Treasury, directs to be taken for granting a visa, entry certificate or entry permit to a national or citizen of that State

except where a United Kingdom visa is issued on a foreign passport held by a person who is a British citizen".

G. I. de Deney,
Clerk of the Privy Council.

(a) 1980 c.23.   **(b)** S.I. 1983/1518.   **(c)** S.I. 1984/1819.

EXPLANATORY NOTE

(This Note is not part of the Order.)

This Order amends the Consular Fees Order 1983 so as to introduce as from 1st January 1985 a fee for issuing an entry certificate. The Order also removes the exemption from paying a fee for a United Kingdom visa in cases where such a visa is issued on a foreign passport held by a person who is a British Dependent Territories citizen, British Overseas citizen or British Protected person.

STATUTORY INSTRUMENTS

1984 No. 1980

INTERNATIONAL IMMUNITIES AND PRIVILEGES

The EUTELSAT (Immunities and Privileges) Order 1984

Laid before Parliament in draft

Made - - - *19th December* 1984

Coming into Operation *On a date to be notified in the London, Edinburgh and Belfast Gazettes*

At the Court at Buckingham Palace, the 19th day of December 1984

Present,

The Queen's Most Excellent Majesty in Council

Whereas a draft of this Order has been laid before Parliament in accordance with section 10(1) of the International Organisations Act 1968(a) (hereinafter referred to as the Act) and has been approved by resolution of each House of Parliament:

Now, therefore, Her Majesty, by virtue and in exercise of the powers conferred on Her by section 1 of the Act(b) or otherwise in Her Majesty vested, is pleased, by and with the advice of Her Privy Council, to order, and it is hereby ordered, as follows:—

1. This Order may be cited as the EUTELSAT (Immunities and Privileges) Order 1984. It shall come into operation on the date on which the Convention establishing the European Telecommunications Satellite Organization "EUTELSAT"(c) (hereinafter referred to as the Convention) enters into force in respect of the United Kingdom. That date shall be notified in the London, Edinburgh and Belfast Gazettes.

2. The European Telecommunications Satellite Organization (hereinafter referred to as EUTELSAT) is an organisation of which the United Kingdom and other sovereign Powers are members.

3. EUTELSAT shall have the legal capacities of a body corporate.

4. Within the scope of activities authorised by the Convention, EUTELSAT shall have exemption from taxes on income and capital gains.

(a) 1968 c.48.
(b) As amended by section 1 of the International Organisations Act 1981 (c.9).
(c) Cmnd. 9069, amended by a Protocol of 15th December 1983 (Cmnd. 9154).

5. Within the scope of activities authorised by the Convention, EUTELSAT shall have exemption from duties (whether of customs or excise) and taxes on the importation by or on behalf of EUTELSAT of communications satellites, their component parts and all equipment for use in the EUTELSAT space segment defined in Article I(h) of the Convention, such exemption to be subject to compliance with such conditions as the Commissioners of Customs and Excise may prescribe for the protection of the Revenue.

G. I. de Deney,
Clerk of the Privy Council.

EXPLANATORY NOTE
(This Note is not part of the Order.)

This Order will enable the United Kingdom to give effect to Articles IV and XVII(b) of the Convention on the European Telecommunications Satellite Organization (EUTELSAT) (Cmnd. 9069), which was signed by the United Kingdom on 28th September 1982, by conferring the legal capacities of a body corporate and certain fiscal privileges on EUTALSAT. It will come into operation on the date on which the Convention enters into force in respect of the United Kingdom.

STATUTORY INSTRUMENTS

1984 No. 1981

INTERNATIONAL IMMUNITIES AND PRIVILEGES

The Inter-American Development Bank (Immunities and Privileges) (Amendment) Order 1984

Laid before Parliament in draft

Made - - - - -	19*th December* 1984
Coming into Operation	20*th December* 1984

At the Court at Buckingham Palace, the 19th day of December 1984

Present,

The Queen's Most Excellent Majesty in Council

Whereas a draft of this Order has been laid before Parliament in accordance with section 10(1) of the International Organisations Act 1968(a) (hereinafter referred to as the Act) and has been approved by a resolution of each House of Parliament:

Now, therefore, Her Majesty, by virtue and in exercise of the powers conferred on Her by section 1 of the Act or otherwise in Her Majesty vested, is pleased, by and with the advice of Her Privy Council, to order, and it is hereby ordered, as follows:—

1. This Order may be cited as the Inter-American Development Bank (Immunities and Privileges) (Amendment) Order 1984 and shall come into operation on the day after the day on which it is made.

2. The Inter-American Development Bank (Immunities and Privileges) Order 1976(b) shall be amended by the addition of a new Article as follows:—

"14. Officers and employees of the Bank shall enjoy, unless they are British citizens, British Dependent Territories citizens or British Overseas citizens or permanently resident in the United Kingdom:

(*a*) the like exemption from duties and taxes on the importation of

---

(**a**) 1968 c. 48.   (**b**) S.I. 1976/222.

furniture and personal effects (including one motor car each) which—

(i) at the time when they first enter the United Kingdom to take up their post, are imported for their personal use or for their establishment, and

(ii) were in their ownership or possession or which they were under contract to purchase immediately before they so entered the United Kingdom,

as in accordance with paragraph 1 of Article 36 of the 1961 Convention Articles is accorded to a diplomatic agent; and

(b) exemptions whereby, for the purposes of the enactments relating to social security, including enactments in force in Northern Ireland—

(i) services rendered for the Bank by them shall be deemed to be excepted from any class of employment in respect of which contributions or premiums under those enactments are payable, but

(ii) no person shall be rendered liable to pay any contribution or premium which he would not be required to pay if those services were not deemed to be so excepted.".

G. I. de Deney,
Clerk of the Privy Council.

EXPLANATORY NOTE

(This Note is not part of the Order.)

This Order confers exemptions from certain taxes and duties on importation and exemptions in respect of social security contributions on officers of the Inter-American Development Bank who are not British citizens, British Dependent Territories citizens or British Overseas citizens or permanently resident in the United Kingdom. It enables the United Kingdom to give effect to two Exchanges of Notes between Her Majesty's Government and the Inter-American Development Bank (Cmnd. 7567 and Cmnd. 8047).

STATUTORY INSTRUMENTS

1984 No. 1982

INTERNATIONAL IMMUNITIES AND PRIVILEGES

The International Lead and Zinc Study Group (Immunities and Privileges) (Amendment) Order 1984

Laid before Parliament in draft

Made - - -	19*th December* 1984
Coming into Operation	20*th December* 1984

At the Court at Buckingham Palace, the 19th day of December 1984

Present,

The Queen's Most Excellent Majesty in Council

Whereas a draft of this Order has been laid before Parliament in accordance with section 10(1) of the International Organisations Act 1968(**a**) (hereinafter referred to as the Act) and has been approved by a resolution of each House of Parliament:

Now, therefore, Her Majesty, by virtue and in exercise of the powers conferred on Her by section 1(5) of the Act or otherwise in Her Majesty vested, is pleased, by and with the advice of Her Privy Council, to order, and it is hereby ordered, as follows:—

1. This Order may be cited as the International Lead and Zinc Study Group (Immunities and Privileges) (Amendment) Order 1984 and shall come into operation on the day after the day on which it is made.

2. The International Lead and Zinc Study Group (Immunities and Privileges) Order 1978(**b**) shall be amended by the addition to Article 14 (which relates to officers of the International Lead and Zinc Study Group) of a new paragraph as follows:

"(*d*) unless they are British citizens, British Dependent Territories citizens or British Overseas citizens or permanently resident in the United Kingdom, and provided that the Group has established its own social security scheme or has joined that of another international organisation, exemptions whereby, for the purposes of the enactments relating to social security, including enactments in force in Northern Ireland —

(**a**) 1968 c.48.　　　　　　　　(**b**) S.I. 1978/1893.

(a) services rendered for the Group by them shall be deemed to be excepted from any class of employment in respect of which contributions or premiums under those enactments are payable, but

(b) no person shall be rendered liable to pay any contribution or premium which he would not be required to pay if those services were not deemed to be so excepted.".

G. I. de Deney,
Clerk of the Privy Council.

EXPLANATORY NOTE

(This Note is not part of the Order.)

This Order confers exemptions in respect of social security contributions on officers of the International Lead and Zinc Study Group who are not British citizens, British Dependent Territories citizens or British Overseas citizens or permanently resident in the United Kingdom. It enables the United Kingdom to give effect to an Exchange of Notes between Her Majesty's Government and the International Lead and Zinc Study Group concerning the Group Staff Social Security Arrangements (Cmnd. 7592).

STATUTORY INSTRUMENTS

1984 No. 1985

MERCHANT SHIPPING

The Merchant Shipping Acts 1983 and 1984 (Isle of Man) Order 1984

Made - - - -	*19th December* 1984
Laid before Parliament	*8th January* 1985
Coming into Operation	*19th January* 1985

At the Court at Buckingham Palace, the 19th day of December 1984

Present,

The Queen's Most Excellent Majesty in Council

Her Majesty, in pursuance of section 8(1) of the Merchant Shipping Act 1983 (**a**) and section 13 of the Merchant Shipping Act 1984 (**b**), is pleased, by and with the advice of Her Privy Council, to order, and it is hereby ordered, as follows:—

1. This Order may be cited as the Merchant Shipping Acts 1983 and 1984 (Isle of Man) Order 1984 and shall come into operation on 19th January 1985.

2. It is hereby directed that—

(a) sections 5 and 7, section 9 so far as it relates to any ship registered under section 5, and sections 10 and 11 of, and the Schedule to, the Merchant Shipping Act 1983 (**c**) ; and

(b) sections 12 and 14 of, and Schedule 2 to, the Merchant Shipping Act 1984,

shall extend to the Isle of Man with the exceptions, adaptations and modifications specified in the Schedule to this Order.

G. I. de Deney,
Clerk of the Privy Council.

(**a**) 1983 c.13.   (**b**) 1984 c.5.
(**c**) Section 9 was amended by Schedule 2 to the Merchant Shipping Act 1984.

Article 2   SCHEDULE

EXCEPTIONS, ADAPTATIONS AND MODIFICATIONS TO PROVISIONS OF THE MERCHANT SHIPPING ACTS 1983 AND 1984 AS EXTENDED TO THE ISLE OF MAN

1. Any reference to an enactment shall be construed, unless the contrary intention appears, as a reference to it as it has effect in the Isle of Man.

THE MERCHANT SHIPPING ACT 1983

2. In section 5(1) of the 1983 Act—

    (a) for "Secretary of State" there shall be substituted "Isle of Man Harbour Board";

    (b) for "United Kingdom" in the first place where those words occur there shall be substituted "Isle of Man";

    (c) for "United Kingdom" in the second place where those words occur there shall be substituted "British Islands".

3. In section 5(3) of the 1983 Act, for "United Kingdom" there shall be substituted "Isle of Man".

4. In section 5(6) of the 1983 Act, "determined with the approval of the Treasury" shall be omitted.

5. In section 5(9) of the 1983 Act, for "Act 1970" there shall be substituted "(Isle of Man) Act 1974 (an Act of Tynwald)".

6. For section 7 of the 1983 Act there shall be substituted the following provision:—

    "7. Regulations made under section 5 shall not come into operation until they are approved by Tynwald.".

7. Sections 10(3) and 11(3) and (4) of the 1983 Act shall be omitted.

8. In paragraph 2 of the Schedule to the 1983 Act—

    (a) in sub-paragraph (j), the words from "being fees" to the end of the sub-paragraph shall be omitted;

    (b) in sub-paragraph (k), for "Secretary of State" there shall be substituted "Isle of Man Harbour Board".

9. In paragraph 3(3) and (4) of the Schedule to the 1983 Act, "(a) in England and Wales and Scotland," and sub-paragraph (b) shall be omitted.

10. In paragraph 4(2) of the Schedule to the 1983 Act, for "Secretary of State" there shall be substituted "Isle of Man Harbour Board".

11. In paragraph 5 of the Schedule to the 1983 Act, for "United Kingdom" there shall be substituted "Isle of Man".

THE MERCHANT SHIPPING ACT 1984

12. In section 12—

    (a) in subsection (1), after "a surveyor of ships"; and

    (b) in subsection (2), after "a surveyor of ships appointed for the purposes of the Merchant Shipping Act 1894",

there shall be inserted "or a surveyor appointed under section 2 of the Merchant Shipping (Registration) Act 1984 (an Act of Tynwald)".

13. Section 14(3), (5) and (6) shall be omitted.

EXPLANATORY NOTE

(This Note is not part of the Order.)

This Order extends to the Isle of Man certain provisions of the Merchant Shipping Acts 1983 and 1984. The provisions extended are principally, as regards the 1983 Act, those concerned with setting up a special register for small ships and, as regards the 1984 Act, those amending certain other enactments relating to ascertainment of tonnage.

STATUTORY INSTRUMENTS

1984 No. 1987

COPYRIGHT

The Copyright (International Conventions) (Amendment No. 2) Order 1984

Made - - - -	19*th December* 1984
Laid before Parliament	20*th December* 1984
Coming into Operation	21*st January* 1985

At the Court at Buckingham Palace, the 19th day of December 1984.

Present,
The Queen's Most Excellent Majesty in Council

Her Majesty, by and with the advice of Her Privy Council, and by virtue of the authority conferred upon Her by sections 31, 32 and 47 of the Copyright Act 1956(**a**) and of all other powers enabling Her in that behalf, is pleased to order, and it is hereby ordered, as follows:—

1. This Order may be cited as the Copyright (International Conventions) (Amendment No. 2) Order 1984 and shall come into operation on 21st January 1985.

2. The Copyright (International Conventions) Order 1979(**b**) shall be amended as follows:—

(*a*) in Schedule 3 (which names countries in whose case copyright in sound recordings includes exclusive right to perform in public and to broadcast) there shall be included a reference to the Philippines;

(*b*) in Schedules 4 and 5 (which name countries whose broadcasting organisations have copyright protection in relation to sound broadcasts and television broadcasts respectively) there shall be included a reference to the Philippines with a related reference in each Schedule to 25th September 1984.

3.—(1) This Order, except for paragraph (*b*) of Article 2, shall extend to all the countries mentioned in the Schedule hereto.

(2) Paragraph (*b*) of Article 2 shall extend to Bermuda and Gibraltar.

G. I. de Deney,
Clerk of the Privy Council.

(**a**) 1956 c. 74.
(**b**) S.I. 1979/1715, amended by S.I. 1980/1723, 1983/1708, 1984/549.

SCHEDULE *Article 3(1)*

COUNTRIES TO WHICH THIS ORDER (EXCEPT ARTICLE 2(*b*)) EXTENDS

Bermuda
British Indian Ocean Territory
British Virgin Islands
Cayman Islands
Falkland Islands
Falkland Islands Dependencies
Gibraltar

Hong Kong
Isle of Man
Montserrat
St Helena
St Helena Dependencies
    (Ascension, Tristan da Cunha)

EXPLANATORY NOTE

(*This Note is not part of the Order.*)

This Order further amends the Copyright (International Conventions) Order 1979 to take account of the accession of the Philippines to the International Convention for the Protection of Performers, Producers of Phonograms and Broadcasting Organisations.

The Order extends to the dependent countries of the Commonwealth to which the 1979 Order now extends.

STATUTORY INSTRUMENTS

1984 No. 1988

CIVIL AVIATION

The Air Navigation (Third Amendment) Order 1984

Made - - -		*19th December* 1984
Laid before Parliament		*8th January* 1985
Coming into Operation		*1st February* 1985

At the Court at Buckingham Palace, the 19th day of December 1984

Present,

The Queen's Most Excellent Majesty in Council

Her Majesty, in exercise of the powers conferred on Her by sections 60 and 102 of the Civil Aviation Act 1982(**a**) and of all other powers enabling Her in that behalf, is pleased, by and with the advice of Her Privy Council, to order, and it is hereby ordered, as follows:—

1. This Order may be cited as the Air Navigation (Third Amendment) Order 1984 and shall come into operation on 1st February 1985.

2. The Air Navigation Order 1980(**b**) shall be amended by inserting in paragraph 1 of Article 93, after the definition of "Flight visibility", the following new definition —

" "Foreign country" shall, for the purposes of Articles 80 and 81, include Hong Kong;".

G. I. de Deney,
Clerk of the Privy Council.

(**a**) 1982 c.16.
(**b**) S.I. 1980/1965, to which there are amendments not relevant to this Order.

EXPLANATORY NOTE

(This Note is not part of the Order.)

This Order amends the Air Navigation Order 1980 by providing that, for the purposes of Articles 80 and 81 of that Order, Hong Kong shall be treated as a foreign country. The effect of this is that aircraft registered in Hong Kong will from 1st February 1985, when the Order comes into operation, require permission from the Secretary of State before taking on board or discharging passengers or cargo carried or to be carried for hire or reward in the United Kingdom (Article 80) or from making any flight over the United Kingdom for the purpose of aerial photography or aerial survey (Article 81).

STATUTORY INSTRUMENTS

1984 No. 1989

DESIGNS

The Designs Rules 1984

Made - - - -	18*th December* 1984
Laid before Parliament	20*th December* 1984
Coming into Operation	4*th March* 1985

ARRANGEMENT OF RULES

61. Costs of proceedings.

The Secretary of State, in exercise of powers conferred by sections 1(4), 3(1) and (4), 5(2), 8(2), 11(1), 17(1) and (2), 18(1), 19(1) and (2), 20(3) and (4), 21(2), 22(2) and (3), 23, 31(1), 32(1), 36, 39(1) and 40 of the Registered Designs Act 1949(a) and now vested in him (b), and after consultation with the Treasury pursuant to section 40 of that Act and with the Council on Tribunals pursuant to section 10(1) of the Tribunals and Inquiries Act 1971(c) and as regards rule 3 hereof, with the consent of the Treasury, hereby makes the following Rules:—

PRELIMINARY

Citation and commencement

1. These Rules may be cited as the Designs Rules 1984 and shall come into operation on 4th March 1985.

(a) 1949 c.88.
(b) S.I. 1970/1537.
(c) 1971 c.62.

Interpretation

2. In these Rules, unless the context otherwise requires—

"the Act" means the Registered Designs Act 1949, and "section" means a section of the Act;

"United Kingdom" includes the Isle of Man;

"Convention application" means an application in the United Kingdom under section 14;

"Office" means the Designs Registry of the Patent Office;

"Register" means the register of designs kept under section 17;

"Specimen" means an article with the design applied to it;

"Textile article" means textile and plastics piece goods, handkerchiefs, shawls and such other classes of articles of a similar character as the Registrar may from time to time decide, for which the protection required is limited to features of pattern and ornament only.

Fees

3. The fees to be paid in respect of any matters arising under the Act shall be those specified in Schedule 1 to these Rules and in any case where a form specified in that Schedule as the corresponding form in relation to any matter is required to be used that form shall be accompanied by the fee specified in respect of that matter.

Forms

4. The forms mentioned in these Rules are those set out in Schedule 2 to these Rules. Replicas of the forms complying with these Rules shall be used wherever required by these Rules. The forms shall not be modified without the consent of the Registrar.

DOCUMENTS

Size and presentation of documents

5. Subject to any directions that may be given by the Registrar in any particular case, all applications, notices, papers having representations affixed, and other documents filed under the Act or these Rules shall be upon strong paper and, except where otherwise required, on one side only, of a size approximately 297 mm by 210 mm (11¾ inches by 8¼ inches) or approximately 330 mm by 200 mm to 210 mm (13 inches by 8 inches to 8¼ inches) and having on the left hand part thereof a margin of approximately 50 mm (2 inches).

Documents filed by firms and bodies corporate

6.— (1) A document filed by a firm acting for itself and not as an agent shall contain the names of the partners in full and shall be signed by all the partners or by any partner stating that he signs on behalf of the partnership or by any other person who satisfies the Registrar that he is authorised to sign the document.

(2) A document filed by a body corporate acting for itself and not as an agent shall be signed by a director or by the secretary of such body corporate or

by any other person who satisfies the Registrar that he is authorised to sign the document.

Documents sent by post

7. Any notice, application or other document sent to the Office by posting it in the United Kingdom shall be deemed to have been given, made or filed at the time when the letter containing it would be delivered in the ordinary course of post.

ADDRESS

Address for service

8.— (1) Every applicant in any proceedings to which these Rules relate, and every person registered as proprietor of, or as having an interest in, a registered design, shall furnish to the Registrar in addition to his full residential or business address an address for service in the United Kingdom.

(2) Such address may be treated, for all purposes connected with such proceedings or design, as the actual address of such applicant or person and shall, in the case of a registered proprietor, be entered on the register as the address for service of such proprietor.

(3) Any written communication addressed to an applicant in any proceedings, or to any person registered as proprietor of, or as having an interest in, a registered design, at his address for service shall be deemed to be properly addressed.

Provision where no address for service furnished

9. Where an address for service has not been furnished to the Registrar, the Registrar may treat the residential or business address as the address for service, unless such residential or business address is out of the United Kingdom, in which case the Registrar need not proceed with the examination of the application until an address for service in the United Kingdom has been furnished to him.

AGENTS

Appointment and recognition of agents

10.— (1) Anything required or authorised by these Rules to be done by or in relation to any person may be done by, or in relation to, his agent.

(2) Where after a person has become a party to proceedings before the Registrar he appoints an agent for the first time, or appoints one agent in substitution for another, the newly appointed agent shall file Form Designs No. 1A in duplicate on or before the first occasion when he acts as agent.

(3) The Registrar may refuse to recognise as such an agent in respect of any business under the Act—

(a) any individual whose name has been erased from, and not restored to,

the register of patent agents kept in pursuance of rules made under the Patents Act 1977(**a**), or who is for the time being suspended from acting as a patent agent; or

(b) any person who is found by the Secretary of State to have been convicted of any offence or to have been guilty of any such misconduct as, in the case of an individual registered in the register of patent agents aforesaid would render him liable to have his name erased from it; or

(c) any company or firm, if any person whom the Registrar could refuse to recognise as agent in respect of any business under the Act is acting as a director or manager of the company or is a partner in the firm.

(4) In any particular case the Registrar may, if he thinks fit, require the personal signature or presence of an applicant or other person.

APPLICATIONS FOR REGISTRATION

Signature of application

11. An application for registration of a design shall be signed by the applicant for registration or by his agent.

Forms for applications

12.— (1) Applications to register designs shall be made—

(a) in the case of applications relating to single articles (except those referred to in sub-paragraph *(b)* below), on Form Designs No. 2;

(b) in the case of applications made pursuant to section 14, on Form Designs No. 3A; and

(c) in the case of applications relating to sets of articles, on Form Designs No. 3A.

(2) In the case of textile articles, if any question arises as to whether a design consists substantially of checks or stripes only, or lace, it shall be decided by the Registrar.

Application for same design in respect of more than one article

13. Where it is desired to register the same design in respect of more than one article other than sets of articles, a separate application shall be made in respect of each article and each application shall be numbered separately and shall be treated as a separate and distinct application.

Statement of article to which design is applied

14. Every application shall state the article to which the design is to be applied and that the applicant claims to be the proprietor thereof.

(**a**) 1977 c.37.

Statement of novelty on representations or specimens

15. Except in the case of an application to register the pattern or ornament of a design to be applied to a textile article, to wallpaper or similar wall covering or to lace or to sets of textile articles or lace, a statement satisfactory to the Registrar of the features of the design for which novelty is claimed shall appear on each representation or specimen of the design.

Registration of same design in respect of other articles etc.

16. If the application is for the registration of a design which has already been registered in respect of one or more articles, or consists of a registered design with modifications or variations not sufficient to alter the character or substantially to affect the identity thereof, and it is desired to claim the protection of section 4 for such application, it shall contain the number or numbers of the registration or registrations already effected.

REPRESENTATIONS AND SPECIMENS

Supply of representations and specimens

17. Except as regards applications for registration of designs to be applied to sets of articles, there shall be furnished in connection with an application three identical representations of the design, in a form satisfactory to the Registrar, or three specimens. Where representations are supplied the Registrar may at any time before registration require specimens or additional representations.

Representations and specimens for sets of articles

18.— (1) There shall be furnished in connection with an application for the registration of a design to be applied to a set of articles four identical representations of the design in a form satisfactory to the Registrar, or four specimens.

(2) The representations shall show the design as applied to each different article included in the set.

Size and presentation of representations

19.— (1) Each representation of the design, whether to be applied to a single article or to a set of articles, shall be upon paper of the size prescribed by rule 5 above and not on cardboard, and shall appear on one side only of the paper. The figure or figures shall be placed in an upright position on the sheet except where the Registrar is satisfied that it is impracticable. When more figures than one are shown, these shall where reasonably practicable be on one and the same sheet, and each shall be designated perspective view, front view, side view, plan or otherwise as the case may be.

(2) Each sheet shall bear in the top left hand corner the name of the applicant and in the top right hand corner the number of sheets comprising the representation and the consecutive number of each sheet.

Drawings or tracings

20. When the representations furnished are drawings or tracings, they shall be in ink, and if on tracing cloth or tracing paper shall be mounted on paper of the size prescribed by rule 5 above.

Replacement of specimens by representations

21. When specimens are furnished and are not, in the Registrar's opinion, of a kind which can be conveniently mounted in a flat position by means of an adhesive upon paper, or by stitching on linen-backed sheets of paper of the size prescribed by rule 5 above and stored without damage to other documents, representations shall be furnished in place of specimens.

Words, letters or numerals

22. In an application where words, letters or numerals appear in the design, the Registrar may require that a disclaimer of any right to their exclusive use shall appear on each representation or specimen.

Repeating surface patterns

23. Each representation or specimen of a design which consists of a repeating surface pattern shall show the complete pattern and a sufficient portion of the repeat in length and width, and shall not be of less size than 180 mm by 130 mm (7 inches by 5 inches).

Use of portrait of a member of the Royal Family or armorial bearings etc.

24. Where a portrait of Her Majesty or of any member of the Royal Family, or a reproduction of the armorial bearings, insignia, orders of chivalry, decorations or flags of any country, city, borough, town, place, society, body corporate, institution or person appears on a design, the Registrar, before proceeding to register the design, shall, if he so requires, be furnished with a consent to the registration and use of such portrait or reproduction from such official or other person as appears to the Registrar to be entitled to give consent, and in default of such consent he may refuse to register the design.

Use of portrait of living or recently dead person

25. Where the name or portrait of a living person appears on a design, the Registrar shall be furnished, if he so requires, with consent from such person before proceeding to register the design and, in the case of a person recently dead, the Registrar may call for consent from his personal representative before proceeding with the registration of a design on which the name or portrait of the deceased person appears.

DESIGNS EXCLUDED FROM REGISTRATION UNDER SECTION 1(4)

Exclusion of designs to be applied to certain articles

26. There shall be excluded from registration under the Act designs to be applied to any of the following articles, namely—

(1) works of sculpture other than casts or models used or intended to be used as models or patterns to be multiplied by any industrial process;

(2) wall plaques, medals and medallions;

(3) printed matter primarily of a literary or artistic character, including bookjackets, calendars, certificates, coupons, dressmaking patterns, greetings cards, leaflets, maps, plans, postcards, stamps, trade advertisements, trade forms and cards, transfers, playing cards, labels and the like.

CONVENTION APPLICATIONS

Declarations

27. An application for registration under section 14 shall contain a declaration that the application in a convention country upon which the applicant relies is the first application made in a convention country in respect of the design, whether by the applicant or by any person of whom he claims to be the personal representative or assignee, and shall specify the convention country in which such foreign application was made, or is to be deemed under section 14(4) to have been made, and the official date thereof.

Copies and translations

28.— (1) In addition to the representations or specimens filed with every convention application there shall be filed with the application or within three months thereafter, a copy of the representation of the design filed or deposited in respect of the first application in a convention country, duly certified by the authority with which it was filed or otherwise verified to the satisfaction of the Registrar.

(2) If any certificate or other document relating to the application is in a language other than English, a translation thereof into English verified to the satisfaction of the Registrar as corresponding to the original text shall be annexed thereto.

PROCEDURE ON RECEIPT OF APPLICATION

Statement of objections by the Registrar

29. If upon consideration there appears to the Registrar to be any objection to the application, a statement of those objections shall be sent to the applicant in writing, and unless within two months thereafter the applicant applies for a hearing or makes observations in writing on those objections, he shall be deemed to have withdrawn his application.

Decision of Registrar to be communicated in writing

30. If the applicant applies for a hearing, the decision of the Registrar at the hearing shall be communicated to the applicant in writing, together with an indication in general terms of the grounds for that decision.

Appeal from Registrar's decision

31. If the applicant desires to appeal from the Registrar's decision, he shall within one month from the date of the decision apply to the Registrar, upon Form Designs No. 7, requesting him to state in writing the grounds of, and the materials used by him in arriving at, his decision. Upon receipt of such application, the Registrar shall send to the applicant a statement as aforesaid in writing and the date when the statement is sent shall be deemed to be the date of the Registrar's decision for the purpose of an appeal.

CERTIFICATE OF REGISTRATION

Form of certificate

32. The certificate of registration of a design shall be in the Form D.R. No. 1, 1A, 1C or 1D set out in Schedule 3 to these Rules, whichever is applicable, and may be modified as directed by the Registrar.

NON-COMPLETION

Time limits

33. The time prescribed for the purposes of section 3(4), which relates to non-completion of an application, shall be twelve months from the date of the application:

> Provided that the application may be completed at any time after twelve months but within fifteen months of the date aforesaid, if a request for an extension of time is made on Form Designs No. 8 accompanied by the prescribed fee.

DEATH OF APPLICANT

Substitution

34. In case of the death of any applicant for the registration of a design after the date of his application, and before registration of the design has been effected, the Registrar may, on being satisfied of the applicant's death, enter in the Register, in place of the name and address of such deceased applicant, the name and address of the person owning the design on such ownership being proved to the satisfaction of the Registrar.

EXTENSION OF PERIOD OF COPYRIGHT

Extension of second period

35. An application for extension of the period of copyright for a second period shall be made on Form Designs No. 9 not more than three months before the expiry of the first period of five years.

Extension for third period

36. An application for extension of the period of copyright for a third period shall be made on Form Designs No. 10 not more than three months before the expiry of the second period of five years.

Enlargement of time for payment of fees

37. A request for an enlargement of time for payment of any fee payable for an extension of the period of copyright shall be made on Form Designs No. 11.

REGISTRATION OF ASSIGNMENTS ETC

Procedure for application for registration

38.— (1) An application for the registration of the title of any person becoming entitled by assignment, transmission or operation of law to a registered design or to a share in a registered design, or becoming entitled as mortgagee, licensee or otherwise to any interest in a registered design, shall be made—

(a) in the case of an application under section 19(1) by the person becoming so entitled on Form Designs No. 12,

(b) in the case of an application under section 19(2) by the assignor, licensor or other party conferring the interest on Form Designs No. 13.

(2) Application may be made on Form Designs No. 14 for entry in the Register of notification of any other document purporting to affect the proprietorship of a registered design.

Documents and copies

39.— (1) An official or certified copy of any instrument or other document which is referred to in an application under rule 38 and is a matter of record in the United Kingdom shall be produced to the Registrar with the application.

(2) Any other document so referred to shall, unless the Registrar otherwise directs, be produced to him with the application and a certified copy of any such document shall be filed.

Particulars to be provided

40. An application under rule 38(1) shall contain the name and address of the person claiming or stated to be entitled together with full particulars of the instrument, if any, under which title is claimed or given.

Cancellation of claim to be mortgagee or licensee

41. Where the name of a person is entered in the Register as mortgagee or licensee, such person may on making an application for the purpose on Form Designs No. 15 have a note entered in the Register that he no longer claims to be mortgagee or licensee, as the case may be.

Alteration of name and address

42.— (1) An application by the registered proprietor, mortgagee or licensee of a design for the alteration of a name, address or address for service entered on the Register in respect of his design shall be made on Form Designs No. 16.

(2) Before acting on a request to alter a name, the Registrar may require such proof of the alteration as he thinks fit.

(3) If the Registrar is satisified that the request may be allowed, he shall cause the Register to be altered accordingly.

CORRECTION OF ERRORS

Application for correction

43. Where an applicant for registration or the registered proprietor of a design desires, under the provisions of section 21, to correct an error, he shall make the application on Form Designs No. 18.

CANCELLATION UNDER SECTION 11(1)

Application for cancellation

44. Where the registered proprietor of a design desires to cancel his registration, he shall make the application on Form Designs No. 19.

DISCRETIONARY POWER

Notice of hearing

45. The Registrar shall, before exercising any discretionary power vested in him by the Act or these Rules adversely to any party to a proceeding before him, give that party at least fourteen days' notice of the time when he may be heard.

SEARCHES

Procedure when registration number known

46. Where any person desires to obtain the information which he is entitled to obtain under section 23 and can furnish the registration number of the design, he shall apply on Form Designs No. 20 and the Registrar shall thereafter furnish him with the information aforesaid.

Procedure when registration number unknown or general search

47. The Registrar shall, upon application for the purpose made on Form Designs No. 21, accompanied by a representation or specimen (in duplicate) of the design applied to an article, cause such search as may be reasonably practicable to be made among registered designs and state whether the design as applied to that article appears to be identical with, or closely to resemble, any registered design applied to that or any other article, and shall furnish such information as can properly be given.

DISPENSATION BY REGISTRAR

Registrar's power to dispense from Rules

48. Where under these Rules any person is required to do any act or thing, or any document or evidence is required to be produced or filed and it is shown to the satisfaction of the Registrar that from any reasonable cause that person is unable to do that act or thing, or that document or evidence cannot be produced or filed the Registrar may, upon the production of such evidence and subject to such terms as he thinks fit, dispense with the doing of any such act or thing, or the production or filing of that document or evidence.

AMENDMENTS

Registrar's power to allow amendments and rectify irregularities in procedure

49. If the Registrar thinks fit any document or drawing or other representation of a design may be amended, and any irregularity in procedure may be rectified, on such terms as the Registrar may direct.

ENLARGEMENT OF TIME

Registrar's power to enlarge times prescribed by Rules

50. The times or periods prescribed by these Rules for doing any act or taking any proceeding thereunder may be enlarged by the Registrar if he thinks fit, upon such notice and upon such terms as he may direct, and such enlargement may be granted although the time or period for doing such act or taking such proceeding has already expired.

CERTIFICATE BY REGISTRAR

Registrar's power to provide certificate

51. Where a certificate is required for the purpose of obtaining registration of a design in any country or territory outside the United Kingdom, or of any legal proceeding, or other special purpose, as to any entry, matter or thing which the Registrar is authorised by the Act or these Rules to make or do, the Registrar may, on the making of a request on Form Designs No. 23, give such certificate.

DESIGNS NOT OPEN TO PUBLIC INSPECTION

Direction by Registrar under section 5(1)

52. Where the Registrar has given a direction under section 5(1) prohibiting or restricting the publication of a design, the representation or specimen of the design shall not be open to public inspection while such direction remains in force.

Prohibition on inspection under section 22(2)

53. The period under section 22(2) during which a design shall not be open to inspection, except as provided in that section, shall be, as regards designs to be applied to textile articles, three years and as regards designs to be applied to wallpaper and similar wall covering and lace, two years from the date of the registration thereof.

APPLICATION FOR COMPULSORY LICENCE UNDER SECTION 10

Procedure for application

54. An application for the grant of a compulsory licence under section 10 shall be made on Form Designs No. 25. Such application shall be accompanied by a copy thereof and a statement in duplicate setting out fully the nature of the applicant's interest and the facts upon which he bases his case. Copies of the application and the statement of case shall be transmitted by the Registrar to the registered proprietor.

Opposition by registered proprietor

55. If the registered proprietor desires to oppose the application he shall, within such time as the Registrar may allow, file a counterstatement fully setting out the grounds on which the application is to be opposed and shall deliver to the applicant a copy thereof.

Evidence of applicant

56. The applicant may, within such time as the Registrar may allow after receipt of the counterstatement, file evidence in support of his case and shall deliver to the registered proprietor a copy of any evidence so filed.

Evidence of registered proprietor and evidence in reply

57. Within such time as the Registrar may allow, the proprietor may file evidence in support of his case and shall deliver to the applicant a copy thereof; and within such time as the Registrar may allow, the applicant may file evidence confined to matters strictly in reply and shall deliver to the proprietor a copy thereof.

Prohibition on further evidence

58. No further evidence shall be filed by either party except by leave or on direction of the Registrar.

Procedure for hearing

59.— (1) On completion of the evidence, if any, or at such other time as he may see fit, the Registrar shall appoint a time for the hearing of the case, and shall give the parties at least fourteen days' notice of the appointment.

(2) If either party desires to be heard he shall give notice to the Registrar on Form Designs No. 27 and the Registrar may refuse to hear either party who has not filed that Form prior to the date of the hearing.

(3) The hearing before the Registrar of any dispute between two or more parties relating to any matter in connection with a registered design shall be in

public unless the Registrar, after consultation with those parties to the dispute who appear in person or are represented at the hearing, otherwise directs.

(4) Nothing in this rule shall prevent a member of the Council on Tribunals or of its Scottish Committee from attending a hearing in his capacity as such.

CANCELLATION OF REGISTRATION OF DESIGNS

Procedure for cancellation under section 11(2)

60.— (1) An application for the cancellation of the registration of a design under section 11(2) shall be made on Form Designs No. 26, and shall be accompanied by a copy thereof and a statement in duplicate setting out fully the nature of the applicant's interest and the facts on which he relies.

(2) A copy of the application shall be sent by the Registrar to the registered proprietor and thereupon the provisions of rules 55 to 59 shall apply.

Costs of proceedings

61. In the event of an application for the grant of a compulsory licence or for the cancellation of the registration of a design being uncontested by the proprietor, the Registrar in deciding whether costs should be awarded to the applicant shall consider whether proceedings might have been avoided if reasonable notice had been given by the applicant to the registered proprietor before the application was filed.

COPY OF CERTIFICATE OF REGISTRATION

Procedure for application

62. An application under section 18(2) for a copy of a certificate of registration shall be made on Form Designs No. 6 and shall be accompanied by evidence setting out in full and verifying the circumstances in which the original certificate of registration was lost or destroyed or cannot be produced.

EVIDENCE BEFORE REGISTRAR

Evidence by statutory declaration or affidavit

63. Where under these Rules evidence is required to be filed, it shall be by statutory declaration or affidavit, unless otherwise expressly provided in these Rules.

Form and content of statutory declaration or affidavit

64.— (1) The statutory declarations and affidavits required by these Rules, or used in any proceedings thereunder, shall be headed in the matter or matters to which they relate, and shall be divided into paragraphs consecutively numbered, and each paragraph shall, so far as possible, be confined to one subject.

(2) Every statutory declaration or affidavit shall state the description and true place of abode of the person making the same, and shall be written, typed, lithographed, or printed.

Making and subscription of statutory declaration or affidavit

65. Any statutory declaration or affidavit filed under the Act or these Rules shall be made and subscribed as follows—

(a) in the United Kingdom, before any justice of the peace, or any commissioner or other officer authorised by law in any part of the United Kingdom to administer an oath for the purpose of any legal proceedings;

(b) in any other part of Her Majesty's dominions, or in any dependent territory as defined in the British Nationality Act 1981(a) or in the Republic of Ireland, before any court, judge, justice of the peace, or any officer authorised by law to administer an oath there for the purpose of any legal proceedings; and

(c) elsewhere, before a British Minister, or person exercising the functions of a British Minister, or a Consul, Vice-Consul, or other person exercising the functions of a British Consul, or before a notary public, or before a judge or magistrate.

Authentication of seal or signature

66. Any document purporting to have affixed, impressed, or subscribed thereto or thereon the seal or signature of any person authorised by rule 65 above to take a declaration in testimony that the declaration was made and subscribed before him, may be admitted by the Registrar without proof of the genuineness of the seal or signature, or of the official character of the person or his authority to take the declaration.

Registrar's power to require documents, information or evidence

67. At any stage of any proceedings before the Registrar, he may direct that such documents, information or evidence as he may require shall be filed within such period as he may fix.

HOURS OF BUSINESS AND EXCLUDED DAYS

Hours of business

68. The Patent Office shall be deemed to be closed at the following hours for the transaction of business of the classes specified—

(a) on weekdays, other than Saturdays, at midnight for the filing of applications, forms and other documents, and at four p.m. for all other business,

(b) on Saturdays, at one p.m. for the filing of new applications for the registration of designs which are not Convention applications.

Excluded days

69.— (1) All Sundays and such days as may, from time to time, be notified by a notice posted in a conspicuous place in the Office shall be excluded days

(a) 1981 c.61.

for the purposes of the transaction by the public of business under the Act of all classes or such class or classes as may be specified in the notice.

(2) All Saturdays other than those falling within paragraph (1) above shall be excluded days for purposes of the transaction of all classes of business other than the filing of new applications for the registration of designs which are not Convention applications.

Calculation of times or periods

70.— (1) Subject to the provisions of paragraphs (2) and (3) below, where any period of time specified in the Act or these Rules for the giving, making or filing of any notice, application or other document expires on a day certified by the Registrar as being one on which there is a general interruption or subsequent disclocation in the postal services of the United Kingdom, the period shall be extended to the first day following the end of the period of interruption or dislocation.

(2) Where, in or in connection with an application under section 14 of the Act for registration of a design ("the application in suit"), the period of six months from the date of the application, or the first application, for protection in a convention country ends on a day which is an excluded day for the purposes of section 39 of the Act, such period shall, if the application in suit is made on the first following day on which the Patent Office is open for the transaction of such business, be altered so as to include both the date of the application or the first application for protection in a convention country and the date on which the application in suit is made.

(3) Where it is desired to make such an application and the said period of six months from the date of the application, or the first application, for protection in a convention country ends on a day certified under paragraph (1) above as being one on which there is a general interruption or subsequent dislocation in the postal services of the United Kingdom, the period shall, if the said application is made on the first day following the end of the period of interruption or dislocation, be altered so as to include both the date of the application, or the first application, for protection in a convention country and the date on which the application in suit is made.

(4) Where an application for registration of a design is filed upon the day immediately following a day which is certified under paragraph (1) above as being one on which there is a general interruption or subsequent dislocation in the postal services of the United Kingdom or which is an excluded day for the purposes of section 39 of the Act the period of six months specified in section 6 of the Act shall be computed from the day following the next proceding day which is neither so certified nor so excluded.

ORDERS OF THE COURT

Service of application on Registrar

71. Where application to the court under section 20 for rectification of the register has been made, the applicant shall forthwith serve an office copy of the application on the Registrar, who shall enter a notice of the application in the register.

Filing of order with Registrar

72. Where an order has been made by the court in any case under the Act, the person in whose favour such order has been made shall forthwith file Form Designs No. 28 accompanied by an office copy of the order. The Register shall, if necessary, thereupon be rectified by the making of any entry therein or the variation or deletion of any entry therein.

REVOCATION

Revocation of rules in Schedule 4

73. The rules mentioned in Schedule 4 below are hereby revoked.

Geoffrey Pattie,
Minister of State,
Department of Trade and Industry.

17th, December 1984.

We consent to the making of rule 3 of these Rules.

Ian B. Lang,
A. G. Hamilton,
Two of the Lords Commissioners
of Her Majesty's Treasury.

18th, December 1984.

SCHEDULE 1   Rule 3

LIST OF FEES PAYABLE

Subject or Proceeding	Amount	Corresponding Form
	£	
1. On application to register one design to be applied to a single article made of lace or a design of checks or stripes to be applied to a single textile article	10	Designs No. 2 (or 3A if application made under section 14)
2. On application to register one design to be applied to a single article not falling within item 1	37	Designs No. 2 (or 3A if application made under section 14)
3. On application to register one design to be applied to a set of articles made of lace or a design of checks or stripes to be applied to a set of textile articles	17	Designs No. 3A
4. On application to register one design to be applied to a set of articles not falling within item 3	72	Designs No. 3A
5. On application for a copy of certificate of registration	5	Designs No. 6.
6. On application to Registrar to state grounds of decision and materials used under Rule 31	47	Designs No. 7.
7. On request for enlargement of time to complete an application for registration of a design:—		
Not exceeding one month	10	Designs No. 8.
Not exceeding two months	20	Designs No. 8.
Not exceeding three months	30	Designs No. 8.
8. On application for extension of copyright under section 8(2) for second period	87	Designs No. 9.
9. On application for extension of copyright under section 8(2) for third period	130	Designs No. 10.
10. On request for enlargement of time for payment of fee for extension of copyright:—		
Not exceeding one month	10	Designs No. 11.
Not exceeding two months	20	Designs No. 11.
Not exceeding three months	30	Designs No. 11.
Not exceeding four months	40	Designs No. 11.
Not exceeding five months	50	Designs No. 11.
Not exceeding six months	60	Designs No. 11.

Rule 3 SCHEDULE 1

LIST OF FEES PAYABLE (*Cont'd.*)

Subject or Proceeding	Amount	Corresponding Form
	£	
11. On application to enter subsequent proprietorship, &c. under Rule 38 made within six months from date of acquisition of proprietorship, &c.:—		
In respect of one design..................	11	Designs No. 12 or 13.
Made after six but within twelve months from date of acquisition of proprietorship, &c.:—		
In respect of one design..................	23	Designs No. 12 or 13.
Made after expiration of twelve months from the date of acquisition of proprietorship, &c:—		
In respect of one design..................	39	Designs No. 12 or 13.
On application covering more than one design, for each additional design similarly acquired....................................	2	—
12. On application for entry of notification of document in the register made within six months of date of document:—		
In respect of one design..................	11	Designs No, 14.
Made after six months but within twelve months from date of document:—		
In respect of one design..................	23	Designs No. 14.
Made after expiration of twelve months from date of document:—		
In respect of one design..................	39	Designs No. 14.
On application covering more than one design, for each additional design referred to in the same document as the first design....................................	2	—
13. On application of mortgagee, licensee, or other person for entry that he no longer claims such interest:—		
In respect of each design..................	2	Designs No. 15.
14. On application by registered proprietor to alter name, address or address for service in the Register:—		
In respect of each design..................	2	Designs No. 16.

SCHEDULE 1

Rule 3

LIST OF FEES PAYABLE (*Cont'd.*)

Subject or Proceeding	Amount	Corresponding Form
	£	
15. On request under section 21 to correct error..	16	Designs No. 18.
On a request covering more than one design, the error being the same as with the first design, for each additional design...................	2	Designs No. 18.
16. On application by proprietor for cancellation	—	Designs No. 19.
17. On request for search under section 23 when registration number is supplied.............................	4	Designs No. 20.
18. On request for search under section 23 when registration number is not supplied.......................	17	Designs No. 21.
19. On request for certificate of Registrar for use in obtaining registration in a country or territory outside the United Kingdom and the Isle of Man or for use in legal proceedings or other special purpose.........................	5	Designs No. 23.
20. On application for compulsory licence under section 10	27	Designs No. 25.
21. On application for cancellation of registration under section 11(2)......................................	17	Designs No. 26.
22. On notice that hearing of an application for cancellation or compulsory licence will be attended...	11	Designs No. 27.
23. On application for entry of Order of Court in Register	—	Designs No. 28.
24. Inspection of Register or design where inspection is permitted other than inspection under the second paragraph of section 22(2).....................................	1	—
25. For certifying Office copies...............	2	—

Rule 4

SCHEDULE 2

GENERAL FORMS

FORM DESIGNS NO. 1A
(Please file in duplicate)
(Rule 10)

REGISTERED DESIGNS ACT 1949

Form of Declaration of Authorisation where an Agent is
appointed during the progress of an Application or where
one Agent is substituted for another.

NOTES:

(a) Enter name and address in the United Kingdom of agent.

(b) Enter the full name and address of applicant, proprietor or other person who has authorised agent.
The full names of all the partners in a firm must be entered.

(c) State the particular matter for which agent is appointed, quoting application or registration number
appropriate.

I/We *(a)* ....

of ....

....

declare that I/we have been authorised by *(b)* ....

....

of ....

....

to act as agent in the matter of *(c)* ....

....

....

and request that all communications relating thereto be sent to me/us at my/our address given above.

Signature ....

Dated this ....day of ....19 ....

To The Registrar
     Designs Registry, The Patent Office

FORM DESIGNS NO. 2   (Revised 1984)

| FEE: ITEM
1 OR 2 | (Rule 12) |

FOR OFFICIAL USE ONLY

REGISTERED DESIGNS ACT 1949

Application for Registration of Design

NOTES

(a) Insert the name and address of each applicant. Names of individuals should be indicated in full and the surname or family name should be underlined. The names of all partners in a firm must be given in full. Bodies corporate should be designated by their present corporate name and the country of incorporation and, where appropriate, the state of incorporation within that country should be inserted where provided. Full corporate details, eg, "a corporation organised and existing under the laws of the State of Delaware, United States of America," nationality, and former names, eg "formerly [known as] ABC Ltd," are *not* required and should *not* be given.

(b) Delete words which do not apply. For textile articles see definition given in Rule 2 of the Designs Rules 1984. If "other article", state the article to which the design is to be applied as shown in the representations.

(c)
(d) Delete one or both paragraphs, if inapplicable.

(e) If the applicant has appointed an agent to act on his behalf, the agent's name and address should be indicated at (e) and (f).

(f) An address for service in the United Kingdom to which documents may be sent must be inserted.

(g) Attention is directed to Rules 10 and 11 of the Designs Rules 1984.

Application is made for registration of the accompanying design in the name of (a) ....
....
....Country ....State ....
Address ....
....

who claim(s) to be the proprietor(s) thereof.
The design is to be applied to (b) a textile article *or* wallpaper or similar wall covering *or* lace *or* other article ....
....

(c) The design has been previously registered for one or more other articles under No. ....

(d) The design consists of the design previously registered under No. ....with modifications or variations not sufficient to alter the character or substantially to affect the identity thereof.

(e) Name of agent, if any:— ....

(f) Address for service in the United Kingdom:— ....
....

(g) Signature ....

Dated this ....day of ....19 ....

Please note Three identical representations or specimens of the design should accompanying this Form, and except in the case of an application in respect of a textile article, wallpaper (or similar wall covering), or lace, each representation or specimen should carry a statement of the features of the design for which novelty is claimed. If words, letters or numerals appear in the design the Registrar will normally require a disclaimer of any right to their exclusive use to appear on each representation or specimen.

To   The Registrar
     Designs Registry, The Patent Office.

FORM DESIGNS NO. 3A (Revised 1984)

FEE: ITEM 1 TO 4	(Rule 12)

REGISTERED DESIGNS ACT 1949

Application for Registration of Design
Under Section 14*
To be applied to a set of Articles*   (*Delete if inapplicable)

(PLEASE READ THE NOTES OVERLEAF)

Application is made for the registration of the accompanying design (for a set of articles)* in the name of (a)

....

....Country ....State ....

Address ....

....

who claim(s) to be the proprietor(s) thereof (b) ....

....

....

....

The design is to be applied to (c) a textile article *or* wallpaper or similar wall covering *or* lace *or* other article

....

(d)   The design has been previously registered for one or more other articles under No. ....

(e)   The design consists of the design previously registered under No. ....with modifications
or variations not sufficient to alter the character or substantially to affect the identity thereof.

Application for protection of the design has been made in (f) ....

on the following official date, viz (g) ....

Such application is the first application made in a Convention country in respect of the design, whether by the applicant(s) or by any person of whom he (they) claim(s) to be the legal representative(s) or assignee(s) and I (we) request that the design may be registered as of the date (g) ....

(h)   Name of agent, if any:— ....

(i)   Address for service in the United Kingdom:— ....

....

(j)   Signature ....

      Dated this ....day of ....19 ....

Please note THREE (or, where the design is to be applied to a set of articles, FOUR) identical representations or specimens of the design should accompany this Form and, except in the case of an application in respect of a textile article, wallpaper (or similar wall covering), or lace, each representation or specimen should carry a statement of the features of the design for which novelty is claimed. If words, letters or numerals appear in the design, the Registrar will normally require a disclaimer of any right to their exclusive use to appear on each representation or specimen.

To   The Registrar
      Designs Registry, The Patent Office

M67C

OTES:

)   Enter the name and address of each applicant. Names of individuals should be indicated in full and the surname or family name should be underlined. The names of all partners in a firm must be given in full. Bodies corporate should be designated by their present corporate name and the country of incorporation and, where appropriate, the state of incorporation within that country should be inserted where provided. Full corporate details, eg "a corporation organised and existing under the laws of the State of Delaware, United States of America," nationality, and former names, "formerly [known as] ABC Ltd," are *not* required and should *not* be given.

)   If the applicant is not the person who made the application in the Convention country, the words "by virtue of", followed by particulars of the instrument under which he claims should be inserted here.

)   Delete words which do not apply. For textile articles see definition given in Rule 2 of the Designs Rules 1984. If "other article", state the article or set of articles, and also if appicable, the trade description of each of the articles comprised in the set, to which the design is to be applied as shown in the representations.

) to (g)   Complete entries if applicable or delete paragraphs if inapplicable.

*   Enter the name of the Convention country in which the *first* application was made.

)   Enter the official date of the *first* application in a Convention country.

)   If the applicant has appointed an agent to act on his behalf the agent's name and address should be indicated at (h) and (i).

*   An address for service in the United Kingdom to which all documents may be sent must be inserted here.

*   Attention is directed to Rules 10 and 11 of the Designs Rules 1984.

FORM DESIGNS NO. 6 (Revised 1984)

FEE: ITEM 5   (Rule 62)

REGISTERED DESIGNS ACT 1949

Application for copy Certificate of
Registration of Design

(A representation identical with that attached to the original
Certificate of Registration should accompany this form.)

NOTES:

(a) State whether "has been lost" or "has been destroyed" or "cannot be produced", as the case may be,
and state in full the circumstances of the case, which must be verified by statutory declaration or
affidavit.

(b) State interest possessed by applicant in the design (e.g. proprietor).

I/We inform you that the Certificate of Registration of Design No. ....

(a) ....

....

....

My/Our interest in the design is *(b)* ....

....

I/We apply for the issue of a copy of the certificate.

Address in the United Kingdom to which the certificate should be sent ....

....

Signature ....

Dated this ....day of ....19 ....

To   The Registrar
       Designs Registry, The Patent Office

ORM DESIGNS NO. 7   (Revised 1984)

FEE: ITEM 6   (Rule 31)

REGISTERED DESIGNS ACT 1949

Application for Statement of Grounds
of Decision under Rule 31

NOTE: *Attention is directed to Rules 10 and 11 of the Designs Rules 1984.

Application for Design No. ....

Application is made under Rule 31 of the Designs Rules, 1984, for a statement in writing of the grounds of the

decision dated the ....

day of ....after the hearing on the ....

day of ....and the materials used in arriving at such decision.

Address ....

....

*Signature ....

Dated this ....day of ....19 ....

To   The Registrar
     Designs Registry, The Patent Office

FOR OFFICIAL USE ONLY

FORM DESIGNS NO. 8 (Revised 1984)

FEE: ITEM 7   (Rule 33)

REGISTERED DESIGNS ACT 1949

Request for Extension of Time to complete an Application
for the Registration of a Design

NCTES: *(a)*   Enter name and full address to which receipt is to be sent.
            (b)   Attention is directed to Rules 10 and 11 of the Designs Rules 1984.

I/We apply for ....month's extension of time to complete the application No. ....
for the registration of a Design.

(a) Name ....

Address ....

(b) Signature ....

To   The Registrar
Designs Registry, The Patent Office

FORM DESIGNS NO. 9 (Revised 1984)

FEE: ITEM 8

(Rule 35)

FOR OFFICIAL USE ONLY

REGISTERED DESIGNS ACT 1949

Application for Extension of Copyright in
Design for the second period*

NOTE:
*(a) Enter name and full address to which certificate is to be sent.

I/We apply for the extension of the period of copyright in Design No. ....
for a second period.*

(a)   Name ....

         Address ....

         ....

         Signature ....

To The Registrar
     Designs Registry, The Patent Office

(This part of the form to be completed by the Patent Office)

**CERTIFICATE OF EXTENSION OF COPYRIGHT IN DESIGN
FOR THE SECOND PERIOD***

This is to certify that ....

did on ....19............................ make application and pay the

prescribed fee for the extension of copyright in the Design No. ....and that the copyright

is   extended   for   a   second   period*   until   ....19..............

*The second period of copyright is normally five years. However, in the case of an associated design registered by
virtue of Section 4 copyright will expire when copyright in the original design expires. The extended period of
copyright may thus be less than the full five years.

Designs Registry, The Patent Office

M307

FORM DESIGNS NO. 10 (Revised 1984)

FEE: ITEM 9   (Rule 36)

FOR OFFICIAL USE ONLY

REGISTERED DESIGNS ACT 1949

Application for Extension of Copyright in Design for the third period*

NOTE:
(a) Enter name and full address to which certificate is to be sent.

I/We apply for the extension of the period of copyright in Design No. ....
for a third period.*

(a) Name ....

Address ....

....

Signature ....

To   The Registrar
Designs Registry, The Patent Office

(This part of the form to be completed by the Patent Office)

CERTIFICATE OF EXTENSION OF COPYRIGHT IN DESIGN
FOR THE THIRD PERIOD*

This is to certify that ....

did on ....19 ....make application and pay the

prescribed fee for the extension of copyright in the Design No. ....and that the copyright

is extended for a third period* until ....19......

*The third period of copyright is normally five years. However, in the case of an associated design registered by virtue of Section 4 copyright will expire when copyright in the original design expires. The extended period of copyright will thus be less than the full five years.

Designs Registry, The Patent Office

FORM DESIGNS NO. 11   (Revised 1984)

| FEE: ITEM 10 | (Rule 37) |

REGISTERED DESIGNS ACT 1949

Request for Enlargement of Time for
Payment of Fee for Extension of
Copyright in Design

NOTE:
a) Enter name and full address to which certificate is to be sent.

I/We request ....months enlargement of time for the payment of the copyright

extension fee for Design No. ....

(a) Name ....

   Address ....

   ....

   Signature ....

The Registrar
Designs Registry, The Patent Office

V5064

FORM DESIGNS NO. 12   (Revised 1984)

| FEE: ITEM 11 | (Rule 38) |

REGISTERED DESIGNS ACT 1949

Application under Rule 38(1)(a) by Assignee, Mortgagee, or Licensee, etc, to enter subsequent proprietorship or interest in Design in the Register

NOTES:
Delete words which do not apply

a) The instrument under which the applicant claims and a certified copy of that instrument should accompany this form.

b) Enter name and address. Bodies corporate should be designated by their corporate name and the country of incorporation and, where appropriate the state of incorporation within that country should be inserted where provided.

c) Enter full particulars of the instrument.

d) If the applicant has appointed an agent to act on his behalf, the agent's name and address should be indicated at d) and e).

e) An address for service in the United Kingdom to which all documents may be sent must be inserted here.

f) Attention is directed to Rules 10 and 11 of the Designs Rules 1984.

I/We *(b)* ....

Country .... State ....

Address ....

....

request that you enter my/our name(s) in the register as *proprietor(s) *or *mortgagee(s), *or *licensee(s)

of the design No ....

I am/We are entitled to *the said design (*or* to *a share *or *an interest in the said design) in pursuance of

(c) ....

....

(d) Name of agent, if any ....

....

(e) Address for service in the United Kingdom ....

....

....

(f) Signature ....

....

Dated this .... day of .... 19 ....

To   The Registrar
     Designs Registry, The Patent Office

FORM DESIGNS NO. 13   (Revised 1984)

FEE: ITEM
11

(Rule 38)

REGISTERED DESIGNS ACT 1949

Application under Rule 38(1)(b) by Assignor, Mortgagor,
Licensor, etc, to enter subsequent Proprietorship or
Interest in the Design in the Register.

* *Delete words which do not apply*
NOTES:
(a) The instrument referred to in the application and a certified copy of that instrument should accompany
this form.
(b) Enter name and address.
(c) Enter name and address of assignee etc. Bodies corporate should be designated by their corporate name
and the country of incorporation, and where appropriate the state of incorporation within that country
should be entered where provided.
(d) Enter full particulars of the instrument.
(e) Enter the address for service in the United Kingdom of the subsequent proprietor, mortgagee, licensee,
etc.
(f) Attention is directed to Rules 10 and 11 of the Designs Rules 1984.

I/We *(b)* ....
....
....

request that you enter the name(s) of *(c)* ....
....Country ....State ....
Address ....
....

in the Register as subsequent *proprietor(s) *or* *mortgagee(s) *or* *licensee(s) of the design No. ....
....

He is/they are entitled to *the said design (*or* to *a share *or* *interest in the said design) by virtue of
(d) ....
....

The address for service in the United Kingdom of the subsequent proprietor, mortgagee, or licensee,
etc, is *(e)* ....
....

Name of agent, if any ....

(f) Signature ....
Dated this ....day of ....19 ....

To   The Registrar
Designs Registry, The Patent Office

V5032

FORM DESIGNS NO. 14   (Revised 1984)

FEE: ITEM 12	(Rule 38)

REGISTERED DESIGNS ACT 1949

Application for Entry of Notification of

Document in Register

NOTES

a) Enter a description of the nature of the document, giving its date and the names and addresses of the parties.

b) Enter full name and address of the party benefiting under the document.

c) If the applicant has appointed an agent to act on his behalf, the agent's name and address should be indicated at c) and d).

d) An address for service in the United Kingdom to which all documents may be sent must be inserted here.

e) Attention is directed to Rules 10 and 11 of the Designs Rules 1984.

I/We transmit an attested copy of *(a)* ....

....

relative to Design No. ....as well as the original document for verification,

and I/we apply that a notification may be entered in the Register.

(b) ....

....

(c) Name of agent (if any) ....

(d) Address for service in the United Kingdom ....

....

....

(e) Signature ....

Dated this ....day of ....19 ....

To   The Registrar
      Designs Registry, The Patent Office

V5033

FOR OFFICIAL USE ONLY

ORM DESIGNS NO. 15   (Revised 1984)

| FEE: ITEM 13 | (Rule 41) |

REGISTERED DESIGNS ACT 1949

pplication by Mortgagee or Licensee under Rule 41 for Entry
in Register of Note that he no longer claims such Interest

* Delete whichever does not apply

NOTES:
(a) If the applicant has appointed an agent to act on his behalf, the agent's name and address should be indicated at (a) and (b).
(b) An address for service in the United Kingdom to which all documents may be sent must be inserted here.
(c) Attention is directed to Rules 10 and 11 of the Designs Rules 1984.

Design No ....

Name of Registered Proprietor ....

....

Place of Business ....

I/We the undersigned ....

of ....

apply for the entry in the register that I/we no longer claim to be *mortgagee *or* *licensee in respect of the Design No. ....

(a) Name of agent, if any ....

(b) Address for service in the United Kingdom ....

....

....

(c) Signature ....

Dated this ....day of ....19 ....

To   The Registrar
      Designs Registry, The Patent Office

V5034

FORM DESIGNS NO. 16   (Revised 1984)

| FEE: ITEM 14 | (Rule 42) |

REGISTERED DESIGNS ACT 1949

Application to Enter Alteration of Name of Registered
Proprietor, Mortgagee or Licensee of Design or of
Address for Service in Register

NOTES:

     † *Delete words which do not apply*

(a) Enter registered design number.

(b) Enter name and address of registered proprietor of design and of mortgagee or licensee if appropriate.

(c) Enter particulars of alteration.

(d) Enter reason for desired change.

(e) Enter revised address.

(f) If the applicant has appointed an agent to act on his behalf, the agent's name and address should be indicated at (f) and (g).

(g) An address for service in the United Kingdom to which all documents may be sent must be inserted here.

(h) Attention is directed to Rules 10 and 11 of the Designs Rules 1984.

(a)   Design No. ....

(b)   ....

....

....

*Delete or
complete
entries in
square
brackets
as
appropriate.*

* ⌈ I/We, the †registered proprietor(s) *or* †mortgagee(s) *or* †licen-
see(s), apply that my/our names(s) in the register may be
altered to *(c)* ....
There has been no change in the actual proprietorship of the
Design or the Mortgage or Licence, but *(d)* .... ⌋

* ⌈ I/We, the †registered proprietor(s) *or* †mortgagee(s) *or* †licen-
see(s), of the Design numbered as above, apply that
my/our address/address for service in the register may be altered
to *(e)* .... ⌋

(f)   Name of agent, if any ....

....

(g)   Address for service in the United Kingdom (unless entered at *(e)*) ....

....

....

(h)   Signature ....

Dated this ....day of ....19 ....

Please note. If alteration of name is required a certified copy of the Certificate of Incorporation upon change of name or equivalent document should be supplied with this form.

To   The Registrar
     Designs Registry, The Patent Office

FOR OFFICIAL USE ONLY

ORM DESIGNS NO. 18   (Revised 1984)

FEE: ITEM 15	(Rule 43)

REGISTERED DESIGNS ACT 1949

Request under Section 21 for correction of error

NOTES:

a) Enter a brief description of the error for which correction is required.
b) State whether in application, representation or entry in register.
c) If an agent has been appointed to act in these proceedings, the agent's name and address should be indicated at c) and d).
d) An address for service in the United Kingdom to which all documents may be sent must be inserted here.
e) Attention is directed to Rules 10 and 11 of the Designs Rules 1984

I request that the following error *(a)* ....
....
....
....
....
....

in the *(b)* ....
....

of Design No. ....may be corrected.

(c) Name of agent, if any ....
....

(d) Address for service in the United Kingdom ....
....
....

(e) Signature ....
Dated this ....day of ....19 ....

To   The Registrar
     Designs Registry, The Patent Office

FORM DESIGNS NO. 19 (Revised 1984)

FEE: ITEM
16   (Rule 44)

REGISTERED DESIGNS ACT 1949

Application by Registered Proprietor of Design to Cancel Entry
in Register

NOTES:

a) Enter name and address of individual or organisation responsible for completion of this Form if different from that of registered proprietor entered above.

b) Attention is directed to Rules 10 and 11 of the Designs Rules 1984.

Design No. ....

Name of Registered Proprietor ....

....

Address ....

....

I/We, the undersigned *(a)* ....

of ....

....

....

apply that the entry in the Register of the Design No. ....

may be cancelled.

(b) Signature ....

Dated this ....day of ....19 ....

To   The Registrar
      Designs Registry, The Patent Office

V5038

FOR OFFICIAL USE ONLY

RM DESIGNS NO. 20   (Revised 1984)

| FEE: ITEM 17 | (Rule 46) |

EGISTERED DESIGNS ACT 1949

quest for Information under Section 23 when Registration
Number is Supplied

I/We request that I/we be given such information as I/we may be entitled to under Section 23 with respect
to the design registered under the No ....

Signature ....

Name ....

Address ....

....

....

Dated this ....day of ....19 ....

To   The Registrar
     Designs Registry, The Patent Office

V5039

FORM DESIGNS NO. 21 (Revised 1984)

| FEE: ITEM 18 | (Rule 47) |

REGISTERED DESIGNS ACT 1949

Request for search under Section 23 when Registration
Number is not supplied

NOTE:
a) Enter name of article

I/We request that a search be made in respect of the Design (a representation or specimen of which is annexed in duplicate) applied to *(a)* ....

....

....

and that I/we be informed whether the design is registered or closely resembles any registered design, and if so, in respect of what articles, and whether any extension of the period of copyright has been granted. The date of registration and the name and address of the registered proprietor are also requested.

Signature ....

Name ....

Address ....

Dated this ....day of ....19 ....

To   The Registrar
     Designs Registry, The Patent Office

FOR OFFICIAL USE ONLY

)RM DESIGNS NO. 23   (Revised 1984)

FEE: ITEM
19   (Rule 51)

EGISTERED DESIGNS ACT 1949

Request for Certificate for use in obtaining registration in a
country or territory outside the United Kingdom or for use
in legal proceedings or other special purpose

NOTES:
a) Where particulars of an application are to be certified, a representation of the design as originally filed must accompany this form; the representation should otherwise be identical with that attached to the Certificate of Registration.
b) If the Registry is required to prepare photocopies for any documents or representations for incorporation into the requested certificates then the appropriate photocopy charges must be paid separately from and in addition to the fee paid on this form.
c) This form can be used for a single design number only. One form suffices where certificates are required for use in more than one country or territory. The countries or territories should be entered at (h) and the fee payable is the product of their number and the basic Form Fee.
d) This form is not to be used for the certification of the application form or other documents (certified office copies) when the usual official certificate is not also required.
e) Enter number of design and name of proprietor(s).
f) Enter name and address to which certificate is to be supplied.
g) Set out the particulars which the Registrar is requested to certify. State whether the certificate is required to certify the circumstances of the original filing of the design or of the particulars of its registration if that has been effected.
h) State the purpose for which the certificate is required, ie whether for use in obtaining registration in another country (if so, name the country and see Note (c) above if more than one country) or for use in legal proceedings (if so, state title of proceeding(s) or for what other purpose).
i) Attention is directed to Rules 10 and 11 of the Designs Rules 1984.

*   *Delete as appropriate and see Notes a—d.*
  *Design Application
            No *(e)* ....in the name of
  *Registered Design

....
....
....

I/We *(f)* ....
of ....
....

request you to furnish me/us with your Certificate *(g)* ....
....
....

for use in *(h)* ....
....
....

(i) Signature ....
Dated this ....day of ....19 ....

To   The Registrar
     Designs Registry, The Patent Office

FORM DESIGNS NO. 25 (Revised 1984)

| FEE: ITEM 20 | (Rule 54) |

REGISTERED DESIGNS ACT 1949

Application for the grant of a Compulsory Licence under
Section 10

NOTES:

a) If the applicant has appointed an agent to act on his behalf, the agent's name and address should be indicated at a) and b).

b) An address for service in the United Kingdom to which all documents may be sent must be inserted here.

c) Attention is directed to Rules 10 and 11 of the Designs Rules 1984

Design No. ....

I/We ....

of ....

apply for the grant of a compulsory licence in respect of Design No. ....

on the ground that the design is not applied in the United Kingdom by any industrial process or means

to the article in respect of which it is registered to such an extent as is reasonable in the circumstances

of the case.

(a) Name of Agent, if any ....

....

(b) Address for service in the United Kingdom ....

....

....

(c) Signature ....

Dated this ....day of ....19 ....

To   The Registrar
      Designs Registry, The Patent Office

FORM DESIGNS NO. 26   (Revised 1984)

| FEE: ITEM |
| 21 |

(Rule 60)

REGISTERED DESIGNS ACT 1949

Application for Cancellation of Registration under
Section 11(2)

NOTES:
a) State ground(s) on which cancellation is requested.
b) If the applicant has appointed an agent to act on his behalf, the agent's name and address should be indicated at b) and c).
c) An address for service in the United Kingdom to which all documents may be sent must be inserted here.
d) Attention is directed to Rules 10 and 11 of the Designs Rules 1984.

Design No. ....

I/We ....

of ....

apply for cancellation of the registration of Design No. ....

on the ground(s) that *(a)* ....

....

....

....

(b) Name of agent, if any ....

....

(c) Address for service in the United Kingdom ....

....

....

(d) Signature ....

Dated this ....day of ....19 ....

To   The Registrar
     Designs Registry, The Patent Office

V5046

FORM DESIGNS NO. 27 (Revised 1984)

| FEE: ITEM 22 | (Rule 59) |

REGISTERED DESIGNS ACT 1949

Notice that Hearing of Application for Cancellation
of Registration of a Design or for the Grant of a
Compulsory Licence will be Attended.

NOTES:
(a)　　　Enter full name and address.
(b) and (c)　Delete the words which are not applicable to the case.

I/We *(a)* ....

....

....

give notice that the hearing relating to the application *(b)* to cancel the registration *(c)* for the grant
of a compulsory licence, in respect of Design No. ...., will be attended by myself/ourselves
or by some person on my/our behalf.

Signature ....

Dated this ....day of ....19 ....

To　The Registrar
　　Designs Registry, The Patent Office

FORM DESIGNS NO. 28   (Revised 1984)

| FEE: ITEM 23 | (Rule 72) |

FOR OFFICIAL USE ONLY

REGISTERED DESIGNS ACT 1949

Application for Entry of Order of the Court in Register

NOTES:

a) State (in full) name and address of applicant.
b) State the purport of the order.
c) If the applicant has appointed an agent to act on his behalf, the agent's name and address should be indicated at c) and d).
d) An address for service in the United Kingdom to which all documents may be sent must be inserted here.
e) Attention is directed to Rules 10 and 11 of the Designs Rules 1984.

Design No. ....

(a) I/We ....

....

....

transmit an office copy of an Order of the Court with reference to *(b)* ....

....

....

(c) Name of agent, if any ....

....

(d) Address for service in the United Kingdom ....

....

....

(e) Signature ....

Dated this ....day of ....19 ....

To   The Registrar
      Designs Registry, The Patent Office

Rule 32   **SCHEDULE 3**

FORMS OF CERTIFICATE OF REGISTRATION OF DESIGN

UNITED KINGDOM OF GREAT BRITAIN AND NORTHERN IRELAND
AND THE ISLE OF MAN

D.R. No.

REGISTERED DESIGNS ACT, 1949

Certificate of Registration of Design

Number of Registration

Date of Registration

Date of Issue of Certificate

This is to certify that, in pursuance of and subject to the provisions of the Registered Desig
Act, 1949, the Design, of which a representation is annexed, has been registered as of the abc
registration date in the name of

in respect of the application of such Design to

Designs Registry,
The Patent Office

Registrar

UNITED KINGDOM OF GREAT BRITAIN AND NORTHERN IRELAND
AND THE ISLE OF MAN

D.R. No. 1A

REGISTERED DESIGNS ACT, 1949

Certificate of Registration of Design

Number of Registration

Date of Registration

Date of Issue of Certificate

This is to certify that, in pursuance of and subject to the provisions of the Registered Designs Act, 1949, the Design, of which a representation is annexed, has been registered as of the above registration date in the name of

in respect of the application of such Design to

This design has been registered under the provisions of Section 4 in association with Registered Design number

Designs Registry
The Patent Office

Registrar

UNITED KINGDOM OF GREAT BRITAIN AND NORTHERN IRELAND
AND THE ISLE OF MAN

D.R. No. 1C

REGISTERED DESIGNS ACT, 1949

Certificate of Registration of Design

Number of Registration

Date of Registration

Date of Issue of Certificate

This is to certify that, in pursuance of and subject to the provisions of the Registered Designs
Act, 1949, the Design, of which a representation is annexed, has been registered as of the above
registration date (being the date on which application was made for protection of the Design in a
Convention country, viz.

in the name of

in respect of the application of such Design to

Designs Registry
The Patent Office

Registrar

UNITED KINGDOM OF GREAT BRITAIN AND NORTHERN IRELAND
AND THE ISLE OF MAN

D.R. No. 1D

REGISTERED DESIGNS ACT, 1949

Certificate of Registration of Design

Number of Registration

Date of Registration

Date of Issue of Certificate

This is to certify that, in pursuance of and subject to the provisions of the Registered Designs
Act, 1949, the Design, of which a representation is annexed, has been registered as of the above
registration date (being the date on which application was made for protection of the Design in a
Convention country, viz.

in the name of

in respect of the application of such Design to

This design has been registered under the provision of Section 4 in association with Registered
Design number

Designs Registry
The Patent Office

Registrar

Rule 73

SCHEDULE 4

REVOCATIONS

Number	Title
S.I. 1949/2368	The Designs Rules 1949
S.I. 1955/116	The Designs (Amendment) Rules 1955
S.I. 1964/229	The Designs (Amendment) Rules 1964
S.I. 1965/1551	The Designs (Amendment) Rules 1965
S.I. 1967/393	The Designs (Amendment) Rules 1967
S.I. 1974/2043	The Designs (Amendment No. 2) Rules 1974
S.I. 1975/890	The Designs (Amendment No. 2) Rules 1975
S.I. 1980/1794	The Designs (Amendment No. 2) Rules 1980
S.I. 1981/71	The Designs (Amendment) Rules 1981

EXPLANATORY NOTE

(This Note is not part of the Rules.)

These Rules consolidate with modifications the Designs Rules 1949, as amended.

The principal modifications are—

(a) the Manchester Branch of the Designs Registry of the Patent Office is to be closed. Consequently all references to the Manchester Branch have been deleted from the Rules, and forms designed for use at that Branch have been incorporated into Form Designs No. 2;

(b) the number of forms has been reduced by rationalising application forms and forms requesting searches, certificates of the Registrar and changes of name and address on the Register;

(c) rule 10 modifies the present requirements for an agent in all cases to produce evidence of his authority to act by providing for him to do so where, after his principal has become a party to proceedings before the Registrar, he is appointed for the first time or there is a change of agent;

(d) rule 29 is modified by extending from one month to two months the period within which an applicant for registration may apply for a hearing;

(e) rule 45 is modified by extending from ten days to fourteen days the period of notice to be given to a party to a proceeding of the time when that party may be heard by the Registrar before the Registrar exercises any discretionary power adversely to that party;

(f) rule 50 is modified to make all times prescribed by the Rules extendible by the Registrar;

(g) rule 56 is modified by removing the mandatory requirement for an applicant for a compulsory licence to lodge evidence;

(h) rule 57 is modified by giving a registered proprietor the option of filing evidence whether or not evidence has been filed under rule 56;

(i) rule 59(1) is modified by extending from ten days to fourteen days the period of notice to be given of an appointment of a time for hearing an application for a compulsory licence under section 10 of the Registered Designs Act 1949;

(j) rule 70 introduces provisions to allow for general interruption or subsequent dislocation in the postal services of the United Kingdom; and

(k) Schedule 2 contains revised forms.

STATUTORY INSTRUMENTS

1984 No. 1990

BANKS AND BANKING

The Deposit Protection Fund (Excluded Institutions) (No. 2) Order 1984

Made	- - -	19th December 1984
Laid before Parliament		20th December 1984
Coming into Operation		9th January 1985

Whereas the Treasury are satisfied, after consultation with the Deposit Protection Board, that sterling deposits with the United Kingdom offices of the institutions listed in the Schedule to this Order (all of which are bodies corporate formed under the law of countries outside the United Kingdom) are as well protected under the law of those countries as they would be under Part II of the Banking Act 1979(a):—

Now, therefore, the Treasury, in exercise of the powers conferred on them by section 23(2) of the Banking Act 1979 and of all other powers enabling them in that behalf, hereby make the following Order:—

1. This Order may be cited as the Deposit Protection Fund (Excluded Institutions) (No. 2) Order 1984 and shall come into operation on 9th January 1985.

2. The institutions listed in the Schedule to this Order are hereby excluded from Section 23(1) of the Banking Act 1979.

T. Garel-Jones,
A. G. Hamilton,
Two of the Lords Commissioners
of Her Majesty's Treasury.

19th December 1984.

(a) 1979 c.37.

THE SCHEDULE   *Article 2*

<small>INSTITUTIONS EXCLUDED FROM SECTION 23(1) OF THE BANKING ACT 1979</small>

Kansallis—Osake—Pankki
Barbados National Bank
Union Bank of Finland Ltd.

EXPLANATORY NOTE

(*This Note is not part of the Order.*)

This Order excludes the three institutions listed in the Schedule to the Order from section 23(1) of the Banking Act 1979 thus exempting them from the requirement to contribute to the Deposit Protection Fund established by section 21 of the Act, and removing deposits with them from the protection afforded by section 28 in the event of insolvency.

STATUTORY INSTRUMENTS

1984 No. 1991

SOCIAL SECURITY

The Social Security (Adjudication) Amendment (No. 2) Regulations 1984

Made	- - -	*19th December* 1984
Laid before Parliament		*7th January* 1985
Coming into Operation		*28th January* 1985

The Secretary of State for Social Services, after consultation with the Council on Tribunals(a) so far as is required, and the Social Security Advisory Committee having agreed that the proposals for the regulations need not be referred to them(b), in exercise of the powers conferred on him by sections 6(1) and 10 of the Family Income Supplements Act 1970(c), sections 112(5), 114(1) and (2) and 115 of, and Schedules 13 and 20 to, the Social Security Act 1975(d) and sections 2(1) and 34(1) of the Supplementary Benefits Act 1976(e) and of all other powers enabling him in that behalf, hereby makes the following regulations:—

Citation and commencment
1. These regulations may be cited as the Social Security (Adjudication) Amendment (No. 2) Regulations 1984 and shall come into operation on 28th January 1985.

Amendment of the Social Security (Adjudication) Regulations 1984
2. The Social Security (Adjudication) Regulations 1984(f) shall be amended as follows:—

(*a*) in regulation 2(2)(*b*) after the words "any person" there shall be inserted "(except a person undergoing training as an adjudication officer or, in the case of a medical appeal tribunal, as an adjudicating medical practitioner)";

(*b*) in regulation 6(2) after the word "Act" in the first place where it appears there shall be inserted the word "or" and for sub-paragraphs (*a*) and (*b*) there shall be substituted the following sub-paragraphs —

(a) *See* Tribunals and Inquiries Act 1971 (c.62), section 10.
(b) *See* Social Security Act 1980 (c.30), section 10(2).
(c) 1970 c.55; section 6(1) was substituted by the Health and Social Services and Social Security Adjudications Act 1983 (c.41), Schedule 8, paragraph 16.
(d) 1975 c.14.
(e) 1976 c.71; section 2(1) was substituted by the Health and Social Services and Social Security Adjudications Act 1983, Schedule 8, paragraph 14.
(f) S.I. 1984/451; relevant amending instrument is S.I. 1984/613.

"(a) before the hearing begins, with the consent in writing of —

(i) in a case which originated in a decision of or a reference by an adjudication officer (other than a reference pursuant to section 109(3) of the Act), the adjudication officer; or

(ii) in any other case, the Secretary of State,

and, in any case, of any other party to the proceedings; or

(b) after the hearing has begun, with the leave of the adjudicating authority or, in the case of a tribunal or board, its chairman, at any time before the determination is made.";

(c) paragraph (2) of regulation 8 is revoked;

(d) in regulation 19(2)(b) for the words "grounds of" there shall be substituted the words "the reasons for";

(e) in regulation 26(4), after the word "practicable" there shall be inserted the words "to the clerk, or person acting as clerk, to the tribunal from which the appeal or application was brought or by which the reference was made,";

(f) for regulation 29 there shall be substituted the following regulation:—

"Time limits for making written observations

29.—(1) Unless otherwise directed by the Commissioner and subject also to regulation 92(8), a party to an application, appeal or reference to a Commissioner may submit written observations thereon —

(a) in the case of proceedings which lie only on a question of law, within 4 weeks; and

(b) in any other case, within 3 months,

beginning in either case, with the day on which notice of the application, appeal or reference was received by him.

(2) Unless otherwise directed by a Commissioner and subject also to regulation 92(8), a party to an application, appeal or reference to a Commissioner may submit written observations on the written observations submitted by another party —

(a) in the case of observations on observations submitted pursuant to paragraph (1), within 6 weeks; and

(b) in any other case, within 4 weeks,

beginning, in either case, with the day on which the document to which the observations are directed was received by him.

(3) Without prejudice to the provisions of paragraphs (1) and (2), the Commissioner may direct any party to any proceedings before him to make such written observations or further written observations as may seem to him necessary to enable the question at issue to be determined and may specify the time within which they are required to be made.

(4) Any time limit imposed by or under this regulation may be extended by the Commissioner for special reasons.

(5) For the purposes of this regulation the receipt of any notice, observations or directions at a local office shall be treated as receipt by the Secretary of State or an adjudication officer as the case may be and where any notice, observations or directions are addressed to any other party and delivered (by post or otherwise) to his ordinary or last known address they shall be treated as being received by him at the date of such delivery.";

(g) in regulation 60(3) after the word "them" where it first appears there shall be inserted the words ", except that on such review any medical question arising in connection with a person's entitlement to an allowance shall be determined as at the date when the application for review is made"; and

(h) in paragraph 1 of columns (3) and (4) of Schedule 4 for the word "None" there shall be substituted "Sections 101 and 104 apply subject to the modifications made by this Schedule and regulations 67 and 71 apply instead of sections 99, 100 and 103.".

Saving

3. The amendments made by regulation 2(f) (time limits for making written observations) shall not apply to the submission of observations on observations received before the amendments come into operation.

Signed by authority of the Secretary of State for Social Services.

Tony Newton,
Minister of State,
Department of Health and Social Security.

19th December 1984.

EXPLANATORY NOTE

(This Note is not part of the Regulations.)

These regulations further amend the Social Security (Adjudication) Regulations 1984. In so far as they consist of procedural rules for tribunals the Council on Tribunals has been consulted. In so far as they do not so consist, the requirement of section 10(1) of the Social Security Act 1980, that proposals for the regulations be referred to the Social Security Advisory Committee, is dispensed with because that Committee has agreed, under section 10(2), that the proposals need not be referred to them.

The main amendments provides for a new regulation 29 which imposes time limits for making written observations in proceedings before the Commissioner and makes such limits subject to any contrary direction by the Commissioner.

STATUTORY INSTRUMENTS

1984 No. 1992

PUBLIC HEALTH, ENGLAND AND WALES

The Control of Noise (Codes of Practice for Construction and Open Sites) Order 1984

Made - - - -	17*th December* 1984
Laid before Parliament	7*th January* 1985
Coming into Operation	29*th January* 1985

The Secretary of State, in exercise of his powers under sections 71 and 104(1) of the Control of Pollution Act 1974(**a**), and of all other powers enabling him in that behalf, hereby makes the following Order:—

Citation, commencement and extent

1.—(1) This Order may be cited as the Control of Noise (Codes of Practice for Construction and Open Sites) Order 1984 and shall come into operation on 29th January 1985.

(2) This Order shall extend to England and Wales.

Codes of practice

2. The Secretary of State approves the following British Standards Institution Codes of Practice relating to noise control on construction and open sites:—

(*a*) the Code of Practice for basic information and procedures for noise control published on 31st May 1984 under the number BS 5228: Part 1: 1984 (which is concerned, inter alia, with the carrying out of works to which section 60 of the Control of Pollution Act 1974 applies), and

(*b*) the Code of Practice for noise control applicable to surface coal extraction by opencast methods published on 31st May 1984 under the number BS 5228: Part 3: 1984.

(**a**) 1974 c. 40.

Revocation

3. The Control of Noise (Code of Practice for Construction Sites) Order 1975(**a**) is revoked.

Patrick Jenkin,
Secretary of State for the Environment.
17th December 1984.

Nicholas Edwards,
Secretary of State for Wales.
17th December 1984.

EXPLANATORY NOTE

(This Note is not part of the Order.)

Under section 71 of the Control of Pollution Act 1974 the Secretary of State may give guidance on appropriate methods for minimising noise by approving codes of practice. He is required to approve a code for the carrying out of works to which section 60 of the Act applies. These include building and roadworks, demolition, dredging and other works of engineering construction.

This Order (which extends to England and Wales) approves the two codes mentioned in article 2. The Code of practice for basic information and procedures for noise control mentioned in article 2(*a*) covers all construction sites and other open sites.

The Order replaces The Control of Noise (Code of Practice for Construction Sites) Order 1975 which is revoked.

Both the approved Codes of Practice are obtainable from the British Standards Institution at the following addresses—

(*a*) by post from Linford Wood, Milton Keynes MK14 6LE, and

(*b*) in person from Hampden House, 61 Green Street, London W1 and 195 Pentonville Road, London N1.

(**a**) S.I. 1975/2115.

STATUTORY INSTRUMENTS

1984 No. 1993

CABLE PROGRAMME SERVICES

The Cable (Excepted Programmes) Order 1984

Made - - - - -	19*th December* 1984
Coming into Operation	1*st January* 1985

In exercise of the powers conferred upon me by section 13(1) of the Cable and Broadcasting Act 1984(a), and after consultation with the Cable Authority, the British Broadcasting Corporation and the Independent Broadcasting Authority, I hereby make the following Order:—

1. This Order may be cited as the Cable (Excepted Programmes) Order 1984 and shall come into operation on 1st January 1985.

2. The duty imposed on the Cable Authority by section 13 of the Cable and Broadcasting Act 1984 to do all that they can to secure that every licensed diffusion service includes, by the reception and immediate re-transmission of the broadcasts, the programmes included in the broadcasting services mentioned in that section is subject to the exceptions specified in the Schedule to this Order.

Home Office.

19th December 1984.

Leon Brittan,
One of Her Majesty's Principal
Secretaries of State.

(a) 1984 c. 46.

SCHEDULE   Article 2.

Exceptions to the duty imposed on the Cable Authority by section 13

1.—(1) The exceptions for programmes included in television broadcasting services
are—

(*a*) in the case of a diffusion service in respect of which there was, immediately
prior to 1st January 1985, a licence granted(**a**), or having effect as if granted(**b**),
by the Secretary of State under section 58 of the Telecommunications Act 1984(**c**),
the programmes included in any television broadcasting service which the licensee
was not licensed to include in his service;

(*b*) in the case of any other diffusion service provided over a restricted capacity
telecommunication system and in respect of which there is a licence granted by
the Cable Authority, if the licensee—

(i) was, prior to the date on which the licence takes effect, providing by means
of that system, cable programme services consisting of the reception and immediate re-transmission of programmes included in television broadcasting services;
and

(ii) has made available to the persons to whom such services were provided
facilities for the reception, otherwise than by means of the system, of the
programmes included in those services,

the programmes included in those services.

(2) In paragraph (*b*) above, "restricted capacity telecommunication system" means
a system which—

(*a*) prior to 1st January 1985 was run wholly or mainly for the purpose of relaying
at High Frequency television broadcasting services; and

(*b*) is not capable of conveying visual images on more than six channels of 8 MHz
simultaneously.

2. The exceptions for programmes included in sound broadcasting are—

(*a*) in the case of a prescribed diffusion service, where—

(i) a sound broadcasting service consists of two or more programme schedules
broadcast from time to time on different frequencies; and

(ii) the licensee includes in his service the programmes contained in one of
those schedules,

the programmes contained in any other programme schedule forming part of that sound
broadcasting service;

(*b*) in the case of any other diffusion service, the programmes included in all
sound broadcasting services, but—

(i) if the licensee includes in his service, at a time when he is also including
services in sounds and visual images, a service in sound only provided otherwise
than by a broadcasting authority, he should include the programmes included in at
least one sound broadcasting service provided by a broadcasting authority, in
which case paragraph (*a*) above shall apply as it applies in the case of a prescribed
diffusion service;

(**a**) By virtue of section 58(2) of the Cable and Broadcasting Act 1984, such a licence has effect
as if granted by the Cable Authority.
(**b**) Paragraph 8(2) of Schedule 5 to the Telecommunications Act 1984 (c. 12).
(**c**) 1984 c. 12.

(ii) if the licensee includes in his service, at a time when he is also including services in sounds and visual images, two or more services in sound only provided otherwise than by a broadcasting authority, the exception in this paragraph shall not apply, but paragraph (*a*) above shall apply as it applies in the case of a prescribed diffusion service.

EXPLANATORY NOTE

(This Note is not part of the Order.)

Under section 13 of the Cable and Broadcasting Act 1984 the Cable Authority are required to do all that they can to secure that every licensed diffusion service provided in any area includes, by the reception and immediate retransmission of the broadcasts, the programmes included in each television and radio service intended for reception in that area, subject to such exceptions as the Secretary of State may by Order specify. The Schedule to this Order specifies those exceptions.

By virtue of paragraph 1 of the Schedule the Authority are not required to secure the inclusion of programmes included in any BBC or IBA television broadcasts in services in respect of which there was before 1st January 1985 a licence granted by the Secretary of State to provide only programmes other than those included in such broadcasts. In relation to services provided over restricted capacity telecommunication systems and licensed by the Cable Authority after that date, the obligation is to secure the inclusion of only those programmes included in television broadcasts which have not been made available off-air to subscribers, who were previously provided with such programmes by means of the system.

Paragraph 2 of the Schedule provides that the Authority is not required to secure the inclusion of any BBC or IBA sound broadcasting service in more than one form, where it is broadcast in more than one form from separate transmitters. In addition, diffusion services do not have to include BBC or IBA radio broadcasts at all unless they include (at a time when they are also including television services) a sound service provided otherwise than by the BBC or IBA, in which case they must include at least one BBC or IBA service, but only in one form. If they include two or more such services provided otherwise than by the BBC or IBA, they must include, at least in one form, all appropriate BBC and IBA radio broadcasts.

STATUTORY INSTRUMENTS

1984 No. 1994

CABLE PROGRAMME SERVICES

The Cable (Prescribed Diffusion Service) Order 1984

Made - - - - - 19th December 1984

Coming into Operation 1st January 1985

In exercise of the powers conferred upon me by section 2(3) of the Cable and Broadcasting Act 1984(a), and after consultation with the Cable Authority, I hereby make the following Order:—

1. This Order may be cited as the Cable (Prescribed Diffusion Service) Order 1984 and shall come into operation on 1st January 1985.

2.—(1) For the purposes of Part I of the Cable and Broadcasting Act 1984, "prescribed diffusion service" means a diffusion service consisting of sounds and visual images sent by means of a telecommunication system which—

(a) is connected to apparatus by means of which the service is received; and

(b) is capable of conveying simultaneously visual images on at least 16 channels of 8 MHz from the place from which it is run.

(2) For the purposes of paragraph (a) above, a system shall not be regarded as connected to apparatus unless it would be so regarded for the purposes of section 4 of the Telecommunications Act 1984(b).

Home Office.

19th December 1984.

Leon Brittan,
One of Her Majesty's Principal
Secretaries of State.

(a) 1984 c. 46.   (b) 1984 c. 12.

EXPLANATORY NOTE

(This Note is not part of the Order.)

Under the Cable and Broadcasting Act 1984 the Cable Authority are charged with a number of duties in relation to "prescribed diffusion services", the most important of which is their duty, under section 4(9), to exercise their licensing powers in the manner which they consider is best calculated to promote the provision of such services. By virtue of section 2(3) a "prescribed diffusion service" means a diffusion service of such description as the Secretary of State, after consultation with the Cable Authority, may by order prescribe. This Order describes a "prescribed diffusion service" as a diffusion service in which sound and television programmes are relayed direct to the home by means of a wideband cable system capable of carrying at least 16 video channels simultaneously.

STATUTORY INSTRUMENTS

1984 No. 1995
WATER, ENGLAND AND WALES
The Water Authorities (Return on Assets) Order 1984

Made - - - -	17th December 1984
Laid before Parliament	7th January 1985
Coming into Operation	29th January 1985

The Secretary of State for the Environment, with the approval of the Treasury, in exercise of the powers conferred on him by section 29(2)(a) of the Water Act 1973(a) and of all other powers enabling him in that behalf, hereby makes the following order:—

Title, commencement and application of powers

1.—(1) This order may be cited as the Water Authorities (Return on Assets) Order 1984 and shall come into operation on 29th January 1985.

(2) This order applies to the water authorities mentioned in the Schedule.

Interpretation

2.—(1) In this order "the relevant period" means the period beginning with the commencement of this order and ending on 31st March 1985.

(2) In construing, for the purposes of this order, "current cost" and "current cost operating profit" regard shall be had to the requirements for the preparation of current cost accounts contained in the publication entitled "Statement of Standard Accounting Practice No. 16" issued in March 1980 by the bodies represented on the Consultative Committee of Accountancy Bodies.

Definition of "the value of their net assets" for the purposes of section 29 of the Act

3. In relation to any water authority "the value of their net assets" is defined, for the purposes of section 29 of the Water Act 1973, as the mean between the total net value, at current cost, of the assets held by the authority for the purposes of their functions (other than functions relating to land drainage) on 1st April 1984 and of the assets so held on 31st March 1985.

Return on value of net assets

4.—(1) In this article, in relation to any water authority—

"their 1984 balance" means the amount by which that authority's 1984 achievement, as defined in the Water Authorities (Return on Assets) Order 1983(b), exceeded or fell short of the rate of return specified for that authority in the Schedule to that order; and

"their 1985 achievement" means the aggregate of—

(a) 1973 c. 37; section 29(2)(a) was amended by section 11(3) of, and Schedule 5 to, the Water Act 1983 (c. 23).
(b) S.I. 1983/1592.

(a) their 1984 balance,

(b) the current cost operating profit of the authority earned for the financial year 1984–85 from the authority's functions other than functions relating to land drainage, and

(c) any amount transferred to their appropriation account in respect of that year from any tariff equalisation fund maintained by the authority.

(2) The Secretary of State specifies as the rate of return on the value of their net assets which he considers it reasonable for each of the water authorities mentioned in the Schedule hereto to achieve in the relevant period, such rate as results in that authority achieving for the financial year 1984–85 a rate of return on those assets equal to the rate specified in the Schedule hereto in relation to that authority.

(3) It is hereby directed that during the relevant period each water authority mentioned in the Schedule to this order shall discharge their functions with a view to securing that for the financial year 1984–85 the ratio of their 1985 achievement to the value of their net assets, expressed as a percentage, is not less than the relevant rate specified in that Schedule.

Article 4   SCHEDULE

SPECIFIED RATE OF RETURN ON VALUE OF NET ASSETS IN RESPECT OF THE YEAR 1984–85

Water authority	Rate of return for 1984/5
	per cent.
Anglian Water Authority	1.36
Northumbrian Water Authority	1.25
North West Water Authority	0.95
Severn-Trent Water Authority	1.25
Southern Water Authority	0.91
South West Water Authority	1.26
Thames Water Authority	0.50
Wessex Water Authority	0.61
Yorkshire Water Authority	1.00

Patrick Jenkin,
Secretary of State for the Environment.

14th December 1984.

We approve the making of this order,

John Major,
Donald Thompson,
Two of the Lords Commissioners
of Her Majesty's Treasury.

17th December 1984.

EXPLANATORY NOTE

(This note is not part of the order.)

This order gives directions to the nine English water authorities. It specifies the rate of return on the value of their net assets which the Secretary of State considers each water authority can reasonably achieve and directs those authorities to discharge their functions for the rest of the financial year 1984–85 with a view to achieving for that year the appropriate rate of return specified in the Schedule.

The Publication entitled "Statement of Standard Accounting Practice No. 16", which is mentioned in article 2 of the order, is obtainable from the Institute of Chartered Accountants in England and Wales, Silbury Boulevard, Witan Gate East, Central Milton Keynes, Buckinghamshire MK9 2HL.

STATUTORY INSTRUMENTS

1984 No. 1996

ROAD TRAFFIC

The Motor Vehicles (Payments in Respect of Applicants for Exemption from Wearing Seat Belts) Order 1984

Made - - - - -	19th December 1984
Laid before Parliament	10th January 1985
Coming into Operation	1st February 1985

The Secretary of State for Transport, in exercise of his powers under section 70(3) of the Transport Act 1982(a) and all other powers enabling him in that behalf, hereby makes the following Order:—

1. This Order may be cited as the Motor Vehicles (Payments in Respect of Applicants for Exemption from Wearing Seat Belts) Order 1984 and shall come into operation on 1st February 1985.

2. Section 70(2)(a) of the Transport Act 1982 (which specifies certain classes relating to payments in respect of applicants for exemption from wearing seat belts) shall be amended so as to add, after sub-sub-paragraph (iv) the following:

"(v) a mobility supplement under a scheme made under the Personal Injuries (Emergency Provisions) Act 1939(b) or under an Order in Council made under section 12 of the Social Security (Miscellaneous Provisions) Act 1977(c) (war pensioners mobility supplement); or

(vi) a disability pension paid by the Secretary of State for Defence on account of disability attributable to injury sustained after 30th September 1921 but before 3rd September 1939 together with a mobility supplement paid under the Naval and Marine Pay and Pensions (Disablement Awards) (No. 2) Order 1984 or under Royal Warrant dated 30th December 1949 or under Queen's Regulations for the Royal Air Force.".

Nicholas Ridley,
Secretary of State for Transport.

19th December 1984.

(a) 1982 c.49. (b) 1939 c.82. (c) 1977 c.5.

EXPLANATORY NOTE

(This Note is not part of the Order.)

This Order amends section 70 of the Transport Act 1982 so as to enable the Secretary of State to make payments in respect of those applicants for exemption from wearing seat belts who are in receipt of war pensioners' mobility supplement.

The Naval and Marine Pay and Pensions (Disablement Awards) (No. 2) Order 1984 is an Order in Council made under Section 11 of the Naval and Marine Pay and Pensions Act 1865 (c. 73); it is not published. Queen's Regulations for the Royal Air Force 4th Edition 1971 is published by HMSO. The Royal Warrant dated 30 December 1949 (as amended) is not published.

STATUTORY INSTRUMENTS

1984 No. 1998

OFFSHORE INSTALLATIONS

The Offshore Installations (Safety Zones) (Revocation) (No. 72) Order 1984

Made - - - -	*19th December* 1984
Coming into Operation	*21st December* 1984

The Secretary of State, in exercise of the power conferred on him by section 21(1) of the Oil and Gas (Enterprise) Act 1982(a), and of all other powers enabling him in that behalf, hereby makes the following Order:—

1. This Order may be cited as the Offshore Installations (Safety Zones) (Revocation) (No. 72) Order 1984 and shall come into operation on 21st December 1984.

2. The Offshore Installations (Safety Zones) (No. 80) Order 1984(b) is hereby revoked.

Alick Buchanan-Smith,
Minister of State,
Department of Energy.

19th December 1984.

EXPLANATORY NOTE

(This Note is not part of the Order.)

This Order revokes the Offshore Installations (Safety Zones) (No. 80) Order 1984. The installation known as Treasure Swan which was protected by the safety zone established by that Order has been removed and accordingly that Order is no longer required.

(a) 1982 c.23.   (b) S.I. 1984/1724.

STATUTORY INSTRUMENTS

1984 No. 1999

OFFSHORE INSTALLATIONS

The Offshore Installations (Safety Zones) (Revocation) (No. 73) Order 1984

Made - - - - -	19*th December* 1984
Coming into Operation	21*st December* 1984

The Secretary of State, in exercise of the power conferred on him by section 21(1) of the Oil and Gas (Enterprise) Act 1982(a), and of all other powers enabling him in that behalf, hereby makes the following Order:—

1. This Order may be cited as the Offshore Installations (Safety Zones) (Revocation) (No. 73) Order 1984 and shall come into operation on 21st December 1984.

2. The Offshore Installations (Safety Zones) (No. 56) Order 1984(b) is hereby revoked.

Alick Buchanan-Smith,
Minister of State,
Department of Energy.

19th December 1984.

EXPLANATORY NOTE

(*This Note is not part of the Order.*)

This Order revokes the Offshore Installations (Safety Zones) (No. 56) Order 1984. The installation known as Sovereign Explorer which was protected by the safety zone established by that Order has been removed and accordingly that Order is no longer required.

(**a**) 1982 c. 23.   (**b**) S.I. 1984/1138.

STATUTORY INSTRUMENTS

1984 No. 2000

OFFSHORE INSTALLATIONS

The Offshore Installations (Safety Zones) (No. 98) Order 1984

Made - - - -	*19th December* 1984
Coming into Operation	*21st December* 1984

The Secretary of State, in exercise of the powers conferred on him by section 21(1), (2) and (3) of the Oil and Gas (Enterprise) Act 1982(a) (hereinafter referred to as "the Act"), and of all other powers enabling him in that behalf, hereby makes the following Order:—

1. This Order may be cited as the Offshore Installations (Safety Zones) (No. 98) Order 1984 and shall come into operation on 21st December 1984.

2.—(1) A safety zone is hereby established around the installation specified in Column 1 of the Schedule hereto (being an installation maintained in waters in an area designated under section 1(7) of the Continental Shelf Act 1964(b)) having a radius of five hundred metres from the point as respects that installation which has the co-ordinates of latitude and longitude according to European Datum (1950) specified in Columns 2 and 3 of the Schedule.

(2) The prohibition under section 21(3) of the Act on a vessel entering or remaining in a safety zone without the consent of the Secretary of State shall not apply to a vessel entering or remaining in the safety zone established under paragraph (1) above—

(*a*) in connection with the laying, inspection, testing, repair, alteration, renewal or removal of any submarine cable or pipe-line in or near that safety zone;

(*b*) to provide services for, to transport persons or goods to or from, or under the authority of a government department to inspect, any installation in that safety zone;

(*c*) if it is a vessel belonging to a general lighthouse authority performing duties relating to the safety of navigation;

(*d*) in connection with the saving or attempted saving of life or property;

(*e*) owing to stress of weather; or

(*f*) when in distress.

Alick Buchanan-Smith,
Minister of State,
Department of Energy.

19th December 1984.

(**a**) 1982 c. 23.   (**b**) 1964 c. 29.

SCHEDULE   Article 2(1)

SAFETY ZONE

1	2	3
Name or other designation of the offshore installation	Latitude North	Longitude East
Glomar Arctic III	57° 52′ 11·84″	01° 16′ 59·13″

EXPLANATORY NOTE

(This Note is not part of the Order.)

This Order establishes, under section 21 of the Oil and Gas (Enterprise) Act 1982, a safety zone, having a radius of 500 metres from a specified point, around the installation known as Glomar Arctic III maintained in waters in an area designated under section 1(7) of the Continental Shelf Act 1964.

Vessels (which includes hovercraft, submersible apparatus and installations in transit) are prohibited from entering or remaining in the safety zone except with the consent of the Secretary of State or in the circumstances mentioned in Article 2(2) of the Order.

STATUTORY INSTRUMENTS

1984 No. 2001

OFFSHORE INSTALLATIONS

The Offshore Installations (Safety Zones) (No. 99) Order 1984

Made	- - -	19*th December* 1984
Coming into Operation		21*st December* 1984

The Secretary of State, in exercise of the powers conferred on him by section 21(1), (2) and (3) of the Oil and Gas (Enterprise) Act 1982 (**a**) (hereinafter referred to as "the Act"), and of all other powers enabling him in that behalf, hereby makes the following Order:—

1. This Order may be cited as the Offshore Installations (Safety Zones) (No. 99) Order 1984 and shall come into operation on 21st December 1984.

2.—(1) A safety zone is hereby established around the installation specified in Column 1 of the Schedule hereto (being an installation maintained in waters in an area designated under section 1(7) of the Continental Shelf Act 1964(**b**)) having a radius of five hundred metres from the point as respects that installation which has the co-ordinates of latitude and longitude according to European Datum (1950) specified in Columns 2 and 3 of the Schedule.

(2) The prohibition under section 21(3) of the Act on a vessel entering or remaining in a safety zone without the consent of the Secretary of State shall not apply to a vessel entering or remaining in the safety zone established under paragraph (1) above—

   (*a*) in connection with the laying, inspection, testing, repair, alteration, renewal or removal of any submarine cable or pipe-line in or near that safety zone;

   (*b*) to provide services for, to transport persons or goods to or from, or under the authority of a government department to inspect, any installation in that safety zone;

   (*c*) if it is a vessel belonging to a general lighthouse authority performing duties relating to the safety of navigation;

   (*d*) in connection with the saving or attempted saving of life or property;

   (*e*) owing to stress of weather; or

   (*f*) when in distress.

Alick Buchanan-Smith,
Minister of State,
Department of Energy.

19th December 1984.

(**a**) 1982 c.23.   (**b**) 1964 c.29.

SCHEDULE Article 2(1)

SAFETY ZONE

1	2	3
Name or other designation of the offshore installation	Latitude North	Longitude East
Ocean Benloyal	59° 45′ 30·38″	01° 37′ 17·99″

EXPLANATORY NOTE

(*This Note is not part of the Order.*)

This Order establishes, under section 21 of the Oil and Gas (Enterprise) Act 1982, a safety zone, having a radius of 500 metres from a specified point, around the installation known as Ocean Benloyal maintained in waters in an area designated under section 1(7) of the Continental Shelf Act 1964.

Vessels (which includes hovercraft, submersible apparatus and installations in transit) are prohibited from entering or remaining in the safety zone except with the consent of the Secretary of State or in the circumstances mentioned in Article 2(2) of the Order.

STATUTORY INSTRUMENTS

1984 No. 2002 (C.47)

POLICE

The Police and Criminal Evidence Act 1984 (Commencement No. 1) Order 1984

Made - - - *20th December* 1984

In exercise of the powers conferred on me by section 121(1) of the Police and Criminal Evidence Act 1984(a), I hereby make the following Order:—

1. This Order may be cited as the Police and Criminal Evidence Act 1984 (Commencement No. 1) Order 1984.

2.—(1) So much of section 1 of the Police and Criminal Evidence Act 1984 as relates to search for stolen articles shall come into force on 1st January 1985 for the purpose of conferring powers on constables in localities to which this paragraph applies.

(2) Paragraph (1) applies to any locality in which there was in force on 31st December 1984 an enactment conferring power on a constable to search for stolen or unlawfully obtained goods, other than an enactment contained in a public general Act or an enactment relating to statutory undertakers.

3. The provisions of the Police and Criminal Evidence Act 1984 specified in the Schedules to this Order shall come into force on the dates mentioned in the headings to those Schedules.

Leon Brittan,
One of Her Majesty's Principal
Secretaries of State.

Home Office,
20th December 1984.

(a) 1984 c.60.

SCHEDULE 1

PROVISIONS OF THE POLICE AND CRIMINAL EVIDENCE ACT 1984 COMING INTO FORCE ON
1ST JANUARY 1985

1 Provisions of the Act	2 Subject matter of provisions
Section 7(2)(*b*).	Power of constables employed by statutory undertakers to search for stolen or unlawfully obtained goods.
Section 7(3).	Meaning of "statutory undertakers".
Section 23.	Meaning of "premises", etc.
Section 59.	Legal aid for persons at police stations.
Section 66.	Codes of practice.
Section 67.	Codes of practice—supplementary.
Section 106.	Arrangements for obtaining the views of the community on policing.
Section 109(*c*).	Authorisation of Police Federations to make rules relating to their constitution and proceedings.
Section 112.	Metropolitan police officers.
Section 113(3) to (13).	Application of Act to Armed Forces.
Section 115.	Expenses.
Section 118.	General interpretation.

SCHEDULE 2

PROVISIONS OF THE POLICE AND CRIMINAL EVIDENCE ACT 1984 COMING INTO FORCE ON
1ST MARCH 1985

Provisions of the Act	Subject matter of provisions
Section 108.	Deputy chief constables.
Section 110.	Functions of special constables in Scotland.
Section 111.	Regulations for police forces and police cadets—Scotland.
Section 119 to the extent necessary to bring into operation the provisions of Schedules 6 and 7 respectively specified in Appendix A and Appendix B hereto.	•Amendments and repeals.
So much of Schedule 6 as is specified in Appendix A hereto.	Minor and consequential amendments.
So much of Schedule 7 as is specified in Appendix B hereto.	Miscellaneous repeals.

APPENDIX A

So much of Schedule 6 as amends the following enactments:—
Section 7(1) and section 29(2) of the Police Act 1964 (c.48).
Police (Scotland) Act 1967 (c.77).

APPENDIX B

REPEALS TAKING EFFECT FROM 1ST MARCH 1985

Chapter	Short title	Extent of repeal
1967 c.77.	Police (Scotland) Act 1967.	Section 5(3).

EXPLANATORY NOTE

(This Note is not part of the Order.)

Article 2 of the Order brings section 1 of the Police and Criminal Evidence Act 1984 into force on 1st January 1985 for the limited purpose of replacing constabulary powers of stop and search for stolen or unlawfully obtained goods exercisable under local enactments referred to in section 7(1) and (2) of the Act (which expire at the end of 1984) by the equivalent powers, in the localities to which those enactments apply, to search for stolen articles under section 1 of the Act.

Article 3 brings into force on 1st January 1985 and 1st March 1985 respectively the provisions of the Police and Criminal Evidence Act 1984 set out in Schedules 1 and 2 to the Order. As provided by section 120, those provisions extend to England and Wales only, except for sections 7, 108(1) and (6) and 109 (which extend throughout Great Britain); sections 108(4) and (5), 110, 111, 112(1), the amendments to the Police (Scotland) Act 1967 in paragraphs 30 to 33 of Schedule 6, and the repeal in Schedule 7 of section 5(3) of that Act (which extend to Scotland only); section 112(2) (which extends to Northern Ireland only); and section 113(3) to (13), section 115, the definition of "document" in section 118 and section 119 in so far as they have effect in relation to any provision other than a provision extending to England and Wales only.

STATUTORY INSTRUMENTS

1984 No. 2004

INDUSTRIAL TRAINING

The Industrial Training Levy (Construction Board) Order 1984

Laid before Parliament in draft

Made - - - - 20*th December* 1984

Coming into operation
on the fourteenth day
after the day on which
it is made.

Whereas proposals made by the Construction Industry Training Board for the raising and collection of a levy have been submitted to, and approved by, the Manpower Services Commission under section 11(1) of the Industrial Training Act 1982(a) ("the 1982 Act") and thereafter submitted by the said Commission to the Secretary of State under that subsection;

And whereas in pursuance of section 11(3) of the 1982 Act the said proposals include provision for the exemption from the levy of employers who, in view of the small number of their employees, ought in the opinion of the Secretary of State to be exempted from it;

And whereas the proposals are made in pursuance of section 11(4)*(b)* of the 1982 Act, and the Secretary of State is satisfied that those proposals falling within section 11(5)*(b)* of the said Act ("the relevant proposals") are necessary as mentioned in the said section 11(5), and that the condition mentioned in section 11(6)*(b)* of the 1982 Act is satisfied in the case of the relevant proposals;

And whereas the following Order falls within section 11(7)*(b)* of the 1982 Act;

And whereas a draft of the following Order was laid before Parliament in accordance with section 12(6) of the 1982 Act and approved by resolution of each House of Parliament;

Now, therefore, the Secretary of State in exercise of the powers conferred by sections 11(2), 12(3) and 12(4) of the 1982 Act and of all other powers enabling him in that behalf hereby makes the following Order:—

(a) 1982 c. 10.

Citation and commencement

1. This Order may be cited as the Industrial Training Levy (Construction Board) Order 1984 and shall come into operation on the fourteenth day after the day on which it is made.

Interpretation

2.—(1) In this Order unless the context otherwise requires:—

(a) "assessment" means an assessment of an employer to the levy;

(b) "the Board" means the Construction Industry Training Board;

(c) "business" means any activities of industry or commerce;

(d) "construction establishment" means an establishment in Great Britain engaged wholly or mainly in the construction industry for a total of twenty-seven or more weeks in the period of twelve months that commenced on 6th April 1983 or, being an establishment that commenced to carry on business in the said period, for a total number of weeks exceeding one half of the number of weeks in the part of the said period commencing with the day on which business was commenced and ending on the last day thereof;

(e) "the construction industry" does not include any activities of an establishment which have been transferred from the industry of the Board to the industry of another industrial training board by one of the transfer orders, but save as aforesaid means any one or more of the activities which, subject to the provisions of paragraph 2 of the Schedule to the industrial training order, are specified in paragraph 1 of that Schedule as the activities of the construction industry or, in relation to an establishment whose activities have been transferred to the industry of the Board by one of the transfer orders, any activities so transferred;

(f) "the twentieth levy period" means the period commencing with the day upon which this Order comes into operation and ending on 31st March 1985;

(g) "employer" means a person who is an employer in the construction industry at any time in the twentieth levy period;

(h) "the industrial training order" means the Industrial Training (Construction Board) Order 1964(a);

(i) "the levy" means the levy imposed by the Board in respect of the twentieth levy period;

(j) "notice" means a notice in writing;

(k) "the transfer orders" means—

(i) the Industrial Training (Transfer of the Activities of Establishments) Order 1975(b);

(ii) the Industrial Training (Transfer of the Activities of Establishments) (No. 2) Order 1975(c);

(a) S.I. 1964/1079, amended by S.I. 1980/1274, 1982/922.
(b) S.I. 1975/434.
(c) S.I. 1975/1157.

(iii) the Industrial Training (Transfer of the Activities of Establishments) Order 1976(**a**);

(iv) the Industrial Training (Transfer of the Activities of Establishments) (No. 2) Order 1976(**b**);

(v) the Industrial Training (Transfer of the Activities of Establishments) (No. 3) Order 1976(**c**);

(vi) the Industrial Training (Transfer of the Activities of Establishments) Order 1977(**d**);

(vii) the Industrial Training (Transfer of the Activities of Establishments) Order 1978(**e**);

(viii) the Industrial Training (Transfer of the Activities of Establishments) (No. 2) Order 1978(**f**);

(ix) the Industrial Training (Transfer of the Activities of Establishments) (No. 3) Order 1978(**g**);

(x) the Industrial Training (Transfer of the Activities of Establishments) Order 1979(**h**);

(xi) the Industrial Training (Transfer of the Activities of Establishments) (No. 2) Order 1980(**i**); and

(xii) the Industrial Training (Transfer of the Activities of Establishments) Order 1981(**j**).

(2) Any reference in this Order to an establishment that commences to carry on business or that ceases to carry on business shall not be taken to apply where the location of the establishment is changed but its business is continued wholly or mainly at or from the new location, or where the suspension of activities is of a temporary or seasonal nature.

Imposition of the levy

3.—(1) The levy to be imposed by the Board on employers in respect of the twentieth levy period shall be assessed in accordance with the provisions of this Article and of the Schedule to this Order.

(2) The levy shall be assessed by the Board separately in respect of each construction establishment of an employer, but in agreement with the employer one assessment may be made in respect of any number of such establishments, in which case those establishments shall be deemed for the purposes of that assessment to constitute one establishment.

Assessment notices

4.—(1) The Board shall serve an assessment notice on every employer assessed to the levy, but one notice may comprise two or more assessments.

(**a**) S.I. 1976/396.
(**b**) S.I. 1976/1635.
(**c**) S.I. 1976/2110.
(**d**) S.I. 1977/1951.
(**e**) S.I. 1978/448.
(**f**) S.I. 1978/1225.
(**g**) S.I. 1978/1643.
(**h**) S.I. 1979/793.
(**i**) S.I. 1980/1753.
(**j**) S.I. 1981/1041.

(2) An assessment notice shall state the amount of the levy payable by the person assessed to the levy, and that amount shall be equal to the total amount of the levy assessed by the Board under the provisions of this Order in respect of each establishment included in the notice.

(3) An assessment notice shall state the Board's address for the service of a notice of appeal or of an application for an extension of time for appealing.

(4) An assessment notice may be served on the person assessed to the levy either by delivering it to him personally or by leaving it, or sending it to him by post, at his last known address or place of business in the United Kingdom or, if that person is a corporation, by leaving it, or sending it by post to the corporation, at such address or place of business or at its registered or principal office.

Payment of the levy

5.—(1) Subject to the provisions of this Article and of Articles 6 and 7 the amount of the levy payable under an assessment notice served by the Board shall be due and payable to the Board one month after the date of the assessment notice.

(2) The amount of an assessment shall not be recoverable by the Board until there has expired the time allowed for appealing against the assessment by Article 7(1) of this Order and any further period or periods of time that the Board or an industrial tribunal may have allowed for appealing under paragraph (2) or (3) of that Article or, where an appeal is brought, until the appeal is decided or withdrawn.

Withdrawal of assessment

6.—(1) The Board may, by a notice served on the person assessed to the levy in the same manner as an assessment notice, withdraw an assessment if that person has appealed against that assessment under the provisions of Article 7 of this Order and the appeal has not been entered in the Register of Appeals kept under the appropriate Regulations specified in paragraph (5) of that Article.

(2) The withdrawal of an assessment shall be without prejudice—

(a) to the power of the Board to serve a further assessment notice in respect of any establishment to which that assessment related; or

(b) to any other assessment included in the original assessment notice, and such notice shall thereupon have effect as if any assessment withdrawn by the Board had not been included therein.

Appeals

7.—(1) A person assessed to the levy may appeal to an industrial tribunal against the assessment within one month from the date of the service of the assessment notice or within any further period or periods of time that may be allowed by the Board or an industrial tribunal under the following provisions of this Article.

(2) The Board by notice may for good cause allow a person assessed to the levy to appeal to an industrial tribunal against an assessment at any time within the period of four months from the date of the service of the assessment notice or within such further period or periods as the Board may allow before such time as may then be limited for appealing has expired.

(3) If the Board shall not allow an application for extension of time for appealing, an industrial tribunal shall upon application made to the tribunal by the person assessed to the levy have the like powers as the Board under the last foregoing paragraph.

(4) In the case of an establishment that ceases to carry on business in the twentieth levy period on any day after the date of the service of the relevant assessment notice, the foregoing provisions of this Article shall have effect as if for the period of four months from the date of the service of the assessment notice mentioned in paragraph (2) of this Article there were substituted the period of six months from the date of the cessation of business.

(5) An appeal or an application to an industrial tribunal under this Article shall be made in accordance with the Industrial Tribunals (England and Wales) Regulations 1965(a) except where the establishment to which the relevant assessment relates is wholly in Scotland, when the appeal or application shall be made in accordance with the Industrial Tribunals (Scotland) Regulations 1965(b).

(6) The powers of an industrial tribunal under paragraph (3) of this Article may be exercised by the President of the Industrial Tribunals (England and Wales) or by the President of the Industrial Tribunals (Scotland) as the case may be.

Evidence

8.—(1) Upon the discharge by a person assessed to the levy of his liability under an assessment the Board shall if so requested issue to him a certificate to that effect.

(2) The production in any proceedings of a document purporting to be certified by the Secretary of the Board or any other person, being a member, officer or servant of the Board authorised to act in that behalf, to be a true copy of an assessment or other notice issued by the Board or purporting to be a certificate such as is mentioned in the foregoing paragraph of this Article shall, unless the contrary is proved, be sufficient evidence of the document and of the facts stated therein.

Signed by order of the Secretary of State.

Peter Morrison,
Minister of State,
Department of Employment.

20th December 1984.

(a) S.I. 1965/1101, amended by S.I. 1967/301.
(b) S.I. 1965/1157, amended by S.I. 1967/302.

Article 3 SCHEDULE

Interpretation

1. In this Schedule unless the context otherwise requires:—

(a) "agriculture" has the same meaning as in section 109(3) of the Agriculture Act 1947(a) or, in relation to Scotland, as in section 86(3) of the Agriculture (Scotland) Act 1948(b);

(b) "average number" in relation to any category and description of persons employed at or from a construction establishment of an employer means the number that is equal to the average of the numbers of the persons of that category and description specified in the first and second columns of the Appendix to this Schedule employed, or treated as employed under the provisions of paragraph 2(c) of this Schedule, at or from the establishment by the employer on the relevant dates or, in the case of an establishment that commenced to carry on business after the first of the relevant dates but before the second, the number of persons of that category and description specified as aforesaid and employed by the employer at or from the establishment on the second of the relevant dates;

(c) "charity" has the same meaning as in section 360 of the Income and Corporation Taxes Act 1970(c);

(d) "clerical or miscellaneous worker" includes—

  (i) a clerk and other office staff, including those working in sales, computers and stores, and supervisors of these staff;

  (ii) a storeman;

  (iii) a transport worker (but not a motor mechanic);

  (iv) an operative or conversion fitter (excluding a gas fitter, a plumber or a heating and ventilating fitter), engaged in the conversion of appliances to natural gas or in the preliminary work;

  (v) a terrazzo worker, including a terrazzo layer;

  (vi) any other person (including a foreman, a ganger and a charge-hand) mainly employed as a manual worker not comprised in any other category and description of worker specified in this Schedule or the appendix thereto;

(e) "craftsman (building)" means—

  (i) a bricklayer, including a specialist bricklayer;

  (ii) a carpenter joiner, including a carpenter, a joiner, a formwork carpenter, a joiner bench hand, a woodworking machinist or woodworking operative and a setter out;

  (iii) a mason, including a monumental mason, a stone carver and a stone polisher;

  (iv) a mason pavior, including a person involved in cutting and carving stone and who is following or has completed a course of further education being the City and Guilds of London Institute Course No. 588 on Masonry at Craft Level;

(a) 1947 c. 48.
(b) 1948 c. 45.
(c) 1970 c. 10.

(v) a painter, including a painter and decorator, an industrial painter, a french polisher and a signwriter;

(vi) a plasterer, including a solid or fibrous plasterer, a moulder and a dry-lining or partition operative;

(vii) a roof slater and tiler;

(viii) any other person (including a foreman, a ganger and a chargehand) mainly employed as a manual worker, otherwise than as a labourer or general operative, in any of the trades specified in this sub-paragraph;

(f) "craftsman (mechanical engineering services)" means—

(i) a gas fitter;

(ii) a heating and ventilating fitter, including a heating fitter;

(iii) an oil burner mechanic;

(iv) a pipe fitter;

(v) a plumber, including a chemical plumber, a plumber welder and a hot water fitter;

(vi) a refrigeration mechanic;

(vii) a welder, including an oxy-acetylene, metallic-arc or shielded-arc welder;

(viii) any other person (including a foreman, a ganger and a chargehand) mainly employed as a manual worker, otherwise than as a labourer or general operative, in any of the trades specified in this sub-paragraph;

(g) "craftsman (electrical engineering services)" means—

(i) an electrician, including a cable jointer;

(ii) any other person (including a foreman, a ganger and a chargehand) mainly employed as a manual worker, otherwise than as a labourer or general operative, in any of the trades specified in this sub-paragraph;

(h) "craftsman (miscellaneous)" means—

(i) a thermal insulation operative or ductwork erector;

(ii) any other person (including a foreman, a ganger and a chargehand) mainly employed as a manual worker, otherwise than as a labourer or general operative, in either of the trades specified in this sub-paragraph or in any other trade not specified in this Schedule or the appendix thereto;

(i) "specialist building operative" means—

(i) a floor or wall tiler, including a mosaic worker and a tile fixer;

(ii) a ceiling fixer, including a suspended ceiling erector and a metal fixer (ceiling systems);

(iii) a mastic asphalter, including a mastic asphalt spreader;

(iv) a floor coverer, including a parquet floorer and a vinyl, linoleum or carpet layer;

(v) a floorer, including a granolithic or other in situ floor finisher;

(vi) a glazier, including a double glazier, a window fixer, a patent glazier, a leaded light worker and a glass production or processing worker;

(vii) a demountable partition erector;

(viii) a steeplejack, including a lightning conductor erector;

(ix) a demolisher, including a general labourer using a compressed air drill or pneumatic punching machine or spade, a sorter, an improver, a mattockman, a topman, a burner topman, a burner groundsman, a shorer (timber) and a shorer's mate;

(x) any other person (including a foreman, a ganger and a chargehand) mainly employed as a manual worker otherwise than as a labourer or general operative, in any of the trades specified in this sub-paragraph;

(j) "a labour-only agreement" means any agreement, not being a contract of service or of apprenticeship, made between an employer and any other person or persons whereby the services (including any incidental use of tools) of such person or persons, or of any other person or persons were rendered to the employer in his trade or business;

(k) "the relevant dates" means 6th October 1983 and 5th April 1984;

(l) "skilled building and civil engineering worker" means—

(i) a concretor, including a bar bender and fixer, a pre-cast concrete erector and fixer, a pre-stressing or pre-tensioning operative, a concrete placer, vibrator or finisher;

(ii) a diver, including a surface, demand or helmet diver and a life linesman;

(iii) an excavation operative, including a heading driver, a manhole builder, a pipe layer, a pipe jointer and a timberman;

(iv) a mechanical plant operator, including a mechanical equipment, compressor, air tool or paving machine operator, a mixerman, a potman, a banksman, a slinger, a plant driver, a dumper driver, a crane driver, an excavation plant operator, an earthmoving plant operator, a pumpman, an oiler and a greaser;

(v) a piling or well drilling operative, including a borer driver, a vibrator or specialist piling operative, a well or rock driller and a shaft sinker;

(vi) a tunnel miner, including a soft-heading miner;

(vii) a blacksmith, including a marker-out;

(viii) a steel erector;

(ix) a repetitive process factory worker;

(x) a gas distribution mains layer, including a service layer;

(xi) a plant mechanic, including a plant maintenance mechanic, a contractors' plant mechanic and a motor mechanic;

(xii) a tar pavior;

(xiii) a labourer or general operative mainly employed in any of the trades specified in this sub-paragraph or in sub-paragraph *(e)*, *(f)*, *(g)*, *(h)*, *(i)* or *(n)* of this paragraph who was entitled to extra payment for skill or responsibility under a Working Rule Agreement;

(xiv) any other person (including a foreman, a ganger and a chargehand) mainly employed as a manual worker, otherwise than as a labourer or general operative, in any of the trades mentioned in this sub-paragraph;

(m) "a person employed in a managerial, administrative, professional or technical capacity" includes—

(i) a manager, including a contracts, site, area, sales or office manager;

(ii) an accountant or company secretary;

(iii) an estimator, surveyor or buyer;

(iv) an engineer or architect;

(v) a technical, planning or laboratory assistant, a draughtsman, a tracer or a design detailer;

(vi) a work study officer;

(vii) a personnel officer, a training officer or an instructor;

(viii) a person occupying the position of foreman or of works supervisor being a person who is not mainly employed as a manual worker whether in handling materials or otherwise;

(n) "a roof sheeter or felter" includes—

(i) a roof sheeter and cladder, an asbestos roofer, a galvanised or protected steel sheeter or an aluminium sheeter;

(ii) a roofing felt fixer and a roofing felt layer;

(iii) any other person (including a foreman, a ganger and a chargehand) mainly employed as a manual worker, otherwise than as a labourer or general operative, in any of the trades specified in this sub-paragraph;

(o) "trainee" means a person (including an apprentice) who is learning a managerial, administrative, professional, technical or manual skill and whose employer has undertaken to provide training for him in that skill for a specified period of not less than twelve months;

(p) "Working Rule Agreement" means any agreement as to pay, being an agreement between—

(i) parties who are or represent employers or organisations of employers or associations of such organisations; and

(ii) parties who are or represent organisations of employees or associations of such organisations;

but includes also any award modifying or supplementing such an agreement.

2. For the purposes of this Schedule, except, in relation to *(c)* below, for the purposes of paragraph 3 below, the following provisions shall have effect—

(a) no regard shall be had to any person employed wholly in the supply of food or drink for immediate consumption or in agriculture or who was normally working for an aggregate of less than 8 hours weekly;

(b) no regard shall be had to a company director remunerated solely by fees but, save as aforesaid, the provisions of this Schedule shall apply to a company director (including a person occupying the position of director by whatever name he is called) as they apply to other persons and accordingly such a person shall be taken to be comprised in the category appropriate to the work in which he was mainly engaged;

(c) in the case of a construction establishment that is taken over (whether directly or indirectly) by an employer in succession to, or jointly with, another person, the person or persons carrying on the establishment on the day upon which this Order comes into operation shall be treated as the employer of any person who was employed on either or both of the relevant dates, or at any time in the period of twelve months that commenced on 6th April 1983 at or from the establishment under a contract of service or of apprenticeship or under a labour-only agreement, by the person then carrying on the establishment;

Basic assessment rules

3.—(1) Subject to the exemptions in paragraphs 4 and 5(1) below, the amount to be assessed by way of levy in respect of a construction establishment, other than a brick-manufacturing establishment, (being an establishment carrying on business in the twentieth levy period) shall be the aggregate of the amount (if any) by which 2% of the labour-only payments exceeds 2% of labour-only receipts and the amount of the occupational levy.

(2) For the purposes of sub-paragraph 3(1) above:—

(a) "2% of labour-only payments" means the sum which (rounded down where necessary to the nearest £1) represents 2% of all payments made to any persons by the employer during the period of 12 months that commenced on 6th April 1983 under labour-only agreements in respect of work carried out at or from the establishment;

(b) "2% of labour-only receipts" means the sum which (rounded down where necessary to the nearest £1) represents 2% of all payments received by the employer during the period of 12 months that commenced on 6th April 1983 from any other employers in the construction industry under labour-only agreements in respect of work carried out at or from the establishment;

(c) "the amount of the occupational levy" means the sum of the amounts (rounded down in each case where necessary to the nearest £1) produced by multiplying the appropriate amount in the third column of the appendix to this Schedule by the average number of persons employed by the employer at or from the establishment under contracts of service or apprenticeship in each relevant category and description of employment less the amount (if any) by which 2% of labour-only receipts exceeds 2% of labour-only payments provided that the amount of the occupational levy shall not exceed an amount equal to 1% of the aggregate of the emoluments and payments intended to be disbursed as emoluments which have been paid or are payable by the employer to or in respect of persons employed in the industry in respect of the period of twelve months which commenced on 6th April 1983.

(3) Subject to the exemptions in paragraphs 4 and 5(2) below, the amount to be assessed by way of levy in respect of a brick-manufacturing establishment

(being an establishment carrying on business in the twentieth levy period) shall be equal to 0.1% of the aggregate of the emoluments and payments intended to be disbursed as emoluments which have been paid or are payable by the employer to or in respect of persons employed at or from the establishment under contracts of service or apprenticeship in respect of the period of 12 months which commenced on 6th April 1983.

(4) For the purposes of this paragraph and paragraph 5 below "a brick-manufacturing establishment" means a construction establishment engaged wholly or mainly in the manufacture of bricks from clay or calcium silicate for building purposes but excluding bricks made for refractory purposes.

Exemption of charities

4. A charity shall be exempt from the levy.

Exemption of small employers

5.—(1) There shall be exempt from the levy an employer in whose case the aggregate amount of—

(a) the sum of the emoluments of all the persons employed at or from the construction establishment or establishments of the employer (not being a brick-manufacturing establishment or brick-manufacturing establishments) in the period of 12 months that commenced on 6th April 1983, and

(b) all such sums (if any) as were paid in the said period by the employer to any person under a labour-only agreement at or from the said establishment or establishments,

was less than £15,000.

(2) There shall be exempt from the levy, in respect of brick-manufacturing establishments, an employer in whose case the sum of the emoluments of all the persons employed at or from the brick-manufacturing establishments of the employer in the period of 12 months that commenced on 6th April 1983 was less than £100,000.

(3) For the purposes of sub-paragraphs (1)(a) and (2) above "emoluments" means all emoluments assessable to income tax under Schedule E (other than pensions), being emoluments from which tax under that Schedule is deductible, whether or not tax in fact falls to be deducted from any particular payment thereof.

(4) For the purposes of sub-paragraphs (1) and (2) above, Article 3(2) of this Order shall be disregarded.

Cessation of business

6. The amount of the levy imposed in respect of a construction establishment that ceases to carry on business in the twentieth levy period shall be in the same proportion to the amount that would otherwise be due in accordance with the foregoing provisions of this Schedule as the number of days between the commencement of the said levy period and the date of cessation of business (both dates inclusive) bears to the number of days in the said levy period.

APPENDIX

Category	Description	Amount Per Capita
1.	A person employed in a managerial, administrative, professional or technical capacity	£42
2.	A clerical or miscellaneous worker	NIL
3.	A craftsman (building)	£71
4.	A craftsman (mechanical engineering services)	£85
5.	A craftsman (electrical engineering services)	£75
6.	A skilled building and civil engineering worker	£25
7.	A labourer or general operative not entitled to extra payment for skill or responsibility under a Working Rule Agreement	£18
8.	A craftsman (miscellaneous)	£20
9.	A specialist building operative	£45
10.	A roof sheeter or felter	£50
11.	A scaffolder	£54
12.	A cavity wall insulation operative, a fencer or fence erector	£30
13.	A trainee in any of the categories 1–6 and 8–12 above	NIL

EXPLANATORY NOTE

(This Note is not part of the Order.)

This Order gives effect to proposals of the Construction Industry Training Board which were submitted to and approved by the Manpower Services Commission, and thereafter submitted by the Manpower Services Commission to the Secretary of State. The proposals are for the imposition of a levy on employers in the construction industry for the purpose of raising money towards meeting the expenses of the Board.

A levy is to be imposed on employers limited to 1 per cent of payroll in respect of employees employed by them under contracts of service or apprenticeship and to 2 per cent of payments made by the employers to persons under labour-only agreements.

A levy of 0.1 per cent of payroll is to be imposed on employers with brick-manufacturing establishments in respect of employees employed by them there under contracts of service or of apprenticeship.

This levy is in respect of the twentieth levy period commencing with the date on which this order comes into operation and ending on 31st March 1985.

The levy will be assessed by the Board, and there will be a right of appeal against an assessment to an industrial tribunal.

STATUTORY INSTRUMENTS

1984 No. 2005

AGRICULTURE

The Sheep Annual Premium Regulations 1984

Made - - - - -	20th December 1984
Laid before Parliament	21st December 1984
Coming into Operation	1st January 1985

The Minister of Agriculture, Fisheries and Food and the Secretary of State, being Ministers designated(a) for the purposes of section 2(2) of the European Communities Act 1972(b) in relation to the common agricultural policy of the European Economic Community, acting jointly in exercise of the powers conferred upon them by that section, and of all other powers enabling them in that behalf, hereby make the following regulations:—

Title, commencement and application

1.—(1) These regulations may be cited as the Sheep Annual Premium Regulations 1984 and shall come into operation on 1st January 1985.

(2) These regulations shall apply where an application is made for a premium in respect of any marketing year commencing after 1st January 1985.

Interpretation

2.—(1) In these regulations unless the context otherwise requires—

"authorised officer" means—

(a) in relation to England, an authorised officer of the Minister,

(b) in relation to Scotland or Wales, an authorised officer of the Secretary of State,

(c) in relation to Northern Ireland, an authorised officer of the Department of Agriculture for Northern Ireland,

acting in each case on behalf of the competent authority in connection with the discharge of the competent authority's functions under the first Council Regulation, the second Council Regulation, the Commission Regulation and these regulations;

(a) S.I. 1972/1811.
(b) 1972 c. 68; section 2 is subject to Schedule 2 to that Act and is to be read, as regards England and Wales, with sections 37, 40 and 46 of the Criminal Justice Act 1982 (c. 48) and S.I. 1984/447, as regards Scotland, with sections 289F and 289G of the Criminal Procedure (Scotland) Act 1975 (c. 21), as inserted by section 54 of the Criminal Justice Act 1982 and S.I. 1984/526 and, as regards Northern Ireland, with S.I. 1984/703 (N.I. 3) and S.R.(N.I.) 1984 No. 253.

"the Commission Regulation" means Commission Regulation (EEC) No. 3007/84**(a)** laying down detailed rules for the application of the premium for producers of sheepmeat;

"the first Council Regulation" means Council Regulation (EEC) No. 1837/80**(b)** on the common organisation of the market in sheepmeat and goatmeat, as amended**(c)**;

"the second Council Regulation" means Council Regulation (EEC) No. 872/84**(d)** laying down general rules for the granting of premiums to sheepmeat producers and repealing Regulation (EEC) No. 2643/80**(e)**;

"the competent authority" has the meaning assigned to it by regulation 3;

"the Minister" means the Minister of Agriculture, Fisheries and Food;

"premium" means the premium provided for under Article 5 of the first Council Regulation;

"producer" means a producer of sheepmeat.

(2) Other expressions used in these regulations have, in so far as the context admits, the same meanings as in the first Council Regulation, the second Council Regulation and the Commission Regulation.

(3) In these regulations, unless the context otherwise requires, any reference to a numbered regulation is a reference to the regulation so numbered in these regulations.

Appointment of competent authority

3. For the purposes of the first Council Regulation, the second Council Regulation and the Commission Regulation, the competent authority shall be—

(*a*) in relation to England and Northern Ireland, the Minister;

(*b*) in relation to Scotland or Wales, the Secretary of State.

Application for premium

4.—(1) An application for a premium shall be in such form and shall contain such particulars as the competent authority may require.

(2) An application for a premium in respect of a marketing year shall be delivered to the competent authority on or after 1st January in the calendar year in which that marketing year commences and not later than—

(*a*) 10th April in that calendar year, or

(*b*) 9th April in that calendar year, if a leap year, or

(*c*) if 10th April or, in a leap year, 9th April is a Saturday, Sunday or public holiday, the next following working day.

(a) O.J. No. L283, 27.10.1984, p. 28.

(b) O.J. No. L183, 16.7.80, p.1.

(c) The amending instruments are Council Regulations (EEC) Nos 3446/80 (O.J. No. L359, 31.12.80, p. 16), 899/81 (O.J. No. L90, 4.4.81, p. 26) and 871/84 (O.J. No. L90, 1.4.84, p. 35).

(d) O.J. No. L90, 1.4.84, p. 40.   **(e)** O.J. No. L275, 18.10.80, p. 6.

Powers of Inspection

5.—(1) Where a producer has made an application for a premium, an authorised officer may, at all reasonable times and on production of his authority on demand, enter on any land occupied, or otherwise used, by the producer for the rearing of animals of the ovine species and may—

(*a*) inspect and count any such animals kept by the producer on that land, and

(*b*) require the producer to furnish for inspection any bill, account, voucher or record in his possession or under his control relating to any such animals kept or formerly kept by him.

(2) An authorised officer may be accompanied by such other persons acting under his instructions as appear to him to be necessary to enable him to exercise the powers conferred upon him by the preceding paragraph and may make such copies or take such extracts as he thinks fit of or from any document furnished for inspection.

(3) The producer and any person in charge of animals of the ovine species on the land shall render all reasonable assistance to an authorised officer to enable him to exercise the powers conferred upon him by this regulation.

Recovery of premiums

6.—(1) Where any person with a view to obtaining the payment of a premium to himself or any other person—

(*a*) makes any statement which is untrue or misleading in a material respect, or

(*b*) furnishes to the competent authority any inaccurate information,

the competent authority shall be entitled to recover on demand as a civil debt the whole or any part of any premium paid to him or to such other person.

(2) Where any producer, having undertaken pursuant to Article 2 of the Commission Regulation to keep a number of ewes, fails in any way to comply with that undertaking, the competent authority shall be entitled, subject to Articles 6 and 7 of the Commission Regulation, to recover on demand as a civil debt the whole or any part of any premium paid to him.

(3) Where any producer or any person in charge of his animals—

(*a*) intentionally obstructs an authorised officer in the exercise of the powers conferred on him by regulation 5 or a person accompanying and acting under the instructions of an authorised officer, or

(*b*) fails without reasonable excuse to comply with a requirement under regulation 5(1)(*b*), or

(*c*) fails to render all reasonable assistance pursuant to regulation 5(3),

the competent authority shall be entitled to recover on demand as a civil debt the whole or any part of any premium paid to that producer.

Offences

7. Any person who—

   (*a*) knowingly or recklessly makes a false statement for the purpose of obtaining the payment of a premium to himself or to any other person, or

   (*b*) intentionally obstructs an authorised officer in the exercise of the powers conferred by regulation 5 or a person accompanying and acting under the instructions of an authorised officer, or

   (*c*) fails without reasonable excuse to comply with a requirement under regulation 5(1)(*b*),

shall be guilty of an offence and liable on summary conviction to a fine not exceeding £2000.

In Witness whereof the Official Seal of the Minister of Agriculture, Fisheries and Food is hereunto affixed on 20th December 1984.

(L.S.)

Michael Jopling,
Minister of Agriculture,
Fisheries and Food.

George Younger,
One of Her Majesty's Principal
Secretaries of State.

20th December 1984.

EXPLANATORY NOTE

(This Note is not part of the Regulations.)

These regulations implement Commission Regulation (EEC) No. 3007/84 which lays down new detailed rules for the payment of an annual premium to sheepmeat producers and repeals the previous detailed rules. The premium was introduced by Article 5 of Council Regulation (EEC) No. 1837/80 (now amended by Council Regulation (EEC) No. 871/84) and general rules for its payment are laid down by Council Regulation (EEC) No. 872/84.

The present regulations make provision for those matters which the Commission Regulation leaves to Member States and which are necessary for the proper implementation of the annual premium scheme in the United Kingdom for the 1985/6 and subsequent marketing years. They appoint the "competent authority" responsible for administering the scheme in the various parts of the United Kingdom (regulation 3), stipulate the manner and time of making an application under it (regulation 4), and confer on authorised officers powers to inspect and count sheep and examine relevant documents (regulation 5).

Regulation 6 provides that the competent authority may recover premiums paid under the circumstances there specified and regulation 7 creates offences (making a false statement, intentional obstruction of authorised officers, failure to produce relevant documents) which are punishable on summary conviction by a fine not exceeding £2000.

Article 11 of the Commission Regulation permits certain Member States (including the United Kingdom) to deal with applications for premium submitted in respect of the 1984/5 marketing year in accordance with national provisions in force at the end of the 1983/4 marketing year. The Sheep Annual Premium Regulations 1980 (S.I. 1980/1577) thus remain in force and continue to apply to the payment of premium for the 1984/5 marketing year.

STATUTORY INSTRUMENTS

1984 No. 2006

CUSTOMS AND EXCISE

The Customs Duties (ECSC) (Quota and Other Reliefs) Order 1984

Made - - - - - - - - -	*21st December* 1984
Laid before the House of Commons	*21st December* 1984
Coming into Operation - - - -	*1st January* 1985

The Secretary of State, in exercise of the powers conferred on him by sections 1 and 4 of the Customs and Excise Duties (General Reliefs) Act 1979(a) and of all other powers enabling him in that behalf, hereby makes the following Order:—

1.— (1) This Order may be cited as the Customs Duties (ECSC) (Quota and Other Reliefs) Order 1984 and shall come into operation on 1st January 1985.

(2) In this Order—

reference to a heading or subheading are references to a heading or subheading in the common customs tariff of the European Economic Community;

references to customs duty are references to duty charged by the Customs Duties (ECSC) Order 1981(b) in relation to the goods.

2.— (1) Up to and including 31st December 1985, no customs duty shall be charged on goods—

(a) which fall within a heading or subheading specified in Part I of Schedule 1 hereto (certain iron and steel products) and

(b) which originate in any country named in Schedule 2 hereto other than a country named in column 2 of Part III of Schedule 1 hereto in relation to that heading or subheading as specified in column 1 thereof.

This paragraph shall not apply in respect of any goods falling within headings 73.08, 73.10 or 73.13 originating in China nor in respect of any goods originating in Yugoslavia.

(2) Up to and including 31st December 1985, no customs duty shall be charged on goods—

(a) 1979 c.3.
(b) S.I. 1981/1769, amended by S.I. 1982/1773, 1983/342, 1782, 1802, 1984/1306, 1452.

(a) which fall within a heading or subheading specified in Part II of Schedule 1 hereto (certain iron and steel products) and

(b) which originate in a country named in Schedule 2 hereto.

(3) Paragraphs (1) and (2) above shall only apply to goods in respect of which an importer delivers a perfect entry thereof for home use (within the meaning of section 37 of the Customs and Excise Management Act 1979(a) and Regulation 13 of the Customs Warehousing Regulations 1979(b) containing an application for relief from customs duty in the United Kingdom on or after 1st January 1985 accompanied by such documents as may be required under the provisions of Regulations of the Commission of the European Communities of 23rd December 1980 (hereinafter referred to a "the Regulations" (c). This paragraph shall not apply in respect of any goods falling within the subheadings 73.12 A, 73.12 B.1, 73.12 C.III.a), 73.12 C.V.a) 1 originating in Yugoslavia.

3.— (1) Up to and including 31st December 1985, no customs duty shall be charged on goods falling within a heading or subheading specified in column 1 of Part III of Schedule 1 hereto (certain iron and steel products) which originate in a country named in column 2 in relation to that heading or subheading if they form part of the relevant quota.

(2) For the purposes of paragraph (1) of this Article the "relevant quota" in relation to any heading or subheading means the amount (expressed as a value in pounds) of goods specified in column 3 of Part III of Schedule 1 hereto in relation to the heading or subheading in respect of each of the countries named in column 2 in relation to that heading or subheading.

(3) Article 4 of the Customs Duties Quota Relief (Administration) Order 1976(d) shall apply for the purposes of this Article subject to the modification that the application for relief from customs duty shall be accompanied by such documents as may be required under the provisions of the Regulations.

4. For the purpose of this Order goods shall be treated as originating in a country named in column 2 of Part III of Schedule 1 or in Schedule 2 hereto if they are to be regarded as so originating by virtue of the Regulations.

Paul Channon,
Minister for Trade,
Department of Trade and Industry.

21st December 1984.

(a) 1979 c.2.
(b) S.I. 1979/207.
(c) Regulations (EEC) Nos. 3510/80 to 3513/80 (OJ No. L368, 31.12.80).
(d) S.I. 1976/2105.

SCHEDULE 1

Article 2(1)

PART I

TARIFF HEADING AND SUBHEADINGS

73.07 A.I.	73.15 A.V.b)
73.07 B.I	73.15 AV.d)1.aa)
73.08	73.15 A.VI.a)
73.10 A	73.15 A.VI.c)1.aa)
73.10 D.I.a)	73.15 A.VII.a)
73.11 A.I.	73.15 A.VII.b)2
73.11 A.IV.a)1.	73.15 A.VII.c)
73.11 B.	73.15 A.VII.d)1
73.13 A	73.15 B.I.b)2.
73.13 B.I	73.15 B.III.
73.13 B.II.b)	73.15 B.IV.
73.13 B.II.c)	73.15 B.V.b)
73.13 B.III.	73.15 B.V.d)1.aa)
73.13 B.IV.b)	73.15 B.VI.a)
73.13 B.IV.c)	73.15 B.VI.c)1.aa)
73.13 B.I V.d)	73.15 B.VII.a)
73.13 B.V.a)2.	73.15 B.VII.b)1.
73.15 A.I.b)2	73.15 B.VII.b)2.bb)
73.15 A.III.	73.15 B.VII.b)3.
73.15 A.IV.	73.15 B.VII.b)4.aa)

Article 2(2)

PART II

TARRIFF HEADINGS AND SUBHEADINGS

73.09	73.16 A.II
73.12 A.	73.16 B.
73.12 B.I	73.16 C.
73.12 C.III.a)	73.16 D.I.
73.12 C.V.a)1.	
73.13 B.II.a)	
73.15 B.I.b)2.	

PART III   Article 3

Tarriff headings and subheadings	Country of Origin (2)	Amount of Quotas (3)
73.07 A.I 73.07 B.I	Brazil	£413,374
73.08	Brazil Republic of Korea Venezuela	£402,537
73.10 A. 73.10 D.I.a)	Argentina Brazil Republic of Korea Venezuela	£249,483
73.13 A. 73.13 B.I. 73.13 B.II.b) 73.13 B.IIc) 73.13 B.III. 73.13 B.IV.b) 73.13 B.IV.c) 73.13 B.IV.d) 73.13 B.V.a)2.	Argentina Brazil Republic of Korea	£683,858
73.15 A.I.b)2 73.15 A.III. 73.15 A.IV. 73.15 A.V.b) 73.15 A.V.d)1.aa 73.15 A.VI.a) 73.15 A.VI.c)1.aa) 73.15 A.VII.a) 73.15 A.VII.b)2. 73.15 A.VII.c) 73.15 A.VII.d)1 73.15 B.I.b)2 73.15 B.III. 73.15 B.IV. 73.15 B.V.b) 73.15 B.V.d)1.aa) 73.15 B.VI.a) 73.15 B.VI.c)1.aa) 73.15 B.VII.a) 73.15 B.VII.b)1. 73.15 B.VII.b)2.bb) 73.15 B.VII.b)3 73.15 B.VII.b)4.aa)	Brazil Republic of Korea	£691,828

SCHEDULE 2

PART I

INDEPENDENT COUNTRIES

Afghanistan
Algeria
Angola
Antigua and Barbuda
Argentina
Bahamas
Bahrain
Bangladesh
Barbados
Belize
Benin
Bhutan
Bolivia
Botswana
Brazil
Brunei Durassalam
Burkina Fasso
Burma
Burundi
Cambodia
Cameroon
Cape Verde Islands
Central African Republic
Chad
Chile
China
Colombia
Comoros
Congo, People's Republic of
Costa Rica
Cuba
Cyprus
Djibouti
Dominica
Dominican Republic
Ecuador
Egypt
El Salvador
Equatorial Guinea
Ethiopia
Fiji
Gabon
Gambia
Ghana
Grenada
Guatemala
Guinea
Guinea Bissau
Guyana
Haiti
Honduras
India
Indonesia
Iran
Iraq
Ivory Coast
Jamaica
Jordan
Kenya
Kiribati
Korea, Republic of
Kuwait
Lao's, People's Democratic
  Republic

Lebanon
Lesotho
Liberia
Libya
Madagascar
Malawi
Malaysia
Maldive Islands
Mali
Mauritania
Mauritius
Mexico
Morocco
Mozambique
Nauru
Nepal
Nicaragua
Niger
Nigeria
Oman
Pakistan
Panama
Papua New Guinea
Paraguay
Peru
Philippines
Qatar
Rwanda
Samoa
Sao Tome and Principe
Saudi Arabia
Senegal
Seychelles and Dependencies
Sierra Leone
Singapore
Solomon Islands
Somalia
St Kitts and Nevis
Sri Lanka
St Lucia
St Vincent
Sudan
Surinam
Swaziland
Syria
Tanzania
Thailand
Togo
Tonga
Trinidad and Tobago
Tunisia
Tuvalu
Uganda
United Arab Emirates
Uruguay
Vanuata
Venezuela
Vietnam
Yemen, Democratic
Yemen Arab Republic
Yugoslavia
Zaire
Zambia
Zimbabwe

PART II

COUNTRIES OR TERRITORIES DEPENDENT OR ADMINISTERED OR FOR WHOSE
EXTERNAL RELATIONS MEMBER STATES OF THE COMMUNITY OR THIRD
COUNTRIES ARE WHOLLY OR PARTLY RESPONSIBLE

American Oceania (a)
Australian Antarctic Territory
Bermuda
British Antarctic Territories
British Indian Ocean Territory
Cayman Island
Christmas Island, Cocos (Keeling) Islands, Heard Island and McDonald Islands,
    Norfolk Island
Falkland Islands
Falkland Islands Dependencies
French Polynesia
French Southern and Antarctic Territories
Gibraltar
Hong Kong
Greenland
Macao
Mayotte
Netherlands Antilles
New Caledonia and Dependencies
New Zealand Oceania (Cook Islands, Niue Islands, Tokelau Islands)
Pitcairn
St Helena
St Helena Dependencies
Turks and Caicos Islands
Virgin Islands of the United States
Wallis and Futuna Islands
West Indies

(a) American Oceania includes: Guam, American Samoa (including Swain's Island), Midway
Islands, Johnston and Sand Islands, Wake Island and the Trust Territory of the Pacific Islands (the
Caroline, Marianas and Marshall Islands).

EXPLANATORY NOTE
(This Note is not part of the Order.)

This Order, which comes into operation on 1st January 1985, provides for reliefs from customs duty on certain iron and steel products originating in the developing countries named in Schedule 2 to the Order in accordance with a Decision of the representatives of the governments of the Member States of the European Coal and Steel Community meeting in Council of 18 December 1984. The reliefs are provided under the Community's Generalised Tariff Preference Scheme for Developing Countries.

The Order provides for exemption from duty for goods specified in Part I of Schedule 1 originating in the countries named in Schedule 2 other than those countries also named in column 2 of Part III of Schedule 1 in relation to the relevant goods. Such exemption does not however apply to goods falling within tariff headings 73.08, 73.10 or 73.13 originating in China nor to goods originating in Yugoslavia (Article 2(1)). The Order also provides for exemption from duty for goods specified in Part II of Schedule 1 originating in the countries named in Schedule 2. Such exemption does not however apply to goods falling within tariff subheadings 73.12A, 73.12B.I., 73.12C.III.a), 73.12.C.V.a) 1 originating in Yugoslavia (Article 2(2)). These exemptions apply with effect from 1st January 1985 up to and including 31st December 1985. The Order also provides for duty-free tariff quotas for the same period for goods listed in Part III of Schedule 1 originating in certain countries named in column 2 of Part III of Schedule 1 (Article 3).

1984 No. 2007

COMPANIES

The Companies (Share Premium Account) Regulations 1984

Laid before Parliament in draft

Made - - - *21st December* 1984

Coming into operation in accordance with Regulation 1

Whereas a draft of these Regulations has been laid before Parliament and approved by resolution of each House of Parliament in pursuance of section 41(3) of the Companies Act 1981(a).

Now, therefore, the Secretary of State, in exercise of his powers under section 41 of the Companies Act 1981, hereby makes the following Regulations —

1. These Regulations may be cited as the Companies (Share Premium Account) Regulations 1984 and shall come into operation forthwith.

2. For the existing section 38 of the Companies Act 1981 there shall be substituted a new section 38 in the terms set out in the Schedule hereto.

Alexander Fletcher,
Parliamentary Under-Secretary of State,
Department of Trade and Industry.
21st December 1984.

SCHEDULE

RELIEF FROM SECTION 56 IN RESPECT OF GROUP RECONSTRUCTIONS

38.—(1) This section applies where the issuing company —

(a) is a wholly-owned subsidiary of another company ("the holding company"); and

(b) allots shares to the holding company or to another wholly-owned subsidiary of the holding company in consideration for the transfer to the issuing company of assets other than cash being assets of any company ("the transferor company") which is a member of the group of companies which comprises the holding company and all its wholly-owned subsidiaries.

(2) Where the shares in the issuing company allotted in consideration for the transfer are issued at a premium, the issuing company shall not be required by section 56 of the 1948 Act to transfer any amount in excess of the minimum premium value to the share premium account.

(a) 1981 c.62.

(3)   In subsection (2) above, "the minimum premium value" means the amount (if any) by which the base value of the consideration for the shares allotted exceeds the aggregate nominal value of those shares.

(4)   For the purposes of subsection (3) above, the base value of the consideration for the shares allotted shall be the amount by which the base value of the assets transferred exceeds the base value of any liabilities of the transferor company assumed by the issuing company as part of the consideration for the assets transferred.

(5)   For the purposes of subsection (4) above —
 (a)   the base value of the assets transferred shall be taken as —
   (i)   the cost of those assets to the transferor company, or
   (ii)   the amount at which those assets are stated in the transferor company's accounting records immediately before the transfer,
  whichever is the less; and
 (b)   the base value of the liabilities assumed shall be taken as the amount at which they are stated in the transferor company's accounting records immediately before the transfer.

(6)   Section 37 of this Act shall not apply in any case to which this section applies.

EXPLANATORY NOTE

(This Note is not part of the Regulations.)

1.   These Regulations extend the relief afforded by section 38 of the Companies Act 1981 from the requirements of section 56 of the Companies Act 1948 (c.38). The extension is achieved by substituting a new section for the existing section 38.

2.   The general requirement of section 56 of the Companies Act 1948 is that any premium received by a company on the issue of its shares be carried to a share premium account. The relief afforded by section 38 of the Companies Act 1981 is available only in the case of a group reconstruction involving the issue of shares by a wholly-owned subsidiary to another such subsidiary or to the holding company. The relief is that the premium to be carried to the share premium account is to be based on the cost or book value of the consideration for the shares issued and not on the fair value of that consideration.

3.   The extension of the relief is that, under the new section 38, it will be available where the consideration for the issue of the shares consists of any non-cash assets of the company providing the consideration and not merely of shares in another subsidiary of the holding company.

STATUTORY INSTRUMENTS

1984 No. 2008

INCOME TAX

The Income Tax (Sub-contractors in the Construction Industry) (No. 2) Regulations 1984

Made - - -	*20th December* 1984
Laid before the House of Commons	*21st December* 1984
Coming into Operation	*1st February* 1985

The Commissioners of Inland Revenue, in exercise of the powers conferred on them by section 70 and Schedule 12 of the Finance (No. 2) Act 1975(**a**) and of all the powers enabling them in that behalf, hereby make the following Regulations:—

1. These Regulations may be cited as the Income Tax (Sub-contractors in the Construction Industry) (No. 2) Regulations 1984 and shall come into operation on 1st February 1985.

2. For paragraph 8 of each of the forms of guarantee prescribed by Schedule 2 to the Income Tax (Sub-contractors in the Construction Industry) Regulations 1982(**b**) there shall be substituted:—

"8. The liability of the Guarantor under this Guarantee shall not be impaired or discharged by reason of any time or other indulgence granted by the Commissioners or by reason of any arrangement entered into or composition accepted by the Commissioners modifying (by operation of law or otherwise) their rights and remedies in respect of the said tax or taxes or by any other act, omission or thing whatsoever whereby the Guarantor as surety or Guarantor only would have been so released or the liability of the Guarantor impaired."

J. M. Green,
J. H. Gracey,
Two of the Commissioners
of Inland Revenue

20th December 1984.

(**a**) 1975 c.45; section 70 and Schedule 12 were amended by section 43 and Schedule 8 of the Finance Act 1980 (c.48) and further amended by section 47 and Schedule 8 of the Finance Act 1982 (c.39).
(**b**) S.I. 1982/1391.

EXPLANATORY NOTE

(This Note is not part of the Regulations.)

These Regulations amend one paragraph in each of the two forms of bank Guarantee prescribed in the Income Tax (Sub-contractors in the Construction Industry) Regulations 1982, which enable a sub-contractor in the construction industry holding a certificate by reason of such a guarantee to obtain payments up to a specified limit without deduction. The new paragraphs 8 omit a provision previously included treating the guarantor bank as a principal debtor to the Revenue in respect of sums becoming due from the bank to the Revenue under the terms of the Guarantee. This provision was thought to raise technical accounting difficulties for the banks though the effect of the amended paragraph remains in substance unchanged.

STATUTORY INSTRUMENTS

1984 No. 2009

VETERINARY SURGEONS

The Veterinary Surgeons and Veterinary Practitioners Registration (Amendment) Regulations Order of Council 1984

Made - - - *21st December* 1984

At the Council Chamber, Whitehall, the 21st day of December 1984

By the Lords of Her Majesty's Most Honourable Privy Council

Whereas in pursuance of section 11 of the Veterinary Surgeons Act 1966(a) the Council of the Royal College of Veterinary Surgeons have made regulations entitled "The Veterinary Surgeons and Veterinary Practitioners Registration (Amendment) Regulations 1984";

And whereas by section 25(1) of the said Act such regulations shall not have effect unless approved by Order of the Privy Council:

Now, therefore, Their Lordships, having taken the said regulations into consideration, are hereby pleased to approve the same as set out in the Schedule to this Order.

This Order may be cited as the Veterinary Surgeons and Veterinary Practitioners Registration (Amendment) Regulations Order of Council 1984.

G. I. de Deney,
Clerk of the Privy Council.

SCHEDULE

THE VETERINARY SURGEONS AND VETERINARY PRACTITIONERS
REGISTRATION (AMENDMENT) REGULATIONS 1984

The Council of the Royal College of Veterinary Surgeons, in exercise of their powers under section 11 of the Veterinary Surgeons Act 1966, hereby make the following Regulations —

1. These Regulations may be cited as the Veterinary Surgeons and Veterinary Practitioners Registration (Amendment) Regulations 1984.

2. Regulation 16 of the Veterinary Surgeons and Veterinary Practitioners Registration Regulations 1967(b) as amended, (hereinafter referred to as "the principal Regulations") shall be further amended by the deletion of the second sentence and the substitution of the following therefor —

(a) 1966 c.36.
(b) S.I. 1967/395, amended by S.I. 1975/70, 2212, 1978/1809.

"This fee shall be paid at the time of the application for registration and shall be £52.50 for names entered on the register before 31st March 1985 and £80 for names entered on the register on 31st March 1985 and thereafter."

3. Regulation 20 of the principal Regulations shall be amended by the deletion in paragraphs (a), (b), (c), (d) and (e) of the amounts "£45.00", "£13.00", "£1.00", "£8.50" and "£4.50" and the substitution therefor of the amounts "£70.00", "£20.50", "£5.00", "£13.00" and "£7.00" respectively.

4. Regulation 22 of the principal Regulations shall be amended by the deletion of the amounts "£6.00" and "£3.00" and the substitution therefor of the amounts "£10.00" and "£5.00" respectively.

5. Regulation 23 of the principal Regulations shall be amended by the deletion in the first and third sentence of paragraph (b) of the amount "£52.50" and the substitution therefor in each case of the amount "£80.00".

PURSUANT to a resolution passed at a Meeting of the Council of the Royal College of Veterinary Surgeons on the 1st day of November 1984, the Common Seal of the said Royal College was affixed hereto on the said 1st day of November in the presence of:

(L.S.)

E. J. L. Soulsby,
President.

John Parry,
Don Haxby,
Members of Council.

EXPLANATORY NOTE

(This Note is not part of the Order.)

The regulations approved by this Order further amend the Veterinary Surgeons and Veterinary Practitioners Registration Regulations 1967 by increasing by about 15% the fees payable in respect of the registration and retention of names in, or the restoration of names to, the registers kept by the Royal College of Veterinary Surgeons. The existing fees were fixed in 1981.

STATUTORY INSTRUMENTS

1984 No. 2010

DENTISTS

The General Dental Council Health Committee (Procedure) Rules Order of Council 1984

Made - - - - *21st December* 1984

Coming into Operation *1st January* 1985

At the Council Chamber, Whitehall, the 21st day of December 1984

By the Lords of Her Majesty's Most Honourable Privy Council

Whereas in pursuance of paragraph 2 of Schedule 3 to the Dentists Act 1984 (a), the General Dental Council have made the General Dental Council Health Committee (Procedure) Rules 1984:

And whereas by sub-paragraph (4) of the said paragraph such Rules shall not come into force until approved by order of the Privy Council:

Now, therefore, Their Lordships, having taken the said Rules into consideration, are pleased to approve the same as set out in the Schedule to this Order.

This Order may be cited as the General Dental Council Health Committee (Procedure) Rules Order of Council 1984, and shall come into operation on 1st January 1985.

G. I. de Deney,
Clerk of the Privy Council.

(a), 1984 c.24.

SCHEDULE

THE GENERAL DENTAL COUNCIL HEALTH COMMITTEE (PROCEDURE) RULES 1984

PART I

PRELIMINARY

PART II

ARRANGEMENTS FOR THE INITIAL CONSIDERATION OF CASES

PART III

INITIAL HEARING BY THE HEALTH COMMITTEE

PART IV

RESUMED HEARINGS BY THE HEALTH COMMITTEE

FIRST SCHEDULE

Provisions as to meetings of the Committee

SECOND SCHEDULE

Medical examiners and medical assessors

PART I

PRELIMINARY

Citation and commencement

1. These rules may be cited as the General Dental Council Health Committee (Procedure) Rules 1984, and shall come into operation on 1st January 1985.

Interpretation

2. In these rules, unless the context otherwise requires:

"the Act" means the Dentists Act 1984;

"the Committee" means the Health Committee constituted in accordance with the provisions of section 2 of the Act;

"complainant" means the body or person providing information to the Council which raises a question whether the fitness of a dentist to practise is seriously impaired by reason of his physical or mental condition;

"the Council" means the General Dental Council;

"defence society" means the Medical Defence Union, the Medical Protection Society, or the Medical and Dental Defence Union of Scotland;

"dentist" means a registered dental practitioner whose fitness to practise is the subject of inquiry under these rules;

"the Legal Assessor" means an assessor appointed by the Council under paragraph 5(1) of Schedule 3 to the Act;

"medical adviser" means, in relation to the dentist as defined in this rule, any registered medical practitioner (but not more than one) whom the dentist has consulted as a patient in regard to his own health and whom the dentist elects to treat as his medical adviser for the purpose of proceedings under these rules;

"medical assessor" means a person chosen by the President as provided in the Second Schedule to the rules to give advice under these rules;

"medical examiner" means a person chosen as provided in the Second Schedule to the rules either by the President to examine and report on a dentist under rules 6, 7 and 8, or by the Committee under rule 20 or 25;

"person acting in a public capacity" means an officer of a Health Authority, Health Board or Board of Governors of a Hospital, or of a Local Medical or Dental Committee or Hospital Medical Staff Committee, or of a Government Department or of a local or public authority, or of any of the dental authorities (i.e. university or other body granting dental diplomas) acting as such, or any person holding judicial office, or any officer attached to a Court, or the Solicitor;

"Preliminary Proceedings Committee" and "Professional Conduct Committee" respectively mean the Committees of those names constituted under Part II of Schedule 3 to the Act;

"the President" means the President of the Council and includes any other member appointed under rule 5(2);

"the Register" means the Dentists Register;

"the Registrar" means the Registrar of the Council;

"the Solicitor" means the person who for the time being holds the appropriate office on behalf of the Council.

Times of meetings of the Committee

3. The provisions of the First Schedule to these rules shall have effect as to the times of meetings of the Committee, and the mode of summoning members.

Appointment of medical assessors and medical examiners

4. The provisions of the Second Schedule to these rules shall have effect as to the nomination of medical assessors and medical examiners and the selection of a particular person to act as a medical assessor or medical examiner in any case, and the duties of medical assessors.

PART II

ARRANGEMENTS FOR THE INITIAL CONSIDERATION OF CASES

Appointment of member to conduct initial consideration of cases

5.—(1) No case shall be considered by the Committee unless it has been referred either:

(a) by the President; or

(b) by the Preliminary Proceedings Committee in accordance with paragraph 3(2) of Schedule 3 to the Act; or

(c) by the Professional Conduct Committee in accordance with paragraph 3(2) of Schedule 3 to the Act.

(2) The Council shall appoint the President or, if he does not wish to be so appointed, some other member nominated by him, to undertake the initial consideration of cases under rules 6 to 8. Where a member of the Council has been appointed in place of the President for the purpose of this rule, references in these rules to the President shall be construed as references to such member.

(3) Without prejudice to the generality of the foregoing paragraph, if at any time the President is absent or unable to act, anything authorised or required by these rules to be done by the President may be done by any other member of the Council authorised in that behalf by the President or (if the President be unable to give authority) authorised by the Council.

Information raising a question as to a dentist's fitness to practise

6.—(1) Where information in writing is received by the Registrar about any dentist which raises a question whether the fitness to practise of the dentist is seriously impaired by reason of his physical or mental condition the Registrar shall submit the information to the President.

(2) If the information has not been received from a person acting in a public capacity the President may require the informant to supply one or more statutory declarations or other affidavits in support thereof; and may require such declaration or affidavit to state the address and description of the deponent and the grounds for his belief in the truth of any fact therein which is not within his personal knowledge.

(3) On receipt of the information the President may cause such inquiries to be made in relation to the matter as he may think fit. The President may, if he considers it necessary to assist him in arriving at a decision, obtain an opinion from a medical assessor selected by him on the information and evidence which he has received.

(4) Unless it appears to the President that the matter need not proceed further he shall, subject to the provisions of paragraphs (5) to (7) of this rule, direct the Registrar to send a notice by recorded delivery to the dentist:

(*a*) informing him that information has been received which appears to raise a question as to whether his fitness to practise is seriously impaired by reason of his physical or mental condition and indicating the nature of the alleged condition;

(*b*) inviting him to agree within 14 days to submit to examination by at least two medical examiners to be chosen by the President and to agree that such examiners should furnish to the President reports on his fitness to practise;

(*c*) informing him that it is also open to him to nominate other medical practitioners to examine him and report to the President on his fitness to practise;

(*d*) inviting him to submit any observations or other evidence which he may wish to offer as to his fitness to practise; and

(*e*) informing him that if he does not reply within 28 days or fails without proper cause to submit to medical examination, the matter may be referred to the Committee forthwith.

(5) If in any case the information received by the Council includes reports on the dentist by two or more medical practitioners who have recently examined him, and it appears to the President that such reports afford sufficient medical evidence that the dentist's fitness to practise may be seriously impaired by reason of a physical or mental condition, paragraph 4*(b)* of this rule shall not apply and the President shall instead cause the Registrar to include with the notice sent to the dentist under paragraph (4) copies of these reports.

(6) Subject to the provisions of paragraph (7) of this rule the President may direct the Registrar to enclose with any notice sent under paragraph (4) of this rule a summary of the information received by the Council and copies of any reports on the dentist by medical practitioners who have recently examined him.

(7) If in the opinion of the President such reports contain any material which is not relevant to the present fitness to practise of the dentist, or which it would not be in the best interests of the dentist to see, the President may direct the Registrar to exclude such material from the documents sent to the dentist under this rule. Any material so excluded shall not subsequently be presented to the Committee.

(8) If the dentist:

(a) does not within 28 days (or such further period as the President may allow) reply to any notice sent to him under paragraph (4) above, or

(b) has refused or failed without proper cause to submit to a medical examination in accordance with paragraph (4)*(b)* of this rule,

the President may, subject to the provisions of paragraph (7) of this rule, refer the case to the Committee.

Medical examination

7.—(1) If the dentist agrees to submit to medical examination in response to an invitation sent under rule 6(4)*(b)* and *(c)* the Registrar shall make arrangements for such examination. The medical examiners shall be chosen by the President.

(2) The Registrar shall send to the chosen medical examiners and to any other medical practitioners nominated under rule 6(4)*(c)* the information received by the Council and shall ask them to report on the fitness of the dentist to engage in practice, either generally or on a limited basis, and on the management of his case which they recommend.

Action following reports of medical examination

8.—(1) Subject to the provisions of paragraph (2) of this rule the President shall cause the Registrar to send copies of the reports received from the medical examiners, including any reports by medical practitioners nominated by the dentist under rule 6(4)*(c)*, to the dentist.

(2) If in the opinion of the President the reports, other than any made by a medical practitioner nominated by the dentist under rule 6(4)*(c)*, contain any material which is not relevant to the present fitness to practise of the dentist or which it would not be in the best interests of the dentist to see, the President may direct the Registrar to delete such material from the reports. No material so excluded shall subsequently be presented to the Committee.

(3) Where in any case it appears to the President that there is insufficient evidence that the dentist is not fit to practise, or is not fit to practise except on a limited basis, or under medical supervision the dentist and the complainant shall be so informed.

(4)(*a*) If the medical practitioners who have examined the dentist report unanimously that he:—

    (i) is not fit to practise, or

    (ii) is not fit to practise except on a limited basis or under medical supervision or both, or

    (iii) suffers from a recurring or episodic physical or mental condition which, although at the time of the examination is in remission, is liable in future to render him unfit to practise or unfit to practise except on a limited basis or under medical supervision or both,

the President shall refer the matter to the Committee and shall direct the Registrar to inform the dentist by letter of the opinion reached as to his physical or mental condition, and to invite him to attend a meeting of the Committee.

(*b*) The foregoing sub-paragraph shall also have effect notwithstanding any difference of opinion among the medical practitioners who have reported if it appears to the President, after considering their reports, that the dentist may not be fit to practise or may not be fit to practise except on a limited basis or under medical supervision or both, or suffers from a recurring or episodic physical or mental condition which can be expected in future to render him unfit to practise.

(*c*) A letter under paragraph (4)(*a*) shall be sent by registered post or by personal service to the dentist at his address on the Register or to his last known or any other address if it appears to the Registrar that a letter so addressed is more likely to reach him.

(5) Before referring a case to the Committee under this rule the President may, if he considers it necessary to assist him in arriving at a decision, obtain an opinion from a medical assessor selected by him on the information and evidence which he has received: provided that if the President considers that in the public interest it is urgent that any such case should be referred to the Committee, he may refer the case before consulting a medical assessor.

Provisions applying when a case has been referred to the Committee by the Preliminary Proceedings Committee or by the Professional Conduct Committee

9.—(1) Where a case has been referred to the Committee by the Preliminary Proceedings Committee or by the Professional Conduct Committee the President may, if he thinks fit, direct the Registrar to invite the dentist to submit to examination, before his case is considered by the Committee, by at least two medical examiners to be chosen by the President and to agree that such examiners should furnish to the Committee reports on his fitness to practise, and to inform him that it is also open to him to nominate another medical practitioner to examine him and to report to the Committee on him.

(2) If the dentist agrees to submit to examination as aforesaid the Registrar shall make arrangements for such examination and any reports received shall be referred to the Committee, together with the information on which the Preliminary Proceedings Committee or the Professional Conduct Committee, as the case may be, decided to refer the case.

PART III

INITIAL HEARING BY THE HEALTH COMMITTEE

Notice of referral

10.—(1) Subject to the foregoing rule, as soon as may be after a case has been referred to the Committee, the Registrar shall send to the dentist a "notice of referral" which shall:

(a) indicate the physical or mental condition by reason of which it is alleged that his fitness to practise is seriously impaired;

(b) state the day, time and place at which the Committee will meet to consider the matter;

(c) indicate that it is open to him to be represented as provided in rule 16(2) and also to be accompanied by his medical adviser;

(d) invite the dentist to state whether he proposes to attend the inquiry; and

(e) inform him that he may call witnesses in his defence with or without notice.

(2) Subject to the provisions of paragraph (3) the Registrar shall send with any notice of referral a copy of these rules and copies of any reports and other information which it is proposed to present to the Committee, other than reports of which copies have already been sent to the dentist under rules 6(6) and 8(1).

(3) The provisions of rule 8(2) shall apply to any reports or information sent under the foregoing paragraph.

(4) Except with the agreement of the dentist no case shall be referred for consideration at any date earlier than 28 days after the date of posting the notice of referral.

(5) A notice of referral shall be sent by registered post or by personal service to the dentist at his address on the Register or to his last known or any other address if it appears to the Registrar that a notice so addressed is more likely to reach him.

(6) The Registrar shall notify the complainant of the day, time and place of the hearing, and inform him of his rights to be heard, and represented.

Evidence to be given orally

11. Subject to rule 10(4) above, not less than 28 days before the date on which the case is to be considered the Registrar shall inform the dentist in writing:

(a) what part or parts of the information or of the findings or opinions contained in the medical reports the Solicitor will require to be given orally in evidence before the Committee (either on behalf of the Council or on behalf of the dentist); and

(b) that he will be required to state not less than 14 days before the date when the case is to be considered by the Committee what part or parts of the information or of the findings and opinions contained in the medical reports he will require to be given orally in evidence before the Committee, regardless of whether the Solicitor has indicated under paragraph 11(a) above that he wishes to call evidence orally.

Medical assessors

12. The President shall arrange for one or more medical assessors to attend the meeting of the Committee called to consider a case.

Preliminary circulation of evidence

13. Before the meeting of the Committee the Registrar shall send to each member of the Committee, and to the medical assessors chosen to advise the Committee on the case, copies of the notice of referral, of the information and report sent to the dentist under rule 10(2), of any medical reports received in accordance with rules 8 and 9, and of any observations or other evidence submitted by or on behalf of the dentist.

Postponement of inquiry

14.—(1) The President may if he thinks fit postpone the holding of the first hearing of a case to such later date or such later meeting of the Committee as he may determine.

(2) The Registrar shall, as soon as may be, send notification to the dentist and complainant of any decision to postpone a hearing, and shall inform him at that time or subsequently of the date of the postponed hearing.

Cancellation of inquiry

15.—(1) If it appears to the President, after a case has been referred to the Committee, that the inquiry should not be held, he may make a direction to this effect provided that in any case referred to the Committee by the Preliminary Proceedings Committee or the Professional Conduct Committee the President shall so direct only after consultation with the present members of the committee which referred the case and in accordance with the opinion of those members, or the majority of their opinions (including his own opinion).

(2) Where the opinions of the members of the Preliminary Proceedings Committee or the Professional Conduct Committee (including the opinion of the President) are equally divided the question shall be deemed to have been resolved in favour of the dentist, and the President shall direct that the inquiry shall not be held.

(3) Where the President directs that the inquiry should not be held and at the time of the direction no notice of referral or resumed hearing has been sent, rules 10 and 28 shall not have effect.

(4) As soon as may be after the giving of any such direction the Registrar shall send notification thereof to the dentist and to the complainant. Such notification may, at the discretion of the President, include reasons for the cancellation of the inquiry.

Opening of Inquiry

16.—(1) The Committee shall sit in private.

(2) The dentist shall be entitled to be present while his case is considered, and may also be represented or accompanied by an officer of his defence society or of any other organisation of which he is a member, or by counsel or solicitor, or by any member of his family, and may be accompanied by his medical adviser. Provided that this paragraph shall not entitle the dentist to

be represented or accompanied by any person from whom oral evidence is to be required under rules 17 to 19.

(3) The Registrar shall inform the Committee:

(a) if the dentist has failed to reply within 28 days to a notice sent to him under rule 6(4) or to a letter sent to him for the purpose of rule 9(1); or

(b) if the dentist has failed to submit to examination under rule 6(4) or under rule 9(1).

(4) Where the dentist is neither present nor represented the Registrar shall give the Committee such information he may have as to whether or not the notice of referral has been effectively served on the dentist. If the Committee are satisfied that the notice has been served the inquiry may proceed if the Committee think fit. If the Committee are not satisfied that the notice has been served they may

(a) if in their opinion all reasonable efforts have been made to serve the notice, proceed with the inquiry; or

(b) if they are of the opinion that further efforts should be made to serve the notice, adjourn the meeting to a later date for this purpose; or

(c) in any other case, adjourn the meeting indefinitely, or refer the case back to the President, or decide to cancel the inquiry.

(5) The Solicitor may be represented by counsel.

(6) The complainant shall be entitled to be present while the case is considered and may be represented by a solicitor or by counsel.

Presentation of the case

17.—(1) If the Committee have determined to proceed with the inquiry the Chairman shall invite the Solicitor to open the case and to present the evidence by reason of which it is alleged that the dentist's fitness to practise is seriously impaired.

(2) If in any case before the opening of the inquiry the Solicitor has under rule 11(a) required, or the dentist has within the period indicated in rule 11(b) required, that all or part of the information or reports be supported by oral evidence, then the persons on whose testimony or opinion such information or reports depend shall be called as witnesses. Such witnesses shall be examined by the Solicitor, may be examined by the complainant or his representative, may be cross-examined by the dentist or his representative, may be questioned by the Committee and, with the leave of the Chairman, by any medical assessor.

Calling of witnesses where no previous notice has been given

18. If in any case where no prior notice has been given by or on behalf of the dentist that he will require all or part of the evidence forming part of the case against him to be given orally, the dentist or his representative nevertheless indicates at the hearing that he requires witnesses to appear to give such evidence, the Committee shall consult the Legal Assessor whether in the interests of justice they should adjourn the hearing in order to secure the attendance of such persons as witnesses or whether they may properly proceed with the hearing without taking such oral evidence.

Presentation of the dentist's case

19.—(1) At the conclusion of any oral evidence given as aforesaid the Chairman shall invite the dentist or his representative to address the Committee and to adduce evidence as to the dentist's fitness to practise. Any witnesses called on behalf of the dentist shall be examined by the dentist, may be cross-examined by the complainant or the Solicitor, may be questioned by the Committee and, with the leave of the Chairman, by any medical assessor.

(2) Where any evidence has been called on behalf of the dentist (including any evidence given by the dentist himself) the Chairman shall invite the complainant or the Solicitor to address the Committee.

(3) The dentist or his representative may then address the Committee for a second time.

Adjournment for further medical reports

20. At the conclusion of proceedings under the foregoing rules the Committee may adjourn the case in order to obtain further medical reports or other evidence as to the physical or mental condition of the dentist or for any other reason.

Postponement of finding

21. If the Committee do not think fit to adjourn the case under the foregoing rule they shall consider whether to postpone their finding as to the dentist's fitness to practise.

Determination of the Committee

22.—(1) If the Committee do not think fit to adjourn the case or postpone their finding under rules 20 and 21 they shall consider and determine whether they judge the fitness to practise of the dentist to be seriously impaired by reason of his physical or mental condition.

(2) In reaching their judgement the Committee shall be entitled to take account of the dentist's current physical and mental condition, or a continuing and episodic condition, or a condition which, although currently in remission, may be expected to cause recurrence of serious impairment.

(3) Where the practitioner has refused or, in the opinion of the Committee has failed without reasonable cause to submit to medical examination in accordance with rule 6(4)*(b)* or rule 9 the Committee shall be entitled, if they think fit, to find that the dentist's fitness to practise is seriously impaired on the basis of the information before them and the dentist's refusal or failure to submit to medical examination.

(4) If the Committee judge the dentist's fitness to practise to be seriously impaired, they shall next consider and determine whether it shall be sufficient to direct that the registration of the dentist shall be conditional on his compliance, during such period not exceeding three years as the Committee may specify, with such requirements as the Committee may think fit to impose for the protection of members of the public or in his interests.

(5) If the Committee so determine they shall then consider and decide what conditions (of whatever nature) shall be imposed in accordance with section 28(1)*(b)* of the Act and the Committee may impose more than one condition under this paragraph.

Direction for suspension of registration

23.—(1) If the Committee decide that it is not sufficient to impose conditions on the dentist's registration they shall direct that the registration of the dentist shall be suspended in accordance with section 28(1)*(a)* of the Act for such period not exceeding 12 months as the Committee may determine.

(2) If in any case the Committee determine to suspend the registration of a dentist, the Committee shall also consider and determine whether in accordance with section 30(3) of the Act, it is necessary for the protection of members of the public or would be in the best interests of the dentist to order that his registration shall be suspended forthwith.

Announcement of determination

24. The Chairman shall announce the determination or determinations of the Committee under rules 22 and 23 in such terms as the Committee may approve.

Provision for resumed hearings

25.—(1) In any case in which the Committee have adjourned the case or postponed their finding or imposed conditions on, or suspended, the registration of the practitioner for a period they shall, when announcing such decision, intimate that they will, at a meeting to be held before the end of such period, resume consideration of the case.

(2) The Committee may also indicate the medical evidence of the dentist's fitness to practise, or other evidence, which they will require at the resumed hearing. Such evidence may include one or more reports from medical or dental practitioners who have treated and/or supervised the dentist since the time of the original hearing.

(3) The Committee may also require the dentist to submit to examination by one or more medical examiners chosen by or on behalf of the Committee.

Cases referred by the Preliminary Proceedings Committee or the Professional Conduct Committee: dentist's fitness to practise found not to be seriously impaired

26. If in any case referred by the Preliminary Proceedings Committee or the Professional Conduct Committee, the Committee judge that the fitness to practise of the dentist is not seriously impaired by reason of his physical or mental condition they shall certify such opinion to the Committee that made the reference, and notify the dentist.

PART IV

RESUMED HEARINGS BY THE HEALTH COMMITTEE

Direction for resumed hearing

27.—(1) If, in any case where the Committee have suspended the registration of the dentist, or imposed conditions upon his registration or have adjourned the case or postponed their finding, it appears to the President that the Committee should resume consideration of the case at an earlier meeting or date than that specified by the Committee, the President may direct the Registrar to notify the dentist that the Committee will resume consideration of the case at such earlier meeting or date as the President shall determine.

(2) Without prejudice to the generality of the foregoing paragraph, where in any case the Committee have imposed conditions upon a dentist's registration, and it appears to the President from information subsequently received that the dentist is in a material respect not complying with such conditions, the President may exercise his powers under the foregoing paragraph.

(3) Before exercising his powers under paragraph (1) above, the President may invite the dentist to submit to further medical examination as provided in rule 25(2).

(4) In any case in which the President has given a direction under paragraph (1) of this rule, the Committee shall then resume consideration of the case at the meeting determined by the President notwithstanding their earlier decision.

Notice of resumed hearing

28.—(1) Where under any of the foregoing rules the Committee have adjourned the case (except in the case of adjournment for less than 28 days), or have postponed their finding or have imposed conditions upon the registration of the dentist or have directed that his registration shall be suspended, or where the President has given a direction under rule 27, the Registrar shall send to the dentist a notice which shall:

(a) specify the date, time and place at which the proceedings are to be resumed and invite him to appear thereat;

(b) in any case where the President has exercised his powers under rule 27 state the nature of the information in consequence of which he has exercised his powers;

(c) if the Committee or the President have so directed, invite the dentist to submit to examination by the medical examiners chosen by the Committee or by the President;

(d) if the Committee have so directed, invite the dentist to furnish the names and addresses of medical practitioners or other persons to whom the Committee will be able to apply for confidential information as to their knowledge of his fitness to practise since the time of the original inquiry.

(2) Except with the agreement of the dentist, the proceedings shall not be resumed at any date earlier than 28 days after the date of posting the notice of resumed proceedings.

(3) Paragraphs (1)(c) to (e), (2), (5) and (6) of rule 10 shall apply to the sending of notices under this rule.

(4) A request under rule 11 shall only apply to evidence which has not previously been considered by the Committee.

Medical assessors at resumed hearing

29. In choosing medical assessors to assist the Committee at any resumed hearing the President shall have regard to any opinion expressed by the Committee at the previous hearing as to the nature of the matters on which medical advice would be useful.

Procedure at resumed hearing

30. At any resumed hearing the procedure shall be that provided by rules 12 to 24 for the original hearing and the Committee may exercise any power which under those rules they could have exercised at the original hearing save that:

(a) the Committee shall not extend any period of conditional registration for more than 12 months on any resumed hearing; and

(b) the Committee may revoke any previous direction for conditional registration or revoke or vary the conditions previously imposed on the dentist's registration.

Validity of proceedings

31. Subject to the provisions of the Act, the validity of any resumed proceedings of the Committee shall not be called into question by reason only that members of the Committee who were present at any former meeting were not present at the resumed meeting, or that members present at the resumed meeting were not present at any former meeting.

PART V

GENERAL

Adjournment of proceedings

32. The Committee may adjourn any of their proceedings or meetings from time to time as they think fit.

Deliberation in camera

33. Subject to the provisions of these rules the Committee may deliberate in camera at any time and for any purpose during any proceedings and for such purpose may exclude the dentist, his representatives and his medical adviser and the complainant and his representatives.

Evidence

34.—(1) Subject to the provisions of rules 11, 17(2) and 18 the written evidence sent to the dentist in accordance with rule 10(2) shall be admissible in documentary form without the necessity of calling witnesses to give that evidence orally.

(2) Subject to paragraph (1) above the Committee may at their discretion at any hearing receive oral, documentary or other evidence of any fact or matter which appears to them relevant to the inquiry into the case before them and the time limits imposed by rule 11 shall not apply to such evidence:

Provided that, where any fact or matter is tendered as evidence which would not be admissible as such if the proceedings were criminal proceedings in England, the Committee shall not receive it unless, after consultation with the Legal Assessor, they are satisfied that its reception is desirable to enable them to perform their duty.

Voting

35. The following provisions shall have effect as to the taking of the votes of the Committee on any question to be determined by them:

(1) The Chairman of the Committee shall call upon the members present to signify their votes by raising their hands, signify his own vote, and declare the way in which the question appears to him to have been determined.

(2) If the result so declared by the Chairman is challenged by any member, the Chairman shall:

(a) call upon each member individually to declare his vote,

(b) announce his own vote, and

(c) announce the number of members of the Committee who have voted each way and the result of the vote.

(3) If the votes are equal, the question shall be deemed to have been resolved in favour of the dentist.

Postal service of documents

36. Without prejudice to any requirement of these rules as to the service of documents by registered post, any notice authorised or required by these rules may be sent by post.

Notes and transcript of proceedings

37.—(1) A shorthand writer shall be appointed by the Registrar to take shorthand notes of the proceedings of the Committee.

(2) The dentist shall, on application to the Registrar and on payment of the proper charges, be furnished with a transcript of the shorthand notes of any part of the proceedings at which the dentist was entitled to be present, whether he was present or not.

FIRST SCHEDULE

Provisions as to meetings of the Committee

1. The Committee shall meet on such days as the Chairman, Committee or Council may determine and at such time as the Chairman may determine.

2. Members of the Committee shall be summoned to meetings of the Committee by the Registrar, by notice addressed to each member. Except in the case of a meeting held to resume the hearing of a case which has been adjourned or postponed for less than 28 days such notice shall be sent out not less than 7 days before the meeting to which it relates.

SECOND SCHEDULE

Medical examiners and medical assessors

1. Subject to paragraph 3 of this Schedule medical examiners and medical assessors shall be chosen by the President or by the Committee from persons nominated by the following Bodies as appropriate:

The Royal Colleges and their Faculties

The Central Committee for Hospital Medical Services of the British Medical Association

The General Medical Services Committee of the British Medical Association

2. The Council may from time to time determine the minimum number of persons to be nominated in respect of each branch of medicine, the periods for which nominations shall be made, and the intervals at which the lists of those nominated shall be revised, and may give directions as to the nomination of persons on a geographical basis. The Council may also determine from time to time the scale of remuneration of medical examiners and medical assessors.

3. In choosing medical examiners and medical assessors to act in relation to particular cases, the President or Committee shall have regard to the nature of the physical or mental condition which is alleged to impair the dentist's fitness to practise.

4.   (a) It shall be the duty of the medical assessors to be present at the proceedings before the Committee for which they have been chosen to act and to advise the Committee on the medical significance of the evidence before the Committee.

    (b) Medical assessors shall give such advice on questions referred to them by the Committee, and shall also advise the Committee of their own motion if it appears to them that, but for such advice, there is a possibility of a mistake being made in judging the medical significance of such evidence (including the absence of evidence) on any particular matter relevant to the fitness to practise of the dentist.

EXPLANATORY NOTE

(This Note is not part of the Order.)

The Rules approved by this Order provide for the reference of cases to the Health Committee established under section 2(4) of the Dentists Act 1984 and for the procedure to be followed and the rules of evidence to be observed in proceedings before the Committee. They also provide for the times and places of meetings of the Committee, the mode of summoning the members, for the selection of medical examiners and assessors to advise the Committee, and to assist the President in the initial consideration of cases.

STATUTORY INSTRUMENTS

1984 No. 2011

OFFSHORE INSTALLATIONS

The Offshore Installations (Safety Zones) (No. 100) Order 1984

Made - - - -	*20th December* 1984
Coming into Operation	*22nd December* 1984

The Secretary of State, in exercise of the powers conferred on him by section 21(1), (2) and (3) of the Oil and Gas (Enterprise) Act 1982(a) (hereinafter referred to as "the Act"), and of all other powers enabling him in that behalf, hereby makes the following Order:—

1. This Order may be cited as the Offshore Installations (Safety Zones) (No. 100) Order 1984 and shall come into operation on 22nd December 1984.

2.—(1) A safety zone is hereby established around the installation specified in Column 1 of the Schedule hereto (being an installation maintained in waters in an area designated under section 1(7) of the Continental Shelf Act 1964(b)) having a radius of five hundred metres from the point as respects that installation which has the co-ordinates of latitude and longitude according to European Datum (1950) specified in Columns 2 and 3 of the Schedule.

(2) The prohibition under section 21(3) of the Act on a vessel entering or remaining in a safety zone without the consent of the Secretary of State shall not apply to a vessel entering or remaining in the safety zone established under paragraph (1) above—

(*a*) in connection with the laying, inspection, testing, repair, alteration, renewal or removal of any submarine cable or pipe-line in or near that safety zone;

(*b*) to provide services for, to transport persons or goods to or from, or under the authority of a government department to inspect, any installation in that safety zone;

(*c*) if it is a vessel belonging to a general lighthouse authority performing duties relating to the safety of navigation;

(*d*) in connection with the saving or attempted saving of life or property;

(*e*) owing to stress of weather; or

(*f*) when in distress.

Alick Buchanan-Smith,
Minister of State,
Department of Energy.

20th December 1984.

(**a**) 1982 c. 23.   (**b**) 1964 c. 29.

Article 2(1)

SCHEDULE

SAFETY ZONE

1	2	3
Name or other designation of the offshore installation	Latitude North	Longitude East
Transworld 58	56° 16′ 05·14″	02° 39′ 49·05″

EXPLANATORY NOTE

(This Note is not part of the Order.)

This Order establishes, under section 21 of the Oil and Gas (Enterprise) Act 1982, a safety zone, having a radius of 500 metres from a specified point, around the installation known as Transworld 58 maintained in waters in an area designated under section 1(7) of the Continental Shelf Act 1964.

Vessels (which includes hovercraft, submersible apparatus and installations in transit) are prohibited from entering or remaining in the safety zone except with the consent of the Secretary of State or in the circumstances mentioned in Article 2(2) of the Order.

STATUTORY INSTRUMENTS

1984 No. 2019

TERMS AND CONDITIONS OF EMPLOYMENT

The Employment Protection (Variation of Limits) Order 1984

Laid before Parliament in draft

Made - - -	*21st December* 1984
Coming into Operation	*1st April* 1985

Whereas in accordance with section 148 of the Employment Protection (Consolidation) Act 1978(**a**) ("the 1978 Act") the Secretary of State has reviewed the limits referred to in sections 15 and 122(5) of, and the limits imposed by paragraph 8(1) of Schedule 14 to, the 1978 Act(**b**):

And whereas the Secretary of State having regard to the considerations mentioned in section 148(2) of the 1978 Act has determined that certain of those limits shall be varied as hereinafter provided:

And whereas a draft of the following Order was laid before Parliament in accordance with section 148(3) of the 1978 Act and approved by resolution of each House of Parliament:

Now, therefore, the Secretary of State in exercise of the powers conferred on him by sections 15(5), 122(6), 148, 154(3) and 154(4) of, and paragraph 8(2), (3) and (4) of Schedule 14 to, the 1978 Act(**c**) and of all other powers enabling him in that behalf, hereby makes the following Order:—

Citation, commencement and revocation

1.—(1) This Order may be cited as the Employment Protection (Variation of Limits) Order 1984 and shall come into operation on 1st April 1985.

(2) Subject to Article 3(6) below, the Employment Protection (Variation of Limits) Order 1983(**d**) is revoked.

(**a**) 1978 c.44.　　　　　　　　　　(**b**) These limits were last varied by S.I. 1983/1962.
(**c**) Paragraph 8(3) was amended by paragraph 30(3) of Schedule 3 to the Employment Act 1982 (c.46).
(**d**) S.I. 1983/1962.

Variation of Limits

2. Subject to Article 3 below, each limit specified in columns 1 and 2 of the Table below is varied by the substitution of the new figure in column 3 for the old figure in column 4.

Column 1 Provision	Column 2 Nature of Limit	Column 3 New figure	Column 4 Old figure
1. Section 15(1) of the 1978 Act.	Limit on amount of guarantee payment payable to an employee in respect of any day.	£10.50	£10.00
2. Section 122 (5) of the 1978 Act.	Limit on amount payable to an employee in respect of any debt mentioned in section 122(3) of the 1978 Act where that debt is referable to a period of time.	£152.00	£145.00
3. Paragraph 8(1)(*a*)of Schedule 14 to the 1978 Act.	Limit on amount of "a week's pay" for the purpose of calculating additional award of compensation where employer fails to comply with order for reinstatement or re-engagement under section 69 of the 1978 Act.	£152.00	£145.00
4. Paragraph 8(1)(*b*) of Schedule 14 to the 1978 Act.	Limit on amount of "a week's pay" for the purpose of calculating basic award of compensation for unfair dismissal under section 73 of the 1978 Act.	£152.00	£145.00
5. Paragraph 8(1)(*c*) of Schedule 14 to the 1978 Act	Limit on amount of "a week's pay" for the purpose of calculating redundancy payment.	£152.00	£145.00

Supplementary and transitional provisions

3.—(1) The variation specified in item 1 of the Table in Article 2 above shall have effect as respects any day in respect of which an employee becomes entitled to a guarantee payment after this Order comes into operation.

(2) The variation specified in item 2 of the Table in Article 2 above shall have effect where the relevant date (as defined in section 122(2) of the 1978 Act(**a**)) falls after this Order comes into operation.

(**a**) Section 122(2) was amended by paragraph 3 of Schedule 3 to the Employment Act 1982.

(3) The variation specified in item 3 of the Table in Article 2 above shall have effect as respects an employer's failure to comply with an order for reinstatement or re-engagement where the date (specified under section 69(2)(c) or, as the case may be, section 69(4)(f) of the 1978 Act) by which the order must be complied with falls after this Order comes into operation.

(4) The variation specified in item 4 of the Table in Article 2 above shall have effect where the effective date of termination as defined in section 55(4) or, where applicable, section 55(5) or 55(6) of the 1978 Act(**a**) falls after this Order comes into operation.

(5) The variation specified in item 5 of the Table in Article 2 above shall have effect —

   (*a*) as respects a lay-off or a keeping on short-time where the relevant date (as defined in section 90(2) of the 1978 Act) falls after this Order comes into operation; and

   (*b*) as respects a dismissal where the relevant date (as defined in section 90(1) or 90(3) of the 1978 Act) falls after this Order comes into operation.

(6) Nothing in this Order affects any limit otherwise than as provided by the foregoing provisions of this Article and accordingly the limits operative under the Order mentioned in Article 1(2) above continue to apply in cases not falling within those provisions.

Signed by order of the Secretary of State.

Peter Bottomley,
Joint Parliamentary Under Secretary of State,
Department of Employment.

21st December 1984.

(**a**) Section 55(5) was amended, and section 55(6) inserted, by paragraph 1 of Schedule 3 to the Employment Act 1982.

EXPLANATORY NOTE

(This Note is not part of the Order.)

This Order, which comes into operation on 1st April 1985, varies certain of the limits which are required to be reviewed annually by the Secretary of State under section 148 of the Employment Protection (Consolidation) Act 1978. The limit on the amount of guarantee payment payable under section 15(1) of the 1978 Act in respect of any day is increased from £10 to £10.50. The limit on the amount for the purpose of calculating the sum payable by the Secretary of State under section 122 of the 1978 Act in respect of a debt due to an employee whose employer becomes insolvent is increased from £145 to £152. The limits on the amount of "a week's pay" for the purposes of calculating redundancy payments and basic and additional awards of compensation for unfair dismissal are increased from £145 to £152.

STATUTORY INSTRUMENTS

1984 No. 2020

TERMS AND CONDITIONS OF EMPLOYMENT

The Unfair Dismissal (Increase of Compensation Limit) Order 1984

Laid before Parliament in draft

Made - - - - -	*21st December* 1984
Coming into Operation	*1st April* 1985

Whereas a draft of the following Order was laid before Parliament in accordance with section 75(2) of the Employment Protection (Consolidation) Act 1978(a) ("the 1978 Act") and approved by resolution of each House of Parliament:

Now, therefore, the Secretary of State, in exercise of the powers conferred on him by sections 75(2), 154(3) and 154(4) of the 1978 Act and all other powers enabling him in that behalf, hereby makes the following Order:—

Citation, commencement and revocation

1.—(1) This Order may be cited as the Unfair Dismissal (Increase of Compensation Limit) Order 1984 and shall come into operation on 1st April 1985.

(2) Subject to Article 4(2), the Unfair Dismissal (Increase of Compensation Limit) (No. 2) Order 1982(b) ("the second 1982 Order") is revoked.

Interpretation

2. In this Order, "effective date of termination" has the same meaning as in section 55(4) of the 1978 Act except in a case in which section 55(5) or (6) of that Act would have effect so as to treat a later date as the effective date of termination, in which case that later date shall be the effective date of termination for the purposes of this Order.

(a) 1978 c. 44; section 55 was amended by section 21(2) of and paragraph 1 of Schedule 3 to the Employment Act 1982 (c. 46).

(b) S.I. 1982/1868.

Increase of compensation limit
3. Subject to Article 4, the limit on compensation specified in section 75(1) of the 1978 Act**(a)** is increased to £8,000.

Transitional provisions
4.—(1) The increase specified in Article 3 shall have effect where the effective date of termination falls on or after 1st April 1985.

(2) Notwithstanding the revocation of the second 1982 Order, the limits of compensation set by, or, as the case may be, preserved by, Articles 3 and 4 of that Order shall continue to have effect as provided by that Order where the effective date of termination falls before 1st April 1985.

Signed by order of the Secretary of State.

Peter Bottomley,
Joint Parliamentary Under Secretary of State,
Department of Employment.
21st December 1984.

EXPLANATORY NOTE

(This Note is not part of the Order.)

This Order, which comes into operation on 1st April 1985, increases from £7,500 to £8,000 the limit on the amount of compensation which can be awarded by an industrial tribunal in claims for unfair dismissal as the compensatory award or as compensation for failure fully to comply with the terms of an order for reinstatement or re-engagement.

(a) The limit of compensation specified in section 75(1) of the 1978 Act was increased from £5,200 to £5,750 by S.I. 1978/1778, from £5,750 to £6,250 by S.I. 1979/1723, from £6,250 to £7,000 by S.I. 1982/76 and from £7,000 to £7,500 by S.I. 1982/1868.

STATUTORY INSTRUMENTS

1984 No. 2021

TERMS AND CONDITIONS OF EMPLOYMENT

The Unfair Dismissal (Increase of Limits of Basic and Special Awards) Order 1984

Laid before Parliament in draft

Made - - -		*21st December* 1984
Coming into Operation		*1st April* 1985

Whereas a draft of the following Order was laid before Parliament in accordance with sections 73(4B) and 75A(7) of the Employment Protection (Consolidation) Act 1978(a) ("the 1978 Act") and approved by resolution of each House of Parliament:

Now, therefore, the Secretary of State, in exercise of the powers conferred on him by sections 73(4B), 75A(7) and 154(3) of the 1978 Act and all other powers enabling him in that behalf, hereby makes the following Order:—

Citation and commencement

1. This Order may be cited as the Unfair Dismissal (Increase of Limits of Basic and Special Awards) Order 1984 and shall come into operation on 1st April 1985.

Interpretation

2. In this Order, "effective date of termination" has the same meaning as in section 55(4) of the 1978 Act except in a case in which section 55(5) or (6) of that Act would have effect so as to treat a later date as the effective date of termination, in which case that later date shall be the effective date of termination for the purposes of this Order.

Increase of limits

3.—(1) Subject to Article 4, the minimum award of £2,000 provided for by section 73(4A) of the 1978 Act is increased to £2,100.

(2) Subject to Article 4, the sum of £10,000 specified in section 75A(1) of the 1978 Act is increased to £10,500.

(a) 1978 c.44; sections 73(4A) and 73(4B) were inserted by section 4(1) of the Employment Act 1982 (c.46), and section 75A was inserted by section 5(3) of the Employment Act 1982.

(3) Subject to Article 4, the sum of £20,000 specified in section 75A(1) of the 1978 Act is increased to £21,000.

(4) Subject to Article 4, the sum of £15,000 specified in section 75A(2) of the 1978 Act is increased to £15,750.

Transitional provision
4. The increases specified in Article 3 shall have effect where the effective date of termination falls on or after 1st April 1985.

Signed by order of the Secretary of State.

Peter Bottomley,
Joint Parliamentary Under Secretary of State,
Department of Employment.

21st December 1984.

EXPLANATORY NOTE

(This Note is not part of the Order.)

This Order, which comes into operation on 1st April 1985, increases from £2,000 to £2,100 the minimum basic award (before appropriate reductions) and increases the limits of £10,000, £20,000 and £15,000 to £10,500, £21,000 and £15,750 respectively, applicable to calculation of the special award. These limits and the minimum basic award are only relevant to dismissals which are to be regarded as unfair by virtue of section 58 or 59(a) of the Employment Protection (Consolidation) Act 1978.

STATUTORY INSTRUMENTS

1984 No. 2022

ORDNANCE FACTORIES AND MILITARY SERVICES

The Royal Ordnance Factories (Extinguishment of Public Dividend Capital) Order 1984

| Made | - | - | - | 20th December 1984 |

Coming into Operation   2nd January 1985

Whereas—

(1) by virtue of a provision contained in a scheme made under section 1(1)(a) of the Ordnance Factories and Military Services Act 1984(a) property has been transferred to Royal Ordnance public limited company (hereinafter referred to as "the company") being property which was immediately before the transfer appropriated as an asset of the fund (hereinafter referred to as "the fund") established by the Royal Ordnance Factories Trading Fund Order 1974(b);

(2) shares have been issued by the company in consideration of that transfer by virtue of a provision contained in the scheme under section 1(2) of that Act;

(3) the value of the liabilities which subsist in respect of public dividend capital designated in respect of the fund under section 2(2) of the Government Trading Funds Act 1973(c) and ranking as an asset of the Consolidated Fund does not exceed the nominal value of the shares so issued;

Now, therefore, the Secretary of State, in exercise of the powers conferred upon him by section 10(2) of the Ordnance Factories and Military Services Act 1984 and of all other powers enabling him in that behalf, hereby makes the following Order:—

Citation and commencement

1. This order may be cited as the Royal Ordnance Factories (Extinguishment of Public Dividend Capital) Order 1984 and shall come into operation on 2nd January 1985.

Extinguishment of Public Dividend Capital

2. All liabilities which subsist in respect of public dividend capital designated in respect of the fund under section 2(2) of the Government Trading Funds Act 1973 and ranking as an asset of the Consolidated Fund are hereby extinguished.

Michael Heseltine,
One of Her Majesty's Principal
Secretaries of State.

20th December 1984

(a) 1984 c.59.   (b) S.I. 1974/1106.   (c) 1973 c.63.

EXPLANATORY NOTE

(This Note is not part of the Order.)

This Order extinguishes all liabilities in respect of public dividend capital designated under section 2(2) of the Government Trading Funds Act 1973 in respect of the Royal Ordnance Factories Trading Fund.

STATUTORY INSTRUMENTS

1984 No. 2024

AGRICULTURE

The Hill Livestock (Compensatory Allowances) Regulations 1984

Laid before Parliament in draft

Made - - - -	*20th December* 1984
Coming into Operation	*1st January* 1985

The Minister of Agriculture, Fisheries and Food and the Secretary of State, acting jointly, being Ministers designated (a) for the purposes of section 2(2) of the European Communities Act 1972 (b) in relation to the common agricultural policy of the European Economic Community, in exercise of the powers conferred upon them by the said section 2(2) and of all other powers enabling them in that behalf, hereby make the following regulations, a draft of which has been approved by resolution of each House of Parliament:—

Citation, extent and commencement

1. These regulations may be cited as the Hill Livestock (Compensatory Allowances) Regulations 1984, shall apply throughout the United Kingdom, and shall come into operation on 1st January 1985.

Interpretation

2.—(1) In these regulations, unless the context otherwise requires—

"agriculture" includes horticulture, fruit growing, seed growing, dairy farming and livestock breeding and keeping, the use of land as grazing land, meadow land, osier land, market gardens and nursery grounds, and the use of land for woodlands where that use is ancillary to the use of land for other agricultural purposes, and "agricultural" shall be construed accordingly;

"the appropriate Minister" means—

(a) in relation to England and Northern Ireland, the Minister of Agriculture, Fisheries and Food, and

(b) in relation to any other part of the United Kingdom, the Secretary of State;

"approved breed" means any hardy breed or cross breed of sheep approved by the appropriate Minister for the purposes of these regulations, being a breed or cross breed which is suitable for breeding and rearing on land in respect of which the severity of the permanent natural handicaps affecting the breeding and rearing of sheep on that

---

(a) S.I. 1972/1811.
(b) 1972 c.68; section 2 is subject to Schedule 2 to that Act and is to be read, as regards England and Wales, with section 40 of the Criminal Justice Act 1982 (c.48) and S.I. 1984/447, as regards Scotland, with section 289F and 289G of the Criminal Procedure (Scotland) Act 1975 (c.21), as inserted by section 54 of the Criminal Justice Act 1982, and S.I. 1984/526, and, as regards Northern Ireland, with S.I. 1984/703 (N.I. 3) and S.R. (N.I.) 1984 No. 253.

land is greater than that affecting the breeding and rearing of sheep on severely disadvantaged land generally;

"breeding cow" means a female bovine animal, comprised in a regular breeding herd, which is not maintained primarily for the production of milk and which, on or before the qualifying day—

(a) has borne a calf, or

(b) has been brought into the herd primarily for the purpose of replacing an animal which has borne a calf, and is, in the opinion of the appropriate Minister, suitable for the purpose of bearing a calf during the year following the qualifying day;

"designated maps" means—

(a) in relation to England, the 3 volumes of maps numbered 1 to 3, each such volume being marked "volume of maps of less-favoured farming areas in England" and with the number of the volume, dated 3rd April 1984, signed and sealed by the Minister of Agriculture, Fisheries and Food and deposited at the offices of the Ministry of Agriculture, Fisheries and Food at Great Westminster House, Horseferry Road, London SW1P 2AE;

(b) in relation to Wales, the 2 volumes of maps numbered 1 and 2, both volumes being marked "volume of maps of less-favoured farming areas in Wales" and with the number of the volume, dated 29th March 1984, signed by the Secretary of State for Wales and deposited at the offices of the Welsh Office Agriculture Department at Plas Crug, Aberystwyth, Dyfed SY23 1NG;

(c) in relation to Scotland, the 4 maps numbered 1 to 4, each such map being marked "map of less-favoured farming areas in Scotland" and with the number of the map, dated 2nd April 1984, signed by the Secretary of State for Scotland and deposited at the offices of the Department of Agriculture and Fisheries for Scotland at Chesser House, Gorgie Road, Edinburgh EH11 3AW;

(d) in relation to Northern Ireland, the map marked "map of less-favoured farming areas in Northern Ireland", dated 4th April 1984, signed by the Secretary of State for Northern Ireland and deposited at the offices of the Department of Agriculture for Northern Ireland at Dundonald House, Upper Newtownards Road, Belfast BT4 3SB;

"disadvantaged land" means land—

(a) which is, in the opinion of the appropriate Minister, inherently suitable for extensive livestock production but not for the production of crops in quantity materially greater than that necessary to feed such livestock as are capable of being maintained on such land, and

(b) whose agricultural production is, in the opinion of the appropriate Minister, restricted in its range by, or by any combination of, soil, relief, aspect or climate,

which land is within the area shaded blue or shaded pink on the designated maps;

"eligible land" means an area of land of not less than three hectares, being land—

(a) which is situated in an area included in the list of less-favoured farming areas adopted by the Council or the Commission of the European Communities under Article 2(2) of Council Directive No. 75/268/EEC on mountain and hill farming and farming in certain less-favoured areas (a) , and

(b) which is severely disadvantaged land or disadvantaged land;

"ECU" means the unit of account used for the purposes of the common agricultural structures policy of the European Economic Community, and any reference in these regulations to a specified number of ECU in relation to a compensatory allowance shall be taken to be a reference to the sterling equivalent of that number of ECU converted into sterling at the agricultural exchange rate applicable on the qualifying day in the year in which the compensatory allowance is paid;

"ewe" means a female sheep which, on the qualifying day, is more than one year old;

"hill sheep land" in relation to Scotland means severely disadvantaged land suitable for use for the maintenance of sheep of a hardy breed, but not of sheep of other breeds;

"occupier" includes a person who has a right to use eligible land for the purpose of grazing cattle or sheep;

"qualified flock" means a flock of ewes which is kept on eligible land, or on eligible land and other land used with it, for the breeding and rearing of lambs, and which is, in the opinion of the appropriate Minister, maintained and managed in accordance with sound husbandry practice;

"the qualifying day" means, in respect of any year in which a compensatory allowance may be paid under these regulations, 1st January in that year;

"regular breeding herd" means a herd of cattle which is kept on eligible land, or on eligible land and other land used with it, and which—

(a) has, on the qualifying day, been in existence for a period of at least six months,

(b) is, in the opinion of the appropriate Minister, maintained primarily for the purpose of breeding and rearing calves, and

(c) is, in the opinion of the appropriate Minister, reasonably constant in its composition and maintained and managed in accordance with sound husbandry practice;

"retirement pension" means—

(a) in relation to Great Britain, a category A and category B pension within the meaning of section 12(1)(f) of the Social Security Act 1975 (b) , and a category C and category D pension within the meaning of section 34(1)(e) of that Act;

(b) in relation to Northern Ireland, a category A and category B pension within the meaning of section 12(1)(f) of the Social Security (Northern Ireland) Act 1975 (c) , and a category C and category D pension within the meaning of section 34(1)(e) of that Act;

(a) O.J. No. L128, 19.5.1975, p.1. Council Directive 75/268/EEC was amended by Council Directive 80/666/EEC (O.J. No. L180, 14.7.1980, p. 34).
(b) 1975 c.14; section 12(1)(f) was amended by the Social Security Pension Act 1975 (c.60), Schedule 4, paragraph 37.
(c) 1975 c.15.

"severely disadvantaged land" means—
   (a) land—
      (i) which is, in the opinion of the appropriate Minister, inherently suitable for extensive livestock production but not for the production of crops in quantity materially greater than that necessary to feed such livestock as are capable of being maintained on such land, and
      (ii) whose agricultural production is, in the opinion of the appropriate Minister, severely restricted in its range by, or by any combination of, soil, relief, aspect or climate, or
   (b) land situated in the Isles of Scilly,
which land is within the area shaded pink on the designated maps;

"specially qualified flock" means a qualified flock in which all, or in the opinion of the appropriate Minister substantially all, of the ewes comprised in the flock are of an approved breed, and which—
   (a) in England, Wales and Northern Ireland is maintained on severely disadvantaged land or on severely disadvantaged land and other land used with it;
   (b) in Scotland is maintained or substantially maintained on hill sheep land.

(2) Where in Scotland any agricultural unit consists in part only of eligible land, that land or any part thereof shall be deemed for the purposes of these regulations not to be eligible land unless, in the opinion of the appropriate Minister, such land or such part thereof would be suitable to be dealt with as a separate unit which is capable, having regard to the number of other animals normally grazed thereon, of maintaining a regular breeding herd or a qualified flock.

Compensatory allowances

3.—(1) Subject to the provisions of these regulations, the appropriate Minister may, in respect of the year 1985 and each succeeding year, pay to any person who is on the qualifying day in that year the occupier of eligible land, a compensatory allowance for cattle and sheep maintained by him on that day, being cattle comprised in a regular breeding herd and sheep comprised in a qualified flock.

(2) Subject to regulations 3(4) and 4 below, a compensatory allowance for cattle shall be payable in respect of the number of breeding cows comprised in a herd on the qualifying day at the following rates—
   (a) in the case of cows maintained by a person whose only eligible land is severely disadvantaged land, £44.50 or 97 ECU per cow, whichever is the less;
   (b) in the case of cows maintained by a person whose eligible land comprises severely disadvantaged land and disadvantaged land—
      (i) £44.50 or 97 ECU per cow, whichever is the less, up to an amount calculated by multiplying the number of hectares of severely disadvantaged land available to that person in accordance with regulation 3(4)(a) below by £60 or 97 ECU, whichever is the less, and deducting from the resulting figure any allowances payable in respect of sheep maintained by that person under paragraph (3) below (other than such allowances payable at the rate of £2.12 or 14.55 ECU per ewe); and

(ii) thereafter £22.25 or 97 ECU per cow, whichever is the less;

(c) in the case of cows maintained by a person whose only eligible land is disadvantaged land, £22.25 or 97 ECU per cow, whichever is the less.

(3) Subject to regulations 3(4) and 5 below, a compensatory allowance for sheep shall be payable in respect of the number of ewes comprised in a flock on the qualifying day at the following rates—

(a) in the case of ewes of an approved breed comprised in a specially qualified flock, £6.25 or 14.55 ECU per ewe, whichever is the less;

(b) in the case of ewes not referred to in sub-paragraph (a) above maintained by a person—

(i) whose only eligible land is severely disadvantaged land, £4.25 or 14.55 ECU per ewe, whichever is the less;

(ii) whose eligible land comprises severely disadvantaged land and disadvantaged land, £4.25 or 14.55 ECU per ewe, whichever is the less, for a number of ewes calculated by multiplying the number of hectares of severely disadvantaged land available for the maintenance of the flock in accordance with regulation 5(2)(c) by 6, and thereafter for additional ewes £2.12 or 14.55 ECU per ewe, whichever is the less;

(iii) whose only eligible land is disadvantaged land, £2.12 or 14.55 ECU per ewe, whichever is the less.

(4) Notwithstanding the provisions of paragraphs (2) and (3) above, the total amount of a compensatory allowance which may be paid in respect of any year—

(a) to the occupier of severely disadvantaged land, shall not exceed £60, or 97 ECU, whichever is the less, for each hectare of such land which appears to the appropriate Minister to have been available to that occupier in the preceding year for the maintenance of his herd or flock;

(b) to the occupier of disadvantaged land, shall not exceed £45 or 97 ECU, whichever is the less, for each hectare of such land which appears to the appropriate Minister to have been available to that occupier in the preceding year for the maintenance of his herd or flock.

(5) A compensatory allowance in respect of any year shall only be paid to an occupier of eligible land if (except in the case of such an occupier who is in receipt of a retirement pension) he enters into a written undertaking in such form as the appropriate Minister may require to the effect that he will, for a period of five years from the qualifying day in that year, continue to use eligible land for agricultural purposes.

Provisions with respect to cattle

4.—(1) Subject to the following provisions of this regulation, where the appropriate Minister is of the opinion that the number of breeding cows comprised in a regular breeding herd on the qualifying day is greater or less than the number of breeding cows which he is satisfied has been the number normally comprised in that herd throughout the preceding year or, in the case of a herd newly established or re-established in that year, throughout such shorter period as the appropriate Minister may determine (including, as breeding cows for this purpose heifers which have become, or would in his opinion have become, breeding cows by that qualifying day), a compensatory allowance shall be payable in relation to that qualifying day in respect of the number of breeding cows which the appropriate Minister is satisfied is the number of breeding cows which has been normally so comprised in the herd.

(2) For the purposes of paragraph (1) above, the appropriate Minister may disregard any temporary reduction in numbers where he is satisfied that such reduction was or is due to deaths or disposals of cows, and that those cows have been or will be suitably replaced as soon as reasonably practicable.

(3) Where the appropriate Minister is satisfied that—

(a) the number of breeding cows comprised in a regular breeding herd on a qualifying day is less than the number normally comprised in that herd, and that the reduction is due to the slaughter of cows in the herd in the course of brucellosis eradication, and

(b) the person to whom a compensatory allowance in respect of that herd may be paid will make satisfactory arrangements for those animals to be suitably replaced in the herd as soon as reasonably practicable, and for repayment of any compensatory allowance paid in respect of any such animal in the event of its not being so replaced,

a compensatory allowance shall be payable in relation to that qualifying day in respect of such number of breeding cows as would, in the opinion of the appropriate Minister, have been comprised in that herd on that qualifying day had its numbers not been reduced by reason of such slaughter.

(4) Where, in the opinion of the appropriate Minister, an appreciable quantity of milk has been produced by a regular breeding herd in the period of 12 months immediately preceding the qualifying day, and such milk has been sold or used for the manufacture of milk products for sale, a compensatory allowance shall be payable in relation to that qualifying day in respect of the number of breeding cows comprised in the herd on that day, reduced by such number as appears to the appropriate Minister to be the number of cows in the herd required to produce that quantity of milk in that period.

(5) Notwithstanding the foregoing provisions of these regulations, the number of breeding cows in respect of which compensatory allowance may be paid in relation to any qualifying day shall not exceed either of the following numbers, that is to say—

(a) where the number of calves produced by the herd in the year preceding that day is, in the opinion of the appropriate Minister, unusually low for a herd of its size, such number of breeding cows as he considers to be reasonable, regard being had to the number of calves so produced; or

(b) the number of breeding cows which, in the opinion of the appropriate Minister, the land on which the herd was substantially grazed and maintained in the year preceding that day was capable of carrying without overgrazing it, taking into account the number of other animals grazed and maintained on that land in that year.

Provisions with respect to sheep

5.—(1) A compensatory allowance for sheep shall not be paid in respect of any ewe the use of which for breeding would not, in the opinion of the appropriate Minister, be in accordance with sound husbandry practice.

(2) Subject to paragraph (1) above, and notwithstanding the foregoing provisions of these regulations, the number of ewes in respect of which compensatory allowance may be paid in relation to any qualifying day may not exceed—

(a) the number of ewes which the appropriate Minister may determine as the number of ewes which he is satisfied has been comprised in the flock throughout the greater part of the year preceding that day or, in the case of a flock newly established or re-established in that year, throughout such shorter period thereof as the appropriate Minister may determine, disregarding—

   (i) any seasonal variation in number, and

   (ii) any losses which he is satisfied have been or will be made good, or cannot reasonably be made good, within a reasonable period;

(b) the number of ewes which, in the opinion of the appropriate Minister, is reasonable, having regard to the number of lambs produced in the year preceding the qualifying day;

(c) a number calculated at the rate of—

   (i) six ewes for each hectare of severely disadvantaged land, and

   (ii) nine ewes for each hectare of disadvantaged land,

   being land which the appropriate Minister is satisfied was available for the maintenance of the flock throughout the greater part of the year preceding that day, or throughout such shorter period of that year as is referred to in sub-paragraph (a) above; or

(d) the number of ewes which the appropriate Minister determines to be the number which the land on which the flock was substantially grazed and maintained in the year preceding that day was, in his opinion, capable of carrying without overgrazing, taking into account the number of other animals grazed and maintained on the land in that year.

Power of appropriate Minister to apportion eligible land in certain cases

6. Where is appears to the appropriate Minister that on the qualifying day in any year, or during the year immediately preceding that qualifying day, any land was available for the maintenance of—

(a) more than one regular breeding herd,

(b) more than one qualified flock, or

(c) breeding cows comprised in a regular breeding herd and ewes comprised in a qualified flock,

he may, for the purpose of determining any person's entitlement under the foregoing provisions of these regulations, apportion that land among the occupiers or former occupiers thereof as he thinks reasonable in the circumstances.

Applications for compensatory allowances

7.—(1) Payment of a compensatory allowance shall not be made unless an application for that payment has been submitted to the appropriate Minister in such form and at such time as he may require.

(2) If a person authorised by the appropriate Minister so requires, the herd or flock to which an application relates shall be gathered together at a convenient place for the purpose of counting and inspection, and such

documents or records as may be required by the appropriate Minister shall be produced for inspection in support of any application.

(3) In any counting of sheep, a reasonable allowance may be made for dead or ungathered animals.

Release from undertaking

8. A person in receipt of a compensatory allowance under these regulations shall be released from the undertaking referred to in regulation 3(5) above where—

(a) he ceases farming in accordance with the provisions of Article 2(1) of Council Directive No. 72/160/EEC concerning measures to encourage the cessation of farming and the re-allocation of utilised agricultural areas for the purposes of structural improvement (a);

(b) he is in receipt of a retirement pension; or

(c) he is prevented from continuing to discharge that undertaking by reason of—

(i) any material circumstances beyond his control, or

(ii) the compulsory purchase of his eligible land, or the eligible land used by him for the grazing of animals, or its purchase in the public interest.

Recovery of compensatory allowances

9. Where any person—

(a) with a view to obtaining payment to himself or to any other person of a compensatory allowance under these regulations makes any statement which is untrue or misleading in a material particular, or

(b) having given an undertaking under regulation 3(5) above, which has not been released in accordance with regulation 8 above, fails in any way to comply with the terms thereof, or

(c) fails to replace animals in accordance with regulation 4(2) or (3) above in respect of which a compensatory allowance has been paid under the provisions of these regulations, or

(d) being a person in receipt of a compensatory allowance under these regulations, fails to comply with a requirement by a person authorised by the appropriate Minister to gather a herd or flock for counting and inspection or to produce documents or records required by the appropriate Minister in accordance with regulation 7(2),

the appropriate Minister shall be entitled to recover on demand as a civil debt the whole or any part of any compensatory allowance paid to him or to such other person.

False statements

10. If any person for the purpose of obtaining for himself or any other person a compensatory allowance under these regulations knowingly or recklessly makes a false statement, he shall be liable on summary conviction to a fine not exceeding £1,000.

(a) O.J. No. L96, 23.4.72, p. 9.

Revocations

11. The regulations listed in the Schedule hereto are hereby revoked.

In Witness whereof the Official Seal of the Minister of Agriculture, Fisheries and Food is hereunto affixed on 20th December 1984.

Michael Jopling,
Minister of Agriculture, Fisheries
and Food.

George Younger,
One of Her Majesty's Principal
Secretaries of State.

20th December 1984.

SCHEDULE   Regulation 11

REVOCATIONS

Regulations revoked	References
The Hill Livestock (Compensatory Allowances) Regulations 1979	S.I. 1979/1748
The Hill Livestock (Compensatory Allowances) (Amendment) Regulations 1980	S.I. 1980/2028
The Hill Livestock (Compensatory Allowances) (Amendment) Regulations 1981	S.I. 1981/1843
The Hill Livestock (Compensatory Allowances) (Amendment) Regulations 1982	S.I. 1982/1886

EXPLANATORY NOTE

(This Note is not part of the Regulations.)

These regulations, which apply throughout the United Kingdom, consolidate with amendments the Hill Livestock (Compensatory Allowances) Regulations 1979, (as amended), which implemented part of Council Directive 75/268/EEC on mountain and hill farming and farming in certain less favoured areas (O.J. No. L128, 19.5.75, p. 1), as amended by Council Directive 80/666/EEC (O.J. No. L180, 14.7.80, p. 34). The main provisions of the regulations are as follows—

Provision continues to be made for the payment of an annual compensatory allowance for cattle and sheep maintained by the occupier of "eligible land". Eligible land is defined by reference to land in a less favoured farming area included in the list of such areas adopted under Article 2 of Council Directive 75/268/EEC (the full list of less favoured farming areas is contained in Council Directive No. 84/169/EEC (O.J. No. L82, 26.3.84, p. 67)), which is "severely disadvantaged land" or "disadvantaged land" (as defined in the regulations). Severely disadvantaged land and disadvantaged land must be respectively within the area shaded pink, or within the area shaded blue or pink on designated maps referred to in the regulations. (Severely disadvantaged land corresponds to eligible land under the previous regulations, but the regulations have not previously applied to disadvantaged land (regulations 2(1) and 3(1)).)

The existing rates of allowance (£44.50 per cow, £6.25 per ewe in a specially qualified flock or £4.25 for other ewes) are payable for eligible animals kept on severely disadvantaged land, subject to an overall financial limit of £60 per hectare of land available for the herd or flock and a stocking limit of 6 ewes per hectare of such land. For eligible animals kept on disadvantaged land, allowances are introduced at a rate of £22.25 per cow and £2.12 per ewe, subject to an overall financial limit of £45 per hectare of available land a stocking limit of 9 ewes per hectare of such land. Where both severely disadvantaged and disadvantaged land is occupied, provisions are made for allocating allowances at the higher and lower rates among the cows and ewes maintained on the two categories of land (regulation 3(2)–(4)). Further provisions affecting the number of cattle and sheep in respect of which an allowance may be paid are set out in regulations 4 and 5.

Knowingly or recklessly making a false statement for the purpose of obtaining an allowance is now punishable on summary conviction by a maximum fine of £1,000 (regulation 10).

The designated maps referred to in these regulations are available for inspection during normal office hours at the addresses specified in the definition of "designated maps" (regulation 2(1)). Copies of the maps may be inspected during normal office hours at any Regional or Divisional Office of the Ministry of Agriculture, Fisheries and Food, at the Welsh Office Agriculture Department at Plas Crug, Aberystwyth or any of its Divisional Offices, at any Area Office of the Department of Agriculture and Fisheries for Scotland or at any County Agricultural Executive Office or selected Area Offices of the Department of Agriculture for Northern Ireland.

STATUTORY INSTRUMENTS

1984 No. 2028 (S. 159)

EDUCATION, SCOTLAND

The Teachers' Superannuation (Scotland) Amendment Regulations 1984

Made - - - -	*17th December* 1984
Laid before Parliament	*14th January* 1985
Coming into Operation	*4th February* 1985

In exercise of the powers conferred on me by sections 9 and 12 of the Superannuation Act 1972 (**a**) and of all other powers enabling me in that behalf, after consulting with representatives of education authorities and of teachers and with such representatives of other persons likely to be affected as appear to me to be appropriate in accordance with section 9(5) of the said Act and with the consent of the Treasury (**b**), I hereby make the following regulations:—

Citation and commencement

1.—(1) These regulations may be cited as the Teachers' Superannuation (Scotland) Amendment Regulations 1984, and the Teachers' Superannuation (Scotland) Regulations 1977 to 1980 (**c**) , Part V of the Teachers' Superannuation (War Service, Etc.) (Scotland) Regulations 1983 (**d**), the Teachers' Superannuation (Scotland) Amendment Regulations 1983 (**e**) and these regulations may be cited together as the Teachers' Superannuation (Scotland) Regulations 1977 to 1984.

(2) These regulations shall come into operation on 4th February 1985 and shall have effect—

(a) for the purposes of regulations 5 and 11 as from 7th September 1977;

(b) for all other purposes as from 4th February 1985.

Interpretation

2. In these regulations a reference to "the principal regulations" is a reference to the Teachers' Superannuation (Scotland) Regulations 1977 (**f**) .

Definitions

3. In regulation 3 of the principal regulations in the definition of "child" after the words "disqualifying income;" there shall be inserted the words "or a person who has not attained the age of 19 and who is not engaged in remunerative full-time work and who is not entitled to supplementary benefit by reason that he is treated as receiving relevant education for the purposes of section 6(2) of the Supplementary Benefits Act 1976 (**g**) ;".

(**a**) 1972 c.11.
(**b**) The function was transferred to the Treasury by S.I. 1981/1670.
(**c**) S.I. 1977/1360, 1808, 1978/1507, 1980/344.
(**d**) S.I. 1983/639.
(**e**) S.I. 1983/1431.
(**f**) S.I. 1977/1360, amended by S.I. 1977/1808, 1978/1507, 1980/344, 1983/639, 1431.
(**g**) 1976 c.71; section 6(2) was amended by section 6(1) of and Part I of Schedule 2 to, the Social Security Act 1980 (c.30).

Reckonable service

4. In regulation 4(1) of the principal regulations sub-paragraph *(f)* shall be deleted and sub-paragraph *(g)* shall be renumbered *"(f)"*.

Pensionable salary

5. In regulation 8(5) of the principal regulations in the definition of "salary" there shall be inserted after the word " "salary" " the following words:—

"in relation to a teacher whose salary is reduced during absence on sick or maternity leave means salary at the annual rate at which it would have been paid but for such reduction, and".

Calculation where reckonable service is less than 20 years

6. In regulation 50*(c)* of the principal regulations after the figure "60" there shall be inserted the following words:—

"or ceases to be employed in reckonable service in such circumstances as regulation 46(2)*(c)* applies".

Allocation of annual pension

7. After regulation 53(7) of the principal regulations there shall be inserted the following paragraph:—

"(8) Where a teacher, having given notice of his intention to retire within four months, delivers a declaration under this regulation to the Secretary of State on or after 4th February 1985 and thereafter the annual pension to which the declaration refers is increased, apart from an increase under the Pensions Increase Act 1971 **(a)**, the amount allocated shall be increased by the same proportion as the increase in the annual pension bears to the former amount of the pension, the result being rounded down to the nearest pound; and the amount of the pension payable to the teacher shall be reduced by the amount of the increased allocation and, in the case falling within paragraph (1)*(b)*, the rate of annuity there mentioned shall be increased to take account of the increase in the amount allocated as from the date on which the increase in the pension takes effect; and on the subsequent death of the teacher the amount of the pension payable in accordance with his declaration shall similarly be increased.".

Death gratuities

8.—(1) In regulation 57(1) of the principal regulations for the words "personal representatives" there shall be substituted the words "spouse, whom failing, to the legal personal representatives".

(2) In regulation 57(2) of the principal regulations for the words "personal representatives" there shall be substituted the words "spouse, whom failing, to the legal personal representatives".

Commutation of benefits

9.—(1) In paragraphs (1) and (2) of regulation 84A of the principal regulations the words "or family pension" shall be deleted.

(2) After regulation 84A(2) of the principal regulations there shall be inserted the following paragraph:—

(a) 1971 c.56.

"(3) Where a family pension, payable under these regulations, is an annual sum of an amount not exceeding £104 the Secretary of State may discharge his liability in respect thereof by the payment of a lump sum representing the capital value of that annual sum.".

Payments in respect of deceased persons

10. In regulation 85 of the principal regulations for the sum of "£1,500" there shall be substituted the sum of "£5,000".

Short-term pensions

11. In Tables 1 and 2 of Schedule 7 to the principal regulations in end columns "Rate of pension (all categories)" and "Rate of pension" respectively there shall be inserted after the words "reckonable service" the words—

"or, where on that date the teacher was absent on sick or maternity leave and the teacher's salary was in consequence reduced, at the annual rate at which it would have been payable but for such reduction".

Modification relating to National Insurance

12.—(1) In paragraph 13*(a)* of Schedule 12 to the principal regulations for the words "employed in" there shall be substituted the words "retired from".

(2) After paragraph 13*(b)* of the said Schedule 12 for the words "such service as aforesaid" there shall be substituted the words "reckonable service".

Revocations

13. The provisions of the enactments set out in columns (1) and (2) of the Schedule to these regulations are revoked to the extent indicated in column (3).

Right to opt out

14. No provision of these regulations shall apply to any person to whom at any time before 4th February 1985 any benefit including a return of contributions was or may become payable if—

(a) he is placed by that provision in a worse position than he would have been in if it had not applied in relation to that benefit; and

(b) that provision relates to a benefit paid or payable in respect of a person who—

(i) ceased before 4th February 1985 to be in reckonable service; or

(ii) died before that date while employed in reckonable service; and

(c) the person first mentioned in this regulation elects by giving notice in writing to the Secretary of State within 6 months after 4th February 1985, that the provision shall not apply to him.

George Younger,
One of Her Majesty's Principal
Secretaries of State.

New St Andrew's House, Edinburgh.
12th December 1984.

We consent,

John Major,
A. G. Hamilton,
Two of the Lords Commissioners of
Her Majesty's Treasury.

17th December 1984.

SCHEDULE

REVOCATIONS

Column 1 Legislation revoked	Column 2 References	Column 3 Extent of revocation
The Teachers' Pensions (National Service) (Scotland) Rules 1952.	S.I. 1952/518.	The whole instrument.
Teachers' Superannuation (Scotland) Act 1968.	1968 c.12.	Section 13.

EXPLANATORY NOTE

(This Note is not part of the Regulations.)

These regulations amend the Teachers' Superannuation Regulations 1977. In so far as they do so with retrospective effect, this is authorised by section 12(1) of the Superannuation Act 1972. In addition to certain corrections and clarification, the following changes are made.

The definition of "child" in regulation 3 of the 1977 Regulations is amended to permit the extended payment of child pensions to school leavers up to the date on which they become entitled to claim supplementary benefit (regulation 3).

The reference to the Teachers' Pensions (National Service) (Scotland) Rules 1952 in regulation 4(1)*(f)* of the 1977 Regulations is removed as these provisions are spent (regulations 4 and 13).

Regulation 8(5) and Tables 1 and 2 of Schedule 7 of the 1977 Regulations are amended to require the "pensionable salary" of a teacher for superannuation purposes and the rate of a short term pension to be based on full salary without any deduction to reflect a deduction in that salary during sick or maternity leave (regulations 5 and 11).

Regulation 50*(c)* of the 1977 Regulations is amended to take account of premature retirement for the purposes of calculating awards where reckonable service is less than 20 years (regulation 6).

Regulation 53 of the 1977 Regulations enables a teacher to allocate a portion of the annual allowance payable on his retirement to provide benefits for his widow or other dependant. Provision is made for the amount of allocation to be automatically increased in line with any increase (except an increase under the Pensions (Increase) Act 1971) in the amount of the allowance, with a corresponding increase in the amount of the benefits payable (regulation 7).

Regulation 57 of the 1977 Regulations is amended to clarify the position that where a death gratuity is payable it is paid first to a surviving spouse (where the marriage was extant at date of death) or the legal personal representative(s) where there is no spouse (regulation 8).

Regulation 84A of the 1977 Regulations is amended to increase the commutation level on personal benefits and to distinguish between personal and family benefits (regulation 9).

Regulation 85 of the 1977 Regulations permits payment to be made, without probate or other proof of title, of any sum due under those regulations not exceeding £1,500. This figure is increased to £5,000 in relation to deaths occurring after 4th February 1985 (regulation 10). This increase is in accordance with the provisions of the Administration of Estates (Small Payments)(Increase of Limit) Order 1984 (S.I. 1984/539).

Schedule 12 to the 1977 Regulations is revised to cover the situation of bare equivalent pension benefits (regulation 12).

Section 13 of the Teachers' Superannuation (Scotland) Act 1968 is revoked; this power to pay deferred annuities is superseded by the provisions of the Superannuation Act 1972 (regulation 13).

STATUTORY INSTRUMENTS

1984 No. 2029 (S.160)

POLICE

The Police Cadets (Scotland) Amendment Regulations 1984

Made - - - -	20th December 1984
Laid before Parliament	10th January 1985
Coming into Operation	31st January 1985

In exercise of the powers conferred on me by section 27 of the Police (Scotland) Act 1967(a), and of all other powers enabling me in that behalf, and after taking into consideration the recommendations made by the Police Negotiating Board for the United Kingdom and furnishing the said Board with a draft of the regulations in accordance with section 2(1) of the Police Negotiating Board Act 1980(b), I hereby make the following regulations:—

Citation

1. These regulations may be cited as the Police Cadets (Scotland) Amendment Regulations 1984.

Interpretation

2. In these regulations any reference to "the principal regulations" is a reference to the Police Cadets (Scotland) Regulations 1968(c).

Operation and effect

3. These regulations shall come into operation on 31st January 1985 and shall have effect—

(a) for the purposes of regulations 4, 7, 8 and 9(b), as from 31st January 1985;

(b) for the purposes of regulation 5, as from 25th October 1984;

(c) for the purposes of regulations 6 and 9(a), as from 1st September 1984.

Amendments

4. For paragraphs (1) and (1A) of regulation 16 of the principal regulations (Uniform and equipment) there shall be substituted the following paragraph:—

"(1) Subject to the following provisions of this regulation, the police authority shall supply a police cadet with 2 pairs of boots or shoes annually for the purposes of normal duty and with such other items of uniform and equipment as are requisite in his case, and shall provide for the dry cleaning of uniform and the repair of footwear.".

5. In paragraph (1B) of regulation 16 of the principal regulations, for the sum "£22" there shall be substituted the sum "£25".

(a) 1967 c.77.　　　　　　　　　(b) 1980 c.10.
(c) S.I. 1968/208; the relevant amending instruments are S.I. 1972/778, 1974/1248, 1977/1131, and 1983/1368.

6. For the Table in Schedule 1 to the principal regulations (which contains scales of pay) there shall be substituted the following table:—

"
                                    TABLE

Age	Annual Pay
Under 17 years	£2,646
17 years	£2,805
18 years or over	£3,123

."

7. In Schedule 2 to the principal regulations (which relates to charges for board and lodging), for the sum "£354" there shall be substituted the sum "£369".

Revocations

8. Regulation 5(1) of the Police Cadets (Scotland) Amendment Regulations 1974 (**a**) and regulation 5 of the Police Cadets (Scotland) Amendment Regulations 1977 (**b**) (which relate to the footwear allowance) are hereby revoked.

9. The following regulations of the Police Cadets (Scotland) Amendment (No. 2) Regulations 1983 (**c**) are hereby revoked:—

(*a*) regulation 4 (which relates to scales of pay) and

(*b*) regulation 5 (which relates to charges for board and lodging).

George Younger,
One of Her Majesty's Principal
Secretaries of State.

New St Andrew's House,
Edinburgh.
20th December 1984.

(**a**) S.I. 1974/1248.   (**b**) S.I. 1977/1131.
(**c**) S.I. 1983/1368.

EXPLANATORY NOTE

(This Note is not part of the Regulations.)

These regulations further amend the Police Cadets (Scotland) Regulations 1968.

Regulation 4 amends regulation 16 of the 1968 Regulations, with effect from 31st January 1985, so as to provide for the issue of footwear to all cadets and for the withdrawal of the footwear allowance.

Regulation 5 increases the stockings allowance for woman police cadets from £22 per year to £25 per year with effect from 25th October 1984.

Regulation 6 increases the pay of police cadets with effect from 1st September 1984. The retrospective effect of these regulations is authorised by section 27(2) of the Police (Scotland) Act 1967.

Regulation 7 increases the charges payable by cadets for board and lodging provided by police authorities from £354 per annum to £369 per annum with effect from 31st January 1985.

STATUTORY INSTRUMENTS

1984 No. 2031

RESTRICTIVE TRADE PRACTICES

The Restrictive Trade Practices (Approval of Standards and Arrangements) Order 1984

Made -   -   -   -   21st *December* 1984
Coming into Operation   15th *January* 1985

Whereas section 9(5) of the Restrictive Trade Practices Act 1976(a) ("the Act") provides for the approval by the Secretary of State of standards of dimension, design, quality or performance or of arrangements as to the provision of information or advice to purchasers, consumers or users prescribed or adopted by any trade association or other body:

Now, therefore, the Secretary of State in exercise of the powers conferred on him by section 9(5) of the Act hereby makes the following Order:—

1. This Order may be cited as the Restrictive Trade Practices (Approval of Standards and Arrangements) Order 1984 and shall come into operation on 15th January 1985.

2. The Secretary of State hereby approves the standards and arrangements specified in the Schedule hereto.

Eric Wright,
An Under Secretary of the
Department of Trade and Industry.

21st December 1984.

SCHEDULE

Standards of dimension, design, quality or performance and arrangements as to the provision of information or advice to purchasers, consumers or users, contained in Decision XV–7 (as amended by Decision XVI–4) taken pursuant to the Convention for the Reciprocal Recognition of Proof Marks for Small Arms(b) done at Brussels on 1st July 1969 by the Permanent International Commission for the Reciprocal Recognition of Proof Marks for Small Arms.

The standards and arrangements were adopted by the Worshipful Company of Gunmakers on 1st March 1983 and by the Birmingham Gun Barrel Proof House on 24th February 1983.

(a) 1976 c. 34.   (b) Cmnd. 5942.

EXPLANATORY NOTE

(This Note is not part of the Order.)

This Order is made under section 9(5) of the Restrictive Trade Practices Act 1976. This provides for certain terms in an agreement to be disregarded in deciding whether the Act applies to the agreement. The terms to be disregarded are those by which the parties to the agreement (e.g. manufacturers or suppliers of goods) agree to comply with—

(a) standards of dimension, design, quality or performance; or

(b) arrangements as to the provision of information or advice to purchasers, consumers or users.

Such standards or arrangements, unless approved by the British Standards Institution, must have been prescribed or adopted by a trade association or other body and must be approved by order of the Secretary of State made by statutory instrument.

By this Order, the Secretary of State approves the standards and arrangements contained in Decision XV–7 (as amended by Decision XVI–4) taken pursuant to the Convention for the Reciprocal Recognition of Proof Marks for Small Arms done at Brussels on 1st July 1969 by the Permanent International Commission for the Reciprocal Recognition of Proof Marks for Small Arms.

The effect of the Order is thus to allow manufacturers and suppliers of commercial ammunition to agree to comply with these standards and arrangements without the agreement needing to be registered under the Act and investigated by the Restrictive Practices Court.

Copies of the Decisions containing the standards and arrangements are available for public inspection during working hours and without payment at the offices of the Worshipful Company of Gunmakers, The London Proof House, 48–50 Commercial Road, London E1 1LP and the Birmingham Gun Barrel Proof House, Banbury Street, Birmingham B5 5RH.

Copies of the Decisions may be obtained from either address.

STATUTORY INSTRUMENTS

1984 No. 2034

SOCIAL SECURITY

The Supplementary Benefit (Requirements) Amendment and Temporary Provisions Regulations 1984

Laid before Parliament in draft

Made - - - - - - - -	*20th December* 1984

Coming into operation in accordance with regulation 1(1)

The Secretary of State for Social Services, with the consent of the Treasury(a), in pursuance of paragraph 2 of Schedule 1 to the Supplementary Benefits Act 1976(b) and in the exercise of powers conferred by sections 2(1A) and (2), 33(5) and 34(1)(c) of that Act and sub-paragraphs (1), (3) and (4) of that paragraph and of all other powers enabling him in that behalf, after agreement by the Social Security Advisory Committee that proposals to make these regulations should not be referred to it(d), hereby makes the following regulations of which a draft has, in accordance with section 33(3) of that Act, been laid before Parliament and approved by resolution of each House of Parliament:—

Citation, commencement and interpretation

1.—(1) These regulations may be cited as the Supplementary Benefit (Requirements) Amendment and Temporary Provisions Regulations 1984 and shall come into operation forthwith.

(2) In these regulations the "1983 Regulations" means the Supplementary Benefit (Requirements) Regulations 1983(e) and expressions used in regulation 3 of these regulations which are also used in the 1983 Regulations shall have the same meaning as in the 1983 Regulations.

(a) *See* section 33(3) of the Supplementary Benefits Act 1976 (c. 71).

(b) 1976 c. 71, as amended by section 6(1) of and Part I of Schedule 2 to the Social Security Act 1980 (c. 30) and section 25 of and Part III of Schedule 8 to the Health and Social Services and Social Security Adjudications Act 1983 (c. 41).

(c) *See* the definitions of "prescribed" and "regulations".

(d) *See* section 10(1) of the Social Security Act 1980.

(e) S.I. 1983/1399; the relevant amending instruments are S.I. 1984/282, 1102.

Amendment of the 1983 *Regulations*

2.—(1) The 1983 Regulations shall be amended in accordance with the following provisions of this regulation.

(2) In regulation 2(1) (interpretation) in the definition of "qualifying benefit" for the words "or non-contributory invalidity pension" there shall be substituted the words "non-contributory invalidity pension or severe disablement allowance".

(3) In regulation 9(8) (modification of normal requirements of boarders) for "£30.70" there shall be substituted "£32.30".

(4) In regulation 22(5)(*h*)**(a)** (reduction in amounts applicable for certain occupants of the home) for the words "non-contributory invalidity pension" there shall be substituted the words "non-contributory invalidity pension or severe disablement allowance" and for the words "a pension" there shall be substituted the words "a pension or an allowance".

Temporary provisions as to boarders

3.—(1) Until 1st May 1985 the maximum amount in respect of the assessment unit as a whole referred to in paragraph (1)(*a*) of regulation 9 (modification of normal requirements of boarders) of the 1983 Regulations shall be an amount ascertained in accordance with the following provisions of this regulation; and until that date—

   (*a*) those provisions shall accordingly apply in place of the provisions contained in paragraph (6) of that regulation; and

   (*b*) any reference in the 1983 Regulations to regulation 9 or 9(6) of those regulations shall accordingly be construed and have effect as if the following provisions of this regulation had been substituted for the said regulation 9(6).

(2) Subject to paragraphs (7) and (16) of regulation 9 of the 1983 Regulations the maximum amount in respect of the assessment unit as a whole referred to in paragraph (1)(*a*) of that regulation shall be the aggregate of the following amounts—

   (*a*) in respect of each member of the assessment unit who is a dependent aged less than 11, $1\frac{1}{2}$ times the amount referred to in paragraph (5)(*c*) of that regulation; and

   (*b*) in respect of each other member of the assessment unit, an amount determined under paragraph (3) below as appropriate in respect of the weekly charge in the relevant area for full board and lodging of a standard suitable for a claimant resident in the type of accommodation provided for the claimant in that assessment unit.

(a) Added by regulation 2(12)(*c*) of the Supplementary Benefit (Requirements and Resources) Amendment Regulations 1984.

(3) Any question as to the amount appropriate for the purposes of paragraph (2)(*b*) above shall be determined by the Secretary of State in his discretion; and his decision of such a question—

(*a*) may be given either generally or in relation to a particular case;

(*b*) may be revised from time to time as he considers desirable;

(*c*) if it is not given in relation to a particular case—

(i) may make different provision for different cases or classes of case or otherwise for different circumstances;

(ii) shall be published in such form as he considers suitable; and

(*d*) shall be conclusive for the purposes of regulation 9 of the 1983 Regulations.

Signed by authority of the Secretary of State for Social Services

Tony Newton,
Minister of State,
Department of Health and Social Security.
19th December 1984.

We consent,

Ian B. Lang,
A. G. Hamilton,
Two of the Lords Commissioners
of Her Majesty's Treasury.
20th December 1984.

EXPLANATORY NOTE

(*This Note is not part of the Regulations.*)

These regulations amend the Supplementary Benefit (Requirements) Regulations 1983 ("1983 Regulations") by suspending the provisions of regulation 9(6) on a temporary basis and providing, amongst other things, that until 1st May 1985 the board and lodging maximum in respect of persons over 11 years of age which is, under the suspended provisions, an amount estimated by an adjudication officer to be a reasonable charge for the relevant area, shall instead be an appropriate amount determined by the Secretary of State. The regulations also make minor amendments consequent upon the introduction of severe disablement allowance by the Health and Social Security Act 1984 (c. 48) and increase the amount specified in regulation 9(8) of the 1983 Regulations to £32.30.

STATUTORY INSTRUMENTS

1984 No. 2035

MENTAL HEALTH

The Court of Protection Rules 1984

Made - - - -	*18th December* 1984
Laid before Parliament	*10th January* 1985
Coming into Operation	*1st February* 1985

ARRANGEMENT OF RULES

PART I

PRELIMINARY

PART II

EXERCISE OF JURISDICTION

PART III

APPLICATIONS

PART IV

SERVICE

PART V

EVIDENCE

PART VI

HEARING OF PROCEEDINGS

PART VII

RECEIVERS

PART VIII

ENTRY AND ENFORCEMENT OF ORDERS

PART IX

SUMMONSES AND ORDERS FOR ATTENDANCE OF WITNESSES AND OTHER PERSONS

47. Summoning of witnesses.
48. Powers of court where undue delay, etc.
49. Order for examination of patient.

PART X

AMENDMENT

50. Amendment of application.
51. Clerical mistakes and slips.
52. Endorsements of amendment.

PART XI

APPEALS

53. Appeal from Master or nominated officer.
54. Appeal from order not made on appointment for a hearing.

PART XII

SECURITY

55. Receiver to give security.
56. Manner of giving security.
57. Lodgment of security.
58. Discharge of security where new security given.
59. Maintenance of security by bond.

PART XIII

ACCOUNTS

60. Passing of accounts.
61. Application of balance due from receiver.
62. Default by receiver.
63. Payment of maintenance and costs.
64. Final accounts.
65. Accounting by other persons.

PART XIV

INQUIRIES

PART XV

CUSTODY AND DISPOSAL OF FUNDS AND OTHER PROPERTY

PART XVI

SETTLEMENT AND APPROVAL OF DEEDS

PART XVII

COPIES OF DOCUMENTS

PART XVIII

FEES

PART XIX

COSTS

PART XX

REVOCATION

The Lord Chancellor, in exercise of the powers conferred on him by sections 106, 107 and 108 of the Mental Health Act 1983(a) and section 54 of the Trustee Act 1925(b) and with the consent of the Treasury so far as is required by section 106(5) of the said Act of 1983, hereby makes the following Rules:—

PART I

PRELIMINARY

Citation and commencement

1. These Rules may be cited as the Court of Protection Rules 1984 and shall come into operation on 1st February 1985.

Interpretation

2.— (1) In these Rules, unless the context otherwise requires—

expressions used in the Supreme Court Act 1981(c) shall have the same meaning as they have for the purposes of that Act;

"the Act" means the Mental Health Act 1983;

"court" means the Court of Protection;

"entered" means entered in the books of the Court of Protection;

"filed" means filed in the court office;

"judge" means the Lord Chancellor or a nominated judge;

"Master" means the Master of the Court of Protection;

"officer of the court" means an officer of the Court of Protection;

"order" includes a certificate, direction or authority under seal;

"patient" includes a person who is alleged to be or who the court has reason to believe may be incapable by reason of mental disorder of managing and administering the property and affairs;

"receiver" means a receiver appointed under section 99(1) of the Act;

"seal" means an official seal of the Court of Protection and "sealed" shall be construed accordingly;

"stock" includes shares and also any fund, annuity or security transferable in the books kept by any body corporate or unincorporated company or society, or by an instrument of transfer either alone or accompanied by other formalities and "dividends" shall be construed accordingly;

"Visitor" means one of the Lord Chancellor's Visitors.

(2) Where any discretion, power or other function is (in whatever words) expressed by these Rules to be exercisable by "the court" then subject to the provisions of the Act, that discretion, power or other function may be exercised—

(a) 1983 c. 20.
(b) 1925 c. 19; section 54 was substituted by the Mental Health Act 1959 (c.72), Schedule 7.
(c) 1981 c. 54.

(a) by a judge;

(b) by the Master;

(c) to the extent to which he is authorised to exercise it by and under section 94 of the Act, by any nominated officer.

(3) In these Rules a form referred to by letter means the form so designated in the Schedule 1 to these Rules or a form to the like effect with such variations as the circumstances may require or the court may approve.

Computation of time

3.— (1) Where the time limited by these Rules or any order or direction of the court for doing any act or taking any proceedings is less than six days, Saturday, Sunday, Christmas Day, Good Friday, Tuesday in Easter Week, any bank holiday or day appointed for public thanksgiving or mourning and any other day on which the court office is closed shall not be included in the computation of that time.

(2) Where the time so limited expires on a day on which the court office is closed and by reason thereof the act or proceeding cannot be done or taken on that day, the act or proceeding shall be in time if done or taken on the next day on which the court office is open.

(3) Where the time so limited is a particular number of days not expressed to be clear days, it shall be reckoned exclusively of the first day and inclusively of the last day.

Power to vary time

4. The court may extend or abridge the time limited by these Rules or any order or direction of the court for doing any act or taking any proceeding upon such terms as the court thinks fit and notwithstanding, in the case of an extension, that the time so limited has expired.

PART II

EXERCISE OF JURISDICTION

Exercise of jurisdiction

5. Except where these Rules otherwise provide, the jurisdiction of the court may be exercised—

(a) without fixing an appointment for a hearing;

(b) by the court of its own motion or at the instance or on the application of any person interested;

(c) whether or not any proceedings have been commenced in the court with respect to the patient.

PART III

APPLICATIONS

Forms of application

6.— (1) Subject to the following provisions of this rule, a first application to the court for the appointment of a receiver shall be in Form A and an application to the court respecting the exercise of any of its other jurisdiction in relation to a patient may be by letter unless the court directs that a formal application shall be made, in which case it shall be made in Form B.

(2) On grounds of urgency the court may dispense with the need for an application in writing.

(3) An application relating to the committal of a person for contempt of court shall be made to a judge by motion.

Short procedure

7.— (1) Without prejudice to the generality of rule 5, if it appears to the court that—

    (a) the property of the patient does not exceed £5,000 in value; or

    (b) it is otherwise appropriate to proceed under this rule,

and that it is not necessary to appoint a receiver for the patient, the court may make an order under this rule whether or not an application has been made for the appointment of a receiver for the patient.

(2) An order under this rule is an order directing an officer of the court or some other suitable person named in the order to deal with the patient's property, or any part thereof, or with his affairs, in any manner authorised by the Act and specified in the order.

Date for hearing

8.— (1) Upon receiving an application under rule 6 the court shall fix a date for the hearing of the application unless it considers that the application can properly be dealt with without a hearing, and upon the same ground the court may cancel any hearing fixed under this paragraph.

(2) Where a hearing is fixed under paragraph (1) an officer of the court shall endorse the date and time thereof on the application form, shall seal it and shall retain a copy.

Consolidation of proceedings

9. The court may allow one application to be made in respect of two or more patients or may consolidate applications relating to two or more patients, if in the opinion of the court the proceedings relating to them can be more conveniently dealt with together.

Power to direct application by officer of court or Official Solicitor

10. Where in the opinion of the court an application ought to be made for the appointment or discharge of a receiver or for the exercise of any other power conferred on the court with respect to the property and affairs of a patient, and there appears to the court to be no other suitable person able and willing to make the application, or the court for any other reason thinks fit, the court may direct that the application be made by an officer of the court or, if he consents, by the Official Solicitor.

Representation of patient by receiver

11.— (1) An application on behalf of a patient for whom a receiver has been appointed shall, unless the court otherwise directs, be made by the receiver in his own name.

(2) Subject to any directions given by the court, a patient for whom a receiver has been appointed may be represented by the receiver at any hearing relating to the patient or of which the patient has been given notice.

Representation of patient by Official Solicitor

12. Where in any proceedings the court considers that the interests of a patient for whom a receiver has been appointed are not adequately represented by the receiver, the court may if he consents direct that the Official Solicitor shall act as solicitor for the patient either generally in the proceedings or for any particular purpose connected with the proceedings, so, however, that it shall not be necessary to appoint the Official Solicitor to be receiver or guardian ad litem for the patient.

Persons under disability

13.— (1) In this rule "person under disability" means a minor or a patient for whom no receiver has been appointed.

(2) A person under disability shall not make an application in proceedings relating to another person except by his next friend and shall not resist, or attend the hearing of, an application in any such proceedings except by his guardian ad litem.

(3) Where a person is to be appointed next friend or guardian ad litem of a person under disability in substitution for the person previously acting as next friend or guardian ad litem, the appointment shall be made by the court but, except as aforesaid, an order of the court appointing a next friend or guardian ad litem of a person under disability shall not be necessary.

(4) Before the name of any person is used in any proceedings as next friend or guardian ad litem of a person under disability there shall be filed—

   (a) a written consent of the first-mentioned person to act as next friend or guardian ad litem, as the case may be, of the person under disability in the proceedings, and

   (b) a certificate by the solicitor acting for the person under disability certifying—

   (i) that he knows or believes that the person to whom the certificate relates is a minor or patient giving (in the case of a patient) the grounds of his knowledge or belief, and

(ii) except where the person named in the certificate as next friend or guardian ad litem is the Official Solicitor, that the person so named has no interest in the proceedings adverse to that of the person under disability.

Application under section 54 of the Trustee Act 1925

14. An application to the court with respect to the jurisdiction referred to in section 54(2) of the Trustee Act 1925 may be made only by—

(a) the receiver for the patient, or

(b) any person who has made an application for the appointment of a receiver which has not yet been determined, or

(c) a continuing trustee, or

(d) any other person who, according to the practice of the Chancery Division, would have been entitled to make the application if it had been made to the High Court.

Application under section 36(9) of the Trustee Act 1925

15. No application may be made to the court under section 36(9) of the Trusee Act 1925 for leave to appoint a new trustee in place of a patient unless the person intending to make the appointment is an applicant.

Application under section 96(1)(k) of the Act

16. The provisions of rule 14 shall apply with such modifications as may be necessary to an application under section 96(1)(k) of the Act for an order for the exercise of any power vested in a patient of appointing trustees or retiring from a trust.

Application for settlement or gift of patient's property or for execution of will of patient

17. An application under section 96(1)(d) of the Act for an order for the settlement or gift of any property of a patient, or an application under section 96(1)(e) of the Act for an order for execution for a patient of a will, may be made only by—

(a) the receiver for the patient, or

(b) any person who has made an application for the appointment of a receiver which has not yet been determined, or

(c) any person who, under any known will of the patient or under his intestacy, may become entitled to any property of the patient or any interest therein, or

(d) any person for whom the patient might be expected to provide if he were not mentally disordered, or

(e) any other person whom the court may authorise to make it.

was effected shall be filed as soon as practicable after service of a document has been effected in accordance with these Rules.

(2) The court may if it thinks fit order that instead of, or in addition to, a certificate of service, an affidavit of service shall be filed.

(3) The provisions of paragraphs (1) and (2) of this rule shall apply to the giving of notification under rule 23 as they apply to the service of documents and references in paragraphs (1) and (2) to service and the effecting of service shall accordingly be construed as including references to notification and the giving of notification respectively.

PART V

EVIDENCE

Affidavit evidence

25.— (1) Except where these Rules otherwise provide, evidence in proceedings under these Rules shall be given by affidavit.

(2) An affidavit for use in proceedings under these Rules may be sworn—

(a) in England or Wales, before any person authorised to take affidavits under the Commissioners for Oaths Acts 1889 and 1891(a) or under the Solicitors Act 1974(b) or before any officer of the court of, or above, the rank of higher executive officer;

(b) outside England and Wales, before any person before whom an affidavit may be sworn for use in the Supreme Court.

Unsworn evidence

26.— (1) Notwithstanding rule 25(1), the court may accept and act upon a statement of facts or such other evidence, whether oral or written, as the court considers sufficient, although not given on oath and whether or not it would be admissible in a court of law apart from this rule.

(2) The court may give directions as to the manner in which a statement of facts or other written evidence under paragraph (1) above is to be given but subject to such directions any such statement or other evidence shall—

(a) be drawn up in numbered paragraphs and dated; and

(b) be signed by the person by whom it is made or given.

Written questions to Visitors

27.— (1) Where a Visitor's report, or information contained in such a report, has been disclosed to any person in pursuance of section 103(8) of the Act, the court may, on the application of any person who appears to the court to be

---

(a) 1889 c. 10, 1891 c. 50.
(b) 1974 c. 47.

interested, give leave for written questions relevant to the issues before the court to be put to the Visitor by whom the report was made.

(2) The questions sought to be put to the Visitor shall be submitted to the court, which may put them to the Visitor with such amendments, if any, as it thinks fit and the Visitor shall give his replies in writing to the questions so put.

(3) The court may disclose the replies given by a Visitor under this rule to any person who appears to the court to be interested, or to his legal or medical adviser, on such conditions, if any, as it thinks fit.

Cross-examination of deponent

28. Any person who has made an affidavit or given a certificate or other written evidence for use in proceedings under these Rules may be ordered by the court to attend for cross-examination.

Administration of oaths

29. The court may direct that an oath be administered to any witness or interpreter in any proceedings before the court.

Filing of written evidence

30.— (1) Before an affidavit, certificate or other written evidence is used in any proceedings under these Rules it shall be filed but the court may make an order on the basis of such evidence before it is filed if the person tendering it undertakes to file it before the order is drawn up.

(2) There shall be endorsed on every affidavit, certificate or other written evidence the name and address of the solicitor, if any, for the person on whose behalf it is filed.

Use of evidence in subsequent proceedings

31.— (1) Except where the court otherwise directs, evidence which has been used in any proceedings relating to a patient may be used at any subsequent stage of those proceedings or in any other proceedings relating to the same patient or to another member of the patient's family.

(2) Without prejudice to paragraph (1) above, the Master may, upon application being made for the purpose, authorise the use of any such evidence in any legal proceedings that the Master may specify.

Evidence to be filed on a first application for receiver, etc.

32.— (1) On the issue of a first application for the appointment of a receiver for a patient or for an order authorising any person to do any act or carry out any transaction on behalf of a patient without appointing him receiver, the applicant shall, unless the court otherwise directs, file a medical certificate and evidence of family and property.

(2) In this rule—

"a medical certificate" means a certficate by a medical practitioner that the patient is incapable, by reason of mental disorder, of managing and administering his property and affairs; and

"evidence of family and property" means a certificate or, if the court so orders in a particular case, an affidavit, giving particulars of the patient's relatives, property and affairs and of the circumstances giving rise to the application.

(3) Rule 26(2) above applies to unsworn evidence of family and property as it applies to unsworn evidence generally.

Evidence of patient's death or recovery

33. Where at any stage of proceedings relating to a patient the court has reason to believe that the patient has died or recovered, the court may require evidence of the death or recovery to be furnished by such person as the court thinks appropriate.

Consent to act as trustee

34. Where in any proceedings it is proposed to appoint a person to act as trustee, a written consent in Form C signed by him and verified by some other person shall be evidence of his consent so to act, but not such consent shall be required where the person to be appointed is an applicant in the proceedings or the proceedings are brought under section 36(9) of the Trustee Act 1925.

Proof of amount due to public authority

35. The amount due to any public authority for the past maintenance of a patient may, unless the court otherwise directs, be proved by the filing of an account certified under the hand of the proper officer of the authority.

PART VI

HEARING OF PROCEEDINGS

Applications to be heard in chambers

36. Every application shall be heard in chambers unless, in the case of an application for hearing by the judge, the judge otherwise directs.

Persons attending hearing

37. The court may determine what persons are to be entitled to attend at any stage of the proceedings relating to a patient.

Representation at hearing

38. Where two or more persons appearing at a hearing are represented by the same legal representative, the court may, if it thinks fit, require any of them to be separately represented.

Reference of proceedings to judge

39. The Master shall, after giving such directions as he thinks fit, refer to the judge any proceedings or any question arising in any proceedings which ought by virtue of any enactment or in the opinion of the Master, to be considered by the judge.

Reference of proceedings to Master

40. The judge may refer any proceedings before him or any question arising therein to the Master for inquiry and report.

PART VII

RECEIVERS

Interim provision

41.— (1) Where in the opinion of the court it is necessary to make immediate provision in relation to the property and affairs of a patient for any of the matters referred to in section 95(1) of the Act, the court may

   (a) by certificate direct or authorise any person named therein to do any act or carry out any transaction specified in the certificate; or

   (b) by order appoint a receiver ad interim for the patient and, subject to any direction given by the court, such appointment shall continue until further order.

(2) An order appointing a receiver ad interim shall, unless the court otherwise directs, be served upon the patient within such time as the order may specify and the patient may, within such further time as the order may specify, apply under rule 54 for the reconsideration of the order by the court or, if the order was made by a judge, apply to have the order set aside.

Remuneration of receiver

42.— (1) Where a receiver is appointed for a patient, the court may, during the receivership, allow the receiver remuneration for his services at such amount or at such rate as the court considers reasonable and proper and any remuneration so allowed shall constitute a debt due to the receiver from the patient and his estate.

(2) No request by a receiver to have the sum payable for his remuneration fixed after the death or recovery of the patient shall be entertained unless the court has during the receivership directed that remuneration be allowed and the request is made within six years from the date of the receiver's discharge.

Appointment of receivers with survivorship

43. Where in the opinion of the court two or more persons ought to be appointed receivers for the same patient and one or more of them ought to continue to act after the death or discharge of any of the others, the court may when appointing them receivers direct that the receivership shall continue in favour of the surviving or continuing receiver or receivers.

PART VIII

ENTRY AND ENFORCEMENT OF ORDERS

Sealing and filing of orders

44. Every order, certificate, direction or authority of the court which is drawn up shall, when entered, be sealed and filed.

Entry of orders after notification to patient

45.— (1) Where—

(a) an order is made on a first application appointing a receiver for a patient or directing or authorising any person to do any act or carry out any transaction on behalf of a patient without appointing him receiver, or

(b) an order with respect to a patient's property is made under rule 7,

the order shall not be entered until the expiration of ten clear days after the patient has been notified in accordance with rule 23(1) unless such notification is dispensed with.

(2) Nothing in paragraph (1) above shall prevent the entry of an interim order for the protection of a patient's property or for the application of a patient's property for his benefit.

Enforcement of orders

46. Every writ of execution or other process for the enforcement of an order of the court shall be issued out of the Central Office of the Supreme Court.

PART IX

SUMMONSES AND ORDERS FOR ATTENDANCE OF WITNESSES AND OTHER PERSONS

Summoning of witnesses

47.— (1) In any proceedings under these Rules the court may allow or direct any party or the Official Solicitor to take out a witness summons in Form D requiring the person named therein to attend before the court and give oral evidence or produce any document.

(2) An application by a person to be allowed to take out a witness summons shall be made by filing a statement giving—

(a) the name and address of the person making the application and of his solicitor, if any;

(b) the name, address and occupation of the proposed witness;

(c) particulars of any document which the proposed witness is to be required to produce; and

(d) the grounds on which the application is made.

(3) A witness summons shall be served on the witness personally a reasonable time before the day fixed for his attendance and he shall be entitled to the like conduct money and payment for expenses and loss of time a if he had been summoned to attend the trial of an action in the High Court.

Powers of court where undue delay, etc.

48.— (1) If the court is dissatisfied with the conduct of any proceedings or the carrying out of any order or direction of the court whether by reason of undue delay or otherwise, the court may require the person having the conduct of the proceedings, or any other person appearing to be responsible, to explain the delay or other cause of dissatisfaction, and may thereupon make such order for expediting the proceedings or otherwise as may be appropriate.

(2) For the purpose of the last foregoing paragraph the court may direct any person to make any application and to conduct any proceedings and carry out any directions which the court may specify; and the court may, if it thinks fit, and if he consents appoint the Official Solicitor to act as solicitor for the patient in the proceedings in the place of any solicitor previously acting for him.

Order for examination of patient

49. In any proceedings relating to a patient a judge or the Master may make an order for the patient's attendance at such time and place as he may direct for examination by the Master, a Visitor or any medical practitioner.

PART X

AMENDMENT

Amendment of application

50.— (1) The court may allow or direct an applicant, at any stage of the proceedings, to amend his application in such manner and on such terms as to costs or otherwise as may be just.

(2) The amendment may be effected by making in writing the necessary alterations of the application, but if the amendments are so numerous or of such a nature or length that written alterations would make it difficult or inconvenient to read, a fresh application amended as authorised or directed may be issued.

Clerical mistakes and slips

51. The court may at any time correct any clerical mistakes in an order or any error arising in an order from any accidental slip or omission.

Endorsement of amendment

52. Where an application or order has been amended under rule 50 or 51, a note shall be placed on it showing the date on which it was amended and the alterations shall be sealed.

PART XI

APPEALS

Appeal from Master or a nominated officer

53.— (1) Subject to rule 54, any person aggrieved by an order or decision of the court may, within eight days from the date of entry of the order or, as the case may be, from the date of the decision, appeal therefrom to a nominated judge.

(2) The appellant shall, within the said period of eight days—

    (a) serve a notice of appeal in Form E on—

        (i) every person who is directly affected by the appeal, being a person who appeared, or was represented before, the court when the order or decision was made or given, and

        (ii) any other person whom the court may direct; and

    (b) leave a copy of the notice at the court office.

(3) The time and place at which the appeal is to be heard shall be fixed by the court in consultation with the judge, and the court shall cause notice of the time and place so fixed to be sent to the appellant who shall forthwith send notice thereof to every person who has been served with notice of the appeal.

(4) No further evidence shall be filed in support of or in opposition to the appeal without leave of the court.

Appeal from order not made on appointment for a hearing.

54.— (1) No appeal shall lie—

    (a) from any order or decision of the court which is not made or given on an appointment for a hearing; or

    (b) at the instance of a patient from any order of the court appointing a receiver ad interim for the patient,

except in accordance with the following provisions of this rule.

(2) No appeal shall lie from any decision of the court in relation to the exercise of its powers under rule 83 of these Rules.

(3) Any person who is aggrieved by such an order or decision as is mentioned in paragraph (1)*(a)*, or a patient who is aggrieved by such an order as is mentioned in paragraph (1)*(b)*, may apply to the court to reconsider the order or decision, and the court shall fix an appointment for a hearing.

(4) No further evidence shall be filed in support of or in opposition to the application without the leave of the court.

(5) On the hearing of the application the court may either confirm or revoke its previous order or decision or make or give any other order or decision which it thinks fit.

(6) Any person aggrieved by any order or decision made or given on the

hearing of the application may appeal therefrom to a nominated judge in accordance with rule 52.

PART XII

SECURITY

Receiver to give security

55.— (1) Where an order is made appointing a person other than the Official Solicitor as receiver for a patient—

    (a) the person appointed shall, unless the court otherwise directs, give such security for the due performance of his duties as the court may approve and shall give it before acting as receiver unless the court allows it to be given subsequently; and

    (b) the order shall not be entered until the person appointed has given to the satisfaction of the court any security required to be given by him before acting.

(2) The court may from time to time vary any security required.

Manner of giving security

56.— (1) Subject to any directions of the court, security may be given in any of the following ways or partly in one of those ways and partly in another—

    (a) by a bond approved by the court and given by the person giving security and also by—

        (i) an insurance company, group of underwriters or bank approved by the court; or

        (ii) with the approval of the court, two personal sureties; or

    (b) by lodging in court a sufficient sum of money or stock; or

    (c) in such other manner as the court may approve.

(2) A person desiring to give security in whole or in part by lodging money or stock in court shall file a form of request in Form F and the court may thereupon give leave to make the lodgement and direct how any such money is to be invested and how any dividends are to be applied.

Lodgement of security

57. Any security given by lodgement of money or stock shall be dealt with in accordance with the terms of the request filed when the lodgement was made.

Discharge of security where new security given

58. Where a receiver is authorised or directed to give new security, and—

    (a) the new security has been completed, and

    (b) he has paid or secured to the satisfaction of the court any balance due from him,

the former security shall, unless the court otherwise directs, be discharged.

Maintenance of security by bond

59. Every person who has given security by a bond shall, whenever his accounts are passed or the court so directs, satisfy the court—

(a) that any premiums payable in respect of the bond have been duly paid, or

(b) if the bond was given by personal sureties, that each surety is living and within the jurisdiction and has neither been adjudicated bankrupt nor compounded with his creditors,

and, if the court is not so satisfied, it may require new security to be given or may give such other directions as it thinks fit.

PART XIII

ACCOUNTS

Passing of accounts

60.— (1) Every receiver shall annually, or at such other intervals as the court may direct, deliver his accounts to the court and attend at or within such time as the court may appoint to have the accounts taken and passed.

(2) On the passing of any accounts the court shall make all proper allowances out of the patient's estate, including an allowance in respect of the reasonable and proper costs of the receiver of passing the accounts and of any other person allowed to attend.

(3) The court may, if it thinks fit, direct that a receiver need not account under this rule or may dispense with the passing of any accounts at any time at which they would otherwise require to be passed.

Application of balance due from receiver

61. The balance found due from a receiver on the passing of his accounts or so much thereof as the court may direct, shall—

(a) be paid by the receiver into court to the credit of the proceedings and invested in such manner as the court may direct, or

(b) be invested or otherwise dealt with by the receiver in such manner as the court may direct.

Default by receiver

62. Where a receiver fails to comply with rule 60 or fails to pay into court or invest or otherwise deal with any money in accordance with any direction of the court, the court may disallow any remuneration which would otherwise be due to the receiver and, if he has made default in paying into court or investing or otherwise dealing with any money, may charge him with interest thereon at such rate as the court may fix, for the period of his default.

Payment of maintenance and costs

63. Unless otherwise directed, any money ordered to be paid by a receiver for maintenance shall be paid out of income and any costs ordered to be paid by a receiver may, when taxed or fixed, be paid out of any moneys coming into his hands, after providing for any maintenance and fees payable under these rules.

Final accounts

64.— (1) On the discharge or death of a receiver or on the death or recovery of a patient for whom a receiver has been appointed, the court shall take and pass the accounts of the receiver from the foot of his last account or, if no account of his has previously been passed, from the date of his appointment, unless in the opinion of the court the taking and passing of such accounts may properly be dispensed with.

(2) If a balance is found due from the receiver or his estate, he or his personal representatives, as the case may be, shall pay it into court or otherwise deal with it as the court may direct.

(3) If a balance is found due to the receiver or his estate, it shall be paid to him or his personal representatives, as the case may be, by the patient or out of the patient's estate.

(4) On payment of any balance found due from the receiver, or if no balance is found due from him or the passing of his accounts has been dispensed with under paragraph (1) above, the security of the receiver shall, unless the court otherwise directs, be discharged.

Accounting by other persons

65. Rules 60 to 64 shall also apply, to the extent directed by the court, to any person who is—

    (a) directed to deal with the patient's property or affairs under rule 7;

    (b) directed or authorised to act under rule 41(1)*(a)*; or

    (c) appointed a receiver ad interim under rule 41(1)*(b)*,

as they apply to a receiver.

PART XIV

INQUIRIES

Inquries as to desirability of appointment of receiver, etc.

66.— (1) Where the court has reason to believe that a receiver should be appointed for a patient or that any other power conferred on the court should be exercised with respect to the property and affairs of a patient, the court may direct—

    (a) an officer of the court or a Visitor or, if he consents, the Official Solicitor to make inquiries and report to the court whether it is

desirable in the interests of the patient that an application should be made for that purpose; or

(b) a Medical Visitor to visit the patient and report to the court on the capacity of the patient to manage and administer his property and affairs.

(2) On receiving any report pursuant to paragraph (1) above, the court may, if it thinks fit—

(a) direct an application to be made pursuant to rule 10; or

(b) if the report is by a Medical Visitor and the court is satisfied that the patient is incapable, by reason of mental disorder, of managing and administering his property and affairs, make an order appointing a receiver or exercising any other power conferred on the court with respect to the patient's property and affairs.

Inspection of patient's property

67. For the purpose of any proceedings relating to the property of a patient, the court may if it thinks fit, inspect the property or direct an officer of the court or, if he consents, the Official Solicitor to inspect the property, make any necessary inquiries and report to the court.

Inquiries as to prior dealing with the patient's property

68. In any proceedings relating to a patient the court may make or cause to be made such inquiries as it thinks fit as to any dealing with the patient's property before the commencement of the proceedings and as to the mental capacity of the patient at the time of such dealing.

Inquries as to testamentary documents executed by patient

69. The court may make or cause to be made inquiries whether any person has in his possession or under his control or has any knowledge of any testamentary document executed by a patient, and may direct that person to answer the inquries on oath and to produce any such document which is in his possession or under his control and deal with it in such manner as the court may direct.

Power to direct other inquiries

70. The court may make or cause to be made any other inquiries which it may consider necessary or expedient for the proper discharge of its functions under the Act or these Rules.

PART XV

CUSTODY AND DISPOSAL OF FUNDS AND OTHER PROPERTY

Statement of property retained or deposited.

71. Where under a direction of the court any furniture or effects of a patient are allowed to remain in the possession of, or deposited with, any person, that person shall, unless the court otherwise directs, sign and file a statement of the furniture or effects and an undertaking not to part with them except on a direction under seal.

Stock in name of patient or receiver

72.— (1) Where any stock—

(a) is standing in the name of a patient beneficiary entitled thereto; or

(b) is standing in the name of a receiver in trust for a patient, or as part of his property, and the receiver dies intestate or himself becomes incapable by reason of mental disorder of acting as receiver, or is out of the jurisdiction of the court, or it is uncertain whether he is still alive, or he neglects or refuses to transfer the stock or to receive and pay over the dividends thereof as the court directs,

the court may order some proper person to transfer the stock into the name of the receiver or, as the case may be a new receiver for the patient or into court or otherwise deal with it as the court may direct and also to receive and pay over the dividends thereof as the court may direct.

(2) Where an order is made under paragraph (1) above or under section 100 of the Act directing stock to be transferred into court, the person required to effect the transfer shall be—

(a) in the case of stock standing in the stock register kept by the Bank of England or any other bank or by the Crown Agents for Overseas Governments and Administrations, some proper officer of the bank or the Crown Agents;

(b) in any other case, some proper officer of the company or other body, whose stock is to be transferred;

and the said person shall, if so ordered, receive any sum accrued due before the transfer by way of dividend, bonus or periodical payment in respect of the stock and pay it into court to the general account of the patient or to a separate account or otherwise deal with it as the court may direct.

Disposal of property on patient's death or recovery

73.— (1) On the death or recovery of a patient the court may order any money, securities or other property belonging to the patient, or forming part of his estate, or remaining under the control of, or held under the directions of the court, to be paid, transferred, delivered or released to the person who appears to be entitled thereto.

(2) If no grant of representation has been taken out to the estate of a deceased patient and it appears to the court that the assets of the estate, after deduction of debts and funeral expenses, do not exceed £5,000 in value, the court may, if it thinks fit, provide for payment of the funeral expenses out of any funds in court standing to the credit of the deceased and order that any such funds, or the balance thereof, or any other property of the patient remaining under the control, or held under the directions, of the court, be paid, transferred, delivered or released either to the personal representative of the deceased when constituted or to the person who appears to be entitled to apply for a grant of representation to his estate.

(3) The court may at any time, pending notification to the court of the grant of representation to the estate of a patient, direct that any money or securities which belonged to the patient when he died and were not already in court shall be transferred into court.

PART XVI

SETTLEMENT AND APPROVAL OF DEEDS

Documents to be settled by court

74. All mortgages, leases and other dispositions of a patient's land and such other deeds and documents relating to his estate as may be directed shall be settled and approved by the court.

Authentication by seal

75.— (1) The seal of the court on any deed or other document shall be evidence that it has been settled and approved by the court.

(2) Unless otherwise directed, no deed or other document shall be sealed for the purpose aforesaid unless—

(a) it bears a certificate by the person tendering it that it is an exact copy of a draft settled and approved by the court, and

(b) in the case of a deed or document containing a recital that any money has been lodged in court, a certificate of the Accountant General is produced stating that the logment has been made.

PART XVII

COPIES OF DOCUMENTS

Copies of documents in court

76.— (1) Any person who has filed an affidavit or other document shall, unless the court otherwise directs, be entitled, on request, to be supplied by the court with a copy of it.

(2) The person having the conduct of any proceedings shall, unless the court otherwise directs, be entitled, on request, to be supplied by the court with a copy of any order, certificate, authority, direction of other document made, given or prepared by the court in the proceedings.

(3) Any other person may, on request, be supplied by the court with a copy of any such document as it mentioned in paragraph (1) or (2), if the court is satisfied that he has good reason for requiring it and that it is not reasonably practicable for him to obtain it from the person entitled to bespeak a copy from the court.

(4) Any copy of a document supplied under paragraph (1), (2) or (3) above shall, if so required, be marked as an office copy.

PART XVIII

FEES

Appendix of fees

77.— (1) The Appendix to these Rules, in this Part of these Rules described as the "Appendix", shall apply so as to fix the fees payable pursuant to the following provisions of this part of these Rules.

(2) Subject to paragraph (3), the fees set out in column 2 of the Appendix shall be taken in respect of the event referred to in column 1.

(3) The fees prescribed by rules 79 and 80 and the corresponding provisions of the Appendix shall not be payable where an officer of the court has been appointed and is acting as receiver for the patient.

(4) Unless the court otherwise directs, all fees shall be taken in cash.

(5) Subject to paragraph (6) below, the person by whom any fee (other than a fee payable under rule 81) is payable shall, unless the court otherwise directs, make the payment out of the income of the patient or, if he is dead, out of his estate.

(6) Where the court directs that a fee is to be paid by the Accountant General wholly or partly out of funds in court, then, unless the court directs payment to be made out of capital, the Accountant General shall meet the fee out of the income arising from the fund.

Commencement fee

78.— (1) A commencement fee shall be payable on any first application for the appointment of a receiver or other originating process in respect of any patient except where the clear annual income at the patient's disposal is less than the exemption for small estates specified in item 1 of the Appendix.

(2) An additional fee on commencement shall be payable by personal applicants for the issue of process.

Administration fee

79.— (1) An annual administration fee shall be payable in respect of the clear annual income at the disposal of the patient from the date of issue of the first application for the appointment of a receiver or other originating process until the termination of the proceedings.

(2) The court shall annually, or at such other intervals as may be convenient, issue a certificate in respect of each patient in which there shall be stated—

    (a) the amount of the administration fee payable in respect of the patient at the date of the certificate;

    (b) the period in respect of which the administration fee is payable; and

    (c) the name of the person by whom the payment is to be made.

(3) The court may, if it thinks fit, issue a certificate for the payment of an estimated administration fee.

(4) Upon the issue of a certificate under this rule the amount of the fee shall be charged upon the patient's estate, and the payment shall be made within such time (not exceeding one month from the date of the certificate) as the court may allow.

(5) In any case in which it appears to the court that the amount of the fee certified under this rule has been wrongly assessed, the court may direct that the fee is to be adjusted upon the passing of the receiver's accounts or at such other time as appears to the court to be convenient.

(6) Without prejudice to the generality of rule 83—

    (a) no administration fee may be taken where the proceedings are terminated before any order is made, and

    (b) the clear annual income at the patient's disposal for the purposes of this rule does not include income which accrued and became payable to him more than six months prior to the date of the first application for the appointment of a receiver or other originating process but which was received after that date.

Transaction fee

80.— (1) A transaction fee shall be payable in respect of any order made in exercise of the specific powers conferred on the court by—

    (a) paragraphs *(b)*, *(c)*, *(d)*, *(e)*, *(h)* and *(k)* of section 96(1) of the Act;

    (b) section 100 of the Act;

    (c) sections 36(9) and 54 of the Trustee Act 1925; and

    (d) section 1(3) of the Variation of Trusts Act 1958(a)

(2) In a special case, the standard fee payable in accordance with the Appendix shall be increased in accordance with the Appendix where there is readily ascertainable pecuniary consideration in the nature of capital arising to or provided by the patient (otherwise than by way of loan to, or repayment of a loan by, the patient), no account being taken of the possible capitalisation of the value of rents or interest or other income payments.

(3) Where a transaction is to be approved under an order mentioned in paragraph (1) above, the fee shall be taken on the approval of the transaction and the court shall issue a certificate stating the amount payable.

(4) Except where the court otherwise directs, no fee shall be payable under this rule upon the sale or purchase of personal chattels or any investment for the time being authorised by law for the investment of trust property or in securities quoted on any stock exchange in the United Kingdom.

(5) In this rule, "special case" means an order made by the court—

    (a) under paragraph *(b)*, *(c)*, *(d)* and *(h)* of section 96(1) of the Act;

(a) 1958 c. 53.

(b) relating to the sale or purchase by a patient in exercise of his powers as a tenant for life under the Settled Land Act 1925(a); or

(c) under section 1(3) of the Variation of Trusts Act 1958.

Fee on taxation

81.— (1) A fee shall be payable in respect of the taxation of a bill of costs.

(2) On the withdrawal of a bill of costs which has been lodged for taxation there shall be payable such a fee (not exceeding the amount which would have been payable under paragraph (1) above if the bill had been allowed in full) as appears to the taxing officer to be fair and reasonable.

Receivership fees

82.— (1) An appointment fee shall be payable, as set out at paragraph 5 of the Appendix, upon the appointment of an officer of the court as receiver for a patient.

(2) In cases where an officer of the court is receiver an annual fee shall be payable in respect of the clear annual income at the disposal of the patient.

(3) The said annual fee shall be payable—

(a) upon the annual passing of the account by an officer of the court; and

(b) on the scale set out at paragraph 6 of the Appendix.

(4) The clear annual income at the patient's disposal for the purpose of this rule does not include income which accrued and became payable to him more than six months prior to the date when the court's jurisdiction was first exercised in relation to him.

(5) No annual fee shall be taken where the proceedings are terminated less than four weeks from the date of issue of the first application for the appointment of a receiver.

Remission, postponement and exemption

83.— (1) The court may remit or postpone the payment of the whole or part of any fee where in its opinion hardship might otherwise be caused to the patient or his dependants or the circumstances are otherwise exceptional.

(2) The court may remit the payment of the whole or part of any fee where the cost of calculation and collection would be disproportionate to the amount involved.

(a) 1925 c. 18.

(3) No fee shall be payable pursuant to rules 78(2), 79 and 82 on any income by way of a war pension or war injuries (civilian) pension in respect of—

(a) service in the armed forces of the Crown to which section 2 of the War Pensions Act 1920(a) applies; or

(b) service in the armed forces of the Crown after 2nd September 1939; or

(c) service before the 15th August 1945 to which the Pensions (Polish Forces) Scheme 1964(b) applies; or

(d) detention, capture, war injury or war risk injury within the meaning of any scheme (other than that mentioned in paragraph *(c)* above made under the Pensions (Navy, Army, Air Force and Mercantile Marine) Act 1939(c), or under that Act as amended and applied by the Pensions (Mercantile Marine) Act 1942(d); or

(e) war service injury within the meaning of the Personal Injuries (Civilians) Scheme 1983(e) as amended in the case of a civil defence volunteer to whom that Scheme applied.

Part XIX

Costs

Costs generally

84.— (1) All costs incurred in relation to proceedings under these Rules, and not provided for by way of remuneration under rule 42, shall be in the discretion of the court and the court may order them to be paid by the patient or charged on or paid out of his estate or paid by any other person attending or taking part in the proceedings.

(2) Every order made under the last foregoing paragraph shall be enforceable in the same manner as an order as to costs made by the High Court.

(3) An order that costs incurred during the lifetime of a patient be paid out of or charged on his estate may be made within six years after his death.

(a) 1920 c. 23.
(b) S.I. 1964/2007.
(c) 1939 c. 83.
(d) 1942 c. 26.
(e) S.I. 1983/686.

Applications under sections 36(9) and 54 of the Trustee Act 1925

85. The court may make any such order with respect to the costs of an application under section 36(9) or 54 of the Trustee Act 1925 as the High Court could make under section 60 of that Act in relation to any matter mentioned in that section.

Supreme Court costs rules to apply

86. Subject to the provisions of these Rules, Order 62 of the Rules of the Supreme Court 1965 shall apply, with such modifications as may be necessary to costs incurred in relation to proceedings under these Rules as they apply to costs incurred in relation to proceedings in the Chancery Division and may be taxed where required accordingly.

Costs of unnecessary employment of solicitor etc., not to be allowed

87.— (1) No receiver for a patient other than the Official Solicitor, shall, unless authorised by the court, be entitled at the expense of the patient's estate to employ a solicitor or other professional person to do any work not usually requiring professional assistance.

(2) Where two or more persons having the same interest in relation to the matter to be determined attend any hearing by separate legal representatives, they shall not be allowed more than one set of costs of that hearing unless the court certifies that the circumstances justify separate representation.

Costs of Official Solicitor

88. Any costs incurred by the Official Solicitor in relation to proceedings under these Rules or in carrying out any directions given by the court, and not provided for by way of remuneration under rule 42, shall be paid by such person or out of such funds as the court may direct.

Ascertainment of prior costs, etc.

89. Where in proceedings relating to a patient a claim is made against his estate in respect of any costs alleged to have been incurred by him or on his behalf otherwise than in relation to the proceedings, the court may refer the claim to a Taxing Master of the Supreme Court so that the amount due to the claimant may be ascertained by him or under his direction.

Part XX

Revocation

Revocation of previous Rules

90. The Court of Protection Rules 1982(a) are hereby revoked.

Dated 17th December 1984.   *Hailsham of St. Marylebone,* C.

We concur.

Dated 18th December 1984.   *Ian B. Lang,*
                                                   Donald Thompson,
                                       Two of the Lord Commissioners of
                                             Her Majesty's Treasury

---

(a) S.I. 1982/322.

SCHEDULE

FORMS

FORM A: FIRST APPLICATION FOR THE APPOINTMENT OF A RECEIVER

COURT OF PROTECTION

19   no

Rule 6

IN THE MATTER OF ....

.... A PATIENT

I...

of...

....

NOTES

Complete EITHER paragraph 1, OR paragraph 2. Delete the one which does not apply.

apply to the Court of Protection for:

1. my own appointment as receiver for the patient

   a. I am not related to the patient*

   b. I am the.. of the patient (state relationship)*

2. the appointment of...

*Delete whichever does not apply.

of...

.... as receiver for the patient

   a. He/She is the .... of the patient (state relationship)*

DO NOT DELETE

paragraph 3.

Where any other order in addition to that at paragraphs 1, 2 and 3 is sought, a general form of application should be used.

OR

3. the appointment of some other suitable person.

Applicant's signature...

Date...

OR Solicitors for the applicant:

of:

TO BE COMPLETED BY THE COURT,

THE COURT WILL CONSIDER THIS APPLICATION ON THE .... DAY

OF .... 19.......... AT .... O'CLOCK

FORM B: GENERAL FORM OF APPLICATION

COURT OF PROTECTION

19   no

Rule 6

IN THE MATTER OF ....

.... A PATIENT

I..

of...

NOTES

Where the application is one to
which rules 16
or 17 applies, give details of
your authority to make the
application e.g. Receiver,
Trustee, etc.

Give details of the order you
are asking the court to make

apply to the Court of Protection for an order that:

....

....

....

....

....

....

....

....

....

and for any directions which are necessary as a result of my
application.

Applicant's signature ....

Date ....

OR Solicitors for the applicant:

of:

TO BE COMPLETED BY THE COURT,

THE COURT WILL CONSIDER THIS APPLICATION ON THE .... DAY
OF .... 19......... AT .... O'CLOCK

FORM C: CONSENT OF PROPOSED NEW TRUSTEE TO ACT

COURT OF PROTECTION

19   no

Rule 34

IN THE MATTER OF ....

.... A PATIENT

I ....

of ....

....

give my consent to:

a. act as the trustee of the will of

NOTE

If paragraph a does not
apply delete and give details
of what is being consented to
in paragraph b.

OR

b. ....

....

....

....

....

....

....

....

Signed ....

Date ....

I ....

of ....

....

certify that the signature written above is the signature of
the person mentioned in the above consent.

Signed ....

Date ....

FORM D: WITNESS SUMMONS

COURT OF PROTECTION

19   no

Rule 47

IN THE MATTER OF ....

.... A PATIENT

To..

of...

....

You are ordered to attend before

....

at...

....

on the............................ day of............................ 19.........

at .... o'clock, to:

a. give evidence in this matter

b. bring with you and produce at the hearing the documents listed below:

....

....

....

....

....

....

Date ....

THIS SUMMONS WAS ISSUED AT THE REQUEST OF

....

.... SOLICITORS FOR THE

.... of...

....

....

FORM E: NOTICE OF APPEAL

COURT OF PROTECTION

19   no

Rule 53(2)

IN THE MATTER OF ....

.... A PATIENT

I..

of ....

....

wish to appeal to a Judge against the order/decision* of the Court made in this matter on the .... day of ....

.... 19 .... that:

....

NOTE

If you are appealing against only part of the order/decision write down which part.

....

....

....

....

....

*Delete whichever does not apply

I intend to ask that the order/decision* may be:

a. discharged*

b. varied in the following way*

Give details of new order/decision you are asking to be made

....

....

....

....

YOU WILL BE SENT NOTICE OF THE TIME, DATE AND PLACE OF THE HEARING OF THIS APPEAL

Signed.. Appellant

Date ....

Solicitors for the Appellant ....

of ....

....

FORM F: REQUEST FOR LEAVE TO GIVE SECURITY BY LODGMENT IN COURT.

COURT OF PROTECTION

19   no

Rule 56(2)

IN THE MATTER OF ....

.... A PATIENT

I... Receiver

for the above named patient, of....................................

....

....

NOTE

If the security is not money, give details of what it is, and its value

ask the court to allow me to give my security to the court

a. in the sum of £...............

b. ....

....

....

....

....

....

I agree that if the court decides that I have failed to pay or account to the patient's estate for any money or security which I have received on his/her behalf in carrying out my duties as receiver, the money or security I have lodged with the court may immediately be transferred to the patient's account, or used as the court decides for the benefit of the patient; but if I prove that the loss, including any costs, is smaller than the amount of money or the value of the securities originally lodged, the balance will be returned to me.

Signed .... Receiver

Date...

APPENDIX

COURT OF PROTECTION FEES

Rule 77

Column 1	Column 2
Item	Fee

Commencement fee (rule 78)

1.— (1) On a first application for the appointment of a receiver or other originating process, except where it appears that the patient's clear annual income is less than £1,000   £50.00

(2) On commencement pursuant to a request by a personal applicant, in addition to Fee (1) above, for every £100 or fraction of £100 above £1,000 of the income which the patient's estate might be expected to yield if duly administered by the court.   £4.00 but not exceeding a total of £50.00

Annual administration fee (rule 79)

2. On a certificate issued by the court   In accordance with Table 1

Transaction fee (rule 80)

3.— (1) On any order (or, as the case may be, on any approval given by the court under an order) made by the court in the exercise of powers conferred by—

  (i) section 96(1)—

    (b) (sale, exchange, etc. of property)

    (c) (acquisition of property)

    (d) (settlement or gift of property)

    (h) (carrying out of contract) or

    (k) (exercise of powers as guardian or trustee)

of the Act;

  (ii) section 100 of the Act (vesting of stock in curator appointed outside England and Wales);

  (iii) section 36(9) of the Trustee Act 1925 (appointment of new trustee);   £50.00 or, in a "special case", $\frac{1}{4}$% of the pecuniary consideration as defined in rule 80 if greater than £50

  (iv) section 54 of the Trustee Act 1925 (concurrent jurisdiction with High Court over trusts);

  (v) section 1(3) of the Variation of Trusts Act 1958 (variation of trusts for benefit of patient),

provided that no fee under this item shall be taken if the property is worth less than £50.00 and no such fee shall exceed £500.00.

APPENDIX *(continued)*

COURT OF PROTECTION FEES

Column 1	Column 2
Item	Fee
(2) On the making by the court of any order or authority under section 96(1)*(e)* of the Act (execution of will)	£100.00

Taxation (rule 81)

4. On the taxation of a bill of costs, for every £1 or fraction of £1 allowed.	£0.05

Receivership fees (rule 82)

5. On the appointment of an officer of the court as receiver, except where it appears that the patient's clear annual income is less than £1,000	£150.00
6. On passing an account	In accordance with Table 2

TABLE 1 (Fee No. 2)

Income Band	Clear Annual Income		Fee	
	Exceeding	Not exceeding		
(i)		£ 1,000	None	
(ii)	£ 1,000	£ 2,000	£ 75	
(iii)	£ 2,000	£ 3,000	£150	
(iv)	£ 3,000	£ 5,000	£225	
(v)	£ 5,000	£ 7,000	£375	
(vi)	£ 7,000	£10,000	£600	
(vii)	£10,000	£15,000	£850	
(viii)	£15,000		£850	plus 5% of income exceeding £15,000

TABLE 2 (Fee No. 6)

Income Band	Clear Annual Income		Fee	
	Exceeding	Not exceeding		
(i)		£ 1,000	None	
(ii)	£ 1,000	£ 2,000	£ 200	
(iii)	£ 2,000	£ 3,000	£ 400	
(iv)	£ 3,000	£ 5,000	£ 600	
(v)	£ 5,000	£ 7,000	£1,000	
(vi)	£ 7,000	£10,000	£1,475	
(vii)	£10,000	£15,000	£2,100	
(viii)	£15,000		£2,100	plus 5% of income exceeding £15,000

NOTES

1. In relation to fees numbers 2 and 6, and their corresponding Tables, where income exceeds the lower limit of a band by less than the difference between the fees for that band and the next lower band, the fee charged shall be the fee for the lower band plus the amount by which the income exceeds the upper limit of that band. For example, in calculating fee No. 2 on a clear annual income of (£2,050 (which exceeds the lower limit (£2,000) on Band (iii) by less than the difference (£75) between the fee (£150) on Band (iii) and the fee (£75) on Band (ii)), the fee payable is—

£ 75	(the fee on Band (ii))
+£ 50	(the amount by which the income exceeds £2,000)
£125	

2. In accordance with rule 77(3), fees numbers 2 and 3 are not payable where an officer of the court is acting as receiver for the patient.

EXPLANATORY NOTE
(*This Note is not part of the Rules.*)

These Rules consolidate with a substantial number of amendments the existing Rules relating to the management of the property and affairs of patients and the fees to be taken in the Court of Protection. The main changes are:—

(1) The manner in which the Court of Protection's powers under the Mental Health Act may be exercised is made clearer (rule 5), and the provisions for the making of applications are shortened and clarified (Part III of the Rules).

(2) The provisions for the giving of notice of hearings are set out in a single rule (rule 18) and the minimum notice required for the hearing of a first application for the appointment of a receiver is extended from seven to ten days.

(3) Modifications are made to take account of the transfer from the Official Solicitor to the Management Division of the Court of the responsibility of acting as receiver for the majority of those patients for whom no other suitable receiver can be found who is able and willing to act.

(4) Where certain kinds of application to the court are made (rule 23) the patient will in future be given informal notification by letter instead of formal notice.

(5) The usual form of written evidence as to:—

    (a) service of process; and

    (b) family and property

will be in future be by signed certificate rather than by affidavit and the requirements as to the form of certificate and certain other documents are less closely defined; but the court will retain a discretion to order an affidavit in a particular case if it thinks fit.

(6) Rule 49 enables the Master of the Court of Protection as well as a judge to order the attendance of a patient for examination.

(7) No appeal shall lie against the decision of the Chief Clerk of the Court under rule 83 as to whether to remit or postpone payment of any court fee.

(8) The rule (rule 73) enabling the Court to take certain steps in relation to the estate of a deceased patient even if no grant of representation is taken out is updated by increasing from £1,500 to £5,000 the maximum value of estates to which it applies. This is in line with the changes made in April 1984 by the Administration of Estates (Small Payments) (Increase of Limit) Order 1984 (S.I. 1984/539).

(9) The new Appendix of Fees makes certain changes to the court fees payable. In particular:—

    (a) annual fees are introduced in respect of the services of the Principal of the Management Division of the Court as receiver;

(b) fees for copies of documents are abolished;

(c) the requirement of the Rules that documents be marked when fees are taken is abolished.

(10) References to the Mental Health Act 1959 are replaced by references to the Mental Health Act 1983 and various drafting improvements are made, in particular to omit obsolete and unnecessary material and to modernise the wording of the forms prescribed in the Schedule.

STATUTORY INSTRUMENTS

1984 No. 2036

CROWN AGENTS FOR OVERSEA GOVERNMENTS AND ADMINISTRATIONS

The Crown Agents Commencing Capital Debt Order 1984

Laid before the House of Commons in draft

Made - - -	12*th December* 1984
Coming into Operation	13*th December* 1984

Whereas it is provided in section 17 of the Crown Agents Act 1979(a) ("the Act") that the Crown Agents shall assume a commencing capital debt in respect of which for an initial period interest shall be payable only if the Minister so determines;

And whereas it is provided in section 17(9) of the Act that "the initial period" means a period of five years or seven years if the Minister by order so provides;

And whereas a draft of this Order has been laid before the House of Commons in accordance with section 17(10) of the Act and has been approved by a resolution of that House;

Now, therefore, the Secretary of State, in exercise of the powers conferred by section 17(9) of the Act and now vested in him(b), hereby makes the following Order:—

1. This Order may be cited as the Crown Agents Commencing Capital Debt Order 1984 and shall come into operation on the day after the day on which it is made.

2. For the purposes of section 17 of the Act "the initial period" means the period of seven years beginning with the appointed day.

Geoffrey Howe,
One of Her Majesty's Principal
Secretaries of State.

12th December 1984.

(a) 1979 c.43.
(b) By virtue of Article 2(1) of the Ministry of Overseas Development (Dissolution) Order 1979 (S.I. 1979/1451).

EXPLANATORY NOTE

(This Note is not part of the Order.)

This Order extends from five years to seven years the period, beginning on 1st January 1980 (the "appointed day" prescribed in the Crown Agents Act 1979 (Appointed Day) Order 1979 (S.I. 1979/1672)), during which the Secretary of State has the power to determine whether and, if so, at what rate, interest is payable on the Crown Agents' commencing capital debt.

STATUTORY INSTRUMENTS

1984 No. 2037

TERMS AND CONDITIONS OF EMPLOYMENT

The Statutory Sick Pay Up-rating Order 1984

Laid before Parliament in draft

Made - - - -	*28th December* 1984
Coming into Operation	*6th April* 1985

Whereas, the Secretary of State for Social Services having made a review under section 7 of the Social Security and Housing Benefits Act 1982(**a**), a draft of the following Order was laid before Parliament in accordance with the provisions of section 7(5) of that Act and approved by resolution of each House of Parliament:

Now, therefore, the Secretary of State for Social Services, in exercise of the powers conferred upon him by section 7(5), (6) and (10) of the above-mentioned Act, and of all other powers enabling him in that behalf, hereby makes the following Order:—

Citation and commencement

1. This Order may be cited as the Statutory Sick Pay Up-rating Order 1984 and shall come into operation on 6th April 1985.

Increase of specified sums

2.—(1) The sums specified in section 7(1) of the Social Security and Housing Benefits Act 1982(**b**) (relationship between rates of payment of statutory sick pay and employees' normal weekly earnings) shall be increased in accordance with the provisions of this article with effect from 6th April 1985.

(2) The sums specified in section 7(1)(*a*) shall be increased from £42.25 and £68 to £44.35 and £71 respectively.

(3) The sums specified in section 7(1)(*b*) shall be increased from £35.45, £68 and £50.50 to £37.20, £71 and £53 respectively.

(4) The sum specified in section 7(1)(*c*) shall be increased from £28.55 to £30.

(**a**) 1982 c. 24.
(**b**) The sums specified in section 7(1), as enacted, were increased by the Statutory Sick Pay Up-rating Order 1983 (S.I. 1983/123), and the Statutory Sick Pay Up-rating (No. 2) Order 1983 (S.I. 1983/1947).

Transitional provision

3. Where a period of entitlement as between an employer and an employee is running at 6th April 1985—

(*a*) in a case where the employee's normal weekly earnings under his contract of service with that employer are not less than £68 they shall be treated as not less than £71 for the remainder of that period;

(*b*) in a case where the employee's normal weekly earnings under his contract of service with that employer are less than £68 but not less than £50.50 they shall be treated as less than £71 but not less than £53 for the remainder of that period.

Revocation

4. The Statutory Sick Pay Up-rating (No. 2) Order 1983(**a**) is hereby revoked.

Norman Fowler,
Secretary of State for Social Services.

28th December 1984.

EXPLANATORY NOTE

(This Note is not part of the Order.)

A draft of this Order has been laid before Parliament and approved by resolution of each House. The Order is made in consequence of a review carried out by the Secretary of State under section 7 of the Social Security and Housing Benefits Act 1982 ("the 1982 Act") for the purpose of determining whether the sums payable in respect of statutory sick pay and the weekly earnings limits have retained their value in relation to the general level of prices obtaining in Great Britain. For the purposes of the review the Secretary of State estimated the general level of prices by reference to the movement in the Retail Price Index in the year to the end of October 1984, during which the index rose by 5 per cent.

The Order increases further the sums specified in section 7(1) of the 1982 Act so that with effect from 6th April 1985 statutory sick pay payable by an employer will be at the weekly rate of £44.35 where the employee's normal weekly earnings under his contract of service with that employer are not less than £71, at the weekly rate of £37.20, where those earnings are less than £71 but not less than £53, or at the weekly rate of £30 in any other case. The Order contains a transitional provision for cases where a period of entitlement is running at 6th April 1985.

(**a**) S.I. 1983/1947.

STATUTORY INSTRUMENTS

1984 No. 2040

IMMIGRATION

The Immigration Appeals (Notices) Regulations 1984

Made - - - - -	21st December 1984
Laid before Parliament	11th January 1985
Coming into Operation	1st March 1985

In exercise of the powers conferred upon me by section 18(1) of the Immigration Act 1971 (a), I hereby make the following Regulations:—

Citation, commencement and revocation
1.—(1) These Regulations may be cited as the Immigration Appeals (Notices) Regulations 1984 and shall come into operation on 1st March 1985.

(2) The Immigration Appeals (Notices) Regulations 1972 (b) are hereby revoked.

Interpretation
2.—(1) In these Regulations—

"the Act" means the Immigration Act 1971;

"appeal" means an appeal under Part II of the Act and

"appealable" shall be construed accordingly;

"entry clearance officer" means a person having authority to grant an entry clearance on behalf of the Government of the United Kingdom.

(2) In these Regulations any reference to a Regulation shall be construed as a reference to a Regulation contained in these Regulations; and any reference in a Regulation to a paragraph shall be construed as a reference to a paragraph of that Regulation.

Notice of decisions and actions appealable under Part II of the Act
3.—(1) Subject to the following provisions of this Regulation, written notice of any decision or action which is appealable (or would be appealable but for the grounds of the decision or action) shall as soon as practicable be given in accordance with the provisions of these Regulations to the person in respect of whom the decision or action was taken.

(a) 1971 c. 77.   (b) S.I. 1972/1683, amended by S.I. 1982/1027.

(2) Any such notice as is referred to in paragraph (1) shall be given—

(a) in the case of a decision or action taken by an immigration officer in the exercise of powers conferred on him as such, by the immigration officer;

(b) in the case of a refusal of an application for the grant of an entry clearance or certificate of entitlement, where the decision was taken otherwise than in the United Kingdom and Islands, by the entry clearance officer who refused the application;

(c) where the officer required by sub-paragraph (a) or (b) of this paragraph to give the notice is for any reason unable to do so, by such an immigration officer or entry clearance officer as may be designated for the purpose by the Secretary of State;

(d) in the case of a decision or action other than one mentioned in sub-paragraph (a) or (b) of this paragraph, by the Secretary of State.

(3) Where any such decision or action as is mentioned in paragraph (1) is taken as a result of an application made or submitted by a person on behalf of another person, or where a person in respect of whom such decision or action is taken (herein referred to as "the applicant") has, subsequent to the making of the application, appointed a person to act on his behalf in connection with the application, the provisions of paragraph (1) shall be deemed to be satisfied if notice in compliance with those provisions is given to the person who made or submitted the application or, as the case may be, to the person appointed to act on behalf of the applicant.

(4) It shall not be necessary for notice to be given in compliance with the provisions of paragraph (1) if the officer or authority required by paragraph (2) to give it has no knowledge of the whereabouts or place of abode of the person to whom it is to be given.

(5) Where notice is given in compliance with the provisions of paragraph (1) of a decision to refuse leave to a person to enter the United Kingdom, it shall not be necessary in addition for notice to be given of the decision that he requires leave unless he claims or has claimed that leave is not required.

Contents of notice
4.—(1) Subject to the provisions of paragraph (2), any notice given under Regulation 3 shall—

(a) include a statement of the reasons for the decision or action to which it relates;

(b) if it relates to the giving of directions for the removal of any person from the United Kingdom to a country or territory specified in the directions, include a statement of that country or territory; and

(c) be accompanied by a statement informing the person in respect of whom the decision or action has been taken of—

(i) his right of appeal if any and the relevant provisions of the Act;

(ii) the manner in which the appeal should be brought and the address to which a notice of appeal should be sent;

(iii) the time within which an appeal should be brought; and

(iv) the facilities available for advice and assistance in connection therewith.

(2) In the case of a notice which relates to any decision to vary the limited leave of a person to enter or remain in the United Kingdom, it shall not be necessary to comply with the requirements of paragraph (1) if the decision was taken at the request of the person to whom notice is given and was not less favourable to him than that which was requested.

Certain notices under the Act deemed to comply with Regulations

5.—(1) Subject to the provisions of paragraph (2), where any power to refuse leave to enter or to give a limited leave to remain in or to vary leave to enter or remain in the United Kingdom is exercised by notice in writing in accordance with section 4 of or paragraph 6 of Schedule 2 to the Act (notice of decisions as to leave to enter or remain) the provisions of these Regulations shall, if the statements required by Regulation 4 are included in or accompany the notice, be deemed to have been complied with in relation to the exercise of that power.

(2) Paragraph (1) shall not apply in the case of a notice given to a person in charge of a party in accordance with sub-paragraph (4) of the said paragraph 6.

Service of notice

6. Any notice required by Regulation 3 to be given to any person may be delivered, or sent by post in a registered letter or by recorded delivery service to—

(*a*) that person's last known or usual place of abode; or

(*b*) an address provided by him for receipt of the notice.

Leon Brittan,
One of Her Majesty's Principal
Secretaries of State.

Home Office.
21st December 1984.

EXPLANATORY NOTE

(This Note is not part of the Regulations.)

These Regulations re-enact the Immigration Appeals (Notices) Regulations 1972 with amendments. The changes of substance are as follows:—

   (*a*) the circumstances in which a notice of a decision or action may be given to an applicant's representative are extended to include the case where the representative was appointed after the application was made (Regulation 3(3));

   (*b*) the means by which a notice may be served are extended (Regulation 6).

STATUTORY INSTRUMENTS

1984 No. 2041

IMMIGRATION

The Immigration Appeals (Procedure) Rules 1984

Made - - - -	*21st December* 1984
Laid before Parliament	*11th January* 1985
Coming into Operation	*1st March* 1985

ARRANGEMENT OF RULES

PART I

INTRODUCTION

In exercise of the powers conferred upon me by section 22 of the Immigration Act 1971(**a**) and paragraph 25 of Schedule 2 thereto, after consultation with the Council on Tribunals, I hereby make the following Rules:—

PART I

INTRODUCTION

Citation, commencement and revocation

1.— (1) These Rules may be cited as the Immigration Appeals (Procedure) Rules 1984 and shall come into operation on 1st March 1985.

(2) The Immigration Appeals (Procedure) Rules 1972(**b**) are hereby revoked; but where appeal proceedings were commenced in accordance with the provisions of the aforementioned Rules of 1972 before 1st March 1985 then those provisions continue to apply to those proceedings and nothing in these Rules affects those provisions.

(3) For the purposes of paragraph (2) above, appeal proceedings shall be regarded as having been commenced prior to 1st March 1985 if, before that date—

(a) notice of appeal relating to the proceedings in question was given in due form and to the appropriate officer, in accordance with Rule 6 of the Rules of 1972; or

(b) pursuant to Rule 5 of the Rules of 1972, a written petition was served on the appropriate officer specified in Rule 6(2) of those Rules.

Interpretation

2.— (1) In these Rules, unless the context otherwise requires:—

"the Act" means the Immigration Act 1971;

"appeal" means, subject to Rules 3 and 13, any appeal under Part II of the Act;

"appellate authority" means an adjudicator or the Tribunal;

"chairman" means any member of the Tribunal qualified as mentioned in paragraph 7 of Schedule 5 to the Act;

"entry clearance officer" means a person having authority to grant an entry clearance on behalf of the Government of the United Kingdom;

"officer" means an immigration officer or an entry clearance officer;

"the president" means the president of the Tribunal;

"the Tribunal" means the Immigration Appeal Tribunal for the purposes of the Act.

(2) Without prejudice to section 11 of the Interpretation Act 1978(**c**), the following expressions have the same meanings as in the Act:—

(**a**) 1971 c.77.
(**b**) S.I. 1972/1684, amended by S.I. 1982/1026.
(**c**) 1978 c.30.

"adjudicator";

"aircraft";

"certificate of entitlement";

"entry clearance";

"immigration officer";

"limited leave".

(3) Any reference in these Rules to a Rule is a reference to a Rule contained therein.

(4) Any reference in these Rules to a form is a reference to a form set out in the Schedule thereto.

PART II

APPEAL TO ADJUDICATOR OR TRIBUNAL AT FIRST INSTANCE

Application of Part II

3. This Part applies to appeals at first instance to an adjudicator or to the Tribunal, and references in this Part to—

(a) an appeal, an appellant, the appropriate appellate authority or proceedings shall be construed accordingly;

(b) the respondent, shall be construed as references to the person, other than the appellant, who is a party to the appeal by virtue of Rule 7(1).

Time limit for appealing

4.— (1) Notice of appeal under section 13(1) of the Act by a person refused leave to enter the United Kingdom may be given—

(a) where, by virtue of section 13(3) of the Act, he is not entitled to appeal so long as he is in the United Kingdom, after the departure of the ship or aircraft in which he leaves the United Kingdom but not later than 28 days thereafter;

(b) in any other case, before or after the departure of the ship or aircraft in which he is to be removed from, or leaves, the United Kingdom but not later than 28 days thereafter.

(2) Notice of appeal under section 13(2) of the Act by a person refused a certificate of entitlement, on an application duly made to an entry clearance officer, may be given not later than 3 months after the refusal.

(3) Notice of appeal under section 13(2) of the Act by a person refused a certificate of entitlement, on an application duly made to the Secretary of State, may be given not later than 14 days after the refusal.

(4) Notice of appeal under section 13(2) by a person refused an entry clearance may be given not later than 3 months after the refusal.

(5) Notice of appeal under section 14(1) of the Act by a person who has a

limited leave to enter or remain in the United Kingdom, against any variation of the leave or any refusal to vary it, may be given not later than 14 days after the variation or refusal to vary.

(6) Notice of appeal under section 14(2) of the Act by a person given a limited leave to remain in the United Kingdom in the circumstances there mentioned, against any provision limiting the duration of the leave or attaching any condition to it, may be given not later than 14 days after the giving of the limited leave.

(7) Notice of appeal under section 15(1)*(a)* of the Act by a person against whom the Secretary of State has decided to make a deportation order by virtue of section 3(5), against that decision, may be given not later than 14 days after the decision.

(8) Notice of appeal under section 15(1)*(b)* of the Act by a person against whom a deportation order is in force, against a refusal by the Secretary of State to revoke the order, may be given not later than 28 days after the refusal.

(9) Notice of appeal under section 16(1) of the Act by a person for whose removal from the United Kingdom such directions as are there mentioned have been given, against those directions, may be given—

> *(a)* where, by virtue of section 16(2) of the Act, he is not entitled to appeal so long as he is in the United Kingdom, after the departure of the ship or aircraft in which he leaves the United Kingdom but not later than 28 days thereafter;

> *(b)* in any other case, before or after the departure of the ship or aircraft in which he is to be removed from, or leaves, the United Kingdom but not later than 28 days thereafter.

(10) Notice of appeal under section 17(1) of the Act by a person for whose removal from the United Kingdom directions have been given, on the ground that he ought to be removed (if at all) to a different country or territory specified by him, may be given—

> *(a)* where the directions have been given on his being refused leave to enter the United Kingdom, at any time before the departure of the ship or aircraft in which he is to be removed from the United Kingdom;

> *(b)* in any other case, before such departure but not later than 14 days after the giving of the directions.

(11) Where notice in writing of an action or decision is required by the Immigration Appeals (Notices) Regulations 1984(a) to be given then, for the purposes of this Rule, that action or decision shall be deemed to have been taken—

> *(a)* where the notice is sent by post, on the day on which it was sent;

> *(b)* in any other case, on the day on which the notice was served.

(a) S.I. 1984/2040.

Further opportunity to appeal

5.— (1) Where a person gives, to the appropriate officer specified in Rule 6(2), notice of appeal after the expiry of the period permitted by Rule 4 for the giving of such notice, the appropriate officer may, subject to paragraph (3) below, treat the notice as if it had been given in accordance with Rule 4 if he is of the opinion that, by reason of special circumstances, it is just and right so to do, and in such a case the notice in question shall, as from the day on which the aforementioned power is exercised, be treated for all purposes as if it had been given in accordance with Rule 4.

(2) No steps shall be taken under this Rule in the case of a person in respect of whom a deportation order is for the time being in force.

(3) Rule 6(8) shall apply for the purposes of this Rule as it applies for the purposes of Rule 6.

Notice of appeal

6.— (1) Notice of appeal shall be given by furnishing, in writing, and serving on the appropriate officer specified in paragraph (2) below, the particulars specified in paragraph (3) below:

Provided that notice of appeal under section 13(1) of the Act by a person refused leave to enter, against the refusal (unless, by virtue of section 13(3) of the Act, he is not entitled to appeal so long as he is in the United Kingdom) or against the decision that he requires leave, may, if the appellant is in the United Kingdom, be given orally to any immigration officer (whether or not responsible for the decision or action in question) by him or by a person duly authorised by him in that behalf or, in the case of an appellant who is a minor or who is for any reason incapable of acting, by any person acting on his behalf.

(2) For the purposes of paragraph (1) above the appropriate officer is—

(a) in the case of an appeal under section 13(1), 16(1) or 17(1) of the Act, against an action or a decision for which an immigration officer is responsible, that officer;

(b) in the case of an appeal under section 13(2) of the Act by a person refused an entry clearance or a certificate of entitlement on an application duly made to an entry clearance officer, that officer;

(c) in the case of any other appeal, the Secretary of State,

except that, in the case of such an appeal as is mentioned in sub-paragraph (a) or (b) above, where the Secretary of State is satisfied that, by reason of special circumstances, it is impracticable or impossible for notice of appeal to be served on the immigration or entry clearance officer concerned, the appropriate officer shall be the Secretary of State or such immigration or entry clearance officer as he may designate to accept service of the notice.

(3) The particulars referred to in paragraph (1) above shall consist of—

(a) the full name, address, date of birth and nationality or citizenship of the appellant;

(b) particulars of the decision or action to which the notice relates; and

(c) the grounds of appeal on which the appellant intends to rely.

Without prejudice to paragraph *(c)* above, where the notice of appeal relates to a right of appeal under section 17 of the Act, the notice shall include a statement which specifies the reasons why the appellant objects to removal to the country or territory specified by the respondent, identifies the country or territory to which the appellant claims he ought to be removed (if at all) and refers to evidence which demonstrates or tends to show that the country or territory so identified would admit the appellant if he were to be removed there.

(4) The grounds of an appeal particularised in a notice of appeal may be varied or amplified at any time during the course of the appeal.

(5) The notice of appeal shall be signed by the appellant or by a person duly authorised by him in that behalf or, in the case of an appellant who is a minor or who is for any reason incapable of acting, by any person acting on his behalf.

(6)*(a)* Subject to paragraph (7) below, an officer to whom notice of appeal has been given in accordance with these Rules shall, unless the appellant subsequently gives that officer written notice of the withdrawal of his appeal, take such steps as are necessary to ensure that the notice of appeal is referred to the appropriate appellate authority together with such particulars relating to the nature and grounds of the appeal as have been given by the appellant.

(b) The steps required by sub-paragraph *(a)* above shall be taken, in the case of an immigration officer, as soon as practicable after the giving of the notice of appeal or, in any other case, as soon as practicable after the written statement of facts required by Rule 8 has been prepared.

(7) Where notice of appeal has been given to an officer in accordance with these Rules but the decision or action to which it relates has subsequently been reversed, withdrawn or varied, the officer shall ascertain whether the appellant wishes to pursue the appeal and—

(a) unless he does, no action shall be taken on the notice;

(b) if he does, he shall be afforded an opportunity to amend the notice or to substitute a fresh notice therefor.

(8) Where a written notice of appeal directed to an immigration officer or an entry clearance officer has in accordance with Rule 44 been sent to, or delivered at, the address mentioned in Rule 44(1)*(d)* then, if that officer is for any reason unable to receive the notice, it shall, on being received at that address, be deemed to have been served on him; and in any such case the Secretary of State shall cause the steps required by paragraph (6) above to be taken by another officer in accordance with that paragraph.

Parties

7.— (1) The parties to an appeal shall be the appellant and—

(a) in the case of an appeal under section 13(1), 16(1) or 17(1) of the Act against an action or a decision for which an immigration officer is responsible, that officer;

(b) in the case of an appeal under section 13(2) of the Act by a person refused an entry clearance or a certificate of entitlement on an application duly made to an entry clearance officer, that officer;

(c) in the case of any other appeal, the Secretary of State,

except that, in the case of such an appeal as is mentioned in sub-paragraph *(a)* or *(b)* above, where the Secretary of State is satisfied that, by reason of special circumstances, it is impracticable or impossible for the immigration or entry clearance officer concerned to take part in the proceedings, the Secretary of State may direct that he, or such immigration or entry clearance officer as he may designate for the purpose, shall be treated as a party to the appeal in place of the officer concerned; and thereupon any notice or other document sent or given by or to the officer concerned for the purposes of the appeal shall be deemed to have been sent or given by or to the Secretary of State or the designated officer.

(2) The Secretary of State shall be treated as a party to any appeal, where he would not otherwise be a party to it by virtue of this Rule, upon giving written notice to the appellate authority at any time during the course of the appeal stating that he desires to be so treated.

(3) If any party to an appeal is or claims to be a refugee within the competence of the United Nations High Commissioner for Refugees, the United Kingdom Representative of the High Commissioner shall be treated as a party to the appeal upon giving written notice to the appellate authority at any time during the course of the appeal stating that he desires to be so treated.

Explanatory statement by respondent

8.— (1) Subject to the provisions of paragraphs (2) and (3) below, the respondent in an appeal shall, as soon as practicable after the notice of the appeal is given, cause to be prepared a written statement of the facts relating to the decision or action in question and the reasons therefor and take such steps as are necessary to ensure that the statement is referred to an adjudicator or the Tribunal, as appropriate, and that a copy thereof is given to the appellant.

(2) It shall not be necessary for an immigration officer who is the respondent in an appeal to comply with the requirements of paragraph (1) above if he is of the opinion that it is not practicable to do so, having regard to the time available before the hearing of the appeal; but he shall then, as soon as practicable after notice of the appeal is given, give written notice to the appellate authority and the appellant that he is of that opinion and that a statement of the facts relating to the decision or action in question and the reasons therefor will be given orally at the hearing of the appeal.

(3) Where the respondent to an appeal alleges that—

    (a) the appellant is not entitled to appeal—

        (i) by virtue of a provision of the Act specified by the respondent, or

        (ii) by reason that a passport or other travel document, certificate of entitlement, entry clearance or work permit (or any part thereof or entry therein) on which the appellant relies is a forgery or was issued to, and relates to, a person other than the appellant, or

        (iii) by reason that notice of appeal has not been signed by the appellant or by a person duly authorised by him in that behalf or, in the case of an appellant who is a minor or who is for any reason incapable of acting, by any person acting on his behalf; or *(b)* the notice of appeal was not given within the period permitted by Rule 4,

the written statement referred to in paragraph (1) above shall include that allegation but it shall not be necessary for the respondent to include in the statement facts which are not relevant to the allegation.

(4) Where a written statement has been given in accordance with paragraph (1) above, then at the commencement of any hearing before an appellate authority, the authority shall give to the respondent an opportunity to amplify orally the statement of the facts relating to the decision or action in question and the reasons therefor contained in the written statement; if no such written statement has been given, then at the commencement of any hearing before an appellate authority, the authority shall obtain from the respondent an oral statement of the facts relating to the decision or action in question and the reasons therefor.

Appeal against removal on objection to destination

9.— (1) This Rule shall apply where an appellant objects to removal to a particular country or territory and claims that he ought to be removed (if at all) to a different country or territory—

(a) on appeal under section 17(1) of the Act; or

(b) by virtue of section 17(2) of the Act, on appeal under section 13(1) thereof, or

(c) by virtue of section 17(3) of the Act, on appeal under section 15 thereof.

(2) The appellant shall submit with his notice of appeal a statement in writing of the matters put forward in support of his objection and claim.

Supply of documents

10. Subject to the provisions of Rule 30(2) (cases involving forgery of documents) the appellate authority shall cause copies of all notices and other documents required for an appeal to be supplied to every party to the appeal.

Determination of preliminary issues

11.— (1) Where the respondent to an appeal makes such an allegation as is mentioned in Rule 8(3), the appellate authority may, and at the request of the respondent shall, determine the validity of the allegation as a preliminary issue.

(2) Unless in consequence of the determination of such a preliminary issue the appellate authority determines that—

(a) it has no jurisdiction to proceed, or

(b) the appeal should be dismissed,

the respondent shall, by such time as the appellate authority directs, submit to that authority a written statement of the facts relating to the decision or action in question to the extent that by virtue of the provisions of Rule 8(3) those facts have not already been furnished, and a copy of such a statement shall be given to the appellant.

(3) Save where, in consequence of a determination of a preliminary issue, an appellate authority makes a further determination to the effect specified in subparagraph *(a)* or *(b)* of paragraph (2) above, in any hearing before the authority, at the commencement of the proceedings subsequent to the determination of the preliminary issue, the appellant authority shall give to the respondent an opportunity to amplify orally the written statements given in accordance with Rule 8(1) or paragraph (2) above.

(4) Where the respondent to an appeal makes such an allegation as is mentioned in Rule 8(3)(b) and the appellate authority determines, as a preliminary issue, that the notice of appeal was not given within the period permitted by Rule 4, then, except where a deportation order is for the time being in force in respect of the appellant, the appellate authority shall not be required to dismiss the appeal but may allow it to proceed if the authority is of the opinion that, by reason of special circumstances, it is just and right so to do; and, in such case, the notice of appeal shall be treated for all purposes as if it had been given in accordance with Rule 4.

Determination of appeal without hearing

12.— (1) An appellate authority may determine an appeal without a hearing if—

(a) no party to the appeal has requested a hearing; or

(b) the appellate authority has decided, after giving every other party to the appeal an opportunity of replying to any representations submitted in writing by or on behalf of the appellant, to allow the appeal; or

(c) the appellate authority is satisfied that the appellant is outside the United Kingdom or that it is impracticable to give him notice of a hearing and, in either case, that no person is authorised to represent him at a hearing; or

(d) the appellate authority is satisfied that no matter arises on the appeal other than an objection by the appellant to removal to a particular country or territory or a claim by him that he ought to be removed (if at all) to a different country or territory and is of opinion that matters put forward in support of the appeal in pursuance of Rule 9 do not warrant a hearing; or

(e) such a preliminary issue as is referred to in Rule 11 arises and the appellate authority has afforded the appellant a reasonable opportunity to submit a statement in writing of matters put forward in rebuttal of the respondent's allegation, and—

(i) the appellant has not submitted such a statement, or
(ii) the appellate authority is of the opinion that matters put forward by the appellant in such a statement do not warrant a hearing; or

(f) the decision appealed against has been withdrawn or reversed by the respondent, and the appellate authority is satisfied that written notice of the withdrawal or reversal, as appropriate, has been given to the appellant by the respondent.

PART III

APPEAL TO TRIBUNAL FROM ADJUDICATOR

Application of Part III

13. This Part applies to appeals to the Tribunal from the determination of an adjudicator under section 20 of the Act, and, except where the context otherwise requires, references in this Part to an appeal, an appellant or proceedings shall be construed accordingly.

Leave to appeal

14.— (1) An appeal shall lie only with the leave of the adjudicator or of the Tribunal.

(2) In addition to the circumstances in which leave to appeal must be granted by virtue of section 22(5) of the Act (existence of certificate of entitlement or entry clearance), an appellate authority to whom application for leave to appeal as aforesaid is duly made shall grant it—

(a) if the authority is satisfied that the determination of the appeal involves an arguable point of law, except that where leave to appeal is sought from the Tribunal on the ground that an adjudicator misdirected himself on a point of law then the Tribunal may, notwithstanding that it is of the opinion that the point of law raised in the application might be decided in favour of the applicant, refuse leave to appeal if it considers that even if the adjudicator had not misdirected himself on the point in question, he could properly have made the determination he did; or

(b) where an adjudicator has dismissed an appeal by a person who is in the United Kingdom, if the authority is satisfied that the country or territory to which he is to be removed is one to which he is unwilling to go owing to a well founded fear of being persecuted there for reasons of race, religion, nationality, membership of a particular social group or political opinion.

Time limit for appealing

15.— (1) Application to an adjudicator for leave to appeal shall be made forthwith after the determination in question.

(2) Application to the Tribunal for leave to appeal or notice of appeal may be made or given not later than 14 days after the determination in question.

(3) Where the applicant or the appellant, as the case may be, is the person against whom the decision or action in question was taken and he is not in the United Kingdom, the Isle of Man, the Channel Islands or the Republic of Ireland, paragraph (2) above shall have effect as if for the words "14 days" there were substituted the words "42 days".

(4) In this Rule any reference to a determination is a reference—

(a) where it is pronounced at a hearing in the presence of the appellant or his representative, to its pronouncement;

(b) in any other case, to the sending to the appellant in accordance with Rule 44, or to the delivery to the appellant, of a copy of the document, referred to in Rule 39(3), recording the determination.

Notice of appeal and application for leave to appeal

16.— (1) Subject to the following provisions of this Rule, notice of appeal or an application for leave to appeal from an adjudicator to the Tribunal shall, respectively, be given or made by furnishing, in writing, and serving on an adjudicator or the Tribunal, as appropriate, the particulars specified in paragraph (2) below.

(2) The particulars referred to in paragraph (1) above shall consist of—

(a) the full name, address, date of birth and nationality or citizenship of the appellant or applicant, as the case may be;

(b) particulars of the determination of the adjudicator to which the notice or application, as the case may be, relates; and

(c) the grounds on which the appellant, or applicant, as the case may be, intends to rely.

(3) The notice or application shall be signed by the appellant or applicant, as the case may be, or by a person duly authorised by him in that behalf or, in the case of an appellant or applicant who is a minor or who is for any reason incapable of acting, by any person acting on his behalf.

(4) The grounds of an appeal or application contained in particulars furnished in accordance with paragraph (1) above may be varied or amplified during the course of the appeal or application.

(5) Notwithstanding the provisions of paragraph 1 above, an application to an adjudicator for leave to appeal may be made orally by the applicant or by a person duly authorised by him in that behalf or, in the case of an applicant who is a minor or who is for any reason incapable of acting, by any person acting on his behalf: but, if leave is granted, the requirements of paragraph (1) above; relating to the giving of notice of appeal shall be complied with, in accordance with the time-limits specified in paragraphs (2) and (3) of Rule 15 above, except that the notice of appeal shall be served on the adjudicator instead of on the Tribunal.

(6) An application for leave to appeal shall be disposed of without a hearing unless the adjudicator or, as the case may be, the Tribunal to whom the application is made considers that special circumstances render a hearing desirable.

(7) Where an adjudicator grants leave to appeal he shall endorse on or attach to the written application made in accordance with paragraph (1) above or, as the case may be, the notice of appeal served on him in pursuance of paragraph (5) above, notice in writing of his decision, and he shall transmit the application or notice of appeal, together with the endorsement or notice of his decision, to the Tribunal; and in any such case notice of appeal shall be deemed to have been duly given to the Tribunal.

(8) Where the Tribunal grants leave to appeal on an application made in accordance with paragraph (1), notice of appeal shall be deemed to have been duly given to the Tribunal.

Parties

17.— (1) On any appeal against the determination of an adjudicator, the persons who were the parties to the appeal before the adjudicator shall be the parties to the appeal before the Tribunal.

(2) The Secretary of State shall be treated as a party to any appeal, where he would not otherwise be a party to it by virtue of paragraph (1) above, upon giving written notice to the Tribunal at any time during the course of the appeal stating that he desires to be so treated.

(3) If any party to an appeal is or claims to be a refugee within the competence of the United Nations High Commissioner for Refugees, the United Kingdom Representative of the High Commissioner shall be treated as a party to the appeal, where he would not otherwise be a party to it by virtue of paragraph (1) above, upon giving written notice to the Tribunal at any time during the course of the appeal stating that he desires to be so treated.

(4) If the Secretary of State is satisfied that an officer is for any reason unable to take part in the proceedings of any appeal to which he would otherwise be a party by virtue of paragraph (1) above, the Secretary of State may direct that he, or such immigration or entry clearance officer as he may designate for the purpose, shall be treated as a party to the appeal in place of the officer; and thereupon any notice or other document sent or given by or to the officer for the purpose of the appeal shall be deemed to have been sent or given by or to the Secretary of State or the designated officer.

Evidence

18.— (1) In any proceedings on an appeal the Tribunal shall receive as evidence the summary or record taken or kept in accordance with Rule 40 of any evidence received—

- *(a)* by the adjudicator in the course of the proceedings to which the appeal relates, or

- *(b)* by an adjudicator to whom the appeal has been remitted in pursuance of paragraph (3)*(c)*(i) below.

(2) If any party to the appeal wishes to adduce evidence before the Tribunal further to that to be received in accordance with paragraph (1) above, he shall give notice in writing to that effect to the Tribunal indicating the nature of the evidence; and any such notice shall—

- *(a)* in the case of the appellant, be given with the notice of appeal or as soon as practicable after notice of appeal is given or is deemed to have been given;

- *(b)* in the case of any other party, as soon as practicable after he has been notified of the appeal.

(3) In any proceedings on an appeal—

- *(a)* the Tribunal may, in its discretion, receive or decline to receive further evidence of which notice has been given in accordance with paragraph (2) above;

- *(b)* if, to enable it to arrive at a proper determination of the appeal, the Tribunal requests the furnishing of further evidence relating to specified matters, it shall receive such further evidence;

(c) where such further evidence as is mentioned in sub-paragraph *(a)* or *(b)* above falls to be received it shall be given, as the Tribunal may direct, either—

    (i) orally, in which case the Tribunal may take the further evidence itself or remit the appeal to the same or another adjudicator for the taking of that evidence, or

    (ii) in writing, in which case it shall be given in such manner and at such time as the Tribunal may require.

Supply of documents

19. Subject to the provisions of Rule 30(2) (cases involving forgery of documents), the Tribunal shall cause copies of all notices and other documents required for an appeal, other than those already supplied in accordance with Rule 10, to be supplied to every party to the appeal.

Determination of appeal without hearing

20. The Tribunal may dispose of an appeal without a hearing if—

(a) no party to the appeal has requested a hearing; or

(b) where the appellant is the person against whom the decision or action in question was taken, the Tribunal is satisfied that he is outside the United Kingdom or that it is impracticable to give him notice of a hearing and, in either case, that no other person is authorised to represent him at a hearing; or

(c) leave to appeal to the Tribunal is granted pursuant to section 22(5) of the Act and the Tribunal is of the opinion, after giving the appellant an opportunity of responding to any evidence submitted in writing by the respondent, that the matters put forward in support of the appeal do not warrant a hearing.

Remittal of appeal for determination by adjudicator

21.— (1) The Tribunal may, if in the circumstances of a particular appeal it thinks it appropriate so to do, remit that appeal to an adjudicator for determination by him in accordance with any directions given to him by the Tribunal.

(2) The adjudicator to whom an appeal is remitted under this Rule may be either the adjudicator whose determination is the subject matter of the appeal or some other adjudicator.

(3) Subject to any necessary adaptations, Rules 17, 18 and 19 shall apply in relation to any proceedings on an appeal remitted to an adjudicator under this Rule as they apply in relation to proceedings before the Tribunal.

PART IV

GENERAL PROCEDURE

Application of Part IV

22.— (1) This Part shall apply in relation to—

(a) proceedings to which Part II applies (appeal at first instance to an adjudicator or the Tribunal);

(b) proceedings to which Part III applies (appeal to the Tribunal from an adjudicator), and

(c) an application for bail.

(2) References in this Part to the appellant shall be construed—

(a) in relation to proceedings to which Part II applies, in accordance with Rule 3;

(b) in relation to proceedings to which Part III applies, as references to the person who was the appellant before the adjudicator, notwithstanding that he may not be the appellant before the Tribunal, and

(c) in relation to an application for bail, as references to the person to whom the application relates, notwithstanding that he may not have an appeal pending.

Bail

23.— (1) An application by an appellant to be released on bail under paragraph 22 or 29 of Schedule 2 to the Act—

(a) if made to an immigration officer or police officer, shall be made orally; or

(b) if made to an appellate authority, shall be made either orally or in writing.

(2) Where an application is made in writing pursuant to paragraph (1)(b) above, it shall contain the following particulars—

(a) the full name of the appellant;

(b) the address of the place where the appellant is detained at the time when the application is made;

(c) the address where the appellant would reside if his application for bail were to be granted;

(d) the amount of the recognizance in which he would agree to be bound;

(e) the full names, addresses and occupations of two persons who might act as sureties for the applicant if his application for bail were to be granted, and the amounts of the recognizances in which those persons might agree to be bound; and

(f) the grounds on which the application is made.

(3) An application made in writing pursuant to paragraph (1)(b) above shall be signed by the applicant or by a person duly authorised by him in that behalf, or, in the case of an applicant who is a minor or who is for any reason incapable of acting, by any person acting on his behalf.

(4) The recognizance of an appellant shall be in Form 1 and that of a surety in Form 2.

(5) Where an appellate authority directs the release of an appellant on bail and the taking of the recognizance is postponed under paragraph 22(3) or 29(6)

of Schedule 2 to the Act, the authority shall certify in writing that it has granted bail in respect of the appellant, and shall include in the certificate particulars of the conditions to be endorsed on the recognizance with a view to the recognizance being taken subsequently, the amounts in which the appellant and any sureties are to be bound and the date of issue of the certificate.

(6) The person having custody of an appellant shall—

(a) on receipt of a certificate signed by the secretary of the Tribunal or by the adjudicator stating that the recognizances of any sureties required have been taken, or on being otherwise satisfied that all such recognizances have been taken; and

(b) on being satisfied that the appellant has entered into his recognizance,

release the appellant.

(7) Paragraphs (4) and (5) above shall not apply to Scotland, and in its application to Scotland paragraph (6) above shall have effect as if for the references to recognizance of sureties having been taken there were substituted references to bail having been taken and for the references to a recognizance there were substituted references to a bail bond.

Notice of time and place of hearing

24.— (1) Subject to the provisions of paragraph (2) below, as soon as practicable after notice of appeal has been given, or is deemed to have been given, or an appeal has been remitted to an adjudicator in accordance with Rule 18(3)(c)(i) or 21 the appellate authority shall, if there is to be a hearing, give notice in writing to every party to the appeal stating the time and place of the hearing.

(2) Where an appellant is detained under paragraph 16 of Schedule 2 to the Act (detention pending examination or removal), the appellate authority may, instead of giving notice in writing as aforesaid, cause any immigration officer to be notified orally of the time and place of the hearing; and thereupon that officer shall take such steps as are necessary to ensure that every party to the appeal is notified accordingly and that the appellant is produced at the hearing.

(3) Where a hearing is adjourned, the appellate authority shall give notice, either orally or in writing, to every party to the appeal of the time and place of the adjourned hearing except in the case of a party who has been absent throughout the preceding proceedings on the appeal or where the authority is satisfied that it is impracticable to give such notice.

Power to require particulars

25. An appellate authority may at any time request any party to the appeal to furnish any particulars which appear to be requisite for the determination of the appeal and thereupon that party shall send the particulars to the appellate authority.

Representation

26.— (1) In any proceedings on an appeal, a party to the appeal may act in person or be represented or may appear—

(a) in the case of the appellant, by counsel or a solicitor, a consular officer or a person performing functions corresponding to those of a consular officer, a person appointed in that behalf by any voluntary organisation for the time being in receipt of a grant under section 23 of the Act or, with the leave of the appellate authority, by any other person appearing to the authority to be acting on behalf of the appellant;

(b) in the case of the Secretary of State or any officer, by counsel or a solicitor or any officer of the Home Department;

(c) in the case of the United Kingdom Representative of the United Nations High Commissioner for Refugees, by a person appointed by him in that behalf.

(2) A person representing a party to an appeal in accordance with paragraph (1) above may take all such steps and do all such things relating to the proceedings as the person whom he represents is by these Rules required or authorised to take or do.

Summoning of witnesses

27.— (1) An appellate authority may, for the purposes of any appeal, by summons require any person in the United Kingdom to attend as a witness at a hearing of the appeal at such time and place as may be specified in the summons and, subject to the provisions of Rule 29(2), at the hearing to answer any questions or produce any documents in his custody or under his control which relate to any matter in question in the appeal:

Provided that no person shall be required, in obedience to such a summons, to go more than 10 miles from his place of residence unless the necessary expenses of his attendance are paid or tendered to him, and, when the summons is issued at the request of a party to the appeal, those expenses are so paid or tendered by that party.

(2) Any such summons shall be in Form 3.

Conduct of proceedings at hearings

28. Subject to the provisions of Rules 18 and 34 at any hearing by an appellate authority—

(a) the appellate authority shall give to each party to the appeal an opportunity to address the authority, to give evidence and to call witnesses, and any party to the appeal may put questions to any person giving evidence before the authority;

(b) the appellate authority shall give to each party to the appeal an opportunity of making representations on the evidence (if any) and on the subject matter of the appeal generally but, where evidence is taken, such opportunity shall not be given before the completion of the taking of evidence,

but, save as aforesaid and after complying where appropriate with the provisions of Rule 8(5) or 11(3), the appellate authority shall conduct the proceedings in such manner as it considers appropriate in the circumstances for ascertaining the matters in dispute and determining the appeal.

Evidence

29.— (1) An appellate authority may receive oral, documentary or other evidence of any fact which appears to the authority to be relevant to the appeal, notwithstanding that such evidence would be inadmissible in a court of law.

(2) In any proceedings before an appellate authority, no person shall be compelled to give any evidence or produce any document which he could not be compelled to give or produce on the trial of an action in that part of the United Kingdom in which the proceedings are conducted.

(3) An appellate authority may require any witness to give evidence on oath or affirmation, and for that purpose an oath or affirmation in due form may be administered.

Inspection of documentary evidence

30.— (1) Subject to paragraph (2) below, when an appellate authority takes into consideration documentary evidence the authority shall give every party to the appeal an opportunity of inspecting that evidence and taking copies thereof.

(2) Where on an appeal it is alleged—

    (a) that a passport or other travel document, certificate of entitlement, entry clearance or work permit (or any part thereof or entry therein) on which a party relies is a forgery, and

    (b) that the disclosure to that party of any matters relating to the method of detection would be contrary to the public interest,

then, if supply of a document to that party would involve such disclosure, that document shall not be supplied to, or made available for inspection by, that party.

Burden of proof

31.— (1) If in any proceedings before an appellate authority a party thereto asserts that a decision or action taken against him under any provisions of the Act ought not to have been taken on the grounds that he is not a person to whom those provisions apply, it shall lie on him to prove that he is not such a person.

(2) If in any proceedings before an appellate authority a party thereto asserts any fact of such a kind that, if the assertion were made to the Secretary of State or any officer for the purposes of any of the provisions of the Act or any immigration rules, it would by virtue of those provisions or rules be for him to satisfy the Secretary of State or officer of the truth thereof, it shall lie on that party to prove that the assertion is true.

(3) In paragraph (2) above, "immigration rules" means the rules for the time being laid down as mentioned in section 3(2) of the Act.

Exclusion of public

32.— (1) Subject to the provisions of this Rule, any hearing by an appellate authority shall take place in public.

(2) Subject to the provisions of paragraph (4) below, where in accordance with section 22(4) of the Act (cases involving forgery of documents) an appellate authority is required to arrange for the proceedings to take place in the absence of a party and his representatives, the authority shall exclude all members of the public from those proceedings.

(3) Subject to the provisions of paragraph (4) below, an appellate authority may exclude any member of the public or members of the public generally from any hearing by the authority or from any part of such a hearing—

(a) at the request of a party; or

(b) where, in the opinion of the authority, a member of the public is behaving in a manner likely to interfere with the proper conduct of the proceedings and, to prevent such interference, that member or members of the public generally should be excluded; or

(c) where, in the opinion of the authority, such evidence relating to a person other than a party is likely to be given as, subject to the interests of the parties, should not be given in public and no party requests that it be given in public.

(4) Nothing in this Rule shall prevent a member of the Council on Tribunals or of its Scottish Committee from attending a hearing in his capacity as such.

Transfer of proceedings

33.— (1) Where any proceedings before an adjudicator have not been disposed of by the adjudicator and the chief adjudicator, or any person for the time being carrying out the functions of the chief adjudicator, is of the opinion that it is not practicable without undue delay for the proceedings to be completed by that adjudicator, he shall make arrangements for them to be dealt with by another adjudicator; and any adjudicator to whom any proceedings are transferred as aforesaid shall have power to deal with them as if they had been commenced before him.

(2) Where an adjudicator dealing with an appeal considers that it is expedient that it should be dealt with by another adjudicator—

(a) at a place elsewhere by reason of the existence there of facilities for the medical examination or further medical examination of the appellant; or

(b) by reason of the first-mentioned adjudicator's personal connection with, or interest in, the circumstances of the appeal,

the first-mentioned adjudicator may make arrangements for it to be dealt with by that other adjudicator; and any other adjudicator to whom an appeal is transferred as aforesaid shall have power to deal with it as if it had been commenced before him.

(3) Where any proceedings are transferred to an adjudicator in accordance with paragraph (1) or (2) above, any notice or other document sent or given by

or to the adjudicator from whom the proceedings were transferred shall be deemed to have been sent or given by or to the first-mentioned adjudicator.

Hearing of appeal in absence of appellant or other party

34.— (1) An appellate authority may, where in the circumstances of the case it appears to the authority proper so to do, hear an appeal in the absence of the appellant—

(a) if satisfied that he is not in the United Kingdom; or

(b) if satisfied that he is suffering from a communicable disease or from a mental disorder; or

(c) if satisfied that by reason of illness or accident he cannot attend the hearing; or

(d) if satisfied that it is impracticable to give him notice of the hearing and that no person is authorised to represent him at the hearing.

(2) Without prejudice to paragraph (1) above but subject to paragraph (3) below, an appellate authority may proceed with the hearing of an appeal in the absence of a party (including the appellant) if satisfied that, in the case of that party, such notice of the time and place of the hearing, or of the adjourned hearing, as is required by Rule 24, has been given.

(3) The appellate authority shall not, unless in the circumstances of the case it appears to the authority proper so to do, proceed with the hearing in pursuance of paragraph (2) above if the absent party has furnished the authority with an explanation of his absence.

(4) Where in pursuance of this Rule an appellate authority hears an appeal or proceeds with a hearing in the absence of the appellant or some other party, the authority may determine the appeal upon such evidence as has been received.

(5) For the purposes of this Rule—

(a) notice of the time and place of a hearing, or an adjourned hearing, shall be presumed to have been given, unless the contrary be shown, if notice was sent by post in accordance with Rule 44 not later than 7 days before the date thereof;

(b) a reference to a party (including an appellant) includes a reference to his representative.

Summary determination of appeals

35.— (1) Subject to the provisions of paragraph (2) below, where it appears to an appellate authority that the issues raised on an appeal have been determined—

(a) in the case of an appeal before an adjudicator, by the same or another adjudicator or by the Tribunal, or

(b) in the case of an appeal before the Tribunal, by the Tribunal,

under Part II of the Act in previous proceedings to which the appellant was a party, on the basis of facts which did not materially differ from those to which the appeal relates, the authority may forthwith determine the appeal without a hearing.

(2) Before an appellate authority determines an appeal without a hearing in accordance with paragraph (1) above, the authority shall give the parties an opportunity of making representations to the effect that the appeal ought not to be so determined.

(3) Where an appeal is determined without a hearing in accordance with paragraph (1) above, the appellate authority shall give written notice to the parties that the appeal has been so determined, and any such notice shall contain a statement of the issues raised on the appeal and specify the previous proceedings in which those issues were determined.

Combined hearings

36. Where in the case of two or more appeals it appears to the appellate authority—

> *(a)* that some common question of law or fact arises in both or all of them; or

> *(b)* that they relate to decisions or action taken in respect of persons who are members of the same family; or

> *(c)* that for some other reason it is desirable to proceed with the appeals under this Rule,

the appellate authority may, with the agreement of all the parties to those appeals, decide that the appeals should be heard together.

Miscellaneous powers

37. An appellate authority may—

> *(a)* postpone the time fixed for the hearing of an appeal;

> *(b)* give directions on any matter arising in connection with an appeal to any party who requests them;

> *(c)* if the parties to an appeal agree in writing upon the terms of a determination to be made by the appellate authority, determine the appeal accordingly;

> *(d)* adjourn the hearing of any evidence or representations or the consideration of an appeal to such date as the authority may determine; and

> *(e)* subject to the provisions of the Act and of these Rules, regulate its own procedure.

Irregularities

38. Any irregularity resulting from failure to comply with these Rules before an appellate authority has reached its decision shall not by itself render the proceedings void, but the appellate authority may, and shall if it considers that any person may have been prejudiced, take such steps as it thinks fit before reaching its decision to cure the irregularity, whether by amendment of any document, the giving of any notice or otherwise.

Promulgation of determination and reasons therefor

39.— (1) Where there is a hearing of an appeal and the appellate authority does not reserve the determination on the appeal, the authority shall pronounce the determination and the reasons therefor at the conclusion of the hearing, and shall send to every party to the appeal, as soon as practicable, a copy of the document recording the determination, referred to in paragraph (3) below.

(2) Where there is a hearing of an appeal but the appellate authority reserves the determination on the appeal, the appellate authority shall as soon as practicable notify every party to the appeal of its determination by sending to each party a copy of the document recording the determination referred to in paragraph (3) below.

(3) The determination on any appeal shall be recorded by the appellate authority in a document signed by the adjudicator or, as the case may be, the president or presiding chairman of the Tribunal; and the reasons for the determination shall be set out therein.

Record of proceedings

40. The appellate authority shall cause a summary of the proceedings before it to be taken, except insofar as a record of them is kept by means of shorthand notes or by mechanical means.

PART V

MISCELLANEOUS

References by the Secretary of State

41. An appellate authority shall consider any matter referred to it by the Secretary of State for consideration under section 21 of the Act in whatever manner it thinks appropriate.

Performance of functions of Tribunal

42. The following functions may be performed by the president of the Tribunal or a chairman thereof acting alone—

(a) any function conferred on the Tribunal by Part II of Schedule 2 to the Act;

(b) any function conferred on the Tribunal relating to applications for leave to appeal;

(c) any function conferred on the Tribunal to—

(i) determine a preliminary issue, or to make a determination in consequence thereof, pursuant to Rule 11 above;

(ii) remit an appeal to an adjudicator pursuant to Rule 21(1) above; or

(iii) require the attendance of witnesses at the hearing of an appeal, pursuant to Rule 27 above.

Time

43.— (1) Where the time provided by these Rules for doing any act expires on a Saturday. a Sunday or a public holiday and by reason thereof the act cannot be done on that day. the act shall be in time if done on the next working day.

(2) Where. under these Rules. an act is to be done not later than a specified period after any event. the period shall be calculated from the expiry of the day on which the event occurred.

Notices etc.

44.— (1) Any notice or other document required or authorised by these Rules to be sent or given to any person or authority may be sent by post in a registered letter or by the recorded delivery service or delivered—

(a) in the case of a document directed to the Tribunal. to the secretary of the Tribunal:

(b) in the case of a document directed to an adjudicator. to any person employed as his clerk:

(c) in the case of a document directed to the Secretary of State. to the Immigration and Nationality Department (Appeals Section). the Home Office;

(d) in the case of a document directed to an immigration officer or entry clearance officer, to the address specified in the statement issued in relation to the decision or action in question under Regulation 4 of the Immigration Appeals (Notices) Regulations 1984 or, if no such statement has been issued, to the address specified in sub-paragraph (c) above;

(e) in the case of a document directed to any other person. to his address for service specified in any notice given under these Rules, or to his last known or usual place of abode,

and, if sent or given to a person representing a party to an appeal in accordance with Rule 26(1), shall be deemed to have been sent or given to that party.

(2) A party to an appeal may at any time by notice to the appellate authority change his address for service under these Rules.

Variation of forms

45. The forms set out in the Schedule to these Rules or forms substantially to the like effect may be used with such variations as the circumstances may require.

Leon Brittan,
One of Her Majesty's Principal
Secretaries of State.

Home Office.
21st December 1984.

SCHEDULE

FORMS   Rule 45

FORM 1   Rule 23(4)

IMMIGRATION ACT 1971

Recognizance of appellant

I,..(hereinafter called the appellant) acknow-
ledge that I owe to Her Majesty The Queen the sum of £..........................., payment
thereof to be enforced against me by due process of law if I fail to comply with the
condition[s] endorsed hereon.

Signed...

Address at which appellant proposes to reside pending appeal:

....

....

....

Taken before me the...........day of ....19......

at..

Signed...

Office ....

(*Endorsement*)

Condition[s]

The condition[s] of this recognizance is [are] that if the appellant appears before
....(appellate authority) at...(time
and place) unless the appellate authority otherwise orders, then this recognizance shall
be void, but otherwise shall remain in full force (*see Note below*).

Note:
   Conditions appearing to the appellate authority to be likely to result in the appellant's
appearance at the time and place required may be added.

Rule 23(4)

FORM 2

IMMIGRATION ACT 1971

Recognizance of appellant's surety

I,...acknowledge that I owe to Her Majesty

The Queen the sum of £................................., payment thereof to be enforced against

me by due process of law if...................................... detained in......................................
fails to comply with the condition endorsed hereon.

Signed ....

Address ....

....

....

Taken before me the............................. day of................................. 19........ at...........

Signed ....

Office ....

(*Endorsement*)

Condition

The condition of the recognizance is that if the said..

appears before.. (appellate authority) at................. (time
and place) unless the appellate authority otherwise orders, then this recognizance shall
be void, but otherwise shall remain in full force.

FORM 3   Rule 27(2)

IMMIGRATION ACT 1971

Summons to witness

To.. (name)

of...(address)

An appeal has been lodged by...

against the   *\{ decision

                *\{ action   of ....

                *\{ determination

to the effect that:—

....⎡State shortly the

                                           |particulars of the

....⎨decision, action or

                                           |determination

....⎣appealed against

And I, the undersigned, am satisfied that you are likely to be able to [give material evidence] [and] [produce the undermentioned document[s] likely to be material evidence] therein.

You are therefore summoned to attend as a witness at the hearing of the appeal at ....(time and place) and at the hearing to [answer any questions] [and] [produce the following document[s]]:—

Signed ....
(President/Chairman of the Tribunal/
Adjudicator)

Date..

*Delete words which are inapplicable.

Note:
    Failure to comply with this summons without reasonable excuse is an offence carrying a fine not exceeding level 3 on the standard scale (s.22(6) Immigration Act 1971).

EXPLANATORY NOTE
(This Note is not part of the Rules.)

These Rules replace the Immigration Appeals (Procedure) Rules 1972 relating to the practice and procedure to be followed on or in connection with appeals under Part II of the Immigration Act 1971.

The substantive changes introduced by these Rules (which, in the main, reproduce the substance of the 1972 Rules without amendment) are described below.

Provision for an appellant to petition for a further opportunity to appeal notwithstanding the expiry of the period permitted for giving notice of appeal (which existed under Rule 5 of the 1972 Rules) is not provided for under these Rules. Under Rule 5 of the 1972 Rules generally the petition had to be referred to the appellate authorities for their consideration. Under Rule 5 of these Rules, provision is instead made so that a respondent is able to accept a notice of appeal given out of time, without reference to the appellate authorities. In the event that a respondent refuses to accept a notice which he alleges was given out of time, the appellate authorities may determine the validity of the allegation as a preliminary issue, and may allow the appeal to which the notice relates to proceed notwithstanding that they determine the allegation is well-founded, if of the opinion, by reason of special circumstances, that it is right and just so to do (Rule 11).

Rules 6, 16 and 23 each contain changes, similar in nature, from the corresponding provisions of the 1972 Rules. Rules 6, 16 and 23 of the 1972 Rules made reference respectively to Form 1 (Notice of appeal to adjudicator or Tribunal at first instance), Form 2 (Notice of appeal or application for leave to appeal from adjudicator), and Forms 3 (Application to an appellate authority for bail), 6 (Certificate of conditions of bail) and 7 (Certificates that all recognisance taken). Rules 6, 16 and 23 make no equivalent reference. Instead, the essential information previously contained in the forms referred to above (which were set out in the Schedule to the 1972 Rules) is particularised in the text of the Rules, and is required to be supplied in accordance with them.

Rule 8 differs from the corresponding provisions of the 1972 Rules in that paragraph (3)*(a)* (ii) and (iii) make provision for two additional circumstances the existence of which qualifies the application of paragraph (1) of the Rule (provision of a written statement of facts by the respondent to an appeal).

Sub-paragraph *(a)* of Rule 11(2) provides for an additional circumstance (namely, where the appellate authority has determined, in consequence of its determination of a preliminary issue, that it has no jurisdiction to proceed), the existence of which excepts the respondent from any requirement to supplement in a written statement facts previously furnished by him in connection with the proceedings relating to the determination of the preliminary issue.

Rule 12(1)*(f)* extends the range of appeals that may be determined at first instance without a hearing. It enables an appellate authority, in certain circumstances, to determine an appeal without a hearing where the decision appealed against has been withdrawn or reversed by the respondent.

Under Rule 14(1) an appeal to the Tribunal from an adjudicator will only lie with leave. Under Rule 14(1) of the 1972 Rules, certain appellants exercising the right of appeal under section 14 of the Immigration Act 1971 could appeal from an adjudicator to the Tribunal without first having to obtain leave to appeal.

Rule 14(2)*(a)* sets out more fully than the corresponding provision of the 1972 Rules the circumstances in which an appellate authority is obliged to grant leave to appeal from the determination of an adjudicator to the Tribunal where the authority is satisfied that the determination of the appeal involves an arguable point of law.

Under Rule 16(5), where leave to appeal is granted in accordance with that provision, subsequent notice of appeal must be given within specified time-limits. Under the corresponding provision of the 1972 Rules (Rule 16(4)), notice of appeal had to be given "as soon as practicable" after the grant of leave.

Rule 20*(c)* makes provision for an additional circumstance the existence of which enables the Tribunal to determine an appeal without a hearing. The circumstance relates to appeals where leave to appeal has been granted pursuant to section 22(5) of the Immigration Act 1971.

Rule 34 adds a further circumstance on the basis of which an appellate authority may hear an appeal in the absence of an appellant, namely, where it is satisfied that it is impracticable to give the appellant notice of the hearing and that no person is authorised to represent him at the hearing.

Rule 39(2) provides that in the case of a reserved determination, promulgation of the determination shall be effected by sending to each party a copy of the document recording the determination.

Rule 42 generally increases the range of functions which may be performed by the president of the Tribunal or a chairman of the Tribunal, acting alone. (The Rule does, however, reflect a diminution of the tasks which may be undertaken by the president or a chairman in one respect. Under these Rules, the Tribunal has no function corresponding to that which it had under Rule 5 of the 1972 Rules, in respect of which the president or a chairman were empowered to act independently.)

Rule 43 now provides that in addition to Sundays and public holidays, where the time provided by the Rules for doing any act expires on a Saturday, and for that reason the act cannot be done on that day, the act shall be in time if done on the next working day.

The Schedule to these Rules sets out forms for use concerning the recognizance of an appellant, the recognizance of an appellant's surety, and the summoning of a witness. (The corresponding forms were, respectively, set out in Forms 4, 5 and 8 of the Schedule to the 1972 Rules.)

STATUTORY INSTRUMENTS

1984 No. 2043

EDUCATION, ENGLAND AND WALES

The Remuneration of Teachers (Further Education) (Amendment) Order 1984

Made - - - - -	*28th December* 1984
Coming into Operation	*31st December* 1984

WHEREAS—

(1) in pursuance of section 3(1) of the Remuneration of Teachers Act 1965(a) ("the Act") certain matters in respect of which agreement had not been reached in the Committee constituted under section 1 of the Act for the purpose of considering the remuneration payable to teachers paid by local education authorities who are employed in establishments of further education and to other teachers employed by such authorities for the purpose of their functions relating to further education (excluding teachers seconded to bodies which reimburse the employing authorities the amount of their salaries) ("the Committee") were referred to arbitration, and in pursuance of section 4(1) of the Act the recommendations of the arbitrators with respect to those matters have been transmitted to the Secretary of State;

(2) there is in force an Order made under section 2(4) of the Act with respect to the remuneration of the teachers in question, namely the Remuneration of Teachers (Further Education) Order 1983(b);

(3) it appears to the Secretary of State that effect can most conveniently be given to the recommendations of the arbitrators by amending the scales and other provisions set out in the document referred to in the said Order, namely the document published by Her Majesty's Stationery Office on 7th October 1983 entitled "Scales of Salaries for Teachers in Further Education, England and Wales 1983"(c) ("the 1983 Document");

(4) in pursuance of section 2(5) of the Act the Secretary of State has prepared a draft Order setting out the amendments to the 1983 Document which, in his opinion, are requisite for giving effect to the recommendations of the arbitrators; and

(5) the Secretary of State, as required by section 2(6) of the Act, has consulted the Committee with respect to the draft Order and the Committee have made no representations with respect thereto:

(a) 1965 c. 3.   (b) S.I. 1983/1464.   (c) ISBN 0 11 270467 0.

Now, therefore, the Secretary of State, in pursuance of sections 2(6) and 7(3) of the Act, hereby makes the following Order, which is in the form of the draft:—

1.—(1) This Order may be cited as the Remuneration of Teachers (Further Education) (Amendment) Order 1984.

(2) This Order shall come into operation on 31st December 1984 and shall have effect as from 1st April 1984.

2. The Scales and other provisions contained in the 1983 Document are hereby amended, with effect from 1st April 1984, in the manner specified in the Schedule to this Order.

SCHEDULE

Amendments effective from 1st April 1984

1. In section 13—

   (*a*) in sub-section (1) for the sum of £444 there shall be substituted the sum of £465 and for the date 1 April 1983 there shall be substituted the date 1 April 1984.

   (*b*) in sub-section (2) for the sum of £1266 there shall be substituted the sum of £1323 and for the words "Individual allowances payable on 31 March 1983 shall be increased by 4.5 per cent, rounded to the nearest multiple of £3, from 1 April 1983" shall be substituted the words "Individual allowances payable on 31 March 1984 shall be increased by 4.6 per cent, rounded to the nearest multiple of £3, from 1 April 1984.";

   (*c*) in sub-section (3) for the sums of £1278 and £1953 there shall be substituted the sums of £1338 and £2043 respectively and for the words "Individual allowances payable on 31 March 1983 shall be increased by 4.5 per cent, rounded to the nearest multiple of £3, from 1 April 1983." shall be substituted the words "Individual allowances payable on 31 March 1984 shall be increased by 4.6 per cent, rounded to the nearest multiple of £3, from 1 April 1984.";

   (*d*) in sub-section (4) for the sums of £1125 and £894 there shall be substituted the sums of £1176 and £936 respectively, and for the words "Individual allowances payable on 31 March 1983 shall be increased by 4.5 per cent, rounded to the nearest multiple of £3, from 1 April 1983." there shall be substituted the words "Individual allowances payable on 31 March 1984 shall be increased by 4.6 per cent, rounded to the nearest multiple of £3, from 1 April 1984."

2. In Appendix IA—

(a) in paragraph 1, for the date 1 April 1983 there shall be substituted the date 1 April 1984.

(b) In paragraph 2 for the table there set out shall be substituted the following table:—

2. Lecturer Grade I, Lecturer Grade II, Senior Lecturer, Principal Lecturer and Reader.

Incremental Point	Lecturer Grade I	Lecturer Grade II	Senior Lecturer	Principal Lecturer	Reader
	£	£	£	£	£
0	5,910	7,548	11,175	13,095	13,095
1	6,153	8,010	11,634	13,569	13,569
2	6,405	8,463	12,099	14,043	14,043
3	6,657	8,910	12,609	14,580	14,580
4	6,906	9,348	13,128	15,048	15,048
5	7,176	9,771	13,599	15,525	15,525
6	7,434	10,251	14,061	15,999	15,999
7	7,734	10,686		16,467	16,467
8	8,037	11,175	See (b)	See (c)	
9	8,334	11,634	and (d)	and (d)	
10	8,634	12,099	below	below	
11	8,925				
12	9,213	See (a)			
13	9,498	and (d)			
14	9,777	below			
15	10,512				

(c) In paragraph 2(c)(ii) for the date 31 March 1983 shall be substituted the date 31 March 1984 and for the percentage 4.5 per cent shall be substituted the percentage 4.6 per cent and for the date 1 April 1983 shall be substituted the date 1 April 1984.

(d) In paragraph 3, for the table there set out shall be substituted the following table:—

3. Heads of Department and academic posts above Reader.

| Incremental Point | Grade | | | | | |
	I	II	III	IV	V	VI
	£	£	£	£	£	£
0	10,902	12,522	13,692	14,799	16,098	17,397
1	11,280	12,918	14,094	15,237	16,533	17,844
2	11,658	13,320	14,481	15,690	16,989	18,285
3	12,036	13,713	14,889	16,131	17,427	18,723
4	12,414	14,115	15,282	16,578	17,877	19,170
	See (a) below					See (b) below

(e) In paragraph 4 for the table there set out there shall be substituted the following table:—

4. Vice-Principals and Principals.
   (i) The ranges referred to in Section 7 and Appendix IIA, Part V(B), paragraphs 4 and 8 are as follows—

Group	Ranges of Salaries for Vice-Principals	Ranges of Salaries for Principals
	£ £	£ £
1	12,210–13,191	14,313–15,483
2	13,374–14,352	15,765–16,938
3	14,631–15,615	17,265–18,462
4	15,966–16,944	18,975–20,154
5	17,199–18,189	20,448–21,489
6	18,330–19,311	21,822–22,869
7	19,515–20,502	22,911–23,958
8	20,589–21,459	24,072–25,116
9	21,651–22,527	25,122–26,175
10	22,551–23,424	26,205–27,243
11	23,451–24,327	27,501–28,560
12	24,348–25,227	28,806–29,877

3. In Appendix IB—

  (a) In paragraph 1 for the date 1 April 1983 shall be substituted the date 1 April 1984.

  (b) In paragraph 2 for the table there set out shall be substituted the following table:—

2. Lecturer Grade IA and Lecturer Grade IB.

Incremental point	Lecturer Grade IA	Lecturer Grade IB
	£	£
0	5,910	6,636
1	6,153	6,888
2	6,405	7,140
3	6,657	7,386
4	6,906	7,647
5	7,176	7,911
6	7,434	8,169
7	7,734	8,469
8	8,037	8,763
9	8,334	9,069
10	8,634	9,366
11	8,925	9,657
12	9,213	9,948
13	9,498	10,272
14	9,777	10,557
15	10,512	10,968

(c) In paragraph 3 for the table there set out shall be substituted the following table:—

3. Lecturer Grade II, Vice-Principal and Principal.

The scales of salaries for these teachers shall be determined by local education authorities from the following ranges—

Salary point	Lecturer Grade II	Vice-Principal	Principal
	£	£	£
0	10,287	11,310	14,526
1	10,632	11,649	14,868
2	10,968	11,991	15,222
3	11,310	12,444	15,624
4	11,649	12,783	16,089
5	11,991	13,128	16,494
6	12,339	13,476	16,887
7	12,783	13,827	17,295
8	13,128	14,175	17,691
9	13,476	14,526	18,093
10	13,827	14,868	18,492
11	(a) 14,175	15,222	19,050
12	(a) 14,526	15,624	19,452
13		16,089	19,863
14		16,494	20,271
15		16,887	20,679
16		17,295	
17		17,691	
	See (a) below	See (b) below	

4. In Appendix III—

(a) For paragraph 6 there shall be substituted the following paragraph—

"6. (1) In paragraphs 9, 13A, 13B, 14, 15 and 18 of this Appendix incremental credit to be calculated in accordance with this paragraph shall be calculated as follows:—

(a) Where the point payable on the relevant former scale is below the minimum point on the relevant new scale, $1\frac{1}{2}$ times the difference between that minimum point and the next point above rounded up in accordance with sub-paragraph (2).

(b) Where the point payable on the relevant former scale coincides with a point on the relevant new scale, $1\frac{1}{2}$ times the difference between that latter point and the next point above rounded up in accordance with sub-paragraph (2).

(c) Where the point payable on the relevant former scale falls between two points on the relevant new scale, $1\frac{1}{2}$ times the difference between those two points rounded up in accordance with sub-paragraph (2).

(2) Incremental credit in all calculations under this paragraph or under paragraphs 7 to 17 inclusive and 19(*b*) of this Appendix shall unless they result in an exact incremental point, be rounded up to the minimum incremental point or to the next higher incremental point on the appropriate scale.".

(*b*) In paragraph 9(2) there shall be substituted for the words "equal to $1\frac{1}{2}$ increments on the Lecturer Grade I or Grade IA scale" the words "by way of incremental credit calculated in accordance with paragraph 6 of this Appendix".

(*c*) In paragraph 13A(4) for the words "equal to $1\frac{1}{2}$ increments on the new scale," there shall be substituted the words "by way of incremental credit calculated in accordance with paragraph 6 of this Appendix,".

(*d*) In paragraph 13B(1) for the sum of £217 shall be substituted the sum of £227.

(*e*) In paragraph 13B(2) for the words "equal to $1\frac{1}{2}$ increments on the new scale" the words "by way of incremental credit calculated in accordance with paragraph 6 of this Appendix".

(*f*) For paragraph 14 there shall be substituted the following paragraph:—

"14. A Senior Lecturer appointed in that capacity on or after 1 April 1984 shall enter the appropriate scale—

(1) either

(*a*) at the minimum to which shall be added incremental credit up to and including point 4 in respect of time spent as a Senior Lecturer to whom the Further Education Salaries Documents under the Remuneration of Teachers Act 1965(**a**) or a Pelham Report applied, or in other educational service or commercial, professional or research work which in the opinion of the local education authority should be regarded as equivalent to service as a Senior Lecturer, or

(*b*) where the Senior Lecturer is appointed after teaching service to which this document or the corresponding document relating to teachers at maintained schools(**b**) applies, at the salary payable in the former post (excluding any "London Area" allowance) plus (except where the salary scale applicable to his former post had the same or a higher maximum) an additional sum by way of incremental credit calculated in accordance with paragraph 6 of this Appendix but so that no such addition shall cause his salary to exceed point 4 on the scale

whichever, except where sub-paragraph (3) below applies, is the higher.

(2) Except where sub-paragraph (3) below applies, where the Senior Lecturer is appointed after service other than teaching service to which this document or the corresponding document relating to teachers at maintained schools applies, and the salary calculated under sub-paragraph (1)(*a*) above is considered by the local education authority to be inadequate, at such point up to and including point 4, as the local education authority deem appropriate having regard to the entitlement of former teachers under sub-paragraph (1)(*b*) above.

(**a**) 1965 c. 3.   (**b**) ISBN 0 11 270550 2.

(3) Where the salary corresponding to point 4 on the Senior Lecturer scale is less than the teacher's former salary (excluding any "London Area" allowance) in the post he held immediately before appointment and he is entitled, under the provisions of Appendix IA of this document to proceed beyond point 4 of the Senior Lecturer scale, at such incremental point above the said former salary as the local education authority deem appropriate.".

(g) For paragraph 15 there shall be substituted the following paragraph:—

"15. A Principal Lecturer appointed in that capacity on or after 1 April 1984 shall enter the appropriate scale—

(1) either

 (a) at the minimum to which shall be added incremental credit up to and including point 3 in respect of time spent as a Principal Lecturer to whom the Further Education Salaries Documents under the Remuneration of Teachers Act or a Pelham Report applied, or in other educational service or commercial, professional or research work which in the opinion of the local education authority should be regarded as equivalent to service as a Principal Lecturer, or

 (b) where the Principal Lecturer is appointed after teaching service to which this document or the corresponding document relating to teachers at maintained schools applies, at the salary payable in the former post (excluding any "London Area" allowance) plus (except where the salary scale applicable to his former post had the same or a higher maximum) an additional sum by way of incremental credit calculated in accordance with paragraph 6 of this Appendix but so that no such addition shall cause his salary to exceed point 3 on the scale

whichever, except where sub-paragraph (3) below applies, is the higher.

(2) Except where sub-paragraph (3) below applies, where the Principal Lecturer is appointed after service other than teaching service to which this document or the corresponding document relating to teachers at maintained schools applies, and the salary calculated under sub-paragraph (1)(a) above is considered by the local education authority to be inadequate, at such point up to and including point 3 as the local education authority deem appropriate having regard to the entitlement of former teachers under sub-paragraph (1)(b) above.

(3) Where the salary corresponding to point 3 on the Principal Lecturer scale is less than the teacher's former salary (excluding any "London Area" allowance) in the post he held immediately before appointment and he is entitled, under the provisions of Appendix IA of this document to proceed beyond point 3 of the Principal Lecturer scale, at such incremental point above the said former salary as the local education authority deem appropriate.".

(h) In paragraph 18(2) for the words "equivalent to $1\frac{1}{2}$ increments on the appropriate Head of Department scale" shall be substituted the words "by way of incremental credit calculated in accordance with paragraph 6 of this Appendix".

5. In Appendix III Annex B—

(a) For paragraph 1 thereof there shall be substituted the following paragraph:—

"1.(i) A course leading to the degree of Bachelor of Education, the Certificate in Education, the Post-graduate Certificate in Education or a comparable academic award of a university in the United Kingdom or of some other institution and validated by the Council for National Academic Awards provided that such course is approved as a course for the initial training of teachers in schools by the Secretary of State for Education and Science for the purposes of paragraph 2(a) of Schedule 5 to the Education (Teachers) Regulations 1982**(a)**.

(ii) A course leading to a Certificate of Education (Further Education) validated by the Council for National Academic Awards".

(b) Paragraphs 5 and 6 shall be deleted.

6. In Appendix IV for the sums £12.15, £10.63 and £7.58 there shall be substituted the sums of £12.70, £11.12 and £7.96 respectively.

7. In Appendix V, paragraph 2, for the words "Where a Lecturer Grade I, Lecturer Grade II, Senior Lecturer or Principal Lecturer employed in teaching on a course of teacher training is seconded to a school for the purpose of research or of refreshing his experience of school teaching or is seconded to any other occupation approved by the seconding authority," there shall be substituted the words "Where, for the purposes of their functions relating to further education, a local education authority seconds a Lecturer Grade I, Lecturer Grade II, Senior Lecturer or Principal Lecturer employed in teaching on a course of teacher training to a school or to any other occupation".

Keith Joseph,
Secretary of State for Education and Science.

28th December 1984.

EXPLANATORY NOTE

(*This Note is not part of the Order.*)

This Order amends with effect from 1st April 1984, provisions contained in the document setting out the scales and other provisions for determining the remuneration of teachers employed in further education establishments who are paid by local education authorities and of other further education teachers employed by such authorities. This document, entitled "Scales of Salaries for Teachers in Establishments for Further Education, England and Wales 1983" may be obtained from Government Bookshops or through booksellers. The Order gives effect to the recommendations of the arbitrators appointed under section 3 of the Remuneration of Teachers Act 1965. The restrospective effect of the Order is authorised by section 7(3) of that Act.

(a) S.I. 1982/106.

STATUTORY INSTRUMENTS

1984 No. 2048

TERMS AND CONDITIONS OF EMPLOYMENT

The Land Authority for Wales (Compensation for Premature Retirement) Regulations 1984

Made - - - - -	*17th December* 1984
Coming into Operation	*25th January* 1985

The Secretary of State for Wales, in exercise of the powers conferred upon him by paragraph 6(3) of Schedule 22 to the Local Government, Planning and Land Act 1980(a) and of all other powers enabling him in that behalf, with the consent of the Treasury(b) hereby makes the following regulations:—

Citation and commencement

1. These regulations may be cited as the Land Authority for Wales (Compensation for Premature Retirement) Regulations 1984 and shall come into operation on 25th January 1985

Interpretation

2. Unless the context otherwise requires, in these regulations any reference to a regulation shall be construed as a reference to a regulation contained in these regulations, any reference to a paragraph shall be construed as a reference to a paragraph in the same regulation and any reference to a sub-paragraph shall be construed as a reference to a sub-paragraph contained in the same paragraph.

Definitions

3. In these regulations:—

"employment" includes office and service; and

"material date" in relation to a person means the date upon which he ceased to be in the employment of the Land Authority for Wales.

"the 1978 Act" means the Employment Protection (Consolidation) Act 1978(c);

"the 1982 Regulations" means the Local Government (Compensation for Premature Retirement) Regulations 1982(d) as amended by Part III of the 1984 Regulations;

(a) 1980 c. 65.

(b) *See* the Transfer of Functions (Minister for the Civil Service and Treasury) Order 1981. (S.I. 1981/1670).

(c) 1978 c. 44; relevant amendments are made by the Redundancy Payments (Local Government) (Modification) Order 1983 (S.I. 1983/1160).

(d) S.I. 1982/1009.

"the 1984 Regulations" means the Local Government (Compensation for Redundancy and Premature Retirement) Regulations 1984**(a)**; and

"pensionable employee" "qualifying service" and "reckonable service" have the same meanings as in the Local Government Superannuation Regulations 1974**(b)**.

Persons to whom the Regulations apply

4. These regulations shall apply to a pensionable employee who on or after 30th November 1980 and before the end of three years from the coming into operation of these regulations ceases to be in the employment of the Land Authority for Wales as a result of the changes in the Authority's functions arising from Part XII of the Local Government, Planning and Land Act 1980.

Compensation

5.—(1) A person described in regulation 4 who on the material date is entitled to a redundancy payment under Part VI of the 1978 Act and who on the material date has not attained the age of 41 years shall be paid the compensation specified in Part II of the 1984 Regulations.

(2) A person described in regulation 4 who on the material date is entitled to a redundancy payment under Part VI of the 1978 Act and who on the material date has attained the age of 50 years but has not attained the age of 65 years and whose reckonable service and qualifying service entitled to be aggregated is not less than 5 years shall be subject to the provisions of the 1982 Regulations and of Part II of the 1984 Regulations.

(3) A person described in regulation 4 who on the material date is entitled to a redundancy payment under Part VI of the 1978 Act and who on the material date either:—

(*a*) has attained the age of 41 years but has not attained the age of 50 years; or

(*b*) has attained the age of 50 years but not attained the age of 65 years and whose reckonable service and qualifying service entitled to be aggregated is less than 5 years

shall be paid the compensation specified in regulation 6.

(4) For the purpose of the application of the 1982 Regulations and of the 1984 Regulations to the provisions of paragraph (2), a person described in paragraph (2) shall be deemed to be "an eligible person" and the Land Authority for Wales shall be deemed to be an "employing authority" within the meaning of those phrases in the 1982 Regulations.

Duty of Land Authority for Wales to pay compensation

6.—(1) Without prejudice to any other power in that behalf, the Land Authority for Wales shall pay a pensionable employee described in regulation 5(3) such compensation for such loss of employment as is specified in paragraphs (2) and (3).

(a) S.I. 1984/740.
(b) S.I. 1974/520; the amending instruments are not relevant to the subject matter of these regulations.

(2) The compensation which shall be paid in pursuance of paragraph (1) shall not exceed the difference between—

  (a) the redundancy payment to which he is entitled under Part VI of the 1978 Act; and

  (b) the redundancy payment to which he would have been so entitled if that Act had been amended as provided in paragraph (3).

(3) For the purposes of paragraph (2)(b) the 1978 Act shall be treated as if it had been amended as hereinafter provided, that is to say—

  (a) as if for subparagraphs (a), (b) and (c) of paragraph 2 of Schedule 4 (calculation of redundancy payments) there had been substituted the following provisions:—

  "(a) four weeks' pay for each such year of employment up to a maximum of 8 years which consists wholly of weeks (within the meaning of Schedule 13) in which the employee was not below the age of forty-one; and

  "(b) two weeks' pay for each such year of employment not falling within the preceding sub-paragraph which consists wholly of weeks (within the meaning of Schedule 13) in which the employee was not below the age of eighteen."

  (b) as if in paragraph 3 of Schedule 4 for the words "twenty years", in both places where they occur, there had been substituted the words "twenty-five years", and

  (c) as if paragraph 8(1)(c) of Schedule 14 (weekly pay in excess of specified limit to be disregarded in calculating redundancy payments) had been repealed.

Nicholas Edwards,
Secretary of State for Wales.

17th December 1984.

EXPLANATORY NOTE

(*This Note is not part of the Order.*)

These regulations require the payment of compensation to persons who suffer loss of employment in the Land Authority for Wales during a period beginning on 30th November 1980 and ending three years after the coming into operation of these regulations as a result of changes in the Authority's functions arising from Part XII of the Local Government, Planning and Land Act 1980. (regulation 4).

Regulation 5 makes different provisions for the calculation of such compensation according to whether or not on the termination of the employment an employee is entitled to receive an immediate pension under the Local Government Superannuation Regulations 1974, as amended.

Regulation 5(1) applies to an employee aged under 41 at the time of the termination of his employment. Such employee is not entitled to an immediate pension, but is entitled to a redundancy payment if he comes within the provisions of Part VI of the Employment Protection (Consolidation) Act 1978. If such a person is entitled to a redundancy payment then he is also to be given compensation by the Land Authority for Wales under the provisions of Part II of the Local Government (Compensation for Redundancy and Pre-mature Retirement) Regulations 1984. The maximum compensation payable under Part II of the 1984 Regulations is the difference between the redundancy payment to which the person is entitled under Part VI of the 1978 Act and that to which he would have been entitled if the provisions in Part VI of the 1978 Act relating to the weekly earnings limit in the calculation of redundancy payments under Part VI had been waived.

By regulation 5(2) and (4) an employee aged 50 or over who has completed 5 or more years service at the time of the termination of his employment, the years of service being calculated according to the provisions of the Local Government Superannuation Regulations 1974, as amended, is entitled to be compensated in the form of additional amounts to his immediate pension benefits. The calculation of these additional amounts is set out in the Local Government (Compensation for Premature Retirement) Regulations 1982 as amended which are applied to such a person by regulations 5(2) and (4). In addition if such an employee is also entitled to redundancy payments in the same way as an employee aged under 41, then similar provisions are made in respect of him as regards the calculation of his redundancy payment by applying the provisions of Part II of the 1984 Regulations.

Regulation 5(3) applies to an employee who at the time of the termination of his employment is aged between 41 and 49 or is aged 50 or over and has not completed at least 5 years' service calculated in accordance with the 1974 Superannuation Regulations. Such a person is entitled to a redundancy pay-ment under the provisions of the Employment Protection (Consolidation) Act 1978. Regulation 6 treats Part VI of the 1978 Act as if it were amended so that the person is entitled to be paid by the Land Authority for Wales firstly such a sum in supplementation of his entitlement to a redundancy payment under Part VI of the 1978 Act as shall bring his total compensation to a maximum sum equivalent to 66 weeks' pay, depending upon the length of service, and secondly such sum comprising the difference between the redundancy payment to which the person is entitled under Part VI of the 1978 Act and that to which he would have been entitled if the provisions in Part VI of the Act relating to the weekly earnings limit in the calculation of redundancy payments under Part VI had been waived.

STATUTORY INSTRUMENTS

1984 No. 2056

POULTRY

HUMANE SLAUGHTER

The Slaughter of Poultry (Humane Conditions) Regulations 1984

Made - - - -	*20th December* 1984
Laid before Parliament	*21st January* 1985
Coming into Operation	
Regulations 8 *and* 11	*11th February* 1986
Remainder	*11th February* 1985

The Minister of Agriculture, Fisheries and Food, the Secretary of State for Scotland and the Secretary of State for Wales, acting jointly, in exercise of the powers conferred by section 3 of the Slaughter of Poultry Act 1967 (**a**) and now vested in them (**b**), and of all other powers enabling them in that behalf, after consultation with such persons and bodies as seem to them representative of the interests concerned in accordance with subsection (6) of the said section 3, hereby make the following regulations:—

Title and commencement

1.—(1) These regulations may be cited as the Slaughter of Poultry (Humane Conditions) Regulations 1984 and, subject to paragraph (2) below, shall come into operation on 11th February 1985.

(2) Regulation 8 (operation of shackle-line) and regulation 11 (manual back-up of automatic machinery) shall come into operation on 11th February 1986.

Interpretation

2.—(1) In these regulations—

"approved instrument" means an instrument of a kind approved by the Minister of Agriculture, Fisheries and Food, the Secretary of State for Scotland and the Secretary of State for Wales, acting jointly, under section 1(1) of the Slaughter of Poultry Act 1967;

"bird" means a turkey kept in captivity or a domestic fowl, guinea-fowl, duck, goose or quail so kept.

(2) Any provision of these regulations which applies to a bird awaiting slaughter applies until the bird is dead.

Scope

3.—(1) These regulations shall not apply in relation to the slaughter of a bird—

(a) for a purpose other than a commercial purpose;

(**a**) 1967 c.24; section 3 was substituted by section 6 of the Animal Health and Welfare Act 1984(c.40).
(**b**) In the case of the Secretary of State for Wales, by virtue of S.I.1978/272.

(b) in pursuance of powers conferred by, or by any instrument made or having effect as if made under, the Animal Health Act 1981 (a);

(c) in the course of an experiment in respect of which restrictions are imposed by the Cruelty to Animals Act 1876 (b), being an experiment performed subject to any restrictions so imposed; or

(d) by a person registered in the register of veterinary surgeons or the supplementary veterinary register, or a person acting under his direction, where the person so registered is acting in the exercise of his profession.

(2) A bird is slaughtered for a commercial purpose if slaughtered—

(a) in the course or furtherance of a business or for reward; or

(b) by, or on behalf of, the purchaser of the bird on premises belonging to, occupied by or under the control of, the seller of the bird; or

(c) in a market place.

Requirements prior to slaughter

4. No person shall cause unnecessary pain or unnecessary distress to any bird awaiting slaughter, or permit any such pain or distress of which he knows or may reasonably be expected to know.

5. The occupier or person in charge of any premises shall ensure that any bird on those premises awaiting slaughter—

(a) is slaughtered as soon as is practicable;

(b) is protected from the direct rays of the sun and from adverse weather;

(c) is provided with adequate ventilation;

(d) is, if found, because of injury or any other cause, to be in a condition in which it may reasonably be supposed to be suffering unnecessary pain or unnecessary distress, immediately slaughtered.

Requirements as to lighting

6. The occupier of any premises at which birds are slaughtered shall provide—

(a) in those parts of the premises where birds are awaiting slaughter, lighting which is adequate for the inspection of such birds, and

(b) in those parts of the premises where birds are slaughtered, at all times when birds are being slaughtered, lighting which is adequate for the efficient carrying out of such slaughter.

Placing of birds in shackles

7. No person shall, in connection with the slaughter of any bird, place or cause or permit to be placed the bird in a shackle—

(a) in such a manner as to cause it unnecessary pain or unnecessary distress; or

(b) if the bird, because of injury or any other cause, is in a condition in which it may reasonably be supposed it will suffer unnecessary pain or unnecessary distress if placed in the shackle.

(a) 1981 c.22.   (b) 1876 c.77.

Operation of shackle-line

8.—(1) No person shall operate or cause or permit to be operated any shackle-line unless—

(a) each bird suspended from it is kept clear of any object which may cause it unnecessary pain or unnecessary distress until it is stunned by means of an approved instrument or slaughtered;

(b) adequate provision is made for action to be taken for the purpose of relieving any unnecessary pain or unnecessary distress which a bird suspended from the shackle appears to be suffering or for removing such bird from the shackle; and

(c) the shackle-line is operated at such a speed that any act or operation intended to be performed in relation to or on any bird suspended from it can be performed without causing the bird unnecessary pain or unnecessary distress.

(2) No person shall, in connection with the slaughter of any bird, use or cause or permit to be used any shackle-line, machine or other equipment unless—

(a) there is unimpeded access to its control mechanism, and

(b) except in an emergency to relieve suffering, it is used in connection with the slaughter of birds of the type, size and weight for which it was designed.

Requirements as to slaughter

9. No person shall suspend, or cause or permit to be suspended, any turkey kept in captivity or any domestic fowl so kept for more than 6 minutes in the case of a turkey, or for more than 3 minutes in the case of a domestic fowl before such turkey or fowl is slaughtered or is stunned by means of an approved instrument for the purpose of slaughter.

10. No person shall cause or permit any turkey kept in captivity or any domestic fowl so kept which has had severed one or more of the major blood vessels of its neck to be immersed in a scalding tank or to be plucked before a period of not less than 2 minutes in the case of a turkey or of not less than 90 seconds in the case of a domestic fowl has elapsed after such severance.

Manual back-up of automatic machinery

11.—(1) No person shall, in connection with the slaughter of any bird, operate or cause or permit to be operated any machine or other equipment the function of which is, by automatic means, to slaughter birds or to sever one or more of the major blood vessels of the neck with the object of causing death unless a person is present when the machine or other equipment is operated who is able to ascertain whether or not it has been effective in slaughtering the bird or, as the case may be, in severing one or more of the major blood vessels of its neck.

(2) In the event of the machine or other equipment not being effective in slaughtering the bird or, as the case may be, in severing one or more of the major blood vessels of its neck, the occupier or the person in charge of the premises on which the machine or other equipment is situated shall ensure that the bird is immediately slaughtered.

Penalties

12. A person who contravenes or fails to comply with any of the provisions of these regulations shall, unless he proves that by reason of an accident or other emergency such contravention or non-compliance was necessary for preventing physical injury or suffering to any person or bird, be guilty of an offence against these regulations, and liable, on summary conviction, to a fine not exceeding £400(a).

Revocation

13. The Slaughter of Poultry (Humane Conditions) Regulations 1971 (**b**) and the Slaughter of Poultry (Humane Conditions) (Amendment) Regulations 1983 (**c**) are revoked.

In Witness whereof the Official Seal of the Minister of Agriculture, Fisheries and Food is hereunto affixed on 12th December 1984.

Michael Jopling,
Minister of Agriculture, Fisheries and Food.

George Younger,
Secretary of State for Scotland.

18th December 1984.

Nicholas Edwards,
Secretary of State for Wales.

20th December 1984.

(**a**) The amount of fine which may be specified under section 3(2) *(e)* and (4) of the Slaughter of Poultry Act 1967 was increased to £400 (level 3) by S.I. 1984/447 in relation to England and Wales and by S.I. 1984/526 in relation to Scotland.
(**b**) S.I. 1971/661.
(**c**) S.I. 1983/687.

EXPLANATORY NOTE

(This Note is not part of the Regulations.)

These regulations re-enact the Slaughter of Poultry (Humane Conditions) Regulations 1971 with amendments.

The regulations continue to protect poultry awaiting slaughter against unnecessary pain or distress (regulation 4) and against bad weather, direct sunshine, lack of ventilation and delays in slaughtering (regulation 5). The requirements as to lighting (regulation 6) and as to the maximum periods during which birds may be suspended before being slaughtered or stunned (regulation 9) and the minimum periods which must elapse before the birds are immersed in a scalding tank or plucked after slaughter (regulation 10) are also continued.

The changes of substance are—

1.   The scope of the regulations is no longer confined to the slaughter of poultry for the purposes of preparation for sale for human consumption (regulation 3).

2.   The regulations have been extended to apply to guinea fowls, ducks, geese and quails in addition to turkeys and domestic fowls (regulation 2(1)).

3.   The regulations now include provisions concerning the placing of birds in shackles, the operation of shackle-lines, and manual back-up of automatic machinery (regulations 7, 8 and 11).

4.   The maximum fine which may be imposed for an offence against the regulations has been increased from £200 to £400 (regulation 12).

STATUTORY INSTRUMENTS

1984 No. 2058 (S. 162)

PRISONS

The Prison (Scotland) Amendment Rules 1984

Laid before Parliament in draft

Made - - - -	*31st December* 1984
Coming into Operation	
Except for Rule 4	*1st January* 1985
Rule 4	*1st June* 1985

In exercise of the powers conferred on me by section 35 as read with section 7 of the Prisons (Scotland) Act 1952(**a**), and of all other powers enabling me in that behalf, considering that a draft of the following Rules has been laid before Parliament, that the period of 40 days has expired and that neither House has resolved that the Rules be not made, I hereby make the following Rules:—

Citation and commencement

1. These Rules may be cited as the Prison (Scotland) Amendment Rules 1984 and shall come into operation on 1st January 1985 except for rule 4 which shall come into operation on 1st June 1985.

Interpretation

2. In these Rules the expression "the principal Rules" means the Prison (Scotland) Rules 1952(**b**).

Amendment of the principal Rules

3. For paragraph (3) of Rule 187 of the principal Rules there shall be substituted the following paragraphs:—

"(3) The member or members of a Visiting Committee to be appointed by a regional or district council shall be so appointed at a meeting of the council held in the month of May 1985 and thereafter shall be so appointed at a meeting of that council held—

(*a*) in the case of a regional council, in the month of May after the ordinary election of councillors to that council in 1986 and every four years thereafter; and

(*b*) in the case of a district council, in the month of May after the ordinary election of councillors to that council in 1988 and every four years thereafter.

(**a**) 1952 c. 61.
(**b**) S.I. 1952/565; the relevant amending instrument is S.I. 1979/1630.

(3A) The members of a Visiting Committee in office at 1st May 1985 shall remain in office until 31st May 1985.

(3B) Subject to paragraph (3A) above, any member of a Visiting Committee appointed by a regional or district council in accordance with paragraph (3) above shall take office on 1st June following his appointment and shall hold office, unless he earlier resigns, until the 31st day of the month in May in which the next appointment of a member or members by that council is required to be made under that paragraph.".

4. For paragraphs (4) to (9) of Rule 187 of the principal Rules there shall be substituted the following paragraphs:—

"(4) The Visiting Committee constituted for each prison shall meet at the prison at such times as may be determined by the Committee.

(5) A Visiting Committee shall appoint a chairman for such a period as the Committee may determine.

(6) Members of a Visiting Committee shall frequently visit and inspect the prison and for this purpose shall arrange a rota of attendance at the prison.

(7) If for any reason the requisite number of members of a Visiting Committee is not appointed at the proper time in terms of paragraph (3) above, or if for any cause a vacancy occurs in a Visiting Committee, the appointing authority may at any time appoint a person to fill the vacancy, and any person so appointed shall hold office until the same day as if he had been appointed at the proper time.

(8) A Visiting Committee shall fix a quorum of not less than three for the purpose of carrying out their duties, and this shall also be the quorum for any sub-committee appointed under paragraph (10) below.".

5. Rule 188 of the principal Rules shall be deleted.

6. In the Schedule to the principal Rules, after the entry relating to Inverness Prison, there shall be inserted the following entry:—

"

Name of Prison	Names of Appointing Authorities	Numbers of members to be appointed
Low Moss	Strathclyde Regional Council	3
	Fife Regional Council	1
	Lothian Regional Council	1
	City of Glasgow District Council	3
	Strathkelvin District Council	3
	Minimum number of women 3	11

"

New St Andrew's House,   *George Younger,*
Edinburgh.   One of Her Majesty's Principal
31st December 1984.   Secretaries of State.

EXPLANATORY NOTE

(This Note is not part of the Rules.)

These Rules amend the provisions of the Prison (Scotland) Rules 1952 regarding the times when members of Visiting Committees for prisons are appointed by regional and district councils and the period for which they serve. Previously all such members were appointed annually during the month of May in each year. These Rules provide for all members to be appointed in May 1985. Thereafter members appointed by regional councils will be appointed in May after the regional council elections in 1986 and every four years thereafter. Members appointed by district councils will be appointed in May after the district council elections in 1988 and every four years thereafter. Thus members of visiting committees will normally serve for a four years term (Rule 3).

In consequence on this change, the requirement for a Visiting Committee to hold a "first meeting" in June each year is abolished and provisions relating to such meeting consequentially amended (Rules 4 and 5).

The Rules also provide for the constitution of a Visiting Committee for Low Moss Prison (Rule 6).

STATUTORY INSTRUMENTS

1984 No. 2060

INCOME TAX

The Capital Allowances (Vehicles for the Disabled) (Similar Payments) Order 1984

Made - - - -	*19th December* 1984
Coming into Operation	*1st February* 1985

The Treasury, in exercise of the powers conferred on them by section 43(3) of the Finance Act 1971(**a**) and section 64(12) of the Finance Act 1980(**b**), both as amended by section 61(1) of the Finance Act 1984(**c**), hereby make the following Order:—

1. This Order may be cited as the Capital Allowances (Vehicles for the Disabled) (Similar Payments) Order 1984 and shall come into operation on 1st February 1985.

2. In this Order

"army inter-war pensioners" means former members of Her Majesty's military forces in receipt of a disability pension paid by the Secretary of State for Defence on account of disability attributable to injury sustained after 30th September 1921 but before 3rd September 1939.

3. The following payments are hereby specified as appearing to be of a similar kind to payments within paragraphs (*a*), (*b*) and (*c*) of subsection 3 of the said section 43 and of subsection 12 of the said section 64 for the purposes of the making of first-year allowances in respect of capital expenditure on the provision of mechanically propelled road vehicles, that is to say—

(1) mobility supplement paid under the Naval and Marine Pay and Pensions (Disablement Awards) Order 1984 or under the Naval and Marine Pay and Pensions (Disablement Awards) (No. 2) Order 1984;

(2) mobility supplement paid under Queen's Regulations for the Royal Air Force; and

(3) supplementary allowance paid under Royal Warrant dated 30th December 1949 to army inter-war pensioners equivalent to the mobility supplement provided for by Article 26A of the Naval Military and Air Forces etc (Disablement and Death) Service Pensions Order 1983(**d**).

(**a**) 1971 c. 68. (**b**) 1980 c. 48. (**c**) 1984 c. 43.
(**d**) S.I. 1983/883, as amended by S.I. 1983/1116, 1521, 1984/1154, 1687.

4. This Order has effect in relation to expenditure incurred on or after 21st November 1983.

A. G. Hamilton,
Donald Thompson,
Two of the Lords Commissioners of
Her Majesty's Treasury.

19th December 1984.

EXPLANATORY NOTE

(This Note is not part of the Order.)

Section 43(3), Finance Act 1971, and section 64(12), Finance Act 1980, both as amended by section 61, Finance Act 1984, empower the Treasury to specify payments as being similar to certain mobility allowances payable under social security legislation and certain war pension mobility supplements, with the consequence that first-year capital allowances are available for expenditure incurred in providing mechanically propelled vehicles wholly or mainly for the use of persons in receipt of such payments.

This Order, which applies to expenditure incurred (that is to say when the sums in question become payable) on or after 21st November 1983, so prescribes mobility supplements payable to former members of the armed services on account of disability attributable to injury sustained after 30th September 1921 but before 3rd September 1939.

The Naval and Marine Pay and Pensions (Disablement Awards) Order 1984, its amending instrument the Naval and Marine Pay and Pensions (Disablement Awards) (Amendment) Order 1984 and the Naval and Marine Pay and Pensions (Disablement Awards) (No. 2) Order 1984 are Orders in Council made under Section 11 of the Naval and Marine Pay and Pensions Act 1865; they are not published. Queen's Regulations for the Royal Air Force 4th Edition 1971 is published by HMSO. The Royal Warrant dated 30th December 1949 (as amended) is not published.

STATUTORY INSTRUMENTS

1984 No. 2063 (S. 163)

ANIMALS

ANIMAL HEALTH

The Tuberculosis (Scotland) Order 1984

Made- - - -	19*th December* 1984
Laid before Parliament	25*th January* 1985
Coming into Operation	15*th February* 1985

In exercise of the powers conferred by sections 1, 7(1), 8(1), 10(1) and (2), 15(4), 25, 32(2), 72, 83(2), 87(2) and 88(2) as read with section 86(1) of the Animal Health Act 1981(a) , and of all other powers enabling me in that behalf, I hereby make the following order:—

Title extent and commencement

1. This order which may be cited as the Tuberculosis (Scotland) Order 1984 shall apply to Scotland only and shall come into operation on 15th February 1985.

Interpretation

2.—(1) In this order, unless the context otherwise requires—

"the Act" means the Animal Health Act 1981;

"affected animal" means a cow which is affected with tuberculosis of the udder or is giving tuberculous milk, or a bovine animal which is affected with tuberculous emaciation, or is excreting or discharging tuberculous material, or is affected with a chronic cough and shows clinical signs of tuberculosis and includes a reactor;

"appropriate officer" means a veterinary inspector, an officer of the Secretary of State, or an officer of the Minister;

"approved disinfectant" means a disinfectant listed in the Diseases of Animals (Approved Disinfectants) Order 1978(b) as being approved for the time being for use against tuberculosis;

"bovine animal" means a bull, cow, steer, heifer or calf;

"carcase" means the carcase of a bovine animal, and includes part of a carcase and the meat, bones, hide, skin, hooves, offal or other part of a bovine animal, separately or otherwise, or any portion thereof;

"cow" includes a heifer that has calved;

"Divisional Veterinary Officer" means the veterinary inspector appointed by the Minister to receive information about animals or carcases affected or suspected of being affected with specified diseases, for the area in which the animal or carcase is;

"milk" includes cream and separated or skimmed milk;

(a) 1981 c.22.
(b) S.I. 1978/32; relevant amending instruments are S.I. 1984/55, 1338.

"the Minister" and "the Ministry" mean respectively the Minister and the Ministry of Agriculture, Fisheries and Food;

"premises" includes land with or without buildings but unless expressly so provided does not include any part or parts of any premises used for the temporary detention of animals, as a market, sale-yard, fairground, slaughterhouse, lair or place of exhibition;

"reactor" means a bovine animal which gives rise to a reaction consistent with it being affected with tuberculosis when tested for that disease;

"slaughterhouse" means a slaughterhouse or knacker's yard as defined in section 22 of the Slaughter of Animals (Scotland) Act 1980(a) ;

"suspected animal" means an animal suspected of being an affected animal;

"veterinary surgeon" means a person registered in the register of veterinary surgeons or the supplementary veterinary register.

(2) References in this order to notices served in Form A or Form B shall be construed as references to notices served in the forms respectively so headed in Schedule 1 to this order, or in forms substantially to the like effect.

Extension of definition of "disease" and power to slaughter on account of tuberculosis

3. For the purposes of the Act, the definition of "disease" in section 88(1) of the Act is hereby extended so as to include tuberculosis, and section 32 of the Act (power to slaughter animals) shall apply to that disease.

Application of the order

4. The provisions of this order shall not apply in relation to approved premises, within the meaning of the Importation of Animals Order 1977(b) , and shall apply in relation to imported animals only—

(a) from the time specified in the licence issued in respect of those animals under article 11(5) of that order; or

(b) where the existence or suspected existence of disease in any part of Great Britain makes it expedient that such licence should be issued for the time being, from the time when those animals have completed the period of detention in quarantine required under the provisions of that order or, as the case may be, have been rested at an approved reception centre for the period so required.

Notification of disease in bovine animals

5,—(1) A person who has in his possession or under his charge on any premises a suspected or affected animal other than a reactor, and a veterinary surgeon who, in the course of his practice, examines any such animal shall, with all practicable speed, give notice of the fact to a constable of the police force for the area in which the animal is or to an inspector of the local authority or to the Divisional Veterinary Officer.

(2) Where notice under paragraph (1) above is given to a constable or to an inspector of the local authority, he shall immediately transmit the information contained therein by the most expeditious means to the Divisional Veterinary Officer.

(a) 1980 c.13.   (b) S.I. 1977/944.

(3) A person who has in his possession or under his charge a suspected or affected animal other than a reactor shall forthwith detain it on the premises where it then is and isolate it as far as practicable from other bovine animals, and shall adopt precautions with respect to milk produced by the affected or suspected animal as if a notice in Form A had already been served upon him under article 7 below in respect of that animal.

Notification of disease in carcases

6.—(1) A person who has in his possession or under his charge on any premises a carcase which is affected with or suspected of being affected with tuberculosis, and—

(a) a veterinary surgeon who, in the course of his practice, examines any such carcase, and

(b) a person who in the course of his duties under the Food (Meat Inspection) (Scotland) Regulations 1961(a), or whilst inspecting meat for any other purpose, inspects any such carcase,

shall with all practicable speed give notice of the fact to the Divisional Veterinary Officer.

(2) A person who has in his possession or under his charge a carcase to which paragraph (1) above applies shall detain it, or so much of it as is affected with or suspected of being affected with tuberculosis on the premises where it then is until it has been examined by a veterinary inspector.

Veterinary enquiry as to the existence of disease

7.—(1) Where by reason of information received, whether under article 5 or article 6 above or otherwise, there is reason to believe that there is on any premises a suspected or affected animal other than a reactor or a carcase which is affected with or suspected of being affected with tuberculosis, a veterinary inspector shall, with all practicable speed, take such steps as may be necessary to establish the correctness of that information. For the purpose of carrying out his duties under the foregoing provisions of this paragraph a veterinary inspector may examine any bovine animal or carcase on the premises and take such samples as may be required for the purpose of diagnosis from any such bovine animal or carcase.

(2) A veterinary inspector shall serve on the owner or person in charge of any bovine animal examined by him which in his opinion is an affected or suspected animal a notice in Form A requiring the detention and isolation of affected or suspected animals and the adoption of precautions with respect to milk, and prohibiting movement of bovine animals.

(3) The person on whom a notice in Form A has been served under this article shall comply with the notice and such notice shall remain in force until—

(a) the animal to which it relates has died, or has been slaughtered pursuant to section 32 of the Act; or

(b) withdrawn by a notice in writing served by a veterinary inspector on the person on whom the notice in Form A was served.

(a) S.I. 1961/243, to which there are amendments not relevant to this order.

Tuberculin tests and valuation

8.—(1) The owner or person in charge of any bovine animal shall comply with all reasonable requirements of an appropriate officer with a view to facilitating the examination of that animal by a veterinary inspector, or the application to it of any diagnostic test for tuberculosis or the valuation of the animal in a case where the Secretary of State intends to cause it to be slaughtered under section 32 of the Act in its application to tuberculosis, and in particular shall arrange for the collection, penning and securing of any such animal if so required.

(2) No person shall test a bovine animal with tuberculin except with the consent of the Secretary of State and a person to whom any such consent is given shall, as soon as he knows the result of the test, forthwith report it to the Secretary of State.

(3) If any person fails to comply with any reasonable requirement of an appropriate officer made in accordance with the provisions of paragraph (1) above the Secretary of State may, without prejudice to any proceedings for an offence arising out of such default, take or cause to be taken all such steps as may be necessary to facilitate the examination and valuation of such animal, or the application to it of any diagnostic test for tuberculosis, and the amount of any expenses reasonably incurred by the Secretary of State for the purpose of making good the default shall be recoverable by him as a civil debt from the person in default.

Prohibition on vaccination and therapeutic treatment

9.—(1) No person shall vaccinate a bovine animal against tuberculosis.

(2) No person shall treat a bovine animal for tuberculosis.

Notification of intended slaughter of animals

10.—(1) Where the Secretary of State intends to cause a bovine animal to be slaughtered under section 32 of the Act in its application to tuberculosis, a veterinary inspector may serve a notice in Form B on the owner or person in charge of the animal informing him of the intended slaughter and requiring him to detain the animal pending such slaughter (or pending its surrender and removal for such slaughter) on such part of the premises as is specified in the notice and to isolate it as far as practicable from such other animals as are so specified.

(2) The person on whom such a notice has been served—

    (a) shall comply with the notice; and

    (b) shall not move the animal, or cause or permit it to be moved, off that part of the premises on which it is required to be detained, except under the authority of a licence issued by an appropriate officer.

Precautions against spread of infection

11.—(1) Where the Secretary of State is satisfied that any bovine animal kept on any premises is an affected animal or a reactor—

    (a) a veterinary inspector may, by notice in writing, served on the owner or person in charge of any such animal, require him to take such steps as may be reasonably practicable to prevent any bovine animal kept on the premises from infecting by contact any bovine animal kept on any adjoining premises; and

  (b) an appropriate officer may by notice in writing served on the owner or person in charge of any such animal, require him—

   (i) to arrange for the isolation of any animal or animals which may be specified in the notice on any part or parts of the premises so specified;

   (ii) to ensure that any part or parts of the premises specified in the notice shall not be used by any animal on the premises, or by such animal or animals as may be so specified;

   (iii) at his own expense, and within such time and in such manner as may be specified in the notice, to cleanse and disinfect such part or parts of the premises as may be so specified;

   (iv) to treat and store manure or slurry from any place which has been used by such animal in accordance with the requirements of the notice;

   (v) not to spread any manure or to spread or spray any slurry from any place which has been used by any such animal otherwise than in accordance with the requirements of the notice;

   (vi) to cleanse and wash all utensils and other articles used for or about an animal to which the notice relates within such time and in such manner as may be specified in the notice.

(2) Where an appropriate officer reasonably believes that any bovine animal which is on, or which has been on, any premises which are used for any show, exhibition, market, sale or fair, is an affected animal or has been exposed to the infection of tuberculosis, he may, by notice in writing served on the occupier of such premises, require him—

  (a) to ensure that any part or parts of the premises specified in the notice shall not be used by any other bovine animal for such period as may be specified in the notice;

  (b) at his own expense, and within such time and in such manner as may be specified in the notice—

   (i) to cleanse and disinfect such part or parts of the premises as may be specified in the notice;

   (ii) to dispose of any manure, slurry or other animal waste, straw, litter or other matter which has or might have come into contact with such animal.

(3) If any person on whom a notice is served under paragraphs (1) or (2) above fails to comply with the requirements of the notice, the Secretary of State may, without prejudice to any proceedings arising out of such default, carry out or cause to be carried out the requirements of the notice, and the amount of any expenses reasonably incurred by the Secretary of State for the purpose of making good the default shall be recoverable by him as a civil debt from the person in default.

(4) A notice served under paragraph 1*(b)* (i) or (ii) above shall remain in force until withdrawn by a further notice in writing served by an appropriate officer on the owner or person in charge of the bovine animal to which that notice relates.

Prohibition on movement of bovine animals

 12.—(1) A veterinary inspector may by notice in writing served on the owner or person in charge of bovine animals kept on such premises as are specified in the notice, prohibit the movement of bovine animals on to or off such premises, except under the authority of a licence issued by an appropriate officer and in accordance with any conditions subject to which the licence is issued.

(2) Such notice shall remain in force until withdrawn by a further notice in writing served by a veterinary inspector on the owner or person in charge of the bovine animals to which that notice relates.

Manure, slurry, etc.

13. Where a notice has been served on the owner or person in charge of bovine animals kept on any premises under the provisions of article 12(1) above which prohibits the movement of bovine animals off such premises except under the authority of a licence, no manure, slurry or other animal waste shall be removed from such premises except under the authority of a licence issued by an appropriate officer and in accordance with any conditions subject to which such licence is issued.

Suspected animals in markets, fairs and sales

14.—(1) Where a veterinary inspector reasonably believes that a bovine animal on any premises at which a show, exhibition, market, sale or fair is being held, is infected with or has been exposed to the infection of tuberculosis, he may require that animal to be removed from those premises, and (as the owner or person in charge of the animal may elect) taken either—

(a) to a slaughterhouse for immediate slaughter; or

(b) back to the premises from which the animal was brought to the show, exhibition, market, sale or fair or to such other premises as may be approved by the appropriate officer for the purpose, provided the premises to which the animal is to be taken are not used for any show, exhibition, market, sale or fair.

(2) A bovine animal shall only be moved in accordance with the provisions of subparagraph *(b)* of paragraph (1) above on condition that it is immediately put into isolation for a period to be terminated by a notice in writing served on the owner or person in charge of the said animal by an appropriate officer.

Control of infection from other animals

15.—(1) Where a veterinary inspector reasonably believes that an animal kept on any premises is, or may be, infected with tuberculosis, he may by notice in writing served on the occupier of such premises, require him to keep the animal under control in such manner as may be specified in the notice or to confine it to such part of the premises as may be so specified.

(2) A notice served under paragraph (1) above in respect of an animal kept on any premises shall remain in force until such time as the animal dies or the notice is withdrawn by a further notice in writing served by a veterinary inspector on the occupier of such premises.

(3) For the purposes of paragraphs (1) and (2) above "animal" means any kind of mammal except man.

Identification of bovine animals

16.—(1) Subject to paragraph (2) below, the owner of a bovine animal kept on any premises shall mark or identify the animal in a manner approved by the Secretary of State and shall thereafter maintain such mark or identification so as to be clearly legible.

(2) The requirement in paragraph (1) above shall not apply in relation to any bovine animal less than 14 days old that is not removed, or is removed only to a slaughterhouse from such premises, within such period of 14 days.

(3) No person shall alter, remove, obliterate or deface or attempt to alter, remove, obliterate, or deface any such mark as is referred to in paragraph (1) above.

Restriction on the movement or sale of unidentified bovine animals

17. The owner of a bovine animal other than one which falls within article 16(2) above, shall not—

(a) move or cause or permit the movement of that animal to any premises including any place used for any show, exhibition, market, sale or fair; or

(b) expose for sale or cause or permit to be exposed for sale that animal,

unless the animal has been marked or identified in accordance with the provisions of article 16(1) above and such mark or identification is still clearly legible.

Marking of bovine animals

18.—(1) If so required in writing by an appropriate officer the owner or person in charge of bovine animals kept on any premises shall mark such animals in the manner required by the appropriate officer.

(2) The appropriate officer may paint, stamp, clip, tag or otherwise mark bovine animals kept on any premises.

(3) No person shall alter, remove, obliterate, or deface, or attempt to alter, remove, obliterate or deface any such mark as is referred to in the foregoing provisions of this article.

Production of licences

19. Where a bovine animal is moved under the authority of a licence issued under this order—

(a) the animal shall be accompanied throughout such movement by the licence; and

(b) the person in charge of the animal being so moved shall, on demand made under this order by an appropriate officer, or by an inspector of the local authority or a constable, furnish his name and address and shall produce the licence and allow a copy thereof or extract therefrom to be taken.

Enforcement by local authority

20. This order shall, except where otherwise expressly provided, be executed and enforced by the local authority.

Offences

21. Any person who, without lawful authority or excuse, proof of which shall lie on him—

(a) contravenes any provision of this order or of a licence issued or of a notice served under this order; or

(b) fails to comply with any such provision or with any condition of any such licence or notice or with any requirement made under this order; or

(c) causes or permits any such contravention or non-compliance,

commits an offence against the Act.

Revocation

22. The orders listed in Schedule 2 are hereby revoked.

George Younger,
One of Her Majesty's Principal
Secretaries of State.

New St Andrews House,
Edinburgh.
19th December 1984.

Article 7

SCHEDULE 1
FORM A
ANIMAL HEALTH ACT 1981
Department of Agriculture and Fisheries for Scotland

TUBERCULOSIS (SCOTLAND) ORDER 1984

Notice requiring detention and isolation of affected or suspected animals, adoption of precautions with respect to milk and prohibiting movement of bovine animals.

To   of
I, the undersigned, being a veterinary inspector appointed by the Minister of Agriculture, Fisheries and Food hereby give you notice as the owner/person in charge* of the following bovine animal, namely, ... on the under-mentioned premises which is an affected or suspected animal for the purposes of the above Order, requiring you—

(1) to detain the animal on the said premises and to keep the animal isolated as far as practicable from other bovine animals,

(2) to take steps to ensure that the milk produced by the animal shall not be mixed with other milk and to ensure that all such milk shall forthwith be boiled or otherwise sterilised, and that any utensil with which such milk has been in contact before being so treated shall be thoroughly cleansed and scalded with steam or boiling water before being used again; and

(3) to ensure that no bovine animals are moved on to or off the premises except under the authority of a licence issued by a veterinary inspector and in accordance with any conditions subject to which the licence is issued.

This notice remains in force until the animal to which it relates has died or has been slaughtered pursuant to the above-mentioned Act, or until it is cancelled by a subsequent notice served by a veterinary inspector on the owner or person in charge of the animal.

Signed ....   Official Address
             (*Veterinary Inspector*)

Name in Block
Capitals ....

Date ....

Description of premises on which the animal is to be detained and isolated

Note. The veterinary inspector is with all practicable speed to send a copy of this notice to the Divisional Veterinary Officer, and to the local authority.

*Delete as appropriate

FORM B   Article 10

ANIMAL HEALTH ACT 1981

Department of Agriculture and Fisheries for Scotland

TUBERCULOSIS (SCOTLAND) ORDER 1984

NOTICE OF INTENDED SLAUGHTER

To ....   Herd Ref. No. ....

of ....

....

....

....

I, the undersigned, being a Veterinary Inspector appointed by the Minister of Agriculture, Fisheries and Food, hereby give notice that the Secretary of State proposes to cause the following bovine animals to be slaughtered with all convenient speed under the powers conferred by section 32 of the above Act in its application to tuberculosis, namely—

     (a) affected animals and reactors *(see Note 1 below)*

....

....

     (b) other animals *(see Note 1 below)*

....

....

I require you, pending such slaughter (or pending surrender and removal for such slaughter), to detain the animal(s) specified above in ....

....

being part of the premises where it is/they are* now kept, and to keep it/them* isolated as far as practicable from other bovine animals *(see Note 2 below)*.

Signed ....   Official Address
      (Veterinary Inspector)

Name in Block
Capitals ....

Date ....

*Delete as appropriate

Note 1: The Brucellosis and Tuberculosis Compensation (Scotland) Order 1978 (a) fixes rates of compensation for affected animals and reactors and for other bovine animals which are slaughtered as a result of being exposed to the infection of tuberculosis.

Note 2: In accordance with article 11(1) of the Tuberculosis (Scotland) Order 1984 you are required to take such steps as may be reasonably practicable to prevent the infection of bovine animals kept on adjoining premises by contact with bovine animals kept on your premises.

(a) S.I. 1978/1485, amended by S.I. 1981/1448.

Article 22

SCHEDULE 2

Orders revoked	References
The Tuberculosis (Scotland) Order 1964	S.I. 1964/1109
The Tuberculosis (Scotland) Amendment Order 1973	S.I. 1973/2101
The Tuberculosis (Scotland) Amendment Order 1977	S.I. 1977/957

EXPLANATORY NOTE

(This Note is not part of the Order.)

This order consolidates with amendments the provisions of the Tuberculosis (Scotland) Order 1964 and its amending instruments.

Articles 3, 5, 6 and 7(1) of this order continue in force the provisions of the 1964 Order as now applied by section 32 of the Animal Health Act 1981 (power to slaughter animals) in respect of tuberculosis, the compulsory notification of the disease and the investigation by a veterinary inspector into the existence of the disease.

Also continued are the provisions enabling a veterinary inspector to require precautionary measures to be taken when a bovine animal is affected, or suspected of being affected, with tuberculosis (article 7(2) and (3)); prohibiting the vaccination of a bovine animal for, or treating it against, tuberculosis (article 9); and, with minor additional controls, enabling precautions to be taken against the spread of tuberculosis (articles 10, 11, 12, 13 and 14).

Changes of substance made by the order are—

(a) the inclusion of a default power enabling the Secretary of State to carry out the requirements of a notice served on the occupier of premises used for any show, exhibition, market, sale or fair and on which there is or has been an animal suspected of being infected with tuberculosis, where such person fails to comply with its requirements, and to recover the cost of doing so from the person in default (article 11(3));

(b) the empowering of a veterinary inspector to require animals of any species to be kept under control or confined to certain parts of the premises on which they are kept in order to prevent the risk of spread of the disease; this power applied previously only in respect of goats and swine (article 15);

(c) the inclusion of a prohibition on the movement or exposure for sale of a bovine animal by its owner unless it has been marked or identified in accordance with the provisions of the order and the mark or identification is clearly legible (article 17).

A person who contravenes the order without lawful authority or excuse is guilty of an offence against the Act, and, by virtue of section 75 of the Act is liable in summary conviction to a fine not exceeding level 5 on the standard scale (presently £2,000) or in some cases a fine not exceeding level 3 on the standard scale (at present £400) for each animal or quantity of substance involved.

STATUTORY INSTRUMENTS

1984 No. 2065

PARLIAMENT

Resolution of the House of Commons, dated 17th December 1984, passed in pursuance of the House of Commons Members' Fund Act 1948, s.3 (11 and 12 Geo. 6 c.36) and the House of Commons Members' Fund and Parliamentary Pensions Act 1981, s.2 (1981 c.7).

Resolved

That, in pursuance of the provisions of section 3 of the House of Commons Members' Fund Act 1948 and of section 2 of the House of Commons Members' Fund and Parliamentary Pensions Act 1981 the maximum annual amounts of the periodical payments which may be made out of the House of Commons Members' Fund under the House of Commons Members' Fund Act 1939(a), as amended(b), and the annual rate of any payments made under section 1 of the said Act of 1981 shall be varied as from 1st December 1984, as follows:

(a) for paragraph 1 of Schedule 1 to the said Act of 1939, as amended, there shall be substituted the following paragraph:

"1. The annual amount of any periodical payment made to any person by virtue of his past membership of the House of Commons shall not exceed £2,199 or such sum as, in the opinion of the trustees, will bring his income up to £4,067 per annum, whichever is the less:

Provided that if, having regard to length of service and need, the trustees think fit, they may make a larger payment not exceeding £4,245 or such sum as, in their opinion, will bring his income up to £6,113 per annum, whichever is the less";

(b) for paragraph 2 of that Schedule there shall be substituted the following paragraph:

"2. The annual amount of any periodical payment to any person by virtue of her being a widow of a past Member of the House of Commons shall not exceed £1,101 or such sum as, in the opinion of the trustees, will bring her income up to £2,969 per annum, whichever is the less:

Provided that if, having regard to her husband's length of service or to her need, the trustees think fit, they may make a larger payment not exceeding £2,118 or such sum as, in the opinion of the trustees, will bring her income up to £3,986 per annum, whichever is the less";

(a) 1939 c.49.
(b) S.I. 1956/1668, 1957/388, 1961/988, 1965/718, 1971/770, 1972/1181, 1974/2061, 1975/2038, 1979/1667, 1980/1899, 1981/1848, 1982/1827, 1983/1823.

(*c*) in paragraph 2A of that Schedule, for the words "the annual amount of any periodical payment" to the end of the paragraph, there shall be substituted the words:

"the annual amount of any periodical payment made to any such widower shall not exceed £1,101 or such sum as, in the opinion of the trustees, will bring his money up to £2,969 per annum, whichever is the less:

Provided that if, having regard to his wife's length of service or to his needs, the trustees think fit, they may make a larger payment not exceeding £2,118 or such sum as, in the opinion of the trustees, will bring his income up to £3,986 per annum, whichever is the less";

(*d*) in section 2(1) of the said Act of 1981, for the words from the beginning to the end of paragraph (*b*), there shall be substituted the words;

"the annual rate of any payments made under section 1 shall be —

(*a*) £1,282 if the payments are made to a past Member; and

(*b*) £641 if payments are made to the widow or widower of a past Member".

APPENDIX

CERTAIN INSTRUMENTS NOT REGISTERED AS STATUTORY INSTRUMENTS

Orders in Council
Letters Patent
and Royal Instructions

relating to the Constitutions etc. of
Overseas Territories or to appeals to the Judicial
Committee

Royal Proclamations etc.

BY THE QUEEN

A PROCLAMATION

CALLING IN ALL COINS OF THE DENOMINATION OF ONE HALFPENNY

ELIZABETH R.

Whereas under section 3(1)(*e*) of the Coinage Act 1971, We have power by Proclamation made with the advice of Our Privy Council to call in coins of any denomination:

And Whereas it now appears to Us desirable to call in all coins of the denomination of one halfpenny:

We, therefore, with the advice of Our Privy Council and in pursuance of section 3(1)(*e*) of the Coinage Act 1971, do hereby call in by the thirty-first day of December One thousand nine hundred and eighty-four all coins of the denomination of one halfpenny, and accordingly after such thirty-first day of December One thousand nine hundred and eighty-four such coins shall not be current or legal tender within Our United Kingdom of Great Britain and Northern Ireland.

Given at Our Court at Buckingham Palace, this twenty-second day of November in the year of our Lord One thousand nine hundred and eighty-four and in the thirty-third year of Our Reign.

GOD SAVE THE QUEEN

CLASSIFIED LIST

OF THE

LOCAL

STATUTORY INSTRUMENTS

REGISTERED DURING

1984

TABLE OF CONTENTS

CLASS 1. ROADS, BRIDGES, ROAD TRAFFIC AND RIGHTS OF WAY

(1) *Bridges and Tunnels*   (2) *Establishment as Highways*
(3) *Traffic Regulation*   (4) *Roads and Bridges, Scotland*

(1) Bridges and Tunnels

Mersey Tunnels (Revision of Traffic Classification) Order 1984 Confirmation Instrument *made under the County of Merseyside Act 1980 (c. cx) s. 92* .... (1894)

Confirmation Instruments made under the Highways Act 1980 (c. 66) s. 106(3) and, where indicated, s. 325
Cambridgeshire County Council (River New Bedford Mepal By-Pass Bridge) Scheme 1983 (1341)
Cheshire County Council (River Dee (Afon Dyfrdwy) Bridge) Scheme 1983 (1591)
County Council of—
　Buckinghamshire H7 Milton Keynes (Canal Bridge) Scheme 1982 [*s. 325*] (696)
　South Glamorgan (Peripheral Distributor Road Grangetown Link) Bridges Scheme 1982 (1626)
　Surrey (Guildford St. Catherine's—River Wey Bridge) Scheme 1982 (1646)
　West Sussex (Stopham: River Arun Bridge) Scheme 1983 (1432)
Greater—
　London Council (Grand Union Canal Bridge) Scheme 1983 (1743)
　Manchester County Council (Welch Hill Canal Bridge) Scheme 1984 (874)
North Yorkshire County Council (Rawcliffe Bridge) Scheme 1982 (25)
Northamptonshire County Council—
　(A428 Britannia Inn Improvement, Northampton Classified Road) (New Bridge) Scheme 1984 (1864)
　(Oundle Bypass New A605 Classified Road) (New Bridges) Scheme 1983 (11)
　(Southern Approach Road, Northampton Classified Road) New Bridge Scheme 1983 (1373)
Warrington (River Mersey New Bridge) Scheme 1983 (700)

(2) Establishment as Highways

(a) TRUNK ROADS

Orders made under the Highways Act 1980 (c. 66) s. 106
A13 London to Tilbury Trunk Road (River Roding Bridge) (1381)
M63 Motorway (Barton Bridge) (1476)

Orders made under one or more of the following sections of Highways Act 1980 (c. 66): ss. 10, 12, 41 and, where indicated, ss. 106, 108, Sch. 23, para. 4

A5 London—Holyhead Trunk Road (Cerrigydrudion Diversion) (1567)
(A6) London—Carlisle—Glasgow—Inverness Trunk Road—
　(Kegworth Bypass) (Revn.) 848
　(Mountsorrel By-Pass) (Revn.) [*Sch. 23, para. 4*] (1707)
　(Quorn Bypass) (Revn.) [*Sch. 23, para. 4*] (616)
A11 London—Norwich Trunk Road (Barton Mills Bypass) (1676)

A12 London—Great Yarmouth Trunk Road—
  (Chelmsford Bypass and Slip Roads) [ss. *106, 108*] (53)
  (Margaretting—Boreham) Detrunking (54)
A13 London to Tilbury Trunk Road (Roundabout near Gooseley Lane and Slip Roads) (1380)
(A38) Exeter—Leeds Trunk Road (Cappers Lane Link) (Trunking) (1090)
A43 Oxford—Market Deeping Trunk Road (Gosford Bypass Section and Slip Roads) (1929)
(A46) Bath—Lincoln Trunk Road and the (A17) King's Lynn—Newark Trunk Road (Newark Relief Road) No. 1 (1549)
(A49) Shrewsbury—Warrington and the (A51) North of Newcastle-under-Lyme—Tarvin Trunk Roads (A49/51 Tarporley Bypass) (427)
(A64) Leeds—Scarborough Trunk Road—
  (Seamer and Crossgates Bypass) (1544)
  (Spital Road to Musham Bank De-Trunking) (1679)
(A69) Carlisle—Sunderland Trunk Road—
  (Cross Lane Enterprise Zone Junction) Slip Roads (1734)
  (Kingsway Roundabout Grade Separated Junction) (476)
A406—
  London North Circular Trunk Road (Great Cambridge Road (A10) Junction Improvement Trunk Road and Slip Roads) (1812)
  South Woodford to Barking Relief Road and Slip Roads (1382)
(A446) Little Packington—Weeford Trunk Road (De-trunking at Bassetts Pole) (531)
(A453) North East of Birmingham—Nottingham Trunk Road (De-trunking at Bassetts Pole) (532)
Bath—Lincoln Trunk Road—
  (A46)—
    (Coventry Eastern Bypass and Slip Roads) (1604)
    (Stratford-upon-Avon to Marraway) Detrunking (73)
  (Avon County Boundary to Culver Hill, Woodchester) (Detrunking) (1093)
  (Bear Hill, Woodchester to Dudbridge Road, Stroud) (Detrunking) (1092)
  (Culver Hill to Bear Hill, Woodchester) (Detrunking) (1091)
  (Dudbridge Road to Stratford Road, Stroud) (Detrunking) (1089)
  (Stratford Road, Stroud to Sandford Road, Cheltenham) (Detrunking) (1088)
  (Stratford-upon-Avon Northern Bypass) [ss. *106, 108*] (72)
  (Walsgrave-on-Sowe, Coventry to M6) Detrunking (1605)
Birmingham—Great Yarmouth Trunk Road (A47) (Billesdon Bypass Improvement) (1127)
Chester—Bangor Trunk Road A55 (Bodelwyddan Improvement and Slip Roads) (1225)
East of Birmingham—Birkenhead Trunk Road (A41) (Tong) and the Worcester—Wolverhampton—South of Stafford Trunk Road (A449) (Coven Heath) Trunking (1764)
Exeter—Launceston—Bodmin Trunk Road (Exeter to Okehampton Diversion and Slip Road) (Variation) (968)
Felixstowe—Weedon Trunk Road (A428) (Bromham Bypass) [s. *106*] (589)
Folkestone—Honiton Trunk Road—
  (A27 Brighton Bypass and Slip Roads) (956)
  (A27) (Old Shoreham Road De-Trunking) (1520)

Ipswich—Newmarket—Cambridge—St. Neots—Bedford—Northampton—
Weedon Trunk Road (Bromham Bypass) (Revn.) (590)

Leeds—Exeter Trunk Road (Westwood Main Road) (404)

Levens Bridge—Carlisle Trunk Road (Thursby Bypass) (428)

Liverpool—Sheffield—Skegness Trunk Road—
(Stocksbridge to M1 and Slip Roads) (403)
(Underbank to Middlewood De-Trunking) (405)

London—
—Edinburgh—Thurso Trunk Road (A1) (Baldersby Junction Improvement) (1869)
—Holyhead Trunk Road—
(A5) (Rhoswiel to Weirbrook) De-Trunking (1616)
(Rhoswiel to Weirbrook) A5 Improvements and the Swansea—
Manchester Trunk Road (A483) (Oswestry Bypass) (1615)

Newport—Shrewsbury Trunk Road (A49) Leominster (By-Pass) [s. 106] (414)

North of Oxford—South of Coventry Trunk Road (A423) (Ladbroke By-Pass) (289)

North West of Wolverhampton—Oakengates Trunk Road (A464) and the
East of Birmingham—Birkenhead Trunk Road (A41) De-Trunking (1736)

St. Clears—Nash (South Pembrokeshire) Trunk Road (Pen y Bont to West of
Begelly Cross) Detrunking (962)

Swansea—Manchester Trunk Road
(A54 Kelsall Bypass) (790)
(A483) (Gobowen to Sweeney) De-Trunking (1617)

Taunton—Fraddon Trunk Road (A361) (Wiveliscombe Relief Road)
(Trunking) and (West Road, West Street, The Square and High Street,
Wiveliscombe) (Detrunking) (1942)

West of Maidenhead—Oxford Trunk Road (Crowmarsh Bypass) (729)

(b) SPECIAL ROADS

Special Road (Llanddulas to Colwyn Bay) Regulations *made under the Road
Traffic Regulation Act 1984 (c. 27) s. 17(2)(3)* .... (1719)

*Instrument and Schemes confirming Schemes made under one or more of the
following sections of the Highways Act 1980 (c. 66): ss. 16, 17, 19 and,
where indicated, s. 326*

Cheshire and Merseyside County Councils (M53 Ellesmere Port Motorway)
Revn. Scheme 1984 Confirmation Instrt. (1852)

M1 Motorway (Aston—Sheffield—Leeds Special Road) Connecting Roads
(No. 5) (Hood Hill Interchange) Scheme (410)

M4 London—South Wales Motorway (Heathrow Spur to M25 Interchange)
Scheme (579)

M5 Birmingham—Exeter Motorway (Rashwood Junction) Connecting Roads
Scheme (1425)

M11 London—Cambridge Motorway (Redbridge—Stump Cross Section)
Partial Revn. Scheme [s. 326] (1383)

M25 Motorway (Micklefield Green to South Mimms Section) and Connecting
Roads Supplementary No. 2 Scheme (1630)

M40 London—Oxford—Birmingham Motorway (Waterstock to Warwick
Section) and Connecting Roads (No. 1) Scheme (1934)

M63 Motorway (Eccles Interchange to the A57 Junction at Peel Green) and
Connecting Roads Scheme (1477)

M69 Coventry—Leicester Motorway (Southerly Ext.) Scheme (1606)

(3) Traffic Regulation

(i) *General Regulations*

Trunk Road (A406) (North Circular Road, Brent) Restriction of Traffic Order *made under the Road Traffic Regulation Act 1984 (c. 27) s. 6* .... (1583)

Trunk Road (A446) (North of Dunton Roundabout) (Restriction of Traffic) Order *made under the Road Traffic Regulation Act 1984 (c. 27) s. 14(1)(7)* .... (1730)

Orders made under one or more of the following provns. of the Road Traffic Regulation Act 1967 (c. 76): ss. 1(1)–(3)(3A)(3B)(6), 84D and, where indicated, ss. 9(1)(4) and 12(1)(12)

(A17) King's Lynn—Sleaford—Newark Trunk Road Heckington Bypass (24-Hour Main Carriageway Clearway) (106)

King's Lynn—Sleaford—Newark Trunk Road (A17) (London Road, Long Sutton) (Prohibition of Waiting, Loading and Unloading) (438)

Liverpool—
—Leeds—Hull Trunk Road (A63) (Hessle Road, Hull) (Prohibition of use of gap in Central Reservation)—
    O. (745)
    (No. 2) O. (1545)
—Preston—Leeds Trunk Road (A660)—
    (Gay Lane and Leeds Road, Otley) (Prohibition and Restriction of Waiting) (74)
    (Leeds Road, Bramhope) (Bus Stop Clearway) (143)

London—
—Bristol Trunk Road (A4) (24 Hour Main Carriageway Clearway) (3)
—Edinburgh—Thurso Trunk Road (A1) (Kneeton, Scotch Corner) (Prohibition of Waiting) (1073)
—Great Yarmouth Trunk Road (A12) (Prohibition of Use of Gap in Central Reservation, Hughes Corner, East Bergholt) (1481)

North Orbital Trunk Road (A405) (Prohibition of Use of Gap in Central Reservation) (163)

Penrith—Middlesbrough Trunk Road (A66) (Sedbury Lodge Lay-by) (Prohibition and Restriction of Waiting) (1546)

Sheffield—Grimsby Trunk Road (A180) (Brocklesby Interchange—Pyewipe Roundabout) (24 Hour Main Carriageway Clearway) (680)

Stanningley and Seacroft (Leeds Ring Road) Trunk Road (A6120) (Shadwell Lane, Moortown Ring Road Junction) (Prohibition of Right Turn) (Prohibition of U-Turns) (Prescribed Route) (Box Junction) (555)

Trunk Road(s)—
(A1)—
    (24-Hour Main Carriageway Clearway) (592)
    (Kate's Cabin, Alwalton) (Prohibition of U-turns) (784)
(A5) (Dunstable) (Prohibition of 'U' Turn) (827)
(A6) (Various Roads, Market Harborough) (Prohibition and Restriction of Waiting, Loading and Unloading) (139)
(A11) London—Norwich (Wymondham, South Norfolk) (Direction of Traffic) (1344)

Trunk Road(s)—

(A17) (Bridge Road, Sutton Bridge) (Prohibition of Waiting) (512)

(A27) (Beddingham Level Crossing) (Prohibition of Waiting) (Laybys) (395)

(A38) (Alrewas, Staffordshire) (One Way Traffic and Prohibition of Left-Hand Turn) (1129)

(A40)—

> (Carmarthen, Dyfed) (Prohibition of Traffic) [s. 12(1)(12)] (669)
>
> (Gloucester Northern Bypass, Gloucestershire) (Longford to Over) (Clearway) (191)
>
> (Layby at Wilton Road, Ross-on-Wye) (Restriction of Waiting) (439)
>
> (New Road, Llandeilo, Dyfed) (Prohibition of Waiting) (482)

(A47) (Dereham Road, Norwich) (Restriction of Waiting) (270)

(A48) (Llanvaches, Gwent) (Traffic Regulation) (1458)

(A49)—

> (High Street, Tarporley) (Prohibition of Waiting) (1550)
>
> (Whitchurch Road, Shrewsbury) (Prohibition and Restriction of Waiting) (1524)

(A55)—

> (Bodellwyddan, Clwyd)—
>
> > (Prohibition of Overtaking) [s. 12(1)(12)] (479)
> >
> > (Prohibition of Waiting) [s. 12(1)(12)] (478)
>
> (Coed-y-Cra, Halkyn, Clwyd) (Prescribed Routes) (154)

(A55/A494) (Hawarden By-Pass, Clwyd) (Clearway) (1474)

(A63) (Welton) (Prohibition of Driving) (944)

(A64) (Prohibition of Right Turn) (80)

(A167) (Prohibition of Right Turn) (491)

(A259) (Various Roads Hythe) (Prohibition and Restriction of Waiting) (Amdt.) (4)

(A405) (Hertfordshire) (24-Hour Main Carriageway Clearway) (287)

(A423) (Henley-on-Thames) (Various Roads) (Traffic Regulation) (752)

(A428) (St. Loyes Street, Bedford)—

> (Prohibition of Loading and Unloading) [s. 9(1)(4)] (765)
>
> (Prohibition of Right Turn) (Revn.) [s. 9(1)(4)] (764)

(A449) (Penkridge, Staffordshire) (Prohibition and Restriction of Waiting) (1252)

(A453)—

> (Upper Gungate, Tamworth)—
>
> > (Prohibition of Right and "U"-Turns) (1032)
> >
> > (Prohibition of "U"-Turns at Junction with Eastern Loop Road) (1076)

(A458/A483) Welshpool, Powys (Prohibition and Restriction of Waiting) (Variation) (1563)

(A465) (Clydach Gorge, Gwent) (Prohibition of Right-Hand Turn) [s. 12(1)(12)] (79)

(A465/A40/A449/A4042) (Clearways) (480)

(A470) (Blaenau Ffestiniog, Gwynedd) (Prohibition and Restriction of Waiting) (121)

(A487) (Dublin Street, Tremadog, Gwynedd) (Prohibition of Waiting) (961)

(A487 and A44) (Various Roads, Aberystwyth) (Prohibition and Restriction of Waiting) [s. 9] (976)

Trunk Road(s)—
  (A500)—
    (Hanford—Hanchurch Link, Stafford and Stoke-on-Trent) (Clearway)
      (1409)
    (Queensway, Newcastle-under-Lyme) (Clearway) (1407)
  (A565) (Hemer Terrace and Trent Street) (Prohibition of use of gap in
    Central Reservation) (339)
  (A622) Accrington Easterly Bypass Northern Section (Prohibition of Wait-
    ing) (Clearway) (314)
  (A696)—
    (Newcastle upon Tyne and Castle Morpeth) (Clearway) (610)
    (Prestwick Terrace, Castle Morpeth) (Prohibition of Entry) (17)
  (A4123)—
    (Birmingham New Road, Tipton) (Prohibition of Waiting) (556)
    (Junction with Pound Road, Causeway Green) (Prohibition of Right
      Turns and of Use of Gaps in Central Reservation) (38)
  (Picket Post) (Prohibition of U-turns) (1343)
  (Route A7) (Galashiels) (Prohibition of Waiting) (1136)
  (Route A78) (Loans Bypass—Meadowhead Roundabout to Monkton
    Roundabout) (Clearways) (624)
  (Route A83) (Lochgilphead) (Bus Stops Clearway) (706)
  (Route A96) (Kintore) (Prohibition of Waiting) (1462)
  (Route A929/A94) (Forfar) (Prohibition of Waiting) (1422)
  (Thurso) (Prohibition of Waiting) (1198)
  (Various Roads, Selby) (Prohibition and Restriction of Waiting) (1513)
Winchester—Preston Trunk Road (A34) (Sandleford Priory, Newbury)
  (Prohibition of Right Hand Turns) (1413)
York—Hull Trunk Road (A1079) (Hull City Boundary to Ings Bridge
  Roundabout) (Clearway) (983)

*Orders made under the Road Traffic Regulation Act 1967 (c. 76) s. 6 and,
  where indicated, s. 84D*
Trunk Road—
  (A1) (Barnet Way, Barnet) (Prescribed Routes) (1128)
  (A4) (Great West Road, Hounslow) (Restriction of Traffic) (70)
  (A10) (Great Cambridge Road, Enfield) (Prescribed Routes) (1004)
  (A12) (Colchester Road, Havering) (Prescribed Routes) [*s. 84D(1)*] (114)
  (A40)—
    (Western Avenue, Ealing) (Prescribed Routes) (622)
    (Western Avenue, Hillingdon) (Prescribed Routes) (268)

*Orders made under one or more of the following provns. of the Road Traffic
  Regulation Act 1984 (c. 27): ss. 1(1)(2), 2(1)—(3), 4(1)(2), 14(1)(7) and,
  where indicated, Sch. 9, Pt. IV, para. 27*
(A6) Trunk Road (Loughborough Road/High Street/Leicester Road, Quorn)
  (Prohibition of Waiting) (1753)
East of Snaith—Sunderland Trunk Road (A19) (Ingleby Arncliffe, North
  Yorkshire) (Prohibition of U-Turns) (1612)
Liverpool—Leeds—Hull Trunk Road (A63) (Commercial Road Roundabout,
  Mytongate, Hull) (One-Way Traffic) (Prohibition of Right Turns and Left
  Turns) (1638)
London North Orbital Trunk Road (A405) (Prohibition of U-Turns) (1709)
North-West of Doncaster—Wakefield—Bradford—Skipton—Kendal Trunk
  Road (A638) (Wakefield Road, Ackworth) (Restriction of Waiting) (1949)

Trunk Road(s)—

(A3) (London Road, Clanfield) (Prohibition of Use of Gaps in Central Reservation) (1950)

(A38) (Green Lane Junction, Burnaston, Derbyshire) (Prohibition of U-Turns) (2017)

(A38 and A358) (Taunton, Somerset) (One Way Traffic and Prohibition and Restriction of Waiting, Loading and Unloading) (Variation) [*Sch. 9, Pt. IV*] (1951)

(A40)—

(Bancyfelin, Dyfed)—

(One-Way Traffic) (1712)

(Prohibition of U-Turns and Prohibition of Traffic) (1711)

(A48) (Western Avenue, Cardiff) (Prescribed Routes) (1746)

(A487) (Porthmadog, Gwynedd) (Prohibition and Restriction of Waiting) [*Sch. 9, Pt. IV, para. 27*] (1758)

(A487/A470/A489) (Various Roads, Machynlleth, Powys) (Prohibition and Restriction of Waiting) [*Sch. 9, Pt. IV, para. 27*] (1656)

(Musselburgh) (Box Junction) (1831)

(Route A9) (Dunblane) (Prohibition of Right Hand Turn) (1777)

(Route A82) (Prohibition of Specified Turns) (Dunglass Roundabout to Kilbowie Roundabout) [*Sch. 9, Pt. IV, para. 27*] (2057)

(Route A96) (Elgin) (Prohibition of Waiting) [*Sch. 9, Pt. IV, para. 27*] (1779)

(ii) *Miscellaneous Restrictions*

Orders made under one or more of the following provns. of the Road Traffic Regulation Act 1967 (c. 76): ss. 72(3), 73(1)(2), 74(1)(2), 84D(1)

A16 Trunk Road (Surfleet Road, Pinchbeck) (De-Restriction) (1272)

A47 Birmingham—Great Yarmouth Trunk Road (De-restriction) (585)

East of Snaith—Sunderland Trunk Road (A1041) (De-restriction) (1069)

Leeds—Exeter Trunk Road (A61) (De-restriction) (1234)

Liverpool—Leeds—Hull Trunk Road (A63) (De-restriction)—

O. (804)

(No. 2) O. (805)

North West of Doncaster—Kendal Trunk Road (A65) (Ingleton, North Yorkshire) (Derestriction) (762)

Trunk Road(s)—

(A1) (Bedfordshire) (De-Restriction) (1532)

(A5)—

(Bedfordshire) (De-Restriction) (1533)

(Hertfordshire) (De-Restriction) (509)

(Llanfairpwllgwyngyll By-pass, Gwynedd) (De-restriction) (172)

(A6) (Bedfordshire) (De-Restriction) (1534)

(A40, A423 and A34) (Various Roads) (De-Restriction) (1023)

(A55) (Hawarden By-Pass Clwyd) (De-restriction) (1475)

(A59)—

(Liverpool—Preston—Leeds)—

(Balderstone, Lancashire) (De-Restriction) (315)

(Longton Bypass, Lancashire) (De-Restriction) (313)

(Sollom, Lancashire) (De-Restriction) (317)

(Whalley—Clitheroe Bypass, —

Lancashire) (De-Restriction) (319)

Pendleton Junction) (De-Restriction) (1293)

Trunk Road(s)—
  (A66)—
    (Workington—Penrith—Middlesbrough)—
      (Fitz Cottage Junction, Cumbria) (De-restriction) (890)
      (Lamplugh Road Junction, Cockermouth) (De-Restriction) (1514)
  (A405) Hertfordshire (De-Restriction) (508)
  (A477) (Kilgetty, Dyfed) (De-restriction) (1139)
  (A483) (Swansea—Manchester) (Chester, Cheshire) (De-Restriction) (777)
  (A556) (Swansea—Manchester) (Northwich By-pass, Rudheath, Cheshire)
    (De-Restriction) (369)
  (A570) (North of St. Helens—Southport) (De-Restriction) (312)
  (A585) (South side of the Roundabout Junction of the M55 Motorway—
    Dock Street, Fleetwood) (De-Restriction) (320)
  (A622) (Accrington Easterly Bypass Northern Section) (De-Restriction)
    (318)
  (A646) (Leeds—Halifax—Burnley—Blackburn—East of Preston)
    (De-Restriction) (34)
  (A679) (Leeds—Halifax—Burnley—Blackburn—East of Preston) (De-
    Restriction) (311)
  (Carlisle—Sunderland Trunk Road) (A69) (De-Restriction) (1531)
  (East of Snaith—York—Thirsk—Stockton-on-Tees—Sunderland Trunk
    Road (A19)) De-restriction—
      (No. 1) (305)
      (No. 2) (560)
  (London—Edinburgh—Thurso Trunk Road) (A1) (De-restriction) (1236)
  (Route A96) (Kintore) (De-restriction) (1241)
  (Sheffield—Grimsby Trunk Road) (A180) (Derestriction)—
    O. (535)
    (No. 2) O. (536)

*Orders made under the Road Traffic Regulation Act 1984 (c. 27) ss. 82(2),
83(1) and, where indicated, Sch. 9, para. 27*
Trunk Road(s)—
  (A1) (Bedfordshire) (Various Roads) (De-Restriction) (2052)
  (A5) (Bedfordshire) (Various Roads) (De-Restriction) (2053)
  (A6) (Bedfordshire) (Various Roads) (De-Restriction) (2054)
  (A41 Newport By-Pass) (De-Restriction) (2018)
  (A51) (Tarvin South-West Bypass, Cheshire) (De-Restriction) (1798)
  (A428) (Bedfordshire) (Various Roads) (De-Restriction) (2055)
  (A483) (Swansea—Manchester) (Belgrave, South of Chester, Cheshire)
    (De-restriction) (2062)
  (A6119) (Blackburn Ring Road) (De-restriction) (1759)
  (Routes A96 and A98) (Restricted Road) (Fochabers) [Sch. 9, para. 27]
    (1607)

*Orders made under one or more of the following provns. of the Road Traffic
Regulation Act 1967 (c. 76): ss. 72(3), 73(1)(a)(2), 74(1)(2), 84D(1)*
Northwest of Doncaster—Kendal Trunk Road (A638) (Restricted Roads)
  (1412)
Trunk Road(s)—
  (A470) (Glan Conwy, Gwynedd) (Restricted Roads) (1565)
  (A483) (Gresford, Clwyd) (Restricted Roads and 40 mph Speed Limit) (798)

Trunk Road(s)—
  (A487)—
    (Aberaeron, Dyfed), (Restricted Roads) (824)
    (Lower Town, Fishguard, Dyfed) (Restricted Roads) (515)
  (Restricted Roads)—
    O. (772)
    (Ross and Cromarty) Amdt. (782)
  (Route A9) (Restricted Road) (Dunblane) (1113)
  (Route A78) (Restricted Road) (Fairlie) (1521)

Orders made under one or more of the following provns. of the Road Traffic
Regulation Act 1967 (c. 76): ss. 74(1)(2), 84D and, where indicated,
ss. 72(3), 73(1)(2)

East of Snaith—Sunderland Trunk Road (A1041) (40 mph Speed Limit) (1070)
North West of Doncaster—Kendal Trunk Road (A638) (Ackworth) (40mph
  Speed Limit) (No. 3) (82)
Trunk Road(s)—
  (40mph Speed Limit)—
    (No. 1) (75)
    (No. 2) (57)
    (No. 4) (409)
    (No. 5) (505)
  (A38 Traffic Island, Minworth, West Midlands) (40mph Speed Limit)
    (1407)
  (A40) (Carmarthen, Dyfed) (40mph Speed Limit) (7)
  (A48) (Cowbridge Road West, Cardiff) (40mph Speed Limit) (26)
  (A52) (Bottesford, Leicestershire) (40mph Speed Limit) (384)
  (A66) (Workington—Penrith—Middlesbrough) (Great Clifton, Allerdale,
    Cumbria) (40mph Speed Limit) (1440)
  (A449 at Coven Heath, Staffordshire) (40mph Speed Limit) (644)
  (A470) (Llandinam, Powys) (40mph Speed Limit) (690)
  (A487) (Penrhyndeudraeth, Gwynedd) (40mph Speed Limit) (153)
  (Route A82)—
    (Drumnadrochit) (40mph Speed Limit) (537)
    (Onich) (40mph Speed Limit) (196)
  (Route A92) (Admiralty Road, Inverkeithing) (40mph Speed Limit) (801)
  (Tutshill, Gloucestershire) (40mph Speed Limit) [*ss. 72(3), 73(1)(2)*] (1516)
  (50mph Speed Limit) (A140) (Stonham Parva and Earl Stonham) (873)
  (A12) (Colchester Road, Havering) (50mph Speed Limit) (965)
  (Montague Road (Brielle Way) West Minster) (60mph Speed Limit) (646)
  (A13) (Newham, Barking and Dagenham, and Havering)
    (Speed Limit) [*72(3), 73(1)(2)*] (615)
  (A40) (Western Avenue, Ealing) (Speed Limits) [*72(3), 73(1)(2)*] (621)
  Speed Limits (No. 1) Order 1972 (Variation) (728)

Orders made under one or more of the following provns. of the Road Traffic
Regulation Act 1984 (c. 27): ss. 84(1)(2), 88(1) and, where indicated, Sch. 9,
Pt. IV

Trunk Road(s)—
  (A34 Birmingham Road, Stratford-upon-Avon) (40mph Speed Limit)
    [*Sch. 9, Pt. IV*] (1893)
  (A40 at Weston under Penyard) (40mph Speed Limit) (1854)
  (A483) (Ruabon, Clwyd) (40mph Speed Limit) (1876)
  (Route A87) (Balmacara) (40mph Speed Limit) (1868)

(iii) *Temporary Restrictions*

Orders made under one or more of the following provns. of the Road Traffic Regulation Act 1967 (c. 76): s. 12(1)(4)(5)(12)

A1(M) Motorway—
(Hertfordshire) (Temp. Prohibition of Traffic) (316)
(Sliproads at Warmsworth Junction) (Temp. Prohibition of Traffic) (1253)
(South Mimms Roundabout) (Temp. Prohibition of Traffic) (1238)
(Stevenage Bypass) (Temp. Prohibition of Traffic) (502)

A12 London—Great Yarmouth Trunk Road—
(Temp. Prohibition of Traffic and of Waiting and One-way Traffic) (735)
(Temp. Restriction of Traffic) (523)

(A16) Trunk Road (Littleworth Station Level Crossing) (Temp. Prohibition of Traffic) (1484)

A41(M) Motorway (Tring Bypass) (Temp. Prohibition of Traffic) (1537)

A45 Felixstowe—Weedon Trunk Road (Temp. Restriction of Traffic) (1463)

(A50) Trunk Road (Market Street, Ashby De La Zouch) (Temp. Prohibition of Traffic and Waiting) (1535)

Brigg—Ulceby Trunk Road (A180) (Temp. Prohibition of Traffic) (326)

East of Snaith—Sunderland Trunk Road (A19)—
(Gate Lane Bridge to Three Tuns Bridge, Borrowby) (Temp. Prohibition of Traffic) (710)
(Tontine Bridge to Pasture House Bridge) (Temp. Prohibition of Traffic) (636)

Felixstowe—Weedon Trunk Road (A428) (Bromham Bridge) (Temp. Prohibition of Traffic) (1282)

Leeds—York—Scarborough Trunk Road (A64)—
(Headley Bar Interchange) (Temp. Prohibition of Traffic) (1235)
(York Bypass) (Temp. Prohibition of Traffic) (943)

Liverpool—Leeds—Hull Trunk Road (A63)—
(Boothferry Road, Hessle) (Temp. Prohibition of Use of Gap in Central Reservation) (645)
(Myton Bridge) (Temp. Prohibition of Traffic) (1460)
(North Ferriby By-Pass) (Temp. Prohibition of Traffic) (1410)

London—
—Cambridge—King's Lynn Trunk Road (A10) (Temp. Prohibition of Traffic) (914)
—Edinburgh—Thurso Trunk Road (A1)—
(Holtby Cottages to Leases Grange) (Temp. Prohibition of Traffic) (773)
(Leases Bridge—Cowfold Grange) (Temp. Prohibition of Traffic) (1539)
(South of Dishforth Roundabout) (Temp. Prohibition of Traffic) (1541)
(Temp. Restriction of Speed) (88)
(Wyboston) (Temp. Prohibition of Traffic) (663)
—King's Lynn Trunk Road (A10) (Hoddesdon Bypass, Hertfordshire) (Temp. Prohibition of Traffic) (1255)
—Yorkshire Motorway (M1)—
(Bedfordshire)—
(Temp. Prohibition of Traffic)—
O. (394)
(No. 2) O. (506)
(No. 3) O. (741)
(Crick—Heyford) (Temp. Prohibition and Restriction of Traffic) (259)

London—
  Yorkshire Motorway (M1)—
    (Junction 15 to Buckinghamshire Boundary) (Temp. Prohibition of Traffic) (851)
    (Junction 21–23) (Temp. Prohibition and Restriction of Traffic) (372)
    (Junction 22) (Temp. Prohibition and Restriction of Traffic) (583)
    (Junctions 23–24) (Temp. Prohibition of Traffic) (86)
    (Junctions 24 to 25) (Temp. Prohibition of Traffic) (635)
    (Junctions 25 to 26) (Temp. Prohibition of Traffic) (492)
M1 Motorway—
  (Bedfordshire) (Temp. Prohibition of Traffic) (351)
  (Hertfordshire)—
    (Junction 6, Waterdale) (Temp. Prohibition of Traffic) (608)
    (M25 Interchange) (Temp. Prohibition of Traffic) (437)
    (Junction 13 Bedfordshire) (Temp. Prohibition of Traffic) (1265)
    (Leeds—Wakefield) (Kirkhamgate) (Temp. Prohibition of Traffic) (23)
    (London Borough of Barnet) (Temp. Prohibition of Traffic) (495)
    (Milton Keynes, Buckinghamshire) (Temp. Prohibition of Traffic) (1389)
    (River Rother Bridge) (Temp. Prohibition of Traffic) (800)
    (Temp. Prohibition of Traffic) (654)
    (Thorpe Hesley—Tankersley) (South Yorkshire) (Temp. Restriction of Traffic) (507)
    (Thorpe Hesley to Haigh) (Temp. Prohibition of Traffic)—
      O. (883)
      (No. 2) O. (951)
M1 and M10 Motorways (Hertfordshire) (Temp. Prohibition of Traffic) (657)
M2 Motorway (Medway Towns) (Temp. Restriction of Traffic) (753)
M3 Motorway—
  (Popham to Bar End) (Temp. Restriction of Traffic) (1420)
  (Ravenswood Overbridge to Lightwater Interchange) (Temp. Restriction of Traffic) (597)
  (Sunbury Cross) (Temp. Restriction of Traffic) (1251)
M4 Motorway—
  (Aust to Newhouse) (Temp. Speed Limit)—
    O. (525)
    (No. 2) O. (1498)
  (Brynglas Tunnels, Newport) (Temp. Traffic) (78)
  (London—
    Borough of Hounslow) (Temp. Prohibition of Traffic)—
      O. (105)
      (No. 2) O. (440)
    —South Wales Motorway) (Temp. Restriction of Traffic) (271)
  (Pencoed, Mid Glamorgan) (Temp. Traffic) (1275)
  (Port Talbot, West Glamorgan) (Temp. Traffic) (1569)
  (Severn and Wye Bridges, Footway and Cycle Track) (Temp. Prohibition of Traffic) (205)
  (Stanton St Quintin to Wooton Bassett, Wilts) (Temp. Restriction of Traffic) (642)
M5 Motorway—
  (Almondsbury, Avon) (Temp. Prohibition of Traffic) (1496)
  (at Junction with M6 Motorway) (Temp. Restriction of Traffic) (559)
  (Avonmouth Bridge Cycle Track) (Temp. Prohibition of Traffic) (511)

M5 Motorway—
  (County of Hereford and Worcester) (Temp. Restriction of Traffic)—
    O. (370)
    (Junction 4 to Junction 7) O. (1482)
  (Dunball Interchange, Somerset) (Temp. Prohibition of Traffic) (952)
  (Frocester to Stinchcombe, Gloucestershire) (Temp. Restriction of Traffic)
    (1525)
  (Haresfield to Frocester, Gloucestershire) (Temp. Restriction of Traffic)
    (591)
  (Junction 1, West Bromwich) (Temp. Restriction of Traffic) (889)
  (South West of Cribbs Causeway to Lower Almondsbury, Avon) (Temp.
    Prohibition of Traffic) (441)
M6 Motorway—
  (Birmingham—Preston—Carlisle)—
    (Between Junctions 33 and 32) (Temp. Prohibition of Traffic) (371)
    (Carlisle Bypass) (Between Marker Post 482/5 and 491/0) (Junctions 42
      and 43) (Temp. Restriction of Traffic) (327)
    (Junction 9, Bescot) (Temp. Restriction of Traffic) (1405)
    (Preston Bypass) (Between Pope Lane Bridge and Longbridge Road
      Bridge) (Temp. Prohibition of Traffic) (496)
    (South of Junction 22 to North of Junction 25) (Temp. Restriction of
      Traffic) (712)
    (Southbound entry slip road at Junction 5, Castle Bromwich) (Temp.
      Prohibition of Traffic) (58)
    (Warwickshire) (Temp. Restriction of Traffic) (916)
M6 and M42 Motorways Slip Roads at Gravelly Hill, Great Barr, Coleshill and
  Bickenhill) (Temp. Restriction of Traffic) (915)
M10 Motorway—
  (Hertfordshire) (Temp. Prohibition of Traffic)—
    O. (1018)
    (No. 2) O. (1465)
M18 Motorway—
  (North of M1 Interchange) (Temp. Prohibition of Traffic) (1294)
  (St. Catherine's Interchange) (Temp. Prohibition of Traffic) (1388)
  (Sliproads at Junction 1, Bramley) (Temp. Prohibition of Traffic) (1031)
M18 and M1 Motorways (Thurcroft Interchange) (Temp. Prohibition of
  Traffic) (1455)
M25 Motorway (A1(M) South Mimms—A111) and the A1(M) Motorway
  (Hertfordshire) (Temp. Prohibition of Traffic) (829)
M27 Motorway (Park Gate Interchange) (Temp. Prohibition of Traffic) (717)
M40 Motorway—
  (Beaconsfield, Buckinghamshire) (Temp. Prohibition of Traffic) (1283)
  (Buckinghamshire)—
    (M25 Interchange) (Temp. Prohibition of Traffic)—
      O. (617)
      O. (1439)
    (Temp. Prohibition of Traffic) (742)
  (Stokenchurch to Lewknor) (Temp. Restriction of Traffic) (1367)
M45 Motorway (Dunchurch Spur) (Temp. Prohibition and Restriction of
  Traffic) (263)
M50 Motorway—
  (County of Hereford and Worcester) (Temp. Restriction of Traffic) (1077)

M50 Motorway—
  (Junction 1, Brockeridge Common) (Temp. Closure of Westbound Entry
    Slip Road) (927)
M53 Motorway—
  (Bidston Moss Viaduct) (Temp. Prohibition of Traffic) (157)
  (Mid Wirral) (South of Junction 11) (Temp. Restriction of Traffic) (788)
M54 Motorway (Junction 5, Forge) (Temp. Closure of Eastbound Exit Slip
  Road) (787)
M56 Motorway (North Cheshire) (Between Junctions 12 and 14 and Junctions
  15 and 16) and the M53 Motorway (Mid-Wirral) (Between Junctions 7–10)
  (Temp. Restriction of Traffic) (945)
M61 Motorway—
  (Manchester—Preston)—
    (South of Junction 1) (Worsley Braided Interchange) (Temp. Restriction
      of Traffic) (993)
    ,the M62 Motorway (Liverpool—Hull) and the Trunk Road A580
      (Manchester—Liverpool) (Temp. Restriction of Traffic) (658)
M62 Motorway—
  (Addle Lane Overbridge) (Temp. Prohibition of Traffic) (1485)
  (Chain Bar to Gildersome) (Temp. Prohibition of Traffic) (524)
  (Church Lane to Parkfields) (Temp. Prohibition of Traffic) (744)
  (Langham West Bridge to Kilpin Bridge) (Temp. Prohibition of Traffic)
    (1030)
  (Liverpool—Hull)—
    (Between Junctions 20–22) (Temp. Restriction of Traffic) (674)
    (Greater Manchester and Cheshire) (Junctions 11–12) (Temp. Restriction
      of Traffic) (632)
    (North of Junction 14) (Temp. Restriction of Traffic) (411)
M63 Motorway (Stretford—Eccles Bypass) (Between Junctions 2 and 3)
  (Temp. Prohibition of Traffic) (1515)
M66 Motorway—
  (Bury Easterly By Pass)—
    (Junctions 1–4) (Greater Manchester) (Temp. Restriction of Traffic)
      (991)
    (Northern Section) (between terminal junction with A56 and North side
      of Junction 2) (Temp. Prohibition of Traffic) (1587)
M180 Motorway—
  (Brigg Bypass) (Temp. Prohibition of Traffic)—
    O. (321)
    (No. 2) O. (1487)
  (Scunthorpe Southern Bypass) (Temp. Prohibition of Traffic) (87)
  (Trent Bridge) (Temp. Prohibition of Traffic) (926)
North of Boroughbridge—Thirsk Trunk Road (A168) (Warren Farm Bridge)
  (Temp. Prohibition of Traffic) (799)
Penrith—Middlesbrough Trunk Road (A66) (Sedbury Lodge Lay-by) (Temp.
  Prohibition of Traffic) (149)
Sheffield—Grimsby Trunk Road (A18) (Melton Ross) (Temp. Prohibition of
  Traffic) (1488)
Trunk Road(s)—
  (A1)—
    (Biggleswade, Bedfordshire) (Temp. Prohibition of Traffic) (1464)
    (Fisher Lane Interchange) (Temp. Prohibition of Traffic) (415)

Trunk Road(s)—
  (A1)—
    (Great North Road, Gonerby Moor) (Temp. Prohibition and Restriction
      of Traffic) (1368)
    (Green Lanes Roundabout, Hatfield) (Temp. Prohibition of Traffic)
      (1416)
    (Long Bennington and Foston Bypasses) (Temp. Prohibition and
      Restriction of Traffic) (888)
    (Markham Moor to Tuxford) (Temp. Prohibition and Restriction of
      Traffic) (711)
    (Morpeth Bypass) (Temp. Restriction of Traffic) (639)
    (Newark Bypass) and the Trunk Road (A46) (Temp. Prohibition and
      Restriction of Traffic) (1342)
    (South Mimms Roundabout) (Temp. Prohibition of Traffic) (1237)
    (Testo's Roundabout to White Mare Pool Interchange) (Temp.
      Restriction of Traffic) (662)
  (A1(M))—
    (Havannah Interchange to White Mare Pool Interchange) (Temp.
      Restriction and Prohibition of Traffic) (643)
    (Lime Lane Bridge to Grove Farm Accommodation Bridge) (Temp.
      Restriction of Traffic) (826)
  (A2)—
    (Barham to Lydden) (Temp. Restriction of Traffic) (1417)
      (Crown Woods Way Slip Road, Bexley and Greenwich) (Temp.
        Prohibition of Traffic) (517)
  (A3)—
    (Beverley Way, Merton) (Temp. Restriction of Traffic) (1561)
    (Hook Rise North, Kingston upon Thames) (Temp. Prohibition of
      Traffic) (852)
    (Robin Hood Way and Beverley Way, Kingston upon Thames) (Temp.
      Restriction of Traffic) (946)
  (A5) (Watling Street, Tamworth) (Temp. Restriction of Traffic) (1231)
  (A6)—
    (Ampthill Road, Bedford) (Temp. Restriction of Traffic) (1478)
    (Bedfordshire) (Temp. Prohibition of Traffic) (498)
    (Derby Road/Church Gate/Market Place, Kegworth) (Temp. Prohibition
      of Traffic and of Waiting) (13)
    (Derby Road/Loughborough Road, Hathern) (Temp. Prohibition and
      Restriction of Traffic) (138)
    (Fairfield Road, Buxton) (Temp. Prohibition of Traffic) (1608)
    (Hertsmere, Hertfordshire) (Bell Roundabout) (Temp. Prohibition of
      Traffic) (665)
    (Newton Road, Rushden) (Temp. Prohibition of Traffic) (262)
    (The Bell Roundabout to South Mimms Roundabout) (Temp. Prohibition
      of Traffic) (1239)
  (A10)—
    (High Road, Tottenham, Haringey) (Temp. Suspension of One-Way
      Working and of a Bus Lane) (1418)
    (Kingsmead Viaduct, Ware) (Temp. Prohibition of Traffic) (503)
  (A12)—
    (Darsham Public Level Crossing) (Temp. Prohibition of Traffic) (1065)

Trunk Road(s)—
  (A12)—
    (Gallows Corner Flyover, Havering) (Temp. Prohibition of Traffic)—
      O. (269)
      (No. 2) O. (709)
    (Mountnessing Bypass Slip Road) (Temp. Prohibition of Traffic) (896)
  (A13)—
    (Beckton Flyover, Newham) (Temp. Prohibition of Traffic) (500)
    (Canning Town Flyover, Newham) (Temp. Prohibition of Traffic) (584)
    (Movers Lane and Lodge Avenue Flyovers) (Temp. Prohibition of Traffic) (786)
  (A16)—
    (Bridge Street, Louth) (Temp. Prohibition of Traffic) (1486)
    (High Ferry Level Crossing, Lincolnshire) (Temp. Prohibition of Traffic)—
      O. (12)
      O. (675)
  (A17)—
    (Heckington Bypass, Lincolnshire) (Temp. Prohibition and Restriction of Traffic) (987)
    (Swineshead Level Crossing, Lincolnshire) (Temp. Prohibition of Traffic) (1497)
  (A19)—
    (Billingham Diversion) (Temp. Restriction of Traffic) (928)
    (Mandale Road Interchange Southbound Slip Roads) (Temp. Prohibition of Traffic) (81)
  (A21)—
    (Sevenoaks Bypass) (Temp. Restriction of Traffic) (192)
    (Tonbridge Bypass) (Temp. Restriction of Traffic) (260)
  (A27)—
    Beddingham Level Crossing (Temp. Prohibition of Traffic) (1266)
    (Chichester Bypass and Westhampnett Road) (Temp. Restriction of Traffic) (664)
  (A30) (Camborne Bypass, Cornwall) (Temp. Restriction of Traffic) (1503)
  (A31) (West Moors, Dorset) (Temp. Restriction of Traffic) (46)
  (A33) (Chandlers Ford Bypass) (Temp. Restriction of Traffic) (807)
  (A34)—
    (Birmingham Road, Stratford-upon-Avon) (Temp. One Way Traffic and Prohibition of Left Turn) (290)
    (Hanford to Trentham) (Temp. Restriction of Traffic) (1029)
    (Sandleford Priory Newbury) (Temp. Restriction of Traffic) (169)
    (Stone Road Strongford) (Temp. Restriction of Traffic) (227)
  (A35) (Axminster, Devon) (Temp. Prohibition of Traffic) (164)
  (A38)—
    (Alfreton—South Normanton Bypass) (Temp. Prohibition and Restriction of Traffic) (393)
    (Branston Interchange) (Temp. Restriction of Traffic) (183)
    (Burton-upon-Trent By-Pass) (Temp. Restriction of Traffic) (763)
    (Marsh Mills to Deep Lane, Devon) (Temp. Prohibition of Traffic) (1003)
    (Ripley—Swanwick Bypass) (Temp. Prohibition and Restriction of Traffic) (708)
    (Tideford to Trerulefoot, Cornwall) (Temp. Restriction of Traffic) (656)

Trunk Road(s)—
  (A40)—
    (Cheltenham Gloucestershire) (Temp. Regulation of Traffic) (1453)
    (Mitchel Troy, Gwent) (Temp. Traffic)—
      O. (776)
      (No. 2) O. (1423)
    (Sandhills to Holton) (Temp. Restriction of Traffic)—
      O. (595)
      (No. 2) O. (596)
    (Western Avenue, Ealing) (Temp. Prohibition of Traffic) (1397)
  (A41) (King Edward Avenue, Aylesbury) (Temp. Prohibition of Traffic)
    (1254)
  (A45) (Heyford to Kislingbury) (Temp. Prohibition and Restriction of
    Traffic) (182)
  (A46) (Millgate, Newark) (Temp. Prohibition of Traffic and Suspension of
    One-Way Working) (1461)
  (A47) (Wisbech and West Walton Highway Bypass) (Temp. Restriction of
    Traffic) (1022)
  (A48) (Lydney, Gloucestershire) (Temp. Restriction of Traffic) (1021)
  (A52)—
    (Clifton Bridge, Nottingham) (Temp. Prohibition of Traffic)—
      O. (122)
      O. (982)
  (A61) (Lordsmill Street, Chesterfield) (Temp. Prohibition of Traffic) (34)
  (A66) (Stockton Road) (Temp. Restriction of Traffic) (828)
  (A69)—
    (Bardon Mill Bridge) (Temp. Prohibition of Traffic) (1438)
    (Carlisle—Newcastle) (Temp. Prohibition of Traffic) (44)
  (A158) (Langworth Level Crossing, Lincolnshire) (Temp. Prohibition of
    Traffic) (272)
  (A167) (Ferryhill Cutting) (Temp. Prohibition of Traffic) (158)
  (A259) (Monkbretton Bridge, New Road) (Temp. Restriction of Traffic)
    (695)
  (A303)—
    (Hundred Acre Corner) (Temp. Restriction of Traffic) (1074)
    (London—Penzance) (Compton Pauncefoot, Somerset) (Temp.
      Restriction of Traffic) (750)
  (A339)—
    (Basingstoke Northern Bypass) (Temp. Restriction of Traffic)—
      0.(1068)
      (No. 2) O. (1328)
  (A405)—
    (Chorleywood Interchange to Hunton Bridge Roundabout) (Temp.
      Prohibition of Traffic) (743)
    (Hunton Bridge Roundabout to Long Lane Roundabout) (Temp.
      Prohibition of Traffic) (731)
    (Mount Pleasant Lane) (Temp. Prohibition of Traffic) (609)
  (A406)—
    (North Circular Road—
      Barnet (Temp. Restriction of Traffic) (825)
      Brent and Ealing) (Temp. Prohibition of Traffic and Waiting) (1419)
  (A446) (Stonebridge Road, Coleshill) (Temp. Restriction of Traffic) (1071)

Trunk Road(s)—
 (A449/A40)—
  (Gibraltar Tunnels, Monmouth) (Temp. Traffic) (383)
  (Monmouth, Gwent) (Temp. Traffic) (406)
 (A465)—
  (Rassau, Gwent) (Temp. Prohibition of Overtaking)—
   O. (809)
   O. (1557)
 (A483)—
  (Wind Street, Ammanford) (Temp. Traffic)—
   O. (228)
   (No. 2) O. (1274)
 (A483/A458) (Welshpool, Powys) (Temp. Traffic) (229)
 (A487) (Cardigan, Dyfed) (Temp. Traffic) (49)
 (A523) (Derby—Macclesfield—South of Stockport) (Temp. Prohibition of Waiting) (40)
 (A580) (East Lancashire) (East of Lane Head Junction, Wigan) (Temp. Restriction of Traffic) (1454)
 (A590) (London—Carlisle—Glasgow—Inverness) (Kendal Link, Cumbria) (Temp. Prohibition of Traffic) (1536)
 (A679)—
  (Blackburn—Accrington—Burnley)—
   (Broadway, Accrington) (Temp. Prohibition of Traffic) (634)
   (Junction with the Accrington Northern By-Pass) (A622) (Temp. Prohibition of Traffic) (925)
 (A4042)—
  (Croes-y-Mwyalch, Gwent) (Temp. Traffic)—
   O. (304)
   (No. 2) O. (689)
  (Llanellen, Gwent) (Temp. Traffic) (564)
 (A5111) (Warwick Avenue, Derby) (Temp. Prohibition and Restriction of Traffic) (5)
 (A6119) (Leeds—Halifax—Burnley—Blackburn—East of Preston) (Whitebirk Road, Blackburn) (Temp. Prohibition of Traffic) (789)
 (A6514)—
  (Middleton Boulevard, Nottingham) (Temp. Prohibition of Traffic) (493)
  (Valley Road, Nottingham) (Temp. Prohibition and Restriction of Traffic) (882)
 (Birmingham—Great Yarmouth) (A47) (Temp. Prohibition of Traffic)—
  O. (534)
  .O. (1130)
 (Felixstowe—Weedon) (A45) (Temp. Prohibition of Traffic) (156)
 (Greenham Common) (Temp. Prohibition of Traffic) (420)
 (London—
  —Great Yarmouth) (A12)—
   (Ipswich Eastern Bypass) (Temp. Restriction of Traffic) (1064)
   (Temp. Prohibition of Traffic)—
    O. (18)
    O. (277)
   Temp. Prohibition of U-Turns (Pound Lane to Folly Lane, Copdock) (278)
  —Portsmouth) (A3) (Temp. Restriction of Traffic) (1466)

Trunk Road(s)—
  (M25)—
    (Bell Common Tunnel, Essex) (Temp. Prohibition of Traffic)—
      O. (170)
      (No. 2) O. (1499)
    (Holmesdale Tunnel, Hertfordshire) (Temp. Prohibition of Traffic)—
      O. (171)
      O. (1526)
  (Route A8) (Strathclyde Region) (Temp. Restriction of Traffic) (676)
  (Route A74)—
    (Abington) (Temp. Prohibition of Specified Turns) (747)
    Beattock Summit (Temp. Closure) (450)
    (Crawford)—
      (Temp. Closure) (1415)
      (Temp. Prohibition of Specified Turns) (1242)
    (Dumfries and Galloway Region)—
      (Temp. Prohibition of Overtaking) (659)
      (Temp. Prohibition of Traffic) (754)
    (Maryville Interchange to Fullarton Road) (Temp. Restriction of Traffic) (376)
    (Strathclyde Region)—
      (Temp. Prohibition of Overtaking) (660)
      (Temp. Restriction of Traffic) (533)
  (Route A77)—
    (Ayr Road, Newton Mearns) (Temp. Closure and Prohibition of Right Hand Turns) (931)
    (Giffnock) (Temp. Closure and Waiting and Loading Restrictions) (936)
    (Newton Mearns)—
      (Temp. Closure of North-bound Carriageway) (286)
      (Temp. Closure of Northbound Carriageway and Prohibition of Specified Turns) (375)
  (Route A80)—
    (Bonnybridge—Castle Cary Crossover (B816)) (Temp. Closure of Northbound and Southbound Carriageways) (1322)
    (Strathclyde Region) (Temp. Prohibition of Traffic) (374)
  (Route A82) Barloan Roundabout—Barnhill Road) (Temp. Closure of West-bound Carriageway) (1414)
  (Route A92)—
    (Balfarg—New Inn Glenrothes) (Temp. Closure of North-bound Carriageway) (373)
    (Bankhead Roundabout to Preston Roundabout, Glenrothes) (Temp. Closure) (180)
  (Route A835) (Contin-Maryburgh) (Temp. Weight Restriction) (1335)
  (Route A972) (Kingsway, Dundee) (Temp. Closure) (885)
  (Route M8)—
    (Airport Interchange to Craigton Interchange) (Temp. Closure of West-bound Carriageway) (935)
    (Hillington Interchange) (Temp. Closure of East-bound Carriageway) (1329)
    (Strathclyde Region) (Temp. Restriction of Traffic) (671)

Trunk Road(s)—
  (Route M9)—
    (Charterhall Bridge) (Temp. Closure of North-bound Carriageway) (161)
    (Kinnaird Interchange) (Temp. Prohibition of Traffic) (1377)
    (Plean) (Temp. Closure of East-bound and West-bound Carriageways) (755)
    (Polmont) (Temp. Closure) (934)
  (Route M74) (Maryville Interchange) (Temp. Prohibition of Traffic) (677)
  (Route M80) (Auchenbowie Overbridge) (Temp. Closure of South-bound Carriageway) (1321)
  (Route M90)—
    (Admiralty Interchange) (Temp. Closure) (933)
    (Masterton) (Temp. Closure of North-bound and South-bound Carriageways) (670)
  (Route M876)—
    (Larbert) (Temp. Prohibition of Traffic) (1378)
    (M9 Crossover) (Temp. Closure of North-bound Carriageway) (1320)
    (Wheatlands) (Temp. Prohibition of Traffic) (1379)
  (St. Albans Road, St. Albans) (A405) (Temp. Prohibition of Traffic) (504)
  (Staples Corner Flyover, Barnet and Brent) (Temp. Prohibition of Traffic) (633)
  (Taunton, Somerset) (Temp. Prohibition of Traffic) (56)

Orders made under the Road Traffic Regulation Act 1984 (c. 27) s. 14(1)(5)(7)
A1(M) Motorway (A1001 Interchange) (Temp. Restriction of Traffic) (1666)
A1 Trunk Road (Great North Road/Colsterworth Bypass) (Temp. Prohibition and Restriction of Traffic) (1830)
(A5) Trunk Road (Crick Crossroads, Watling Street) (Temp. Restriction of Traffic) (1768)
(A16) Trunk Road (Littleworth Station Level Crossing) (Temp. Prohibition of Traffic) (1637)
(A38) Trunk Road (Egginton Bridge) (Temp. Prohibition and Restriction of Traffic) (2016)
A406 Trunk Road (Lea Valley Viaduct, Waltham Forest) (Temp. Weight Restriction) (2027)
(A550) Trunk Road (Queensferry—South of Birkenhead) (Welsh Road, Hooton, Ellesmere Port) (Temp. Prohibition of Traffic) (1737)
Chester—Bangor Trunk Road—
  (A55 Diverted at Llanddulas) (Temp. Traffic) (1732)
  (A55 Diverted at Llanddulas to Old Colwyn) (Temp. Traffic) (1731)
Gildersome—Leeds Motorway (M621) (Temp. Prohibition of Traffic) (1883)
London—
  —Edinburgh—Thurso Trunk Road (A1)—
    (Ferrybridge Interchange) (Temp. Prohibition of Traffic) (1884)
    (New Inn Farm to Roxby House) (Temp. Prohibition of Traffic) (1962)
  —Norwich Trunk Road (All) (Temp. Prohibition of Right Turn) (2038)
M4 Motorway—
  (Brynglas Tunnels, Newport) (Temp. Traffic) (No. 2) (1839)
  (Coldra Interchange, Newport) (Temp. Traffic) (1783)
  (Heathrow Spur to M25 Interchange) (Temp. Restriction of Traffic) (1748)
  (London Borough of Hounslow) (Temp. Prohibition of Traffic) (No. 3) (1769)

M4 Motorway—
    (Magor, Gwent) (Temp. Traffic) (1813)
    (Malpas Interchange, Newport) (Temp. Traffic) (1733)
    (Severn and Wye Bridges, Footway and Cycle Track) (Temp. Prohibition of Traffic) (No. 2) (1750)
    (Theale Interchange) (Temp. Restriction of Traffic) (1807)
    (Winnersh to Witley) (Temp. Restriction of Traffic) (1609)
M6 Motorway—
    (Birmingham—Preston—Carlisle)—
        (Between Junctions 17 and 18) (Temp. Restriction of Traffic) (1729)
        (Between Junctions 43 and 44) and the Trunk Road (A74) (London—Carlisle—Glasgow—Inverness) (North of Greymoorhill North Bridge, Carlisle) (Temp. Restriction of Traffic) (1584)
        (Junction 9, Bescot) (Temp. Prohibition of Traffic) (1749)
        (Staffordshire) (Junctions 10A to 11) (Temp. Restriction of Traffic) (1755)
M18 Motorway (Wadworth Intersection) (Temp. Prohibition of Traffic) (1842)
M25 Motorway—
    (A111–A10) (Temp. Restriction of Traffic) (1667)
    (Chertsey—Wisley Section)—
        (Slip Roads) (Temp. Restriction of Traffic) (1806)
        (Temp. Restriction of Traffic) (1610)
        (Temp. Restriction of Traffic) (1961)
M50 Motorway (County of Hereford and Worcester) (Temp. Restriction of Traffic) (No. 2) (1585)
M53 Motorway (Mid Wirral) (Bidston Moss Viaduct) (Temp. Prohibition of Traffic) (1586)
M56 Motorway (North Cheshire) (Junction 3) and (Eastbound Exit Slip Road and Westbound Entry Slip Road at Junction 3) (Temp. Restriction of Traffic) (1588)
M62 Motorway (Junction 13) and (the Southbound Entry Slip Road at Junction 13) (Temp. Restriction of Traffic) (1952)
North-West of Doncaster—Kendal Trunk Road (A629)—
    (Kildwick Level Crossing) (Temp. Prohibition of Traffic) (1681)
    (Skipton Western By-pass) (Temp. Prohibition of Traffic) (1937)
Special Road Llanddulas to Colwyn Bay (A55) (Temp. Traffic) (1931)
Trunk Road(s)—
    (A1)—
        Barnet Bypass (Temp. Restriction of Traffic) (1665)
        (Lay-by at North Charlton) (Temp. Prohibition of Traffic) (2015)
        (Shilbottle Road Bridge, Alnwick) (Temp. Restriction of Traffic) (1744)
    (A1 and A41) (Watford Way Barnet) (Temp. Prohibition of Use of Gaps in Central Reservation) (1595)
    (A11) (Stump Cross Junction—Bourn Bridge Junction) (Temp. Prohibition of Traffic) (1631)
    (A16) (High Ferry Level Crossing, Lincolnshire) (Temp. Prohibition of Traffic) (1781)
    (A21) (Sevenoaks Bypass) (Temp. Restriction of Traffic) (No. 2) (1596)
    (A27) (Beddingham Level Crossing) (Temp. Prohibition of Traffic) (1708)
    (A38) (Monk's Bridge Lay-by, Derbyshire) (Temp. Prohibition of Traffic) (1757)

Trunk Road(s)—
 (A40)—
  (Mitchel Troy, Gwent) (Temp. Traffic) (No. 3) (1556)
  (Over Causeway, Gloucestershire) (Temp. Restriction of Traffic) (1840)
  (Quay Road, Fishguard Harbour, Fishguard) (Temp. Traffic) (1973)
 (A48) (Crick, Gwent) (Temp. Traffic) (1953)
 (A49)—
  (at Ford Railway Bridge) (Temp. Prohibition of Traffic) (1841)
  (Onibury Level Crossing) (Temp. Prohibition of Traffic) (1668)
 (A59) (Liverpool Road, South Ribble) (Penwortham Bypass) (Temp. Prohibition of Traffic) (2059)
 (A69) (Blenkinsop Level Crossing) (Temp. Prohibition of Traffic) (1853)
 (A167) (Ferryhill Cutting) (Temp. Restriction of Traffic and Waiting) (2039)
 (A303) (Hundred Acre Corner) (Temp. Restriction of Traffic) (2042)
 (A361) (Norton Fitzwarren, Somerset) (Temp. Prohibition of Traffic) (1786)
 (A406) (Gunnersbury Avenue, Hounslow) (Temp. Restriction of Traffic) (1742)
 (A419) (Stratton St Margaret, Wiltshire) (Temp. Restriction of Traffic) (1910)
 (A439) (Grove Road and Evesham Place, Stratford-upon-Avon) (Temp. Restriction of Traffic) (1738)
 (A449/A40)—
  (Coldra-Usk, Gwent) (Temp. Traffic) (1655)
  (Gibraltar Tunnels, Monmouth) (Temp. Traffic) (No. 2) (1632)
 (A470) (Abercynon, Mid Glamorgan) (Temp. Traffic) (1580)
 (A4042) (Llantarnam, Gwent) (Temp. Traffic) (1581)
 (Birmingham—Great Yarmouth) (A47) (Carrow Bridge, Norwich) (Temp. Prohibition of Traffic) (1597)
 (Felixstowe—Weedon) (A45) (Temp. Restriction of Traffic) (St. Saviours, Westley and Moreton Hall (Eastern) Interchanges) (1745)
 (London—Great Yarmouth) (A12) Temp. No U Turn (Hughes Corner/Appletree Corner, Stratford St Mary) (1611)
 (Route A9)—
  (Dalreoch—Burnside) (Temp. Prohibition of Overtaking) (1639)
  (Kessock Bridge—Charlestown Junction) (Temp. Closure of Northbound and Southbound Carriageways) (1672)
 (Route A92)—
  (Balquharn, Portlethen) (Temp. Closure of Northbound and Southbound Carriageways) (1928)
  (Stonehaven) (Temp. Prohibition of Traffic) (1882)
 (Routes A929/A94)—
  (Craig O'Loch Road and Dundee Loan) (Temp. Closure)—
   O. (1559)
   O. (1673)
 (Route M8) (Arkleston Road Bridge—Hillington Footbridge) (Temp. Closure of Eastbound and Westbound Carriageways) (1678)
 (Route M90) (Kelty) (Temp. Closure of Northbound and Southbound Carriageways) (1710)

(iv) *Experimental*

Orders made under the Road Traffic Act 1984 (c. 27) s. 9(1)(4) and, where indicated, ss. 4(2), 10(1), Sch. 9, Pt. IV, para. 27

Trunk Road—

(A2) (Wilmington) (Prohibition of Use of Laybys) (Experimental) (1284)

(A35) (Dorchester, Dorset) (Taxi Rank) (Experimental) (24)

(A487) (Great Darkgate Street, Aberystwyth) (Experimental Prohibition and Restriction of Waiting) [*ss. 4(2), 10(1), Sch. 9, Pt. IV, para. 27*] (1613)

(A494) (Chester Street, Mold, Clwyd) (Prohibition of Right-Hand Turn) (Experimental) (1957)

(4) Roads and Bridges, Scotland

Strathclyde Regional Council (Monkland Motorway) (Ramp M) (Connecting Roads) Special Road Scheme 1983 Confirmation Instrument 1984 *made under the Special Roads Act 1949 s. 1*

Orders made under the Trunk Roads Act 1946 (c. 30) s. 1(2)

Carlisle—Glasgow—Inverness Trunk Road (A82) (Eachrain Diversion) (1398)

Edinburgh—Carlisle Trunk Road (A7) (Synton Mossend Diversions) [*s. 1(2) as read with the Trunk Roads Act 1936 (c. 5) s. 13(2) ext. by s. 11(4) of the 1946 Act*] (1657)

Gretna—Stranraer—Glasgow—Stirling Trunk Road—

(A75)—

(Bridge of Dee Diversion) (1954)

(Creetown Bypass) [*as read with ss. 2(5), 6(1)*] (433)

(A77)—

(Doonholm Improvement) (37)

(Glenapp Church Corner Diversion) (598)

London—Edinburgh—Thurso Trunk Road—

(A9)—

(Alness Bypass) (1399)

(Dalreoch to Burnside Diversion) (101)

(Dingwall Relief Road) The Dingwall—Ullapool Trunk Road (A834) (High Street) (Detrunking) (781)

(Mussleburgh Bypass) (1359)

Perth—Aberdeen—Inverness Trunk Road (Banff Bridge and Approach Roads Diversion) (Revn.) [*s. 1(2) as read with the Trunk Roads Act 1936 (c. 5) s. 13(2) ext. by s. 11(4) of the 1946 Act*] (181)

Stirling—Callander—Crianlarich Trunk Road (A84) (Kingshouse Diversion) (1794)

CLASS 2. RAILWAYS, TRAMWAYS AND TROLLEY VEHICLES

(1) *Light Railways*   (2) *Transport Charges*

(1) Light Railways

Orders made under the Light Railways Act 1896 (c. 48), enabling sections in square brackets, and, where indicated, the Transport Act 1968 (c. 73) s.121(2)

Amlwch Light Railway (Amdt.) [*ss. 7, 9–12, 24*] (681)

Cranmore Light Railway (Ext.) [*ss. 7, 9–11; 1968 s. 121(2)*] (557)

Llangollen and Corwen Light Railway [*ss. 7, 9–11; 1968 s. 121(2)*] (558)

Severn Valley Light Railway [*ss. 7, 9–12, 18, 24; 1968 s. 121(2)*] (1202)

(2) Transport Charges

Orders made under the Transport Charges &c. (Misc. Provns.) Act 1954 (c. 64) s. 6
Blyth Ferries (Revision of Charges) (Variation) (2061)
Bournemouth—Swanage Ferry (Revision of Charges) (771)
Dartmouth—Kingswear Higher Ferry (Revision of Charges) (494)

CLASS 3.   RIVERS AND INLAND WATERWAYS

(1) *Land Drainage*   (2) *River, Scotland*

(1) Land Drainage

Orders made under the Land Drainage Act 1976 (c. 70); enabling sections in square brackets
Anglian Water Authy.—
  (Alteration of Boundaries of the Southery and District Internal Drainage District) [*ss. 11(4), 109(6)*] (462)
  (Ancholme Internal Drainage District) [*ss. 11(4), 109(6)*] (497)
  (Variation of the Longstanton and Swavesey Awards) [*ss. 25(4), 109(6)*] (2064)
Northumbrian Water Authy. (Abolition of the Prestwick Carr Internal Drainage District) [*ss. 11(4), 109(6)*] (162)

(2) River, Scotland

Orders made under the Diseases of Fish Act 1937 (c. 33) s. 2(1) as read with s. 11
Salmon and Freshwater Fisheries—
  Diseases of Fish (Infected Area) (*S.*)—
    O. (20)
    (No. 2) O. (424)
    Revn.—
      O. (140)
      (No. 2) O. (141)
      (No. 3) O. (150)
      (No. 4) O. (483)
      (No. 5) O. (484)
      (No. 6) O. (485)

CLASS 4.   SHIPPING, HARBOURS, DOCKS, PORTS, etc.

(1) *Harbours, Docks, Piers and*   (2) *Port Health Authorities,*
       Ferries   *England and Wales*

(1) Harbours, Docks, Piers and Ferries

Revision Orders made under the Harbours Act 1964 (c. 40) s. 14
Aberdeen (1027)
Bridlington (998)
Great Yarmouth Port and Haven (Constitution) (1067)
Harwich (59)
Inverness—
  O. (206)
  (No. 2) O. (207)

Mallaig (803)
Manchester Ship Canal (50)
Mersey Docks and Harbour—
    O. (1878)
    (No. 2) O. (1974)

(2) Port Health Authorities, England and Wales

Orders made under the Public Health Act 1936 (c. 49) ss. 2, 3 and 9
Medway Port Health Authy. (1054)
Whitehaven Port Health Authy. (714)
Workington Port Health Authy. (715)

CLASS 5. LOCAL GOVERNMENT

(1) *Changes in Local Government Areas*
(2) *Clean Air*
(3) *Electoral Arrangements*
(4) *Local Government, Scotland*
(5) *London Government*
(6) *Pensions*
(7) *Powers and Duties of Local Authorities*

(1) Changes in Local Government Areas

Orders made under one or more of the following provns. of the Local Govt. Act 1972 (c. 70): ss. 47, 51(1) (2), 67(4) (5) and, where indicated, Sch. 10, para. 7, as applied by para. 9
(Areas)—
    Basildon and Castle Point (89)
    Bedfordshire (2023)
    Bristol, Wansdyke and Woodspring (66)
    East Hertfordshire and Stevenage (60)
    Humberside and North Yorkshire (1906)
    Sedgemoor and Taunton Deane (1793)
(Communities)—
    Afron [*Sch. 10, para. 7, as applied by para. 9*] (473)
    Alyn and Deeside [*Sch. 10, para. 7, as applied by para. 9*] (1782)
    Blaenau Gwent [*Sch. 10, para. 7, as applied by para. 9*] (1930)
    Delyn [*Sch. 10, para. 7, as applied by para. 9*] (2049)
    Glyndwr [*Sch. 10, para. 7, as applied by para. 9*] (739)
    Meirionnydd [*Sch. 10, para. 7, as applied by para. 9*] (797)
    Ogwr [*Sch. 10, para. 7, as applied by para. 9*] (1562)
    Rhymney Valley [*Sch. 10, para. 7, as applied by para. 9*] (1875)
    Taff-Ely [*Sch. 10, para. 7, as applied by para. 9*] (1441)
(Parishes)—
    Amber Valley (118)
    Bassetlaw (117)
    Bolton (2044)
    Chester-le-Street (1682)
    East Hampshire (2025)
    Gravesham (2026)
    Guildford (411)
    Mid Bedfordshire (2003)

(Parishes)—
  Newcastle-under-Lyme (152)
  North Wiltshire (387)
  Peterborough (258)
  Rushcliffe (151)
  Scarborough (2045)
  South Cambridgeshire (1877)
  South Wight (116)
  Suffolk Coastal District (2046)
  Tandridge (1560)
  Test Valley (348)
  Tunbridge Wells (2047)
  Waverley (115)
  Yeovil (67)

(2) Clean Air

Orders made under the Clean Air Act 1956 (c. 52) s. 11(7) and the Clean Air Act 1968 (c. 68) s. 9(4)
(Suspension of Smoke Control)—
  (North Warwickshire) (2012)
  (Portsmouth) (2033)
  (Preston) (2013)
  (Reading) (2014)

(3) Electoral Arrangements

Orders made under one or more of the following provns. of the Local Govt. Act 1972 (c. 70): ss. 7(6), 51(2), 58(2), 67, 265, 266
Borough of—
  Aberconwy (757)
  Afron (1799)
  Rhondda (758)
City of Leicester (924)
County of—
  Cambridgeshire (1944)
  Leicestershire (119)
  Norfolk (1752)
  Suffolk (538)
  Is. of Scilly (Amdt.) (1720)
  Royal County of Berkshire (120)

(4) Local Government, Scotland

Orders made under the Local Govt. (S.) Act 1973 (c. 65) s. 17(1)(2)
Boundaries Amdt.—
  Central and Tayside Regions and Clackmannan District and Perth and Kinross District (Backhill, Glendevon) (1938)
  East Kilbride and Hamilton Districts (Greenhall Estate, Blantyre and Torrance House, East Kilbride) (1940)
  Inverclyde and Renfrew Districts (Heathmount, Kilmacolm and Knockmountain Farm) (1941)
  Kyle and Carrick District and Cunninghame District (Drybridge and Barassie/Gailes Foreshore) (1856)

Boundaries Amdt.—
  Lothian and Borders Regions and East Lothian and Berwickshire Districts
    (Monynut and Bothwell Valleys) (1855)
  Monklands and Strathkelvin Districts (Gartcosh Steel Works and Whitehill,
    Gartcosh) (1939)
  Nairn and Inverness Districts (Croy) (2030)
(Electoral Arrangements)—
  District of—
    Badenoch and Strathspey Amdt. (68)
    Cumbernauld and Kilsyth (69)
    Dumfries and Galloway Region and Nithsdale Amdt. (448)
    Fife Region and Kirkcaldy Amdt. (382)
    Kyle and Carrick Amdt. (160)
    Moray Amdt. (425)
    Strathclyde Region and Clydesdale District Amdt. (449)

(5) London Government

London Borough of Waltham Forest (Transfer of Housing Accommodation
  etc.) Order *made under the London Govt. Act 1963 (c. 33) ss. 23(3),
  84....* (1390)

(6) Pensions

Scottish Development Agency Pension and Life Assurance Scheme for
  Permanent Staff Modification Order *made under the Social Security Act
  1973 (c. 38) s. 65, as read with ss. 64 and 96....* (2032)

(7) Powers and Duties of Local Authorities

Orders made under the Highways Act 1980 (c. 66) s. 186
Somerset County (Ext. of Operation of New Street Byelaws—
  (Chard)) (99)
  (Shepton Mallet)) (808)

CLASS 6. PUBLIC HEALTH

(1) *Mental Health*   (2) *National Health Service,*
                                            England and Wales

(3) *Public Health, England and*
      and Wales

(1) Mental Health

Mental Health (State Hospital Management Ctee., State Hospital, Carstairs:
  Membership and Procedure) (S.) Regulations *made under the Mental
  Health (S.) Act 1960 (c. 61) Sch. 2A, para. 6 as read with the N.H.S. (S.)
  Act 1978 (c. 29) s. 102(2)....* (389)
Mental Health (State Hospital Management Ctee., State Hospital, Carstairs)
  (S.) Order *made under the Mental Health (S.) Act 1960 (c. 61) s. 90(2) and
  the N.H.S. (S.) Act 1978 (c. 29) s. 102(2)....* (294)

(2) National Health Service, England and Wales

Powys Family Practitioner Ctee. (Membership) Order *made under the N.H.S. Act 1977 (c. 49) ss. 10 and 126(3), Sch. 5, para 7(1)* . . . .(1213)

(3) Public Heath, England and Wales

Orders made under the Caravan Sites Act 1968 (c. 52) s. 12(1)(2)(4)
Gipsy Encampments (Designation of the—
  Borough of Boston) (1469)
  City of Chester) (1958)
  District of—
    Huntingdonshire) (1959)
    Selby) (1797)
    South Derbyshire) (967)
    Wealden and Rother and the Boroughs of Eastbourne and Hastings) (1964)
    West Lindsey) (1780)
  London Borough of Hillingdon)—
    O. (1017)
    (No. 2) (1296)
  Metropolitan Borough of Rochdale) (200)
  Royal Borough of Kingston upon Thames) (16)

CLASS 7.   TOWN AND COUNTRY PLANNING, OPEN SPACES, ACCESS TO THE COUNTRYSIDE

(1) *Defence*   (2) *New Towns*
(3) *Town and Country Planning, Scotland*

(1) Defence

Orders made under the Military Lands Act 1892 (c. 43) Pt. II and, where indicated, the Military Lands Act 1900 (c. 56) s. 2 and the Land Powers (Defence) Act 1958 (c. 30) s. 7
British Underwater Test and Evaluation Centre Byelaws [*1900 s. 2; 1958 s. 7*] (1851)
Bellerby Moor and Wathgill Ranges Byelaws (1770)

(2) New Towns

Central Lancashire New Town (Exclusion of Land) Order *made under the New Towns Act 1981 (c. 64) s. 2(1)* . . . .(84)
Telford New Town Licensed Premises Ctee. Order *made under the Local Govt., Planning and Land Act 1980 (c. 65) s. 132* . . . .(45)

(3) Town and Country Planning, Scotland

Town and Country Planning (Hamilton District Development Plans) Partial Revn. Order *made under the Town and Country Planning (S.) Act 1972 (c. 52) s. 18(3), Sch. 5, para. 6* . . . .(726)

CLASS 8.   WATER SUPPLY

(1) *Water, England and Wales*   (2) *Water Supply, Scotland*

(1) Water, England and Wales

Northumbrian Water Authy. (Exemption from Licensing Control) Order *made under the Northumbrian Water Authy. Act 1981 (c. xxvii) ss. 4, 6....*(209)

Orders made under one or more of the following provns. of the Water Act 1945 (c. 42): ss. 9, 23, 32, 33, 50 and, where indicated, the Water Act 1948 (c. 22) s. 3 and the Compulsory Purchase Act 1965 (c. 56) s. 33(2)
Colne Valley Water (1319)
Eastbounre Water—
   (Catsfield) (1353)
   (Ten Acre Gill) (905)
Severn-Trent Water Authy.—
   (Pershore Airfield) Mains (36)
   (Wymeswold Airfield) Mains (1354)
Three Valleys Water (785)
Welsh Water Authy. (Dunfield Boreholes) [*1948 s. 3; 1965 s. 33(2)*] (806)
Yorkshire Water Authy. (Local Enactments) (108)

Orders made under the Water Resources Act 1963 (c. 38) s. 133
Welsh Water Authy.—
   (Afon-y-bedol) (908)
   (Bryn-Aled Pumping Station) (818)

Drought Orders made under one or more of the following provns. of the Drought Act 1976 (c. 44): ss. 1(1) (3)(a)—(c)(e), 2(3)(a)—(c), 3(4)(5), 5(5)(6)
Bristol Waterworks Company (River Severn) (1362)
North West Water Authy.—

   (Ashworth Moor Reservoir) (821)
   (Blackmoss and Lower Coldwell Reservoirs) (1435)
   (Bottoms and Teggsnose Reservoirs) (1120)
   (Bottoms Lodge Reservoir Longdendale)—
      O. (953)
      (Variation) O. (1436)
   (Coupe and Clowbridge Reservoirs)—
      O. (822)
      (Variation) O. (1187)
   (Delph, Jumbles and Wayoh Reservoirs)—
      O. (823)
      (Variation) O. (1468)
   (Ennerdale Water)—
      O. (783)
      (Variation) O. (1472)
   (Ext. of Period) (1680)
   (Greenbooth Reservoir) (1483)
   (Hurst Reservoir) (1099)
   (Lake Thirlmere) (1448)
   (Lamaload Reservoir) (1119)
   (Laneshaw Reservoir) (923)
   (Langden and Hareden Streams) (1019)

North West Water Authy.—
  (Park Mine, Dalton-in-Furness) (1124)
  (Prescribed Uses) (1323)
  (River Duddon) (1437)
  (River Dunsop) (1020)
  (River Lune) (1228)
  (River Rawthay-Sedbergh) (1449)
  (River Wyre) (1227)
  (Rivington Reservoirs) (1192)
  (Stocks Reservoir) (1063)
  (Swindale, Heltondale and Cawdale Becks) (984)
  (Swineshaw Reservoir) (1101)
  (Ullswater)—
    O. (1229)
    (Variation) O. (1530)
  (Windermere) (1212)
Severn-Trent Water Authy.—
  (Ambergate) (1291)
  (Church Wilne) (1281)
  (Clywedog Reservoir) (1339)
  (Derwent Valley Reservoirs) (1292)
  (Prescribed Uses) (1393)
  (Tittesworth Reservoir) (1194)
South Staffordshire Waterworks Co.
  (River Blithe) (1392)
South West Water Authy.—
  O. (1246)
  (No. 2) O. (1363)
  (Avon Reservoir)—
    O. (1122)
    (Variation) (1262)
  (Burrator Reservoir) (1245)
  (Carwynnen Stream) (1336)
  (Challacombe Reservoir) (948)
  (Colaton Raleigh Stream) (1034)
  (Drift Reservoir)—
    O. (1062)
    (Variation) O. (1450)
  (Fernworthy Reservoir)—
    O. (1226)
    (Variation) O. (1288)
  (Ladock Intake) (1028)
  (Medlyn Moor Stream) (1364)
  (Meldon Reservoir)—
    O. (1035)
    (No. 2) O. (1451)
  (Mill Mehal River) (1394)
  (Pitt Farm Intake) (1186)
  (Prescribed Uses)—
    O. (1083)
    (No. 2)(1084)
    (No. 3)(1085)
    (No. 4)(1123)

South West Water Authy.—
  (Prescribed Uses)—
    (No. 5)(1185)
    (No. 6)(1340)
  (River Axe) (985)
  (River Bray) (1271)
  (River Cober) (1433)
  (River Dart) (1189)
  (River De Lanke) (1191)
  (River Exe-River Taw Transfer and Taw Abstraction) (1395)
  (River Kennall) (1365)
  (River Tamar—River Lamburn/Tavy Transfer) (1193)
  (River Tavy)—
    O. (1036)
    (No. 2) O. (1263)
  (River Taw Below Taw Marsh) (947)
  (River Teign at Teigngrace) (1396)
  (River Torridge at Torrington Intake) (1327)
  (River Yealm) (1100)
  (Stithians Reservoir)—
    O. (850)
    (No. 2) O. (1121)
  (Unnamed Tributary of the River Caen) (1331)
  (Upper Tamar Lake)—
    O. (930)
    (Variation) O. (1188)
  (Venford Brook and River Swincombe)—
    O. (1037)
    (Variation) O. (1264)
Welsh Water Authy.—
  (Abstractions and Discharges)—
    O. (1568)
    (No. 2) O. (1594)
  (Afon Teifi) (1026)
  (Aled Isaf Reservoir and River) (1006)
  (Cray Reservoir) (964)
  (Cwymstradllyn Reservoir)—
    O. (963)
    (Variation) O. (1279)
  (Elan Valley Reservoirs) (1370)
  (Ffynnon Llugwy Reservoir) (1434)
  (Llyn Cwellyn) (1025)
  (Llyn Eiddew Mawr) (1086)
  (Monmouth Abstraction) (894)
  (Parts of Wales)—
    (No. 1)(1087)
    (No. 2)(1276)
    (No. 3)(1278)
    (Emergency Provns.) (1277)
  (Prescelly Reservoir) (1196)
  (Prescribed Uses) (1190)
  (River Eastern Cleddau) (1273)

Welsh Water Authy.—
  (River Usk)—
    O. (884)
    (Llanddetty Abstraction) (1547)
    (River Western Cleddau) (1374)
    (Sudbrook Pumping Station) (2050)
    (Taf Fechan and Llwyn-on Reservoirs)—
      O. (849)
      (No. 2) O. (1195)
    (Talybont Reservoir) (1375)
    (Treforest Industrial Estate) (2051)
Yorkshire Water Authy.—
  (Bradford and Craven) (1510)
  (Harrogate) (1366)
  (Pennine Reservoirs) (1125)
  (Prescribed Uses)—
    O. (1184)
    (No. 2) O. (1324)
  (Richmond) (1337)
  (River Wharfe) (1473)

(2) Water Supply, Scotland

Orders made under the Water (S.) Act 1980 (c. 45); enabling sections in square brackets

Borders Regional Council (Galashiels Mill Lade) (Amdt.) Water (891) [*ss. 17(2), 29(1), 107(1)(b)*]
Central Regional Council (Longhill Weir) (Emergency) Water [*s. 77(1)(b) as read with s. 79*] (1501)
Fife Regional Council (Castlehill Reservoir) (Emergency) Water [*s. 77(1)(b) as read with s. 79*] (1540)
Highland Regional Council (Tomatin Borehole, Tomatin) Water [*ss. 17(2), 29(1)*] (1421)
Strathclyde Regional Council—
  (Camps Water) (Emergency) Water [*s. 77(1)(b)*] (1332)
  (Carradale Water, Kintyre) and (Allt Deucheran and Allt Buidhe) (Amdt.) Water [*ss. 17(2), 29(1), 107(1)(b)*] (989)
  (Daer) (Emergency) Water [*s. 77(1)(b)*] (1333)
  (Loch Lomond) (Emergency) Water [*s. 77(1)(b)*] (1334)
  (Loch Katrine) (Emergency) Water [*s. 77(1)(b)*] (1502)
Western Is. Is. Council (Loch Steisevat, Harris) Water [*ss. 17(2), 29(1)*] (844)

CLASS 9.   EDUCATION

  (1) *Education, England and Wales*   (2) *Education, Scotland*

(1) Education, England and Wales

Educational Endowments Orders made under the Education Act 1973 (c. 16) s. 2(1)(2)
Diocese of—
  Bristol (574)
  Chichester (1614)
  Coventry (791)

Diocese of—
  Ely (937)
  Guildford (1384)
  Lincoln (570)
  Monmouth (1197)
  Newcastle (1706)
  Norwich—
    O. (678)
    (No. 2) O. (1997)
  Oxford (1489)
  Portsmouth (792)

(2) Education, Scotland

Regulations made under the Education (S.) Act 1980 (c. 44) ss. 73(c)(f), 74(1)
Education (Grants) (Newbattle Abbey College) (1183)
John Watson's Trust Scheme (1480)
St Mary's Music School (Aided Places) Amdt. (841)

CLASS 11.   ADMINISTRATION OF JUSTICE

(1) *Coroners' Districts*

(2) *Justices of the Peace, England and Wales*

(3) *Juvenile Courts and Offenders*

(4) *Probation*

(1) Coroners' Districts

Orders made under the Coroners (Amdt.) Act 1926 (c. 59) s. 12
Gwent (Revn.) (454)
Lincolnshire (Amdt.) (1795)
Suffolk (28)

(2) Justices of the Peace, England and Wales

Orders made under the Justices of the Peace Act 1979 (c. 55) s. 23(3)(5)
Petty Sessional Divisions—
  (Cornwall) (391)
  (Dyfed) (1528)
  (Northumberland) (568)

(3) Juvenile Courts and Offenders

Orders made under the Children and Young Persons Act 1933 (c. 12) Sch. 2
Juvenile Ct. Panel—
  Dyfed (1529)
  Felixstowe, Ipswich and Woodbridge (27)
  South East Cornwall (665)
  West Coquetdale Ward and Bamburgh and East Coquetdale (572)

(4) Probation

Orders made under the Powers of Criminal Cts. Act 1973 (c. 62) s. 54(4), Sch. 3, para. 1
Combined Probation Areas—
(Cornwall) (426)
(Dyfed) (1628)
(Gloucestershire) (1204)
(Northumbria) (577)

CLASS 12. AGRICULTURE, FISHERIES AND FORESTRY

(1) *Agriculture*   (2) *European Communities*
(3) *Sea Fisheries*   (4) *Wildlife*

(1) Agriculture

Orders made under the Agricultural Marketing Act 1958 (c. 47) ss. 2, 41(3)
Aberdeen and District Milk Marketing Scheme—
(Application to Banff) Revn. (463)
(Approval) (464)

(2) European Communities

Regulations made under the European Communities Act 1972 (c. 68) s. 2(2)
Western Is. Integrated Development Programme—
(Payments to Outgoing Crofters) (S.) (1313)
(S.) (Amdt.) (1360)

(3) Sea Fisheries

Southampton Water (Chilling) (Oyster) Fishery Order *made under the Sea Fisheries (Shellfish) Act 1967 (c. 83) Sch. 1*....(907)

(4) Wildlife

Orders made under the Wildlife and Countryside Act 1981 (c. 69) ss. 3(1)(4)(5), 26(4)
Berry Head and Berry Head (Southern Redoubt) (Areas of Special Protection) (1471)
Gull Is. and Warren Shore and Needs Ore Point (Areas of Special Protection) (578)

CLASS 13. MISCELLANEOUS

(1) *Children and Young Persons* (2) *Civil Aviation*
(3) *Consumer Credit*   (4) *Customs and Excise*
(5) *Derelict Land*   (6) *Enterprise Zones*
(7) *Protection of Wrecks*   (8) *Public Passenger Vehicles*

(1) Children and Young Persons

Cessation of Approved Institutions (Amdt.) Order *made under the Children and Young Persons Act 1969 (c. 54) s. 46(1)*....(2075)

Revn. of Instrt. of Management Orders made under the Child Care Act 1980 (c. 5) s. 43A(3), except where otherwise indicated

Maryvale Nursery, Manresa Working Girls' Hostel, St Anthony's Working Boys' Hostel, St Vincent's Home for Boys and St Thomas's Home for Boys (2066)

Carlton School [*s. 43(4)*] (2067)

St Etheldreda's (2068)

St Peter's Home (2069)

Our Lady's Convent, Southam (2070)

McClean House (2071)

St Aidan's (2072)

Farringdon House (2073)

Pelham House (2074)

(2) Civil Aviation

Regulations made under the Air Navigation Order 1980 (S.I. 1980/1965) Art. 66

Air Navigation (Restriction of Flying)—
  (Central Electricity Generating Bd. Demonstration) (843)
  (Exhibition of Flying) (563)
  (Farnborough) (1002)
  (Middle Wallop) (759)
  (Pool of London) (1891)
  (Thames Barrier Opening Ceremony) (594)

(3) Consumer Credit

Consumer Credit (Local Acts) Order *made under the Consumer Credit Act 1974 (c. 39) s. 178....* (1107)

(4) Customs and Excise

Designation Orders made under the Customs and Excise Management Act 1979 (c. 2) s. 100A

Free Zone—
  (Belfast Airport) (1206)
  (Birmingham Airport) (1207)
  (Cardiff) (1208)
  (Liverpool) (1209)
  (Prestwick Airport) (1210)
  (Southampton) (1211)

(5) Derelict Land

Derelict Land Clearance Area Order *made under the Derelict Land Act 1982 (c. 42) s. 1(7)(8)(b)....* (778)

(6) Enterprise Zones

Designation Orders made under the Local Govt., Planning and Land Act 1980 (c. 65) Sch. 32, para. 5 and, where indicated, s. 179

Dudley (Round Oak) (1403)

Glanford (Flixborough) (347)

Milford Haven Waterway—
  (North Shore) [*s. 179*] (443)
  (South Shore) [*s. 179*] (444)

(7) Protection of Wrecks

Orders made under the Protection of Wrecks Act 1973 (c. 33) ss. 1(1)(2)(4), 3(2)(a)
Protection of Wrecks—
  (Designation—
    No. 1) O. (521)
    No. 2) O. (1658)
  (Revn.)—
    O. (2)
    No. 2 O. (802)

(8) Public Passenger Vehicles

Passenger Vehicles (Experimental Areas) Designation (Ext. of Duration) Order *made under the Public Passenger Vehicles Act 1981 (c. 14) s. 47(4)(6)*....(204)

TABLES OF EFFECT
of LEGISLATION

TABLE A
A CHRONOLOGICAL TABLE OF ACTS OF PARLIAMENT
WHOSE OPERATION WAS AFFECTED BY
STATUTORY INSTRUMENTS OF 1984

TABLE B
A CHRONOLOGICAL TABLE OF SUBORDINATE LEGISLATION
(S.R. & O. AND S.I.) AND CERTAIN PREROGATIVE INSTRUMENTS
WHOSE OPERATION WAS AFFECTED BY
LEGISLATION OF 1984 (ACTS AND INSTRUMENTS)

TABLES OF EFFECT
TABLE A

NOTES

1. For List of Abbreviations used in this Table, see p. ix in Part I of this Edition.

2. A comprehensive table showing the effect of Acts, Measures and S.I. of 1984 on Acts and Measures is printed in the Annual Volume of Public General Acts.

PART I

EFFECT ON PUBLIC GENERAL ACTS

	Short Title	How affected and Instrument by which affected
1821	Ct. of Session Act (c. 38)	s. 31 **r.**, 1984/253
1825	Ct. of Session Act (c. 120)	s. 4 **r.**, 1984/499
1868	Documentary Evidence Act (c. 37)	**applied**, 1984/1814
1875	Explosives Act (c. 17)	ss. 5, 7, 16(3), 17, 22, 24, 32, 46, 47, 48, 63 **am.**, First Sch., Pt. One, regs. (1)—(7) **am.**, Two, regs. (2), (3), (5), (6) **am.**, 1984/510
	Intestates Widows and Children (S.) Act (c. 41)	s. 3 **am.**, Schs. A, B **am.**, 1984/1848
1876	Small Testate Estates (S.) Act (c. 24)	s. 3 **am.**, Sch. A **am.**, 1984/1848
1887	Coroners Act (c. 71)	ss. 19(1)(2), 23 **am.**, 1984/447
1894	Merchant Shipping Act (c. 60)	s. 460 **applied with mod.**, 1984/1203, 460(1), 692 **mod.**, 1984/408 692 **applied with mod.**, 1984/1203, 1216, 1217
1907	Sheriff Cts. (S.) Act (c. 51)	s. 40 **am.**, 1984/253 First Sch., Rule 3 **re-numbered** 3(1), 3(2)—(6) **inserted**, 5(1) **am.**, 5(2) **re-numbered** 5(3), 5(2) **inserted**, 9(1) **am.**, 9(2)—(5) **re-numbered** 9(3)—(6) respectively, 9(2) **inserted**, 11(1) **am.**, 11A **inserted**, 12(1), 21(2) **am.**, 23 **replaced**, 28 **am.**, 34, headnote **replaced**, 34(1) **am.**, 34(2) **replaced**, 34(3), 56 **am.**,

Short Title	How affected and Instrument by which affected
	59(1) **replaced**,
	59(3), 59A, **inserted**,
	72(1) **replaced**,
	72(5) **am.**,
	72(6) **r.**,
	89(1) **am.**,
	90A **inserted**,
	129(1) **am.**,
	130, headnote, (1) **am.**,
	130(5)—(8) **inserted**,
	131, headnote **am.**,
	131 **re-numbered** 131(1),
	131 (2)—(4) **inserted**,
	132(1)(3), 133(1) **am.**,
	135—143 **inserted**, 1984/255
	144—149 **inserted**, 1984/921
	appx., Form B **am.**,
	B1 **inserted**,
	B2 **am.**,
	C1 **inserted**, 1984/255
	CC **inserted**, 1984/921
	S, heading **am.**,
	S, para. (3) **replaced**,
	S1, S2, S3 **inserted**,
	T **am.**,
	V, W, X, Z, SDA1, SDA2, SDA3, SDA4, SDA5 **inserted**, 1984/255
1913 Bankruptcy (S.) Act (c. 20)	s. 12 **am.**, 1984/1199
1914 Bankruptcy Act (c. 59)	s. 4(1)(*a*) **am.**, 1984/1199
1920 Admin. of Justice Act (c. 81)	Pt. II **am.**, 1984/129
1925 Church of Scotland (Property and Endowments) Act (c. 33)	s. 1(3) **am.**, 1984/253
1937 Diseases of Fish Act (c. 33)	s. 10(1) **am.**, 1984/301
1939 Local Govt. Supn. Act (c. 18) H.C. Members' Fund Act (c. 49)	remainder **r.**, 1984/1232 Sch. 1, paras. 1, 2 **replaced**, 2A **am.**, 1984/2065
1948 Companies Act (c. 38)	Certain provns. **applied with mods.** to unregistered companies, 1984/682 s. 2(4)(*c*), 7(1) **replaced**, 7(2)(3) **r.**, 1984/134 38(1)(3) **am.**, 39 **r.**, 41(1)(*b*)(i) **am.**, 50(7) **r.**, 1984/716 51(6) **am.**, 51(7) **inserted**, 52 **am.**, 106(2), 106K(2) **inserted**, 124(1), 125(2), 126(2), 143, 152 **am.**, 1984/134 152A(2) **am.**, 1984/1169 167(2) **am.**, 1984/134 187(5) **inserted**, 1984/1169 223(*a*) **am.**, 1984/1199 249(4)(5), 320, 322 **am.**, 1984/134 328(4) **inserted**, 1984/1169 348 **replaced**, 372, 374, 384, 385 **am.**, 387A **inserted**, 1984/134

	Short Title	How affected and Instrument by which affected
		399(6)(*a*) **am.**, 1984/1199
		407(1) **replaced,**
		407(2) **am.,**
		407(2A) **r.,**
		409(3) **inserted,**
		415 **am.**, 1984/134
		423(2) **ext.**, 1984/716
		455 **am.**, 1984/134
		Sch. 1 **am.**, 1984/1717
		6 **am.**, 1984/134
		8, 8A **am.**, 1984/134, 1859
1949	Juries Act (c. 27)	s. 26(1) **am.**, 1984/253
1955	Army Act (c. 18)	Sch. 5A, paras. 11(2), 14(1) **am.**, 1984/447
	Air Force Act (c. 19)	Sch. 5A, paras. 11(2), 14(1) **am.**, 1984/447
1956	Clean Air Act (c. 52)	s. 11 **excluded,** 1984/1649
	Valuation and Rating (S.) Act (c. 60)	Sch. 1, table **replaced** (wef 1.1.85), 1984/1112
	Copyright Act (c. 74)	**mod.** in relation to British Indian Ocean Territory as follows:
		ss. 7, 8(1)(2) **am.,**
		8(3) **replaced,**
		8(4)(4)(*a*)(10)(11), 10(2)(3) **am.,**
		10(5) **replaced,**
		12(6) **am.,**
		13(3) **replaced,**
		13(8) **am.,**
		13(11) **r.,**
		15(4) **am.,**
		17(6) **r.,**
		18(1) **am.,**
		18(4) **r.,**
		21(1)(6)(7C)(7D) **am.,**
		21(10) **r.,**
		22(1)—(5) **am.,**
		22(6) **r.,**
		22(7) **replaced,**
		31(1)(2) **r.,**
		31(4) **am.,**
		33(1) **replaced,**
		37(4) **r.,**
		39(8) **am.,**
		40(3) **r.,**
		40(4)(5) **am.,**
		41(7) **r.,**
		43 **am.,**
		46(1) **r.,**
		46(2) **am.,**
		47(1)—(3) **r.,**
		47(4) **am.,**
		48(4), 49(2) **am.,**
		51(2) **replaced,**
		51(3) **r.,**
		Sch. 7, paras. 25, 26, 40, 41 **r.**, 46 **am.**, 1984/541
1957	Naval Discipline Act (c. 53)	Sch. 4A, para. 14(1) **am.**, 1984/447
1958	Prevention of Fraud (Investments) Act (c. 45)	ss. 2(2)(*b*)—(*d*), 14(2)(*a*)(*b*) **am.**, 1984/716
1959	County Cts. Act (c. 22)	ss. 84(1), 157 **am.**, 1984/447

Short Title	How affected and Instrument by which affected
1960 Radioactive Substances Act (c. 34)	Sch. 1, Pt. I (E. & W.), para. 8D **inserted,** II (S.), para. 9B **inserted,** 1984/863
1962 Local Govt. (Financial Provns. etc.) (S.) Act (c. 9)	Sch. 1 **am.,** 1984/193
Transport Act (c. 46)	s. 5(1)(3)(*a*) **r.,** 1984/1747
1963 British Museum Act (c. 24)	Third Sch., Pt. I, paras. 3—5 **inserted,** 1984/1181
Weights and Measures Act (c. 31)	s. 24 **re-applied,** 1984/1318 Sch. 4, Pts. I, II **r.,** 1984/1315 VI **am.,** 1984/1314 VII **am.,** XII **r.,** 1984/1315 remainder of Sch. 4 **r.,** 1984/1316 8, para. 5 **replaced,** 1984/1316
1964 Plant Varieties and Seeds Act (c. 14)	s. 25, 25(1)(4) **mod.,** 26(2)(4)—(9) **excluded,** 1984/412
1965 Admin. of Justice Act (c. 2)	s. 20(3)(*b*) **am.,** 1984/1199
Ministerial Salaries and Members' Pensions Act (c. 11)	s. 14(2) **am.,** 1984/539
Admin. of Estates (Small Payments) Act (c. 32)	ss. 1, 2 **am.,** 1984/539
Merchant Shipping Act (c. 47)	**ext.** to Is. of Man **with mods.,** 1984/1160
Nat. Insurance Act (c. 51)	s. 36(1) **am.,** 1984/1104
1966 N.H.S. Act (c. 8)	s. 6(3) **am.,** 1984/580
1967 Forestry Act (c. 10)	Sch. 1, para. 12 **am.,** 1984/539
Parliamentary Commr. Act (c. 13)	Sch. 2, Note 2 **am.,** 1984/1814
Legal Aid (S.) Act (c. 43)	ss. 2(1), 3(1)(*a*) **am.,** 1984/1865 16(1)(*b*)(i)(2)(4) **r.,** 1984/253
Road Traffic Regulation Act (c. 76)	Sch. 5, paras. 1—26 **replaced,** 1984/325
Companies Act (c. 81)	Certain provns. **applied with mods.** to unregistered companies, 1984/682 ss. 43(1A), 44(1A), 46(3A) **inserted,** 111(1) **am.,** 1984/134
1968 Teachers' Supn. (S.) Act (c. 12)	s. 13 **r.,** 1984/2028
Gaming Act (c. 65)	ss. 20(3), 21(2), 41 **am.,** 1984/247 **am,** (S.), 1984/468 s. 48(3)(*a*)—(*g*)(4)(*a*)(*b*) **replaced,** 1984/166 **replaced** (S.), 1984/338
Medicines Act (c. 67)	s. 52 **excluded,** 1984/1861
Transport Act (c. 73)	s 97(1) **replaced,** 97(7) **am.,** 1984/144
Sea Fisheries Act (c. 77)	s. 8(2)(3) **applied,** 1984/1522, 1523, 1627 8(4) **applied,** 1984/1523, 1627
1969 Children and Young Persons Act (c. 54)	ss. 2(13), 15(2A)(4) **am.,** 1984/447
Synodical Govt. Measure 1969 No. 2	Sch. 3, rule 1(2) **am.,** 1(7)(*d*) **replaced,** 2(3)(4), 4(1) **am.,** 5(3)(*c*) re-lettered (*b*) 5(3)(*c*)(*d*) **inserted,** 8(3) **am.,** 1984/1039 9(1A) **inserted,** 1984/1040 10A(1)(2), 11(1) **am.,** 12(1)(*b*) **replaced,** 16(3)(4) **am.,** 16(5) **replaced,** 16(6) **r.,** 16(7)—(11) re-numbered 16(6)—(10)

Short Title	How affected and Instrument by which affected
	16(9), 17(1) **am.**, 17(4) **replaced,** 17(5)(6) **r.**, 17(7)—(10) **re-numbered** 17(5)—(8) 17(7), 17A(1) **am.**, 17A(4) **replaced,** 17A(5)(6) **r.**, 17A(7)—(9) **re-numbered** 17A(5)—(7) 17B(1)(3) **am.**, 19(2A) **inserted.**, 19(2A) **re-numbered** 19(2B) and **am.**, 19(3)(*d*), 20(1)(4) **am.**, 20A **r.**, 23(1)(*a*), 24(3)(*a*)(iv)(4), 25(6), 26(1)(4)(5), 28(1)(*e*)(*f*) **am.**, 28(1)(*g*) **inserted,** 28(1)(*g*)—(*j*) **re-lettered** (*h*)—(*k*) 28(1)(*i*)(*j*), 29(1)(*b*) **am.**, 30(1) **replaced,** 30(1A) **inserted,** 31(1) **replaced,** 31(1A) **am.**, 31(1B) **inserted,** 33(3) **am.**, 33(4) **replaced,** 35(3), 36(2)(4) **am.**, 35(5) **replaced,** 36(6)(7) **am.**, 37(1)(*e*) **inserted,** 37(2)(3) **replaced** by new paras. (2)—(4) 37(4)(5) **re-numbered** 37(5)(6) 37(5), 39(5)—(7), 43(1)(*c*) **am.**, Appx. I, s. 1, **am.** and Note 4 **inserted,** 2—4, 5(3), 7, 8 **am.**, II, para. 1(*g*) **am.**, 4(*c*) **inserted,** 12(*d*) **am.**, 1984/1039
1970 Merchant Shipping Act (c. 36)	s. 66(2) **am.**, 1984/539
1971 Nat. Savings Bank Act (c. 29) Attachment of Earnings Act (c. 32) Misuse of Drugs Act (c. 38) Prevention of Oil Pollution Act (c. 60) Tribunals and Inquiries Act (c. 62) Town and Country Planning Act (c. 78)	s. 9(1) **am.**, 1984/539 s. 23(3) **am.**, 1984/447 Sch. 2, Pts. I—III **am.**, 1984/859 s. 9 **r.**, 1984/862 ss. 10, 19(4) **applied with mods.**, 1984/1247 Sch. 1, Pt. I **applied with mods.**, 1984/1247 I, II **ext.**, 1984/1094 ss. 27, 30(1)(*a*), 53 **applied with mods.** (Crown Land applications), 1984/1015 87(12) **applied with mods.** (special enforcement notices), 87(14)(15) **applied** (special enforcement notices), 89, 90 **applied with mods.** (special enforcement notices), 92 **applied** (special enforcement notices),

Short Title	How affected and Instrument by which affected
	92A, 93, 110, 177, 243(1)(2), 246 **applied with mods.** (special enforcement notices), 1984/1016
1972 Civil List Act (c. 7)	ss. 1(1), 2(7), 3, 3(1), 4(1)(*b*), 5(1) **am.**, 1984/39
Supn. Act (c. 11)	s. 4(1) **am.**, 1984/539
Road Traffic (Foreign Vehicles) Act (c. 27)	s. 1(1)(*a*)(2)(*a*) **am.**, Schs. 1, 2 **am.**, 1984/748
Parliamentary and other Pensions Act (c. 48)	s. 24(1) **am.**, 1984/539
Legal Advice and Assistance Act (c. 50)	s. 1, 1(*a*) **am.**, 1984/1866 3(3) **am.**, 1984/253 4(2) **am.**, 1984/1677 5(6) **r.**, 1984/253 Sch. 1 **am.**, 1984/1677
Town and Country Planning (S.) Act (c. 52)	ss. 24, 27(1)(*a*), 51 **applied with mods.** (Crown Land applications), 1984/996 84(7A)(*b*)(10) **applied** (special enforcement notices), 84(12), 85(10)(11), 86, 87 **applied with mods.** (special enforcement notices), 87A **applied** (special enforcement notices), 89 **applied with mods.** (special enforcement notices), 89A **applied** (special enforcement notices), 166, 231(3)(*f*) **applied with mods.** (special enforcement notices), 1984/995
Nat. Debt Act (c. 65)	s. 6(1) **am.**, 1984/539
Companies (Floating Charges and Receivers) (S.) Act (c. 67)	s. 11(7) **inserted**, 1984/1169 25 **am.**, 1984/134 32(2) **am.**, 1984/1169
European Communities Act (c. 68)	s. 9(1)—(5), (7) **applied with mods.** to unregistered companies, 1984/682 9(8) **am.**, 1984/134
Local Govt. Act (c. 70)	s. 119(1) **am.**, 1984/539
1973 Statute Law (Repeals) Act (c. 39)	Sch. 1, certain of the repeals **ext.** to Is. of Man, 1984/1692
Fair Trading Act (c. 41)	s. 64(1)(*b*) **am.**, 1984/932 Sch. 7, Pt. I, para. 7 **replaced**, 1984/1887
Powers of Criminal Cts. Act (c. 62)	ss. 6(3)(*a*)(6)(*a*), 16(3)(5), 27(3), 31(3A) **am.**, 1984/447
Local Govt. (S.) Act (c. 65)	ss. 202, 202A—202C, 203, 204 **mod.**, 1984/918
1974 Legal Aid Act (c. 4)	s. 1(1), (1)(*a*) **am.**, 1984/1837 4(2) **am.**, 1984/1715 6(1), (1)(*a*), 9(1)(*a*) **am.**, 1984/1838
Local Govt. Act (c. 7)	s. 6(1)(2)(4) **am.**, 6(4A) **r.**, 6(5)(5A) **replaced** by new (5), 1984/1863
Statute Law (Repeals) Act (c. 22)	Sch., certain of the repeals **ext.** to Is. of Man, 1984/1692
Consumer Credit Act (c. 39)	Sch. 3 **am.**, 1984/436
Control of Pollution Act (c. 40)	ss. 31(1), 32(3) **ext.**, 34 **ext.**, 1984/863 **applied with mods.**, 1984/1200 35 **ext.**, 1984/863 **excluded**, 1984/1200 36, 37 **ext.**, 1984/863 **applied with mods.**, 1984/1200

	Short Title	How affected and Instrument by which affected
		38, 39 **ext.**, 1984/863
		excluded, 1984/1200
		40, 42 **ext.**, 1984/863
		applied with mods., 1984/1200
		54, 55 **ext.**, 1984/863
	Friendly Societies Act (c. 46)	s. 64(1)(*c*)(*d*) **am.**, 1984/513
		66, 67, 68 **am.**, 1984/539
	Trade Union and Labour Relations Act (c. 52)	Sch. 1, Pt. IV, para. 31(1)(*b*)**am.**, 1984/539
	Church of England (Worship and Doctrine) Measure (No. 3)	provns. **ext.** to Channel Is. **with mods.**, 1984/1689
1975	Social Security Act (c. 14)	gen. **mod.**, 1984/1817
		s. 1(5) **am.**, 1984/14, 1904
		7(1)(5), 8(1), 9(2), 10(1) **am.**, 1984/15, 1905
		30(1) **am.**, 1984/1104
		36(2)(3) **mod.**, 1984/1303
		41(2A)—(2D), 47B, 64 (1A)—(1D), 66A **excluded**, 1984/1696
		92—119(2) **mod.**, 1984/451
		Sch. 4, Pts. I, III—V **am.**, 1984/1104
		10, para. 4 **am.**, 1984/1818
	Industrial Injuries and Diseases (Old Cases) Act (c. 16)	ss. 2(6)(*c*), 7(2)(*b*) **am.**, 1984/1104
	Criminal Procedure (S.) Act (c. 21)	ss. 289B(6), 289G(2), 407(1A), 435, 453(3) **am.**, 1984/526
	H.C. Disqualification Act (c. 24)	Sch. 1 **am.**, 1984/705
	Social Security Pensions Act (c. 60)	s. 6(1)(*a*) **am.**, 1984/1104
		41A—41C **mod.**, 1984/1921
	Child Benefit Act (c. 61)	s. 6(3) **mod.**, 1984/1960
	N.I. (Loans) Act (c. 83)	s. 1(2) **am.**, 1984/1915
1976	Nat. Coal Bd. (Finance) Act (c. 1)	s. 2(3)(*b*) **am.**, 1984/456
	Statute Law (Repeals) Act (c. 16)	Sch. 1, certain of the repeals **ext.** to Is. of Man, 1984/1692
	Lotteries and Amusements Act (c. 32)	s. 16(3)(*a*)—(*c*) **am.**, 1984/245
		am. (S.), 1984/465
	Dangerous Wild Animals Act (c. 38)	Sch. **mod.**, 1984/1111
	Finance Act (c. 40)	s. 64(2)(*a*) **am.**, 1984/1635
		64A(2), Tables A, B **replaced**, 1984/1636
		Sch. 7, Pt. I, Tables A—C **replaced**,
		II, para. 1(1) **am.**, 1983/1635
	Armed Forces Act (c. 52)	s. 8(1)(*b*) **am.**, 1984/447
	Companies Act (c. 69)	Certain provns. **applied with mods.** to unregistered companies, 1984/682
		s. 9(2) **replaced**,
		9(3) **am.**,
		29 **replaced**, 1984/134
1977	Statute Law (Repeals) Act (c. 18)	Sch. 1, certain of the repeals **ext.** to Is. of Man, 1984/1692
	N.H.S. Act (c. 49)	Sch. 5, Pt. II **applied**, 1984/1735
1978	Refuse Disposal (Amenity) Act (c. 3)	ss. 2(1)(2), 3(1)—(3)(5)(8), 4(1)—(3) (5)—(7), 5(1)—(4), 6(1)—(4)(6)(8), 11 **am.**, 1984/288
	Employment Protection (Consolidation) Act (c. 44)	s. 15(1) **varied**, 1984/2019
		73(4A) **am.** (wef 1.4.85), 1984/2021
		75(1) **am.** (wef 1.4.85), 1984/2020
		75A(1)(2) **am.** (wef 1.4.85), 1984/2021
		122(5) **varied**, 1984/2019

Short Title	How affected and Instrument by which affected
	Sch. 4, paras. 2(*a*)—(*c*), 3 **mod.**, 1984/2048
	14, para. 8(1)(*a*)(*b*) **varied**, 8(1)(*c*) **varied**, 1984/2019 **mod.**, 1984/2048
Statute Law (Repeals) Act (c. 45)	Sch. 1, certain of the repeals **ext.** to Is. of Man, 1984/1692
1979 Nurses, Midwives and Health Visitors Act (c. 36)	s. 11(3A) **am.**, 1984/1975
Merchant Shipping Act (c. 39)	s. 31 **am.**, 1984/356
	31(1) **ext.** to Is. of Man with **mods.**, 1984/1161
Ancient Monuments and Archaeological Areas Act (c. 46)	s. 35 **excluded**, 1984/1286
Pensioners' Payments and Social Security Act (c. 48)	ss. 1—3 **mod.**, 1984/1082
1980 Companies Act (c. 22)	Certain provns. **applied with mods.** to unregistered companies, 1984/682
	s. 5(1A) **inserted**,
	5(5) **am.**,
	10(2A) **inserted**,
	14(10) **am.**,
	14(11) **inserted**,
	17(13), 24(2A), 37, 48(1), 48(3) **am.**, 1984/134
	53(4) **am.**, 1984/1169
	54(8)(9) **inserted**, 1984/1860
	55 **re-numbered** 55(1) and **am.**, 1984/134, 1860
	55(2) **inserted**, 1984/1860
	57, 63 **am.**, 1984/134
	64(1)(*e*) **inserted**, 1984/1169
	Sch. 1, Pts. I, II, forms **replaced**, 1984/1717
	2 **am.**, 1984/134
Social Security Act (c. 30)	s. 14(8)(*a*) **am.**, 1984/1818
Social Security (No. 2) Act (c. 39)	s. 6(1)(*b*) **am.**, 1984/1800
Magistrates' Cts. Act (c. 43)	ss. 22(1), 24(3)(4), 32(9), 33(1)(*a*) 34(3)(*b*), 36(1)(2), 40(1), 63(3)(*a*), 97(4) **am.**,
	Sch. 4, para. 1 **am.**, 1984/447
Coal Industry Act (c. 50)	s. 3(4) **am.**, 1984/1888
Housing Act (c. 51)	s. 130(2) **am.**, 1984/1803
Civil Aviation Act (c. 60)	provns. **ext.** to the Bailiwick of Guernsey with **mods.**, 1984/130
	provns. **ext.** to the Bailiwick of Jersey with **mods.**, 1984/131
	provns. **ext.** to the Is. of Man with **mods.**, 1984/132
	ss. 3, 10(1) **am.**,
	Sch. 1 **am.**, 1984/355
1981 H.C. Members' Fund and Parliamentary Pensions Act (c. 7)	s. 2(1)(*b*) **replaced**, 1984/2065
Public Passenger Vehicles Act (c. 14)	s. 4(2) **r.**, 1984/31
	6, 12, 18, 22 **applied with mods.**, 1984/748
	22(2), 23(1)(2) **am.**, 1984/31
	30 **applied with mods.**, 1984/748
	52(1)(2) **am.**,
	52(4), 53(2) **r.**,
	55, 56(1)(2) **am.**,
	63 **r.**, 1984/31
Statute Law (Repeals) Act (c. 19)	Sch. 1, certain of the repeals **ext.** to Is. of Man, 1984/1692

Short Title	How affected and Instrument by which affected
Judicial Pensions Act (c. 20)	s. 13(1) **am.**, 1984/1818 21(1)(c)(ii) **am.**, 1984/1625 Sch. 1, Pt. IV, para. 20(1) **am.**, 1984/539
Contempt of Ct. Act (c. 49)	ss. 12(2), 14(2) **am.**, 1984/447
Supreme Ct. Act (c. 54)	ss. 20(1)(2)(5)(6), 21(1)—(7), 22(2)(3)(6)—(8), 24(1) **mod.** (in relation to British Indian Ocean Territory), 1984/540
Companies Act (c. 62)	Certain provns. **applied with mods.** to unregistered companies, 1984/682 s. 4(3)(6)(a) **am.**, 9(7) **inserted**, 1984/1169 12(5) **am.**, 24(3) **replaced**, 26, 31(2)(3) **am.**, 1984/134 38 **replaced**, 1984/2007 43(6), 77(7) **am.**, 1984/134
Betting and Gaming Duties Act (c. 63)	Sch. 3, para. 2(1)(a)(i)(b)(i), 5(2)(a)—(c) **am.**, 1984/431
Trustee Savings Banks Act (c. 65)	s. 27(4) **am.**, 1984/539
1982 Civil Aviation Act (c. 16)	s. 15(2)(a) **replaced**, 1984/65
Social Security and Housing Benefits Act (c. 24)	s. 7(1)(a)—(c) **am.**, 1984/2037
Local Govt. (Misc. Provns.) Act (c. 30)	Sch. 3, paras. 22(1), 23(2) **am.**, 1984/447
Cinematograph (Amdt.) Act (c. 33)	s. 7(4) **am.**, 1984/447, 526
Forfeiture Act (c. 34)	s. 4(2) **am.**, 1984/1818
Finance Act (c. 39)	s. 154(1) **am.**, 1984/194
Civic Govt. (S.) Act (c. 45)	Sch. 1, paras. 8(3), 9(1)(8) **applied**, 1984/922 2, para. 19(3) **am.**, 1984/526
Criminal Justice Act (c. 48)	s. 37(2) **am.**, 1984/447 64 (including Sch. 10) **ext.** to the Bailiwick of Jersey, 1984/1690
Transport Act (c. 49)	s. 70(2)(a)(v)(vi) **inserted**, 1984/1996
1983 Representation of the People Act (c. 2)	Certain provns. **applied, with some mods.**—(E., S. and W.), 1984/137 (N.I.), 1984/198
Merchant Shipping Act (c. 13)	Certain provns. **ext.** to Is. of Man **with mods.**, 1984/1985
Matrimonial Homes Act (c. 19)	0.47, rule 4 **replaced**, 1984/576
Companies (Beneficial Interests) Act (c. 50)	s.1(e) **inserted**, 1984/134
Car Tax Act (c. 53)	s. 2(2)(c) **replaced**, 1984/488
V.A.T. Act (c. 55)	Sch. 1, paras. 1, 2 **am.**, 1984/342 5, Group 9, Note (7) **r.**, 1984/767 10, item 3 **replaced**, Note (2) **am.**, 1984/631 14, item 2(f) **replaced**, 4 **am.**, 7—11 **inserted**, 1984/489 12, Notes (6)(7) **inserted**, 1984/959 16, note (4)(e) **inserted**, 1984/766 6 (exemptions), Group 7 (health), item (1A) **inserted**, 1984/1784
1984 Merchant Shipping Act (c. 5)	Certain provns. **ext.** to Is. of Man **with mods.**, 1984/1985
Prevention of Terrorism (Temp. Provns.) Act (c. 8)	**Ext.** to Is. of Man **with certain exceptions, adaptations and mods.**, 1984/860

Short Title	How affected and Instrument by which affected
	provns. **ext.** to Bailiwick of Guernsey **with mods.**, 1984/1165
	provns. **ext.** to Bailiwick of Jersey **with mods.**, 1984/1166
Telecommunications Act (c. 12)	**Ext.** to Is. of Man **with certain exceptions, adaptations and mods.**, 1984/861
County Cts. Act (c. 28)	0.1, rules 2(2), 3, 6 **am.**,
	3, rule 7(2) **am.**,
	5, rule 14 **am.**,
	6, rules 1(3), 1A, 3(*b*)(i)(e), 4 **am.**,
	8, rule 3 **am.**,
	9, rule 8(1)(*b*) **am.**,
	10, rules 1(1), 11(6) **am.**,
	11, rule 1(8) **am.**,
	13, rule 7(2A) **inserted**,
	13, rule 7(3)(4) **am.**,
	16, rules 6(1), 7(1), 8(1) **am.**,
	19, rules 1, 5(1) **am.**,
	19, rule 6(*c*) **replaced**,
	19, rule 7 **am.**,
	20, rules 14(2)(3), 27(2) **am.**,
	21, rule 5(1)(*b*) **am.**,
	21, rule 5(1)(*c*) **re-lettered** (*d*)
	21, rule 5 new sub-para. (*c*) **inserted**,
	21, rule 5(2A) **inserted**,
	22, rules 8(1)(*a*), 11(1) **am.**,
	25, rule 3(5) **am.**,
	25, rule 11 **replaced**,
	25, rule 13 **inserted**,
	26, rules 10(3), 15(1) **am.**,
	27, rules 15(2), 16(2) **am.**,
	28, rules 4(1), 11(3), 14(2) **am.**,
	30, rule 1(3)(4) **am.**,
	33, rules 1(1)(*a*), (2)(*b*), 6(3)(*d*) **am.**,
	34, rules 1, title, 1(*a*)(*b*), 2, title 2 **am.**,
	37, rule 7 **am.**,
	38, rule 4(4) **am.**,
	38, rule 20(2)(3) **replaced**,
	38, rule 20(3A)(3B) **inserted**,
	38, rule 21(5) **replaced**,
	38, rule 21(5A) **inserted**,
	38, rule 24(7) **am.**,
	39, rules 1, 2(1) **am.**,
	39, rule 4 **r.**,
	39, rules 4(1), 5, 12, 13(2) 14(1)(*b*), 18 **am.**,
	40, rules 4(1)(*a*)(*b*), (*b*)(ii), 17(1) **am.**,
	41, rules 2(1), 3 **am.**,
	43, rule 13(1) **am.**, 1984/878
Food Act (c. 30)	ss. 95(5)(6), 97(1)—(3), 99, 100(1)(2), 102(2), 103 **applied**, 1984/1918

TABLES OF EFFECT

TABLE A

PART II

EFFECT ON LOCAL AND PERSONAL ACTS

	Short Title	How affected and Instrument by which affected
1967	British Railways Act (c. xxx)	s. 47 **r.**, 1984/1747
1981	G.L.C. (General Powers) Act (c. xvii)	s. 4(*a*)(i) **am.**, 5(2A) **replaced**, 1984/1244
	United Reformed Church Act (c. xxiv)	provns. **ext.** to the Is. of Man **with mods.**, 1984/361

TABLE B

A Chronological Table of Subordinate Legislation

(S.R. & O. and S.I. and certain Prerogative Instruments)

WHOSE OPERATION WAS AFFECTED BY

LEGISLATION OF 1984 (ACTS AND INSTRUMENTS)

NOTE

For List of Abbreviations used in this Table, see p. ix in Part I of this Edition.

Year and Number (or date)	Short Title	How affected and Instrument by which affected
1875 5th Aug.	Explosives, classification—O. in C. (No. 1)	Class 7 (proviso) **am.**, 1984/510
27th Nov.	Explosives, Magazines for explosives other than gunpowder—O. in C. (No. 3)	Pts. II, III **am.**, 1984/510
27th Nov.	Small firework factories—O. in C. (No. 4)	Pt. II preamble: para. 3 **am.**, art. 4 **am.**, provisos to art. 4 **am.**, arts. 6, 7 **am.**, III general rules nos. 6, 20 **am.**, 1984/510
27th Nov.	Explosives, stores licensed for mixed explosives—O. in C. (No. 6)	Pt. I preamble: para. 3 **am.**, art. 3(2)(*a*)–(*e*) **am.**, provisos (i)–(iii) to art. 3(2) **am.**, arts. 3(4)–(9), 5 **am.**, III, IV **am.**, 1984/510
27th Nov.	Explosives, sale—O. in C. (No. 9)	art. 1 **am.**, provisos (*a*)(*b*) to art. 1 **am.**,
27th Nov.	Explosives other than gun powder, notice of accidents on conveyance—O. in C. (No. 11)	generally **am.**, 1984/510
1883 20th Apr.	Explosives for private use—O. in C. (No. 12)	preamble **am.**, arts. (2)(*a*)(*c*), (3)(*a*) **am.**, Sch. **am.**, 1984/510
1896 964	Mixed Explosives, registered premises— O. in C. (No. 16)	general rule no. 2(5) **am.**, Pt. IV **am.**, 1984/510
1898 248	Compressed Acetylene in admixture with oil—gas—O. (No. 5)	generally **am.**, 1984/510
1905 1128	Compressed Acetylene in admixture with oil—gas—O.	Condition 4 **am.**, 1984/510
1906 380	Mixed Explosives, registered premises —O. in C. (No. 16A)	preamble **am.**, arts. 1, 2 **am.**, 1984/510
1912 348	Public Trustee Rules	rule 30 **am.**, 1984/109
1861	Mixed explosives on registered premises —O. in C. (No. 16B)	arts. (1)–(3) **am.**, 1984/510

Year and Number (or date)	Short Title	How affected and Instrument by which affected
1919		
809	Compressed Acetylene contained in a porous substance—O. (No. 9)	Condition (6) **am.**, Proviso to condition (6) **am.**, Conditions (7)(11) **am.**, 1984/510
1921		
1394	Admin. of Justice Act 1920 Pt. II, ext. to Cyprus and Gibraltar— O. in C.	r., 1984/129
1692	Admin. of Justice Act 1920 Pt. II, ext. to Sierra Leone Colony and St. Vincent—O. in C.	r., 1984/129
1693	Admin. of Justice Act 1920 Pt. II, ext. to Sierra Leone, Somaliland and Zanzibar Protectorates—O. in C.	r., 1984/129
1806	Admin. of Justice Act 1920 Pt. II, ext. to South Australia—O. in C.	r., 1984/129
1922		
125	Admin. of Justice Act 1920 Pt. II, ext. to Ceylon, Grenada, Trinidad and Tobago—O. in C.	r., 1984/129
126	Admin. of Justice Act 1920 Pt. II, ext. to Western Australia—O. in C.	r., 1984/129
291	Admin. of Justice Act 1920 Pt. II, ext. to Nigeria Protectorate and Tanganyika Territory—O. in C.	r., 1984/129
292	Admin. of Justice Act 1920 Pt. II, ext. to Nigeria Colony and Straits Settlements—O. in C.	r., 1984/129
353	Admin. of Justice Act 1920 Pt. II, ext. to Hong Kong and Basutoland— O. in C.	r., 1984/129
354	Admin. of Justice Act 1920 Pt. II, ext. to Bechuanaland, Swaziland and Wei-hai-wei—O. in C.	r., 1984/129
573	Admin. of Justice Act 1920 Pt. II, ext. to British Guiana, St. Lucia, Seychelles and Gold Coast Colony— O. in C.	r., 1984/129
719	Admin. of Justice Act 1920 Pt. II, ext. to Northern Rhodesia and Uganda Protectorate—O. in C.	r., 1984/129
810	Admin. of Justice Act 1920 Pt. II ext. to British Solomon Is. and Nyasaland Protectorates—O. in C.	r., 1984/129
811	Admin. of Justice Act 1920 Pt. II, ext. to Leeward Is., Dominica and Gilbert and Ellice Is.—O. in C.	r., 1984/129
1206	Admin. of Justice Act 1920 Pt. II, ext. to British Honduras and Barbados—O. in C.	r., 1984/129
1923		
562	Admin. of Justice Act 1920 Pt. II, ext. to Newfoundland—O. in C.	r., 1984/129
563	Admin. of Justice Act 1920 Pt. II, ext. to New Zealand—O. in C.	r., 1984/129
564	Admin. of Justice Act 1920 Pt. II, ext. to Kenya and Southern Rhodesia Protectorates—O. in C.	r., 1984/129
565	Admin. of Justice Act 1920 Pt. II, ext. to Falkland Is. and Fiji, and Gambia and Kenya Colonies— O. in C.	r., 1984/129

Year and Number (or date)	Short Title	How affected and Instrument by which affected
1924 253	Admin. of Justice Act 1920 Pt. II, ext. to Federated Malay States, Johore, and Northern Territories of the Gold Coast—O. in C.	r., 1984/129
254	Admin. of Justice Act 1920 Pt. II, ext. to Ashanti, Bermuda, Jamaica and Mauritius—O. in C.	r., 1984/129
1129	Conveyance of explosives on roads, etc.—O. (No. 11)	byelaw 1 generally **am.**, 2, proviso, paras. (*a*)(*b*) **am.**, 4 generally **am.**, 4, regs. (*k*)–(*q*) **am.**, 1984/510
1220	Admin. of Justice Act 1920 Pt. II, ext. to Bahamas—O. in C.	r., 1984/129
1270	Admin. of Justice Act 1920 Pt. II, ext. to Kedah—O. in C.	r., 1984/129
1271	Admin. of Justice Act 1920 Pt. II, ext. to Victoria—O. in C.	r., 1984/129
1925 449	Admin. of Justice Act 1920 Pt. II, ext. to New Guinea—O. in C.	r., 1984/129
450	Admin. of Justice Act 1920 Pt. II, ext. to Northern Territory of Australia and Norfolk Is.—O. in C.	r., 1984/129
1926 91	Admin. of Justice Act 1920 Pt. II, application to Papua—O. in C.	r., 1984/129
217	Admin. of Justice Act 1920 Pt. II, ext. to New South Wales—O. in C.	r., 1984/129
823	Picric acid and picrates etc.—O. in C. (No. 26)	art. 2(*b*) **am.**, 1984/510
1927 60	Admin. of Justice Act 1920 Pt. II, ext. to St. Helena—O. in C.	r., 1984/129
594	Explosives (Di-nitro-phenol and Di-nitro-phenolate) O.	art. 2(*c*) **am.**, 1984/510
1928 86	Admin. of Justice Act 1920 Pt. II, ext. to Saskatchewan—O. in C.	r., 1984/129
245	Sale of Explosives O.	art. 3 **am.**, 1984/510
252	Admin. of Justice Act 1920 Pt. II, ext. to Queensland—O. in C.	r., 1984/129
1930 987.	Admin. of Justice Act 1920 Pt. II, ext. to Malta—O. in C.	r., 1984/129
1932 127	Admin. of Justice Act 1920 Pt. II, ext. to Tasmania—O. in C.	r., 1984/129
1933 789	Milk Marketing Scheme (Approval) O.	Scheme— paras. 11(1), 13(2)(4)(5)(8), 15(1)(3) **am.**, 39 **replaced**, 43E(2), 48(2), 49(3), 77(1)(*a*)–(*c*)(*ca*), 96(2) **am.**, 1984/330

Year and Number (or date)	Short Title	How affected and Instrument by which affected
1321	Public Service Vehicles (Drivers' and Conductors' Licences) Regs.	reg. 3 definition "The Commissioners", **replaced** 1984/32
1346	London Cab O.	para. 40 **replaced**, 41(1)(2) **am.**,
1935		
488	Sheriff Ct., Solicitors', etc. fees—A.S.	Sch., C.II **am.**, 1984/1134
714	Merchant Shipping Load Line Convention (Is. of Man) O.	**r.**, 1984/1163
1936		
1297	Fowl Pest O.	art. 4, para. (1A) **inserted**, 4, paras. (2)–(4), 12 (1) **am.**, 1984/561
1937		
54	Acetylene, restrictions—O. in C. (No. 30)	First provn. **am.**, proviso (1)(*a*)(*b*) **am.**, 1984/510
1176	Diseases of Fish (S.) Regs.	**r.**, 1984/455
1224	Diseases of Fish Regs.	**r.**, 1984/455
1938		
661	Trade Marks Rules	Sch. I **replaced**, 1984/459
1944		
46	Food Standards (Baking Powder and Golden Raising Powder) O.	**r.**, 1984/1304 **r.** (S.), 1984/1518
1457	Prevention of Fraud (Investments) List Regs.	**r.**, 1984/562
1946		
157	Food Standards (Self-Raising Flour) O.	arts. 1–3 **r.**, 1984/1304 **r.** (S.), 1984/1518 Sch. 1 **r.**, 1984/1304 **r.** (S.), 1984/1518
1948		
366	Merchant Shipping (Fishing Boats) O.	**r.**, 1984/1115
1949		
360	Double Taxation Relief (Taxes on Income) (Falkland Is.) O.	**r.** (with saving), 1984/363
581	Supn. (Local Govt. Staffs) (Nat. Service) (S.) Rules	**r.**, 1984/1232
798	Packing of Explosive for Conveyance Rules	Sch. **am.**, 1984/510
2368	Design Rules	**r.**, 1984/1989
1950		
123	Diseases of Fish Regulations 1937 (Amdt.) Regs.	**r.**, 1984/455
1952		
75	Supn. (Local Govt. Staffs) (Nat. Service) (Amdt.) (S.) Rules	**r.**, 1984/1232
518	Teachers' Pensions (Nat. Service) (S.) Rules	**r.**, 1984/2028

Year and Number (or date)	Short Title	How affected and Instrument by which affected
565	Prison (S.) Rules	rule 187(3) **replaced** 187(3A)(3B) **inserted,** 187(4)–(9) **replaced** by new (4)–(8) 188 **r.,** Sch., entry relating to Low Moss **inserted,** 1984/2058
2113	Bankruptcy Rules	rule 146(1) **am.,** 1984/1371
1953 205 246	Coroners Rules Offals in Meat Products O.	**r.** (with saving), 1984/552 **r.,** 1984/1566 **r.** (S.), 1984/1714
1598	Control of Explosives O.	Sch. **am.,** 1984/510
1954 1258	Supn. (Local Govt. Staffs) (Nat. Service) (S.) Amdt. Rules	**r.,** 1984/1232
1612	Public Service Vehicles and Trolley Vehicles (Carrying Capacity) Regs.	**r.,** 1984/1406
1955 116 990	Designs (Amdt.) Rules Motor Vehicles (Construction and Use) (Track Laying Vehicles) Regs.	**r.,** 1984/1989 reg. 3(1) **am.,** 1984/817, 1811 4A **r.,** 7(2)(*b*) **replaced,** 8, 11(1), 12(*g*) **am.,** 15(2)(*a*)(*d*) **replaced,** 18 **am.,** 1984/1811 21A, 22, 23 **r.,** 1984/817 27(2), 29(1) **am.,** 31 **replaced,** 32(2)(*cc*) **inserted,** 33, proviso, sub-para. (*b*) **am.,** 33, proviso, sub-para. (*c*) **inserted,** 34(*b*), 35, 36(2)(*a*), 37, 39, 40 (proviso) **am.,** 1984/1811 44 **r.,** 1984/817 44(4)(*e*) **am.,** 1984/1811 54A **r.,** 1984/817 78(*b*) **replaced,** 1984/1811 Second Sch. (Direction Indicators) **r.,** Fourth Sch. (Diagram of Trailer Plate) **r.,** Fifth Sch. (Diagram of Trailer Plate) **r.,** 1984/817
1993	Slaughter of Animals (Prevention of Cruelty) (S.) Regs.	reg. 25(2) **am.,** 1984/1205
1956 1691	Coroners Rules	**r.** (with saving), 1984/552
1957 191	Petroleum-Spirit (Conveyance by Road) Regs.	**mod.,** 1984/1244
1265	General Dental Council Disciplinary Ctee. (Procedure) Rules	**r.,** 1984/1517
1879	Nat. Insurance and Industrial Injuries (Israel) O.	Convention **am.,** 1984/354

Year and Number (or date)	Short Title	How affected and Instrument by which affected
1958		
61	Work in Compressed Air Special Regs.	regs. 2(2), 3(2), 7, 8(4), 9(3), 10(1)(4)(5), 12(1), 14(3), 17, 18(1)(2), 19, 20, 21 **am.**, Sch., Pt. I, rules 1, 3 **am.**, II, rule 6, proviso (*b*), 7(1)(2) **am.**, Tables I, III **replaced**, 1984/1593
313	Carbon Disulphide (Conveyance by Road) Regs.	**mod.**, 1984/1244
472	Public Service Vehicles and Trolley Vehicles (Carrying Capacity) (Amdt.) Regs.	**r.**, 1984/1406
1971	Slaughter of Pigs (Anaesthesia) Regs.	reg. 14 **am.**, 1984/1310
1975	Import Duty Reliefs (No. 3) O.	**r.**, 1984/810
1979	Import Duty Reliefs (No. 7) O.	**r.**, 1984/810
2166	Slaughter of Animals (Prevention of Cruelty) Regs.	reg. 36 **am.**, 1984/1311
1959		
763	A.S. (Adoption of Children)	**r.**, 1984/1013
831	Arsenic in Food Regs.	reg. 2(1) **am.**, 1984/1304
928	Arsenic in Food (S.) Regs.	reg. 2(1) **am.**, 1984/1518
1311	Keeping of Fireworks O.	art. 3(2) **am.**, Sch. **am.**, 1984/510
1348	Parking Meters (Description and Testing) (S.) O.	**r.**, 1984/1936
2106	Fluorine in Food Regs.	**r.**, 1984/1304
2182	Fluorine in Food (S.) Regs.	**r.**, 1984/1518
1960		
212	Family Allowances, Nat. Insurance and Industrial Injuries (Finland) O.	**r.**, 1984/125
1347	Explosives (Conveyance) (Private Railways) Byelaws	**r.**, 1984/510
1934	General Optical Council (Disciplinary Ctee. Rules) O. of C.	rule 2(*a*) **am.**, 8, 9 **replaced**, 1984/1250
1935	General Optical Council (Investigating Ctee. Rules) O. of C.	rule 3(*c*)–(*e*) **replaced**, 1984/1248
2195	Legal Aid (S.) General Regs.	reg. 14 **r.**, 1984/519
1961		
195	Town and Country Planning (Control of Advertisements) (S.) Regs.	**r.**, 1984/467
705	Parking Meters (Description and Testing) (E. and W.) O.	**r.**, 1984/1575
1214	Nurses Agencies Regs.	reg. 4(4) **am.**, 1984/1400
1580	Construction (General Provns.) Regs.	regs. 8(1)(*a*), 9(1)(4)(*a*), 13, 27(1)(3), 28 **am.**, 1984/1593
1581	Construction (Lifting Operations) Regs.	regs. 12, 13(1)(2), 14(4)(*c*), 17, 28(1)(2), 29(1)(*b*), 30(4)(*c*), 41(*a*), 42(1), 47(3)(*c*)(ii) **am.**, 1984/1593
1962		
225	Construction (Lifting Operations) Reports O.	Sch., Pt.II, cols. 3, 4 **am.**, IV, col. 2 **am.**, 1984/1593
226	Construction (Lifting Operations) Prescribed Particulars O.	art. 3(2)(*a*)(ii)(*b*)(ii) **am.**, Sch., Pt. I, items 10, cols. (i)–(iv), 11 **am.**, II, Table **am.**, 1984/1593

Year and Number (or date)	Short Title	How affected and Instrument by which affected
227	Construction (Lifting Operations) Certificates O.	Sch., Pt. I, items 10, cols. (i)–(iv), 11 **am.**, II, Table, **am.**, III, items (2)(*a*)(3) **am.**, III, note at end **am.**, V, items 6(*a*)(*b*) **am.**, 1984/1593
613	Mental Health (Forms) (S.) Regs.	**r.**, 1984/1495
614	Mental Health (Guardianship) (S.) Regs.	**r.**, 1984/1494
2045	Building Societies (Forms and Fees) Regs.	reg. 3 **replaced**, Sch. 2 **replaced**, 1984/279
1963		
788	Oil in Navigable Waters (Hong Kong) O.	**r.** (with saving), 1984/1153
848	Oil in Navigable Waters (Hong Kong) Regs.	**r.**, 1984/1153
1435	Bread and Flour Regs.	**r.**, 1984/1304
1461	Bread and Flour (S.) Regs.	**r.**, 1984/1518
1710	Weights and Measures Regs.	regs. 1A, 5(1A)(1B), 8A **inserted**, 140 **am.**, Sch. 2, Pt. I, para. **am.**,
1888	Slaughter of Animals (Stunning Pens) (S.) Regs.	reg. 5(2) **am.**, 1984/1205
1964		
229	Designs (Amdt.) Rules	**r.**, 1984/1989
1109	Tuberculosis (S.) O.	**r.**, 1984/2063
1151	Tuberculosis O.	**r.**, 1984/1943
1386	Control of Harbour Devpt. O.	**r.**, 1984/522
1965		
321	A.S. (Rules of Ct., consolidation and amdt.)	rule 30 **replaced**, 70(2) **inserted**, 74(*e*) **am.**, 74A **inserted**, 1984/472 75B **replaced**, 1984/920 79 heading "Motions for interim orders" **substituted**, 79 **re-numbered** 79(1) 79(2)(3) **inserted**, 1984/499 89(*a*) **am.**, 89(*aa*)(*ab*)(*g*)–(*i*) **inserted**, 1984/472 89B **inserted**, 1984/499 91A, 91B **inserted**, 93A **am.**, 104A, 106A, 111(*f*), 122A, 125(*c*) **inserted**, 1984/472 134A–134D **inserted**, 1984/919 153A–153E **inserted**, 1984/472 170B(6)(*c*) **inserted**, 1984/499 219–230 **replaced**, 230A heading **am.**, 230(A)(1)(3), 230B(2), 230E(2), 230F(6), 230H(1)(*b*), 230I(1)(3)(4), 230J, 230K(*b*) **am.**, 1984/997 236(*b*) **am.**, 236(*f*) **inserted**, 1984/499 265(*c*) **inserted**, 1984/472 277(*k*)(i), 281(3)(*c*), 290(*a*) **am.**, 1984/499

Year and Number (or date)	Short Title	How affected and Instrument by which affected
		340–346 **r.**, 1984/235
		347 **am.**, 1984/256, 499, 1132, 1133
		appx., form 5A **replaced**, 1984/920
		36–39C **replaced**, 1984/997
723	Probation Rules	**r.**, 1984/647
1106	Merchant Shipping (Fire Appliances) Rules	rule 10(1) **replaced**,
		36(4), 64A, 65(4)(5) **inserted**,
		Sch. 5, para. 3(*a*) **am.**, 1984/1222
1551	Designs (Amdt.) Rules	**r.**, 1984/1989
1776	Rules of the Supreme Ct. (Revision)	O.8, rule 3(4) **am.**,
		22, rule 11 **am.**,
		33, rule 4(4) **r.**,
		39, rule 1 **am.**,
		3A **inserted**,
		41, rule 1(5) **replaced**,
		50, rule 9A **inserted**,
		59, rules 4(3), 21(3) **inserted**,
		62, Appx. 2, Pt. VII, para. 4(2) **am.**,
		4(3) **replaced**,
		3, Pt. I, Table A **replaced**,
		71, rule 38(2) **am.**,
		38(7) **replaced**.
		75, rule 2(2) **replaced**,
		3(3), 8(1)(2)(5) **am.**,
		12 **replaced**,
		14, title, 14(1) **replaced**,
		15(1) **am.**,
		16(1) **replaced**,
		16(4) **am.**,
		18(2A) **inserted**,
		21(3), 25(1) **am.**,
		26 **replaced**,
		32(1)(5), 33(2) **r.**,
		33A **inserted**,
		34 **replaced**,
		36(2)–(4) **replaced** by new (2)
		42(1)–(3) **replaced** by new (1)(2)
		43(1)(2), 45, 46(2) **am.**,
		47 **r.**,
		76, rule 2(2) **replaced**,
		15(4) **r.**,
		77, rule 16(1A) **inserted**,
		16(2) **replaced**,
		16(2A)(2B) **inserted**,
		88, rule 5 **am.**,
		5A **inserted**,
		90, rules 6(1), 9(1), 16(4)(*d*) **am.**,
		13 **inserted**,
		97, rule 7(1) **am.**,
		103 **r.**,
		Appx. A, Forms 35, 53, 54, 56 **replaced**,
		B, Form 9 **replaced**,
		11 **am.**, 1984/1051

Year and Number (or date)	Short Title	How affected and Instrument by which affected
1838	Registration of Births, Deaths and Marriages (Misc. Provns.) (S.) Regs.	reg. 9 **am.**, 12(*a*)–(*h*) **replaced** by new reg. 12(*a*)–(*e*) 1984/267
1839	Registration of Births, Still-births, Deaths and Marriages (Prescription of Forms) (S.) Regs.	regs. 26, 27 **replaced**, 1984/266 Schs. 6, 7 form **replaced**, 1984/43 27 form **replaced**, 28 **r.**, 1984/266
1862	Cayman Is. (Appeal to Privy Council) O.	**r.**, 1984/1151
1893	Redundancy Payments Rebates Regs.	**r.** (with saving), 1984/1066
1995	Industrial and Provident Societies Regs.	Sch. 2 **replaced**, 1984/307
2067	Redundancy Payments Rebates (Amdt.) Regs.	**r.** (with saving), 1984/1066
1966		
56	Deer (Close Season) (S.) O.	**r.**, 1984/76
94	Construction (Working Places) Regs.	regs. 13(5), 15(4), 19(13)(*b*)(*b*)(i)(ii) (14)(15), 20(1)(*g*), 21(2)(*a*), 22(1), 24(1)(1)(*a*)(*b*)(3)(*b*), 25(1)(*b*)(5), 26(1)(1)(*a*)–(*f*)(2)(2)(*a*)(3), 27(1)(1)(*a*)(*b*), 28(1)(3)(5)(*a*)(6)(*c*) (i)(*f*), 29(2)(2)(*a*)(*b*), 32(4)(5)(*a*)(i)(8), 33(2)(2)(*a*)(4), 35(4)(*b*)(7), 36(1) **am.**, 1984/1593
99	British Museum (Authorised Repositories) O.	**r.**, 1984/1181
674	Public Service Vehicles and Trolley Vehicles (Carrying Capacity) (Amdt.) Regs.	**r.**, 1984/1406
815	Weights and Measures (Exemption) (Beer and Cider) O.	**r.**, 1984/1314
1967		
112	Work in Compressed Air (Prescribed Leaflet) O.	Sch. **am.**, 1984/1593
393	Designs (Amdt.) Rules	**r.**, 1984/1989
395	Veterinary Surgeons and Veterinary Practitioners (Registration Regulations) O. of C.	Sch., regs. 16, 20(*a*)–(*e*), 22, 23 **am.**, 1984/2009
599	Veterinary Surgeons (Examination of Commonwealth and Foreign Candidates) Regs.	reg. 9 **am.**, 1984/1072
810	Carriage by Air Acts (Application of Provns.) (Overseas Territories) O.	Sch. 2, Pt. I, art. 22(1)–(3) **am.**, 22(5) **replaced**, 1984/701
860	Meat Pie and Sausage Roll Regs.	**r.**, 1984/1566
861	Canned Meat Product Regs.	**r.**, 1984/1566
862	Sausage and Other Meat Product Regs.	**r.**, 1984/1566
1077	Meat Pie and Sausage Roll (S.) Regs.	**r.**, 1984/1714
1078	Sausage and Other Meat Product (S.) Regs.	**r.**, 1984/1714
1079	Canned Meat Product (S.) Regs.	**r.**, 1984/1714
1310	Industrial and Provident Societies Regs.	reg. 5 **am.**, 1984/307
1485	Ammonium Nitrate Mixtures Exemption O.	art. 2 **am.**, 1984/510
1582	Solvents in Food Regs.	reg. 2(1) **am.**, 1984/1304
1884	Probation Rules	**r.**, 1984/647
1968		
97	Imported Food Regs.	**r.**, 1984/1918
98	Imported Food (N.I.) Regs.	**r.**, 1984/1917
139	Sausage and Other Meat Product (S.) Amdt. Regs.	**r.**, 1984/1714

Year and Number (or date)	Short Title	How affected and Instrument by which affected
208	Police Cadets (S.) Regs.	reg. 16(1) **replaced,** 16(1A) **r.,** 16(1B) **am.,** Sch. 1, Table **replaced,** 2, **am.,** 1984/2029
263	Solvents in Food (S.) Regs.	reg. 2(1) **am.,** 1984/1518
430	Fish and Meat Spreadable Products Regs.	**r.,** 1984/1566
575	Double Taxation Relief (Taxes on Income) (Falkland Is.) O.	**r.** (with saving), 1984/363
717	Police (Promotion) (S.) Regs.	reg. 9 **replaced,** 10 **inserted,** 1984/648
1100	Double Taxation Relief (Taxes on Income) (Luxembourg) O.	art. III, para. (2) **r.,** (3) **re-numbered** (2) X **replaced,** XI, para. (1) **replaced,** XII, para. (1) **replaced,** XIIIA **inserted,** XVIII **replaced,** XXII **replaced,** XXV, para. (2) **replaced,** 1984/364
1231	Legal Aid in Criminal Proceedings Regs.	reg. 19(3)(a) **am.,** Third Sch. **am.,** 1984/1716
1558	Customs Duty (Personal Reliefs) (No. 1) O.	Sch. 1, para. (a)(4) **am.,** 1984/718
1604	British Museum (Authorised Repositories) O.	**r.,** 1984/1181
2046	Canned Meat Product (Amdt.) Regs.	**r.,** 1984/1566
2047	Sausage and Other Meat Product (Amdt.) Regs.	**r.,** 1984/1566
2049	Registration of Births, Deaths and Marriages Regs.	reg. 63(1) **am.,** 63(1A), 64A, 64B **inserted,** 65(1), 67(2) **am.,** 69(d) **inserted,** Sch. 1, list of contents **am.,** form 23, Pt. II **am.,** 33−37 **inserted,** 1984/460
1969 326	Canned Meat Product (S.) Amdt. Regs.	**r.,** 1984/1714
327	Sausage and Other Meat Product (S.) Amdt. Regs.	**r.,** 1984/1714
740	Merchant Shipping Act 1965 (Is. of Man) O.	**r.,** 1984/1160
1101	Gaming Machine (Licence Duty) Regs.	**r.,** 1984/1178
1342	Savings Contracts Regs.	reg. 10(1) **am.,** 1984/599
1380	Programme Distribution Systems (Exceptions) O.	**r.,** 1984/980
1493	Nat. Insurance (U.S.A.) O.	**r.** (wef 1.1.1988), 1984/1817
1532	Town and Country Planning (Control of Advertisements) Regs.	**r.** (with saving), 1984/421
1642	Supn. (Local Govt. and Overseas Employment) Interchange (S.) Rules	**r.,** 1984/1232
1970 94	Cheese Regs.	reg. 2(1) **am.,** 11 **replaced,** 1984/649
108	Cheese (S.) Regs.	reg. 2(1) **am.,** 11 **replaced,** 1984/847
294	Merchant Shipping (Certificates of Competency as A.B.) Regs.	regs. 4(1)(d), 7(2)(a)(ii) **am.,** 1984/97
400	Labelling of Food Regs.	**r.,** 1984/1305

Year and Number (or date)	Short Title	How affected and Instrument by which affected
548	Wireless Telegraphy (Broadcast Licence Charges and Exemption) Regs.	r. in pt. (wef 1.8.84), remainder r. (wef 1.9.84), 1984/1053
720	A.S. (Variation and Recall of Orders in Consistorial Causes)	r., 1984/667
781	Gaming Clubs (Hours and Charges) (S.) Regs.	r. (S.), 1984/470
799	Gaming Clubs (Hours and Charges) Regs.	r., 1984/248
887	Act. of Adj. (Fees in the High Ct. of Justiciary)	r., 1984/234
1065	Fish and Meat Spreadable Products (S.) Regs.	r., 1984/1714
1127	Labelling of Food (S.) Regs.	r., 1984/1519
1792	Magistrates' Cts. (Children and Young Persons) Rules	rule 2(1) **am.**, 14A(2)(4)(6)(7) **replaced**, 14B(*a*) **am.**, 14C, 16(3) **inserted**, 20(1)(*a*) **replaced**, 20(1)(*aa*) **inserted**, Pt. IIIA, rules 21A–21E **inserted**, Sch. 2, forms 42A–42D **inserted**, 1984/567
1940	Eurocontrol (Immunities and Privileges) O.	arts. 8–10 **inserted**, 1984/127
1956	British Museum (Authorised Repositories) O.	r., 1984/1181
1971 13	Wireless Telegraphy (Broadcast Licence Charges and Exemption) (Amdt.) (No. 1) Regs.	r., 1984/1053
82	British Museum (Authorised Repositories) O.	r., 1984/1181
90	A.S. (Alteration of Sheriff Ct. Fees)	para. 2A **inserted**, Sch. 2, Table of Fees, c. I, heading **replaced**, para. 2, heading **am.**, Pt. II **inserted**, II para. 2A **inserted**, 1984/471 6(*a*), 11, 12, 13(*a*) **am.**, III para. 2(*a*) **am.**, 1984/1135 3 **am.**, 3A **inserted**, 1984/471
129	Registration of Marriages (Welsh Language) Regs.	reg. 3(1) **am.**, 3(2) **inserted**, 4(1) **am.**, 4(2) **inserted**, 6 **am.**, Sch. 1, list of contents **am.**, form 9, Pt. III **am.**, 10–12 **inserted**, 1984/461
249	Residential Establishments (Payments by Local Authies.) (S.) O.	art. 3 **am.**, 1984/1713
295	Wireless Telegraphy (Broadcast Licence Charges and Exemption) (Amdt.) (No. 2) Regs.	r., 1984/1053
450	Road Vehicles (Registration and Licensing) Regs.	reg. 19 **replaced**, Sch. 2, Pt. II, para. 5A(*a*)(*b*) **replaced**, 3, para. 4 r., 1984/814

Year and Number (or date)	Short Title	How affected and Instrument by which affected
480	Probation (Amdt.) Rules	r., 1984/647
492	Children's Hearings (S.) Rules	rules 2(1), 6(1) am., 7(1)(*aa*) inserted, 7(1)(*aaa*) inserted, 1984/1867 7(1)(*b*) am., 7(1)(*cc*) inserted. 7(2), 8(4), 9(3)(*a*), 13(1), 14(1), 18(2), 21, 22(1) am., 22(1A) inserted, 22(2) am., 22(2A) inserted, 23(1), 25(1) am., 25(1A) inserted, 25(2) am., 25(2A) inserted, 25(3) am., 25(4)(5) inserted, Sch. Forms 8A, 8B, 10A, 11A, 15A, 16A, 17A inserted, 18 replaced, 18A, 19A, 19B inserted, 1984/100
618	Corrosive Substances (Conveyance by Road) Regs.	mod., 1984/1244
661	Slaughter of Poultry (Humane Conditions) Regs.	r., 1984/2056
694	Road Vehicles Lighting Regs.	r., 1984/812
1061	Inflammable Liquids (Conveyance by Road) Regs.	mod., 1984/1244
1062	Inflammable Substances (Conveyance by Road) (Labelling) Regs.	mod., 1984/1244
1158	Registration of Births, Still-births, Deaths and Marriages (Prescription of Forms) (S.) Amdt. Regs.	reg. 10 r., Sch. 8 r., 1984/266
1237	Commonwealth Countries and Republic of Ireland (Immunities and Privileges) O.	art. 8A am., Schs. 1, 2 am., 1984/1977
1861	Blood Tests (Evidence of Paternity) Regs.	reg. 12 replaced, Sch. 2 replaced, 1984/1243
1874	Control of Harbour Devpt. (Amdt.) O.	r., 1984/522
1972		
308	Act of Adj. (Fees in the Inferior Cts.)	Sch. Pt. II r., 1984/232
316	Rules of Procedure (Army)	rule 25(1)(*d*)(iv) replaced, 59(1)(2) am., 81(1)(*a*)–(*f*) replaced, 81(1)(*g*) inserted, 92(2) replaced, 100(2) am., Sch. 2(1) (s. 205(1)(*h*)) am., 2(3) am., 5(1) am., 9, para. 11(5) replaced, 1984/1670
395	Pensions Increase (Federated Supn. Scheme for Nurses and Hospital Officers) (Civil Service) Regs.	reg. 3(1A) inserted, 3(2) replaced, 4(1)(2) am., 4(4) inserted, Sch., paras. 4, 5 am., 1984/1751

Year and Number (or date)	Short Title	How affected and Instrument by which affected
419	Rules of Procedure (Air Force)	rule 25(1)(*d*)(iv) **replaced**, 59(1)(2) **am.**, 81(1)(*a*)–(*f*) **replaced**, 81(1)(*g*) **inserted**, 92(2) **replaced**, Sch. 9, para. 11(5) **replaced**, 1984/1669
489	Town and Country Planning (Control of Advertisements) (Amdt.) Regs.	**r.** (with saving), 1984/421
641	Savings Certificates Regs.	reg. 5(1) **replaced**, 1984/1052 **am.**, 1984/1564 20(1) **am.**, 1984/603
653	British Museum (Authorised Repositories) O.	**r.**, 1984/1181
764	Nat. Savings Bank Regs.	reg. 8(3) **replaced**, new reg. 8(4) **inserted**, 1984/9 8(4), **re-numbered** (5), 8(5), **am.**, 1984/9 40(1) **am.**, 1984/602
765	Premium Savings Bonds Regs.	reg. 13(1) **am.**, 1984/601
1101	Cayman Is. (Constitution) O.	s. 18 **replaced**, 20(3) **am.**, 25 **replaced**, Pt. V, ss. 49, 49A–49G **replaced**, 50 **am.**, Sch. II **inserted**, 1984/126
1178	Gas Safety Regs.	regs. 17–48 **r.**, 49, 50, 51(1)–(5) **am.**, 51(6) **inserted**, 1984/1358
1208	Probation (Amdt.) Rules	**r.**, 1984/647
1391	Bread and Flour (Amdt.) Regs.	**r.**, 1984/1304
1489	Bread and Flour (S.) Amdt. Regs.	**r.**, 1984/1518
1577	Building Societies (Designation for Trustee Investment) Regs.	Sch., para. 3 **am.**, 1984/8
1683	Immigration Appeals (Notices) Regs.	**r.**, 1984/2040
1684	Immigration Appeals (Procedure) Rules	**r.** (with saving), 1984/2041
1813	Immigration (Jersey) O.	Sch., para. 31 **am.**, 1984/1690
1973		
118	General Betting Duty Regs.	reg. 2(1) **am.**, 1984/261
173	V.A.T. (Terminal Markets) O.	arts. 2(2), 3(2)(*b*)(ii) **am.**, 1984/202
327	V.A.T. (Imported Goods) Relief (No. 1) O.	**r.**, 1984/746
334	Income Tax (Employments) Regs.	regs. 28(1), 30(1), 51(5)(6) **am.**, 1984/1858
355	Gaming Charges Regs.	reg. 2(2) **r.**, 1984/248
359	Gaming Charges (S.) Regs.	reg. 2(2) **r.** (S.) 1984/470
390	Legal Advice and Assistance (S.) Regs.	reg. 4(2) **am.**, 5(7), (8), (8A), (9), 7(2)(3) **r.**, 9–12 **inserted**, Sch. re-headed Sch. 1, Sch. 2 **inserted**, 1984/210
747	Motor Vehicles (Variation of Speed Limits) Regs.	**r.**, 1984/325
748	Motor Vehicles (Speed Limits on Motorways) Regs.	**r.**, 1984/325

Year and Number (or date)	Short Title	How affected and Instrument by which affected
797	Misuse of Drugs Regs.	reg. 8(4), 9(1)(*c*) **replaced**, 9(2)(*ff*) **inserted**, 9(4), 10(1)(4) **replaced**, 14(4)(*c*) **am.**, 15(2A) **inserted**, Sch. 2, paras. 1, 6 **am.**, 3, para. 1, list of substances **designated** sub-para. (*a*) **am.**, sub-para. (*b*) **inserted**, 4, para. 1(*a*) **am.**, 1984/1143
798	Misuse of Drugs (Safe Custody) Regs.	Sch. 1, para. 3 **inserted**, 1984/1146
1006	Road Vehicles Lighting (Amdt.) Regs.	**r.**, 1984/812
1268	Redundant Mineworkers and Concessionary Coal (Payments Schemes) O.	Sch.: art. 1, definition of "the Schemes of 1984" **inserted**, 2, 6 **am.**, 7(2)(*f*) **inserted**, 1984/457
1350	Imported Food (N.I.) (Amdt.) Regs.	**r.**, 1984/1917
1351	Imported Food (Amdt.) Regs.	**r.**, 1984/1918
1468	N.H.S. (General Dental Services) Regs.	reg. 2(1) **am.**, 1984/760, 1424 3(*a*) **replaced**, 1984/1424 5A **inserted**, 1984/760 8(4) **inserted**, 1984/1424 Sch. 1, Pt. I, para. 3 **replaced**, 1984/760 IV **inserted**, 1984/1424
1469	Occupational Pension Schemes (Preservation of Benefit) Regs.	**r.**, 1984/614
1784	Occupational Pension Schemes (Preservation of Benefit) (No. 2) Regs.	**r.**, 1984/614
1822	Medicines (Pharmacies) (Applications for Registration and Fees) Regs.	reg. 3(1)–(3) **am.**, 1984/1886
1967	Weights and Measures Act 1963 (Pasta) O.	**r.**, 1984/1316
1968	Weights and Measures Act 1963 (Salt) O.	**r.**, 1984/1316
1979	Merchant Shipping (Metrication) Regs.	provns. **ext.** to Is. of Man with **mods.**, 1984/1164
2030	Tuberculosis (Amdt.) O.	**r.**, 1984/1943
2093	Diseases of Fish O.	art. 3 **r.**, 4 **am.**, 1984/301
2101	Tuberculosis (S.) Amdt. O.	**r.**, 1984/2063
2117	A.S. (Domicile and Matrimonial Proceedings Act 1973)	**r.**, 1984/255
2124	Textile Products (Indications of Fibre Content) Regs.	Sch. 2, Pt. I.— item 1, col. 2 **am.**, 28, col. 1 **am.**, 3, item 28 **am.**, 1984/1640
2221	Organic Peroxides (Conveyance by Road) Regs.	**mod.**, 1984/1244
1974 63	N.H.S. (Amdt. of Trust Instrts.) O.	**am.**, 1984/168
82	Scottish Local Elections Rules	rule 2 **replaced**, Sch. 1, rules 1(2), 2(1), 11(4), 16(1)(*a*), 18, 24(4), 25(1), (3), (4), 26(3) **am.**, 32(1)(*b*) **r.**, 37(1)(*f*) **am.**, 51(1) **r.**, 2, **r.**, 1984/352

Year and Number (or date)	Short Title	How affected and Instrument by which affected
149	General Optical Council (Education Ctee. Rules) O. of C.	rule 4(*b*)(*d*)(*e*) **replaced**, 1984/1249
185	Town and Country Planning (Control of Advertisements) (Amdt.) Regs.	**r.** (with saving), 1984/421
248	N.H.S. (Abolition of Authies.: Consequential Provns.) O.	art. 2(1) **am.**, 1984/168
447	Local Govt. (Allowances) Regs.	regs. 3, 8A **am.**, Sch. 2 **replaced**, 1984/698
505	N.H.S. (General Dental Services) (S.) Regs.	reg. 2(1) **am.**, 3(1)(*a*) **replaced**, 5A, 8(4) **inserted**, Sch. 1, Pt. I, para. 3 **replaced**, II, heading **replaced**, IV, paras. 31–37 **inserted**, 1984/1491
520	Local Govt. Supn. Regs.	reg. C1(3) **inserted**, Sch. 6, para. 2(2) **am.**, 8, para. 5(2) **am.**, 20, Pt. III, para. 4(2) **am.**, 1984/201
618	Slum Clearance Subsidy Regs.	**am.**, 1984/244
768	Watermark Disease (Local Authies.) O.	art. 8 **am.**, 1984/688
812	Local Govt. Supn. (S.) Regs.	reg. A3(1) **am.**, 1984/254, 1232 D1(1)(*g*), 2(*d*), 10C(*c*), E16(1)(*a*) **am.**, J9, L7(3), P2A **inserted**, P3 **replaced**, P5, 7(1), (3)(*a*) **am.**, P7(4) **inserted**, P8(1) **am.**, Q6 **inserted**, R2(2)(*d*)(*e*) **am.**, R3(2)(*f*) **inserted**, R3(4) **am.**, R3(5A)(8A) **inserted**, R4(2) **am.**, R4(5)(*a*) **r.**, R4(5)(*b*)(*c*) **re-lettered** (*a*)(*b*) R4(5)(*a*), 5(1)(*b*) **am.**, R5(1)(*c*) **inserted**, R5(2)(*a*) **am.**, R5(2)(*aa*) **inserted**, R6(1) **am.**, R6(1A)–(1F) **inserted**, R7(1), (2)(*a*) **am.**, Sch. 15, para. (8) **replaced**, 20, Pt. I, para. 1 **am.**, II, para–6 **am.**, III, **inserted**, 26, **inserted**, 1984/1232
1064	Probation (Amdt.) Rules	**r.**, 1984/647
1166	Weights and Measures Act 1963 (Sugar) O.	**r.**, 1984/1316
1248	Police Cadets (S.) Amdt. Regs.	reg. 5(1) **r.**, 1984/2029
1329	Occupational Pension Schemes (Preservation of Benefit) Amdt. Regs.	**r.**, 1984/614
2010	Social Security (Benefit) (Married Women and Widows Special Provns.) Regs.	reg. 1(2), definition of "the determining authority" **replaced**, 1984/458
2034	Agriculture (Tractor Cabs) Regs.	reg. 3A **replaced**, 1984/605
2043	Designs (Amdt. No. 2) Rules	**r.**, 1984/1989
2128	Coroners (Amdt.) Rules	**r.** (with saving), 1984/552
2149	Double Taxation Relief (Taxes on Income) (Falkland Is.) O.	**r.** (with saving), 1984/363

Year and Number (or date)	Short Title	How affected and Instrument by which affected
2211	Rabies (Importation of Dogs, Cats and Other Mammals) O.	art. 4(9)(10) **inserted**, 8(3), 15(1) **am.**, Sch. 2, Pt. I **replaced**, 1984/1182
1975		
133	Civil List (Increase of Financial Provn.) O.	**r.**, 1984/39
205	Friendly Societies Regs.	Sch. 2 **replaced**, 1984/309
239	Road Vehicles Lighting (Amdt.) Regs.	**r.**, 1984/812
245	Road Vehicles (Use of Lights during Daytime) Regs.	**r.**, 1984/812
282	Health and Safety (Agriculture) (Poisonous Substances) Regs.	**r.**, 1984/1114
299	Lands Tribunal Rules	Sch. 2 **replaced**, 1984/793
467	Social Security (Employed Earners' Employments for Industrial Injuries Purposes) Regs.	Sch. 1, Pt. II, para. 4 **am.**, 1984/303
493	Social Security (Benefit) (Members of the Forces) Regs.	reg. 2 **am.**, 1984/1303
494	Social Security (Airmen's Benefits) Regs.	reg. 2 **am.**, 1984/1303
529	Social Security (Mariners' Benefits) Regs.	regs. 4(*a*)(*b*), 5, 6(2) **am.**, 1984/1303
539	A.S. (Commissary Business)	Sch., col. 2 **am.**, 1984/969
555	Social Security (Hospital In-Patients) Regs.	reg. 7(3)(*a*)(i)(*b*)(i) **am.**, 1984/1303 Sch. 1, para. (*a*) **am.**, 1984/1699 2, **am.**, 1984/1303
558	Social Security (Determination of Claims and Questions) Regs.	**r.**, 1984/451
563	Social Security Benefit (Persons Abroad) Regs.	reg. 2(1) **am.**, 1984/1303 5 applied, 1984/1703
572	Social Security (Correction and Setting Aside of Decisions) Regs.	**r.**, 1984/451
597	Companies (Unregistered Companies) Regs.	**r.**, 1984/682
598	Social Security (Attendance Allowance) (No. 2) Regs.	regs. 8–14 **r.**, 1984/451
670	Gaming (Small Charges) O.	art. 3(*b*) **am.**, 1984/246
686	Local Authies. (Allowances) (S.) Regs.	regs. 3(1), (2), 3A(1) **am.**, Sch. 2 **replaced**, 1984/691
717	Legal Aid (S.) (Criminal Proceedings) Regs.	reg. 10 **r.**, 1984/520
788	Gaming (Small Charges) (S.) O.	art. 3(*b*) **am.** (S.), 1984/469
825	Local Authy. Stocks and Bonds (S.) Regs.	reg. 3 **am.**, 3A **inserted**, 4(1)(*a*)(2) **am.**, 6(1)(*a*) **replaced**, 7(1)(*g*)(*h*), 8 **am.**, 25(4) **inserted**, 1984/1652
828	Mental Health (Guardianship) (S.) Amdt. Regs.	**r.**, 1984/1494
890	Designs (Amdt. No. 2) Rules	**r.**, 1984/1989
898	Town and Country Planning (Control of Advertisements) (Amdt.) Regs.	**r.** (with saving), 1984/421
958	Social Security (Determination of Industrial Injuries Questions) Regs.	**r.**, 1984/451
1058	Social Security (Non-Contributory Invalidity Pension) Regs.	**r.**, 1984/1303
1137	Admin. of Estates (Small Payments) (Increase of Limit) O.	**r.**, 1984/539
1166	Social Security (Non-Contributory Invalidity Pension) Amdt. Regs.	**r.**, 1984/1303

Year and Number (or date)	Short Title	How affected and Instrument by which affected
1177	Weights and Measures Act 1963 (Cereal Breakfast Foods and Oat Products) O.	r., 1984/1316
1178	Weights and Measures Act 1963 (Flour and Flour Products) O.	r., 1984/1316
1179	Weights and Measures Act 1963 (Dried Vegetables) O.	r., 1984/1316
1190	Nat. Savings Bank (Amdt.) Regs.	r., 1984/602
1191	Premium Savings Bonds (Amdt.) Regs.	r., 1984/601
1192	Savings Certificates (Amdt.) (No. 2) Regs.	r., 1984/603
1193	Savings Contracts (Amdt.) Regs.	r., 1984/599
1204	Town and Country Planning (Tree Preservation Order and Trees in Conservation Areas) (S.) Regs.	regs. 5(*c*), 9(*a*) **am.**, Sch., art. 1(1) **replaced**, 1984/329
1385	Juvenile Cts. (London) O.	art. 5 **replaced**, Sch. 1 **replaced**, 1984/713
1484	Fluorine in Food (Amdt.) Regs.	r., 1984/1304
1485	Misc. Additives in Food (Amdt.) Regs.	r., 1984/1305
1494	Road Vehicles Lighting (Standing Vehicles) (Exemption) (General) Regs.	r., 1984/812
1543	Nature Conservancy Council (Byelaws) (S.) Regs.	r., 1984/918
1573	Mobility Allowance Regs.	reg. 1(2), definition of "medical authority" **replaced**, 7(1)(*a*) **am.**, 1984/458 regs. 12–20 **r.**, 1984/451
1594	Fluorine in Food (S.) Amdt. Regs.	r., 1984/1518
1596	Misc. Additives in Food (S.) Amdt. Regs.	r., 1984/1519
1803	Supreme Ct. Funds Rules	rules. 31(1), 37A(1) **am.**, 1984/285
1831	Dumping at Sea Act 1974 (Overseas Territories) O.	Sch. 2, cols. 2, 3 **am.**, 1984/542
1927	Occupational Pension Schemes (Certification of Employments) Regs.	r., 1984/380
1960	Income Tax (Sub-contractors in the Construction Industry) Regs.	regs. 9(1), 10(1) **am.**, 1984/1857
2069	Town and Country Planning (Listed Buildings and Buildings in Conservation Areas) (S.) Regs.	reg. 6 **applied with mods.** (Crown Land applications), 1984/996
2101	Occupational Pension Schemes (Contracting-out) Regs.	r., 1984/380
2115	Control of Noise (Code of Practice for Construction Sites) O.	r., 1984/1992
2171	Merchant Shipping (Oil Pollution) (Overseas Territories) O.	Sch. 2, paras. 3B(*a*), 6(*a*), 7(*a*), 8(*a*) **r.**, 9, 13(*a*) **am.**, 3, paras. 3B(*a*), 4(*a*), 6(*a*) **r.**, 1984/543
1976 111	Weights and Measures Act 1963 (Biscuits and Shortbread) O.	r., 1984/1316
140	Occupational Pension Schemes (Preservation of Benefit) Amdt. Regs.	r., 1984/614
143	Contracted-out Employment (Notifications, Premiums Payment and Misc. Provns.) Regs.	r., 1984/380
183	Registration of Restrictive Trading Agreements Regs.	r., 1984/392
222	Inter-American Development Bank (Immunities and Privileges) O.	art. 14 **inserted**, 1984/1981
225	Social Security (Reciprocal Agreements) O.	Sch. 1 **am.**, 1984/125

Year and Number (or date)	Short Title	How affected and Instrument by which affected
409	Social Security (Invalid Care Allowance) Regs.	reg. 16 **r.**, 1984/451
430	Weights and Measures Act 1963 (Edible Fats) O.	**r.**, 1984/1316
431	Weights and Measures Act 1963 (Dried Fruits) O.	**r.**, 1984/1316
455	Merchant Shipping (Fishing Boats) (Amdt.) O.	**r.**, 1984/1115
465	Prevention of Terrorism (Supplemental Temp. Provns.) O.	**r.** (with saving), 1984/418
466	Prevention of Terrorism (Supplemental Temp. Provns.) (N.I.) O.	**r.** (with saving), 1984/417
475	Grant-Aided Secondary Schools (S.) Grant Regs.	definition of "financial year" **replaced,** Sch. 1 **replaced,** 1984/381
541	Cocoa and Chocolate Products Regs.	reg. 2(1) **am.**, 1984/1305
615	Social Security (Medical Evidence) Regs.	reg. 5(1) **am.**, 1984/1303
730	Hallmarking (International Convention) O.	Sch. 2 **am.**, 1984/1131
766	Employment Protection (Offshore Employment) O.	art. 3(*g*) **inserted,** Sch., Pt. VII **inserted,** 1984/1149
772	Prevention of Terrorism (Temp. Provns.) Act 1976 (Guernsey) O.	**r.**, 1984/1165
895	Prevention of Terrorism (Temp. Provns.) Act 1976 (Is. of Man) O.	**r.**, 1984/860
896	Prevention of Terrorism (Temp. Provns.) Act 1976 (Jersey) O.	**r.**, 1984/1166
914	Cocoa and Chocolate Products (S.) Regs.	reg. 2(1) **am.**, 1984/1519
962	Child Benefit (Determination of Claims and Questions) Regs.	**r.**, 1984/451
963	Child Benefit (Residence and Persons Abroad) Regs.	regs. 2(2)(*c*)(i), 4(2)(*c*)(2A)(3) **am.**, 1984/875 8(2)(*a*) **am.**, 8(3) **replaced,** 1984/458 10, 11 **r.**, 1984/875
964	Child Benefit (Claims and Payments) Regs.	**r.**, 1984/1960
965	Child Benefit (General) Regs.	reg. 5 **replaced,** 1984/939 9(2)(3) **r.**, 9(4) **inserted,** 1984/337 15 **am.**, 1984/303 16(5)(*a*) **am.**, 1984/337
1019	Offshore Installations (Operational Safety, Health and Welfare) Regs.	reg. 1(4) **replaced,** 1984/419
1073	Police (S.) Regs.	Sch. 2, para. 1, Table **am.**, 3, Tables A, B **replaced,** 10, para. 1 **am.**, 1984/1651
1120	Weights and Measures (Sale of Wine) O.	**r.**, 1984/1314
1190	Devpt. Land Tax (Disposals by Non-Residents) Regs.	reg. 3(*a*) **am.**, 3(*b*) **r.**, 6(1) **replaced,** 1984/1172
1247	Health and Safety Agriculture (Misc. Repeals and Mods.) Regs.	Sch. 3, entry 8 **r.**, 1984/1114
1267	Child Benefit and Social Security (Fixing and Adjustment of Rates) Regs.	reg. 2(1)(2) **am.**, 1984/1106
1294	Weights and Measures Act 1963 (Tea) O.	**r.**, 1984/1316
1295	Weights and Measures (Flour and Oat Products) (Exemption) O.	**r.**, 1984/1316
1542	Offshore Installations (Emergency Procedures) Regs.	reg. 3 **replaced,** 1984/419

Year and Number (or date)	Short Title	How affected and Instrument by which affected
1644	Adoption (County Ct.) Rules	**r.** (with saving), 1984/265
1645	Adoption (High Ct.) Rules	**r.** (with saving), 1984/265
1758	Child Benefit (Misc. Minor Amdts.) Regs.	reg. 2 **r.**, 1984/1960
1768	Magistrates' Cts. (Adoption) Rules	**r.** (with saving), 1984/611
1779	Assembly Pensions (N.I.) O.	art. 2(2)(3) **am.**, 2(4) **inserted**, 4, 5(1) **replaced**, 5(4)–(6) **r.**, 6(1)(3) **am.**, 6(5)(6) **r.**, 8(1) **am.**, 8(2A)(2B) **inserted**, 8(3) **am.**, 8(4A)(4B), 9(3A) **inserted**, 9(4)(5) **r.**, 9(7) **inserted**, 10(1)(2) **am.**, 11A–11D **inserted**, 12(1)(5), 13(1) **am.**, 14(1)(*a*)(*b*) **replaced**, 15(1) **am.**, 15(1)(*a*)(*b*) **replaced**, 15(1A) **inserted**, 15(3) **am.**, 15(3A) **inserted**, 15(4), 16(2)–(4)(6) **am.**, 16A, 16B **inserted**, 17(1) **am.**, 17(1A)(1B) **inserted**, 17(2) **r.**, 18(1)(2), 19(2)(*a*)–(*c*), 20(*a*) **am.**, 22(1)(*b*) **replaced**, 22(2)(*a*)(*b*) **am.**, 22(2)(*c*) **inserted**, 23(1)(2) **am.**, 23(6)(*a*) **r.**, 23(7)(8) **inserted**, Schs. 3, 4 **inserted**, 1984/358
2012	Nat. Savings Stock Register Regs.	reg. 41(1) **am.**, 1984/600
2020	A.S. (Rules of Ct. Amdt. No. 12) (Intimation under Damages (S.) Act 1976)	**r.**, 1984/920
2105	Customs Duties Quota Relief (Admin.) O.	art. 4 **applied with mod.**, 1984/2006 4(1) **excl.**, 1984/898
2181	A.S. (Damages (S.) Act 1976)	**r.**, 1984/921
2183	Agricultural Land Tribunals (Succession to Agricultural Tenancies) O.	**r.** (with saving), 1984/1301
1977		
73	A.S. (Fees in the Ct. of Teinds)	**r.**, 1984/235
88	Standing Civilian Cts. O.	art. 51(5) **replaced**, 1984/1671
228	Town and Country Planning (Listed Buildings and Buildings in Conservation Areas) Regs.	regs. 3(2), 5 **applied with mods.** (Crown Land applications), 1984/1015
248	Costs in Criminal Cases (Central Funds) (Appeals) Regs.	reg. 4 **am.**, 1984/340 4(10A) **inserted**, 5(2) **replaced**, 6(1A) **inserted**, 1984/330
252	Merchant Shipping (Smooth and Partially Smooth Waters) Rules	Sch. 2 **am.**, 1984/955
271	Prevention of Terrorism (Supplemental Temp. Provns.) (Amdt.) O.	**r.** (with saving), 1984/418

Year and Number (or date)	Short Title	How affected and Instrument by which affected
289	Town and Country Planning General Devpt. O.	arts. 7(3), 7(6A), 20(2) **applied with mods.** (Crown Land applications), 1984/1015
331	Consumer Credit (Entry and Inspection) Regs.	reg. 2(*b*) **replaced**, 1984/1046
342	Social Security (Child Benefit Consequential) Regs.	reg. 16 **r.**, 1984/1303
343	Social Security Benefit (Dependency) Regs.	reg. 1(3)(*a*) **am.**, 1984/1728 3(1) **am.**, 1984/1699 3(5) **inserted**, 4A(2) **r.** (with saving), 4A(4), 4B(1) **am.**, 1984/1698 5(1) **am.**, 1984/1699 10(1)(2) **am.**, 1984/1698 10(2)(*a*) **am.**, 1984/1699 10(2)(*b*)(ii)(*e*) **am.**, 10(2)(*f*) **inserted**, 10(3)(4), 11(1)(1)(*a*)(*b*) **am.**, 1984/1698 12(1) **am.**, 1984/1698, 1728 15A **r.**, 1984/1698 Sch. 2, paras. 2A–2C **inserted**, 1984/1699
344	Matrimonial Causes Rules	rules 2(2), 59(1) **am.**, 65(2), proviso **replaced**, 73(2) **am.**, 73(3), 74(3)–(5) **replaced**, 74(6) **inserted**, 75 **replaced**, 76A **inserted**, 92(2) **replaced**, 92(7) **am.**, 95(3), new (*c*) **inserted**, 95(3), (*c*) **re-lettered** (*d*), 104(3)(5) **am.**, 107 **replaced**, 121(1)(2) **am.**, appx. 1, Form 5, para—5(*b*)(iii) (*c*) **am.**, 9, 10, note **inserted**, 1984/1511
455	Prevention of Terrorism (Supplemental Temp. Provns.) (N.I.) (Amdt.) O.	**r.** (with saving), 1984/417
486	Offshore Installations (Life-saving Appliances) Regs.	reg. 3 **replaced**, 1984/419
558	Weights and Measures Act 1963 (Honey) O.	**r.**, 1984/1316
674	Employment Protection (Recoupment of Unemployment Benefit and Supplementary Benefit) Regs.	reg. 12(2) **am.**, 1984/458
789	Trade Union (Nominations) Regs.	regs. 2(1), 6(1) **am.**, 1984/1290
828	Registration of Title O.	**r.** (wef 1.11.85), 1984/1693
910	Inward Processing Relief Regs.	Sch. 2 **replaced**, 1984/1500
948	Tuberculosis (Amdt.) O.	**r.**, 1984/1943
956	Social Security Benefit (Persons Residing Together) Regs.	reg. 2(2)(*a*) **am.**, 1984/1303
957	Tuberculosis (S.) Amdt. O.	**r.**, 1984/2063
971	Customs Duty Reliefs O.	**r.**, 1984/810
1043	Motor Cars (Driving Instruction) Regs.	reg. 13 **replaced**, 1984/1834
1048	Child Benefit (Determination of Claims and Questions) Amdt. Regs.	**r.**, 1984/451
1074	Dutch Elm Disease (Local Authies.) O.	**r.**, 1984/687
1075	Dutch Elm Disease (Restriction on Movement of Elms) O.	**r.**, 1984/686
1131	Police Cadets (S.) Amdt. Regs.	reg. 5 **r.**, 1984/2029

Year and Number (or date)	Short Title	How affected and Instrument by which affected
1143	Friendly Societies (Life Assurance Premium Relief) Regs.	reg. 3(2) **am.**, Sch. 1, para. 1 **am.**, 1984/323
1144	Industrial Assurance (Life Assurance Premium Relief) Regs.	reg. 3(2) **am.**, Sch. 1, para. 1 **am.**, 1984/322
1173	Sheep Scab O.	arts. 3(1), 13, 14(4) **am.**, 15(3)(*a*)(iii) **am.**, 15(8A)(8B) **inserted**, 16(2)(*a*), 17(3)(*b*), 19(3), 26(1)(*a*) **am.**, Sch., Forms H1, H2 **am.**, M **replaced**, 1984/770
1187	Occupational Pension Schemes (Preservation of Benefit) Amdt. Regs.	**r.**, 1984/614
1188	Contracted-out Employment (Misc. Provns.) Regs.	**r.**, 1984/380
1210	Nat. Savings Bank (Investment Deposits) (Limits) O.	art. 3 **am.**, 1984/640
1229	Mobility Allowance (Vehicle Scheme Beneficiaries) Regs.	reg. 6 heading **replaced**, 6(*b*) **replaced**, 6(*c*) **inserted**, 1984/458
1234	Antarctic Treaty (Contracting Parties) O.	**r.**, 1984/1150
1309	Heavy Goods Vehicles (Drivers' Licences) Regs.	reg. 2(1) **am.**, 4(*b*) **replaced**, 4(*bb*)(*bbb*) **inserted**, 4(*d*), 6 **replaced**, 1984/1925 8 **replaced**, 1984/98 9(5) **inserted**, 10(1)(2) **replaced**, by new para. 10(1), 10(6)(*a*)(i) **r.**, 22(3) **inserted**, 1984/1925 23 **replaced**, 1984/98 29(1) **am.**, 29(1)(*g*)(*h*)(*l*) **replaced**, 29(1)(*o*)(*r*) **am.**, 29(1)(*t*)(2) **replaced**, Sch. 2, Class 1, cols. 2, 3 **am.**, 1A, cols. 2, 3 **am.**, 3, 4 **r.**, 1984/1925
1312	Social Security (Non-Contributory Invalidity Pension) Amdt. Regs.	**r.**, 1984/1303
1332	Weights and Measures Act 1963 (Cocoa and Chocolate Products) O.	**r.**, 1984/1316
1333	Weights and Measures Act 1963 (Sugar) (Amdt.) O.	**r.**, 1984/1316
1335	Weights and Measures Act 1963 (Cheese) O.	**r.**, 1984/1315
1360	Teachers' Supn. (S.) Regs.	reg. 3 **am.**, 4(1)(*f*) **r.**, 4(1)(*g*) **re-lettered** 4(1)(*f*) 8(5), 50(*c*) **am.**, 53(8) **inserted**, 57(1)(2), 84A(1)(2) **am.**, 84A(3) **inserted**, 85 **am.**, Sch. 7, Tables 1, 2, and cols. **am.**, 12, para. 13(*a*)(*b*) **mod.**, 1984/2028
1379	Misuse of Drugs (Designation) O.	Sch., para. 1(*a*) **am.**, 1984/1144
1462	Goods Vehicle Operators (Qualifications) Regs.	**r.** (with saving), 1984/176

Year and Number (or date)	Short Title	How affected and Instrument by which affected
1489	Fertilisers Regs.	reg. 2(3) **inserted**, cross-heading and reg. 11A **inserted**, Sch. 1, table, section A, group 1(a), col. 3, definition of ammonium nitrate **am.**, 1984/1592
1560	Road Vehicles Lighting (Amdt.) Regs.	**r.**, 1984/812
1605	Prevention of Terrorism (Supplemental Temp. Provns.) (Amdt.) (No. 2) O.	**r.** (with saving), 1984/418
1615	Contracted-out Employment (Transitional Arrangements) Regs.	**r.**, 1984/380
1691	Valuation Notice (S.) O.	**r.** (with saving), 1984/1505
1692	Valuation Roll (S.) O.	**r.** (with saving), 1984/1505
1694	Valuation Timetable (S.) O.	**r.** (with saving), 1984/1504
1737	Goods Vehicles (Operators' Licences) Regs.	**r.** (with saving), 1984/176
1774	Race Relations (Prescribed Public Bodies) Regs.	**r.**, 1984/218
1881	Coroners (Amdt.) Rules	**r.** (with saving), 1984/552
2059	Weights and Measures Act 1963 (Bread) O.	**r.**, 1984/1316
1978 32	Diseases of Animals (Approved Disinfectants) O.	art. 6(2) **am.**, 1984/1338 Sch. 1 **replaced**, 1984/55 **am.**, 1984/1338 2 **r.**, 1984/55 new Sch. 2 **inserted**, 1984/1338
105	Antioxidants in Food Regs.	reg. 2(1) **am.**, 1984/1304
186	Arbitration (Foreign Awards) O.	**r.**, 1984/1168
209	Packaging and Labelling of Dangerous Substances Regs.	**r.**, 1984/1244
215	Seed Potatoes Regs.	**r.**, 1984/412
250	Contracted-out Employment (Misc. Provns.) Regs.	**r.**, 1984/380
252	Appeals and Valuation Appeal Ctee. Procedure (S.) Regs.	**r.** (with saving), 1984/1506
257	Agricultural Holdings (Arbitration on Notices) O.	arts. 2(1), 9 **am.**, 9A **inserted**, 11, 14(6) **am.**, 1984/1300
258	Agriculture (Forms of Notices to Remedy) Regs.	**r.**, 1984/1308
259	Agricultural Land Tribunals (Rules) O.	art. 2 **am.**, 1984/1301
415	Redundant Mineworkers and Concessionary Coal (Payments Schemes) O.	Sch.: art. 1, definition of "the Schemes of 1984" **inserted**, 2(1), (2), 6(1)(a)(b), 7(2)(d)(e) **am.**, 7(2)(f) **inserted**, 1984/457
417	Convention Adoption Rules	**r.** (with saving), 1984/265
463	Prepackaging and Labelling of Wine and Grape Must (EEC Requirements) Regs.	**r.**, 1984/1318
492	Antioxidants in Food (S.) Regs.	reg. 2(1) **am.**, 1984/1518
540	Child Benefit (Misc. Amdts.) Regs.	reg. 2 **r.**, 1984/451 3 **r.**, 1984/1960
564	Detergents (Composition) Regs.	reg. 2(1) **replaced**, 3(1)(a) **am.**, 3(2) **replaced**, 3(4) **inserted**, 5(7), 6(1)(a)(2)(b), 10(1) (2) **am.**, 1984/1369
611	Offshore Installations (Fire-fighting Equipment) Regs.	reg. 3 **replaced**, 1984/419

Year and Number (or date)	Short Title	How affected and Instrument by which affected
741	Weights and Measures Act 1963 (Potatoes) O.	r., 1984/1316
795	Merchant Shipping (Crew Accommodation) Regs.	reg. 28(17) **am.**, 1984/41
950	N.H.S. (Dental and Optical Charges) Regs.	regs. 4(1), 6, 7(2), (4) **am.**, Schs. 1, 2 **replaced**, 1984/299
998	Education Authy. Bursaries (S.) Regs.	regs. 4(3)(*c*)(i), (*d*)(i), 8(1)(*c*), **am.**, Sch. A1, para. 1(9) **am.**, 1, para. 1, Table **replaced**, 4(2) **am.**, 4(3) **replaced**, Sch. 2, Pt. 1, para. 1(5) **am.**, 1(6) **replaced**, 1(7)(8) **am.**, 1(10), Table **replaced**, Pt. 2, para. 4(3)(*a*)(*b*) **am.**, 4(4) **replaced**, 6(*a*) **am.**, 6(*b*)(*c*) **replaced**, 1984/990
1005	Medicines (Ctee. on Radiation from Radioactive Medicinal Products) O.	r., 1984/1261
1017	Motor Vehicles (Construction and Use) Regs.	reg. 3(1) **am.**, 1984/813, 1809 4(5A), 5AA **inserted**, 6 **replaced**, 9(1), Table, item No. 6 **am.**, 9(1), Table, item No. 7 **inserted.**, 9(2)(*c*)(6)(*a*)(*b*) **am.**, 9(6)(*c*) **inserted**, 11, proviso **replaced**, 12(*c*) **replaced**, 12(*cc*) **inserted**, 13(3)(*c*) **am.**, 14A(2)(*a*) **replaced**, 14A(2)(*cc*), 17(2)(*c*), 20(*h*), 23(1)(*b*)(2)(*b*) **am.**, 24(2)(*b*) **replaced**, 26(6)(*a*), 28(2), 31A(1)(*a*)(*b*)(iii)(*b*) (*b*)(iii)(*c*), 31C(1), 31D(2)(*c*), 37(2)(3)(*a*) **am.**, 37(3)(*aa*) **r.**, 1984/1809 41 **r.**, 1984/813 42(1)(*a*)(iii)(*b*)(i)(ii) **am.**, 42A **inserted**, 46B(2)(*f*) **am.**, 1984/1809 46B(2)(*j*) **replaced**, 1984/195 46B(2)(*o*) **replaced**, 1984/813 46B(2)(*p*) **am.**, 46B(2)(*q*)(*r*) **inserted**, 1984/195 46B(2)(*r*) **am.**, 1984/1809 46B(4)(*c*) **am.**, 1984/195 46D(2)(*e*) **am.**, 1984/1809 46D(2)(*h*) **replaced**, 46D(2)(*m*)(*n*) **am.**, 1984/195 46D(2)(*o*) **replaced**, 1984/813 46D(2)(*p*) **inserted**, 1984/195 **am.**, 1984/1809 46D(4) **am.**, 46D(5)(*a*)(*c*) **replaced**, 46D(5) **am.**, 46D(7) **inserted**, 1984/195 46E **inserted**, 1984/1543 46E(5)(*j*) **am.**, 1984/1809

Year and Number (or date)	Short Title	How affected and Instrument by which affected
		47(2) **am.**, 1984/195
		51(1) **replaced,**
		51(2A) **r.,**
		52(1) **am.,**
		52(2) **r.,**
		55(1)(1A)(5)(6), 56(1) **am.,**
		56(3) **r.,**
		74(1)(*a*) **am.,**
		74(3) **replaced,**
		75(1) **am.,**
		75(4)(*a*) **replaced,** 1984/1809
		75(4)(*e*)(*f*) **am.,**
		75(4)(*g*) **inserted,** 1984/386
		75(4A) **inserted,**
		75(5) **am.,**
		77(*a*) **replaced,**
		77(*b*) **r.,**
		78(3)(*c*), 79, proviso (*b*)(*c*) **am.,**
		79A−79D and heading **inserted,**
		80 **am.,** 1984/1809
		81 **r.,** 1984/813
		81(4)(*e*), 86(5)(*a*), 87 **am.,**
		92(1) **replaced,**
		94A **inserted,** 1984/1809
		96 **r.,** 1984/331
		96A, 101(1)(*g*)−(*i*) **inserted,** 1984/1809
		105 **r.,** 1984/813,
		105C **inserted,** 1984/1543
		107(3)(*a*)(i)−(v) **replaced** by new (i)-(iv),
		110 (*b*) **replaced,** 1984/1809
		116C **inserted,** 1984/679
		130 **replaced,** 1984/386
		130(1)(*e*)(*v*) **am.,** 1984/679
		131 **r.,** 1984/386
		136(1A), definition of "living van" **replaced,** 1984/331
		136B **inserted,**
		137 **replaced,**
		137A and heading **inserted,**
		138(1)(*b*) **replaced,**
		139(*i*)(*j*) **am.,**
		139(K), 140(12) **inserted,** 1984/1809
		140(6)(*b*), 145(1)(2) **am.,**
		Sch. 5 (Diagram of trailer plate) **r.,**
		8, Pt I, para. 3(*d*)(iii) **am.,** 1984/813
		9, col. 1, item 8 **am.,**
		9A, col. 2, items 8−10 **am.,** 1984/1809
1022	Diseases of Fish O.	**r.,** 1984/301
1081	Weights and Measures Act 1963 (Coffee Extracts and Chicory Extracts) O.	**r.,** 1984/1316
1089	Contracting-out and Preservation (Further Provns.) Regs.	**r.,** 1984/614
1260	Road Vehicles (Rear Fog Lamps) Regs.	**r.,** 1984/812
1261	Road Vehicles Lighting (Amdt.) Regs.	**r.,** 1984/812
1262	Road Vehicles (Use of Lights during Daytime) (Amdt.) Regs.	**r.,** 1984/812
1273	Slaughterhouse Hygiene (S.) Regs.	reg. 36(6)(*b*) **am.,** 1984/842
1340	Social Security (Non-Contributory Invalidity Pension) Amdt. Regs.	**r.,** 1984/1303
1354	Cosmetic Products Regs.	**r.,** 1984/1260

Year and Number (or date)	Short Title	How affected and Instrument by which affected
1461	Medicines (Exemption from Licences) (Importation) O.	**r.**, 1984/673
1518	Adoption (County Ct.) (Amdt.) Rules	**r.** (with saving), 1984/265
1519	Adoption (High Ct.) (Amdt.) Rules	**r.** (with saving), 1984/265
1546	Detergents (Composition) (Amdt.) Regs.	**r.**, 1984/1369
1599	Exchange Control (Authorised Dealers and Depositaries) O.	**r.**, 1984/1459
1689	Social Security (Categorisation of Earners) Regs.	Sch. 1, Pt. I col. (A), para. 4(*a*) **r.**, (B), para. 4 **replaced,** Pt. III col. (B), para. 12(*b*) **am.**, 3, col. (A), para. 6(*a*) **r.**, 1984/350
1698	Social Security Benefit (Computation of Earnings) Regs.	reg. 1(2) **am.**, 1984/1303, 1697
1827	Contracted-out Employment (Misc. Provns.) (No. 2) Regs.	regs. 2, 4 **r.**, 1984/380
1837	Parliamentary Pensions (Purchase of Added Years) O.	art. 3, "definitions" **am.**, 4(1)(i) **replaced,** 7(7) **inserted,** 9(1), 10(1) **am.**, 10(1B)(1C) **inserted,** 10(3)(4) **replaced,** 11 **r.**, 13–15 **inserted,** Sch. **replaced,** 1984/1907
1845	Social Security (Non-Contributory Invalidity Pension) Amdt. (No. 2) Regs.	**r.**, 1984/1303
1893	International Lead and Zinc Study Group (Immunities and Privileges) O.	art. 14(*d*) **inserted,** 1984/1982
1903	European Assembly Constituencies (E.) O.	Sch. **replaced,** 1984/544
1904	European Assembly Constituencies (W.) O.	Sch. **replaced,** 1984/545
1911	European Assembly Constituencies (S.) O.	Sch. **replaced,** 1984/548
1942	Exchange Control (Authorised Dealers and Depositaries) (Amdt.) (No. 2) O.	**r.**, 1984/1459
1979		
45	Medicines (Exemptions from Restrictions on the Retail Sale or Supply of Veterinary Drugs) O.	**r.**, 1984/1861
168	Prevention of Terrorism (Supplemental Temp. Provns.) (N.I.) (Amdt.) O.	**r.** (with saving), 1984/417
169	Prevention of Terrorism (Supplemental Temp. Provns.) (Amdt.) O.	**r.** (with saving), 1984/418
218	Misuse of Drugs (Licence Fees) Regs.	reg. 3(1)(*a*) to (*e*) **am.**, 1984/165
220	European Assembly Elections (Returning Officers) (E. and W.) O.	**r.**, 1984/571
290	Social Security (Reciprocal Agreements) O.	Sch. **am.**, 1984/125
304	Arbitation (Foreign Awards) O.	**r.**, 1984/1168
321	Exchange Control (Authorised Dealers and Depositaries) (Amdt.) O.	**r.**, 1984/1459
322	European Assembly Elections (N.I.) Regs.	**r.**, 1984/198
323	Grants for Guarantees of Bank Loans (Ext. of Period) O.	**spent**
338	European Assembly Elections Regs.	**r.**, 1984/137

Year and Number (or date)	Short Title	How affected and Instrument by which affected
342	Employment Agencies Act 1973 (Exemption) Regs.	r., 1984/978
349	European Assembly Elections (Returning Officers) (S.) O.	r., 1984/623
427	Petroleum (Consolidation) Act 1928 (Enforcement) Regs.	mod., 1984/1244
432	Vaccine Damage Payments Regs.	reg. 7(1) **replaced**, 1984/442
588	European Assembly Elections (Returning Officers' Expenses) Regs.	r., 1984/723
589	European Assembly Elections (Returning Officers' Expenses) (N.I.) Regs.	r., 1984/724
591	Social Security (Contributions) Regs.	reg. 3(1) **am.**, 3(1)(*a*)(2) **replaced**, 3(2A) **inserted**, 3(4), 4 **replaced**, 5(*a*)(*b*), 6(1) **am.**, 6(3) **replaced**, 6(4)(5) **inserted**, 1984/77 7 **am.**, 1984/1756 12(1)(2) **am.**, 15 **replaced**, 19(*b*) **am.**, 19(*f*) **r.**, 27(3)(*b*), 28(2)(*b*) **am.**, 28(2)(*c*) **r.**, 32(1)(3), 35(1)(*b*) **am.**, 35(1A) **inserted**, 38(1A) **inserted**, 38(2)–(5) **am.**, 54(1) **replaced**, 72 **am.**, 1984/77 98(*c*) **am.**, 1984/146 Sch. 1, reg. 13 **am.**, 25 **inserted**, 32(5) **am.**, 1984/77
597	Social Security (Overlapping Benefits) Regs.	regs. 4(2)(*d*), 12, 14(2) **am.**, Sch. 1, para. 4 **am.**, 1984/1303
628	Social Security (Claims and Payments) Regs.	reg. 9(6)(7) **inserted**, 10, 11(1)(*a*)(5)(7)–(9), 15(1)(*h*) **am.**, 1984/1303 15(3) **replaced**, 1984/1699 16(6) **replaced**, 21 **am.**, 1984/550 Sch. 1, paras. 3, 4 **am.**, 1984/1303 5(*c*)(*d*), col. 1 **am.**, 1984/1699 10, 11 **am.**, 1984/550 2, paras. 2, 2A **am.**, 1984/1303 3(1)(2) **am.**, **am.**, 1984/1699 3 **am.**, 1984/1303
638	Dutch Elm Disease (Local Authies.) (Amdt.) O.	r., 1984/687
639	Dutch Elm Disease (Restriction on Movement of Elms) (Amdt.) O.	r., 1984/686
642	Social Security (Widow's Benefit and Retirement Pensions) Regs.	reg. 10(*a*) **replaced**, 1984/1704 17(1)(*f*) **am.**, 1984/1303
705	N.H.S. (Dental and Optical Charges) (S.) Regs.	regs. 6(1)(*a*)(i)(ii)(*b*), 8(*a*)(*b*), 9(2)(4) **am.**, Schs. 1, 2 **replaced**, 1984/293
740	Exchange Control (Authorised Dealers and Depositaries) (Amdt.) (No. 2) O.	r., 1984/1459

Year and Number (or date)	Short Title	How affected and Instrument by which affected
752	Preservatives in Food Regs.	reg. 2(1) **am.**, 4(1)(i) **inserted**, Sch. 2 **am.**, 1984/1304
785	Local Govt. (Compensation for Premature Retirement) (S.) Regs.	reg. 3 **am.**, 3A **inserted**, 6 **replaced**, 9(2), 11(3)(4) **am.**, 12, 13 **replaced**, 14(3), 15(4), 16(4) **am.**, Sch. 2, Pt. III **inserted**, 3 **replaced**, 4, Pt. II, para. 6(2)(*b*) **am.**, 1984/846
803	Road Vehicles Lighting (Amdt.) Regs.	**r.**, 1984/812
837	Assisted Areas O.	**r.** (with saving), 1984/1844
841	Wireless Telegraphy (Broadcast Licence Charges and Exemption) (Amdt.) Regs.	**r.**, 1984/1053
930	Air Navigation (Noise Certification) O.	**r.**, 1984/368
937	Industrial and Provident Societies (Credit Unions) Regs.	Sch. 2 **replaced**, 1984/308
978	Adoption (County Ct.) (Amdt.) Rules	**r.** (with saving), 1984/265
991	Police (Promotion) Regs.	reg. 7 **am.**, 9–11 **replaced**, 1984/1214
1005	Oil and Fibre Plant Seeds Regs.	reg. 3(3) **am.**, 1984/199 Sch. 2, Pt. I, para, 8 **replaced**, 1984/1873
1008	Medicines (Exemptions from Restrictions on the Retail Sale or Supply of Veterinary Drugs) (Amdt.) O.	**r.**, 1984/1861
1073	Preservatives in Food (S.) Regs.	reg. 2(1) **am.**, 4(1)(i) **inserted**, Sch. 2 **am.**, 1984/1518
1086	British Museum (Authorised Repositories) O.	**r.**, 1984/1181
1092	Motor Vehicles (Type Approval) (G.B.) Regs.	**r.**, 1984/981
1145	Road Vehicles (Rear Fog Lamps) (Amdt.) Regs.	**r.**, 1984/812
1163	Social Security (Determination of Claims and Questions) Amdt. Regs.	**r.**, 1984/451
1194	Exchange Control (Authorised Dealers and Depositaries) (Amdt.) (No. 3) O.	**r.**, 1984/1459
1198	Motor Vehicles (Authorisation of Special Types) Gen. O.	arts. 3(1), 7, 7(*b*)(*c*) **am.**, 8 **r.**, 13 **replaced**, 13A–13C **inserted**, 14 **r.**, Sch. 4, 5 **inserted**, 1984/1810
1222	Magistrates' Cts. (Adoption) (Amdt.) Rules	**r.** (with saving), 1984/611
1314	Recovery of Maintenance (U.S.A.) O.	Sch. **am.**, 1984/1824
1338	Exchange Control (Authorised Dealers and Depositaries) (Amdt.) (No. 4) O.	**r.**, 1984/1459
1388	Savings Certificates (Amdt.) Regs.	**r.**, 1984/1052
1426	Imported Food (Amdt.) Regs.	**r.**, 1984/1918
1427	Imported Food (N.I.) (Amdt.) Regs.	**r.**, 1984/1917
1470	Police Regs.	reg. 16(2) **am.**, Sch. 3, para. 1, Table, **am.**, 1984/1590 5, Tables A, B **replaced**, 11, para. 1(1)(*a*)(*b*) **am.**, 1984/1808

Year and Number (or date)	Short Title	How affected and Instrument by which affected
1613	Weights and Measures (Packaged Goods) Regs.	reg. 3 **replaced**, 26(4A) **r.**, Sch. 1, Pts. I, III **replaced**, 3, Pt. I, para. 1(A)(B)(*a*) **replaced**, 1(B)(*b*)(i)–(iii)(*c*) **r.**, 1984/1317
1644	N.H.S. (Vocational Training) Regs.	reg. 5(5)(*a*)(i) **am.**, 1984/215
1684	Social Security (Attendance Allowance) Amdt. (No. 2) Regs.	regs. 4, 5 **r.**, 1984/451
1715	Copyright (International Conventions) O.	Schs. 1, 2 **am.**, 1984/549 3–5 **am.**, 1984/549, 1987 6 **am.**, 1984/549
1726	Pneumoconiosis etc. (Workers' Compensation) (Payment of Claims) Regs.	regs. 5(1), 6(1), 8 **am.**, Sch. **replaced**, 1984/1972
1727	Police Cadets Regs.	reg. 18(1)(2) **replaced** by new reg. 18(1) Sch. 2, Table **replaced**, 3, para. 2 **replaced**, 1984/1633
1732	Goods Vehicles (Operators' Licences) (Fees) Regs.	**r.** (with saving), 1984/176
1741	Employment Agencies Act 1973 (Exemption) (No. 2) Regs.	reg. 2(1)(*a*)(*b*), (2)(*a*) **r.**, Sch. **r.**, 1984/978
1746	Passenger and Goods Vehicles (Recording Equipment) Regs.	reg. 2(2)–(4) **r.**, 4 **replaced**, 1984/144
1748	Hill Livestock (Compensatory Allowances) Regs.	**r.**, 1984/2024
1752	Weights and Measures Act 1963 (Milk) O.	**r.**, 1984/1316
1980		
12	Importation of Embryos, Ova and Semen O.	art. 4(2) **replaced**, 5A **inserted**, 6(1)(3)–(5) **am.**, 1984/1326
15	Child Benefit (Determination of Claims and Questions) Amdt. Regs.	**r.**, 1984/451
30	N.H.S. (Vocational Training) (S.) Regs.	reg. 5(5)(*a*)(i) **am.**, 1984/1258
52	Consumer Credit (Exempt Agreements) O.	art. 5 **replaced**, 1984/434 6(*b*) **replaced**, to be **r.** (wef 1.1.85), 1984/917 Sch., Pts. I, II **am.**, 1984/434
54	Consumer Credit (Advertisements) Regs.	reg. 2(1) **am.**, 2(4)(5) **r.**, 8(1)(*a*) **am.**, 8(2) **r.**, Sch. 3, para. 4(1) **am.**, 4(2) **r.**, 1984/1055
55	Consumer Credit (Quotations) Regs.	reg. 3(2)(3) **r.**, Sch. 3, para. 3(1) **am.**, 3(2) **r.**, 1984/1055
70	Commrs. for Oaths (Fees) O.	**r.** (with saving), 1984/481
76	Public Service Vehicles and Trolley Vehicles (Carrying Capacity) (Amdt.) Regs.	**r.**, 1984/1406
116	Road Vehicles Lighting (Amdt.) Regs.	**r.**, 1984/812
222	Motor Vehicles (Type Approval) (G.B.) (Fees) Regs.	**r.**, 1984/1404
223	Motor Vehicles (Type Approval and Approval Marks) (Fees) Regs.	**r.**, 1984/1404

Year and Number (or date)	Short Title	How affected and Instrument by which affected
283	Medicines (Exemptions from Restrictions on the Retail Sale or Supply of Veterinary Drugs) (Amdt.) O.	**r.**, 1984/1861
330	Seeds (Nat. Lists of Varieties) (Fees) Regs.	Sch. **replaced**, 1984/243
335	Sea Fishing (Specified Western Waters) (Restrictions on Landing) O.	art. 4(b) **am.**, Sch. 2 **am.**, 1984/192
351	Plant Breeders' Rights (Fees) Regs.	Sch. **replaced**, 1984/242
369	N.H.S. (Dental and Optical Charges) (S.) Amdt. Regs.	**r.**, 1984/293
377	Social Security (Industrial Injuries) (Prescribed Diseases) Regs.	regs. 1(2), (7)(1)(b)(4), 8(1), 9(1)(2)(a)–(c) **am.**, 1984/458 22–33 **r.**, 1984/451 38, 39(1), 46 **am.**, 1984/458 49 **r.**, 1984/451 51, 53(2) **am.**, 1984/458 56(2) **replaced**, Sch. 1, Pt. I, col. 2, entry B8 **am.**, 1984/1659 2, **mod.**, 1984/451 3, col. 2, entry B8 **am.**, 1984/1659
420	Import and Export (Plant Health) (G.B.) O.	art. 5 (f) **inserted**, 17 **re-numbered** 17(1), 17(2), 21 **inserted**, 1984/839 Sch. 2, Pt. IB, col. 3, para. (7) **inserted**, VIIB, col. 3, para. (3) **inserted**, 1984/306
442	V.A.T. (Cars) O.	arts. 2, 4 **am.**, 1984/33
449	Import and Export of Trees, Wood and Bark (Health) (G.B.) O.	art. 21(1)(c) **am.**, 1984/688 Sch. 3, 2nd col., entry 3 **replaced**, 8 **r.**, 4, entry 1 **replaced**, 7 **r.**, 5, Pt. II, entry 2 **replaced**, 4 **r.**, III, entry 2 **am.**, 3 **replaced**, 5 **r.**, 6, entry 3 **r.**, 1984/1892
450	Tree Pests (G.B.) O.	art. 10(4) **am.**, 1984/688
509	Deeds of Arrangement Fees O.	**r.** (with saving), 1984/887
529	Merchant Shipping (Radio Installations) Regs.	reg. 1(2) **am.**, 13 **replaced**, 1984/1223 18(3), 26(4) **am.**, 1984/346, 1223 Sch. 4 **inserted**, 1984/346
530	Merchant Shipping (Navigational Equipment) Regs.	regs. 2(4), 8, 10, 12, 20(1), 22(1) **am.**, 23(2)(3), 24 **r.**, 1984/1203
535	Merchant Shipping (Passenger Ship Construction) Regs.	reg. 1(3)(a)(b) **replaced**, 3(1) **am.**, 1984/1220
538	Merchant Shipping (Life-Saving Appliances) Regs.	reg. 1(2) **am.**, 1984/97
544	Merchant Shipping (Fire Appliances) Regs.	regs. 1(3)(a), 39(3) **am.**, 64A, 73(5) **inserted**, 1984/1221
557	Coroners (Amdt.) Rules	**r.** (with saving), 1984/552
637	Goods Vehicles (Operators' Licences) (Temp. Use in G.B.) Regs.	reg. 13(2) **replaced**, 13(3)–(5) **r.**, 32(2) **replaced**, 1984/1835 Sch. 5, Pt. II **replaced**, 1984/179

Year and Number (or date)	Short Title	How affected and Instrument by which affected
668	Coroners (Amdt.) (Savings) Rules	r. (with saving), 1984/552
766	Motorcycles (Sound Level Measurement Certificates) (Fees) Regs.	r., 1984/1404
798	Wireless Telegraphy (Broadcast Licence Charges and Exemption) (Amdt.) Regs.	r., 1984/1053
804	Notification of Accidents and Dangerous Occurrences Regs.	Sch. 2 **mod.**, 1984/1114
879	Motor Vehicles (Type Approval) (G.B.) (Amdt.) Regs.	r., 1984/981
899	Fodder Plant Seeds Regs.	Sch. 2, Pt. I, para. 7 **replaced**, 1984/1872
901	Seeds (Fees) (Regs.)	Schs. 1–6 **replaced**, 1984/910
979	Anti-Competitive Practices (Exclusions) O.	Sch. 1, para. 4(1)(2) **am.**, 4(3) **replaced**, 1984/1919
984	Supplementary Benefit (Transitional) Regs.	reg. 3(3) **replaced**, 4(2) **am.**, 1984/458
1036	Agriculture (Tractor Cabs) (Amdt.) Regs.	r., 1984/605
1058	Measuring Instrts. (EEC Requirements) Regs.	reg. 2(1) **am.**, 4A **inserted**, 7(5) **am.**, 8 **r.**, 9(2) **replaced**, 10 **am.**, 11(2)(*cc*) **inserted**, 11(2)(*d*), 13(2)(*b*), 15 **am.**, 15(*c*) **inserted**, 15(i) **am.**, 20A–20C **inserted**, Sch. 3, paras. 1(*d*), 2(3)(*a*) **am.**, 5, para. 1(*a*) **am.**, 1(*aa*)(*bb*) **inserted**, 1(*d*) **am.**, 4A **inserted**, 1984/1618
1072	Agriculture and Horticulture Grant Scheme	para. 2(1) **am.**, 1984/619 3(1)(*a*) **replaced**, 1984/1923 5(3A) **am.**, 1984/619 6(1) **am.**, 1984/619, 1923 6(1A) **inserted**, 1984/619 7(1) **am.**, 1984/1923 9(1)(*a*)(*b*) **am.**, 1984/619, 1923 9(1)(6A) **inserted**, 1984/619 9(1)(6A)(ii) **am.**, 1984/1923 9(2) **am.**, 1984/619 Sch. **replaced**, 1984/1923
1100	Petroleum (Consolidation) Act 1928 (Conveyance by Road Regulations Exemptions) Regs.	**mod.**, 1948/1244
1136	Social Security (Attendance Allowance) Amdt. Regs.	reg. 5 **r.**, 1984/451
1165	Motor Vehicles (Type Approval) (G.B.) (Amdt.) (No. 2) Regs.	r., 1984/981
1182	Motor Vehicles (Type Approval) Regs.	Sch. 2, Pt. I, item 1, col. 2 **am.**, 2, col. 2 **am.**, 7, col. 2(a) **am.**, 18, col. 2(a) **am.**, 20, col. 2 **am.**, 38, col, 2(a) **am.**, 1984/1927
1221	N.H.S. (Dental and Optical Charges) (S.) Regulations Amdt. (No. 2) Regs.	r., 1984/293

Year and Number (or date)	Short Title	How affected and Instrument by which affected
1227	Merchant Shipping (U.K. Fishing Vessels: Manning) Regs.	r., 1984/1115
1233	Mines and Quarries (Fees for Approvals) Regs.	Schs. 1, 2 **replaced**, 1984/310
1254	Teachers' (Compensation for Premature Retirement) (S.) Regs.	reg. 3 **am.**, 3A **inserted**, 6 **replaced**, 9(2), 10(3) **am.**, 12 **replaced**, 13(4), 14(4), 15(4) **am.**, Sch. 1, Pt. III **inserted**, 2 **replaced**, 1984/845
1298	Agriculture and Horticulture Devpt. Regs.	reg. 2(1) **am.**, 5(3)(*b*)(ii) **replaced**, 5(3B) **inserted**, 1984/618 7(1)(*a*) **replaced**, 1984/1922 8(1)(*a*) **am.**, 8(1)(aA) **inserted**, 8(1)(*c*)(2), 16 **am.**, 1984/618 Sch., para. 1 **am.**, 1984/618, 1922 2 **am.**, 1984/618 7, 8, 10 **am.**, 12 **replaced**, footnote **inserted**, 1984/1922
1321	Social Security Commrs. (Appeals to the Cts.) Regs.	r., 1984/451
1336	Prevention of Terrorism (Supplemental Temp. Provns.) (Amdt.) O.	r. (with saving), 1984/418
1339	Secure Tenancies (Notices) Regs.	Sch.— Pt. I, notes to form, para. 2 **am.**, II, notes to form, para. 3 **am.**, 1984/1224
1388	Right to Purchase (Application Form) (S.) O.	r., 1984/1005
1391	Housing (Right to Buy) (Prescribed Forms) (No. 1) Regs.	r., 1984/1175
1437	Family Income Supplements (General) Regs.	reg. 1(2), definitions of "Appeal Tribunal" and "supplement officer" **r.**, 1(2), definition of "determining authority" **replaced**, 1984/458 3(2)(*a*)−(*d*) **substituted**, 3(5) **r.**, 1984/979 11−13 **r.**, 1984/451
1459	Road Transport (International Passenger Services) Regs.	r., 1984/748
1499	Land Registration (District Registries) O.	r., 1984/1579
1503	N.H.S. (Charges for Drugs and Appliances) Regs.	regs. 3(1)(*b*)(4), 4(1)(*b*), **am.**, 5(1)(*a*) **replaced**, 5(1)(*b*), 9(5) **am.**, Sch. 1 **am.**, 2 **replaced**, 2A **inserted**, 1984/298
1514	Merchant Shipping Act 1979 (Hong Kong) O.	art. 2 **am.**, Sch. **am.**, 1984/356
1536	V.A.T. (General) Regs.	reg. 2 **am.**, 23−25 **replaced**, 25A **inserted**, 26, 29 **replaced**, 1984/155 30(14) **replaced**, 32(*c*) **inserted**, 33 **replaced**, 34−36 **r.**, 37(8), 39A **inserted**, 55(1)(*d*) **replaced**, 1984/929

Year and Number (or date)	Short Title	How affected and Instrument by which affected
1561	Social Security (Determination of Claims and Questions) Amdt. Regs.	r., 1984/451
1614	Savings Certificates (Amdt.) (No. 2) Regs.	reg. (2)(*b*)(i) r., 1984/1052
1622	Social Security (Determination of Claims and Questions) Misc. Amdts. Regs.	r., 1984/451
1640	Child Benefit (Determination of Claims and Questions) Amdt. (No. 2) Regs.	r., 1984/451
1641	Supplementary Benefit (Trade Disputes and Recovery from Earnings) Regs.	reg. 3(2) **am.**, 3A **inserted**, 1984/938 18 **am.**, 1984/458
1643	Supplementary Benefit (Determination of Questions) Regs.	reg. 1(2) **am.**, 1984/458 2–5A **r.**, 1984/451 5B(1)(*c*)(ii) **am.**, 1984/938 6(1), 7(1)(*b*)(i)(*c*) **am.**, 1984/458 7A(4) **replaced**, 1984/938
1650	Medicines (Exemptions from Restrictions on the Retail Sale or Supply of Veterinary Drugs) (Amdt.) (No. 2) O.	r., 1984/1861
1668	Increase of Rent Restriction (Housing Assocn.) (S.) O.	art. 3(1)(*b*), (3) **am.**, 1984/501
1674	N.H.S. (Charges for Drugs and Appliances) (S.) Regs.	regs. 3(1)(*b*), (4), 4(1)(*b*) **am.**, 5(1)(*a*) **replaced**, 5(1)(*b*), 9(5) **am.**, Sch. 1 **replaced**, 1A **inserted**, 2 **replaced**, 1984/292
1697	Rent Act 1977 (Forms etc.) Regs.	regs, 6, 9 **am.**, Sch. 1, forms 5–10, 12, 13 **replaced**, 1984/1391
1743	Education (Assisted Places) Regs.	regs. 2(3), 5(1)(*b*) **am.**, 5(2)(3) **replaced** by (2), 15(1) **am.**, 15, Table **replaced**, 21 **am.**, 24 **replaced**, Sch. paras, 3(i), 5 **replaced**, 1984/147
1779	General Medical Council (Registration (Fees) Regulations) O. of C.	r. (with saving), 1984/62
1784	Companies (Unregistered Companies) (Amdt.) Regs.	r., 1984/682
1787	Goods Vehicle Operators (Qualifications) (Amdt.) Regs.	r. (with saving), 1984/176
1788	Goods Haulage Operators' (Certificates of Qualification) Regs.	r. (with saving), 1984/176
1794	Designs (Amdt. No. 2) Rules	r., 1984/1989
1833	Emulsifiers and Stabilisers in Food Regs.	reg. 2(1) **am.**, 1984/1304 Sch. 2, Pt. II am., 1984/649, 1304
1834	Misc. Additives in Food Regs.	reg. 2(1) **am.**, Sch. 1, Pts. I, II **am.**, 2, **am.**, 1984/1304
1849	Food Labelling Regs.	r., 1984/1305
1855	Road Vehicles Lighting (Amdt.) (No. 2) Regs.	r., 1984/812
1888	Emulsifiers and Stabilisers in Food (S.) Regs.	reg. 2(1) **am.**, 1984/1518 Sch. 2, Pt. II **am.**, 1984/847, 1518
1889	Misc. Additives in Food (S.) Regs.	reg. 2(1) **am.**, Sch. 1, Pts. I, II **am.**, 2 **am.**, 1984/1518

Year and Number (or date)	Short Title	How affected and Instrument by which affected
1898	Legal Advice and Assistance Regs. (No. 2)	reg. 3 **am.**, 1984/241 17(3)(c) **r.**, 1984/637 17(3)(d) **inserted**, 1984/241 20 **am.**, 1984/637 Sch. 3 **am.**, 1984/1715
1922	Medicines (General Sale List) O.	**r.**, 1984/769
1965	Air Navigation O.	art. 93, para. 1, definition "Foreign country" **inserted**, 1984/1988
1990	Butter Subsidy (Protection of Community Arrangements) Regs.	**r.**, 1984/1739
2007	Bankruptcy Fees O.	**r.** (with saving), 1984/880
2008	Companies (Dept. of Trade) Fees O.	**r.** (with saving), 1984/881
2028	Hill Livestock (Compensatory Allowances) (Amdt.) Regs.	**r.**, 1984/2024
1981		
1	Gaming (Small Charges) (Amdt.) O.	**r.**, 1984/246
2	Gaming Act (Variation of Monetary Limits) O.	Sch. **am.**, 1984/247
19	Control of Harbour Devpt. (Amdt.) O.	**r.**, 1984/522
55	N.H.S. (Vocational Training) (S.) Amdt. Regs.	**r.**, 1984/1258
58	Gaming Act (Variation of Monetary Limits) (S.) O.	Sch. **am.**, 1984/468
59	Gaming (Small Charges) (S.) Amdt. O.	**r.**(S.), 1984/469
69	Landlord and Tenant Act 1954 (Appropriate Multiplier) Regs.	**r.**, 1984/1932
71	Designs (Amdt.) Rules	**r.**, 1984/1989
86	Police (Promotion) (S.) Amdt. Regs.	**r.**, 1984/648
121	Trade Descriptions (Origin Marking) (Misc. Goods) O.	arts. 1(2), 2(2) **am.**, 4(4)(c) **r.**, 1984/91
129	Contracting-out and Preservation (Further Provns.) Regs.	regs. 2, 3, 5 **r.**, 1984/380 6 **r.**, 1984/614
137	Food Labelling (S.) Regs.	**r.**, 1984/1519
174	Education (Assisted Places) (Incidental Expenses) Regs.	reg. 2(1) **replaced**, 3(2) **am.**, 3(3)–(5) **replaced** by (3), (4), 4 **replaced**, 5(2), 6(2) **am.**, 1984/148
202	Motor Vehicles (Variation of Speed Limits) (No. 2) Regs.	**r.**, 1984/325
257	Public Service Vehicles (Conditions of Fitness, Equipment, Use and Certification) Regs.	reg. 46 **replaced**, 50(a)–(c) **am.**, 1984/1763
260	Public Service Vehicles and Trolley Vehicles (Carrying Capacity) (Amdt.) Regs.	**r.**, 1984/1406
359	N.H.S. (Dental and Optical Charges and Remission of Charges) (S.) Regs.	regs. 1–6, 8, 10 **r.**, 1984/293
362	Civil Aviation (Navigation Services Charges) Regs.	regs. 2(1), Table, 4(3) **replaced**, 5, 6(1) **am.**, 1984/641
461	Road Transport (International Passenger Services) (Amdt.) Regs.	**r.**, 1984/748
552	Magistrates' Cts. Rules	rule 86(2) **replaced**, 87 **am.**, 110 **inserted**, 1984/1552
553	Magistrates' Cts. (Forms) Rules	Sch. 2, form 35 **replaced**, 35A–35D **inserted**, 36, 42 **replaced**, 97A **inserted**, 1984/1542

Year and Number (or date)	Short Title	How affected and Instrument by which affected
572	Merchant Shipping (Cargo Ship Construction and Survey) Regs.	reg. 1(3)(*a*)(4)(*b*)(*c*)(5) **am.**, 1(6A)(9) **inserted**, 34(1) **am.**, 38(2), 41A−41E **inserted**, 71(1), 72(1)(3), 74(3) **am.**, 74A, 74D, 75 **inserted**, 75(1), 76(1) **am.**, Sch. 2 **inserted**, 1984/1219
670	Savings Certificates (Amdt.) (No. 3) Regs.	**r.**, 1984/1052
675	N.H.S. (Charges for Drugs and Appliances) (S.) Amdt. Regs.	**r.**, 1984/292
696	Motor Vehicles (Type Approval) (G.B.) (Amdt.) Regs.	**r.**, 1984/981
722	Housing Assocn. Grant (Disposal of Dwellings) O.	**r.**, 1984/1803
727	Rampton Hospital Review Bd. (Establishment and Constitution) O.	arts. 1(2), 2 **am.**, 1984/692
728	Rampton Hospital Review Bd. (Functions and Membership) Regs.	regs. 2, 3(*d*), 4(2)(*a*) **am.**, 6, 8 **replaced**, 1984/693
781	Housing Act 1964 (Appropriate Multiplier) Regs.	**r.**, 1984/1629
786	Education (Grants) (Music and Ballet Schools) Regs.	reg. 3(1) **am.**, 5(3) **am.**, Sch. 1, para. 12(2) **am.**, 12, table **replaced**, 13(2)(3), 14(2) **am.**, 15(3) **r.**, 15(4)(5) **replaced**, 16, 17(1)(2) **am.**, 17A **inserted**, 19(1) **am.**, appx., para. 3 **am.**, appx., para 5 **replaced**, 2, para. 8 **replaced**, 1984/113
792	Packaging and Labelling of Dangerous Substances (Amdt.) Regs.	**r.**, 1984/1244
793	Medicines (Exemptions from Restrictions on the Retail Sale or Supply of Veterinary Drugs) (Amdt.) O.	**r.**, 1984/1861
815	Supplementary Benefit (Misc. Amdts.) Regs.	reg. 10(2)−(5) **r.**, 1984/451
829	Town and Country Planning (Devpt. by Planning Authies.) (S.) Regs.	reg. 4, para. 2(*c*) **inserted**, 4, para (3) **replaced**, 5(1)(*b*) **am.**, 1984/238
830	Town and Country Planning (General Devpt.) (S.) O.	art. 2(1) **am.**, 5 **r.**, 7, 10(3) **replaced**, 1984/237 10(6), 16(2)(4) **am.**, 1984/237 **applied with mods.** (Crown land applications), 1984/996 Sch. 2 **replaced**, 3, Pt. IV **replaced**, V, VI **inserted**, 1984/237
859	Traffic Signs Regulations and General Directions	reg. 3(2)(iia) **inserted**, 3(2)(iii) **am.**, 3(2)(iv) **inserted**, 7(1)(*a*) **am.**, 7(1)(*d*) **r.**, 7(1)(*e*) **replaced**,

Year and Number (or date)	Short Title	How affected and Instrument by which affected
		7(2)(*b*) **am.**, 7(2)(*e*) **r.**, 7(2)(*f*) **replaced**, 9(*b*) **am.**, 10 **r.**, 11 **replaced**, 15(3) **am.**, Sch. 1, Pt. II **am.**, direction 34(1)(*c*) **am.**, 1984/966
882	Wireless Telegraphy (Broadcast Licence Charges and Exemption) (Amdt.) Regs.	**r.**, 1984/1053
932	Nursing Homes and Mental Nursing Homes Regs.	reg. 2(1) **am.**, 6(3) **replaced**, 10A **inserted**, 1984/958
952	Motor Vehicles (Driving Licences) Regs.	reg. 4(1)(*h*) **inserted**, 5A, 6(*b*), 7 **replaced**, 1984/274 20, para. (4) **am.**, 1984/737
1026	Butter Subsidy (Protection of Community Arrangements) (Amdt.) Regs.	**r.**, 1984/1739

1034	Fresh Meat Export (Hygiene and Inspection) (S.) Regs.	reg. 2(1) **am.**,
		3 **replaced**,
		4(1)(*a*)(i)(ii)(8) **am.**,
		6(1) **replaced**,
		10(1)(1)(*g*)(2)(i) **am.**,
		10(3) **replaced**,
		10(4) **inserted**,
		11 **am.**,
		11(2) **inserted**,
		18 **am.**,
		Sch. 1, para 2(*a*) **replaced**,
		        2(*b*) **am.**,
		        2(*c*) **replaced**,
		        2(*j*)–(*s*) **inserted**,
		        3 **am.**,
		2, Pt. I, para. 1(*c*)(*f*)(*h*)(*i*)
		        am.,
		        1(1)–(*r*)
		        inserted,
		        2 **am.**,
		   II, paras. (*a*)(*b*)(*j*) **am.**,
		3, para. (*b*) **replaced**,
		        (*d*) **am.**,
		        (*g*)–(*q*) **inserted**,
		        2 **inserted**,
		5, Pt. I, para. 7 **inserted**,
		   II, para. 1(*c*) **am.**,
		   III, para. 1(*e*)(*f*)
		        inserted,
		        3(*e*)
		        inserted,
		6, para. 1 **am.**,
		        3(*d*) **inserted**,
		        4(*b*) **am.**,
		        4(*c*) **inserted**,
		        5(*b*) **am.**,
		7, para. (*c*)(i)–(iii) **am.**,
		        (*d*)(*f*) **replaced**,
		        (*h*)(*i*) **am.**,
		        (*k*)–(*m*) **inserted**,

Year and Number (or date)	Short Title	How affected and Instrument by which affected
		8, Pt. I, para. 2(*a*)(*b*) **am.**, 3 **replaced**, Annex. para. 6 **am.**, II, para. 1(*c*)(i) **am.**, 2(*d*) **replaced**, III, para. 1(*b*) **replaced**, 1(*c*)(*g*)(*i*)–(*k*) **am.**, IV, para. 1(*b*) **replaced**, 1(*c*)(*f*)(*g*)(*i*) **am.**, (*j*) **replaced**, 9, paras. (1)(*d*)(*f*) **am.**, (*j*)–(*l*) **inserted**, 11, paras. 2(*a*), 3–6 **am.**, 12, heading **am.**, Pt. I, paras. 1, 2 **am.**, 5, 6 **inserted**, II, para. 3, 3(*a*) **am.**, 13, para. 3(*a*) **am.**, 14, **replaced**, 15, paras. 1, 3, 5, 6, 8 **am.**, 1984/1885
1042	Road Vehicles Lighting (Amdt.) Regs.	**r.**, 1984/812
1059	Dangerous Substances (Conveyance by Road in Road Tankers and Tank Containers) Regs.	reg. 2(1) **am.**, 1984/1244
1084	Imported Food (N.I.) (Amdt.) Regs.	**r.**, 1984/1917
1085	Imported Food (Amdt.) Regs.	**r.**, 1984/1918
1302	Ancient Monuments (Class Consents) O.	Sch., Class VI **inserted**, 1984/222
1329	Motor Vehicles (Type Approval and Approval Marks) (Fees) (Amdt.) Regs.	**r.**, 1984/1404
1330	Motor Vehicles (Type Approval) (G.B.) (Fees) (Amdt.) Regs.	**r.**, 1984/1404
1372	Motor Vehicles (Variation of Speed Limits and Speed Limits on Motorways) (Metrication) Regs.	**r.**, 1984/325
1373	Road Traffic Acts 1960 and 1972, Road Traffic Regulation Act 1967 and Transport Act 1968 (Metrication) Regs.	Sch., Pt. IIIA **am.**, 1984/177
1472	Merchant Shipping (Passenger Ship Classification) Regs.	reg. 2(1) **r.**, 1984/1220
1482	Savings Certificates (Amdt.) (No. 6) Regs.	**r.**, 1984/1052
1487	Census of Production O.	art. 5(*b*)–(*d*) **excl.**, 1984/1762
1524	Supplementary Benefit (Aggregation) Regs.	reg. 1(2) **am.**, 1A(1)(*b*)(xiiiA) **inserted**, 2, 3(5)(*b*) **replaced**, 3(5)(*d*)(*e*) **am.**, 1984/938
1525	Supplementary Benefit (Claims and Payments) Regs.	reg. 2(1) **am.**, 1984/458 5(2)(*a*) **am.**, 5(2)(*bb*), 5B **inserted**, 1984/938 6(2), 8(*a*)(i), 17(2B) **am.**, 1984/458 23A(1)(3), 29(1)(2)(2)(*b*)(i) **am.**, 29(3) **replaced**, 29(3A) **inserted**, 1984/938

Year and Number (or date)	Short Title	How affected and Instrument by which affected
1526	Supplementary Benefit (Conditions of Entitlement) Regs.	regs. 2(1), 7(5)(*b*), 8(1)(*d*) **am.**, 1984/938 9(1)(*b*) **am.**, 9(3)(*c*) **inserted**, 1984/518 10(1) **am.**, 10(1)(*a*) **replaced**, 10(1)(*b*)(2)(9)(ii) **am.**, 11 **replaced**, 1984/938 12(2A) **inserted**, 12(3)(*a*)(*b*) **am.**, 1984/458
1527	Supplementary Benefit (Resources) Regs.	reg. 2 **am.**, 3(2)(*h*) **inserted**, 4(7)(9)(9)(*a*)(*b*), 6(1)(*k*), 9(1)(*a*)(2)(*d*), 10(3)(*d*)(iv)(5), 11 (2)(*k*) **am.**, 11(2)(*r*) **inserted**, 11(5)(*d*) **am.**, 11(5)(*d*)(i)(ii) **replaced** by new (i)–(iii), 12(1)(*a*)(*b*), 13(3) **am.**, 13(3A) **inserted**, 13(5) **replaced**, 1984/1102
1528	Supplementary Benefit (Single Payments) Regs.	reg. 2(1) **am.**, 8(3)(*a*), 9(i) **replaced**, 10(1)(*a*), (*a*)(i) **am.**, 13(2)(*a*), 21, 22(1)(*a*) **replaced**, 22(1)(1), 23(4) **inserted**, 25(1) **am.**, 25(1)(*a*) **replaced**, 25(1)(*aa*) **inserted**, 25(1)(*b*)(iii) **replaced**, 25(8) **inserted**, 27(1)(*a*) **am.**, Schs. 1, 2 **am.**, 1984/938, 1103
1529	Supplementary Benefit (Urgent Cases) Regs.	reg. 21(1), (1)(*a*) **am.**, 21(1)(*d*)–(*h*), (2)(*d*) **inserted**, Sch. 2, para. (1)(*a*), col.(1) **am.**, 1984/938
1534	Motor Vehicles (Type Approval) (G.B.) (Fees) (Amdt.) (No. 2) Regs.	r., 1984/1404
1535	Motor Vehicles (Type Approval and Approval Marks) (Fees) (Amdt.) (No. 2) Regs.	r., 1984/1404
1596	Building Standards (S.) Regs.	reg. A5(1) **am.**, J3(1), proviso **replaced**, R3, Table, col. (1) **am.**, R4(1), proviso **am.**, R7 **replaced**, R9(1)(*a*) **am.**, R9(1)(*b*) **replaced**, R10, proviso **replaced**, T1–T3 **inserted**, Sch. 2, Table 1, cols. (1)(4) **am.**, 13, Pt. II entry for reg. R7 **inserted**, Pt. T **inserted**, Arrangement of regulations— reg. R7 **am.**, Pt. T **inserted**, Indexes 2, 3 **am.**, 1984/1660

Year and Number (or date)	Short Title	How affected and Instrument by which affected
1619	Motor Vehicles (Type Approval) (G.B.) (Amdt.) (No. 2) Regs.	r., 1984/981
1641	Export of Goods (Control) O.	art. 2(ix) **am.**, 1984/694 2(x) **inserted**, 1984/553 Sch. 1, Pt. 2 **am.**, 1984/90 553, 694, 819
1642	Bankruptcy Fees (Amdt.) O.	r. (with saving), 1984/880
1643	Companies (Dept. of Trade) Fees (Amdt.) O.	r. (with saving), 1984/881
1653	Marine Fish Farming (Financial Assistance) Scheme	r., 1984/341
1687	County Ct. Rules	O. 1, rule 6(*d*) **am.**, 22, rule 12(2) **replaced**, 23, rule 2(1) **am.**, 23, rule 3 **replaced**, 32, rule 3(1)(*a*)–(*c*) **replaced**, by rule 3(1)(*a*)–(*f*), 32, rule 3(2) **replaced**, 32, rule 3(3) **r.**, 1984/878 38, rules 13(2), 14(1) **am.**, Appx. A, entries in last 3 columns **am.**, B: Pt. I, para. 4, Tables of Fixed Costs **replaced**, Fixed Costs **replaced**, II, Table **replaced**, III: item 7, paras. (*a*)(*b*) **replaced**, amounts to be allowed **replaced**, C, para. 2, Table **replaced**, 1984/576
1694	Motor Vehicles (Tests) Regs.	reg. 3(1) **am.**, 1984/815 5(1)(3) **am.**, 1984/1126 20(1) **am.**, 1984/401, 727 20(4) **am.**, 1984/401 20(5) **replaced**, 20(5A)(5B)(7)(*c*)(ia) **inserted**, 1984/1126 20(7)(*c*)(iii)(iv) **replaced**, 1984/815 20(8) **inserted**, 1984/1126 23(2) **am.**, 1984/401 Sch. 2, item 1, col. (2)(*b*) **replaced**, 2, col. (2)(*b*) **replaced**, 3, col. (2)(*b*) **replaced**, 12, col. (2)(*b*)(*c*)(*e*) **replaced**, 3, Pt. I, paras. 1(*b*), 2(1) **replaced**, II, para. 3(*b*) **am.**, III, para. 4(*b*) **am.**, 1984/815
1706	Wireless Telegraphy (Broadcast Licence Charges and Exemption) (Amdt.) (No. 2) Regs.	r., 1984/1053
1707	Farm and Horticulture Devpt. Regs.	reg. 2(1) **am.**, 1984/620 3(1)(*a*) **replaced**, 1984/1924 11(1)(*a*) **replaced**, 11A **inserted**, 12(2)(*a*) **am.**, 12(2)((*a*A) **inserted**, 12(2)(*c*)(7), 18 **am.**, 1984/620

Year and Number (or date)	Short Title	How affected and Instrument by which affected
		Sch. 2, para. 1 **am.**, 1984/620, 1924
		7, 9, 12, 14 **am.**, 1984/1924
		20, 21 **am.**, 1984/620
		footnote **inserted**, 1984/1924
1736	General Betting Duty Regs. (N.I.)	r., 1984/1551
1741	V.A.T. (Special Provns.) O.	art. 8 **replaced**, 1984/736
1765	Fishing Vessels (Acquisition and Improvement) (Grants) Scheme	para. 7(1)(a) **am.**, 1984/1879
1769	Customs Duties (ECSC) O.	art. 2 **am.**, 1984/1969
		6(1) **am.**, 1984/1306, 1452
		Sch. 1, Pt. II **am.**, 1984/1969
1770	Local Govt. (Supplementary Grants for Transport Purposes Specified Descriptions) (W.) O.	r., 1984/1863
1772	Child Benefit (Claims and Payments) Amdt. Regs.	r., 1984/1960
1780	Weights and Measures Act 1963 (Dried Fruit and Vegetables) (Amdt.) O.	r., 1984/1316
1781	Weights and Measures Act 1963 (Grain and Farinaceous Products) O.	r., 1984/1316
1782	Weights and Measures Act 1963 (Coffee and Coffee Mixtures) O.	r., 1984/1316
1817	Mobility Allowance (Amdt.) Regs.	reg. 3 **mod.**, 1984/451
1837	N.H.S. (Determination of Districts) O.	art. 6(1) **am.**, 1984/281
		Sch. 1, Pt. I **am.**, 1984/328
1842	Magistrates' Cts. (Adoption) (Amdt.) Rules	r. (with saving), 1984/611
1843	Hill Livestock (Compensatory Allowances) (Amdt.) Regs.	r., 1984/2024
1854	Milk Prices (E. and W. and N.I.) O.	art. 3(5) **inserted**,
		Schs. 1, 2 **replaced**, 1984/666
		3, table **replaced**, 1984/142
1872	Medicines (Exemptions from Restrictions on the Retail Sale or Supply of Veterinary Drugs) (Amdt.) (No. 2) O.	r., 1984/1861
1982		
3	Adoption (High Ct.) (Amdt.) Rules	r. (with saving), 1984/265
4	Adoption (County Ct.) (Amdt.) Rules	r. (with saving), 1984/265
8	Motor Vehicles (Type Approval) (G.B.) (Amdt.) Regs.	r., 1984/981
26	Medicines (General Sale List) Amdt. O.	r., 1984/769
34	Adoption Agencies (S.) Regs.	r., 1984/988
38	Social Security (Determination of Claims and Questions) Amdt. Regs.	r., 1984/451
39	Child Benefit (Determination of Claims and Questions) Amdt. Regs.	r., 1984/451
75	N.H.S. (Mod. of Enactments and Consequential Provns.) O.	art. 4 **am.**, 1984/168
83	Amusements with Prizes (Variation of Monetary Limits) O.	r., 1984/245
85	Gaming Act (Variation of Monetary Limits) O.	r., 1984/247
131	Gaming Act (Variation of Monetary Limits) (S.) O.	r., 1984/468
132	Amusements with Prizes (Variation of Monetary Limits) (S.) O.	r., 1984/465
166	Bingo Duty (Exemptions) O.	r., 1984/431
176	Deep Sea Mining (Reciprocating Countries) (French Republic) O.	r., 1984/1170

Year and Number (or date)	Short Title	How affected and Instrument by which affected
177	Deep Sea Mining (Reciprocating Countries) (Federal Republic of Germany) O.	r., 1984/1170
178	Deep Sea Mining (Reciprocating Countries) (U.S.A.) O.	r., 1984/1170

194	Rate Support Grant (S.) O.	art. 2, table **replaced**, 1984/102
		   5 **am.**,
		Sch. 3, para. 3(*a*)(*b*) **am.**,
		   4, para. 2 **am.**,
		   5, para. 2(*a*)(*b*) **am.**, 1984/1686

226	Goods Vehicles (Operators' Licences) (Amdt.) Regs.	r. (with savings), 1984/176
249	Social Security (Industrial Injuries) (Prescribed Diseases) Amdt. Regs.	regs. 2(5)–(7)(10), 4 **r.**, 1984/451
276	N.H.S. (Appointment of Consultants) Regs.	reg. 2(1) **am.**, Sch. 2, para. 3 **am.**, 4, para. 12 **am.**, 1984/994

287	N.H.S. Functions (Directions to Authies. and Admin. Arrangements) Regs.	reg. 3, 3(*a*) **am.**,
		   3(*d*) **replaced**,
		   4(6) **am.**, 1984/1577

314	Authies. for London Post-Graduate Teaching Hospitals (Establishment and Constitution) O.	Sch. 1 **am.**, 1984/190
315	Authies. for London Post-Graduate Teaching Hospitals Regs.	reg. 5(5) **r.**, 1984/994
318	Local Govt. (Direct Labour Organisations) (Competition) (S.)	r., 1984/159
322	Ct. of Protection Rules	r., 1984/2035
332	N.H.S. (Charges for Drugs and Appliances) (S.) Amdt. Regs.	r., 1984/292
430	Motor Vehicles (Rear Markings) Regs.	r., 1984/812
488	Savings Certificates (Amdt.) Regs.	reg. 2(*c*) **r.**, 1984/1052
541	Bankruptcy Fees (Amdt.) O.	r. (with saving), 1984/880
542	Companies (Dept. of Trade) Fees (Amdt.) O.	r. (with saving), 1984/881
555	Town and Country Planning (Structure and Local Plans) Regs.	reg. 1 **replaced**, 1984/6
566	Social Security (Industrial Injuries) (Prescribed Diseases) Amdt. (No. 2) Regs.	reg. 2 **r.**, 1984/451
586	County Ct. (Forms) Rules	Form N14 **am.**, certificates of service in Forms N37, N38, N55, N88, N88(1), N89 **replaced**, Sch, Forms N9, N10(HP), N56, N92 **replaced**, 1984/879
622	Legal Advice and Assistance (S.) Amdt. Regs.	r., 1984/210
638	Motor Vehicles (Type Approval for Goods Vehicles) (G.B.) (Fees) Regs.	r., 1984/1404
652	A.S. (Fees for Sheriff Ct.)	r., 1984/233
717	Patents Rules	Sch. 1 **replaced**, 1984/283

719	Public Lending Right Scheme 1982 (Commencement) O.	Appx:—
		   arts. 4, 5, (1), 6(2) **replaced**,
		   6(3) **r.**,
		   9(1)(3)(*b*) **replaced**,
		   9A **inserted**,
		   13 **am.**,
		   17(1)(*c*) **replaced**,
		   17A **inserted**,
		   18, 38(2) **replaced**,

Year and Number (or date)	Short Title	How affected and Instrument by which affected
		42(3) **am.**, 45, 52 **r.**, 46(1)(*a*) **am.**, Sch. 1, Pt. I, paras. 5–7 **replaced**, 8 **inserted**, 3 **r.**, 5 **inserted**, 1984/1847
770	N.H.S. (Vocational Training) (S.) Amdt. Regs.	**r.**, 1984/1258
805	Motorcycles (Sound Level Measurement Certificates) (Fees) (Amdt.) Regs.	**r.**, 1984/1404
809	Employment Agencies Act 1973 (Exemption) Regs.	**r.**, 1984/978
828	Registered Housing Assocns. (Accounting Requirements) O.	arts. 1(2), 2(1)–(3) **am.**, 1984/1833 **mod.** for application to qualifying housing assocns., 1984/1833
859	Bankruptcy Fees (Amdt. No. 2) O.	**r.** (with saving), 1984/880
860	Companies (Dept. of Trade) Fees (Amdt. No. 2) O.	**r.** (with saving), 1984/881
863	N.H.S. (Charges to Overseas Visitors) (No. 2) Regs.	reg. 1(2), definition of "Continental Shelf" **inserted**, 4(*a*) **am.**, Schs. 2, 3 **replaced**, 1984/300
876	Merchant Shipping (Safety Officials and Reporting of Accidents and Dangerous Occurrences) Regs.	regs. 10, 11(2) **am.**, 12 **replaced**, 1984/93
894	Statutory Sick Pay (General) Regs.	regs. 6(1), 7(1)(*a*) **am.**, 1984/385
898	N.H.S. (Charges to Overseas Visitors) (S.) Regs.	regs. 1(2), definition of "Continental Shelf" **inserted**, 4(*a*) **am.**, Schs. 2, 3 **replaced**, 1984/295
914	Supplementary Benefit (Housing Benefits) (Misc. Consequential Amdts.) Regs.	reg. 3(2)(3) **r.**, 1984/451
938	Parochial Fees O.	Sch., Pt. I **replaced**, 1984/1042
939	Legal Officers' Fees O.	Sch., Table II **replaced**, 1984/1041
949	Education (Assisted Places) (S.) Regs.	regs. 2(4), 14(2), 16(5)(*a*)(*b*) **am.**, 17 **replaced**, 18(2) **r.**, 18(3)(4), 19(2), 20(2)(*b*) **am.**, 30 **replaced**, Sch. 1 **am.**, 2 **replaced**, 1984/840
1000	Petroleum (Production) Regs.	regs. 5(1), 9(1), 11(1)(2) **am.**, Sch. 3, Pt. VI **am.**, 1984/397 partially **r.**, 1984/1832
1004	British Citizenship (Designated Service) O.	Sch., paras. 8–11 **inserted**, 1984/1766
1009	Local Govt. (Compensation for Premature Retirement) Regs.	reg. 3 **am.**, 3A **inserted**, 4(1) **am.**, 4(2) **replaced**, 5(*a*) **am.**, 6(3A)–(3C) **inserted**, Sch. 3, para. 2 **am.**, 5 **inserted**, 1984/740
1011	British Nationality (Fees) Regs.	**r.** (with saving), 1984/230
1013	Savings Certificates (Amdt.) (No. 2) Regs.	**r.**, 1984/1052
1016	Assured Tenancies (Approved Bodies) (No. 3) O.	Sch., **am.**, 1984/1443

Year and Number (or date)	Short Title	How affected and Instrument by which affected
1018	Meat (Sterilisation and Staining) Regs.	reg. 3(1) **am.**, 5A, 12(1)(*e*), 15A **inserted**, 17(1), (1)(*a*) **am.**, 17(1)(*c*) **replaced**, 17(1)(*e*), (3) **am.**, 17(3)(*d*) **inserted**, 18(1), 19(1), 20(1)(*d*) **am.**, 20(1)(*e*) **inserted**, 20(2)(*a*)(*b*)(*c*)(3)(*b*) **am.**, 20(3)(*c*) **inserted**, 20(4) **r.**, 25(1) **am.**, 1984/604
1019	Medicines (Exemptions from Restrictions on the Retail Sale or Supply of Veterinary Drugs) (Amdt.) O.	**r.**, 1984/1861
1032	Occupational Pension Schemes (Connected Employers) Regs.	**r.**, 1984/380
1043	Butter Subsidy (Protection of Community Arrangements) (Amdt.) Regs.	**r.**, 1984/1739
1079	N.I. Assembly (Pay and Allowances) O. Crown Ct. Rules	**r.**, 1984/1823
1109	Crown Ct. Rules	rule 7(2)(*d*) **am.**, 8 (*bb*) **inserted**, 9(3) **replaced**, 11(2)(*d*) **am.**, 1984/699 16 **am.**, 1984/340

1124	Housing Benefits Regs.	reg. 2(1) **am.**, 1984/104, 110, 1965
		2(5) **am.**,
		2(6) **replaced**, 1984/104
		6(1) **am.**, 1984/940
		6(2) **replaced**, 1984/1965
		7(1) **am.**, 1984/940
		7(3) **replaced**, 1984/104
		8(1) **am.**, 1984/940
		8(3) **replaced**, 1984/104
		   am., 1984/1965
		8A(2) **r.**,
		9(3A) **am.**,
		9(6) **replaced**, 1984/104
		11(1) **am.**,
		11(3) **inserted**, 1984/1965
		11A **inserted**, 1984/940
		12A **inserted**, 1984/104
		13(1)–(3) **am.**, 1984/1105
		15(2)(3) **am.**,
		15(6)(8) **r.**, 1984/104
		16(2) **am.**, 1984/104.941
		16(3A) **inserted**, 1984/940
		16(4A) **inserted**,
		16(5) **am.**, 1984/104
		16(5A) **inserted**, 1984/110
		16(6)(8)(10) **r.**,
		17(1) **am.**,
		17(4) **inserted**, 1984/104
		18(1)(2) **am.**, 1984/103, 940, 941
		18(3A) **inserted**, 1984/1965
		18(4) **am.**,
		18(5A)(5B) **inserted**, 1984/104
		18(6A) **am.**, 1984/103, 940
		18(6B) **inserted**,
		18(6c) **inserted**, 1984/940 **am.**,
		   1984/1728

Year and Number (or date)	Short Title	How affected and Instrument by which affected
		18(7), 19(1)(4) **am.**, 1984/104
		18A **inserted**, 1984/940
		19(5) **am.**, 1984/103, 104, 940
		19(6) **am.**,
		19(6A) **inserted**, 1984/104
		20(1) **replaced**,
		20(1A) **inserted**, 1984/940
		21(1) **am.**,
		21(1A) **inserted**,
		21(4)–(6) **r.**, 1984/104
		22 **r.**, 1984/110
		23 **replaced**, 1984/1965
		25(3A), 26A **inserted**, 1984/104
		26B **inserted**, 1984/110
		28(1) **am.**, 1984/104
		28(2)(*cc*) **inserted**,
		28A **r.**, 1984/940
		30, 31 **am.**,
		32A **inserted**,
		33 **am.**,
		37 **replaced**,
		39(1)(2) **am.**,
		39(3) **inserted**,
		41 **replaced**,
		42 **am.**,
		47(4), 49(1A), 50A **inserted**, 1984/104
		Sch. 1, Pts. I, II **am.**, 1984/940
		2, para. 4(*a*)(*b*) **am.**, 1984/941
		7A **inserted**,
		10, 12 **am.**, 1984/104
		14 **am.**, 1984/104, 941
		15 **am.**, 1984/104
		16 **am.**, 1984/104, 941
		18 **am.**, 1984/104
		3, para. 3(*a*)(*b*)(*d*) **am.**, 1984/941
		4A **r.**,
		5 **replaced**, 1984/104
		11(*a*)(i)(ii) **am.**, 1984/941
1143	Feeding Stuffs Regs.	reg. 2(1) **am.**,
		6 **replaced**,
		7(*a*) **am.**,
		7A **inserted**,
		8, 14(1) **am.**,
		16A **inserted**,
		19 **replaced**,
		Schs. 1–5 **am.**,
		6, 7 **inserted**, 1984/51
1144	Feeding Stuffs (Sampling and Analysis) Regs.	Sch. 1, Pt. II, para. 8 **am.**,
		2, method 4, para. 6 **am.**,
		7, para. 1 **am.**, 1984/52
1155	Parliamentary Pensions (Purchase of Added Years) (Amdt.) O.	**r.**, 1984/1907
1163	Motorways Traffic (E. and W.) Regs.	reg. 3(1)(*b*) **am.**, 1984/1479
1197	Legal Aid in Criminal Proceedings (Costs) Regs.	reg. 2 **am.**, 1984/112
		5(3) **am.**, 1984/264
		6(4)–(6) **inserted**, 1984/112
		8(2)(*a*) **am.**, 1984/264
		9A **inserted**, 1984/112
		11 **am.**, 1984/340
		Sch. 1, para. 1 **replaced**,
		2, tables 1, 2 **replaced**, 1984/264

Year and Number (or date)	Short Title	How affected and Instrument by which affected
1242	Child Benefit (Claims and Payments) Amdt. Regs.	reg. 2 **r.**, 1984/1960 3 **r.**, 1984/451 4 **r.**, 1984/1960
1271	Motor Vehicles (Type Approval for Goods Vehicles) (G.B.) Regs.	reg. 3(1)(*a*)(ii) **am.**, 3(2)(*e*) **replaced,** 3(2)(*ee*) **inserted,** 3(2)(*h*), 4(1)(*b*)(ii) **am.**, 11 **replaced,** Sch. 1, item 2 **replaced**, 1984/697 4B **replaced** by 4B(1)(2), 4C **replaced** by 4C(1)(2), 4D **replaced** by 4D(1)(2), 1984/1402 6A, 6B, 6D **am.**, 1984/697
1289	Adoption Agencies (S.) (Amdt.) Regs.	**r.**, 1984/988
1391	Income Tax (Sub-contractors in the Construction Industry) Regs.	Sch. 2, para. 8 of forms of guarantee **replaced**, 1984/2008
1408	Social Security (General Benefit) Regs.	reg. 2(2) **am.**, 1984/1303 9(1) **am.**, 1984/458 9(6) **am.**, 9(6A) **inserted**, 1984/1259 16 **am.**, 1984/1703 41(4) **am.**, 1984/458
1432	A.S. (Applications under the Matrimonial Homes (Family Protection) (S.) Act 1981)	rule 9, **inserted**, 1984/255
1457	Restriction on Movement of Spruce Wood O.	art. 6(1) **am.**, 1984/688
1478	Goods Vehicles (Plating and Testing) Regs.	regs. 12(3), 16(1)(2) **am.**, 1984/402 16(3)(*c*)(i)(ii) **replaced**, 1984/816 32, 40(1) **am.**, 1984/402 Sch. 2, para. 20 **replaced,** 20A **inserted**, 1984/178 31 **replaced**, 1984/1024 3, paras. 2–5 **replaced** by new para. 2 6 **re-numbered** 3 and **am.**, 1984/816
1489	Workmen's Compensation (Supplementation) Scheme	art. 5(2) **am.**, 1984/1118 12 **am.**, 1984/452 Sch. 1 **replaced**, 1984/1118 2 **am.**, 1984/452
1496	Notification of New Substances Regs.	reg. 4(1)(*c*)(ii) **am.**, Sch. 3, note **replaced**, 1984/1244
1521	Prevention of Terrorism (Supplemental Temp. Provns.) (Amdt.) O.	**r.** (with saving), 1984/418
1528	Social Security (Reciprocal Agreements) O.	Schs. 1, 2 **am.**, 1984/125
1574	Savings Certificates (Amdt.) (No. 4) Regs.	**r.**, 1984/1052
1590	Distributors of Iron and Steel Products (ECSC Requirements) Regs.	reg. 2(1)(ii) **replaced,** 3(1)(3), 4(1)(*b*) **am.**, 1984/1270 4(2) **am.**, 1984/219 7(1) **am.**, 7(1), new (*a*) **inserted,** 7(1)(*a*)(*b*) **re-lettered** (*b*)(*c*), 9(1)(*b*)(2), 10 **am.**, 1984/1270
1602	Poultry Meat (Water Content) Regs.	**r.**, 1984/1145
1606	Offshore Installations (Safety Zones) O.	Sch. 1, entry 3 **r.**, 1984/1901 21 **r.**, 1984/1352 56 **r.**, 1984/1900

Year and Number (or date)	Short Title	How affected and Instrument by which affected
1725	Butter Subsidy (Protection of Community Arrangements) (Amdt.) (No. 2) Regs.	**r.**, 1984/1739
1732	Social Security and Pensions (Forfeiture Act 1982) (Consequential) Regs.	**r.**, 1984/451
1784	Civil Aviation (Joint Financing) Regs.	reg. 4(1) **am.**, 1984/1916
1785	Bankruptcy Fees (Amdt.) (No. 3) O.	**r.** (with saving), 1984/880
1788	Employment Subsidies Act 1978 (Renewal) (G.B.) O.	(expired, 30-6-84)
1805	Medicines (Exemptions from Restrictions on the Retail Sale or Supply of Veterinary Drugs) (Amdt.) (No. 2) O.	**r.**, 1984/1861
1808	Deposit Protection Fund (Excluded Institutions) O.	Sch. **am.**, 1984/897
1817	British Steel Corporation (Reduction of Capital) O.	art. 3 **r.**, 1984/1110
1868	Unfair Dismissal (Increase of Compensation Limit) (No. 2) O.	**r.** (with saving), 1984/2020
1886	Hill Livestock (Compensatory Allowances) (Amdt.) Regs.	**r.**, 1984/2024
1895	Grants by Local Authies. (Repairs Grants for Airey Houses) (Eligible Expense Limits) O.	**r.** (with savings and mod. of art. 3), 1984/1700
1897	Rate Support Grant (S.) (No. 2) O.	art. 2, table **replaced**, 4(2)(*c*) **inserted**, 1984/102 5 **am.**, Sch. 3, para. 3(*a*)(*b*) **am.**, 4, para. 2 **am.**, 5, para. 2(*a*)(*b*) **am.**, 1984/1686
1983 4	Grants by Local Authies. (Repairs Grants for Airey Houses) O.	**r.** (with saving), 1984/1718
5	Gaming Clubs (Hours and Charges) (Amdt.) Regs.	**r.**, 1984/248
17	Packaging and Labelling of Dangerous Substances (Amdt.) Regs.	**r.**, 1984/1244
80	Gaming Clubs (Hours and Charges) (S.) Amdt. Regs.	**r.** (S.), 1984/470
95	Grants by Local Authies. (Appropriate Percentage and Exchequer Contribution) (Repairs Grants for Airey Houses) O.	**r.** (with savings and **mod.** of art. 4) 1984/1880
104	Child Benefit (Interim Payments) Regs.	definition of "determining authority" **replaced**, 1948/458
127	Gaming Act (Variation of Fees) O.	art. 2 **r.**, Sch. **r.**, 1984/166
136	Pneumoconiosis, Byssinosis and Misc. Diseases Benefit Scheme	art. 12 **am.**, Sch. 3 **am.**, 1984/453
14⊦	Greenwich Hospital School (Regulations) (Amdt.) O.	generally **am.**, 1984/123
180	Patents (Amdt.) Rules	rules 2, 3 **r.**, 1984/283
181	Trade Marks (Amdt.) Rules	**r.**, 1984/459
185	Social Security (Industrial Injuries) (Prescribed Diseases) Amdt. Regs.	reg. 2(2) **mod.**, 2(11)(19) **r.**, 1984/451
186	Social Security (Abolition of Injury Benefit) (Consequential) Regs.	reg. 6 **r.**, 1984/451
201	Civic Govt. (S.) Act 1982 (Commencement) O.	**spent**
202	Local Authies. Licensing and Regulation of Particular Activities (Transitional Provns.) (S.) O.	art. 3 **am.**, 4, 5 **inserted**, 1984/775

Year and Number (or date)	Short Title	How affected and Instrument by which affected
256	Sea Fishing (Enforcement of Community Conservation Measures) O.	art. 2, definition of "the Council Regulation" **replaced**, 4(*a*), 5(*a*), 7(6)(*a*) **am.**, Sch. items 5, 8, 14, col. 3 **am.**, items 11–13 **replaced**, item 13A **inserted**, 1984/1956
257	Sea Fishing (Enforcement of Misc. Community Quota Measures) O.	**r.**, 1984/173
261	Block Grant (Education Adjustments) (E.) Regs.	reg. 3(1) **am.**, 1984/224
274	Medicines (Exemptions from Restrictions on the Retail Sale or Supply of Veterinary Drugs) (Amdt.) O.	**r.**, 1984/1861
296	Local Govt. (Prescribed Expenditure) Regs.	Sch. 1, paras. 2, 5 **am.**, 2, para. 1 **replaced**, 3, para. 6 **replaced**, 1984/223
310	Block Grant (Education Adjustments) (W.) Regs.	reg. 3(1) **am.**, 1984/284
328	Motor Vehicles (Type Approval) (G.B.) (Amdt.) Regs.	**r.**, 1984/981
333	Gaming Act (Variation of Fees) O.	art. 2 **r.**, Sch. **r.**, 1984/338
335	N.H.S. (Dental and Optical Charges and Remission of Charges) (S.) Amdt. Regs.	regs. 1–6, 8 **r.**, 1984/293
338	Contracted-out Employment (Misc. Provns.) Regs.	**r.**, 1984/380
350	Industrial and Provident Societies (Amdt. of Fees) Regs.	**r.**, 1984/307
351	Friendly Societies (Fees) Regs.	**r.**, 1984/309
352	Industrial and Provident Societies (Credit Unions) (Amdt. of Fees) Regs.	**r.**, 1984/308
368	Income Tax (Interest Relief) (Housing Assocns.) Regs.	regs. 3, 5(*a*)(2)(*c*) **am.**, 1984/1653
372	Building Societies (Fees) Regs.	**r.**, 1984/279
373	Industrial Assurance (Fees) Regs.	**r.**, 1984/280
380	Contracted-out Employment (State Scheme Premiums) Regs.	**r.**, 1984/380
382	Restrictive Trade Practices (Approval of Standards and Arrangements) O.	Sch., para. 1 **replaced**, 1984/1269
431	Education (Grants for Teacher Training) Regs.	**r.**, 1984/446
435	Representation of the People Regs.	Certain provns. **applied**, some with **mods.** (E., S. and W.) 1984/137 Sch. 3, Forms D, M, N, O, P, Q, R, T, U **am.**, 1984/137
436	Representation of the People (N.I.) Regs.	Certain provns. **applied**, some with **mods.** 1984/198 Sch. 3, Forms A, B, E, F, G, K, L, N, O **am.**, 1984/198
443	Public Trustee (Fees) O.	art. 17(5) **replaced**, 1984/390
480	Public Lending Right Scheme 1982 (Amdt.) O.	**r.**, 1984/1847
481	Education (Teacher Training Awards) Regs.	reg. 7(1)(*a*)(i)(*b*)(*c*) **am.**, Sch. 2, para. 4 **am.**, 3, para. 3 **am.**, 1984/893
484	Mines and Quarries (Fees for Approvals) (Amdt.) Regs.	**r.**, 1984/310
499	V.A.T. (Health) O.	**r.**, 1984/746

Year and Number (or date)	Short Title	How affected and Instrument by which affected

506	Redundant Mineworkers and Concessionary Coal (Payments Schemes) O.	Sch:—
		art. 5(2) **am.**, 1984/1889
		  10(2)(*d*)(*e*) **am.**,
		  10(2)(*f*) **inserted**, 1984/457
		    am.,
		  10(2)(*g*) **inserted**,
		  10(5)(*a*)(*b*) **am.**,
		  10(6) **inserted**, 1984/1889

536	Motor Vehicles (Type Approval) (G.B.) (Fees) (Amdt.) Regs.	**r.**, 1984/1404
537	Motor Vehicles (Type Approval and Approval Marks) (Fees) (Amdt.) Regs.	**r.**, 1984/1404
544	Seed Potatoes (Fees) (S.) Regs.	Sch., para. 1(*a*)-(*c*) **am.**, 1984/661
548	Representation of the People (S.) Regs.	Certain provns. **applied**, some with **mods.**, Sch. 3, Forms D, M, N, O, P, Q, R, T, U **am.**, 1984/137
574	Local Govt. (Allowances) (Amdt.) Regs.	**r.**, 1984/698
579	Local Authies. (Allowances) (S.) Amdt. Regs.	**r.**, 1984/691
582	Merchant Shipping (Sterling Equivalents) (Various Enactments) (No. 2) O.	**r.**, 1984/1548
586	Prevention of Fraud (Investments) Act Fees Regs.	**r.**, 1984/738
593	Carriage by Air (Sterling Equivalents) (No. 2) O.	**r.**, 1984/1582
669	Offshore Installations (Safety Zones) (No. 13) O.	**r.**, 1984/1297
684	Gas (Meters) Regs.	reg. 5(2)(*b*)(3) **am.**, Sch. 1, col. 2 **am.**, 1984/1785

686	Personal Injuries (Civilians) Scheme	art. 2(7)(*e*)-(*g*) **replaced**,
		  2(8) **r.**,
		  2(10) **am.**,
		  2(21A) (21B) **inserted**,
		  12(2) (Table) (3) **am.**,
		  12(4) **r.**, 1984/1289
		  16 **am.**, 1984/1675
		  18(2) **am.**,
		  18(5)(*a*) **r.**,
		  18(5)(*b*) **replaced**,
		  18(5)(*c*), 23(3) **am.**,
		  25B **inserted**,
		  28, 28(1)(2)(3)(*a*)(i)(ii) **am.**,
		  29 **replaced**,
		  30 **am.**,
		  37 **replaced**,
		  38 **am.**,
		  48A, 48B **inserted**,
		  50 **replaced**,
		  57(1) **am.**,
		  71(1) **replaced**,
		  75(3), 76(3)(*aa*) **inserted**,
		  77(1)(*b*) **am.**,
		Schs. 3, 4 **replaced**, 1984/1289

687	Slaughter of Poultry (Humane Conditions) (Amdt.) Regs.	**r.**, 1984/2056
688	Slaughter of Animals (Prevention of Cruelty) (Amdt.) Regs.	**r.**, 1984/1311
689	Slaughter of Pigs (Anaesthesia) (Amdt.) Regs.	**r.**, 1984/1310
707	Seed Potatoes (Fees) Regs.	**r.**, 1984/445
713	Civil Cts. O.	Schs. 1, 3, 4 **am.**, 1984/297, 1075

Year and Number (or date)	Short Title	How affected and Instrument by which affected
714	Health and Safety (Fees for Medical Examinations) Regs.	**r.**, 1984/569
722	Contracting-out (Mod.) Regs.	**r.**, 1984/380
735	Returning Officers' Expenses (E. and W.) Regs.	**r.**, 1984/720
736	Returning Officers' Expenses (S.) Regs.	**r.**, 1984/721
737	Returning Officers' Expenses (N.I.) Regs.	**r.**, 1984/722
745	Land Registration (S.) Act 1979 (Commencement No. 3) O.	**spent**
762	Merchant Shipping (Distress Signals and Prevention of Collisions) (Overseas Territories) O.	Sch. 1 **am.**, 2 reg. 1(5)(*b*), footnote (*b*) **am.**, 1984/1688
774	Companies (Dept. of Trade) Fees (Amdt.) O.	**r.** (with saving), 1984/881
775	Bankruptcy Fees (Amdt.) O.	**r.** (with saving), 1984/880
814	Offshore Installations (Safety Zones) (No. 15) O.	**r.**, 1984/184
879	Transfer of Functions (Arts, Libraries and Nat. Heritage) O.	arts. 8, 9, 10(2) **r.**, 1984/1814
883	Naval, Military and Air Forces etc. (Disablement and Death) Service Pensions O.	art. 12(2)(*b*) **am.**, 12(4) **r.**, 12(5) **am.**, 1984/1154 16 **am.**, 1984/1687 18(2) **am.**, 18(5)(*a*) **r.**, 18(5)(*b*)(*c*), 30, 31, 31(1)(2), 32, 32(*a*)(ii)(*b*) **am.**, 39 **replaced**, 40, 42(1) **am.**, 66 **re-designated** art. 66(1) 66(2), 67(3)(*aa*) **inserted**, 68(1)(*b*) **am.**, Sch. 1, Pt. II, Tables 1, 3 **replaced**, III, Tables 1, 2 **replaced**, IV **replaced**, 2, Pt. II, Table 1A **replaced**, 1B(3) **am.**, 5 **replaced**, III **replaced**, 4, Pt. II, item 19, third column, paras. (*f*)-(*h*) **replaced**, item 23, third column 24, third column **am.**, 25 **r.**, 29(*a*)(*b*), third column **replaced**, 50A, 51A **inserted**, 1984/1154
973	Education (Fees and Awards) Regs.	regs. 2(1), 7(1)(*a*)-(*c*) **am.**, Sch. 2, para. 3 **replaced**, 3, para. 3(1)(*c*) **am.**, 1984/1201
974	Health and Social Services and Social Security Adjudications Act 1983 (Commencement No. 1) O.	**spent**
981	Social Security (General Benefit) Amdt. Regs.	**r.**, 1984/1703
1000	Supplementary Benefit (Misc. Amdts.) Regs.	reg. 5(2) **r.**, 1984/451
1024	Companies Act 1981 (Commencement No. 5) O.	**spent**

Year and Number (or date)	Short Title	How affected and Instrument by which affected
1025	Road Transport (International Passenger Services) (Amdt.) Regs.	r., 1984/748
1048	Legal Officers' Fees O.	Sch., Table I **replaced**, 1984/1041
1063	Savings Certificates (Amdt.) (No. 2) Regs.	reg. 2(a) r., 1984/1052
1071	Diseases of Animals (Approved Disinfectants) (Amdt.) (No. 2) O.	r., 1984/55
1078	Weights and Measures Act 1963 (Wine and Grape Must) O.	r., 1984/1314
1094	Social Security (Industrial Injuries) (Prescribed Diseases) Amdt. (No. 2) Regs.	regs. 5–7, 16 r., 1984/451 17(3) **replaced**, 1984/1659
1097	Offshore Installations (Safety Zones) (No. 24) O.	r., 1984/332
1098	Butter Subsidy (Protection of Community Arrangements) (Amdt.) Regs.	r., 1984/1739
1101	Income Tax (Cash Equivalents of Car Fuel Benefits) O.	**superseded** by 1984/1636
1102	Income Tax (Cash Equivalents of Car Benefits) O.	**superseded** by 1984/1635
1106	Merchant Shipping (Prevention of Oil Pollution) O.	arts. 3(1), 6 **ext.** to Hong Kong with **mods.**, 1984/1153
1128	Ministerial and other Salaries O.	art. 2(1) r., 1984/1171
1135	Education (Mandatory Awards) Regs.	r., 1984/1116
1156	Medicines (Exemptions from Restrictions on the Retail Sale or Supply of Veterinary Drugs) (Amdt.) (No. 2) O.	r., 1984/1861
1175	Control of Pollution Act 1974 (Commencement No. 15) O. retitled, Control of Pollution Act 1974 (Commencement No. 16) O.	art. **am.**, 1984/853
1185	Education (Students' Dependants Allowances) Regs.	reg. 7(1)(a)(i)(3)(a)(e) **am.**, 1984/1179
1186	Mobility Allowance Amdt. Regs.	reg. 3 r., 1984/451
1201	Family Income Supplements (Computation) Regs.	r., 1984/1081
1212	Medicines (Products Other Than Veterinary Drugs) (Prescription Only) O.	art. 1(2)(a)(3)(c) **am.**, 3(1)(f) **inserted**, Sch. 1, Pt. I am., 1984/756
1213	Medicines (Veterinary Drugs) (Prescription Only) O.	art. 1(2)(a) **am.**, Sch. 1, Pt. I, cols. 1, 3 **am.**, II **am.**, 2, cols. 1–3 **am.**, 3, Pt I, col. 3, entry 4 **replaced**, 1984/1862
1215	Education (Fees and Awards) (S.) Regs.	regs. 2(1), 7(1)(a)-(c) **am.**, Pt. IV **inserted**, Sch. 1, para. 3 **replaced**, 2, para. 3(1)(c) **am.**, 3 **inserted**, 1984/1361
1239	Housing Benefits Amdt. (No. 2) Regs.	r., 1984/941
1242	Housing Benefits (Increase of Needs Allowances) Regs.	r., 1984/1105
1244	Social Security Benefits Up-rating O.	r., 1984/1104
1273	Offshore Installations (Safety Zones) (No. 27) O.	r., 1984/1
1338	Misc. Financial Provns. Act 1983 (Commencement of Provns.) O.	**spent**
1346	Blood Tests (Evidence of Paternity) (Amdt.) Regs.	r., 1984/1243
1353	Trustee Savings Banks (Interest-bearing Receipts) (No. 2) O.	r., 1984/612

Year and Number (or date)	Short Title	How affected and Instrument by which affected
1354	Police (S.) Amdt. (No. 2) Regs.	regs. 5, 6 **r.**, 1984/1651
1368	Police Cadets (S.) Amdt. (No. 2) Regs.	regs. 4, 5 **r.**, 1984/2029
1372	Poultry Meat (Water Content) (S.) Regs.	regs. 2, 9(1)(3) **am.**, 15 **inserted**, Sch. **inserted**, 1984/1576
1382	Warble Fly (E. and W.) (Infected Areas) O.	art. 7(1) **am.**, 10(5) **replaced**, 10(6), 10A **inserted**, 1984/1512
1384	Immature Scallops (W.) O.	**r.**, 1984/1522
1399	Supplementary Benefit (Requirements) Regs.	reg. 2(1) **am.**, 1984/1102, 2034

3(2) **am.**, 1984/1102
5(1)(*c*)(2)(*d*)(3)(*b*)(4)(*b*)
   am., 1984/1103
5(6)(*a*), 9(2) **am.**, 1984/1102
9(4)(*b*)(i)-(iii) (7) **am.**, 1984/1103
9(8) **am.**, 1984/2034
9(12)(*a*)(i)(ii)(*b*)(i)(ii)
   (*c*)(i)-(iv) **am.**, 1984/1103
10(6)(*b*) **am.** 1984/1102
11(2) **am.**
11(2A)(2B) **inserted**,
12(1)(2)(*e*) **am.**, 1984/1103
12(2)(*g*) **am.**, 1984/1102
13(1) **am.**,
13(5)(6) **r.**, 1984/1103
15(1)(3)(4) **am.**, 1984/1102
16(1) **am.**, 1984/1102, 1103
18(1) **am.**,
18(1)(*ff*) **inserted**,
18(3)-(6) **am.**, 1984/1102
19(2)(*b*) **am.**, 1984/282
20(2)(*c*) **inserted**,
22(2) **am.**, 1984/1102
22(4)(*c*) **am.**, 1984/282, 1102, 1103
22(4)(*d*) **am.**, 1984/1102
22(4)(*e*) **am.**, 1984/282, 1103
22(5)(*g*) **inserted**, 1984/282
22(5)(*h*) **inserted**, 1984/1102
   am., 1984/2034
22(6)(*a*)(iv) **r.**, 1984/1102
22(6)(*b*) **am.**, 1984/282, 1102
22(7) **replaced**, 1984/1102
22(7)(*a*) **am.**, 1984/282
22(10)(*a*)(ii) **am.**,
22(10)(*aa*) **inserted**, 1984/1102
   am., 1984/1103
22(10)(*d*) **am.**, 1984/282
23 **am.**, 1984/1103
23(2)(4)(*a*) **am.**, 1984/282
Sch. 1, paras. A, B, 1–3 **am.**,
1984/1103
   3, para. 10 **am.**,
      14 **inserted**,
         1984/1102
   4, Pt. I, paras. 1–3, 6 **am.**,
      1984/1103
            7 **am.**,
      1984/1102, 1103
               8 **replaced**,
      1984/1103
      II, para. 14 **am.**,
      1984/1103
               17, 18 **am.**,
      1984/1102, 1103
               21 **am.**,
      1984/1102

Year and Number (or date)	Short Title	How affected and Instrument by which affected
1407	Offshore Installations (Safety Zones) (No. 33) O.	**r.**, 1984/22
1433	Social Security (No. 2) Act 1980 Specified Sum O.	**r.**, 1984/1800
1442	Act of Adj. (Circuits)	**r.**, 1984/1727
1454	Coroners' Juries Act 1983 (Commencement) O.	**spent**
1459	Supn. (Children's Pensions) (Earnings Limit) O.	**r.**, 1984/1625
1465	Nat. Assistance (Charges for Accommodation) (S.) Regs.	**r.**, 1984/1558
1472	Smoke Control Areas (Exempted Fireplaces) (No. 4) O.	**r.**, 1984/1649
1477	Cosmetic Products (Amdt.) Regs.	**r.**, 1984/1260
1492	Nat. Assistance (Charges for Accommodation) Regs.	**r.**, 1984/1356
1493	Offshore Installations (Safety Zones) (No. 35) O.	**r.**, 1984/379
1507	Offshore Installations (Safety Zones) (No. 36) O.	**r.**, 1984/1059
1518	Consular Fees O.	Sch., Pt. II, item 19A **inserted,** 1984/1155 item 22 **replaced,** 1984/1979
1537	Assured Tenancies (Approved Bodies) (No. 8) O.	Sch. **am.**, 1984/1443
1539	Coroners (Amdt.) Rules	**r.** (with saving), 1984/552
1553	Consumer Credit (Agreements) Regs.	regs. 1(2), 2(1)(3)(4)(7) **am.,** 2(7A) **inserted,** Sch. 8, Pt. II, para. 1, col. 2 **am.,** 1984/1600
1557	Consumer Credit (Cancellation Notices and Copies of Documents) Regs.	reg. 3(2)(*d*) **replaced,** 5(4) **inserted,** 1984/1108
1561	Consumer Credit (Enforcement, Default and Termination Notices) Regs.	Sch. 2, para. 7 **am.**, 1984/1109
1575	Gas Safety (Rights of Entry) Regs.	reg. 8 **am.**, 1984/1358
1576	Offshore Installations (Safety Zones) (No. 37) O.	**r.**, 1984/48
1586	Offshore Installations (Safety Zones) (No. 38) O.	**r.**, 1984/185
1587	Social Security (Sickness and Invalidity Benefit and Non-Contributory Invalidity Pension) Amdt. Regs.	**r.**, 1984/1703
1588	Social Security Benefits Up-rating Regs.	**r.**, 1984/1703
1598	Social Security (Unemployment, Sickness and Invalidity Benefit) Regs.	reg. 3(3) **am.**, 1984/1703 7(1)(*k*)(iii) **am.,** 1984/551
1618	Offshore Installations (Safety Zones) (No. 40) O.	**r.**, 1984/486
1629	Opencast Coal (Rate of Interest on Compensation) O.	**r.**, 1984/607
1646	Home Purchase Assistance (Price-limits) (No. 2) O.	**r.**, 1984/954
1656	Measuring Equipment (Intoxicating Liquor) Regs.	reg. 11 **am.**, 1984/273
1665	Legal Advice and Assistance (S.) (Financial Conditions) (No. 4) Regs.	**r.**, 1984/1677
1683	Social Security (Non-Contributory Invalidity Pension) Amdt. Regs.	**r.**, 1984/1303
1688	Public Lending Right Scheme 1982 (Amdt.) (No. 2) O.	art. 2(*a*) **r.**, 1984/1847
1693	Offshore Installations (Safety Zones) (No. 42) O.	**r.**, 1984/333

Year and Number (or date)	Short Title	How affected and Instrument by which affected
1735	Acquisition of Land (Rate of Interest after Entry) (No. 3) Regs.	**r.**, 1984/1096
1736	Acquisition of Land (Rate of Interest after Entry) (S.) (No. 3) Regs.	**r.**, 1984/1097
1765	Offshore Installations (Safety Zones) (No. 44) O.	**r.**, 1984/1009
1766	Building Societies (Designation for Trustee Investments) (Amdt.) Regs.	**r.**, 1984/8
1773	Race Relations (Prescribed Public Bodies) (Amdt.) Regs.	**r.**, 1984/218
1797	Civil Aviation (Route Charges for Navigation Services) Regs.	**r.**, 1984/1920
1803	Customs Duties (Greece) O.	**r.**, 1984/1754
1813	Offshore Installations (Safety Zones) (No. 45) O.	**r.**, 1984/1620
1814	Offshore Installations (Safety Zones) (No. 46) O.	**r.**, 1984/586
1835	Legal Aid (S.) (Financial Conditions) (No. 2) Regs.	**r.**, 1984/1865
1836	Legal Advice and Assistance (S.) (Financial Conditions) (No. 3) Regs.	**r.**, 1984/1866
1859	Motor Vehicles (Dim-Dip Lighting Devices) Regs.	**r.**, 1984/812
1861	Pneumoconiosis etc. (Workers' Compensation) (Payment of Claims) (Amdt.) Regs.	**r.** (with saving), 1984/1972
1862	Health and Social Services and Social Security Adjudications Act 1983 (Commencement No. 2) O.	**spent**
1865	Banking Act 1979 (Exempt Transactions) Regs.	Sch. 4, Pt. 1 **am.**, 1984/396
1875	Offshore Installations (Safety Zones) (No. 48) O.	**r.**, 1984/1008
1876	Offshore Installations (Safety Zones) (No. 49) O.	**r.**, 1984/528
1880	Sea Fishing (Specified Western Waters) (Restrictions on Landing) (Variation No. 2) O.	**r.**, 1984/92
1886	Civil Aviation (Eurocontrol) Act 1983 (Commencement No. 1) O.	**spent**
1906	Merchant Shipping Act 1981 (Commencement No. 2) O.	**spent**
1920	Mental Health (Amdt.) (S.) Act 1983 (Commencement No. 2) O.	**spent**
1921	Offshore Installations (Safety Zones) (No. 50) O.	**r.**, 1984/587
1922	Offshore Installations (Safety Zones) (No. 51) O.	**r.**, 1984/378
1940	Civil Aviation Act 1980 (Appointed Day) O.	**spent**
1946	Children Act 1975 and the Adoption Act 1976 (Commencement) O.	**spent**
1947	Statutory Sick Pay Up-rating (No. 2) O.	**r.**, 1984/2037
1962	Employment Protection (Variation of Limits) O.	**r.** (with saving), 1984/2019
1984		
1	Offshore Installations (Safety Zones) (Revn.) O.	**spent**
21	Offshore Installations (Safety Zones) O.	**r.**, 1984/211
22	Offshore Installations (Safety Zones) (Revn.) (No. 2) O.	**spent**
29	Offshore Installations (Safety Zones) (No. 2) O.	**r.**, 1984/430

Year and Number (or date)	Short Title	How affected and Instrument by which affected
47	Offshore Installations (Safety Zones) (No. 3) O.	r., 1984/212
48	Offshore Installations (Safety Zones) (Revn.) (No. 3) O.	spent
71	Water Act 1983 (Representation of Consumers' Interests) (Appointed Date) O.	spent
102	Rate Support Grant (S.) O.	art. 4(2) r., 5 am., Sch. 2 r., 1984/1686
107	Occupational Pension Schemes (Contracting-out) (Misc. Provns.) Regs.	r., 1984/380
110	Housing Benefits (Subsidy) O.	art. 5(a)(i) am., 1984/1001
145	Pedal Bicycles (Safety) Regs.	reg. 2(1) am., 1984/1057
175	Transport Act 1982 (Commencement No. 5) O.	spent
184	Offshore Installations (Safety Zones) (Revn.) (No. 4) O.	spent
185	Offshore Installations (Safety Zones) (Revn.) (No. 5) O.	spent
186	Offshore Installations (Safety Zones) (No. 4) O.	r., 1984/970
189	Bd. of Governors of the Eastman Dental Hospital Regs.	reg. 4(3) r., 1984/994
208	Nat. Heritage Act 1983 (Commencement No. 4) O.	spent
211	Offshore Installations (Safety Zones) (Revn.) (No. 6) O.	spent
212	Offshore Installations (Safety Zones) (Revn.) (No. 7) O.	spent
213	Offshore Installations (Safety Zones) (No. 5) O.	r., 1984/833
214	Offshore Installations (Safety Zones) (No. 6) O.	r., 1984/794
216	Health and Social Services and Social Security Adjudications Act 1983 (Commencement No. 3) O.	spent
217	Nat. Heritage Act 1983 (Commencement No. 5) O.	spent
220	Legal Aid Act 1982 (Commencement No. 2) O.	spent
225	Nat. Heritage Act 1983 (Commencement No. 6) O.	spent
231	Air Navigation (Dangerous Goods) Regs.	reg. 2(1) am., 1984/1792
239	Local Govt. and Planning (S.) Act 1982 (Commencement No. 3) O.	spent
240	Occupational Pension Schemes (Contracting-out) Amdt. Regs.	r., 1984/380
253	Divorce Jurisdiction, Ct. Fees and Legal Aid (S.) Act 1983 (Commencement) O.	spent
257	Sheriff Ct. Fees O.	art. 4(1) am., 6A inserted, Sch, Table of Fees, paras. 17, 18 replaced, 18A–18D inserted, 1984/466
302	Diseases of Fish Act 1983 (Commencement) O.	spent
332	Offshore Installations (Safety Zones) (Revn.) (No. 8) O.	spent

Year and Number (or date)	Short Title	How affected and Instrument by which affected
333	Offshore Installations (Safety Zones) (Revn.) (No. 9) O.	**spent**
334	Offshore Installations (Safety Zones) (No. 7) O.	**r.**, 1984/912
335	Offshore Installations (Safety Zones) (No. 8) O.	**r.**, 1984/527
336	Offshore Installations (Safety Zones) (No. 9) O.	**r.**, 1984/650
349	Medicines (Exemptions from Restrictions on the Retail Sale or Supply of Veterinary Drugs) (Amdt.) O.	**r.**, 1984/1861
377	Offshore Installations (Safety Zones) (No. 10) O.	**r.**, 1984/588
378	Offshore Installations (Safety Zones) (Revn.) (No. 10) O.	**spent**
379	Offshore Installations (Safety Zones) (Revn.) (No. 11) O.	**spent**
388	Savings Certificates (Amdt.) Regs.	**r.**, 1984/1052
398	Offshore Installations (Safety Zones) (No. 11) O.	**r.**, 1984/834
399	Offshore Installations (Safety Zones) (No. 12) O.	**r.**, 1984/868
400	Offshore Installations (Safety Zones) (No. 13) O.	**r.**, 1984/836
413	Marriage Act 1983 (Commencement) O.	**spent**
423	Zoo Licensing Act 1981 (Commencement) O.	**spent**
429	Offshore Installations (Safety Zones) (No. 14) O.	**r.**, 1984/734
430	Offshore Installations (Safety Zones) (Revn.) (No. 12) O.	**spent**
451	Social Security (Adjudication) Regs.	regs. 2(2)(*b*), 6(2) **am.**, 6(2)(*a*)(*b*) **replaced**, 8(2) **r.**, 19(2)(*b*), 26(4) **am.**, 29 **replaced**, 1984/1991 29(5) **am.**, 1984/613 60(3) **am.**, 1984/1991 82(1)(*b*) **am.**, 1984/1303 92(6)(*a*) **am.**, 1984/613 Sch. 4, para. 1, cols. (3)(4) **am.**, 1984/1991
457	Redundant Mineworkers and Concessionary Coal (Payments Schemes) O.	Sch., arts. 1, 5(2), 10(2)(*f*) **am.**, 10(2)(*g*) **inserted**, 10(5)(*a*)(*b*) **am.**, 10(6) **inserted**, 1984/1889
458	Social Security Adjudication (Consequential Amdts.) Regs.	reg. 9 **r.**, 1984/1960
470	Gaming Clubs (Hours and Charges) (S.) Regs.	reg. 5(1)(*b*)(*c*) **am.**, 1984/1804
486	Offshore Installations (Safety Zones) (Revn.) (No. 13) O.	**spent**
487	Offshore Installations (Safety Zones) (No. 15) O.	**r.**, 1984/900
490	Employment Agencies Act 1973 (Exemption) Regs.	**r.**, 1984/978
522	Control of Harbour Devpt. (Revn.) O.	**spent**
527	Offshore Installations (Safety Zones) (Revn.) (No. 14) O.	**spent**
528	Offshore Installations (Safety Zones) (Revn.) (No. 15) O.	**spent**

Year and Number (or date)	Short Title	How affected and Instrument by which affected
529	Offshore Installations (Safety Zones) (No. 16) O.	r., 1984/1427
530	Offshore Installations (Safety Zones) (No. 17) O.	r., 1984/913
554	Children Act 1975 (S.) (Commencement No. 4) O.	spent
573	Civic Govt. (S.) Act 1982 (Commencement) Amdt. O.	spent
586	Offshore Installations (Safety Zones) (Revn.) (No. 16) O.	spent
587	Offshore Installations (Safety Zones) (Revn.) (No. 17) O.	spent
588	Offshore Installations (Safety Zones) (Revn.) (No. 18) O.	spent
607	Opencast Coal (Rate of Interest on Compensation) O.	r., 1984/1049
612	Trustee Savings Banks (Interest-bearing Receipts) O.	r., 1984/1971
626	Offshore Installations (Safety Zones) (No. 19) O.	r., 1984/1621
627	Offshore Installations (Safety Zones) (No. 20) O.	r., 1984/1298
629	Offshore Installations (Safety Zones) (No. 22) O.	r., 1984/835
630	Offshore Installations (Safety Zones) (No. 23) O.	r., 1984/1295
650	Offshore Installations (Safety Zones) (Revn.) (No. 19) O.	spent
651	Offshore Installations (Safety Zones) (No. 24) O.	r., 1984/1038
652	Offshore Installations (Safety Zones) (No. 25) O.	r., 1984/1007
653	Offshore Installations (Safety Zones) (No. 26) O.	r., 1984/1060
730	Legal Aid Act 1982 (Commencement No. 3) O.	spent
733	Offshore Installations (Safety Zones) (No. 29) O.	r., 1984/1010
734	Offshore Installations (Safety Zones) (Revn.) (No. 20) O.	spent
749	Telecommunications Act 1984 (Appointed Day) (No. 1) O.	spent
751	Education (Grants for In-service Training of Teachers) (S.) Regs.	Sch. replaced, 1984/1740
794	Offshore Installations (Safety Zones) (Revn.) (No. 21) O.	spent
796	Offshore Installations (Safety Zones) (No. 31) O.	r., 1984/1570
810	Customs and Import Duty Reliefs (Revn.) O.	spent
811	Road Traffic Act 1974 (Commencement No. 8) O.	spent
833	Offshore Installations (Safety Zones) (Revn.) (No. 22) O.	spent
834	Offshore Installations (Safety Zones) (Revn.) (No. 23) O.	spent
835	Offshore Installations (Safety Zones) (Revn.) (No. 24) O.	spent
836	Offshore Installations (Safety Zones) (Revn.) (No. 25) O.	spent
837	Offshore Installations (Safety Zones) (No. 32) O.	r., 1984/1426
853	Control of Pollution Act 1974 (Commencement No. 17) O.	spent

Year and Number (or date)	Short Title	How affected and Instrument by which affected
868	Offshore Installations (Safety Zones) (Revn.) (No. 26) O.	**spent**
869	Offshore Installations (Safety Zones) (No. 33) O.	**r.**, 1984/1257
870	Offshore Installations (Safety Zones) (No. 34) O.	**r.**, 1984/1643
871	Offshore Installations (Safety Zones) (No. 35) O.	**r.**, 1984/1351
872	Offshore Installations (Safety Zones) (No. 36) O.	**r.**, 1984/1601
876	Telecommunications Act 1984 (Appointed Day) (No. 2) O.	**spent**
877	London Regional Transport (Appointed Day) O.	**spent**
900	Offshore Installations (Safety Zones) (Revn.) (No. 27) O.	**spent**
901	Offshore Installations (Safety Zones) (No. 37) O.	**r.**, 1984/1722
904	Offshore Installations (Safety Zones) (No. 40) O.	**r.**, 1984/1061
906	Recreation Grounds (Revn. of Parish Council Byelaws) O.	**spent**
911	Offshore Installations (Safety Zones) (No. 41) O.	**r.**, 1984/1641
912	Offshore Installations (Safety Zones) (Revn.) (No. 28) O.	**spent**
913	Offshore Installations (Safety Zones) (Revn.) (No. 29) O.	**spent**
929	V.A.T. (General) (Amdt.) (No. 2) Regs.	italic heading Coming into Operation **am.**, reg. 1 **am.**, 1984/1376
950	Job Release Act 1977 (Continuation) O.	**spent**
957	Health and Social Services and Social Security Adjudications Act 1983 (Commencement No. 4) O.	**spent**
970	Offshore Installations (Safety Zones) (Revn.) (No. 30) O.	**spent**
972	Offshore Installations (Safety Zones) (No. 43) O.	**r.**, 1984/1771
973	Offshore Installations (Safety Zones) (No. 44) O.	**r.**, 1984/1772
974	Offshore Installations (Safety Zones) (No. 45) O.	**r.**, 1984/1428
975	Offshore Installations (Safety Zones) (No. 46) O.	**r.**, 1984/1299
977	Pool Competitions Act 1971 (Continuance) O.	**spent**
981	Motor Vehicles (Type Approval) (G.B.) Regs.	reg. 3(2)(*e*)(iv) **am.**, Sch. 1, item 4C, cols. (3)(*a*)(*c*)(5) **am.**, 5A, cols. (3)(*a*)(*c*)(5) **am.**, 6, cols. (3)(*a*)(*c*)(5) **am.**, 1984/1761 14B, 14C **replaced**, 1984/1401 18, 18A, 19, 19A, col. 4 **am.**, 1984/1761
1007	Offshore Installations (Safety Zones) (Revn.) (No. 31) O.	**spent**
1008	Offshore Installations (Safety Zones) (Revn.) (No. 32) O.	**spent**
1009	Offshore Installations (Safety Zones) (Revn.) (No. 33) O.	**spent**
1010	Offshore Installations (Safety Zones) (Revn.) (No. 34) O.	**spent**

Year and Number (or date)	Short Title	How affected and Instrument by which affected
1011	Offshore Installations (Safety Zones) (No. 47) O.	r., 1984/1430
1033	N.I. (Emergency Provns.) Act 1978 (Continuance) O.	**spent**
1038	Offshore Installations (Safety Zones) (Revn.) (No. 35) O.	**spent**
1043	Offshore Installations (Safety Zones) (No. 49) O.	r., 1984/1385
1047	Dairy Produce Quotas Regs.	Sch. 5, para. 1 **am.**, 1984/1538, 1787 7 **am.**, 1984/1538
1049	Opencast Coal (Rate of Interest on Compensation) (No. 2) O.	r., 1984/1903
1058	Offshore Installations (Safety Zones) (No. 52) O.	r., 1984/1429
1059	Offshore Installations (Safety Zones) (Revn.) (No. 36) O.	**spent**
1060	Offshore Installations (Safety Zones) (Revn.) (No. 37) O.	**spent**
1061	Offshore Installations (Safety Zones) (Revn.) (No. 38) O.	**spent**
1096	Acquisition of Land (Rate of Interest after Entry) Regs.	r., 1984/1456
1097	Acquisition of Land (Rate of Interest after Entry) (S.) Regs.	r., 1984/1457
1116	Education (Mandatory Awards) Regs.	Sch. 3, para. 4(1) **am.**, 1984/1240
1138	Offshore Installations (Safety Zones) (No. 56) O.	r., 1984/1999
1140	Pensions Commutation Act 1984 (Commencement) O.	**spent**
1142	Admin. of Justice Act 1982 (Commencement No. 2) O.	**spent**
1147	Army, Air Force and Naval Discipline Acts (Continuation) O.	**spent**
1180	Finance Act 1984 (Savings-Related Share Option Schemes) Commencement O.	**spent**
1256	Offshore Installations (Safety Zones) (No. 57) O.	r., 1984/1723
1257	Offshore Installations (Safety Zones) (Revn.) (No. 39) O.	**spent**
1261	Medicines (Ctee. on Radiation from Radioactive Medicinal Products) (Revn.) O.	**spent**
1267	Offshore Installations (Safety Zones) (No. 58) O.	r., 1984/1683
1287	Admin. of Justice Act 1982 (Commencement No. 3) O.	**spent**
1295	Offshore Installations (Safety Zones) (Revn.) (No. 40) O.	**spent**
1297	Offshore Installations (Safety Zones) (Revn.) (No. 41) O.	**spent**
1298	Offshore Installations (Safety Zones) (Revn.) (No. 42) O.	**spent**
1299	Offshore Installations (Safety Zones) (Revn.) (No. 43) O.	**spent**
1302	Health and Social Security Act 1984 (Commencement No. 1) O.	art. 3(4)(*a*)(iii) **replaced**, 1984/1467
1305	Food Labelling Regs.	Sch. 3, col. 2 **am.**, 1984/1566
1347	Health and Social Services and Social Security Adjudications Act 1983 (Commencement No. 5) O.	Sch. **am.**, 1984/1767
1351	Offshore Installations (Safety Zones) (Revn.) (No. 44) O.	**spent**
1357	Mental Health Act 1983 Commencement O.	**spent**

Year and Number (or date)	Short Title	How affected and Instrument by which affected
1385	Offshore Installations (Safety Zones) (Revn.) (No. 45) O.	spent
1386	Offshore Installations (Safety Zones) (No. 60) O.	r., 1984/1622
1387	Offshore Installations (Safety Zones) (No. 61) O.	r., 1984/1642
1426	Offshore Installations (Safety Zones) (Revn.) (No. 46) O.	spent
1427	Offshore Installations (Safety Zones) (Revn.) (No. 47) O.	spent
1428	Offshore Installations (Safety Zones) (Revn.) (No. 48) O.	spent
1429	Offshore Installations (Safety Zones) (Revn.) (No. 49) O.	spent
1430	Offshore Installations (Safety Zones) (Revn.) (No. 50) O.	spent
1444	Offshore Installations (Safety Zones) (No. 62) O.	r., 1984/1896
1456	Acquisition of Land (Rate of Interest after Entry) (No. 2) Regs.	r., 1984/1647
1457	Acquisition of Land (Rate of Interest after Entry) (S.) (No. 2) Regs.	r., 1984/1648
1459	Exchange Control (Authorised Dealers and Depositories) (Revn.) O.	spent
1467	Health and Social Security Act 1984 (Commencement No. 1) Amdt. O.	spent
1492	Social Security Act (Commencement No. 4) O.	spent
1493	Local Govt., Planning and Land Act 1980 (Commencement No. 9) O.	spent
1519	Food Labelling (S.) Regs.	Sch. 3, col. 2 am., 1984/1714
1553	Civil Jurisdiction and Judgments Act 1982 (Commencement No. 1) O.	spent
1570	Offshore Installations (Safety Zones) (Revn.) (No. 51) O.	spent
1573	Offshore Installations (Safety Zones) (No. 69) O.	r., 1984/1721
1575	Parking Meters (Description and Testing) (E. and W.) Order 1961 (Revn.) O.	spent
1589	Matrimonial and Family Proceedings Act 1984 (Commencement No. 1) O.	spent
1598	Baking and Sausage Making (Christmas and New Year) Regs.	spent
1599	Juries (Disqualification) Act 1984 (Commencement) O.	spent
1601	Offshore Installations (Safety Zones) (Revn.) (No. 52) O.	spent
1602	Offshore Installations (Safety Zones) (No. 71) O.	r., 1984/1849
1620	Offshore Installations (Safety Zones) (Revn.) (No. 53) O.	spent
1621	Offshore Installations (Safety Zones) (Revn.) (No. 54) O.	spent
1622	Offshore Installations (Safety Zones) (Revn.) (No. 55) O.	spent
1623	Offshore Installations (Safety Zones) (No. 73) O.	r., 1984/1773
1624	Offshore Installations (Safety Zones) (No. 74) O.	r., 1984/1895
1627	Sole (Bristol Channel and South-east of Ireland) (Prohibition of Fishing) O.	r., 1984/1935
1641	Offshore Installations (Safety Zones) (Revn.) (No. 56) O.	spent

Year and Number (or date)	Short Title	How affected and Instrument by which affected
1642	Offshore Installations (Safety Zones) (Revn.) (No. 57) O.	spent
1643	Offshore Installations (Safety Zones) (Revn.) (No. 58) O.	spent
1647	Acquisition of Land (Rate of Interest after Entry) (No. 3) Regs.	r., 1984/1967
1648	Acquisition of Land (Rate of Interest after Entry) (S.) (No. 3) Regs.	r., 1984/1968
1663	Offshore Installations (Safety Zones) (No. 78) O.	r., 1984/1828
1683	Offshore Installations (Safety Zones) (Revn.) (No. 59) O.	spent
1691	Fuel and Electricity (Control) Act 1973 (Continuation) (Jersey) O.	spent
1695	Merchant Shipping Act 1981 (Commencement No. 3) O.	spent
1701	Housing Defects Act 1984 (Commencement) O.	spent
1718	Grants by Local Authies. (Repairs Grants for Airey Houses) (Revn.) O.	spent
1721	Offshore Installations (Safety Zones) (Revn.) (No. 60) O.	spent
1722	Offshore Installations (Safety Zones) (Revn.) (No. 61) O.	spent
1723	Offshore Installations (Safety Zones) (Revn.) (No. 62) O.	spent
1724	Offshore Installations (Safety Zones) (No. 80) O.	r., 1984/1998
1726	Offshore Installations (Safety Zones) (No. 82) O.	r., 1984/1897
1767	Health and Social Services and Social Security Adjudications Act 1983 (Commencement No. 5) (Amdt.) O.	spent
1771	Offshore Installations (Safety Zones) (Revn.) (No. 63) O.	spent
1772	Offshore Installations (Safety Zones) (Revn.) (No. 64) O.	spent
1773	Offshore Installations (Safety Zones) (Revn.) (No. 65) O.	spent
1774	Offshore Installations (Safety Zones) (No. 83) O.	r., 1984/1911
1828	Offshore Installations (Safety Zones) (Revn.) (No. 66) O.	spent
1849	Offshore Installations (Safety Zones) (Revn.) (No. 67) O.	spent
1895	Offshore Installations (Safety Zones) (Revn.) (No. 68) O.	spent
1896	Offshore Installations (Safety Zones) (Revn.) (No. 69) O.	spent
1897	Offshore Installations (Safety Zones) (Revn.) (No. 70) O.	spent
1911	Offshore Installations (Safety Zones) (Revn.) (No. 71) O.	spent
1998	Offshore Installations (Safety Zones) (Revn.) (No. 72) O.	spent
1999	Offshore Installations (Safety Zones) (Revn.) (No. 73) O.	spent

NUMERICAL AND ISSUE LIST

NOTES

(a) Here are listed all the Statutory Instruments that during the year were issued for the first time by Her Majesty's Stationery Office.

(b) The date in square brackets after the title of an instrument shows when it was first issued by Her Majesty's Stationery Office.

(c) The entry **(n)** against an instrument shows that, although printed and issued by Her Majesty's Stationery Office, it is classified as local. Such instruments are not printed in this edition, but they are listed in the Classified List of Local Statutory Instruments at the end of the edition, together with the local instruments that have not been printed.

(d) An asterisk in the last column shows that the instrument is excluded from this edition for the reason explained in paragraph 4 of the Preface.

NUMERICAL AND ISSUE LIST

1181 British Museum (Authorised Repositories) O. [9 Aug. 1984] .. .. II 3411

1182 Rabies (Importation of Dogs, Cats and Other Mammals) (Amdt.) O. [9 Aug. 1984] .. .. .. II 3413

1183 Education (Grants) (Newbattle Abbey College) Regs. [9 Aug. 1984] .. .. (n) III 6096

1199 Insolvency Proceedings (Increase of Monetary Limits) Regs. [10 Aug. 1984] .. .. II 3416

1200 Control of Pollution (Discharges by Authies.) Regs. [9 Aug. 1984] .. .. II 3418

1201 Education (Fees and Awards) (Amdt.) Regs. [10 Aug. 1984] .. .. II 3423

1202 Severn Valley Light Railway O. [10 Aug. 1984] (n) III 6086

1203 Merchant Shipping (Navigational Equipment) Regs. [10 Aug. 1984] .. .. II 3425

1204 Combined Probation Area (Gloucestershire) O. [10 Aug. 1984] .. .. (n) III 6097

1205 Slaughter of Animals (Revision of Penalties) (S.) Regs. [24 Aug. 1984].. .. .. .. II 3449

1206 Free Zone (Belfast Airport) Designation O. [10 Sept. 1984] .. .. (n) III 6098

1207 Free Zone (Birmingham Airport) Designation O. [10 Sept. 1984] .. .. .. (n) III 6098

1208 Free Zone (Cardiff) Designation O. [10 Sept. 1984] (n) III 6098

1209 Free Zone (Liverpool) Designation O. [10 Sept. 1984](n) III 6098

1210 Free Zone (Prestwick Airport) Designation O. [10 Sept. 1984] .. .. (n) III 6098

1211 Free Zone (Southampton) Designation O. [10 Sept. 1984] .. .. (n) III 6098

1213 Powys Family Practitioner Ctee. (Membership) O. [10 Aug. 1984] .. .. (n) III 6091

1214 Police (Promotion) (Amdt.) Regs. [9 Aug. 1984] .. II 3451

1215 International Organisations (Tax Exempt Securities) O. [14 Aug. 1984].. .. .. II 3454

1216 Merchant Shipping (Passenger Ship Construction and Survey) Regs. [10 Aug. 1984] .. .. .. II 3455

1217 Merchant Shipping (Cargo Ship Construction and Survey) Regs. [10 Aug. 1984] .. .. .. II 3547

1218 Merchant Shipping (Fire Protection) Regs. [10 Aug. 1984] .. .. II 3612

1219 Merchant Shipping (Cargo Ship Construction and Survey) Regulations 1981 (Amdt.) Regs. [10 Aug. 1984] .. .. II 3761

1220 Merchant Shipping (Passenger Ship Construction) (Amdt.) Regs. [10 Aug. 1984] .. .. II 3771

1221 Merchant Shipping (Fire Appliances) (Amdt.) Regs. [10 Aug. 1984] .. .. II 3773

1222 Merchant Shipping (Fire Appliances) (Amdt.) Rules [10 Aug. 1984] .. .. II 3775

1223 Merchant Shipping (Radio Installations) (Amdt. No. 2) Regs. [10 Aug. 1984] .. .. .. II 3777

Index to Part III

*Volume
and page
number*

CRIMINAL LAW, S.
Increase of Criminal Penalties etc. (S.) O. (526)   ..   I, p. 1636
CROWN
Civil List (Increases of Financial Provn.) O. (39)   ..   I, p.   35
**CROWN AGENTS FOR OVERSEA GOVERNMENTS
    AND ADMINISTRATIONS**
Crown Agents Commencing Capital Debt O. (2036)   ..   III, p. 5990
CUSTOMS AND EXCISE
Agricultural Levy Reliefs (Frozen Beef and Veal) O. (10)   I, p.   8
Bingo Duty (Exemptions) O. (431)   ..   ..   II, p. 1284
Control of Movement of Goods Regs. (1176)   ..   II, p. 3387
Customs and—
    Excise Duties (Relief for Imported Legacies) O. (895) ..   II, p. 2607
    Import Duty Reliefs (Revn.) O. (810)   ..   II, p. 2327
Customs Duties—
    (ECSC)—
       (Amdt. No. 5) O. (1306)..   ..   ..   ..   II, p. 4134
       (Amdt. No. 6) O. (1452)..   ..   ..   ..   III, p. 4428
       (Amdt. No. 7) O. (1969)..   ..   ..   ..   III, p. 5747
       (Quota and Other Reliefs) O. (2006)   ..   ..   III, p. 5884
       (Greece) O. (1754)   ..   ..   III, p. 5040
       (Quota Relief) O. (898)   ..   ..   ..   II, p. 2613
Customs Duty—
    (Community Reliefs) O. (719)   ..   ..   ..   II, p. 2099
    (Personnel Reliefs) (No. 1) Order 1968 (Amdt.) O.
       (718)   ..   ..   II, p. 2097
Export of Goods (Control)—
    (Amdt. No. 5) O. (90)   ..   ..   I, p.   117
    (Amdt. No. 6) O. (553)   ..   ..   I, p. 1723
    (Amdt. No. 7) O. (694)   ..   ..   II, p. 2007
    (Amdt. No. 8) O. (819)   ..   ..   II, p. 2447
Free Zone Regs. (1177)   ..   ..   ..   II, p. 3392
Gaming Machine (Licence Duty) Regs. (1178)   ..   II, p. 3401
General Betting Duty Regulations 1973 (Amdt.) Regs.
    (261)   ..   ..   I, p.   699
Inward Processing Relief (Amdt.) Regs. (1500) ..   ..   III, p. 4477

DAMAGES
Admin. of Justice Act 1982 (Commencement No. 3) O.
    (1287)   ..   ..   II, p. 3978
DANGEROUS DRUGS
Misuse of Drugs—
    (Amdt.) Regs. (1143)   ..   ..   II, p. 3264
    (Designation) (Variation) O. (1144) ..   ..   ..   II, p. 3268
    (Licence Fees) (Amdt.) Regs. (165) ..   ..   ..   I, p.   360
    (Safe Custody) (Amdt.) Regs. (1146)   ..   ..   II, p. 3280
    Act 1971 (Mod.) O. (859) ..   ..   II, p. 2507
DEEDS OF ARRANGEMENT
Deeds of Arrangement Fees O. (887) ..   ..   ..   II, p. 2596

*Volume
and page
number*

*Volume
and page
number*